THE RISK MANAGER'S DESK REFERENCE

(Formerly Published As
**Quality & Risk Management in
Health Care: An Information Service)**

Edited by
Barbara J. Youngberg, JD, BSN, MSW
Vice President
Insurance, Risk and Clinical Quality Management
University Hospital Consortium
Oak Brook, Illinois

AN ASPEN PUBLICATION®
Aspen Publishers, Inc.
Gaithersburg, Maryland
1994

Library of Congress Cataloging-in-Publication Data

The risk manager's desk reference / edited by Barbara J. Youngberg
p. cm.
"Formerly published as Quality & risk management in health care."
Includes bibliographical references and index.
ISBN 0-8342-0506-8
1. Hospitals—Risk management. I. Youngberg, Barbara J.
II. Quality & risk management in health care.
RA971.38.Q35 1994
361.1'1'068—dc20   93-11503
CIP

Editorial Resources: Ruth Bloom
Library of Congress Catalog Card Number: 93-11503
ISBN: 0-8342-0506-8

Printed in the United States of America

1 2 3 4 5

This resource is dedicated to all of my colleagues who face each new challenge in hospital risk management with skill and creativity and who are helping to shape the profession of risk management into one that will have a significant impact on the quality of health care in the future.

Table of Contents

Contributors

Harold L. Anderson
Assistant Hospital Director
Medical College of Georgia Hospitals and Clinics
Augusta, Georgia

Judi Barager-Kemper, MPA
Director of Quality Assurance and Utilization Review
University of Kentucky Hospital
Lexington, Kentucky

Donald E. Barker, MD, MS
General Surgeon
Trauma Surgeon
Director of Life Force
Chattanooga, Tennessee

Linda Sue Barmore, JD, LLM
Attorney

Matthew Camden
Director, Methods & Standards
Northwestern University Hospital
Chicago, Illinois

Lynn K. Coffman
Risk Management Analyst
Fairfax Hospital
Falls Church, Virginia

Paul A. Craig, Esq.
Katten, Muchin & Zavis
Chicago, Illinois

Jan Davis, RN, BSN, CEN
Assistant Chief Flight Nurse
Aeromedical Service
University of Kentucky Hospital
Lexington, Kentucky

Marie Anne Dizon
Staff Nurse—Obstetrics
University of Illinois Hospital and Clinics
Chicago, Illinois

Frank Dodero
Assistant Vice President
Alexander & Alexander, Inc.
Chicago, Illinois

Thomas V. Ealy
Vice President
Alexander & Alexander, Inc.
Chicago, Illinois

Jay L. Goldstein, MD
Assistant Professor of Medicine
University of Illinois College of Medicine
Chairman, Department of Medicine
Quality Assurance Committee
Chicago, Illinois

Josephine Goode-Johnson
Executive Director
University of Maryland Medical Service System
Baltimore, Maryland

Kristi Kelsey, RN
Director Staffing Support
    and Supplemental Staffing
Mercy Services Corp.
Phoenix, Arizona

James D. Knight
Safety Manager
HCA Presbyterian Hospital
Oklahoma City, Oklahoma

Deborah Korleski
Risk Manager
Thomas Jefferson University Hospital
Philadelphia, Pennsylvania

Claudette Krizek, Esq.
Tampa, Florida

A. Michele Kuhn
Director, Risk Management
Presbyterian-University Hospital of Pittsburgh
Pittsburgh, Pennsylvania

Vickey Masta-Gornic
Director of Insurance and Risk Management
Albany, Medical Center Hospital
Albany, New York

Paul T. Napolski, Esq.
Assistant General Counsel
Chicago Osteopathic Health Systems
Chicago, Illinois

Carole Runyan Price, Esq.
Risk Manager
Pennsylvania State-Milton S. Hershey
    Medical Center
Hershey, Pennsylvania

Diane Runberg, BSN
Director of Counseling Services
Health Decisions, Inc.
Evergreen, Colorado

Susan Salpeter, RN, MBA
Senior Health Care Risk Services Specialist
Zurich American Insurance Company
Schaumburg, Illinois

Mark Schneider
Director of Risk Management and Insurance
Foster G. McGaw Hospital
Loyola University
Maywood, Illinois

Barbara Grand Sheridan, BSN, MJ
Associate Claims Manager
University of Illinois
Chicago, Illinois

Tina L. Spector, RRA
Assistant Hospital Director
Medical Staff Affairs
University of Illinois Hospital and Clinics
Chicago, Illinois

Steve Straka, MHA
Assistant Hospital Director for Clinical Services
University of Illinois Hospital and Clinics
Chicago, Illinois

Claudia Teich, BSN, MS, MJ
Northfield, Illinois

Kathleen Walsh, RN, MS, Esq.
Hinshaw & Culbertson
Waukegan, Illinois

Susan West, RN
Director of Risk Management
University of Colorado Health Sciences Center
Denver, Colorado

Louise White, RN
Assistant Director Quality Assurance and Utilization Review
University of Kentucky Hospital
Lexington, Kentucky

Elizabeth L. Willey, Esq.
Strong and Hanni
Salt Lake City, Utah

Inge Winer
Director of Quality Assurance and Utilization Review
University of Chicago Hospitals and Clinics
Chicago, Illinois

Barbara J. Youngberg
Vice President
Insurance, Risk, & Clinical Quality Management
University Hospital Consortium
Oak Brook, Illinois

Preface

Risk management is a profession in a constant state of change. From one month to the next a health care risk manager may find his or her job description modified to encompass the many changes in the health care, legislative, and regulatory environment. Often responsibilities traditionally belonging to risk management are shifted elsewhere, while responsibilities traditionally belonging elsewhere suddenly become the risk manager's concern, making the risk managers' domain of responsibility difficult to assess.

Risk managers find themselves frequently meeting with each other to discuss the creative, innovative, and sometimes aggressive approaches they take to effect change and ensure quality in their organizations. They share "magic formulas," statistical validation of their efforts, sample policies and programs, and horror stories—all in an effort to improve health care environments in which they work and to simplify implementation of improvements.

They learn quickly that there are no magic answers to ensure a quality risk management program and that any risk management program, in order to be a success, takes hard work, commitment, and a staff that is flexible, creative, and

respected by its colleagues. Risk managers are facilitators, educators, and often enforcers. They must possess technical and financial skills equal only to strong social and interpersonal skills. They must be able and willing to take positions that are not always popular but that are motivated by the desire to improve the health care environment.

The purpose of this reference is to provide risk managers with a resource that addresses new areas of concern but does not overlook traditional concepts necessary for a strong program foundation. It is not intended to provide a *one best way* to manage risk but rather to offer a number of concepts that can be adopted, modified, or even set aside for future use and analysis when not appropriate for the current status of a risk management program.

This reference supports the fact that many different disciplines must be involved in a successful risk management process. It describes the key roles of governing boards, administration, medical staff, nursing staff, legal counsel, quality assurance staff, and others that are necessary to make the program effective. Certain sections focus on these key people and provide the risk manager with methods for engaging their support and participation.

Acknowledgments

Many persons have contributed their time to make this reference a reality. The value of the contributions by named contributors to this text is readily apparent. However, the value of many others, who continually provide me with the stimulation needed to develop a project of this magnitude, also bears mention. In my position as Vice President of Insurance, Risk, and Quality Management for the University Hospital Consortium I have the good fortune to work with many gifted professionals working in the complex academic medical center environment. These incredibly talented and energetic people freely share with me and with each other their ideas, their knowledge, and the products of their hard work. It is because of their commitment that projects such as this resource are completed.

chapter 1

Introduction to Risk Management

A. Michele Kuhn

THE BEGINNING OF RISK MANAGEMENT

Risk is encountered by everyone on a daily basis. Since the beginning of time humans have had to deal with *risk*. The control and possible elimination of known risk has been an ongoing challenge; this process is known as *risk management*.

Risk management has been important in the industrial work force for more than 50 years. Although risk management activities have always taken place in hospitals, it is only during the past 15 years (since 1974–1975) that risk management has been recognized as a function in the health care field and only during the past 8 years as an essential part of health care administration. Hospital risk management, as it is known today, began during the medical malpractice crisis of the mid-1970s. This crisis emphasized the need for the development of risk management programs in the health care field.

Professional liability insurance was either impossible to obtain, or the premiums were exorbitant. The national economy was severely depressed, and many insurers retreated from the marketplace. Those companies remaining in the business increased their premiums significantly. Hospitals were forced to find alternative methods of financing professional liability risk. Also, the insurance providers continuing to offer coverage to physicians and hospitals had certain requirements for their insurers, including the establishment of risk management programs. In fact, many states passed legislation that set limits of liability for physicians and health care institutions and required ongoing claims and risk management programs. Because of the malpractice crisis and the resulting problems, professional health care risk management came into existence.

Some health care administrators implemented risk management programs only because of the requirements set by the state or the insurer. These programs were not offered the support or commitment necessary for a successful risk management process. In addition, the risk management function was often assigned to a member of the administrative staff who had no prior experience with risk management principles or techniques. This individual may have had responsibility for another department in the health care institution that, in his or her opinion, demanded a greater priority than the risk management function. In this case risk management became a program only on paper, and the emphasis was on insurance.

Chief executive officers and financial executives of health care institutions must realize that insurance is only one method of protecting the assets and the reputation of their institutions from loss. The purpose and function of risk management are still not clear to many health care personnel not directly involved with the process. In fact, the term risk management is often considered to be another way of referring to the purchase of insurance. Insurance, of course, is one method of risk financing, but in health care risk management the risk control techniques are equally as important.

Industrial risk management techniques were adopted by health care institutions when they initially established the risk management function. However, it was not long before those responsible for this function realized that such techniques were not appropriate in the health care industry. The primary goal of industrial risk management is to protect the organization from financial loss. This is also an important objective in health care, but the primary goal of health care risk management is to improve the quality of care through the identification and elimination of potential risks.

DEFINITION OF RISK

Webster defines risk as:

- possibility of loss or injury
- dangerous element
- degree of probability of loss

It is important to understand the meaning of risk as it applies to risk management:

- *Risk* is the uncertainty that a loss or losses will occur.
- *Risk management* is a management function aimed at the identification, evaluation, and treatment of risks that could result in a loss.

Risk management is both a concurrent and retrospective process. The goal of risk management is to create an awareness of possible risks that represent financial threats or that are potentially harmful to patients, visitors, or employees. The risk manager, sometimes viewed as a "watchdog" or a "bearer of bad news," must emphasize the positive side of risk management by being an optimist who is discovering better methods of achieving the desired result.

Quality of care is the primary focus, but the risk manager is also responsible for the identification of problem areas and the provision of appropriate coverage. These areas include:

- destruction of property
- dishonesty of employees
- injuries to visitors
- liability of directors and officers
- garage/motor vehicle liability
- boiler/machinery malfunction
- disability or death of employees

There are basically two types of risks that are faced by health care institutions: speculative and pure.

Speculative Risks

These risks have the probability of gain as well as loss. They are inherent in the health care industry and are intended to result in gains for patients.

The health care "business" is based on these daily risks that include:

- surgical procedures
- administration of medication
- medical diagnosis
- medical treatment
- medical research and experimental procedures
- radiology procedures
- nuclear medicine procedures

Pure Risks

These risks, which have a probability only of loss, can result in the depletion of financial resources to a health care institution. Pure risks are the primary focus of the risk manager. Risk management concerns more than identifying and responding to existing areas of liability. It is essential that the risk manager concentrate on identification of potential liability exposure. The prevention or minimization of problems results in the reduction and elimination of liability claims. Loss prevention is the key issue in health care risk management.

RECOGNITION OF RISK MANAGEMENT

In December 1988 the Joint Commission on Accreditation of Healthcare Organizations (Joint Commission) approved risk management–related accreditation standards. Although a "long time coming," these standards constitute a step in the right direction. This recognition was required by risk managers to gain the attention of the medical staffs and administrations of their institutions.

Medical Staff

To be successful a risk management program must have the support of many disciplines. Active involvement of the medical staff in risk management activities is essential. Physicians are a major component of a risk management program. They are in a good position to predict when problems may result in incidents involving liability. This knowledge allows them to take action to prevent adverse occurrences. As noted before, risk management is a process of identification, analysis, and elimination of possible risks. Physicians always have been involved in this type of review activity. They continuously review and evaluate the quality of care provided according to appropriate standards, and can take necessary action when they observe substandard care.

Physicians should cooperate with the risk management staff beyond routine reporting and investigation of incidents. It is their responsibility to assist in minimizing claims and controlling the cost of those that do occur. Physicians also should be responsible for working with administration and risk management in the following areas:

- medical staff credentialing process
- analysis and correction of identified problem areas
- communication with patients and their families

One effective method of involving physicians in the risk management process is to form a multidisciplinary liability control committee. Each medical service should be represented on this committee, in addition to representatives of the hospital administrative staff.

Administration

Equally as important as the commitment of the medical staff are the support and commitment of senior management and the administrative staff of the health care institution. Ideally, prior to the implementation of a risk management system, senior management and the planning staff will study other institutions' risk management programs, meet with risk management professionals, and assess the specific needs of their facility. However, risk management has been a requirement for more than 15 years, and most institutions have an ongoing risk management program. It is important for top level managers to continue review of the program and to take any necessary action required for its improvement. The institution's governing board and senior management should understand the following factors involved in risk management:

- goals of the risk management program
- benefits of a successful risk management program
- needs of each department to support the risk management program

- importance of being informed about current incidents, claims, and liability suits
- importance of management's commitment and support

A formal, written statement should be issued by the hospital board to declare its support and commitment. Administration and the board must be kept informed of risk management activities, problems, and progress through monthly reports submitted for their review. The risk manager of a health care institution should have direct access to the chief executive officer or chief operating officer. If the risk manager does not report directly to this top officer, there should be an understanding that this line of communication is open when needed.

Department Personnel

Risk management must have not only the commitment of the medical staff, the board, and top level management, but it is imperative that lines of communication with risk management are open and utilized by employees from every department. The risk manager must be aware of everything that is happening in the institution as well as plans for the future. The real challenge of risk management is not insuring against losses but preventing them in the first place. Risk management must be a continuous process that is not possible without the cooperation of all disciplines within the health care institution.

BIBLIOGRAPHY

Health Care Review 2, no. 1 (published on behalf of the University Health Center of Pittsburgh Professional Health Care Provider Committee).

Six Ways to Avoid Failure in Your Hospital, *Healthcare Forum Journal*.

chapter 2

Integrating Quality Assurance and Risk Management

Inge Winer and Claudette Krizek

INTRODUCTION

Many authors have argued for the integration of the quality assurance and risk management functions in recent years. Nevertheless in some hospital settings such a merger is still greeted with as much enthusiasm as a "shotgun wedding." Beginning in January 1989, the Joint Commission on Accreditation of Healthcare Organizations (Joint Commission) required "operational linkages between risk management functions and quality assurance functions, and access of quality assurance functions to risk management information useful in identifying and correcting potential risks in patient care and safety."[1]

This chapter describes how a university hospital assessed its operations and developed a plan for integration of the risk management and quality assurance functions in a way that has proven effective for this institution. Some of the methods developed by the University of Chicago Hospitals, as well as how we overcame obstacles in the path of this "merger," may provide helpful examples for other hospitals struggling with the same issues.

DEFINITIONS

Quality Assurance

Various definitions of quality assurance exist. All of them generally include the description of a system that measures whether patients receive safe, appropriate care leading to the most successful outcomes possible according to the types of illness. When problems are identified that interfere with the delivery of such care, the quality assurance process includes the means to resolve these problems and to ensure that they remain resolved. The University of Chicago Hospitals Quality Assurance Plan (1989) states: "Quality Assurance (QA) is an ongoing planned and comprehensive program designed to objectively and systematically monitor and evaluate the quality and appropriateness of patient care, to pursue opportunities to improve care, and to resolve identified problems."

Risk Management

Risk management has been traditionally "an administrative undertaking intended to protect the financial assets of a health care provider in three ways: by assuring adequate, appropriate insurance coverage against potential liability, by reducing liability when untoward events do occur, and by preventing those events that are most likely to lead to liability."[2] Current definitions of risk management, especially in light of the interest of the Joint Commission, are directed not toward protecting assets, but rather toward protecting patients; protection of assets should follow.

SIMILARITIES AND DIFFERENCES

The patient safety aspect of risk management—preventing those events most likely to lead to patient injury—is the

5

area of greatest interaction between quality assurance and risk management. Poor quality of care that creates a risk of injury to patients poses financial risk both to health care practitioners and to health care facilities. Logically, identification and resolution of problems in patient care will prevent events that may result in patient injury and consequently reduce the potential risk of liability to the health care providers.

In addition to the common aim to ensure patient safety, quality assurance and risk management also use similar methodologies. Both areas depend on the establishment of relevant screening criteria, collection and analysis of data pertaining to those criteria, and correction of identified problems through improvements in the system and individual practices.[3]

Risk management has additional responsibilities to the institution beyond patient safety (see Chapter 1). Quality assurance may deal with improvements in hospital systems that lead to better, more efficient patient care but not necessarily reduce the rate of adverse occurrences.

One obstacle to integration of the two functions often is the need to protect one's "turf." This is usually due to a misunderstanding regarding the differences between the two areas. Risk management may be perceived as the more prestigious area because of its tie to the medical-legal function within the hospital; it also may be viewed with suspicion for the same reason. Further, while quality assurance generally has its organizational linkage through clinical operations, risk management reports to senior administration through medical-legal affairs and the general counsel's office. Although this is not the only model, independence does serve the risk management function.

HISTORY OF QUALITY ASSURANCE

There is a simple black stone in the Louvre Museum in Paris. It is about four feet tall, and covered with cuneiform writing. On this stone Hammurabi's code was written and displayed for the people of Babylonia almost 4,000 years ago. Legal regulations regarding medical practice began with the code that designated extreme sanctions for poor outcomes; a physician could lose a hand if his patient died. (It is uncertain whether extenuating circumstances were taken into account.)

In addition to such legal sanctions, since ancient times the medical profession itself has recognized the potential pitfalls that might tempt physicians and has established ethical guidelines and standards to define professional obligations. The Hippocratic Oath, which includes the promise by the physician "first, do no harm," is still pledged by physicians when they enter the profession.

The twentieth century has seen heightened enhancements in societal expectations of medical care. The physician's liability for malpractice has existed since Hammurabi's stone was carved; hospitals now share direct responsibility for patient care. There has been a change from the *laissez faire* attitude of the nineteenth century, with its charitable immunity for hospitals, to a new theme of corporate responsibility. In the past hospitals saw their function as providing an appropriate environment where physician vendors could render their services; "let the buyer beware" prevailed. Legislation and judicial decisions during the past several decades affirm that hospitals are responsible for the competence and dutiful practice of the physicians whom they accept as members of their medical staffs.

When Dr. Flexner surveyed American medical schools in 1910 on behalf of the Carnegie Foundation to examine medical education, he found many of them to be "diploma mills" that graduated poorly trained, unqualified physicians. No uniform standards or curricula existed.[4] Dr. Flexner's report created a furor, and many of the medical schools were closed as a result.

In 1912 the Third Clinical Congress of Surgeons of North America enacted a resolution stating, "Some system of standardization of hospital equipment and hospital work should be developed, to the end that those institutions having the highest ideals may have proper recognition before the profession and that those of inferior equipment and standards should be stimulated to raise the quality of their work. In this way patients will receive the best type of treatment, and the public will have some means of recognizing those institutions devoted to the highest ideals of medicine." This resolution led to the establishment of the American College of Surgeons (ACS) in 1913.[5]

That same year, Dr. E.A. Codman in a lecture to the Philadelphia Medical Society said, "Every hospital should follow every patient that it treats, long enough to determine whether or not the treatment was successful and then to inquire, if not, why not?"[6] While Dr. Codman was stressing that hospitals were responsible for assessing the care that patients received, the legal climate of the times reflected the belief that "hospitals merely procured physicians for the patient to act on their own responsibility, the workshop idea."[7]

The ACS in 1917 developed a one-page set of minimum standards that stressed the need for an organized medical staff to be responsible for reviewing the care of the patients they treated and presenting cases to a group of peers to further their knowledge and to improve patient care.[8] In 1918, the ACS began a voluntary Hospital Standardization Program providing educational and consultative benefits to hospitals and also demanding compliance with a minimum set of standards for ACS approval.

By 1950 over half of the hospitals in the United States participated in the ACS Hospital Standardization Program. The costs became too great for the ACS to bear alone, and it sought participation of other professional groups. In 1951 the American College of Physicians, the American Medical Association, the American Hospital Association, and the Canadian Medical Association joined with ACS to establish the Joint Commission on Accreditation of Hospitals (Joint Commission). The first Standards for Hospital Accreditation published by the Joint Commission in 1953 were based on the minimum standard of the ACS Hospital Standardization Program.

The Joint Commission in 1966 began to focus on peer review, long a tradition in physician education and training, and initiated requirements for ongoing review through periodic medical "audits." In 1975, explicit and measurable criteria, apart from "medical judgment," were required. In 1979 the Joint Commission dropped the audit requirements and began to emphasize quality assurance in specific problem areas identified by individual hospital medical staffs. The requirement for an organization-wide program to monitor the quality and appropriateness of care was added in 1985. The Joint Commission's more recent "Agenda for Change" calls for specific outcome measures as the preferred indicators of the quality of care that hospitals provide. The early standards of ACS dealt primarily with structural criteria (equipment, an organized medical staff, and requirements for membership), although implicit process criteria were used in the discussion of cases and general outcomes, such as mortality and severe or unusual morbidity, led to the choice of cases to be considered. While Dr. Codman was the first to teach that the outcomes of care should be assessed, the current emphasis on outcomes of care provides a common language for the integration of quality assurance and risk management functions required by the Joint Commission as of January 1989.

Independently, developments in industrial quality control and quality assurance have also influenced current thinking about monitoring and evaluating patient care. W. Edwards Deming's theory of "continuous improvement" applied to industrial production is based on the premise that people are invested in doing their jobs well and gain satisfaction from successful performance. This is a far more acceptable philosophy than the "bad apple"[9] theory apparently promoted by the malpractice crisis of the 1970s. The perception of many physicians that hospitals will extrude rather than educate "problem physicians" has proved to be counterproductive to enthusiastic physician participation in quality assurance and risk management activities.

HISTORY OF RISK MANAGEMENT

The history of risk management is tied to changes in legal precedent more than to the interest of specific health care groups to upgrade professional standards of practice. As previously mentioned, at the same time that Dr. Codman called for a look at physicians' outcomes and ACS re-

quested minimum standards for hospitals and medical staffs, the law upheld the principles of the workshop and *respondeat superior* regarding a hospital's responsibility for patient care. Case law reflects this evaluation.[10]

In a 1965 case, *Darling v. Charleston Community Memorial Hospital*, 211 N.E.2d 253 (Ill. 1965), the court specifically held that the "hospital was liable for direct duties owed to the patients." Again, in *Purcell and Tucson General Hospital v. Zimbelman*, 500 P.2d 335 (Ariz. Ct. App. 1972), the court found that the hospital had failed in its responsibility to the patient and was liable for the acts of the incompetent practitioner on its medical staff through its responsibility for controlling medical staff privileges.

In *Gonzales v. Nork and Mercy Hospital*, 131 Cal. Rptr. 717 (Cal. Ct. App. 1974), the court found that the hospital "was liable for the breach of its duty to the patient to protect him from acts of malpractice by an independent or privately retained physician. The duty was breached if the hospital knew, had reason to know, or should have known of the surgeon's incompetence." Although the hospital argued that it had a medical staff peer review system in place, the court found the system "casual, random, and uncritical."

Although *Darling* was the first case to find a hospital—rather than its physicians—directly responsible for patient care, these cases and others changed the way hospitals discharged responsibility to patients. They clearly established the responsibility of hospitals for a monitoring and evaluation system to identify physicians whose technique, judgment, or motivation is less than optimal. Hospitals are responsible for corrective action in regard to such medical staff members by reducing privileges and imposing other sanctions when necessary to ensure patient safety. Risk management efforts by hospitals were implemented in response to the changing legal climate that culminated in the malpractice crisis of the 1970s.

SAMPLE INTEGRATION PROGRAM

The following describes the quality assurance plan, the risk management activities, and the integration of the two functions at the University of Chicago Hospitals.

Quality Assurance Plan

The quality assurance plan for the University of Chicago Hospitals describes the purpose, objectives, and authority of the quality assurance program. It also outlines the responsibilities of the clinical and hospital departments, the medical staff committees, administrative committees, and mandated hospital-wide quality assurance activities. The organizational structure of the quality assurance program is outlined in Figure 2-1. The plan forms a matrix from which all quality assurance activities within the hospitals evolve.

Figure 2-1
**QUALITY ASSURANCE/RISK MANAGEMENT OPERATIONAL LINKAGE,
UNIVERSITY OF CHICAGO HOSPITALS**

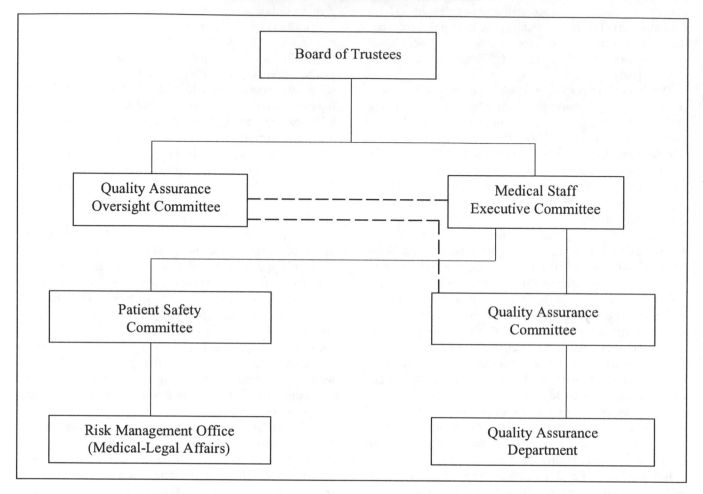

It is revised annually and approved by the president of the University of Chicago Hospitals, the executive vice president of the hospitals, the president of the medical staff organization, and the chairman of the hospitals' Quality Assurance Committee.

The Quality Assurance Oversight Committee is the embodiment of the principle that "quality assurance appears to work best when senior management and senior medical staff members assume responsibility for oversight."[11] This joint administrative and medical staff committee meets twice a month and is chaired by the vice president of the University of Chicago Hospitals. Committee members include the president of the hospitals, the president and vice president of the medical staff, the general counsel for the hospitals, the director of patient safety, the manager of quality assurance, the associate director of the hospitals for nursing, and several other senior managers. The charge of the group is to oversee the quality assurance and risk management pro-

cess and to provide the efforts of the highest clinical and operational authority to the resolution of significant problems affecting patient care. The committee addresses issues related to the following topics:

- compliance with regulatory authorities
- malpractice and potential claims review
- development of quantitative methodology
- review and amendment of policies and procedures for patient care

The Quality Assurance Committee (QAC), as authorized by the Medical Staff Executive Committee, is responsible for all medical staff departmental and committee quality assurance activities. The committee meets twice each month and is chaired by the vice president of the medical staff. Membership includes the chairmen of each medical staff subcommittee: Ambulatory Care Quality Assurance, Committee on Infections and Epidemiology, Medical Records, Pharmacy and Therapeutics, Surgical Case Review, Transfusion and Blood Usage, and Utilization Review. The major clinical departments (medicine, surgery, pediatrics, obstetrics and gynecology, anesthesia and critical care, radiology, and emergency medicine) are represented by physician members. The committee also includes four senior managers, the general counsel for the hospitals, and the director of patient safety. The medical staff administrator and the director of quality assurance provide staff support.

Committee meetings follow a standardized agenda. Subcommittee chairmen report monthly, and each clinical department and medical staff subcommittee presents an annual summary of its activities regarding quality assurance plans, indicators, achievements in improving patient care, and unresolved problems. The summary presentations rotate throughout the year, with several scheduled each month. The QAC assesses the effectiveness of each program and offers recommendations for improvements.

The manager of quality assurance also reviews all departmental and subcommittee minutes and presents any problems remaining unresolved for more than three months to the Quality Assurance Committee. The committee may forward these issues to the Quality Assurance Oversight Committee or the Medical Staff Executive Committee or take other action deemed appropriate. The QAC uses a computerized problem-tracking system to maintain a record of the current status of quality assurance problems. The status report is reviewed monthly by the committee. In addition, other issues are referred to the QAC, such as assessment of Health Care Finance Administration (HCFA) mortality data and the need for improved documentation by the medical staff.

The QAC is also responsible for maintaining medical staff quality assurance activities in compliance with Joint Commission standards. A recent Joint Commission accreditation survey confirmed that the committee has been successful in discharging these duties.

Risk Management Activities

The risk management activities function through the Office of Medical-Legal Affairs of the Hospitals. Patient safety activities are handled by an attorney and three claims investigators. They investigate occurrences and prepare information for the medical and nursing staffs and the administration in accordance with the patient safety plan.

Occurrence Reporting System

The occurrence reporting system was established when the institution formed its own legal office. The reporting system supplies the legal office and the risk management staff with valuable information and insight into the operational aspects of the hospitals.

The patient safety director reports quarterly to the board of trustees on the risk management activities of the hospitals. The profile of incident reports presented as a trending document, along with potential and filed claims and malpractice information, furnishes the trustees with the hospitals' current risk management profile.

Occurrence reports are reviewed daily in the medical-legal affairs office by a claims investigator to obtain an accurate picture of hospital operations from the perspective of patient safety. If an occurrence demands immediate action, it can be reported by telephone and the risk management staff will respond promptly. Specific action is also taken when several reports relate to the same issue. Two recent examples were delays in transferring patients from the recovery room because of lack of beds and difficulties in obtaining supplies from the central supply department. These types of recurring incidents alert the risk management staff to the additional stress occurring on hospital systems during high occupancy and provide risk management the opportunity to inform appropriate staff within the hospital. A monthly report is compiled for each nursing unit and ancillary service with information about the occurrences attributed to it. If a pattern develops that indicates the need for further action, risk management contacts the appropriate hospital committee or medical staff to request resolution of the problem.

Patient Safety Plan

Risk management activities of the hospitals began, as with most hospitals, with occurrence reporting. A broader foundation for the risk management program is now provided by the patient safety plan. Approved nearly a year ago by the hospitals' administration, the Medical Staff Executive Committee, and the board, the plan established a director of patient safety and a Patient Safety Committee. Each is charged with the responsibility of identifying and correcting risks to patients, preferably before harm has occurred.

The Patient Safety Committee meets monthly. It is composed of members of the medical staff who represent the anesthesia and critical care, obstetrics and gynecology, pediatrics, medicine, and surgery departments and members of the nursing staff and hospital administration. The committee's only role is to address risks to patients in an attempt to improve patient care. It makes no decisions on defense, liability, or settlement issues.

Claims Digest. The claims digest is a monthly report of all potential claims received by the medical-legal affairs office. The Patient Safety Committee members review the digest before each meeting. The risk manager informs the committee during the meeting about the disposition of each event and answers questions about the investigation of the cases. The committee is also apprised of corrective steps taken by the risk management office or other staff in situations where ongoing risks are identified. A committee member may request that a case study be prepared for in-depth discussion of patient safety issues.

Case Studies. A case study is a detailed narrative of a particular event described by the patient safety staff, along with patient safety issues amenable to discussion and reso-lution. These individual cases, selected either by the com-mittee or by the patient safety staff because of issues that present ongoing risks to patients, have been fruitful in analyzing actual and present risk. The committee chairman communicates with medical staff members or chairmen of clinical departments and attempts to resolve problems. Members of the committee may also communicate with their respective departments about issues that are relevant to them. A case study often prompts the committee's request for a medical staff member to attend a committee meeting for a discussion of patient safety issues.

Death Review. The Quality Assurance Department com-piles data on all hospital deaths based on an adaptation of HCFA's mortality risk factors. The list of deaths, including the associated risk factors, causes of death, and patients' ages, is given to the Patient Safety Committee for assess-ment. Specific cases may be selected by the committee for further review. This lends an independent and objective oversight to the mortality review process. The mortality figures can be tabulated and compared over time and across ICD9 codes.

Other Risk Indicators. Monitors and other risk indica-tors also may be reported to the committee. Patterns of nursing units (e.g., falls or medication errors from occur-rence reports) and patterns of departments or physicians (morbidity and mortality) can be compared. The patient safety staff has compiled a list of "attributes." When an event is entered into the computer, the tentative cause of the event is included. Approximately 40 attributes are listed; they vary from four kinds of medication errors to problems with supervision of residents or failure to follow hospital practice. Other factors also are documented in patient safety data that are not causes of morbidity or mortality but that may constitute poor practice and create a higher risk of unhappy patients or families or that may make defense of a case more difficult. "Fingerpointing" among members of the staff and poor documentation are included in this category. These attributes can be correlated across depart-ments and over time. This is another attempt to profile for the hospital, through the Patient Safety Committee and the patient safety staff, those areas where risks to patients may be identified.

Review of Responses to Committee Inquiry. A review of responses to the committee's inquiries generally reflects sincere cooperation and a willingness to discuss issues and resolve problems to mutual satisfaction. Examples of issues

in which the committee initiated participation by medical staff members include the role of the attending psychiatrist in competency decision making when the patient refuses lifesaving care and the appropriateness of discharging a minor patient from the emergency room.

Providing Protection for Risk Management Activities

Many traditional risk management materials and occur-rence reporting documents may be held discoverable in litigation involving a reported occurrence. An important aspect of risk management activities is providing protection from admissibility and discoverability in a court case, where possible. The Medical Studies Act of Illinois[12] pro-vides protection to hospital and medical staff committees whose purpose is to improve patient care and reduce mor-bidity and mortality. This is an important reason for the structure of the Patient Safety Committee. Under the plan, the patient safety director acts within the auspices of the committee. Since activities of committees are often cum-bersome and depend upon meetings separated by a month's time, the plan allows the patient safety director, under the auspices of the committee, to act quickly with the consul-tation of the committee chairman. Such actions are then reported and ratified by the committee, so that they remain the committee's responsibility and thus within the protec-tion of the Medical Studies Act. Because the patient safety activities address patient safety, rather than the security of hospital assets, they should fall within the purview of state legislation protecting quality assurance activities.

Therefore, it is crucial to plan the relationship of quality assurance and risk management to make clear that, to the extent possible, risk management activities, like quality assurance, fall within such protection. Where appropriate, the language of the legislation was incorporated into the patient safety plan. Finally, the name of the risk manage-ment program reflects the patient safety aspects of risk management and again conforms to the statute. Other hospitals should consult relevant state legislation for pro-tection of their risk management activities.

Access to Information

Information about events and activities within the hospi-tal, particularly from the medical and nursing staffs, is the risk manager's best tool. Although the risk manager obvi-ously must cultivate his or her own sources of information, the patient safety plan provides that the patient safety director shall have full access to data and information relevant to patient safety throughout the hospitals—from hospital offices and committees and from the medical staff. The plan also specifically indicates certain offices that must furnish such data, including infection control, quality assurance, surgical case review, and credentialing. The close working relationship between quality assurance and risk management facilitates the exchange of information.

Confidentiality

Materials and data prepared for the Patient Safety Committee constitute some of the most confidential information within the hospitals. Protecting this information is an important feature of the patient safety plan. Materials are prepared without names or other identification; printed material is distributed on the day before the committee meeting in a special numbered folder and is returned to the patient safety office at the close of the meeting. The committee is intentionally kept small, and confidentiality is stressed. Committee members, appointed by the president of the hospitals and the president of the medical staff in consultation with the patient safety director, are selected for their ability to view incidents in the context of the protection of patients, the hospitals, and the medical staff, rather than individually or even departmentally.

Quality Assurance and Risk Management Integration

Quality assurance and risk management colleagues from other institutions have reported that the most successful examples of integration of quality assurance and risk management occur where there is a good professional relationship among the people who perform these functions. With open communication, misunderstandings are less likely to occur. This can be fostered through weekly meetings, mutual responsibilities, access to material, information referral, and partnership efforts.

Data Review at Weekly Meetings

The patient safety director and quality assurance manager meet weekly to share information about problems and potential problems in patient care. Data gathered by the quality assurance staff (see Exhibit 2-1) are discussed, as well as information concerning significant occurrences that have been reported to the medical-legal affairs office. If the possibility of a systems problem exists, a joint decision may be made to set up indicators regarding the issue and to have performance monitored by quality assurance staff. The resulting data are summarized and presented to the Patient Safety Committee, the relevant clinical department, or the hospital administrator for appropriate action.

Mutual Committee Responsibilities

Mutual committee responsibilities of the quality assurance and patient safety staffs further enhance the relation-

ship between the two functions. Representatives from both offices serve on all hospital committees that review patient care. These include the Quality Assurance Task Force, the Quality Assurance Committee, the Hospital Safety Committee, and the Patient Safety Committee.

Mutual Access to Material

In interchanges between quality assurance and risk management, the importance of maintaining protection of relevant state legislation (see discussion above) is a priority. The data review and other material requested by risk management through the use of the screening form are generally reviewed orally during the weekly meetings and not committed to writing. The problems that are revealed can be pursued by risk management's preparation of potential claims for the claims digest or by case studies when

---

Exhibit 2-1
PATIENT SAFETY/RISK MANAGEMENT SCREENING FORM

I. Surgical Case Review Committee
   A. All cases determined by the committee to be inappropriately performed

II. Section of Emergency Medicine
   A. All transfers that do not meet the Consolidated Omnibus Budget Reconciliation Act's criteria
   B. All returns to emergency room within seven days that might reflect missed diagnoses

III. Transfusion Committee
   A. Transfusion reactions
   B. Incorrect administration of blood

IV. Infectious Disease Section
   A. Nosocomial infections leading to death
   B. All cases of Legionnaires' disease, Aspergillus, and Fusarium

V. Pharmacy and Therapeutics Committee
   A. Those adverse drug reactions determined by committee review to be level 1 or 2

VI. Department of Medicine
   A. Return to intensive care unit
   B. Cardiopulmonary resuscitation

VII. Department of Anesthesia and Critical Care
   A. Internal criteria developed by the department

VIII. Department of Obstetrics and Gynecology
   A. Mother returned to delivery room or operating room
   B. Infant birth trauma or injury
   C. Standard of care not met according to department's criteria

appropriate. The ability of the risk management office to tap the quality assurance data has proved invaluable. Further, if a problem reported by risk management requires monitoring, the quality assurance staff is able to implement it appropriately as determined through this information exchange.

Cross Referral of Specific Information

Types of specific information referred to patient safety from quality assurance may include "bumps" in the mortality or morbidity data from particular clinical sections or for certain ICD9 codes. This information could prompt patient safety to investigate the data and to prepare appropriate potential claims files for review by the relevant clinical departments and the Patient Safety Committee.

Risk Management Referral of Specific Information

Information referred to quality assurance from risk management for monitoring may involve the existence of a specific event, for example, failure to leave patient on a monitor. Quality assurance can then review the use of patient monitors to determine if the incident reflects an isolated event or a pattern of risk. By monitoring compliance with any stated nursing standard and reporting the data over a period of weeks or months, the quality assurance staff can determine whether a problem actually exists. The appropriate committee or department can then address the problem described by the data.

Partnership Advantages

The patient safety director and the quality assurance director or coordinator are members of the Quality Assurance Task Force and combine their efforts in that group to ensure that problems are addressed as required. Although formal reporting relationships differ for quality assurance and risk management, these differences are viewed as

advantages by both departments. Actual merger of the two departments would not be considered beneficial in this setting. The independence of the risk manager from managerial obligations to clinical operations or departments is viewed as particularly important. It could be in the interest of a clinical operations manager to suppress or understate the significance of an identified risk. The independent reporting obligations of the risk manager to the chief of clinical operations and the general counsel's office, however, ensure appropriate attention. The close and mutual support of risk management and quality assurance enhances the functions of both.

NOTES

1. Joint Commission on Accreditation of Healthcare Organizations, *Accreditation Manual for Hospitals,* Appendix B, MA. 1.8 through MA. 1.8.3 (Chicago: 1989), 290.

2. G. Chapman-Cliburn, ed., *Risk Management and Quality Assurance: Issues and Interactions.* A Special Publication of the *Quality Review Bulletin* (Chicago: Joint Commission on Accreditation of Hospitals, 1986), 5.

3. Chapman-Cliburn, *Risk Management,* 6.

4. A. Flexner, *Medical Education in the United States and Canada.* A Report to the Carnegie Foundation for the Advancement of Teaching. Carnegie Foundation Bulletin No. 4 (New York: Carnegie Foundation, 1910).

5. J.E. Affeldt and R.M. Walczak, The Role of JCAH in Assuring Quality Care, in *Hospital Quality Assurance* (Gaithersburg, Md.: Aspen Publishers, Inc., 1984), 50.

6. L. Davis, *Fellowships of Surgeons: A History of the American College of Surgeons* (Chicago: Charles C Thomas, 1960), 116.

7. Schloendorff v. Society of New York Hospital, 105 N.E. 92 (N.Y. 1914).

8. Davis, *Fellowship of Surgeons,* 65.

9. D.M. Berwick, Continuing Improvement as an Ideal in Health Care, *New England Journal of Medicine* 320 (1989): 53–56.

10. Affeldt and Walczak, *Hospital Quality Assurance,* 52.

11. Affeldt and Walczak, *Hospital Quality Assurance,* 59.

12. Medical Studies Act, Illinois Revised Statutes 1987, Chapter 110, Section 8–2101.

chapter 3

Setting up a Risk Management Department

Barbara J. Youngberg
Thomas V. Ealy

INTRODUCTION

Much has been written about the need to analyze carefully the needs of an institution before determining the configuration, goals, and organizational structure of a risk management department. Important considerations, such as the role the risk manager will play in the institution, the interface and support the risk manager will receive from other hospital departments, and the outside support provided to the risk manager and staff, will influence hiring requirements, program support, and program design.

RISK MANAGEMENT IDENTIFICATION

The purpose of this chapter is to assist the reader in identifying activities that are typically considered part of the risk management discipline. A description is provided of responsibilities involved in each area of risk management that will help the reader determine if a specific function should be included in an individual hospital program. It may, on the other hand, convince the reader that the function is already being handled—and perhaps more appropriately—by another department in the organization. Following this initial program overview and analysis, risk manage-ment structures are provided that address various organizational models. Sample job descriptions (Exhibits 3-1 through 3-5) are provided for several positions that may be required to staff a comprehensive risk management program.

In determining the functions that should come under the purview of a risk management department, it is essential to analyze each suggested function and ask the following questions:

- Is this a function necessary or appropriate for the successful control of risk at this institution?
- Is this function already being handled by another department within the hospital?
- If so, which department is more appropriate for handling this responsibility?
- Are outside consultants performing the work described in this function?
- If outside firms or consultants are being utilized, is this the most efficient and cost-effective method for providing this service?
- What would be the possible negative repercussions from placing this function under the risk management program?
- What would be the benefits of placing this function under risk management?
- What type of risk management staff is needed to support this function?

Exhibit 3-1
SAMPLE JOB DESCRIPTION FOR DIRECTOR OF RISK MANAGEMENT

QUALIFICATIONS

1. Minimum of a Bachelor's degree in business or health-related field
2. Master's degree preferred in business, hospital administration, or other health-related field
3. Excellent oral and written communication skills essential
4. Insurance and claims management experience a plus

REPORTING RELATIONSHIP

Reports directly to the Chief Executive Officer or her or his designee. Reports to legal counsel on matters involving hospital professional liability.

RESPONSIBILITIES

1. Management of insurance program for all hospital coverage:
   —Responsibility of program components, including professional liability, general liability, workers' compensation, motor vehicle liability, property, directors and officers, fiduciary liability (ERISA), electronic data processing coverage
   —Identification and evaluation of markets and options
   —Allocation of risk through the purchase of commercial insurance, deductibles, self-insured funds; evaluation of financial feasibility
   —Allocation of premium among insured entities
   —Oversight of reserves in relation to limits
2. Loss control and claims management:
   —Monitor incidents and claims reporting systems
   —Coordinate with carrier the investigation and defense of all claims and suits
   —Cooperate with medical peer review and institutional committees on issues related to standards of care
   —Develop programs and systems necessary for self-insurance
   —Provide guidance as required to security and environmental safety personnel
3. Coordination with hospital quality assurance programs:
   —Develop a system to share hospital-wide quality of care data with appropriate departments and administrative personnel
   —Develop a system for tracking and trending of generic screening monitors to assist in the identification of potentially high-risk behavior leading to patient, staff, and visitor injuries
   —Develop appropriate operational linkages to correct actual and potential problems that have been identified
4. Resource for education on risk management:
   —Develop a formal program for ongoing education for all hospital staff
   —Respond to crisis situations that have risk management implications and assist staff with problem solving
5. Administrative duties and responsibilities:
   —Supervise all professional and support staff in the Risk Management Department
   —Monitor department budget and assets of self-insurance funds
   —Represent department on appropriate hospital committees as assigned

FUNCTIONS OF RISK MANAGEMENT

Insurance Purchasing

The early theories of risk management are derived from an insurance framework in which risks are transferred through the purchase of insurance. Risk managers were often assigned the responsibility of working with insurance brokers to identify and analyze the available commercial products that would best meet the needs of their organizations. Risk managers also had the responsibility of presenting the risks of the organization in such a way that the underwriter could correctly analyze the risks to be insured. With changes in the insurance marketplace, many risk managers also have been required to analyze the alternatives to the purchase of commercial insurance and to determine which, if any, of these alternatives provide the greatest protection at the least cost to the insured. Often, a large hospital with formal self-insurance and offshore cap-

tive programs may find that it needs additional staff to run what is in essence a small insurance company for the organization.

A hospital that follows the more traditional approach of purchasing commercial insurance should evaluate the services supplied by a carrier or broker and hire risk management staff to support, but not duplicate, the services required. These services may include the following:

- claims handling and litigation support
- computer support
- risk management education
- technical coverage and policy determinations

Claims Handling

The handling of actual and potential lawsuits is frequently assigned to a hospital risk management department. If in-house legal counsel is employed by the hospital, it may also perform or share this responsibility. There are many

Exhibit 3-2
SAMPLE JOB DESCRIPTION FOR SAFETY MANAGER

QUALIFICATIONS

1. Minimum of a Bachelor's degree required
2. Health care and safety experience preferred
3. Knowledge of regulatory and legislative issues and acts related to safety and waste management
4. Excellent interpersonal skills required
5. Good oral and written communication skills essential
6. Ability to make independent judgments and pay close attention to detail required

REPORTING RELATIONSHIP

Reports directly to the Director of Risk Management. Reports indirectly to legal counsel and to senior administrative staff.

RESPONSIBILITIES

Responsibility for all aspects of the hospital safety program, including the following:

1. Review and document employee incidents that relate to safety issues and investigate those with possible negligence, liability, or loss. Discuss incidents with individuals involved and obtain written statements as required. Maintain statistical tabulations and summaries of employee safety-related occurrences and make appropriate reports to various agencies as required by law.
2. Maintain statistical tabulations and summaries of safety-related incidents involving patients and visitors and other occurrences as directed by the risk manager.
3. Review and investigate patient and visitor incident reports as required.

4. Conduct routine physical inspection of the entire hospital plant and grounds to identify existing safety hazards, code violations, and other physical conditions that may represent a threat to the safety of patients, employees, and visitors.
5. Receive and investigate employee complaints concerning possible safety problems within the hospital.
6. Chair and document the proceedings of the Hospital Safety Committee and Disaster Planning Committee.
7. Develop, implement, and maintain educational safety programs for all hospital personnel.
8. Conduct fire drills as required by municipal codes and other standards or requirements. Conduct disaster drills as required by the Joint Commission on Accreditation of Healthcare Organizations.
9. Coordinate revisions of the safety, fire, and disaster planning; bomb threat; laboratory safety; radiation safety; and waste management and disposal policies. Create and update manuals as required.
10. Provide knowledge to staff and enforce the safety rules and regulations as set forth by: Building Officials and Code Administrators (BOCA), National Fire Protection Association (NFPA), Occupational Safety and Health Administration (OSHA), and the Joint Commission on Accreditation of Healthcare Organizations.
11. Act as liaison between the hospital and the fire department, state and local licensing agencies, and insurance carriers.
12. Perform other duties as related to the risk management/safety program as assigned.
13. Prepare formal reports for senior management as required.
14. Act as liaison with the Security Department regarding matters of safety such as bomb threats and civil defense.

Exhibit 3-3
SAMPLE JOB DESCRIPTION FOR WORKERS' COMPENSATION SPECIALIST

QUALIFICATIONS

1. Bachelor of Arts or Sciences or the equivalent in experience
2. Prior workers' compensation claims experience
3. Excellent oral and written communication skills
4. Excellent judgment
5. Ability to work independently

REPORTING RELATIONSHIP

Reports directly to the Director of Risk Management.

RESPONSIBILITIES

Responsibility for processing workers' compensation claims and maintaining insurance requirements mandated by state law and internal hospital guidelines. Specific duties include the following:

1. Coordinate and process work-related incident reports, claims, and related expenses
2. Establish and maintain employee claim files and files related to Occupational Safety and Health Administration (OSHA) requirements.
3. Design reports using the risk management information system for analyses, trend tracking, and interdepartmental communications
4. Assist in the coordination of workers' compensation insurance
5. Serve on committees associated with workers' safety
6. Implement new workers' compensation programs as necessary
7. Act as liaison with health, safety, and security personnel and with the Human Resources Department

Exhibit 3-4 **SAMPLE JOB DESCRIPTION FOR CLAIMS MANAGER**	**Exhibit 3-5** **SAMPLE JOB DESCRIPTION FOR QUALITY MANAGER**

<table>
<tr>
<td>

QUALIFICATIONS:

1. Bachelor's degree in health care, business, or law
2. Minimum of five years of professional liability claims experience
3. Data base management experience desirable
4. Excellent interpersonal skills required
5. Good oral and written communication skills
6. Ability to communicate effectively with physicians, nurses, and other health care professionals
7. Excellent negotiating skills required
8. Working knowledge of insurance coverage a plus

REPORTING RELATIONSHIP

    Reports directly to the Director of Risk Management. Reports indirectly to hospital legal counsel.

RESPONSIBILITIES

    Responsibility for all aspects of claim and lawsuit management, including the following:

1. Evaluate the litigation potential of all incidents and adverse outcomes occurring within the hospital
2. Establish claim files and estimate reserves
3. Coordinate the preparation of staff who may be called as witnesses at trials or depositions
4. Act as a representative of the hospital at selected legal proceedings
5. Assume responsibility for settlement negotiations under the direction of the Director of Risk Management with settlement authority up to $5,000
6. Identify problem areas related to particular claims that may indicate staff educational needs
7. Prepare and review all disbursements for approval from the various self-insurance funds
8. Manage the preparation of a data base to include all claims information
9. Design claims reports for use by hospital department heads, administration, and appropriate committees

</td>
<td>

QUALIFICATIONS

1. Minimum of a Bachelor's degree in nursing
2. Clinical expertise in critical care, obstetrics, or recovery room
3. Minimum of five years of clinical or teaching experience
4. Quality assurance experience desirable
5. Excellent interpersonal skills
6. Good oral and written communication skills

REPORTING RELATIONSHIP

    Reports directly to the Director of Risk Management. Direct working relationship (but not reporting relationship) with the Director of Quality Assurance.

RESPONSIBILITIES

This position focuses on the identification, evaluation, and modification of high-risk clinical activities occurring within the hospital that may give rise to patient injury or suit. The following duties are required to accomplish these goals:

1. Implement an early warning system to identify areas of potential clinical exposure
2. Review all quality assurance data with quality assurance personnel to identify significant risk trends
3. Coordinate communications among various departments and committees to enhance problem resolution, facilitate corrective action, and prevent recurrences
4. Process reports of incidents, claims, suits, and complaints for review by medical staff and quality assurance committees
5. Work closely with individual clinical departments and assist in the development of appropriate department-specific clinical monitors
6. Assess the educational needs of the hospital staff and participate in risk management education programs
7. Serve as a resource to staff and department heads

</td>
</tr>
</table>

advantages to having this function managed within the hospital. They include the following:

- The level of comfort among hospital staff members involved in actual or potential lawsuits is generally greater when they deal with familiar persons who will have the best interests of the hospital and its staff in mind when managing claims. Thus a hospital risk manager may be able to elicit more candid and forth-

right comments about the care rendered than an outside claims adjuster.
- Clinical staff involved in the claims process can conduct a more thorough evaluation of issues that are related to the standard of medical and nursing care rendered in a case.
- The hospital staff is generally committed to presenting the hospital in the most favorable light and may handle claims more aggressively than an outside adjuster.

- Confidentiality issues remain in house if the hospital staff works directly with defense counsel.
- The costs of evaluation and defense are generally less if the bulk of investigations and evaluations occurs internally.

Unfortunately, efficient claims handling requires considerable staff expertise. If risk management is in charge of this function, the staff must have a thorough knowledge of the legal environment. Staff members also should have a working knowledge of the clinical issues relating to alleged injuries. When the risk manager does not have this information, he or she must have access to a committee or list of practitioners within the hospital who can provide this assistance. The risk manager also must be familiar with the legal system and understand the process that takes place when a lawsuit is filed. This part of the function may be assumed by outside adjusters or defense counsel or performed by a claims-handling service. However, the hospital administration must carefully weigh the costs against the benefits if claims handling is not one of the risk manager's responsibilities.

Proactive Clinical Risk Management

Risk management programs today often take a proactive approach to the risk environment. Integrating various aspects of risk management discipline with those of quality assurance has allowed risk managers to identify and manage clinical areas where losses occur and to analyze specific behaviors and practices that frequently result in injury and litigation. The risk manager can then develop educational programs that will increase sensitivity to risk and more readily enable the staff to identify potential threats to the hospital and its personnel.

A proactive risk management program looks at quality-related issues and works diligently with physicians and other staff to help them understand the risk management process and methods of interacting with staff, patients, and their families to minimize the risk of becoming involved in litigation. The types of services and skills required for proactive risk management mandate that their development receive support from within the hospital. Outside consultants are seldom able to operate this type of program successfully, because the hospital staff usually relates more favorably when it deals with in-house risk management personnel. (See Chapter 28 for more details on proactive, clinically specific risk management programs.)

Patient Guest Relations

The operation of a patient guest relations or hospital ombudsman program is often assigned to the risk management department. Because it is generally true that people do not sue people they like, hospital administrators are starting to recognize the importance of a system that listens to and supports patients and their families when questions arise about the quality or adequacy of care. If this service is not directly under the risk management department, at least there should be a mechanism in place to allow for the sharing of information between the two departments.

When the risk manager learns that a patient has been injured, the patient representative can begin working with family members to allow them to vent their frustration and request answers to their questions. Conversely, when a patient representative speaks with a disgruntled patient, he or she can notify the risk manager of the actual or perceived problem; this enables the risk manager to intervene and more fully investigate the situation.

Risk Finance

This aspect of risk management involves a systematic analysis of the cost associated with quantifying risk and funding for it. This responsibility may be delegated to the finance department of an institution, but often the funding associated with a hospital's risk environment is best determined by the risk manager.

The risk manager is able to analyze the exposures (and the dollars associated with them) for each of the high-risk clinical specialties within the hospital and is familiar with its historical loss payout data. Risk financing requires much more than a retrospective cost analysis. At the very least, an active risk management program should have input into financial decisions as they relate to the funding of risk. The risk manager's insight into faculty and staff, high-risk procedures, and claims history is an invaluable addition to this process.

Education

A significant part of the risk manager's job should focus on education. Other hospital departments also play important roles in staff education, but the role of the risk manager in this process cannot be underestimated. The risk manager should interface with the staff education department to coordinate educational programs and determine the topics most relevant to individual staff groups. Whenever possible, the risk manager should participate in new employee orientation and be a part of all staff continuing education. (An example of specific educational programs appropriate for risk management is found in Chapter 23.)

Quality Assurance

Smaller hospitals may wish to establish a single department to handle quality assurance and risk management.

Figure 3-1
SAMPLE ORGANIZATIONAL CHART OF A QUALITY ASSURANCE/RISK MANAGEMENT DEPARTMENT

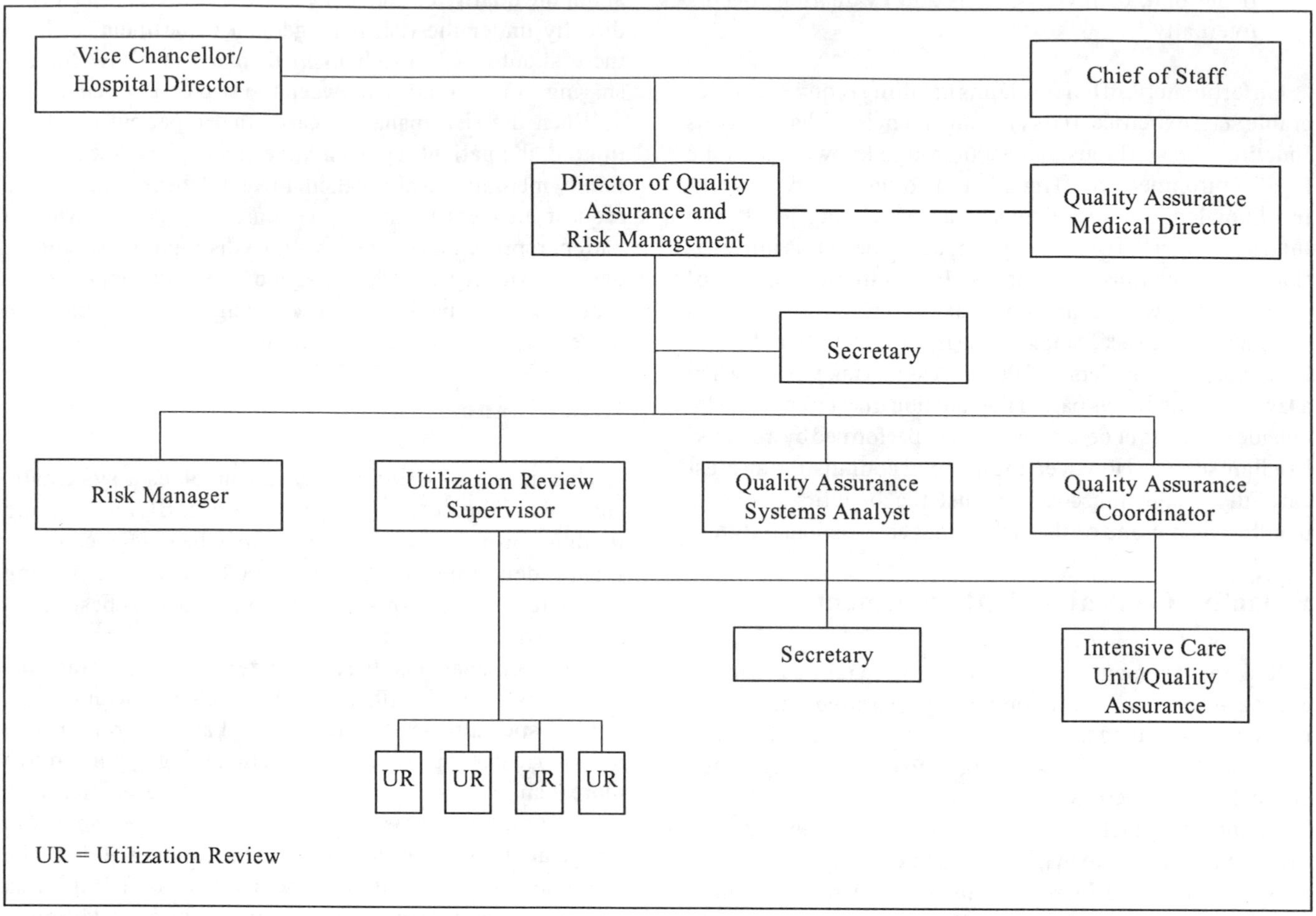

UR = Utilization Review

(See sample organizational and flow charts for this combined activity in Figures 3-1 and 3-2.) This can be more readily accomplished if the right staff person is chosen. Obviously, the ideal person has a clinical background as well as the knowledge and ability to deal with issues related to claims investigation and evaluation. This individual must also possess the ability to relate well with physicians and nurses, because the major focus of a hospital-wide quality assurance program involves quality of care issues.

Other responsibilities of a quality assurance department frequently include the following:

- utilization review and management
- medical staff credentialing and reappointment
- infection control
- discharge abstracting
- concurrent diagnosis and diagnosis-related group (DRG) coding
- severity indexing
- DRG case mix analysis
- medical records

It may be difficult to find someone with expertise in all of these areas. In that case, the hospital may establish a better program by dividing the various responsibilities among several individuals.

PHYSICIAN SUPPORT FOR RISK MANAGEMENT

Many risk managers have complained about physicians' traditional lack of interest in the risk management effort. Risk management also has been viewed negatively by some physicians who may associate it only with litigation, finding of fault, and technical insurance-related issues.

Figure 3-2
SAMPLE FLOW CHART FOR QUALITY ASSURANCE/RISK MANAGEMENT

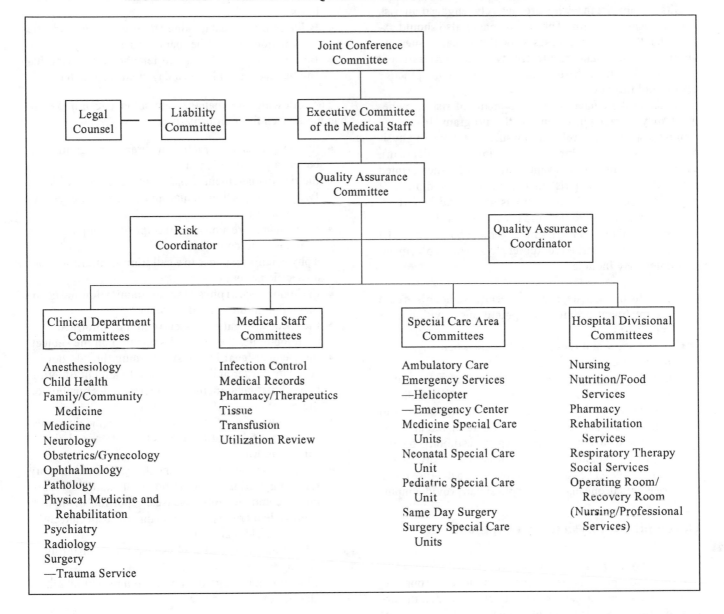

With the change in focus of risk management, physician involvement is no longer a luxury—it is a necessity. Clinically based programs will be endorsed only by departments that have been given the opportunity to assist in their development and to identify risk management factors significant to them. Their active and ongoing involvement in department-specific programs can help to determine potential problems and make necessary changes *before* patients are injured.

When selling the concepts of risk management to physicians, the risk manager must stress that the discipline has changed. The focus is now on offering quality service rather than finding fault. Physicians also should understand the aspect of risk management that addresses the defense of lawsuits and the evaluation of claims and how their involvement in the early investigative stage may actually prevent a suit and aid in a favorable resolution of a claim.

It is often easier to engage physicians who are employees of the hospital in the risk management process, especially when they are appointed to various risk management committees by the hospital chief executive officer or by the chief of staff. However, physicians who have staff privileges at the hospital but are not employees may need to have the values of risk management and their involvement in it "personalized" so that the benefits become more apparent to the individual practitioners. For example, the risk manager may be able to provide these physicians with information from professional liability insurers who offer premium credits to physicians who are actively engaged in risk management programs. The risk manager also should explain that the program focuses on quality of care issues and on helping physicians to identify types of behaviors and practices that have historically resulted in malpractice claims and litigation.

Stressing the educational components of risk management may attract physicians to the program. In-service seminars specifically related to issues that concern physicians (how to avoid malpractice litigation is a popular item), as well as copies of relevant articles and other printed material, may also help risk managers to gain credibility. If physicians perceive the program as useful and important, they are more likely to become involved in it.

A number of important risk management functions can be identified and earmarked for direct physician involvement. Examples may include:

- establishment of department-specific standards of care for treatment provided by practitioners within their specialties
- peer review and required follow-up when physicians fail to meet the standards
- initial review of hospital records when a lawsuit is filed or when the risk manager or physician believes that a suit may address standards of care, in order to identify and support care that was rendered and colleagues who can provide expert testimony on the physician's behalf (leaving litigation solely in the hands of defense counsel can result in a defense much weaker than one in which the physician provides input)

Developing a Physician's Handbook

A handbook or manual for physicians that specifically describes the types of issues and concerns under the purview of risk management can be beneficial to the health care organization. By engaging physicians in the process of working with the risk management department on the project and distributing the handbook to all physicians, a constant risk management "presence" can be enforced.

The following suggestions are typical of the contents that would be helpful to physicians:

- The handbook should be small enough to fit easily into a laboratory coat pocket or readily be available on all hospital units, so that it is readily available in an emergency.
- Information that includes important hospital telephone extensions, the year's calendar, normal laboratory values for common tests, a list of routine preoperative

tests, and other practical data increases the likelihood that physicians will refer to the handbook on a daily basis.
- Brief summary data, rather than extensive didactic information, makes the manual user friendly.
- Emergency and information telephone numbers that can be reached 24 hours a day should be included.

The following risk management subjects can make the handbook even more informative:

- the hospital's malpractice insurance program, if it covers a physician's practice
- the risk management department's system for identifying and reporting actual and potential losses and patient injuries
- a physician's response to receipt of a subpoena or a summons and complaint
- a physician's response to a call from an attorney about a specific patient or case
- the importance of physician communication and documentation in the care of patients
- the medical-legal issues surrounding informed consent, including the hospital's position on the subject
- the medical-legal issues surrounding the "do-not-resuscitate" order and the care and treatment of terminally ill patients, including the hospital's position on these matters
- a brief checklist of issues related to medical records, such as confidentiality, access to records, and disclosure of information
- various state legal requirements related to statutory reporting, testing, and treatment (for example, reporting of communicable diseases, reporting of injuries from violent crimes, and reporting of suspected child, spouse, or elder abuse)
- a brief discussion of a physician's responsibility in dealing with an impaired colleague
- a list of risk management education programs scheduled for the coming year

Obviously, this list can be altered in any manner, according to the perceived needs of the physicians who practice within the organization. Their input into the contents of the handbook can make it a useful and valuable product.

CREATING MEANINGFUL RISK MANAGEMENT REPORTS

When the hospital risk management program becomes effective, the risk manager must collect and measure data to show the value of the risk management effort. This data collection also enables the risk manager to identify areas in need of additional risk management support and to recognize aspects of care that may require modification, additional resources, or termination.

A mechanism is required that will enable the risk manager to communicate the program's statistics in a meaningful way. The development of a good reporting format will greatly enhance the risk manager's ability to prove the value of risk management to the administration and the governing board. This device can also help the risk manager gain the necessary support to make important changes in the program even if they are not initially endorsed or supported by physicians and hospital staff.

Before developing appropriate reports, it is necessary to identify a number of factors. First, the risk manager must decide for whom a specific report is intended. Risk management reports may vary in type of information provided, depending on the groups that will receive them. Generally, risk management reports are reviewed by the following:

- board of trustees
- hospital executive committee
- medical staff
- joint conference committee

Second, the risk manager should determine the purpose of the report. Answers to the following questions may be helpful:

- Is the report prepared in compliance with a regulatory or licensure agency?
- Is the purpose of the report to introduce the goals and functions of the risk management program to the board?
- Is the purpose of the report to demonstrate the value of the risk management program?
- Is the report presented to provide the board with financial information associated with the hospital's professional liability exposure?
- Is the report prepared to enable the board to comply with its public duty and legal obligation to the hospital?
- Is the purpose of the report to assist the hospital's marketing effort or does it focus on particular strengths and weaknesses of the hospital?
- Is systematic, regular reporting by the risk manager to the hospital's governing body and administration required by hospital policy?

Third, the risk manager should evaluate the background and function of the group who will receive the information. For example, if the report is being prepared for hospital administrative officers, they usually require less background information about the day-to-day operation of the risk management program than the governing board. Directors or trustees, however, may need information related not only to the role of risk management within the hospital, but also to their legal responsibilities as they relate to quality of care. This aspect of risk management has emerged with such landmark legal decisions as *Darling v. Charleston Memorial Hospital,* 211 N.E.2d 253 (Ill. 1965), *cert. denied,* 383 U.S. 946 (1966), and *Johnson v. Misericordia,* 301 N.W.2d 156 (Wis. 1981).

Reports should be prepared in a manner that allows recipients to gain necessary information without becoming overburdened by unnecessary details. Graphics are appropriate when presenting statistical data and information showing changes over time. There is limited value in providing raw number data (for example, the number of claims per quarter) to board members without also providing total numbers or denominator data (such as admissions without incident). It is also helpful to provide the board with data that indicate changes (for example, is the hospital improving its care or is it getting worse?). Reports demonstrating changes and improvements are more actionable than those that merely provide numerical information.

Following a basic introduction describing the purpose and goals of the risk management program and its interface with the hospital mission, the risk manager may wish to include such information as listed below:

- the number of incident reports filed during the quarter (include figures for the number of incidents during the prior quarter and during the same quarter of the prior year, if available)
- a breakdown of figures to identify incidents that occurred in "high-risk" areas or those the risk manager believes to be meritorious or likely to result in a claim (these incidents also should be compared to prior quarter and prior year statistics)
- the number of active lawsuits and the dollars reserved for these cases
- the number of claims and suits closed during the quarter with a brief narrative as to how they were resolved (for example, settled, dismissed, or tolling of statute)
- the portion of the hospital budget spent on payment of claims and lawsuits (with comparison figures for prior quarter and year)

Some boards or administrators may wish to see data that compares the hospital with other institutions. The risk manager should stress that such comparative data can be misleading unless the other institutions offer similar services; have the same patient mix and case mix; have a similar incident tracking, reporting, and reserving philosophy; and are located in the same or similar geographic area. It is usually more beneficial to compare the hospital against itself by providing statistical data broken down by quarters and compared with previous years.

The risk manager may wish to highlight specific problem areas or significant improvements that have occurred during the quarter. This type of information helps the board to understand the dynamics of a risk management process and also should help to maintain the board's interest in the program.

COMMUNICATING RISK MANAGEMENT INFORMATION TO THE BOARD*

The stakes in health care risk management have never been higher. With health care spending continuing to spiral upward, consuming an ever greater share of the gross domestic product (GDP), focus has shifted to the health care delivery system and those who provide care within that system. Providing higher quality care at a lower cost and getting people out of the hospital faster places higher demands on providers and exposes them to potentially greater risks. Compounding the challenges faced by risk managers is the higher potential risk of injury to patients resulting from elimination of support services, dwindling staffs, and shrinking health care budgets.

With organizational and personal stakes so high, and resources so precious, it is more important than ever for a risk manager to have a well-defined risk management strategy that articulates to senior managers the vital role played by risk management in helping the organization meet its goals. The challenge is not so much in crafting a risk management strategy that anticipates and advances the organization's objectives and public responsibility to provide quality health care, but in communicating the strategy with data that grab senior management's attention and drive home risk management's acute importance.

One way to express the vitality of health care risk management (and thereby ensure that protecting the organization's assets and revenues, while at the same time providing high quality care, is foremost in the minds of senior managers), is to tightly link the risk management strategy to the organization's mission and strategic vision. This linkage might be best understood by demonstrating risk management's relationship to the organization in the following three key areas:

- competitive strategy—enabling the organization to successfully compete with other providers in its marketplace by developing a system that collects data and analyzes it to proactively address issues related to the quality and efficiency of service

- operating strategy—ensuring that a process is in place to satisfy both internal and external customers in the areas of quality and value
- financial strategy—ensuring continued financial viability in an era where health care spending is tightly controlled and where the costs of malpractice, patient injury, or customer dissatisfaction are substantial.

The benefits of intertwining risk management strategy and organizational strategy are many. For the health care risk manager, linking the two provides an architecture for designing a risk management strategy that is comprehensive, cohesive, and consistent. It also elevates risk management's importance by grounding it in concepts and thought patterns that are second nature to senior managers. Meanwhile, the organization benefits because potentially crippling exposures to loss are more widely understood and better managed, and as a direct result, the quality of service improves.

The balance of this chapter describes a framework that will enable a risk manager to effectively unite a health care organization's risk management and corporate strategies, and communicate the union to senior managers using persuasive logic and familiar language.

While there are many possible definitions for *risk management strategy,* the framework for linking it with the organizational strategy defines it as the sum of the choices risk managers and companies make with respect to (1) risk assessment, (2) risk control, and (3) risk finance. It is the interplay of these three disciplines that determines risk management strategy (see Figure 3-3). No longer can the risk manager view his or her job as merely identifying

Figure 3-3
THE INTERPLAY OF RISK MANAGEMENT DISCIPLINES

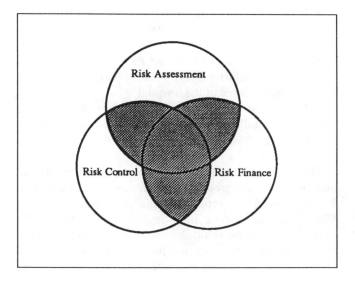

*Source: Reprinted from *Quality and Risk Management in Health Care,* No. 11, March 1993, © Aspen Publishers, Inc.

financing mechanisms to pay for the losses once they occur. Rather, risk management must be part of an aggressive collaborative team effort that continually identifies potential problems and makes necessary modifications before an injury occurs.

The significance of this definition is illuminated by pairing each risk management discipline with the organization's mission and long-term strategic vision:

- risk assessment with competitive strategy
- risk control with operating strategy
- risk finance with financial strategy (see Figure 3-4).

COMPETITIVE STRATEGY AND RISK ASSESSMENT

Risk management strategy begins with risk assessment. In turn, risk assessment—identifying, analyzing, and quantifying the risks of financial loss that can result from patient/visitor/employee injury or a deterioration in the quality of service—is rooted in the hospital's mission and competitive strategy. In the health care setting, because risk is often closely linked to patient injury or harm, the need to identify and correct risks takes on significant importance.

To persuasively communicate risk assessment's relationship to the organization's competitive strategy, a risk manager must strive first to develop a thorough understanding of the organization's mission and strategic vision. Every health care organization consciously seeks to occupy a place within its market that will maximize its value to the community by providing high quality service while maintaining financial viability. Its policies, statements, and

actions that contribute to attaining or preserving this place define the mission and the competitive strategy. Michael Porter, in his book *Competitive Strategy,* identified five forces that influence competitive strategy:

- the threat of new entrants to the industry
- the threat of substitute products or services
- the bargaining power of suppliers
- the bargaining power of customers
- the intensity of rivalry among the industry's existing competitors.[1]

An organization's response to these five forces can take one or a combination of three basic strategic forms:

- *cost leadership.* The health care organization must become increasingly cognizant of the need to provide value as well as quality service to customers. Although in today's market low cost seems to be of paramount importance (especially when negotiating contracts with third party payers), quality is also considered. Furthermore, when quality suffers, not only might a hospital find itself unable to compete with other hospitals in the area but it might also feel the additional financial pressures associated with a rise in insurance costs, a rise in the dollars spent to settle claims (if the hospital self-insures), and a rise in costs associated with defensive medicine, which may not be reimbursed by payers.
- *differentiation.* Instead of striving to achieve cost leadership, the health care organization must set a competitive price for its services and distinguish the institution in the marketplace through superior product features and outcomes and outstanding customer service. Many risk managers are now expected to collect data that can show how proactive risk management initiatives positively impact the quality of care, the volume of lawsuits or patient complaints, and the dollars required to resolve claims or lawsuits. Achieving superior outcomes through quality service at a competitive price is the key to survival of hospitals today and can only be achieved through the collaborative efforts of risk management, quality services, hospital administration, and clinicians.
- *focus.* The health care organization may choose a specific product line—often referred to as a center of excellence. This product line may be targeted toward a particular health care need of the community (e.g., a cancer center or hypertension clinic) or a service that is unique and not available in other local hospitals. The role of risk management in assisting with the proactive analysis of the risks inherent in particular services offered should be stressed.

Figure 3-4
PAIRING OF RISK MANAGEMENT WITH THE ORGANIZATIONAL MISSION

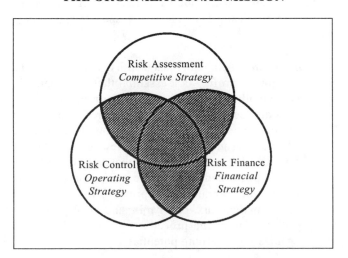

An organization's competitive strategy and mission must drive the assessment of its risks. The central question facing a risk manager when linking competitive strategy and risk assessments is: Given the hospital's strategic focus and corporate mission, what exposures to loss or quality problems are likely to significantly impact its ability to manage its operations? Its earnings? Its assets? Its continued growth? Failing to ask these questions could lead a risk manager to an incomplete assessment of the organization's risks, and potentially an inability to adequately fund for and cover liabilities should they arise. This could place the entire organization in financial peril.

Some examples will help to show how a hospital's competitive strategy influences the assessment of risk. One example is the hospital that seeks to offer a new, technologically superior procedure that requires additional staff training and costly equipment. Although the procedure may be viewed as being very desirable to patients (and to the organization if the procedure is not offered elsewhere), the cost of providing the service or the risks associated with it (when staff is improperly trained or when equipment malfunctions or is used improperly) may lead to a decision not to offer the service. A risk assessment based on this company's competitive strategy would concentrate on issues of competitiveness and need for the service, but would also focus on quality, safety, and liability issues that could arise if the service is performed.

OPERATING STRATEGY AND RISK CONTROL

The second element of a risk management strategy is risk control. After bringing to senior management's attention the magnitudes and probabilities of loss implicit in the organization's competitive strategy, a risk manager should strive to ensure that his or her initiatives to control these risks are grounded in the organization's operating strategy. Doing so will lead not only to measures with a greater likelihood of avoiding and reducing loss, but also to more effective communication of risk control's importance to physicians, nurses, and other health care providers within the organization.

A health care organization's operating strategy has several dimensions:

- the degree of organizational centralization or decentralization, either functionally or by clinical unit or service
- the degree of operational flexibility—in other words, how swiftly the delivery of services can be modified or moved into a setting more convenient to the patient
- the ratio of skilled to unskilled workers in the labor force, as well as the concentration of union versus nonunion workers

To illustrate the effect of a hospital's operating strategy on its risk assessment and risk control strategies, consider the example of a hospital that has two deeply ingrained operational strategies: (a) it employs the technique of stockless inventory, or just-in-time delivery of supplies for surgical services, and (b) it has recently instituted total quality management (TQM).

Risk assessment and risk control efforts for this organization would need to recognize that stockless inventory and TQM techniques create strong webs of interdependency within the hospital as well as between the hospital and its suppliers. Furthermore, a risk assessment rooted in its mission and competitive strategy would pay close attention to the potential interruption of service, losses, or injuries stemming from lack of proper equipment or supplies during unplanned or emergency situations. It also would focus on exposures arising from poor quality—in both the service and product area—that impact the ability to assure high quality care and timely service. These potential risks would be weighed against the benefits of instituting a stockless inventory system within the organization.

Similarly, risk control initiatives grounded in the hospital's operating strategy would center risk avoidance and reduction techniques on supplier-partners. It might take the form of assisting in the risk management efforts of these suppliers, or it could involve seeking multiple suppliers of critical products or supplies. Because of the rigorous requirements placed on suppliers by stockless production and TQM, the pool of qualifying vendors could be limited, making it especially difficult to find suitable alternates.

FINANCIAL STRATEGY AND RISK FINANCE

The third element of any risk management strategy is risk finance. To be truly effective, the financing of a hospital's risks should be tailored to its financial strategy, which in turn influences its ability to survive in the future.

A health care organization's financial strategy is embodied in its policies and decisions with respect to such things as

- *profit goals.* Although most health care organizations are "not for profit," is it essential that they maintain fiscal viability in order to survive. Some organizations stress the need to show an end year "profit" in order to continue to be able to provide community education, indigent care, and other special or new services. Financial strength is critical to ensure that payroll is met and that suppliers and vendors are compensated for the services and products they provide. In the hospital setting, patient mix, payer mix, and appropriate utilization of tests and procedures would influence an organization's earning potential.

- *capital structure.* All organizations establish target ratios for maximum total indebtedness to total capital.
- *tax policy.* Some hospitals seek to maximize current deductions, while others—those experiencing operating losses, for example—do not. Also, some organizations are more willing than others to assume audit risk, or the risk that aggressive deductions will invite IRS scrutiny.
- *investment strategy.* Each organization has a distinct risk personality when it comes to the kinds of businesses, assets (e.g., medical technology), and securities in which it is willing to invest.

Furthermore, each of the decisions health care organizations make regarding profit goals, capital structure, tax policy, and investment strategy helps to determine its overall cost of capital, which is a key yardstick for senior managers when considering the merits of alternative financing decisions.

In designing a risk finance program for a hospital, some tentative conclusions can be made. First, any surprises in the form of large unforeseen losses that might constrain or cripple the hospital's ability to grow would invite senior management's wrath, suggesting the need to transfer significant amounts of risk. Second, increases in total indebtedness, in the form of large self-insured reserves, might conflict with the company's capital structure targets. Third, current deductions for insurance premiums would assist in the sheltering of income. And last, investments in any risk financing vehicle—for example, in the form of funds dedicated to a captive insurer or other alternative risk finance program—would be weighed vis-à-vis other investments the hospital could make. Any scenarios that did not measure up to its cost of capital or other appropriate cost-of-funds benchmark would likely be rejected.

While there are many risk financing schemes that could support the conclusions drawn from this simple example, to fit snugly with the organization's financial strategy, at a minimum its risk finance program would have to transfer significant amounts of risk. Furthermore, while it may be simple, the example reinforces the need to match risk finance with financial strategy, and highlights the framework's usefulness in engineering a risk finance program and communicating its importance to senior management.

In addition to the framework for linking risk management strategy and operational strategy, another way for risk management to gain currency among senior managers is to ensure that its elements—assessment, control, and finance—incorporate the key financial, accounting, tax, and legal considerations employed by the organization when making any strategic or tactical decisions (see Figure 3-5).

Figure 3-5
LINKING RISK MANAGEMENT STRATEGY TO ORGANIZATIONAL CONCERNS

Considerations	Risk Assessment	Risk Control	Risk Finance
Financial	●	◒	●
Accounting	○	◒	●
Tax	○	○	●
Legal	●	●	◒

● Very important ◒ Important ○ Not important

FINANCIAL CONSIDERATIONS

As has been discussed already, financial considerations are very important when assessing a hospital's risks. Identifying and quantifying the potential losses of earnings and resources arising from operational exposures is the first step to building an effective risk management program. They are important, too, when designing and implementing risk control measures. An effective way to measure the success, prospectively or retrospectively, of an investment in risk control is to quantify its cost and its benefit.

ACCOUNTING CONSIDERATIONS

Accounting considerations generally are not important when assessing risk. They are more important when making risk control decisions, inasmuch as the controls imposed by the organization's inside and outside auditors contribute to controlling its fidelity, fiduciary, and directors' and officers' risks.

In contrast to risk assessment and control, however, accounting considerations are very important to risk financing decisions. To be consistent with financial strategy, any proposed risk finance program should recognize and incorporate the organization's tax and financial accounting policies. A basic example of the importance of accounting considerations is that of the organization weighing the benefits of a loss portfolio transfer. If the cash required to transfer the presently self-insured liabilities to an insurer is less than the book value of those liabilities on its balance sheet, the organization can recognize an accounting gain, and thus boost profits. If, however, the book value of the liabilities is less than the cost of risk transfer, the transaction will have an adverse effect on earnings.

TAX CONSIDERATIONS

Tax considerations are not important to risk assessment, and generally are not important to risk control decisions. An exception to this might be if an investment in risk control were to provide an investment tax credit. In this case, a risk control decision should incorporate its relevant tax consequences. Tax considerations are very important to risk finance decisions, as was illustrated when financial strategy and risk finance were discussed earlier.

LEGAL CONSIDERATIONS

Legal considerations are very important in assessing an organization's risks. Key questions include: What is the legal climate in the jurisdictions where the hospital operates? What types of tort reform are available in those jurisdictions? What legal liabilities could arise from the pursuit of new or additional services or marketing strategies, now and in the future (e.g., satellite facilities, state-to-state transfer programs)? Legal considerations are also important when making risk control decisions, especially with respect to the protection of workers, customers, and the environment. Workers' compensation risk control is governed by OSHA regulations. Federal and state medical product safety laws help guide liability risk control, and federal and state EPA requirements drive environmental risk control.

Legal considerations must be taken into account when making risk financing choices. The central question to answer is: What are the state and local legal requirements, restrictions, and opportunities with respect to any proposed risk financing program?

Hospital risk managers, like everyone in today's leaner organizations, must do more with less. Furthermore, with flattened and more decentralized organizational structures, they must influence through persuasion rather than fiat. Therefore, the advantage goes to the risk manager who can craft a potent risk management strategy and communicate its vitality to senior management. In the end, effective risk management is the result of a sound risk management strategy that is grounded in the realities, mission, and culture of the health care organization, and that has top management commitment.

NOTE

1. M. Porter, *Competitive Strategy: Techniques for Analyzing Industries and Competitors* (New York, NY: Free Press, 1980).

chapter 4

Developing a Risk Management Manual

Deborah Korleski

INTRODUCTION

The risk management profession has grown in visibility during the past decade, attracting the attention of regulatory agencies and state legislatures who have established requirements of health care risk management programs. This increased visibility brings with it increasing accountability for program management. Development of a risk management manual can supply evidence of compliance with regulatory requirements, provide an organized compilation of operational procedures, and serve as a ready reference for the orientation and education of new risk management personnel.

The content of a risk management manual is individualistic, depending on the scope and responsibilities of a program. There is no ideal way to compile a manual, but the following discussion provides an approach that may be helpful.

This chapter discusses the manual development process and offers suggestions for manual contents. A generic approach is used so that it can be adapted to the individual needs of any risk manager and to the informational requirements of administrative staff and regulatory agencies.

PURPOSE

A risk management manual is primarily a description of the institution's specific program and related policies and procedures. The scope of the manual depends on the scope and complexity of the risk management program and its intended use. Depending on your preference for specificity and detail, the operational aspects of the risk management department can be delineated beyond an overall description of the program's components to include descriptions of those departments with whom the risk management department interfaces. Further, the level and type of these various interfaces can be described. Identifying the purpose of the manual helps define its breadth.

MANUAL DEVELOPMENT PROCESS

The first step in compiling a manual is the accumulation of existing documents relevant to the risk management program and, where deemed appropriate, its relationship to other hospital departments. Examples of these documents include the risk management program description, organizational charts, information flowcharts, job descriptions, committee charges, descriptions of the safety/security program, insurance program information, and risk management related policies.

The risk management program description provides an overview of the philosophy and scope of the program, the organizational structure, and program components. If no program description exists, consider developing one because it provides the foundation on which the manual is developed. The risk management program description should be written to reflect the value of the risk management service to the organization and the many levels on which the program functions. Risk management related policies include but are not limited to:

- incident reporting
- accident reporting
- informed consent
- confidentiality and release of information
- policies about do-not-resuscitate (DNR) orders or withdrawal of life-sustaining treatment

Additional quality-related policies, such as those governing credentialing and reappointment of medical and other professional staff and the policy indicating the hospital's compliance with the Patient Self-Determination Act, also can be included in this section. Taking the time in advance to pull this information together makes the manual compilation easier and will make the document more of a resource to the department staff. You may find in the process, however, that policies need updating or that policies do not exist and need to be created. Do not let the resulting "to do" list deter you from your goal. Rather, recognize that having appropriate policies and procedures that clearly define what occurs within the hospital is critical to a successful proactive hospital-wide risk management program. Often these policies assist in the development or support of a defense strategy in case specific issues arise in litigation.

MANUAL CONTENTS

Program Description

A program description provides an overview of the philosophy and scope of the program and usually includes a policy statement that reflects the support and commitment given to the risk management program by the governing board, administration, and medical staff. Review the Joint Commission on Accreditation of Healthcare Organizations (Joint Commission) standards regarding risk management before drafting your program description. Then draft your policy statement to comply with the mandated program elements. Your program description establishes the authority for the program and describes its organizational structure and components. In addition, the program description may include a confidentiality statement that describes the protection afforded risk management information. The state statute that delineates this protection should be included as an appendix to the manual.

Policy Statement

A statement reflective of the support and commitment given to the risk management program by the governing board, administration, and medical staff should be established. The purposes of the policy statement are to communicate the commitment and support of the governing board, administration, and medical staff, to define the authority and responsibility of the risk management department, and to emphasize the need for cooperation from all levels in the organization (see Exhibit 4-1).

Organizational Structure

Risk Management Function/Department

Organizational structure refers to the description, organization, and operations of the risk management function. It includes a description of the risk management department, including scope of responsibilities for all staff, hours of operation, access after hours, and job descriptions. This description should identify the risk manager as responsible for the overall coordination of the risk management program. If a specified individual has not been assigned responsibility for the risk management function, then assignment of this responsibility should be explained (i.e., committee oversight). Also, responsibility for the dissemination of risk management information should be addressed in this section.

Organizational Charts

Placement of the risk management function or department within the organization should be depicted in an organizational chart that illustrates the reporting lines to administration and the governing board. Other organizational charts showing the flow of information to and from risk management and the reporting relationships to committees charged with dealing with risk management information also can be devised to enhance the understanding of the risk management role in hospital operations, particularly its integration with quality assurance (see Figures 4-1 to 4-3). (For more sample organizational charts, see Chapter 3, Figures 3-1 and 3-2.)

Committee Structure

The committee structure for addressing risk management issues should be described. Whether the institution has a separate risk management committee or a combined risk management/quality assurance committee, its purpose or charge, membership, meeting frequency, and reporting relationships to other committees should be outlined. Also, additional hospital-wide committees that use risk management information or to which the risk manager might periodically be invited to speak can be included.

Interdepartmental Relationships

According to the Joint Commission risk management standards, operational linkages must exist between the risk management functions related to clinical aspects of patient care and safety and quality assurance. The integration of

Exhibit 4-1
SAMPLE RISK MANAGEMENT POLICY STATEMENT

_____ is committed to providing high quality patient services, enhancing the safety of patients, visitors, and staff, and preserving its financial integrity to continue its mission. To support these objectives, it has established a hospital risk management program as an integral part of the Quality Assurance Program. Risk management is a coordinated hospital-wide process to identify, prevent, or minimize events that may present potential liability exposure. It involves the participation of all hospital employees, house staff, and medical staff.

The hospital has established a risk management department to direct, supervise, and manage the risk management activities. Risk management functions include risk identification and assessment, loss prevention, and claims management.

The Board of Trustees delegates authority and responsibility for the implementation of the risk management program to Hospital Administration and the Medical Staff.

*

_____ is committed to providing a safe and secure environment within its facilities and grounds for all patients, visitors, employees, volunteers, and physicians. A formal risk management program to prevent risks and harm to all persons involved in hospital services will be a part of the hospital's operations.

The hospital's Board of Trustees has delegated authority and responsibility for the operation and maintenance of this risk management program to the hospital President and President of the Medical Staff. The administrative and clinical functions of the program are described in several sources including the Risk Management Policy and Procedure Manual, Quality Assurance Plan, and Safety Manual.

Source: Adapted from _Risk Management for Hospitals: A Practical Approach_ by Bernard L. Brown, p. 61, Aspen Publishers, Inc. © 1979.

Figure 4-1

ORGANIZATION CHART SUPPORTING OPERATIONAL LINK BETWEEN QUALITY ASSURANCE/RISK MANAGEMENT AND ALL HOSPITAL DEPARTMENTS

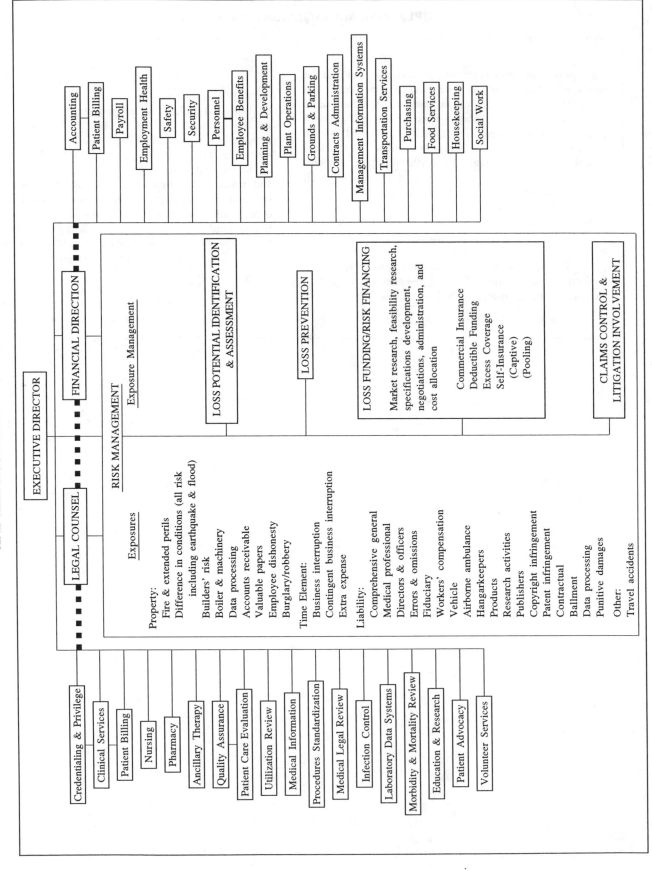

Figure 4-2

QUALITY ASSURANCE/RISK MANAGEMENT INTERFACE

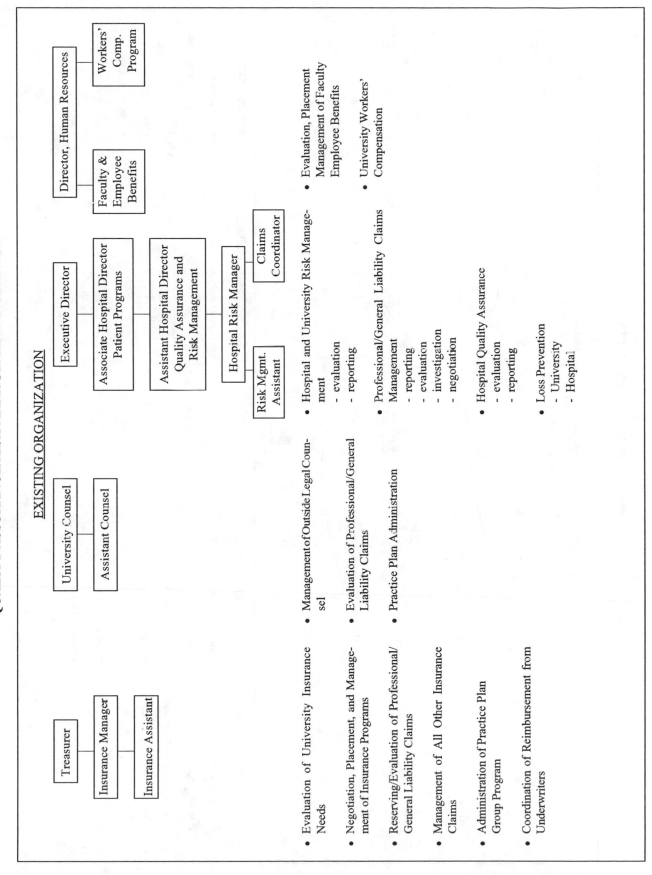

Figure 4-3
QUALITY ASSURANCE/RISK MANAGEMENT INTEGRATION

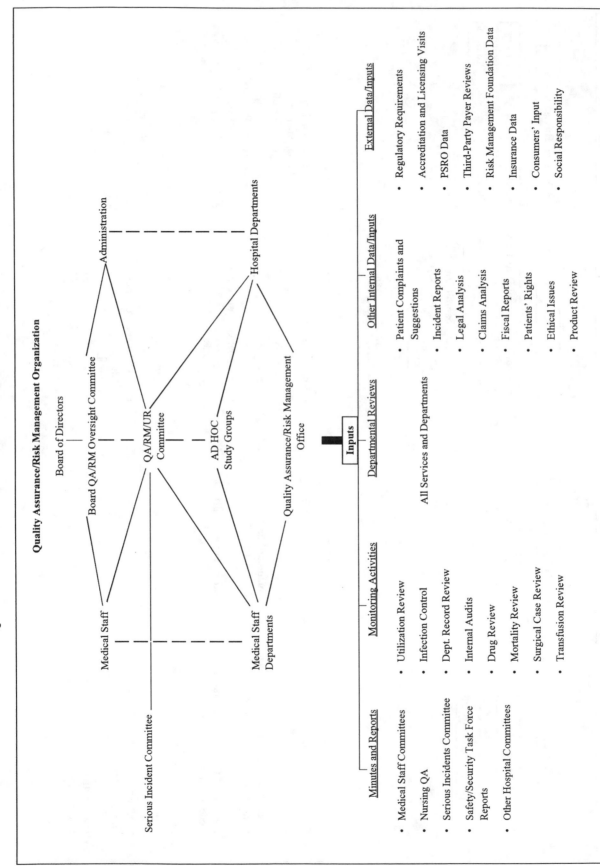

Quality Assurance/Risk Management Organization

Board of Directors

Board QA/RM Oversight Committee

Administration

Medical Staff

QA/RM/UR Committee

AD HOC Study Groups

Hospital Departments

Quality Assurance/Risk Management Office

Serious Incident Committee

Medical Staff Departments

Inputs

Minutes and Reports

- Medical Staff Committees
- Nursing QA
- Serious Incidents Committee
- Safety/Security Task Force Reports
- Other Hospital Committees

Monitoring Activities

- Utilization Review
- Infection Control
- Dept. Record Review
- Internal Audits
- Drug Review
- Mortality Review
- Surgical Case Review
- Transfusion Review

Departmental Reviews

All Services and Departments

Other Internal Data/Inputs

- Patient Complaints and Suggestions
- Incident Reports
- Legal Analysis
- Claims Analysis
- Fiscal Reports
- Patients' Rights
- Ethical Issues
- Product Review

External Data/Inputs

- Regulatory Requirements
- Accreditation and Licensing Visits
- PSRO Data
- Third-Party Payer Reviews
- Risk Management Foundation Data
- Insurance Data
- Consumers' Input
- Social Responsibility

Note: PSRO, Professional Standard Review Organization; QA, quality assurance; RM, risk management; UR, utilization review

risk management and quality assurance can be shown through a description of the organizational structure, accessibility of information, reporting mechanisms, and committee representation. The type and frequency of information shared will depend on the organizational structure and internal communication links. For example, risk management and quality assurance may be separate departments reporting to the same administrator. In this case, integration may be shown through a combined quality assurance/risk management committee. The sharing of information collected by risk management and quality assurance may also be evident through use of a shared data base, routine reporting of incident and occurrence trends, or departmental quality assurance reviews. If the hospital data base has an information system that allows for the integration of this information, a sample report or template of the report may be included in this section, again to enhance the value of this manual as a resource tool.

The involvement and participation of the medical staff in risk management also are required by the Joint Commission. Medical staff participation can be shown through committee action in response to identified areas of potential patient injury, risk management or quality assurance reports, or memoranda describing issues and actions, development of criteria for identifying potential risk areas, and participation in educational programs directed at minimizing patient risk. If the physician who has been assigned this responsibility has a formal job description, it can be included in this section, particularly if the job position is not funded by the risk management department.

Aside from quality assurance and the medical staff, risk management relies on a variety of sources in the identification of potential risk exposures and maintains liaisons with several key departments, such as nursing, patient services, social work, medical records, business office, and utilization management. Describing the particular interfaces with each of these departments can be included in the manual or depicted graphically as discussed earlier.

Program Components

Risk Identification

Incident/Event Reporting Process. Event reporting refers to those systems that provide for the identification and reporting of potentially adverse patient occurrences, unexpected outcomes of treatment, incidents that caused or could have caused injury, and patient complaints about treatment received. Informational sources for identifying potentially reportable events include but are not limited to:

- incident reports
- occurrences screening/reports
- patient complaints

- attorney requests for medical records, x-rays, lab reports
- verbal reports
- quality assurance studies
- licensure/accreditation survey reports
- security reports
- legal complaints and suits
- department/committee reports/minutes

At a minimum, an explanation of the incident reporting and occurrence screening systems should be provided. This includes the mechanics of these systems and how the information is used. For example, the process for investigation of incidents, identification of potentially compensable events, and external reporting requirements would be included. Additionally, specific policies and procedures related to these systems can be included for reference.

Data Management. Data management refers to the mechanism for compiling information on incident data, claims or occurrences for purposes of trending and analysis, and, ultimately, loss prevention. The type, frequency, and distribution of reports should be explained. This includes reports to administration, the governing board, department heads, external agencies, and so forth. Again, if templates are available that highlight important aspects for reporting of specific details to specific groups, they should be included since they will help ensure that the appropriate people are receiving the most beneficial information.

Education

Risk management education for hospital staff is mandated in the majority of states that require risk management programs. Educational programs usually include general orientation for new nursing, hospital, and physician staff and more specific programs geared to a particular specialty or risk issue. The type and frequency of educational programs should be listed in the manual. To enhance this information, a brief description of the educational session, an outline, or syllabus can be included. The process for applying for continuing education credits also should be included, and copies of the forms used for applying for such credit should be provided as samples.

Risk Financing

The components of the risk financing function typically include risk financing techniques for professional, general and other liability areas, broker selection and evaluation, claims management, and workers' compensation program administration. An overview of the management of risk financing activities and the link to hospital or campus risk management should be described. This includes a summary of the insurance program, a schedule of coverages that contains policy periods, coverage limits, policy numbers and insurers, broker selection and evaluation, and claims management.

The responsibilities of risk managers determine the extent of their involvement in risk financing and therefore determine the extent to which it is addressed in the manual. The risk financing function may be the responsibility of the risk manager or of someone else. Although risk managers may not be responsible for risk financing, they may have some involvement in various aspects of the insurance program (e.g., broker selection) and claims management. These limited aspects should be explained. Also, insurance coverage information should be included because it provides a ready reference, if needed, when coverage questions arise.

If advance risk financing techniques are the responsibility of the risk manager, information about loss triangulations may be included with sample copies of these reports.

Claims Management

The role of the risk manager in claims management depends on the type of insurance mechanism employed and whether services are provided in-house or through external organizations (i.e., insurance carriers or claims management firms). For those risk managers whose services are provided in-house, the claims management portion of the manual should be detailed. Suggested topics for inclusion in this part of the manual are:

- acceptance/handling of legal correspondence
- establishing a claims file
- retrieving and securing records
- claims investigation
- assignment of legal counsel
- claims reserving
- notification of excess carriers
- claims confidentiality and security
- litigation management (management of defense counsel)
- settlement authority
- loss runs

For those risk managers whose involvement is limited, the manual may include a description of who accepts legal papers, forwards them to defense counsel, procures medical records, and assists defense counsel with discovery re-

quests. The securing of outside investigators and their management also should be addressed in this section.

Workers' Compensation Program Administration

As applicable, a description of the workers' compensation program should be included as another component of the risk management program. The varied facets of the program can include applicable institutional policies about employee illness and injury, claims management for lost work-time injuries, back-to-work programs to return injured employees to the work force, and loss prevention measures to prevent lost work-time accidents. Any state or federal laws that might impact the operation of this program should be included or referenced.

Safety Management

The responsibilities of the risk manager also can include management of the safety/security program. A safety program description or manual may exist and can be included or referenced in the risk management manual. Components of the safety program include but are not limited to hazardous waste management, right-to-know, accident reporting and investigation, laboratory safety, chemical safety, safety inspections, and responsibilities related to the security of the premises.

Risk Management Related Policies

The risk management manual should include specific policies that have risk management implications. These include but are not limited to informed consent, DNR orders, withdrawal/withholding of life support, patient confidentiality, and release of information. Other policies may include the handling of legal documents, organ donation, brain death determination, child abuse, abusive patients, handling of patients under arrest or in protective custody, and retention of medical records.

Annual Review

As with any policy and procedure manual, it is important that the manual reflects actual practice. An ongoing process of review should be established to keep the manual current.

chapter 5

Risk Management Program Development

Susan West, Kathleen Walsh, and Barbara J. Youngberg

INTRODUCTION

Critical to the success of any risk management program is an organized, easily recognizable program description that carefully delineates goals, objectives, and a process for each staff member to follow. As with most programs within a hospital, two factors can greatly increase the likelihood of a risk management program's success: (1) visibility and accessibility of the program staff, and (2) program guidelines that are easy to follow.

This chapter describes some of the processes and functions of risk management and provides the reader with actual tools to use in assessing the various risks within an organization. Following initial recognition of these risks, the risk manager must develop tools that enable staff members to remain conscious of the potential risks and develop systems to manage the risks.

Many of the tools in this chapter were developed by the risk management staff at the University of Colorado Health Sciences Center as part of its aggressive proactive risk management program. These generic screens, or clinical indicators, were developed to allow the risk management department to interface with the quality assurance department and to engage physicians in the risk management process. Other tools were based on a review of claims data from various sources that identified repetitive behaviors frequently resulting in patient injuries and lawsuits. The risk assessment tools can help a risk manager identify and assess possible areas of exposure within the institution. Following

this process, tools can be developed to address and manage specific risks.

DEVELOPING A COMPREHENSIVE MANUAL

It is advantageous for a risk manager to develop a risk management manual. A copy can be placed on each unit in the hospital to serve as a reference for physicians and staff. The manual need not be voluminous; in fact, an extremely large volume containing countless numbers of policies and procedures is likely to intimidate the staff. Rather, the manual should provide an overview of the program; names of staff members to contact in the event of a risk management issue; relevant policies, procedures, and forms; and educational information deemed appropriate by the risk manager.

Exhibit 5-1 contains a sample table of contents for a risk management manual with appropriate comments. A copy of the institution's organizational flow chart is also helpful to illustrate the flow of information from risk management and the importance of this process to the administration. A clear and concise statement by the hospital administration endorsing the risk management program should be part of the manual. This statement will add credibility to the program and elicit support for the risk management staff. The use of colored paper to indicate specific policies and procedures in the manual can be visually attractive and provide an easy method of reference. Finally, the manual should include

Exhibit 5-1
SAMPLE TABLE OF CONTENTS FOR A
HOSPITAL RISK MANAGEMENT MANUAL

Administrative statement endorsing risk management program and staff participation

Description of the hospital risk management program
Name(s) of risk manager and staff
Brief description of the risk management program, including its many benefits
Location and telephone extension of the risk management office
List of appropriate reasons for contacting the risk management office
Information about after-hours contact
Services provided by the risk management staff
List of risk management educational programs
Sample policies, procedures, and forms that are part of the risk management program (instructions about who completes the forms, what is included in them, where they are routed, when they should be completed, and how they benefit the risk management effort are included)

Basic policies and educational materials (relevant to legal issues)
Informed consent
Withholding and withdrawing life support
Durable power of attorney
Patient confidentiality
Documentation
Malpractice insurance
Child abuse
Attorney contact
Handling of legal documents
Patients' rights and responsibilities
Basic legal glossary
A copy of the state organ donor statute

Other information relating to problems frequently addressed by hospital staff

basic education on issues requiring immediate information that are most often addressed by the staff. Obviously, the most successful risk management program will engage the participation of hospital staff and physicians. The risk manager's ability to identify their needs and tailor the hospital's program to meet them will greatly increase the effectiveness of the program.

INCIDENT TRACKING FORMS

Critical to a successful hospital risk management program is the ability of the staff to gather appropriate data. A form to accomplish this task that does not "compete" with other hospital forms is essential. Since the recent mandate by the Joint Commission on Accreditation of Healthcare Organizations for an integration of quality assurance and risk management functions, many recently developed forms have merged traditional incident forms with department-specific generic quality screens. This is a logical process because much of the identified data has both risk and quality management implications.

The sharing of information by both disciplines through the use of a single form helps to minimize the possibility that information obtained by one department will get lost prior to receipt by the other. (See Exhibits 5-2 and 5-3 for two excellent examples of this type of process.)

Exhibit 5-2
EXAMPLE OF A MANAGEMENT VARIANCE REPORT

UNIVERSITY OF MISSOURI
MANAGEMENT VARIANCE REPORT
(See reverse side for instructions)

FORM NUMBER

1 Addressograph:

Patient Name:

Address:

DOB:

Pt. Number:

NOTE: Space for details or additional information on back of this form

2 Time of Incident

Date: _____ / _____ / _____

Time: _____
use 2400 clock

3 Sex
(circle one)

Male

Female

4 Status
(circle one)
1 - Inpatient
2 - Outpatient
3 - Visitor
4 - Other _____

5 Diagnosis (circle all that apply)
1 Disease or Disorder of the Nervous System
2 Disease or Disorder of the Eye
3 Disease or Disorder of the Ear, Nose, or Throat
4 Disease or Disorder of the Respiratory System
5 Disease or Disorder of the Circulatory System
6 Disease or Disorder of the Digestive System
7 Disease or Disorder of the Hepatobiliary System or Pancreas
8 Disease of the Musculoskeletal System or Connective Tissue
9 Disease of the Skin, Subcutaneous Tissue, or Breast
10 Endocrine, Nutritional, or Metabolic Disease
11 Disease or Disorder of the Kidney or Urinary Tract
12 Disease or Disorder of the Male Reproductive System
13 Disease or Disorder of the Female Reproductive System
14 Pregnancy, Childbirth, or the Puerperium
15 Neonate with Certain Conditions of the Perinatal Period
16 Disease or Disorder of Blood or Blood-Forming Organ or Immunity
17 Certain Neoplasms (Not Elsewhere Classified)
18 Infectious or Parasitic Disease (Systemic)
19 Mental Disorder
20 Substance Use Disorder or Substance Induced Organic Disorder
21 Injury, Poisoning, or Toxic Effect of Drugs
22 Burn
23 Other _____

6 Location of Incident
(circle one and fill in as needed)

1 Patient Room No. _____
2 Bathroom in Patient Room _____
3 Hall _____
4 Bathroom in Hall _____
5 I.C.U. _____
6 Treatment Area _____
7 Waiting Area _____
8 Nursing Station _____
9 OR/L&D Suite
10 Pharmacy
11 Radiology
12 Clinic _____
13 Emergency Room
14 ASU
15 Path. Laboratory _____
16 Helicopter _____
17 Other Location _____

7 Staff Most Closely Involved
(circle one)
1 Attending Physician/Surgeon
2 Resident/Intern
3 Medical Student
4 Nurse Practitioner/PA
5 RN/Graduate Nurse
6 LPN
7 Nursing Technician
8 Nursing Student
9 Dietitian
10 Food Service Worker
11 Housekeeping Staff _____
12 Engineering Staff _____
13 Clerical
14 Volunteer
15 Pharmacy Staff _____
16 Laboratory Staff _____
17 Radiology Staff _____
18 Physical Therapy Staff _____
19 Respiratory Therapy Staff _____
20 OT/Other Rehab Staff _____

8 Patient Condition Prior to Variance (circle one)
1 Alert/Normal
2 Agitated
3 Unconscious
4 Refuses to Cooperate
5 Confused
6 Senile
7 Depressed
8 Suicidal
9 Sedated
10 Anesthetized
11 Substance Abuse
12 Intoxicated
13 Handicapped
14 Mentally Retarded
15 Neurologically Impaired
16 Language Barrier

9 Patient or Family Attitude After Variance (circle one)
Unaware (1)   Cooperative (3)   Angry (5)   Threats of Suit (6)

Circle the Event That Best Describes the Variances

10 Patient Fall (circle one)
1 Ambulating
2 From Bed
3 From Chair
4 From Commode
5 From Stretcher/Gurney
6 From Support Equipment
7 From Wheelchair
8 From Crib/Isolette
9 From Exam Table
10 Other _____

(circle all that apply)
a Rails on Bed Up
b Call Light Not Available
c Call Light On
d Call Light Malfunction
e Floor Slippery
f Struck by Equipment
g Patient Unattended
h Struck by Another Person
i Other _____

11 Medication Variance
(circle one)

1 Medication Missing
2 Adverse Side Effects
3 Medication Given but Not Charted
4 Medication Omitted
5 Duplication/Extra Dose
6 Time Variance
7 Wrong Routing
8 Wrong Dose
9 Wrong Med Administered
10 Rx Filled Wrong
11 Rx Compounded Wrong
12 Wrong Patient

IV VARIANCES
13 IV Compounded Wrong
14 IV Not Checked Properly
15 IV at Wrong Rate
16 Infiltration

12 Procedural Variance
(circle one)

1 Performed on Wrong Patient
2 Improper Preparation of Patient
3 Lost Specimen
4 Spoiled Specimen
5 Patient Did Not Arrive As Scheduled
6 Staff Did Not Arrive As Scheduled
7 Omission of Procedure
8 Performed Wrong
9 Performance Delayed
10 Radiation Exposure
11 NPO Violated
12 Misdiagnosis _____
13 Blood/Blood By-Products Problem (explain) _____
_____
_____
_____
_____
_____

13 Equipment Variance (circle one)
1 Electrical Problem
2 Electrical Shock
3 Equipment Not Available
4 Improper Use
5 Mechanical Problem
6 Operator Unqualified
7 Other Malfunction/Defect
8 Wrong Equipment
9 Other _____

16 Security Variance (circle one)
1 Damage/Loss of Property
(explain on reverse)
2 Code Red
3 Security Problem
4 Drug Count Variance
5 Drug Tampering
6 Drug Keys Variance
7 Other _____

14 OR/ER/L&D Event
(circle one)

1 Consent Problem
2 Break in Sterile Technique
3 Anesthesia Problem
4 Count Discrepancy
5 Foreign Body Left in Patient
6 Unexpected Death
7 Precipitous Delivery
8 Return to OR Same Day
9 Surgical/L&D Procedure Delayed
10 Trauma to Healthy Tissue
11 Unexpected Complications
12 Other _____
_____
_____
_____
_____

15 Miscellaneous Event
(circle one)

1 Fight Among Patients
2 Patient Attacked Staff
3 Patient Abused by Staff
4 Left Without Notice
5 Burn
6 Cardiac Arrest/Code Blue
7 Cross Infection/Code Yellow
8 Diet Problem
9 Patient Left AMA; Refused to Sign AMA Form
10 Trauma to Healthy Tissue
11 Suicide Attempt
12 Patient Denied Treatment
13 Other _____
_____
_____

continues

Exhibit 5–2 continued

UNIVERSITY OF MISSOURI
INSTRUCTIONS FOR VARIANCE REPORT

1. PURPOSE: This form when properly completed provides an effective method of reporting variances to the University risk management, legal counsel, and insurance department. The supervisor and physician should jointly decide if the event warrants the use of a variance report.
2. CONFIDENTIALITY: This report represents a significant component of the confidential communication between University physicians, dentists, nurses, and other health care personnel and their supervisors, legal counsel, risk manager, or insurer.
3. WHO SHOULD REPORT: The immediate supervisor or the staff member most closely associated with the events is responsible for either completing this form or delegating its completion to a party having direct KNOWLEDGE. ANCILLARY DEPARTMENTS involved in variances that may involve more than one department should also complete a report. An example of such multi-department reports is a medication variance involving a nursing unit and the Pharmacy.
4. WHEN AND WHERE THE REPORT SHOULD BE COMPLETED AND FILED: The report should be completed as soon after the event as is practical. It must be completed before the shift ends and the parties depart for the day. If in the opinion of the head nurse or immediate supervisor a physician's examination is indicated, request that it be completed by any physician on the health care team.
5. COMPLETING THE FORM:
   a) Use the patient's addressograph plate, or complete ALL questions in Section 1.
   b) Sections 2 through 9 MUST be completed on all incidents if relevant. Incomplete sections will be returned. Simply circle the relevant section or fill in the blank. Some sections also have sub-parts. Please circle the relevant data.
   c) In the part dealing with the description of the event, the most common variances have been listed for your convenience. Please circle, and if required, furnish the data requested. If the variance you are reporting has not been listed or is not sufficiently descriptive, please describe it in the blank space 18 found below.
   d) If a Follow-Up Examination has been completed, the physician should furnish the results by circling the relevant section or complete the blank space found in 18 below.
   e) Complete Sections 19 through 22. Employee–Supervisor Follow-Up Discussions should be placed in 23. Begin routing the form as soon as it is completed.

MEDICAL FOLLOW-UP (if indicated)

17 Was Doctor Called?
☐ Yes ☐ No   If yes, who? _____ Time called _____ Time arrived _____

18 Circle One: 1 No adverse effect;   2 Minor adverse effect;   3 Major adverse effect, occurrence report required

   Also: Use this space for any additional information about the event and medical care follow-up.

_____
_____
_____
_____
_____
_____

Doctor's Signature _____

19 Print Name and Title of Person Responsible for Variance	**20 Department/Nursing Unit of Person in 19.**

21 Name(s) of Witness(es)—Include Address(es) of Any Non-Employee(s)

Name	Address	Telephone
a		
b		
c		

22 Names of Attending Physician and Primary Resident

Attending: _____ Resident: _____

23 Variance Report Follow-Up

_____
_____
_____
_____
_____
_____
_____
_____
_____
_____

ROUTING ORDER	3 Associate Director _____
1 Immediate Supervisor _____	4 Other Associate Director _____
2 Manager _____	5 Risk Manager _____

Source: Reprinted from *UMUW Form 192* with permission of University of Missouri at Columbia, © 1985.

Exhibit 5–3
EXAMPLE OF A PATIENT/VISITOR OCCURRENCE REPORT AND COMPLETION INSTRUCTIONS

PART A—REPORT FORM

UNIVERSITY OF COLORADO HEALTH SCIENCES CENTER
PATIENT/VISITOR OCCURRENCE REPORT
THIS FORM IS TO BE USED FOR OCCURRENCE WITH ACTUAL OR POTENTIAL INJURY TO PATIENTS OR VISITORS
**IF INJURY OCCURS ALSO NOTIFY RISK MANAGER IMMEDIATELY AT 270-5507 OR 270-5534
AND APPROPRIATE ADMINISTRATOR
CONFIDENTIAL TO RISK MANAGER: UPON COMPLETION PLACE IN BOX OUTSIDE ROOM UH1013**

DO NOT FILE IN MEDICAL RECORD!
RELEVANT FACTS MUST BE DOCUMENTED IN MEDICAL RECORD

INCIDENT DATE   **TIME**   **PATIENT ☐**   **VISITOR ☐**

/   /19   :   AM/PM

LOCATION OF OCCURRENCE

Unit/Dept. _____   ☐ Pt. Room   ☐ Pt. Bathroom

☐ Pt. Shower   ☐ Other: _____

INJURY   PRIOR CONDITION OF PATIENT OR VISITOR'
☐ YES ☐ NO   ☐ Confused   ☐ Language barrier
☐ None Apparent   ☐ Sedated   ☐ Not applicable
                 ☐ Uncooperative ☐ Other: ____

If addressograph unavailable, PRINT NAME, DOB, UNIT, SEX, PATIENT NUMBER, if visitor: give address:

EXTENT OF INJURY
☐ Amputation   ☐ Asphyxia/Anoxia   ☐ Back Injury   ☐ Burn
☐ Concussion   ☐ Decreased level of consciousness ☐ Emotional   ☐ Fracture/Dislocation
☐ Laceration/Bruise/Contusion ☐ Sprain/Strain   ☐ Other _____

FALLS   Bed Height: ☐ Low ☐ High   Bed Rail: ☐ Up ☐ Down ☐ Full ☐ Half
☐ Chair ☐ Bed ☐ Toilet ☐ Ambulating   ☐ Safety device in place before fall   Type: _____
☐ Behavior problem   ☐ Disoriented   ☐ During recreational activity   ☐ Faint   ☐ Sedated
☐ Seizure   ☐ Unconscious   ☐ Weak   ☐ Other _____

MEDICATION/IV ERRORS   Adverse Effect ☐ Yes ☐ No   Drug: _____

Error By: ☐ Nursing   ☐ Pharmacy   ☐ M.D. ☐ Pt. Service Clerk or Other
☐ Omission   ☐ Wrong Dosage   ☐ Wrong Patient   ☐ Wrong Route   ☐ Wrong Drug   ☐ Wrong Time
☐ Duplication   ☐ Order Missing   ☐ Packaging/Labeling ☐ Transcription ☐ Injec. Site Injury ☐ IVPB ☐ IV Push
☐ Wrong IV flow rate ☐ IV Pump Prob. ☐ IV Infiltrate with tissue damage ☐ Central line complication–Type: ____

OR/ANESTHESIA/PACU/DS   Xray Taken   ☐ Yes ☐ No   RESULTS: ____
☐ Incorrect sponge/needle/instrument count ☐ No count   ☐ Break in technique   ☐ Burn   ☐ Allergic to prep.
☐ Specimen not labeled correctly   ☐ Lost specimen ☐ Aspirations   ☐ Neuro deficit   ☐ Inadequate consent
☐ Cor "O" c in 24 hrs of anesthesia   ☐ Death   ☐ Organ/Vessel nicked   ☐ Injured teeth   ☐ Periph nerve damage
☐ Anesthesia problem   ☐ Cor "O"   ☐ Unplanned return to OR ☐ Pump/equip. problems
☐ Unplanned admit from DS to hosp./obs. For: ____   ☐ Unplanned admit to ICU ☐ Other: ____

OBSTETRICS/NURSERY
☐ Impaired newborn   ☐ Outborn infant   ☐ Fetal Death   ☐ Maternal injury
☐ Uncontrolled delivery ☐ Failed C.L. epidural ☐ Maternal death   ☐ Live tab's
☐ Retained placenta sponge ☐ Excessive blood loss (over 500 cc's) ☐ Unplanned return to DR, OR, or RR

PROCEDURE VARIANCE   Procedure: _____
☐ Wrong patient   ☐ Unable to draw   ☐ Performed incorrectly   ☐ IV infiltrate/off/clotted/empty
☐ Lost specimen   ☐ Patient did not arrive as sched'd ☐ Performance delayed ☐ Report missing
☐ Spoiled specimen ☐ Improper preparation of patient ☐ Severe contrast reaction ☐ Other: ____
☐ NPO violated   ☐ Omission of procedure   ☐ Oversedation

continues

Exhibit 5–3 continued

EMERGENCY DEPARMENT

☐ Procedure Treatment error   ☐ E.D. Care s̄ Physician/Nurse Pract.   ☐ Disch c̄ Neuro Deficit   ☐ Missed Diagnosis
    ☐ Unexplained death/Coroner's Case   ☐ Missed or incorrect X-ray lab report EKG

GENERAL

☐ Transfer injury	☐ Patient non-compliant	☐ Transfusion reaction
☐ Equipment injury	☐ Angry hostile patient/family	☐ Excessive blood loss requiring transfusion
☐ Proced./Rx complication	☐ Self inflicted injury	☐ Unplanned readmission within 24 hr
☐ Telemetry problem	☐ AMA	☐ Readmit to ICU within 48 hr of transfer to ward
☐ Unexpected death	☐ AWOL	☐ Transfer to ICU within 24 hr of admission to ward
☐ Coroner's case	☐ No/Improper consent	☐ Other: _____

CONTRIBUTING FACTORS:

☐ Staffing ☐ Communication   ☐ Equipment failure _____   ☐ Other _____

EQUIPMENT FAILURE (if boxed filled above)

Type of equipment _____   I.D. number _____   Disposition _____

DESCRIPTION OF EVENT

FOLLOW-UP/RECOMMENDATIONS:

_____
_____

VISITOR TREATMENT: ☐ Offered   ☐ Refused   ☐ Emergency Department

STAFF INVOLVED AT TIME OF OCCURRENCE   **SHIFT:**

☐ Regular	☐ Non-RN	☐ 8 Hour	☐ Day	☐ Overtime
☐ Float	☐ Outside Agency/Traveler RN	☐ 10 Hour	☐ Evening	☐ Near shift change
☐ Varied Hourly	☐ Student: _____	☐ 12 Hour	☐ Night	☐ Weekend/Holiday
☐ New Graduate Nurse	☐ Physician	☐ Other _____		
☐ New Experienced Nurse	☐ Other: _____			

OTHER PERSONS WITH DIRECT KNOWLEDGE OF OCCURRENCE

Name _____   Name _____

Address (If Visitor) _____   Address (If Visitor) _____

_____   _____

Phone/Bellboy _____   Phone/Bellboy _____

_____ / _____ / _____ / _____

Signature of Reporting Person   Title   Date   Phone/Bellboy

Reviewed by Risk Management _____ on ___ / ___ 19

DO NOT FILE IN MEDICAL RECORD!

continues

Exhibit 5-3 continued

PART B—REPORT FORM COMPLETION INSTRUCTIONS

PURPOSE

The purpose of the Patient/Visitor Occurrence Report is to notify the University of Colorado Health Sciences Center Risk Manager of all occurrences with actual or potential injury to patients and visitors. The Occurrence Report is a *Confidential* communication to the Risk Manager which enables the department to take corrective actions, reducing losses and improving the quality of health care provided at University Hospital. It is also a reporting vehicle to our Self Insured Trust of potential liability claims.

The Occurrence Report enables the Risk Management Department to review circumstances surrounding the occurrence and determine the appropriate course of action. An injury is the most obvious result of an occurrence. An occurrence may also result in the likelihood of a claim. A claim may be made in the absence of an injury. Legitimate claims can be settled fairly and expeditiously. Questionable claims can be investigated on a timely basis and either settled or a defense can be provided.

The Occurrence Report Form must be completed as soon as practical after the occurrence is witnessed or discovered. Several benefits are derived from prompt reporting: corrective actions can be taken, the facts of the occurrence are fresh in the mind of the person who witnesses or discovers the occurrence, and many potential claims against the hospital may be eliminated, or at least controlled.

PROCEDURE

1. The Patient/Visitor Occurrence Report form is to be completed for *all* occurrences with actual or potential injury to patients and visitors. These guidelines for reportable occurrences for each specialty area are referenced as part of this report; see Index.
2. If an injury occurs, the Risk Manager is to be notified at extension 5507 immediately; and the appropriate administrator is to be informed of the incident causing injury immediately. A recorder is on the telephone during the evening, night and weekend.
3. Within 24 hours of the occurrence, the completed form is to be placed in the CONFIDENTIAL TO RISK MANAGER box outside University Hospital Room 1013.
4. The only signature required on the form is that of the person filing the report. The report should be made out by the employee who discovers the occurrence. The personnel involved with the occurrence should be identified; however, the report does not have to be completed by them. It is important that the reports are promptly sent to the Risk Manager.
5. *Do not file or reference this report in the medical record.*
6. The *relevant facts* of the occurrence must be documented in the medical record.

COMPLETION INSTRUCTIONS

OCCURRENCE DATE AND TIME: Write in date and time occurrence actually happened and circle AM or PM if not using military clock.

PATIENT/VISITOR BOX: Check appropriate box. Use addressograph for patient or if unavailable, print patient's name, date of birth, unit, sex and medical record number. If a visitor incident is being reported, print visitor's full name, address and phone number if available.

LOCATION OF OCCURRENCE: Insert unit or area in which occurrence happened and check appropriate box.

INJURY: Check box if an injury occurred in any category.

PRIOR CONDITION OF PATIENT OR VISITOR: Check appropriate box for condition of patient or visitor prior to occurrence of incident. Use "Other" category for a condition not listed which is applicable to the occurrence.

FALLS: Check box(es) which are appropriate to describe the circumstances surrounding an actual or apparent fall.
If an injury did occur, please complete EXTENT OF INJURY section.
Use "Other" section for any applicable information not previously stated.

MEDICATION/IV ERRORS: Check box indicating the error did or did not have an adverse effect on the patient. Check all other applicable boxes in this section. Indicate drug involved.

SPECIALTY AREAS: Operating Room, Anesthesia, Post Anesthesia Care Unit, Day Surgery, Obstetrics, Nursery, and Emergency Department have separate sections. If the occurrence is general in nature (i.e., fall, medication error), use the section of the report that deals with those types of occurrences.

PROCEDURE VARIANCE: Complete this section if cause of occurrence was related to a procedure performed in a department other than nursing (i.e., Laboratory, Radiology, Respiratory Care, Cardiac Catheterization Laboratory, etc.).

continues

Exhibit 5–3 continued

GENERAL: Check appropriate box(es) if applicable. Use "Other" section on any occurrence for which prior sections are not applicable.

EQUIPMENT FAILURE: Complete this section if cause of occurrence was related to equipment.
Identify the equipment involved with the occurrence. Also note the I.D. number from the piece of equipment and the disposition (i.e., sent to Bioengineering, etc.).
Complete patient injury information on front of report.

DESCRIPTION OF EVENT: If additional space is needed to describe the event, include the information in this section. Comments in this section are optional.

FOLLOW-UP/RECOMMENDATIONS: Complete as appropriate. Comments are optional.

STAFF INVOLVED AT TIME OF OCCURRENCE: Check all applicable boxes in this section. If non-RN, write in job classification. If student, write in type of student. If "Other" shift, write in shift specifics.

OTHER PERSONS WITH DIRECT KNOWLEDGE OF OCCURRENCE: If other persons are employees or staff, leave address blank and note phone and/or bellboy number. If other persons are visitors, fill in address and phone number.

PERSON FILING REPORT: Print name, title, phone or bellboy, date of report completion.

As noted in Section 4 (above) the person filing the report may be different from the staff involved in the occurrence. When this happens, list the employee's name who was involved in the occurrence in the "Description of Event Section" (i.e., S. Smith, R.N., working days, discovers a medication error made on the night shift by R. Jones, R.N. S. Smith should make out the report and explain in "Description of Event Section" error made by R. Jones, R.N. S. Smith, R.N. signs as the reporting person).

REPORT SUBMISSION: Place the completed report in the CONFIDENTIAL TO RISK MANAGER box outside University Hospital Room 1013 within 24 hours of occurrence. (Some department managers request that employees give them the occurrence reports and the department manager will get the report to Risk Management in 24 hours. Check with your department manager.)

If an injury occurred, the Risk Manager is to be notified at extension 5507 immediately; also, notify the appropriate administrator.

DO NOT FILE THE REPORT IN THE MEDICAL RECORD.

DO NOT MAKE ANY COPIES OF THIS REPORT FOR ANY REASON.

Document *relevant facts* objectively in the medical record.

_____   _____
Approved   Date

INDEX FOR GUIDELINES FOR DEPARTMENTS

Page

1. Emergency Department
2. Operating Room
3. Post Anesthesia Care Unit (PACU)
4. Intensive Care Units (ICU) For Adults and Pediatrics
5. Medical/Surgical
6. OB/GYN
7. Labor and Delivery
8. Level I Nursery
9. Level II and III Nurseries
10. Pediatric Ambulatory Care and Emergency Department
11. Surgical Outpatient
12. Psychiatric or Colorado Psychiatric Hospital
13. OB/GYN Ambulatory Care
14. University Medical Group Practice (UMGP) and Medical Ambulatory Care

continues

Exhibit 5–3 continued

Guidelines for Emergency Department Reportable Occurrences

1. Return to the Emergency Department within 7 days after discharge or prior visit.
2. Patient injury due to complication of procedure during Emergency Department treatment including cardiac/respiratory arrest.
3. Death in Emergency Department designated as "Coroner's Case."
4. Patient/visitor fall in the Emergency Department or on hospital grounds resulting in injury.
5. Emergency Department patient refuses treatment/hospitalization and leaves A.M.A.
6. Patient discharged from Emergency Department with altered conscious/neurological deficit (e.g., alcohol usage; under influence of parenteral analgesic).
7. Unexpected diagnostic results returned to Emergency Department after patient discharged.
8. Patient discharged from Emergency Department without being seen by an attending MD.
9. Medications/transfusion error in Emergency Department.
10. No written or improper consent for Emergency Department treatment.
11. Misidentification of patient resulting in unnecessary treatment/procedure.
12. Retained sponge post delivery.
13. Triage occurring greater than 30 minutes from the time of arrival in Emergency Department.
14. Transfer to ICU occurring greater than 2 hours from the time the decision has been made to admit and make ICU bed available.

When no patient injury has occurred, interdepartmental problems should be documented on University Hospital Interdepartmental Form. If a patient/visitor injury resulted, then a Patient Occurrence Report should be completed.

Guidelines for Operating Room Reportable Occurrences

1. Incorrect sponge, instrument or needle count.
2. Break in skin integrity.
3. Intubation/extubation injury (i.e., tooth dislodged, aspiration).
4. Postoperative nerve damage or neurological deficit.
5. Instrument breakage during surgery.
6. Wrong patient operated upon.
7. Wrong surgical procedure performed.
8. No written or improper consent for surgical procedures.
9. Unplanned removal or repair of an organ or body part. (Nicked an organ or vessel requiring additional O.R. time or results in patient injury.)
10. Patient injured during transfer to/from the O.R. or Day Surgery.
11. Equipment malfunction causing termination/cancellation of procedure or patient injury (i.e., pump/equipment problems).
12. Uncorrectable break in sterile technique (i.e., a fly landing in the operative wound).
13. Death in O.R.
14. Excessive blood loss.
15. Medication/transfusion error.
16. IV infiltration resulting in tissue damage.
17. Life-threatening complication of anesthesia.
18. Patient burn or allergic reaction to prep.
19. Unplanned return to O.R. or unplanned postoperative admit to ICU.
20. Specimen lost or incorrectly labeled.
21. Retained instrument, sponge, needle, etc.

When no patient injury has occurred, interdepartmental problems should be documented on University Hospital Interdepartmental Form. If a patient/visitor injury resulted, then a Patient Occurrence Report should be completed.

Guidelines for Post Anesthesia Care Unit (PACU) Reportable Occurrences

1. Intubation/extubation injury (i.e., tooth dislodged, aspiration).
2. Patient injured during transfer to/from the PACU.
3. Excessive blood loss.
4. Medication/transfusion error.
5. IV infiltration resulting in tissue damage.
6. Unexpected death in PACU.

continues

Exhibit 5–3 continued

7. PACU incurred trauma (e.g., falls, burns, procedure complications).
8. PACU equipment malfunction or misutilization.
9. Improper airway management resulting in patient injury.
10. Life-threatening complication of anesthesia.
11. Patients leaving from Day Surgery without responsible adult after anesthesia and/or IV sedation.
12. Patients leaving Day Surgery A.M.A.

When no patient injury has occurred, interdepartmental problems should be documented on University Hospital Interdepartmental Form. If a patient/visitor injury resulted, then a Patient Occurrence Report should be completed.

Guidelines for Intensive Care Units (ICU) Reportable Occurrences for Adults and Pediatrics

1. Unexpected death in ICU.
2. ICU incurred trauma (e.g., falls, burns, procedure complications).
3. ICU equipment malfunction or misutilization.
4. Medication/transfusion error in ICU.
5. Patient injured during transfer to/from ICU.
6. Readmit to ICU within 48 hours of transferring to ward.
7. Transfer to ICU within 24 hours of admission to ward.
8. No written or improper consent for procedure.
9. Patients leaving A.M.A.
10. IV infiltration resulting in tissue damage.
11. Hospital acquired infection.
12. Patient/visitor falls resulting in injury.
13. Patient injury due to:
    a) untimely response by MD/RN
    b) failure to carry out MD order appropriately or in timely manner
    c) poor response by ancillary services
    d) complication of procedure (to include postoperative complications)
14. Patient injury due to transcription error (i.e., delays, missed, etc.).

When no patient injury has occurred, interdepartmental problems should be documented on University Hospital Interdepartmental Form. If a patient/visitor injury resulted, then a Patient Occurrence Report should be completed.

Guidelines for Medical/Surgical Reportable Occurrences for Adults and Pediatrics

1. Unexpected death on ward.
2. Patient/visitor falls resulting in injury.
3. Medication/transfusion omissions or errors.
4. Equipment malfunction or absence.
5. Transfer to ICU within 24 hours of transfer or admission to ward.
6. Unplanned return to O.R. within 72 hours postoperatively.
7. Unplanned readmission within 24 hours.
8. No written or improper consent for procedure.
9. Patient leaves A.M.A.
10. Patient injury due to:
    a) untimely response by MD/RN
    b) failure to carry out MD order appropriately or in timely manner
    c) patient noncompliance
    d) poor response by ancillary services
    e) complication of procedure (to include postop complications)
11. IV infiltration resulting in tissue damage.
12. Hospital acquired infection.
13. Patient burn.
14. Patient injury due to transcription error (i.e., delays, missed, etc.).

When no patient injury has occurred, interdepartmental problems should be documented on University Hospital Interdepartmental Form. If a patient/visitor injury resulted, then a Patient Occurrence Report should be completed.

continues

Exhibit 5–3 continued

Guidelines for OB/GYN Reportable Occurrences

1. Medication/transfusion errors.
2. Patient/visitor falls resulting in injury.
3. Precipitous deliveries.
4. Unplanned readmissions within 48 hours.
5. Live TABs.
6. Equipment malfunction or absence.
7. Unexpected death on ward.
8. No written or improper consent for treatment.
9. Refusal of treatment.
10. Patient injury due to:
    a) untimely response by MD/RN
    b) failure to carry out MD order appropriately or in timely manner
    c) poor response by ancillary services
    d) complication of procedure (to include postoperative complications)
11. Unplanned return to O.R.
12. Hospital acquired infection.
13. IV infiltration resulting in tissue damage.
14. Patient leaves A.M.A.
15. Retained sponge.
16. Patient burn.

When no patient injury has occurred, interdepartmental problems should be documented on University Hospital Interdepartmental Form. If a patient/visitor injury resulted, then a Patient Occurrence Report should be completed.

Guidelines for Labor and Delivery Reportable Occurrences

1. Apgar less than 6 at 1 minute or less than 7 at 5 minutes.
2. Maternal injuries/complications related to delivery.
3. Newborn transferred to ICU for complications.
4. Infant injury during delivery.
5. Maternal/infant death in labor/delivery.
6. Emergency C-sections (indicate reason).
7. Mother's unplanned return to delivery room or surgery or ICU.
8. Second stage labor longer than 2.5 hours.
9. Maternal blood loss over 500 cc in O.R. or D.R. or R.R.
10. Complicated bed delivery done by MD/RN.
11. Uncontrolled deliveries resulting in injury.
12. Equipment malfunction or absence.
13. IV infiltration resulting in tissue damage.
14. Medication/transfusion error.
15. Patient/visitor fall resulting in injury.
16. Life-threatening complication of anesthesia.
17. Patient burn.
18. Malignant hyperthermia.
19. Forcep/Silastic deliveries.
20. Failed or difficult C.L.E.
21. "Gut feelings," re: litigious patient.
22. Visitor injury.

When no patient injury has occurred, interdepartmental problems should be documented on University Hospital Interdepartmental Form. If a patient/visitor injury resulted, then a Patient Occurrence Report should be completed.

Guidelines for Level I Nursery Reportable Occurrences

1. Medication/transfusion errors.
2. Falls/injuries/death.

continues

Exhibit 5-3 continued

3. Patient identification issue.
4. Missed PKU/newborn screen.
5. Equipment malfunction or absence.
6. Unplanned readmission within 48 hours; (other than scheduled follow-up).
7. No written or improper consent for procedure.
8. Refusal of treatment/hospitalization.
9. Outborn infants.
10. Apgar less than 6 at 1 minute or less than 7 at 5 minutes.
11. Seizure before discharge.
12. Patient injury due to:
    a) untimely response by MD/RN
    b) poor response by ancillary services
    c) failure to carry out MD order appropriately or in a timely manner
    d) complication of procedure
13. Visitor injury.
14. Treatment/procedure error.

When no patient injury has occurred, interdepartmental problems should be documented on University Hospital Interdepartmental Form. If a patient/visitor injury resulted, then a Patient Occurrence Report should be completed.

Guidelines for Level II and III Nurseries Reportable Occurrences

1. Patient or visitor falls resulting in injury.
2. Medication/transfusion errors.
3. Equipment malfunction or absence.
4. IV infiltration resulting in tissue damage.
5. Patient injury due to:
    a) untimely response by MD/RN
    b) poor response by ancillary services
    c) failure to carry out MD order appropriately or in a timely manner
    d) complication of procedure (to include postoperative complications)
6. Visitor injury.
7. Treatment/procedure error (missed or improper).
8. No written or improper consent for treatment.
9. Unexpected death on ward.
10. Hospital acquired infection.
11. Refusal of treatment/hospitalization.
12. Excessive blood loss.
13. Patient burn.
14. Outborn infants.
15. Apgar less than 6 at 1 minute or less than 7 at 5 minutes.
16. Seizure before discharge.

When no patient injury has occurred, interdepartmental problems should be documented on University Hospital Interdepartmental Form. If a patient/visitor injury resulted, then a Patient Occurrence Report should be completed.

Guidelines for Pediatric Ambulatory Care and Emergency Department Reportable Occurrences

1. Unexpected deaths.
2. Patient injury.
3. Medication errors.
4. Equipment malfunction or absence.
5. Parents taking client A.M.A.
6. Equipment related incidents.
7. Client injury due to delayed response by department other than nursing (including MD).
8. No written or improper consent.
9. IV infiltration resulting in tissue damage.
10. Refusal of treatment or hospitalization.

continues

Exhibit 5–3 continued

11. Adverse reaction to immunization (per National Vaccine Act Guidelines).
12. Alleged violation of privacy (adolescent's parents notified against wishes).
13. Failure to report suspected child abuse or neglect.
14. Request to court for state to act parens patriae (on child's behalf).
15. Failure to diagnose or delay in diagnosis of serious medical condition.
16. Other adverse event.

When no patient injury has occurred, interdepartmental problems should be documented on University Hospital Interdepartmental Form. If a patient/visitor injury resulted, then a Patient Occurrence Report should be completed.

Guidelines for Surgical Outpatient Reportable Occurrences

1. Treatment/procedure error in clinic.
2. Unplanned hospital admission subsequent to an invasive or minor surgical procedure or medication.
3. IV infiltration resulting in tissue damage.
4. Patient or visitor fall or injury in clinic area.
5. Patient refuses treatment/hospitalization and leaves A.M.A.
6. Medication/transfusion error.
7. No written or improper consent for treatment.
8. Cardiac/respiratory arrest/death in clinic.
9. Patient inappropriately discharged from clinic with parenteral analgesics.
10. Excessive blood loss.
11. Equipment malfunction or absence.
12. Retained foreign body identified in patient with history of prior invasive procedure, same day or inpatient surgery.
13. Cancellation of invasive or minor surgical procedure after
    a) premedication, or
    b) local anesthesia administered
14. Patient states desire to establish disability for personal injury claim as a result of the injury prompting health center visit.
15. Adverse results of local anesthesia in the ambulatory setting.
16. Nosocomial infection requiring medical or surgical intervention:
    a) health center acquired
    b) related to same day surgical procedure
    c) related to inpatient surgical procedure
17. Severe depression requiring medical intervention related to prolonged postoperative course.
18. Persistent or recurrent same or similar complaint that prompted recent surgical intervention.
19. Other adverse event or poor outcome (specify event).

When no patient injury has occurred, interdepartmental problems should be documented on University Hospital Interdepartmental Form. If a patient/visitor injury resulted, then a Patient Occurrence Report should be completed.

Guidelines for Psychiatric or Colorado Psychiatric Hospital Reportable Occurrences

1. Unexpected death on ward (i.e., Coroner's case).
2. Patient/visitor falls resulting in injury.
3. Medication/transfusion errors.
4. Equipment malfunction or absence (to include restraints and restraint beds).
5. Transfer to ICU within 24 hours of transfer/admission to ward.
6. Unplanned readmission within 24 hours.
7. No written or improper consent for procedure.
8. Patient's leaving A.M.A. or runaway.
9. Patient injury due to:
    a) untimely response by MD/RN
    b) failure to carry out MD order appropriately or in timely manner
    c) patient noncompliance
    d) poor response by ancillary services
    e) complication of procedure (to include postoperative complications, seclusion, restraints, ECT, etc.)
    f) self-infliction
    g) during recreational activity
10. IV infiltration resulting in tissue damage.

continues

Exhibit 5–3 continued

11. Patient's unplanned transfer to University Hospital.
12. Allegations of sexual misconduct (i.e., between patient and patient; staff and patient; visitor and patient).

When no patient injury has occurred, interdepartmental problems should be documented on University Hospital Interdepartmental Form. If a patient/visitor injury resulted, then a Patient Occurrence Report should be completed.

Guidelines for OB/GYN Ambulatory Care Reportable Occurrences

1. Failure to give antenatal Rhogam.
2. Failure to give one hour glucola screen.
3. Failure to do AFP test.
4. Failure to do HCT and antibody screen.
5. Failure or delay in abnormal lab follow-up.
6. Noncompliance of patient to take prescribed medications.
7. OB patient taking teratogenic drugs.
8. Failure to follow up missed appointments.
9. Excessive bleeding following procedures.
10. Medication reaction.
11. Medication errors.
12. Equipment failure.
13. Patient or visitor falls.
14. Fetal demise.
15. IV infiltration resulting in tissue damage.
16. Injuries or complications related to procedures.
17. Failure to obtain patient consent prior to performing procedures.
18. Failure to obtain patient consent to participate in research study.

When no patient injury has occurred, interdepartmental problems should be documented on University Hospital Interdepartmental Form. If a patient/visitor injury resulted, then a Patient Occurrence Report should be completed.

Guidelines for University Medical Group Practice (UMGP) and Medical Ambulatory Care Reportable Occurrences

1. Patient injury due to complication of procedure during care center visit or:
   a) Missed, inaccurate or untimely diagnosis resulting in delay of treatment or lack of treatment.
   b) Failure to carry out MD order appropriately or in a timely fashion.
   c) Medication error and/or allergic reaction.
2. Patient/visitor falls in and around Care Center A.
3. No written or improper consent for procedure including, but not limited to, sigmoidoscopy, LP, joint aspiration or injection, paracentesis, and I and D.
4. Patient discharged home with potentially life-threatening differential diagnosis not ruled out and follow-up not documented.
5. Patient refuses treatment deemed life threatening or with high mortality, either signing the A.M.A. form or not.
6. Patient admission delay that places patient in jeopardy.
7. Suspected child or senior abuse or failure to report same.
8. Break in confidentiality.
9. Cardiac arrest or death.
10. Failure or delay in abnormal lab follow-up or inability to follow up.
11. Patient states desire to establish workers' compensation and/or personal injury claim as a result of the injury prompting Care Center A, B, or C visit.
12. Medicare/Medicaid patient discharged without attending seeing patient.
13. Patients who express or who are suspected of being dissatisfied with care or who express litigious concerns.
14. Initial diagnosis of breast, colon, or cervical cancer at advanced stage is made in a patient who has had one or more Care Center A visits in past 12 months. (Primary Care Providers)
15. Medication error.
16. IV infiltration with tissue damage.

When no patient injury has occurred, interdepartmental problems should be documented on University Hospital Interdepartmental Form. If a patient/visitor injury resulted, then a Patient Occurrence Report should be completed.

Source: Courtesy of University of Colorado Health Sciences Center, Denver, CO.

INITIAL RISK ASSESSMENT

A risk manager who wants to develop a program that is sensitive to the specific needs of the institution will begin the process by evaluating all potential risk hazards within the designated "high-risk" services and obtain information as to how they are currently managed. The evaluation may begin by reviewing historical claims data and identifying specific practices (or staff) that gave rise to litigation. The standards of professional societies, regional or local standards, and existing hospital policies and procedures also can be reviewed to identify acceptable and appropriate behavior.

The questions in the Self-Assessment Tool (see Exhibit 5-4) can be used by the risk manager to gather baseline data about the hospital, the existing risk management and quality assurance programs, and particular policies that exist in a number of high-risk clinical areas. Risk managers who work in settings with additional high-risk exposure areas can develop similar types of questions. Answers to the questions can be used to drive risk management programs in specific areas where quality of service may be adversely affected or where generally accepted minimal standards of care are not being followed.

PRELIMINARY INCIDENT AND CLAIM MANAGEMENT

The establishment of a basic structure for preliminary incident and claim management focusing on early investigation will assist the risk manager in analyzing incidents identified as having potential for exposure. (The entire subject of claims management is discussed in detail in Chapter 19.)

The risk manager learns of the incidents that will require investigation from various sources, including the following:

- the regular incident reporting or generic screening mechanism of the hospital
- a telephone call from a concerned staff member
- a telephone call or other communication from a patient or a patient's representative describing an incident that resulted in patient or family dissatisfaction
- a telephone call from a physician concerned about a patient outcome
- a rumor or comments overheard in a hospital unit or hallway

If the risk manager believes that the information suggests a patient injury or a legitimate patient dissatisfaction, a preliminary investigation should be instituted. The investigation should consist of a meeting with the patient or family, a meeting with staff members who are in the best position to provide accurate information about the incident, and a meeting with hospital personnel whose function is to address and solve the problem. Continued communication with these persons is necessary until the problem is appropriately resolved. Corrective action, if necessary, also should be identified, established, and documented. When quality of care issues surface during the investigation, the appropriate quality assurance committee and the director of quality assurance should be immediately notified.

If corrective action cannot be taken or if the staff, after diligent effort, is unable to satisfy the patient or other individual who made the complaint, the risk manager may wish to establish an active file and perform additional investigation. This process is detailed in Chapter 19.

The early warning and investigation phase is important in identifying potential areas of disquality and correcting them. This process also enables the risk manager to gather the relevant facts about an incident while they are still fresh in the minds of all parties. When the facts are available prior to the involvement of legal counsel, the hospital is better able to develop a successful defense and to recognize those claims that should be settled as quickly as possible.

Exhibit 5-4
HOSPITAL SELF-ASSESSMENT TOOL

GENERAL QUESTIONS

Does the hospital have a formalized risk management program?

Does the hospital have a designated risk manager with a formal job description?

Does the risk manager have a direct reporting line with hospital administration?

Does the hospital have a mechanism in place for identifying, reporting, and responding to unusual hospital occurrences?

Does the hospital have procedures to monitor the quality of patient care, such as the utilization of generic screens or other clinical indicators?

Does the hospital have a system for concurrent chart review?

Does the risk management effort include clinical chart review? If yes, who participates in the review?

Are credentialing, privilege delineation, and staff reappointment processes well documented?

Does risk management participate in or contribute to these processes?

Are quality of care issues considered during the staff reappointment process?

Does the hospital require professional liability insurance coverage of at least $1 million/$3 million for each physician? Is this coverage verified on an annual basis?

Are contract physicians credentialed in the same manner as staff physicians?

Does the hospital have a system or mechanism for monitoring care rendered in satellite and other off-premises sites?

ANESTHESIA SERVICES

Who is responsible for coordinating and directing the anesthesia service within the hospital?

Does this responsibility also include the management of the recovery room?

Does this responsibility also include the management of off-premises surgicenters?

Are there specific policies to define the activities that occur in these locations?

Are all persons who render general anesthesia board-certified in anesthesia?

Are certified registered nurse anesthetists (CRNAs) used in the operating room? If yes, who supervises them?

How are CRNAs credentialed?

Who provides professional liability coverage for CRNAs?

What are the limits of this coverage?

Is coverage verified on an annual basis?

Is every gas anesthesia apparatus equipped with an oxygen analyzer?

Is pulse oximetry and end-tidal carbon dioxide monitoring used on all patients who receive general anesthesia?

Do the same policies govern inpatient and outpatient surgical areas, especially regarding postanesthesia recovery room care?

Is equipment calibrated prior to the start of each day and is this process documented?

Are preventive maintenance logs maintained on all anesthesia equipment?

Does the anesthesia department have an effective policy that governs the removal from service of defective or potentially defective equipment?

Does the anesthesia service monitor and document systolic and diastolic blood pressure, apical rate, electrocardiogram results, and precordial and esophageal breath sounds on all patients?

Is temperature monitored on all patients who receive general anesthesia during surgery?

Are disconnect and parameter alarms used for all patients who receive general anesthesia?

Is verification of proper endotracheal tube placement always documented?

Are positioning protocols in place and followed to prevent nerve and muscle injury?

Are pre- and postanesthesia visits always made prior to induction and after discharge from the recovery room area? Are these visits documented?

Does the person who administers anesthesia to the patient follow that patient to the recovery room and provide written and oral reports to appropriate recovery room personnel on all facts relevant to operative and perioperative status?

Are anesthesia records completed by the anesthetist prior to the patient's care being assumed by recovery room personnel?

Who is responsible for extubating the patient in the recovery room?

Who is responsible for discharging the patient either home or to the hospital unit?

Does the anesthesia department participate in surgical case reviews or other surgical quality of care committees?

Are gas scavenging systems used to prevent the leaching of nitrous oxide into the operating room?

OBSTETRICAL SERVICES

Is the chief of the obstetrical service board-certified in obstetrics?

Are all patients who present to the obstetrics (OB) department for impending delivery monitored with an external fetal monitor?

Is a baseline electronic fetal monitoring (EFM) strip run on each patient as a part of the initial assessment?

Is this strip maintained as part of the patient's permanent record?

Does the hospital have a written policy that supports baseline fetal monitoring on all obstetrical patients?

Are all high-risk OB patients continuously monitored until delivery?

Is the facility a level III perinatal center? If yes, does it have written policies that describe the transfer of patients to the facility?

continues

Exhibit 5–4 continued

Does the hospital have a perinatal transport team responsible for the pickup of high-risk mothers and neonates?

Is the training of these individuals sufficient to support their ability to care for these patients during transport?

Is a physician part of the transport team and does he or she accompany the team on all transports?

If the facility is not a level III facility, does it have policies in place to govern transfer of patients to level III facilities?

Are there any types of patients routinely transferred out of the facility?

Are protocol procedures well documented for transferring patients in and out of the facility?

Does the hospital have screening criteria to identify high-risk obstetric patients?

Are prenatal records accessible at the time of delivery?

Is an EFM course available for all nurses who care for OB patients?

Is expertise in interpreting EFM strips documented in nurses' continuing education files?

Can a cesarean section be performed within 30 minutes at any time?

Is 24-hour anesthesia coverage available for the obstetrics department?

Is a neonatologist/perinatologist available on a 24-hour basis for difficult and high-risk deliveries?

Is there an interdisciplinary committee that meets routinely to coordinate, evaluate, and monitor the delivery and care of newborns?

Is emergency neonatal resuscitative equipment available in all delivery rooms?

Are cesarean sections performed in the obstetrics department or are patients transferred to surgery for delivery?

Does the hospital operate a neonatal intensive care unit (ICU)?

Does the neonatal ICU unit have 24-hour physician coverage and extra corporeal membrane oxygenation (ECMO) capabilities?

Does the hospital have residency programs in obstetrics, neonatology, and perinatology?

Are ongoing continuing education programs offered in obstetrics for all staff?

EMERGENCY DEPARTMENT

Is the director of the emergency department (ED) board-certified in emergency medicine?

Is the ED staffed by contract physicians?

Does a designated person represent the department within the organized structure of the hospital's medical staff?

If contract physicians are used to staff the ED, are they credentialed pursuant to the hospital's policy for staff physicians?

Is there a defined triage process performed and documented for all patients presenting to the ED for treatment?

Is a responsible physician involved in the care and treatment of each patient examined in the ED?

Does ED policy mandate that a complete set of vital signs (temperature, pulse, respirations, and blood pressure) be obtained for all patients presenting to the ED?

Is a fetal heart rate or a fetal heart monitor strip required for all pregnant patients arriving in the ED for treatment?

Does the policy mandate a repetition of any vital signs taken in the event of initial abnormality prior to discharge?

Is a medical record maintained for each patient examined in the ED?

Has a process been established to identify and communicate discrepancies between initial and final interpretations of laboratory, cardiology, or radiographic findings?

Are all ED staff members required to be certified in cardiopulmonary resuscitation (CPR)?

Are all ED staff members required to be advanced cardiac life support (ACLS) certified?

Does the ED own or operate ambulances?

Is telemetry available for communication between the ambulance staff and the hospital?

Does the hospital own or operate any aircraft (fixed-wing or rotorcraft)?

Who staffs the aircraft and how are these persons trained?

Is the ED a designated regional trauma center?

Do interdisciplinary committees review emergency and trauma care rendered to patients in the ED?

Does the hospital support an ED residency program?

Is an attending physician always present in the ED and does he or she review care rendered to all patients?

Is the ED commonly used as a "holding area" for patients awaiting transfer to intensive care units? If yes, is intensive care protocol related to frequency of monitoring observed by the ED staff?

Does the hospital have a designated trauma service to assume the care of all acute trauma patients?

Does the ED have a department-specific quality review (physician/nursing) process and a committee that meets regularly to discuss issues related to patient care?

Do ED flow sheets parallel those used in intensive care areas of the hospital?

Is pediatric emergency equipment readily available in the ED?

Is a dosage and calculation chart readily available for pediatric emergencies?

PSYCHIATRIC DEPARTMENT

Is the director of the psychiatric service board-certified in psychiatry?

Do the nurses and technicians working in psychiatric units have special training in psychiatric nursing or mental health?

Does the hospital operate both inpatient and outpatient psychiatric services?

Does the psychiatric service include the care of both adults and children?

Are children and adolescents separated from the adult patients on the psychiatric units?

continues

Exhibit 5–4 continued

Are units locked or open?

Does the hospital operate alcohol and chemical dependency units as part of the psychiatric service?

What outpatient psychiatric services are provided by the department?

Are all programs reviewed by a quality review panel of physicians and nurses practicing in the area of psychiatry?

Is there a mechanism in place to allow for the multidisciplinary review of patients who are treated for medical and psychiatric problems?

Are all psychiatric patients who are hospitalized medically cleared during their hospitalization?

Does the hospital have strict procedures for the "leveling" of patients and are these procedures documented in patients' records?

Does the hospital offer a residency program in psychiatry, psychology, or social work?

Does the hospital have specific policies and procedures for the involuntary commitment of patients?

Are seclusion and restraint policies routinely reviewed and evaluated?

Are sharps routinely counted on all psychiatric units?

Is there a mechanism for referral of patients at the time of discharge to outpatient or community-based psychiatric services?

Is electroconvulsive therapy (ECT) performed in the institution?

If ECT is performed, are consents obtained prior to each treatment?

Do strict protocols exist related to the administration of psychopharmacologic drugs (for example, frequent determinations of blood levels and monitoring for side effects that may be related to toxicity)?

Is the unit housing the inpatient psychiatric department designed to prevent injury of suicidal patients (for example, nonbreakable and tamperproof windows, constant observation of potentially suicidal patients, and porches and sunroom areas secured to prevent patients from jumping)?

HOME HEALTH CARE SERVICES

Have specific protocols been developed to identify appropriate patients for home health care services?

Are treatment plans developed for each patient and approved by the supervising physician?

Is home care documented and are summaries of the care periodically sent to the treating physician?

Does the home care program offer hospice or respite service? If yes, is appropriate documentation (for example, living wills and do-not-resuscitate orders) kept in the patients' files?

Is there a preventive maintenance program for all equipment used by patients or their families in the home environment?

Are friends and family members who assist in the care of a patient taught how to troubleshoot equipment used in providing that care?

Are personnel and family members taught how to respond to emergency or life-threatening situations?

AIDS EXPOSURE

Does the hospital have a specific policy addressing employee related issues relative to HIV AIDS?

Does the hospital staff receive up-to-date information about Centers for Disease Control (CDC) guidelines as they relate to the care and treatment of patients with infectious diseases?

Have special consent forms been developed to cover research and experimental treatment available to AIDS and pre-AIDS (ARC and positive human immunodeficiency virus [HIV]) patients?

Does the hospital operate its own blood bank?

Does the blood bank maintain current American Association of Blood Banks and CDC guidelines as they pertain to procurement and distribution of blood and blood products?

Does the hospital have strict guidelines for the handling of confidential information related to HIV testing and the AIDS diagnosis?

Does the hospital have an interdisciplinary committee to address issues (both clinical and ethical) as they relate to the care of patients with AIDS?

RESIDENCY PROGRAMS

Is there a full-time program director for each residency specialty?

Are hospital residents unsupervised in outlying hospitals and clinics?

Is the hospital totally teaching-dependent?

Is there careful delineation of privileges for residents?

Is nursing staff aware of the privilege delineation?

Do resident programs include resident procedure logs?

Does an attending physician see every patient within 24 hours following admission?

Do attending physicians document evidence of continued ongoing supervision of residents?

Is "moonlighting" allowed in residency programs?

Are there controls placed on moonlighting activities?

Who provides insurance coverage for residents who engage in moonlighting activities?

Does the risk manager have an effective procedure to learn about actual and potential litigation against residents that arises from activities occurring away from the main hospital?

Is the chief of each service provided with information about all actual and potential claims pending against residents in his or her program?

chapter 6

Risk Management in the Age of Clinical Service Cutbacks

Lynn K. Coffman

EARLY DISCHARGE

Before the age of cost containment and reimbursement based on diagnosis-related groups, the physician decided when a patient was ready for discharge. However, now that a hospital is frequently reimbursed a fixed amount for each diagnosis or each hospital stay, it has an incentive to discharge a patient as soon as the physician deems the patient is medically cleared. This practice has given rise to claims of inadequate discharge. A patient or the patient's family may allege that the patient suffered injury because he or she was discharged before adequate plans were made for posthospital care.

The American Hospital Association (AHA) states that a patient is medically ready for discharge when two conditions are met: (1) the patient is no longer in need of acute care services, and (2) the patient's needs for post-acute care have been identified and reasonable steps have been taken to formulate and implement a plan to meet these needs.[1]

The Hospital's Obligation in Discharge Planning

The obligation of a hospital to ensure that the post-acute care needs of the patient are met has not been clearly defined. The hospital is obligated to do what a reasonable provider of care would do under the same or similar circumstances. How the hospital chooses to meet this obligation is left to the hospital to decide. The AHA has developed guidelines for discharge planning that provide advice on developing a hospital based discharge planning program (see Appendix 6-A).

The AHA has stated that a hospital fulfills its legal obligation to the patient if it has performed the following:

- assessed the patient's medical status at the time of discharge
- taken steps to identify the appropriate community services and agencies that can meet the patient's post-acute care needs
- made reasonable attempts to make these services known and available to the patient.[2]

Although it is the responsibility of each hospital to define its obligation to the patient for discharge planning in accordance with its own financial and personnel resources as well as available community resources, the AHA has established three factors a hospital should consider in defining this obligation:[3]

1. Who decides the patient is medically ready for discharge? The physician usually is the member of the care team who makes the decision to discharge the patient and signs the discharge order. However, the physician often relies on information provided by social workers, nurses, rehabilitation therapists, and other staff members to provide additional input into the decision-making process. If the other caregivers do not agree with the physician's discharge order, they are obligated to tell the physician of any factors that affect the patient's readiness for discharge.

2. What services is the hospital obligated to provide? The hospital is not obligated to provide the patient with the social services required. Rather, the hospital is obligated to assess the patient to determine what services are required and to formulate and implement a plan to meet these needs. This requires that the hospital be able to identify the appropriate community, state, and federal resources available to the patient and to be able to arrange for these resources to be made available to the patient. The hospital is not obligated to ensure that the ideal resources are available to the patient; the hospital is only obligated to do what a reasonable provider of care would do under the same or similar circumstances.

3. What should the patient be told about the discharge plan? Communication between the patient and those involved in discharge planning is important for the success of the discharge plan and to protect the hospital from future liability. If a patient's and family's expectations of the discharge plan are realistic, future claims of inadequate discharge are less likely to be brought against the hospital. The hospital is obligated to present the patient with alternatives and to involve the patient in the discharge plan. Exhibit 6-1 lists the information that every patient should be given about the discharge plan.

AVOIDING DISCHARGE LIABILITY

Each health care facility must define its discharge obligations to the patient, but there are certain legal principles within which the discharge process should take place in order to avoid claims of inadequate discharge. Potential liability for inadequately discharging a patient from the hospital most likely would be based upon a claim of negligence and its attendant principle of breach of implied contract.

All patients have the right to be free from injuries that are based on careless actions by their caretakers. These caretakers have a duty to the patient to exercise reasonable care in providing treatment, to protect the patient from reasonable or foreseeable harm, and to provide medically necessary care. This balance between the patient's right to be free from harm and the caregivers' duty not to harm the patient forms the basis of the legal theory of negligence.

The doctrine of vicarious liability extends the duty of the caregiver to the hospital. The hospital has a duty to provide the patient with a level of care consistent with the appropriate standard of care against which that care will be judged. This doctrine states that the hospital is responsible for the actions of those it holds out as its employees and agents. Thus, the hospital is responsible for the actions or nonactions of its employees.

Exhibit 6-1
COMMUNICATING THE DISCHARGE PLAN

The American Hospital Association recommends that the following elements of the discharge plan be communicated to the patient and the patient's family to avoid future liability:

1. The post-acute care services needed.
2. The efforts being made to meet the patient's needs.
3. The barriers encountered in trying to meet these needs.
4. The reasonably foreseeable outcome of the discharge plan.
5. The alternatives to the discharge plan that exist.

Source: Adapted from Legal Memorandum Number 9, *Discharging Hospital Patients: Legal Implications for Institutional Providers and Health Care Professionals*, American Hospital Association, Office of General Counsel, June 1987, p. 27.

Under the theory of negligence, the hospital and patient enter into a contractual relationship. This relationship begins at the time the patient presents himself or herself to the hospital in a manner that suggests the patient expects the hospital to provide health care *and* the hospital accepts the patient and offers its services. Because the hospital's duty to provide the patient with a reasonable standard of care is not explicitly written in a contract, the patient and hospital are said to have entered into an *implied* contract.

In the context of patient discharge under this implied contract, the hospital has the duty to provide the patient with a reasonable standard of care and to ensure that reasonable attempts have been made to identify the patient's post-acute discharge needs and formulate and implement a plan to meet these needs. If the hospital does not provide these implied obligations and the patient sustains an injury as a result of this failure, the hospital has breeched the implied contract and may be liable under the theory of negligence.

In addition to breeching an implied contract, the discharge of a patient before he or she is medically ready for discharge may constitute patient abandonment. The hospital's duty to the patient entails providing medically necessary care. If the patient claims that discharge occurred before the patient was medically ready and also claims that he or she was discharged without adequate provision to protect the patient from reasonable and foreseeable harm, the hospital could be liable for abandonment in addition to breech of implied contract.

Discharge Procedures

A hospital can develop several procedures to facilitate the discharge planning process and avoid liability associated with early discharge. These may include the following:

- Use generic screening criteria to identify patients early in their admission who may present potential discharge problems.
- Develop a system for contacting a social worker or discharge planner after regular working hours to handle problems associated with emergency room discharges and unanticipated weekend discharges of inpatients.
- Educate the staff about the correct documentation of the discharge process in the medical record.
- Prepare a hospital policy and procedure for the actions to be taken when a patient wishes to leave "against medical advice" (AMA).
- Educate physicians in the utilization review function and prepare a hospital procedure for challenging termination of third-party payments for continued inpatient care.

Screening Patients

When a physician indicates that a patient is ready for discharge, only one of the discharge conditions outlined by AHA has been met. Prior to this time, the social workers and discharge planning specialists should have identified resources that will satisfy a patient's post-acute care needs in order to meet the second AHA condition. The patient may have problems unrelated to his or her clinical status that should be considered at discharge. It may be necessary to alert the physician to these factors.

In the current environment of scarce resources that are available for patients in need of post-acute care, early identification of patients who will require post-acute care is crucial, so plenty of time is available to plan for their needs. Additionally, the more time spent on planning the discharge, the easier it will be for the discharge planner to cultivate the patient's and family's expectations for a realistic discharge plan. This minimizes the chance that the patient or family will feel as though the patient were rushed out of the hospital without adequate preparation for discharge.

The Washington Adventist Hospital in Takoma Park, Maryland, uses *case-finding criteria* (see Exhibit 6-2) to identify patients at admission who may require post-acute care. Each morning, the social workers screen the admission face sheets for patients on their clinical services who meet one or more of 13 generic criteria. These patients are then further assessed for their discharge planning needs.

Georgetown University Hospital, Washington, D.C., has designed a *high-risk screening protocol* (see Exhibits 6-3 and 6-4) to identify patients at admission who are considered at high risk for continued care after discharge from the acute care setting. The social workers developed generic criteria to identify these patients at admission as well as criteria specific to their clinical services that are used for more thorough reviews of medical records.

After-Hours Discharges

Third-party payers often deny reimbursement when emergency room patients are admitted to the hospital for observation or because their living situations do not provide adequate support for post-acute care. Often these patients can be discharged from the emergency room without exposing the hospital to claims of inadequate discharge if home health or support services are made available to the patients in a timely fashion or if the patients can be temporarily admitted to a facility where they will not be alone.

Many hospitals have a 24-hour, 7-day call system for social workers who assist the medical and nursing staffs in meeting patients' post-acute needs on short notice. The social worker on call can have a resource book that lists the community's shelters, support services, and other facilities,

---

Exhibit 6-2
CASE-FINDING CRITERIA USED AT
WASHINGTON ADVENTIST HOSPITAL

1. All patients over age 80 years and all patients over age 75 years who live alone, except for the following diagnoses that will not be automatically screened:
   A. Cataract
   B. Coronary artery disease
   C. Arteriosclerotic obliterans
2. All cancer patients
3. All AIDS patients
4. All cerebral vascular accident patients
5. All patients with diagnosis of hip fracture or multiple fractures
6. All patients with organic brain disease
7. All patients with progressive degenerative diseases that impair functioning
8. Any problem patient known to the department, including problematic readmissions
9. Any patient admitted from a nursing home or chronic care facility
10. Any patient who is a suspected victim of abuse or neglect
11. All admissions to the psychiatric unit except admissions to the Adult Treatment Unit and patients with insurance coverage under a health maintenance organization (HMO)
12. Any mother under age 14
13. Any patient with a diagnosis of congestive heart failure (CHF), respiratory failure, respiratory insufficiency, or chronic obstructive pulmonary disease (COPD) who does not meet the other screening criteria will be referred for home health services

Source: Courtesy of Washington Adventist Hospital, Takoma Park, MD.

Exhibit 6-3
HIGH-RISK SCREENING PROTOCOL USED AT GEORGETOWN UNIVERSITY HOSPITAL

HIGH-RISK SCREENING PROTOCOL

1. Each social worker will review every admission sheet for his or her service each morning and select those admission sheets that meet predetermined criteria for that particular service.
2. These admission sheets then will be further screened by chart review, discussion with Nursing, or both regarding the appropriateness of social work intervention.
3. If it appears that social work intervention would be required or beneficial, the social worker will then proceed to talk with the patient and family.
4. A social work note will be placed in the chart, either summarizing the determination of why social work will not be involved with the case or stating what the social work plan will be.

Source: Courtesy of the Department of Social Work, Georgetown University Hospital, Washington, D.C.

along with the names of contact persons as well as a description of the services provided, so that he or she can arrange referrals by phone when out of the hospital. Exhibit 6-5 illustrates two sample pages from a social services resource manual.

Staff Education

Communication of the discharge plan to the patient and the patient's family is essential if the patient and family are to participate in the planning process and ultimately accept the discharge plan. Documentation in the medical record of what is communicated to the patient and family is critical if the hospital is ever called upon to demonstrate its planned attempt to avoid foreseeable and reasonable harm to the patient. Exhibit 6-6 outlines the elements that must be included in the discharge planning notes for documentation to be complete.

Documentation of the discharge plan should become a routine part of the medical record. Hospitals can use preprinted sheets that provide space for the necessary elements of documentation. If preprinted forms are not used, cards

Exhibit 6-4
CLINICAL SERVICE-SPECIFIC CRITERIA USED IN HIGH-RISK SCREENING AT GEORGETOWN UNIVERSITY HOSPITAL

ADULT MEDICAL-SURGICAL ONCOLOGY

1. Stage of disease
   A. Newly diagnosed
   B. New protocol
   C. Newly advanced
   D. Terminal
2. Patient adjustment to disease
3. Family/friend adjustment to disease
4. Age of patient in relation to
   A. Stage of disease
   B. Side effects
   C. Body image
   D. Life style
5. No or inadequate support system
6. Poor social/coping skills
7. Level of understanding of disease and its treatment

Environmental
1. Lives alone
2. No family or friends available to help with practical needs
3. Nursing/health aid services
4. Placement
5. Concrete needs (i.e., equipment)
6. Concurrent health problems
7. No income
8. No insurance
9. Lives out of town

CRITICAL CARE AREAS

All patients who:
1. Are under consideration for heart transplant, undergoing heart transplant, or readmitted with complications
2. Are diagnosed with AIDS
3. Are transferred from a hospital from outside metropolitan area
4. Are admitted with no identifying information on face sheet
5. Are admitted as "self-pay"
6. Are known to have previously complicated discharge planning needs

Patients age 75 years or older who meet any one of these criteria:
1. Live alone
2. Transferred from nursing home or retirement facility

NEUROSURGERY
1. Patients with confused or altered mental status
2. Patients with newly diagnosed or exacerbated brain tumor or chronic illness (i.e., Parkinson's, multiple sclerosis, seizure disorder, benign brain tumor, chronic vegetative state from previous cancer or trauma)
3. Newly diagnosed cancer
4. Inability to perform activities of daily living
5. In need of home care

Source: Courtesy of the Department of Social Work, Georgetown University Hospital, Washington, D.C.

Exhibit 6-5
SAMPLE PAGES FROM A SOCIAL SERVICES
RESOURCE MANUAL

Name of community service: Saint Joseph's Parish Home for Men

Address: 2424 Euclid Avenue N.W., Washington, D.C. 20003

Phone: 555-1222

Contact person: Fr. Patrick Harden

Description of services: Provides short-term, overnight shelter for men only. Provides one hot evening meal, sleeping arrangements, bathing facilities. Job counseling available. Will provide temporary shelter while visiting nurse services are necessary, along with additional two meals. No transportation services to and from shelter.

Comments: As space permits, Fathers will monitor patients for changes in mental status, etc. Will not arrange care or supervise its completion. All arrangements must be made prior to patient's arrival.

Name of community service: Spring Village Retirement Home

Address: 2222 Goodhope Road S.W., Washington, D.C. 20018

Phone: 555-3434

Contact person: Maybelle Polk

Description of services: Single- and double-occupancy living units for Medicaid recipients only. Provides house-cleaning services, one hot meal per day in common dining area, emergency medical security services, and transportation services.

Comments: Space limited. Very long waiting list.

Exhibit 6-6
ELEMENTS OF DISCHARGE PLAN NOTES IN
THE MEDICAL RECORD

When documenting the discharge plan in the medical record, the following elements should be included in the discharge notes:

1. Why the patient requires post-acute care
2. What the discharge plan entails
3. What the patient and family were told about the discharge plan
4. An assessment of the patient's and family's levels of understanding the discharge plan
5. Whether the patient and family consent to the discharge plan
6. Why the patient is being discharged
7. What post-acute care is needed
8. What arrangements have been made for post-acute care.

Source: Adapted from "Effective Planning Can Defuse Discharge Risks," by David Burda, in *Hospitals*, February 20, 1987, p. 39, American Hospital Publishing Company.

The hospital should have an AMA policy and procedure in place that indicate the person or persons who are responsible for these discussions with the patient. Documentation of the discussions should be included in the medical record. Additionally, hospital personnel should request the patient to sign a form indicating that the risks of leaving the hospital and the benefits of remaining have been explained and that the patient assumes the risks and consequences of his or her actions and releases the hospital and its personnel from liability. If the patient refuses to sign the form, this should be documented in the medical record. A sample form for discharging a patient AMA is included in Appendix 6-B.

Termination of Third-Party Payment

A hospital requires procedures for challenging termination of third-party payments for continued inpatient care. The procedures should include the education of physicians in utilization review.

Recent case law ruled that the decision to discharge a patient from the hospital is the responsibility of the physician and not that of a third-party provider.[4] In the context of discharge planning, the courts are saying that a third-party payor has the right to determine the number of days it will reimburse a hospital for inpatient care. However, the third party cannot force a physician to discharge a patient against his or her best medical judgment if it is believed the patient will meet reasonably foreseeable harm if discharged at that time. Though the courts assume the physician is solely

can be placed in the front of the medical record or given to the appropriate personnel to carry in their pockets to cue them on the elements to include in the discharge documentation.

Against-Medical-Advice Policy

When a patient wishes to leave against medical advice (AMA), hospital personnel should attempt to discuss the following aspects of this decision with the patient:

- the reasons why the patient wishes to leave
- the risks involved if the patient leaves the hospital
- the benefits of remaining in the hospital
- alternative treatment plans, if applicable

responsible for the discharge decision, through the doctrine of vicarious liability the hospital can be held liable for the physician's actions if the patient sustains an injury because he or she was discharged before medically ready.

A physician who receives a letter of termination of reimbursement for a continued inpatient stay should be instructed in the proper method of contacting the third-party reviewers or the hospital's utilization review committee so that additional reimbursement for the patient may be requested. Efforts should be made to convey to the physician staff that administration will support a request for continuation of benefits if the medical record reflects that discharge at the present time may bring foreseeable harm to the patient. If the physician decides to keep the patient in the hospital despite a termination of benefits, the appropriate hospital personnel should discuss the financial implications of this decision with the patient. Additionally, physician staff should be encouraged to document in the medical record why discharge would be inappropriate at the termination of benefits. Physicians also should be instructed that termination of benefits should never be listed as a factor in the discharge.

THE NURSING SHORTAGE

The nursing shortage may have its impact on the quality of nursing care offered to patients. With high vacancy rates in staff positions and high turnover rates, hospitals are frequently forced to increase their patient-to-nurse ratios and to substitute less experienced nurses for those who are leaving bedside care. The current nursing shortage is not thought to be the result of cyclical forces that have caused the shortages of previous years. Rather, it is forecast as long-term and chronic. It will require hospitals to alter their expectations for the level of nursing experience at the bedside and to adjust the number of nurses available for patient units during each shift. In addition, hospitals will find that nurses cannot be easily deployed from the bedside to attend in-service educational programs and other career-enhancing programs.

The implications for liability are fairly obvious when present responses to the nursing shortage are observed:[5]

- Hospitals are using staff with fewer years of experience than were previously used in highly technical critical care areas.
- Nonprofessional personnel are more frequently utilized to perform direct care activities.
- Nurses who are overstressed and overtired are working overtime schedules.
- Nurses are being floated to unfamiliar areas of the hospital and perhaps using technology with which they are not experienced.

- Hospitals are depending on agency and per-diem nurses, who may not receive the benefits of hospital orientation and in-service education, to fill in the gaps left by the nursing shortage.

A Hospital's Legal Liability

A claim that a nurse acted in a negligent manner is based on a nurse's duty to the patient. A nurse has a duty to perform his or her actions in accordance with the standard of care that would be exercised by any other nurse with similar training or experience under similar circumstances. If the nurse acts in a manner that deviates from this standard, it is said the duty to the patient has been breached. Further, if the patient sustains an injury directly related or proximately caused by this breach in the standard of care, then, and only then, a negligent act has occurred.

A liability claim brought against a hospital that alleges a nurse was negligent in his or her care due to an understaffed or inappropriately staffed nursing unit or because a nurse's action or nonaction caused injury to a patient is usually brought on the theory of either corporate liability or respondeat superior (let the master answer).

The theory of corporate liability holds the hospital liable for the failure of administrators and staff to monitor and supervise properly the delivery of health care within the hospital. In relation to the nursing staff, the hospital must demonstrate that reasonable care was taken in reaching hiring and staffing decisions, evaluating the experience and education of its staff and potential staff, and providing ongoing education for the staff. The hospital also must demonstrate that reasonable care was taken to evaluate the performance of each member of the nursing staff on a continuing basis. Therefore, to hold the hospital responsible for the nurse's negligent action by claiming corporate liability, the patient would have to prove that the hospital was in some way negligent in its hiring, training, supervision, or monitoring the performance of the nurse.

The theory of respondeat superior holds a hospital liable for the actions and nonactions of its employee. It is based on the relationship between the hospital (the employer) and the nurse (the employee). Simply stated, it holds the master, the hospital, liable for the actions of its servant, the employee. Under respondeat superior, a hospital is held liable for the negligent action of its nurse as long as that nurse committed the negligent action while working in the context of the nurse's employment. In a claim against the hospital based on respondeat superior, the patient would not have to prove that the hospital was negligent in its hiring or monitoring of the nurse. The patient would need only to demonstrate that the nurse was negligent in his or her action or nonaction. The hospital's liability is based upon the fact that it employs the nurse and is therefore responsible for the nurse's actions.

The use of agency nurses, who are usually considered employees of their agency and not the hospital, has not protected the hospital from claims of corporate liability or respondeat superior when these nurses have acted in a negligent manner. Hospitals have been found liable under the theory of corporate liability for not properly evaluating the clinical competence and checking the credentials of agency personnel working in the hospitals.[6] In other cases, agency nurses have been viewed as agents or "temporary" employees of the hospital and the hospital was held responsible for their actions under respondeat superior.

AVOIDING LIABILITY DUE TO PERSONNEL SHORTAGES

There are some steps a hospital can take to avoid the liability associated with the nursing shortage. A hospital should consider the following five steps:

1. Assess for reliability the data that are collected for classifying patient and unit acuity levels.
2. Establish a procedure to verify the licensure and credentials of nurses from outside agencies and to evaluate their performance on a continuous basis.
3. Establish an orientation program for agency nurses that includes hospital policies and procedures and the use of new or unfamiliar technologies.
4. Evaluate the competence of the nursing staff in the use of new technology before it is introduced into the clinical setting.
5. Institute a formal float policy outlining the obligations and rights of staff nurses who are assigned to other areas of the hospital.

Reliable Data

Many proprietary patient classification methodologies are available on the market for purchase; many hospitals have designed their own. Regardless of the type of classification methodology used to determine patient care requirements and overall unit staffing needs, quality control practices are essential to assess the accuracy of the collected data on an ongoing basis.

Checking patient classification data for accuracy or inter-rater reliability need not be a complicated statistical analysis. It could simply entail having a second person reclassify the patient's level of care by using the medical record to obtain the necessary information. A system could be implemented in which a sample of patients is chosen for one week of one month out of every quarter and the patients' level of care reclassified for each day the patients were on the unit. The results of the original patient classification level and the reclassified level of care should be compared and deviations between the results investigated. Thresholds for minimum quality control indices (QCI) should be established and education programs or revision of the classification tool implemented as necessary.

Monitoring Agency Nurses

The hospital should check and document the licensure and credentials of nurses from supplemental agencies. Usually agencies are responsible for checking the credentials of their nurse employees. However, incidents arise where a nurse's licensure status is questioned and the hospital finds out too late that the nurse's license has expired or the nurse is unlicensed to practice in that state. When a nurse comes to work in a hospital for the first time, he or she should be required to bring a photocopy of both sides of the nursing license. The status of the license should be verified by hospital personnel and the copies kept on file.

The agency employing a nurse is also responsible for checking the nurse's references. However, a hospital may have little knowledge of how thoroughly these references are checked or what the references actually say. The performance of an agency nurse while working in the hospital should be monitored on a continuous basis.

After each shift the agency nurse's performance should be evaluated by a member of the unit's permanent staff. These performance appraisals should then be reviewed by the staffing coordinator for evidence of unsatisfactory performance. When a nurse is perceived to provide care that is below reasonable standards, the nurse's performance should be discussed with the agency and a determination made as to whether the nurse should be permitted to return to work at the hospital. Appendix 6-C provides a sample performance appraisal form that is simple to fill out at the end of each shift, yet provides an adequate appraisal.

Orientation Program for Agency Nurses

Agency nurses should become familiar with hospital policies and procedures and unfamiliar technology in a formal orientation program before they receive shift assignments. If they are given only a quick orientation to a nursing unit after receiving shift report, they are bound to have difficulty providing patients with reasonable standards of care.

The orientation program should include hospital policies concerning vascular access lines and devices, medication administration and order transcription, order entry methodology, and how to contact the patients' physicians. Additionally, agency nurses who are required to use new technologies or those that may vary from hospital to hospital must be properly trained in their correct application before they use them in patient care.

Orientations for agency nurses should not be viewed as an unnecessary or frivolous expense for a hospital. Under either the corporate liability or respondeat superior theory in legal cases, a hospital is liable for the actions and nonactions of its inadequately trained employees, and it can be held equally responsible for the acts of agency nurses working in the hospital. The financial cost of one negligent action could be greater than the cost of an entire orientation program.

Staff Competence in Technology

Before new technology is introduced into the clinical setting, the competency of the nursing staff in its operation should be evaluated. In-service education is often inadequate for nurses to learn how to use new technology successfully in patient care. Formal mechanisms to evaluate their understanding of the technology are required to ensure that it is used safely. A return demonstration or a post-test may be sufficient to ensure that the technology is understood and can be safely operated and interpreted.

Float Policy

A written "float" policy should outline the obligations and rights of staff nurses who are temporarily assigned to other areas of the hospital. A good patient classification methodology indicates on a daily basis the units with inadequate staff to meet the needs of their total patient acuity and the units with an abundance of staff. Financial considerations, as well as the shortage of available nurses, often preclude the hospital from using per-diem or agency nurses to fill in the gaps on one unit while another unit may have excessive staff. Instead, nurses are increasingly asked to float to other units for the duration of their shifts.

Nurses often object to floating. They claim that it disturbs the continuity of patient care, that they are unqualified to work on a particular nursing unit, or that their unit will need them later in the shift. A written float policy that outlines the nurses' obligation to accept reassignment to another unit when asked is easier to enforce than an informal, unwritten policy.

RISK ISSUES RELATED TO HEALTH MAINTENANCE ORGANIZATIONS

Hospitals are becoming increasingly involved in expansion of services that often include alternative delivery sites and health maintenance organizations (HMOs), either through contract or by direct affiliation. Risk management must be cognizant of the institution's increased liability risk exposure. The nature of these operations often differs significantly from the mission of the acute care facility. The risk manager should verify that care-related concerns are not compromised and that total quality management exists within these alternative types of health care settings. Because they are generally located in areas away from hospital property itself, it may be easy to forget that they incur additional risk exposure for the hospital and its staff.

Monitors and screens to track and trend actual and potential problems should be developed and carefully analyzed by the risk manager to identify potential risk areas. The monitors should parallel those used within the hospital. The risk managers should schedule periodic site visits to evaluate the following:

- completion of clinic records with appropriate documentation and description of care provided
- credentials, appropriate certification, and current licenses for all staff employed by the HMO
- safety and security measures in force with staff demonstrating awareness of policies and procedures related to safety
- emergency equipment in good condition and easily accessible with staff trained in its use

In addition, methods for credentialing and reappointment of physicians and for staff monitoring should be consistent with such procedures within the hospital.

HMO risk and subsequent liability are likely to arise from a number of circumstances. Of critical importance initially is evaluation of the marketing emphasis that has been placed on the center and the methods used to explain its services to the public. Following this analysis, attention should focus on the clinical risk exposures and the types of injuries or allegations that may result from these exposures. Such circumstances often arise due to the unique nature of the HMO setting. Generally the HMO focuses on patient complaints and "wellness" issues. It may seldom address acute emergencies; when they occur, problems may arise regarding failure to diagnose health problems, delays in making a diagnosis, and incorrect diagnosis. Diagnosis-related problems often stem from the fact that the HMO's economic incentive may result in incomplete assessment of a patient's condition and inadequate treatment of symptoms. Because the HMO staff concentrates on "wellness" and illness prevention rather than on critical or emergency medical conditions, it may miss some of the more significant symptomatology that could indicate more serious or life-threatening conditions.

Marketing Issues

Realistic marketing is critical to the maintenance of a risk-free facility. Although a hospital wants to attract clients to a new facility, it must avoid creating the appearance that the satellite facility can provide all of the services that the public expects from the hospital and that it can handle any and all emergencies. Care in naming the facility can also result in a more appropriate public perception of its purpose. For example, including the term "emergicare" or "emergicenter" in its name can create the impression that the facility is indeed equipped to handle any type of emergency. Newspaper advertisements should accurately reflect the strengths and weaknesses of the facility. Policies and procedures of the center should be developed to address the services that the public has a right to expect based on the facility's advertising.

Appropriate Documentation of Care

HMO care presents other areas of potential liability exposure. These additional risks are a result of the possible breakdowns in the continuity of care and communication due to the frequently large number of professionals who see and treat each patient. A triage nurse may speak to the patient to set up the initial appointment, a clinic nurse or receptionist may greet the patient when he or she arrives at the clinic, and several physicians may see the patient during each visit. These patient–staff interactions are all dependent on the quality of the examination provided by the preceding caregiver and the quality of available notes describing previous assessments and treatments. Developing a standardized format for such documentation to identify appropriate aspects of assessment reduces the possibility of inadequate or incomplete assessment and documentation. At the very minimum, this baseline data sheet should contain the following information:

- client's name, address, and telephone number
- alternate telephone number in case of emergency
- client's age
- brief summary of past medical history and statement of reason for client's visit
- recent hospitalizations or emergency department care specifically to determine if this is a follow-up visit
- billing data, including employer, insurer, HMO plan, or other pertinent information (this should be requested *only on the first visit* and maintained as part of the permanent file; focusing on these questions during subsequent visits may give the client the impression that the facility is more concerned about money than his or her health)
- names of additional family members who receive medical care from the facility

The development of additional "form" sheets for specific presenting complaints provides the staff with standardized methods of patient treatment and ensures that appropriate documentation is available in the clinic record. Obviously, the decision to develop these forms should be based on an analysis of the patient population typically receiving care at the facility. Input from nurses, physicians, and clerical staff should be solicited before the forms are developed.

Credentialing and Reappointment

Verifying the credentials of all personnel is critical to the operation of a successful satellite facility. In recruiting staff, the hospital should consider the level of care to be provided. For example, if the center is going to market family health care and "wellness" services, family medicine practitioners and pediatricians must be hired. Nurses should have similar work-related experience and be comfortable in dealing with patients of all ages.

The application and credentialing processes should contain all of the elements governing these processes for the hospital staff. Especially important in this evaluation is the verification of staff certification in basic cardiopulmonary resuscitation. The staff of a satellite facility does not have the luxury of a code team to handle acute emergencies and must be capable of performing first-line care to patients who develop emergency problems.

Staff Orientation

All satellite personnel who are employees of the hospital should receive the same orientation as the hospital staff with an additional focus on the facility where they will be working. If laboratory and x-ray support services are part of the facility and operated by hospital technicians, they must be provided with the hospital's policy and procedure information related to these services.

The orientation process should include information related to risk management incident reporting, disaster planning, and a department-specific quality assurance program that has been developed especially for the facility. The staff also requires information about nearby facilities that can provide the necessary emergency backup support (e.g., the nearest hospital with an obstetrical department, pediatric expertise, or specialization in industrial accidents).

The satellite staff should be provided with information describing available hospital resources, such as education, consultations, and other services, and encouraged to utilize these resources to prevent its isolation from other hospital staff.

NOTES

1. American Hospital Association, Office of General Counsel, Legal Memorandum Number 9, *Discharging Hospital Patients: Legal Implications for Institutional Providers and Health Care Professionals.* (Chicago: American Hospital Association, June 1987): 25.

2. Ibid, 26.

3. Ibid.

4. Wickline v. California, 228 Cal. Rptr. 661 (Ct. App. 1986).

5. K. Fenner, Nursing Shortage: Harbinger of Increased Litigation, *Nursing Management* 19 (November 1988): 44.

6. J.D. Memel and L. Sherwin, Hospital Liability for the Quality of Nursing Care, *Healthcare Executive* 4 (March/April 1989): 40.

Appendix 6-A

Guidelines for Discharge Planning

This guideline document is intended to provide general advice to the membership of the American Hospital Association, as approved by the General Council.

Introduction

The American Hospital Association believes that coordinated discharge planning functions are essential for hospitals to maintain high-quality patient care. Discharge planning is important because it facilitates appropriate patient and family decision making. In addition, it can also help reduce length of stay and the rate of increase of health care costs.

For most patients, discharge planning is a part of routine patient care. For those patients whose posthospital needs are expected to be complex, special discharge planning services are warranted. These guidelines present general information for organizing services for complex discharge planning.

It is recognized that each hospital has different resources and organizes its services differently to meet specific patient needs. It is further recognized that rapid changes in the hospital environment cause rapid changes in discharge planning. These changes, however, have emphasized the importance of discharge planning, and it is in that context that these guidelines are presented.

Definition

Discharge planning is an interdisciplinary hospitalwide process that should be available to aid patients and their families in developing a feasible posthospital plan of care.

Purposes

The purposes of discharge planning are to ensure the continuity of high-quality patient care, the availability of

the hospital's resources for other patients requiring admission, and the appropriate utilization of resources. To ensure the continuity of high-quality care, the hospital will:

- Assign responsibility for the coordination of discharge planning
- Identify as early as possible, sometimes before hospital admission, the expected posthospital care needs of patients utilizing admission and preadmission screening and review programs when available
- Develop with patients and their families appropriate discharge care plans
- Assist patients and their families in planning for the supportive environment necessary to provide the patients' posthospital care
- Develop a plan that considers the medical, social, and financial needs of patients

To ensure the availability of hospital resources for subsequent patients with due regard for prospective pricing, the hospital's procedures should be carried out in such a manner as to accomplish timely discharge.

Principles of Discharge Planning

The discharge planning process incorporates a determination of the patient's posthospital care preferences, needs, the patient's capacity for self-care, an assessment of the patient's living conditions, the identification of health or social care resources needed to assure high-quality posthospital care, and the counseling of the patient or family to prepare them for posthospital care. Discharge planning should be carried out in keeping with varying community resources and hospital utilization activities.

Note: These guidelines were developed by the Society for Hospital Social Work Directors of the American Hospital Association to assist hospitals in evaluating and improving their discharge planning functions. This guidelines document recognizes that each hospital must conduct this function according to its own needs, its resources, and the needs of its patients. It was approved by the General Council on April 11–12, 1984.

Discharge Planning When Multiple Resources Are Required

In addition to discharge instructions for each routine patient discharge plan, the coordination of multiple resources may be required to achieve continued safe and high-quality posthospital care in situations where the patient's needs are complicated.

Essential Elements

The essential elements in accomplishing the hospital's goals for high-quality, cost-effective patient care are:

- Early Identification of Patients Likely to Need Complex Prehospital Care

    There are certain factors that may indicate a need for early initiation of discharge planning, either before admission or upon admission. Screens for automatic early patient identification are developed for each specialty service by the physician and relevant health care providers and used as guidelines to carry out discharge planning.

- Patient and Family Education

    With greater emphasis on self-care, patient and family education is critical to successful discharge planning. The coordination of discharge planning must integrate teaching about physical care to facilitate appropriate self-care in the home.

- Patient/Family Assessment and Counseling

    The psychosocial and physical assessment and counseling of patients and families to determine the full range of needs upon discharge and to prepare them for the posthospital stage of care is a dynamic process. This process includes evaluation of the patient's and the family's strengths and weaknesses; the patient's physical condition; understanding the illness and treatment;

the ability to assess the patient's and family's capacities to adapt to changes; and, where necessary, to assist the persons involved to manage in their continued care. Discharge planning and the coordination of posthospital care plans require an ability to adapt the plans to meet changes in the patient's condition.

- Plan Development

    The discharge plan development should include the results of the assessment and the self-care instructions, including information from the patient, the family, and all relevant health care professionals. Service needs and options are identified, and the patient and family are helped to understand the consequences of whatever plan they choose to adopt. A supportive climate is critical to facilitate appropriate decision making.

- Plan Coordination and Implementation

    The hospital achieves high-quality and effective discharge planning through the delegation of specific responsibilities to the principal and specialized disciplines providing care. In order to minimize the potential for fragmented care and to fulfill the need for a central hospital linkage to the community, there should be assigned responsibility for discharge planning coordination for complex cases.

- Postdischarge Follow-up

    In complex situations requiring coordinated discharge planning, the plans should ensure follow-up with the patient, the family, and/or community service(s) providing continued care to determine the discharge plan outcome.

Quality Assurance

The quality of the discharge planning system should be monitored through the hospitalwide quality assurance program.

Appendix 6-B

Statement Releasing Hospital from Liability When Patient Leaves AMA

ADMITTING AND DISCHARGE

STATEMENT OF PATIENT RELEASING HOSPITAL
FROM LIABILITY UPON LEAVING HOSPITAL
AGAINST MEDICAL ADVICE

_____   _____
Patient's Name   Date

                                                              AM
                                        _____
                                                              PM
                                                   Time

This is to certify that I _____,
                                         Patient's Name
at my own insistence and without the authority of and against the advice of my
personal physician(s) _____ , demand
                                              Name
to leave _____ . I have
                           Hospital's Name
been informed of the dangers to me upon leaving at this time.

I hereby release _____ , its officers and
                                Hospital's Name
personnel, and my personal physician(s) from any responsibility for all consequences caused by my leaving _____
                                                   Hospital's Name
under these circumstances.

_____   _____
Patient's Signature   Witness

                                        _____
                                                     Witness

_____
Source: Reprinted from _Hospital Law Manual,_ p. 56, Aspen Publishers, Inc., © 1988.

Appendix 6-C

Sample Performance Appraisal for Agency Nurses

Factors	Rating	Comments
Application of Skills and Knowledge		
Quality of Work		
Productivity		
Cooperation		
Dependability		

Key to Ratings:
O   = Outstanding
MS = More than satisfactory
S   = Satisfactory
LS = Less than satisfactory
U   = Unsatisfactory

Key to Factors:

Application of skills and knowledge. Consider: application and adaptation of skills to work situation.
Quality of work. Consider: care and attention to detail displayed in work, thoroughness, and accuracy.
Productivity. Consider: amount of work performed, organization, efficiency, and utilization of time.
Cooperation. Consider: interest in work, willingness to assume extra work when necessary, and relationship with other staff members.
Dependability. Consider: reliability and timely completion of tasks.

chapter 7

Education As a Valuable Risk Management Resource

Elizabeth L. Willey and Barbara J. Youngberg

INTRODUCTION

Education is one of the most important aspects of a risk management program. It must be an ongoing process that addresses issues of concern to all hospital personnel. It must deal with problems relevant to the overall hospital environment, as well as timely topics for specific departments and groups. Program promotion is essential for its success, as is providing the audience with relevant printed material to reinforce the content presented. Physicians and nurses practicing in states with mandatory continuing education requirements will be more attracted to risk management sessions where continuing medical education/continuing education units (CME/CEU) credit is provided.

This chapter provides basic information about the educational process and incentives to get the staff involved in the risk management program. Individual educational modules are offered that address various issues of concern within the hospital. Each module is designed to meet the formats of the American Nurses Association and the American Medical Association. Bibliographic information is included with certain modules to assist the presenter in identifying articles for distribution.

THE VALUE OF EDUCATION

Providing educational programs and resource handouts to staff at the hospital can add visibility and credibility to the risk management program, but these resources must be viewed as useful, timely, and professional in nature. Any program that is considered a "waste of staff time" can affect the value and credibility of future programs.

Getting the risk management educational program off to a successful start involves the support and endorsement of highly visible and well-respected administrative and medical staff members. Often these key individuals need information that not only defines the discipline of risk management but also describes its benefits. In addition to providing them with written information, the risk manager should meet with them in order to gain valuable insight into what they believe to be critical elements of risk management in their respective disciplines, such as administration, nursing, surgery, and medicine. Using their ideas to formulate in-service programs can obviously assist in gaining their support and promoting attendance (see Exhibit 7-1). It is also helpful to ask each department manager for a list of dates when the service or department is particularly slow (if that time ever exists!) or a time during the day when the greatest number of staff might be able to attend.

After obtaining support from administration, the chief of the medical staff, and the nursing department, the risk manager should meet with other department heads to learn what educational programs are already offered. For risk management to present the same topics would be repetitive and time-consuming. For example, the infection control department may offer programs on acquired immunodeficiency syndrome (AIDS) and AIDS-related issues, and the biomedical or safety department may present training sessions on equipment or safety.

Exhibit 7-1
CHECKLIST FOR A RISK MANAGEMENT EDUCATIONAL PROGRAM

1. Is the subject of the program relevant to the audience?
2. Has the program been designed to comply with professional society requirements for continuing education credits?
3. Have you included "local" examples (such as particular incidents in your hospital or reported local cases) as part of the presentation? Be sure to maintain confidentiality as appropriate.
4. Have you provided the audience with appropriate handouts to reinforce the presentation?
5. Have you provided the participants with evaluation sheets so they may provide comments for future sessions?
6. Have you prepared a bibliography to enable staff to gain additional information on topics they find especially useful?
7. Have you verified the fact that a similar program has not been offered to staff during the last 12 months?

PLANNING A HOSPITAL-WIDE PROGRAM

Risk management presentations during various orientation sessions are an excellent way to introduce the staff to the risk management process. Such a program can focus on the basics and offer support and additional education as needed. The role of the risk manager as a resource person is stressed in this initial meeting. Basic reporting procedures, litigation management, and educational components of the risk management process are explained. A module for this type of presentation is included in Appendix 7-A.

Following the introductory session, the risk manager may wish to identify those units or practices that pose the greatest threats of risk to the institution and to individual practitioners. Typically, these areas include obstetrics, emergency services, surgery, critical care, and psychiatry. Risk management programs may benefit practitioners of these specialties.

The risk manager also may wish to identify particular subject areas that often present risk management problems. These might include charting, informed consent, the litigation process, do-not-resuscitate orders and policies, AIDS-related issues, and understanding the law of negligence. See Appendixes 7-B through 7-H for sample educational programs in these categories.

To guarantee maximum attendance, risk management in-service programs may be scheduled to coincide with prescheduled meetings (such as monthly grand rounds, staff meetings, or scheduled conferences). It is also helpful to distribute a program agenda prior to the meeting that identifies items to be discussed and that requests attendees to prepare questions for discussion following the presentation. Creative announcements often are very helpful in marketing these programs. Follow-up evaluation forms also should be given to provide the speakers with follow-up for future programs (Exhibit 7-2).

The use of guest speakers at these conferences can also raise interest, particularly if a highly technical or controversial subject is being presented. If legal staff is not employed by the hospital, outside defense counsel should be asked to present an in-service program on malpractice and the litigation process and also on the types of errors made by hospital staff that most often give rise to litigation.

If the hospital has the capabilities, audiotaping or videotaping these presentations will be helpful in educating staff members who work part time and during the evening and night shifts. Obviously, the broader the audience the more effective the hospital's risk management program will be. Copies of the handouts and written material provided as part of specific programs should be kept on file in the risk management office and distributed to appropriate groups who utilize the tapes but cannot attend the regular sessions. This information also should be part of a risk management reference library that is available to all staff.

After the program has been designed and objectives and content agreed upon, the program should be sent to the appropriate professional society for CME/CEU credit. This process often can be facilitated by working with the department of staff education or, when applicable, the medical school or nursing school affiliated with the hospital. The format used in applying for continuing education credits is fairly general. Obviously, it is important to contact the state professional society to learn if there are additional criteria to be met prior to obtaining credit for a particular audience.

Success of the program will be contingent, in great part, on the risk manager's ability to "sell" risk management to the audience. Representations to the staff should stress the goals of risk management—to protect the institution, to protect the staff, and to protect the patient.

Exhibit 7-2
SAMPLE EVALUATION FORM FOR A RISK MANAGEMENT EDUCATIONAL PROGRAM

Title of program _____

Name of presenter _____

Date and time of program _____

Your position and title _____

	Excellent	Good	Fair	Poor
How would you rate the quality of presentation?				
How would you rate the content of the presentation?				
How would you rate the quality of the handouts?				

Did the material presented meet your needs in your current position? _____ Yes _____ No

What do you think could/should have been done to improve the presentation or to make it more useful to you? _____
_____
_____
_____

What subjects would you like to see covered in subsequent risk management presentations? _____
_____
_____

Additional comments: _____
_____
_____
_____

An Introduction to Risk Management

The objective of this presentation is to provide new hospital staff with a brief orientation to the discipline of risk management. It also serves to familiarize the staff with the services and personnel providing risk management support to the hospital. If a risk management manual is part of the hospital's program, it should be available for participants to review at the presentation.

WHAT IS RISK MANAGEMENT?

The risk management department assists the hospital's staff in identifying and controlling problems within the hospital setting that may give rise to patient, staff, or visitor injuries or that may result in the filing of lawsuits against the hospital or any members of its staff. It also seeks to provide staff with educational information on legal issues that may arise within the hospital setting. These issues include:

- problems associated with *informed consent*
- problems associated with *do-not-resuscitate (DNR) orders or living wills*
- problems associated with *confidentiality*
- issues related to *malpractice insurance*
- issues related to appropriate and complete *documentation*
- problems associated with *staffing shortages* and use of agency or float personnel

The risk management department also works with the hospital's staff when a lawsuit is filed to ascertain that the staff is provided with appropriate representation and that it is prepared for every aspect of discovery and trial.

GENERAL INFORMATION

This should include at least the following five aspects of risk management operation:

1. Introduce each staff member and identify his or her areas of responsibility.

2. List telephone extensions of risk management personnel and indicate how to reach the risk manager after office hours or in case of emergency.
3. Note the physical location of the office.
4. Provide a list of programs to be offered by risk management during the coming year.
5. If risk management has developed a sourcebook or manual, describe where it can be found and what information it contains (a copy of the index can be provided to meeting attendees).

INCIDENT REPORT

An introduction and explanation of the incident report should include the following five factors:

1. Explain the use of the report.
2. Explain how, when, and why the report is completed.
3. Describe how information is used and how feedback is provided.
4. Stress that the incident report should not be viewed as a punitive tool, but rather as an aid in identifying problems that could result in staff, patient, or visitor injury.
5. Provide examples of how correct and timely incident reporting has identified and corrected problems within the hospital.

HOSPITAL COMMITTEES

Describe committees that interface with risk management or that operate as part of the risk management department. Identify any of these committees that need additional staff members.

GOOD RISK MANAGEMENT PRACTICES

Describe the nine "Golden Rules" of risk management:

1. Know the hospital policies and procedures that govern your practice. If they are outdated and do not reflect your practice, you should attempt to have them changed. Your failure to follow hospital policies and procedures can be evidence *per se* of negligence.

2. Listen to your patients. If you ignore their concerns or if they perceive you as callous, your chances of being sued increase dramatically. Patients seldom sue people they like!

3. Do not offer patients unrealistic expectations. Choose your words carefully—do not make false promises.

4. Comply with hospital incident reporting to guarantee early intervention and resolution of problems.

5. Learn to recognize patient and family behavior that suggests a litigious propensity. Involve patient relations, social services, and risk management with these persons early in the hospitalization.

6. When in doubt, always err on the side of caution and always draw upon the expertise of others.

7. Treat each of your patients in the same way as you would like yourself or your family treated. Think of how you would react were you in a patient's position.

8. Document patient records as if all of your notes some day will be read by jurors in a court of law. Your notes should create a favorable impression about your level of practice.

9. If you have any questions or concerns regarding any patient care issue, call the risk management department. Chances are that if you *feel* a problem exists, it probably does.

AUDIENCE PARTICIPATION

Reserve time at the end of the session for staff questions and feedback. Allow the staff to become familiar with policies, procedures, and forms described during the lecture so that appropriate questions can be asked.

An Introduction to Malpractice: The Law of Negligence

The objective of this session is to identify for hospital staff those elements of malpractice that must be proven prior to a finding of negligence. Included in the discussion are the standard by which conduct is measured and additional theories that can result in a finding of negligence against a caregiver.

WHY PEOPLE SUE

Among the more common reasons for lawsuits are the following:

- They are dissatisfied with care.
- They feel they have been wronged.
- They have sustained documented injuries or had "less than perfect" results.
- Hospital staff (physicians and nurses) have been rude, unsympathetic, or callous toward them—*people seldom sue people they like!*
- Society has become increasingly litigious and sees lawsuits as a type of lottery or "get rich quick" opportunity.

WHAT IS MALPRACTICE?

Four elements must be proven by a plaintiff for a successful malpractice action:

1. *Duty.* Hospital staff had a responsibility to provide reasonable care to the patient.
2. *Breach of duty.* The caregiver did not fulfill her or his responsibility of providing reasonable care.
3. *Proximate cause of injury.* The patient was injured as a direct result of the breach of duty.
4. *Damages.* The patient suffered damages as a result of the injury.

Duty

Initially, duty must be established between the caregiver and the patient through a contractual relationship. This relationship is presumed to exist when the patient presents himself or herself to the hospital and when the caregiver begins to provide care. It is from this "quasi-contractual" relationship that the duty of a caregiver to a patient arises. After the relationship is established, the caregiver then owes the patient a *duty.* Generally, this duty is defined by the legal term *standard of care.*

Standard of Care

The standard of care is based on what a reasonable person with the same degree of experience and expertise would do in the same or similar circumstances. In more specific terms, the caregiver is expected to possess that degree of knowledge and skill and to exercise that degree of care, skill, and judgment that other caregivers with the same experience and expertise would exercise in the same or similar circumstances.

A board-certified surgeon, for example, is held to the same standard as every other board-certified surgeon. A few states still have a rule known as the locality rule, in which a surgeon in a small rural community would be held to the same standard as another rural surgeon regardless of any type of specialty training that he or she may possess. The modern trend is to move away from this rule, because it is perceived to give rural physicians an unfair advantage over urban physicians.

In a malpractice suit, the best evidence of the standard of care must be shown. Experts will testify as to the standard that the caregiver should have met.

Specialist versus Nonspecialist

The duty imposed by the law upon the caregiver is higher for the specialist than for the nonspecialist. The specialist, by legal definition, is a caregiver who devotes special attention to a particular organ or body region and to the diagnosis and treatment of injuries, diseases, and ailments of that area of the body. The specialist is generally required to possess that degree of knowledge and ability and to exercise that amount of care and skill that are ordinarily possessed and exercised by caregivers of the same specialty.

Degree of Knowledge

The law places upon the caregiver the duty to possess the competence, knowledge, and skill necessary to treat a particular condition. If the caregiver does not possess that knowledge and skill, he or she is under a duty to so inform the patient of the limitation and advise the patient of the desirability of consulting another caregiver or specialist.

Promises of the Caregiver

The caregiver implicitly promises only that he or she will use the degree of skill, knowledge, and care offered by a similarly trained caregiver and will use his or her best judgment in an effort to bring about a good result. The caregiver does not promise, nor is he or she required, to effect a cure or even to obtain a good result in every instance. The failure to effect a cure or obtain a good result does not, in itself, raise an inference of negligence as to the diagnosis made or the treatment adopted.

Breach of Duty

A breach of care, or duty, owed to the patient occurs if the caregiver's quality of care falls below that standard of the reasonable caregiver under like circumstances. Breach of duty is illustrated in the following cases:

- A hospital was liable for the negligence of one of its staff physicians who set a fractured leg in an emergency department. The physician admitted at trial that he had not read a book on orthopedics in 10 years and had not asked for consultation when obvious signs of difficulties developed. *Darling v. Charleston Community Memorial Hospital*, 200 N.E.2d 149 (Ill. 1965).
- A woman had a hysterectomy. The surgeon was a general surgeon, and the operation took place in a hospital with limited facilities. The following day the patient vomited frequently and the surgeon realized she had peritonitis. Six days later he arranged for her transfer to a specialist at a larger hospital. The specialist operated and removed gangrenous bowel, but the patient died of a kidney problem caused by the infec-

tion. In the husband's suit against the surgeon who had performed the hysterectomy, the court held that the failure to send the patient to a specialist as soon as her condition demanded it was negligent. *Richardson v. Holmes*, 525 S.W.2d 293 (Tex. 1975).

Some areas of negligence are so obvious that courts have held that laymen can understand them without expert help and therefore no expert witness is necessary to establish a standard of care. This is the doctrine of *res ipsa loquitor*— "the thing speaks for itself." It may be applied in a case where an injury is one that does not usually occur in the absence of negligence, the apparent cause was within the exclusive control of the caregiver, and the patient could not have contributed to the difficulties. Examples of this doctrine include leaving a sponge or other foreign body in a patient's body after surgery and a baby rolling out of a crib on the pediatrics floor because the side rail was left down.

Breach of duty also can arise under other theories of negligence involving special areas of duty. These include the "Captain of the Ship" doctrine, respondeat superior theory, and borrowed servant doctrine.

Captain of the Ship Doctrine

This doctrine was once the standard for evaluating whether or not a surgeon was negligent. The theory states that the surgeon is the "captain of the ship" (or the person with ultimate responsibility) and can be found negligent if anyone in the operating room makes a mistake that leaves the patient injured. The doctrine has eroded in many jurisdictions, with the result that each caregiver is responsible for his or her own acts of negligence.

Respondeat Superior Theory

The duty arising under this theory allows for the "master" (such as the employer or head nurse) to be held responsible for the torts of his or her "servant" or employee committed in the course of employment. The doctrine places liability on the supervisor or employer for the action of employees. These torts include willful as well as negligent acts of the servant.

The master's liability for his or her servant's torts, however, does not immunize the servant from liability. The injured party may also sue the servant. In addition, the servant may be liable to the master for damages that the latter was compelled to pay to a third person solely because of the servant's negligent or wrongful acts.

Borrowed Servant Doctrine

It is generally recognized that an employee may serve more than one employer. In a borrowed servant case, the lending employer temporarily relinquishes control over his or her worker and the borrowing employer temporarily assumes control. This theory is often applied in cases involving agency and registry nurses and contract physicians.

Proximate Cause of Injury

Even if a patient can prove that a caregiver did not meet the required standard of care, he or she cannot recover damages unless it can be proved that the negligence caused injuries that would not have occurred in the absence of the negligence. No matter how negligent the caregiver may have been, harm must be shown to have resulted for damages to be awarded.

Damages

A complaint filed against a caregiver initially lists the damages in a dollar amount. The jury does not have to award that specific amount. Awards usually cover the following damages:

- cost of medical care to return the patient to his or her condition before the injury occurred, or actual damages (these may include past, present, and future care)
- lost wages
- damages for pain and suffering
- punitive damages (these are designed to punish the caregiver for particularly egregious behavior and have been eliminated or capped in most states)

Appendix 7-C

Do-Not-Resuscitate Orders

The objective of this session is to introduce hospital staff to the do-not-resuscitate (DNR) policy and procedure in effect at the hospital. The session also provides information about the process that should occur prior to the decision to write a DNR order.

The hospital's DNR policy should be the focus of this presentation and a copy handed out to each participant at the beginning of the session. Copies of the state law governing the hospital's practice and addressing the legality of DNR orders also should be distributed.

DEFINITION

When a "no code/DNR" order is in effect, the staff should not take steps to revive the patient. This type of order differs from the withdrawal of life support (e.g., the termination of nasogastric feedings or life-sustaining intravenous therapy or extubation).

GUIDELINES FOR DNR ORDERS

The laws of the state must be followed prior to making a decision to write a DNR order. The patient should be in a permanently vegetative state or be irreversibly and terminally ill. In such cases, further resuscitation would merely delay an inevitable outcome.

Hospital policy must be followed prior to instituting this order. The policy should address the following factors:

- Appropriate communication with the patient or family is required prior to the institution of the order.
- Documentation in the medical record should indicate that this type of interaction has occurred and also list appropriate support persons who were involved in the process (such as the hospital chaplain, social worker, grief counselor, physician, primary nurse, and risk manager).

- If there is a lack of consensus in the above interaction (among family members, treating physicians, and other persons), a court or institutional ethics committee should be consulted. Documentation of this consultation also should be included in the chart.
- If a number of treating physicians or consultants have been involved in the care of this patient, their support of this action also should be documented in the patient's chart.
- The order must be *written, dated, and signed by the treating physician*.
- If the patient's condition changes or if the caregiver has reason to believe that the desires of the patient or family have changed, the treating physician must be consulted and the appropriateness of the order must be re-evaluated.
- A copy of the hospital policy in effect at the time the order is written should be placed in the chart. This helps to protect the hospital in the event questions arise at a later date.

LEGAL TRENDS

In Re Quinlan, 355 A.2d 647 (N.J. 1976), *cert. denied*, 429 U.S. 922 (1976), was one of the first cases to set the stage for dealing with ethical considerations surrounding the patient's and family's rights related to termination of treatment. Subsequent cases have attempted to refine the holding of *Quinlan*; see *In the Matter of Shirley Dinnerstein*, 380 N.E.2d 134 (Mass. App. Ct. 1978); *Superintendent of Belchertown State School v. Saikewicz*, 370 N.E.2d 417 (Mass. 1977); and *Bouvia v. Superior Court of Los Angeles*, 225 Cal. Rptr. 297, (Cal. Ct. App. 1986).

A majority of the case law now relates to the active withdrawal of treatment, rather than DNR orders. Very few cases discuss DNR orders specifically. However, it is clear that if a physician implements a DNR order without the consent of the patient or family, he or she may face both civil and criminal liability.

PATIENT SELF DETERMINATION ACT

In November of 1991 a federal law went into effect that expands the rights of patients to make critical decisions relative to the health care they receive. The law is called the Patient Self Determination Act of 1991. It requires hospitals, nursing homes, home health agencies, hospices, and other institutional Medicare and Medicaid providers to give patients, at the time of their admission, written information concerning their rights under state laws to accept or refuse medical care and to formulate advance directives.

The Importance of Documentation

The objective for this session is to assist the hospital's staff in understanding the importance of thorough and accurate documentation. The discussion includes information about hospital policies and procedures relating to documentation, documentation "dos and don'ts," and the value of documentation in the defense of care.

Sample chart entries highlighting points made during the lecture should be presented for evaluation and comment. Also at the conclusion of the session, examples of documentation can be shown to demonstrate the differences between those that helped and hindered the hospital's defense of cases.

PURPOSES OF DOCUMENTATION

Documentation should accomplish the following purposes:

- provide accurate and complete information about the care and treatment of patients
- provide a basis for planning the course of treatment for each patient
- serve as important legal documents to substantiate care rendered
- provide an ongoing means of communication among all caregivers involved in the treatment of an individual patient

DEFENSIVE DOCUMENTATION

The caregiver must chart with the knowledge that if a lawsuit occurs or if questions arise surrounding the care that was rendered to a patient, the entire hospitalization of the patient will be reconstructed from the medical record. Both plaintiff and defense counsel will review the record carefully in attempts to discover any irregularities. The caregiver will take care of thousands of patients between the time care

is given to a patient who brings litigation and the time trial is set. It is impossible to remember the care rendered to each of these patients. The hospital record may be the only resource available to assist the caregiver in recalling specific instances related to a certain patient and is often the only source of substantiation for the caregiver's testimony.

All procedures noted in the medical records must be in conformance with the hospital's policies and procedures in effect at the time the care was rendered. (Noncompliance may be viewed by courts as negligence.)

Cases in which the medical record can be used as court evidence include the following:

- personal injury cases, including malpractice
- workers' compensation cases
- criminal cases
- probate cases where caregiver notes may provide information as to the mental capacity of the testator

WHAT TO CHART

Many hospitals have developed policies and procedures to provide guidelines for charting in special circumstances, such as obtaining consent, patients leaving against medical advice, and patients refusing treatment. Hospital staff should be aware of these specific policies and of the importance of adhering to them.

Generally, the following 13 suggestions apply to medical records:

1. Date, time, and sign each and every entry.
2. Make entries retrospectively, never prospectively. For example, never chart that a patient tolerated a procedure or medication well until the procedure has been completed or the medication taken. Entries made too early often result in chart errors and corrections.
3. Use only hospital-approved abbreviations. Take special care when using symbols with more than one

meaning, such as BS for both breath sounds and bowel sounds.

4. Note all procedures, diagnoses, and treatments. Make sure that the record is internally consistent.

5. Justify the diagnosis; differentiate rationale for one modality over its alternative.

6. Only chart what actually happened—what you personally observed.

7. Always chart a patient's failure to keep an appointment or refusal of treatment. If appropriate, indicate that you have advised the patient of the possible ill effects of missing appointments or refusing treatment. If letters are sent out to patients about missed appointments, include them in the hospital or clinic file.

8. Always chart in ink. Do not leave spaces between notes where information can be added at a later time.

9. Write as legibly as possible. Sloppy entries are often equated with sloppy care. If handwriting is a serious problem, attempt to have notes typed.

10. If you indicate in notes that certain follow-up is to be provided, make sure that the follow-up is documented.

11. Always sign and complete consent forms. Include the discussion of consent procedure in progress notes, unless the hospital consent form provides space for that discussion.

12. Document all teaching and instruction provided to the patient and to his or her family. Indicate their understanding of this instruction.

13. If the patient speaks a language other than English, be sure to document that appropriate translation was provided for all consents, instructions, and other information. Provide the name and telephone extension of the translator, if available.

HOW AND WHAT NOT TO CHART

It is often as important to know what not to chart as to know the appropriate contents of a medical record. There are also certain rules relating to the actual process. The following six suggestions apply to these areas of documentation:

1. Never erase, "white out," remove pages, or completely obliterate what already has been documented. When an error is made, draw a single line through the entry; date and indicate the reason for the deletion. Altering records to avoid liability is a criminal offense!

2. Maintain fetal heart monitor and electrocardiogram strips as part of the permanent record. In many states if such documents are unavailable at trial, they are "presumed lost for a reason" and are *per se* evidence of negligence.

3. Avoid "jousting" in the record—bickering, belittling, and blaming others.

4. Do not include extraneous information relating to a patient's billing or insurance status. It should not be part of the medical record, except as it appears on the face sheet.

5. Make all entries based on objective data. Never describe a patient in an inflammatory or prejudicial manner. If the patient acts inappropriately, describe the behavior rather than merely labeling the patient. If the patient makes rude, threatening, or inflammatory statements, include them in quotes as part of the medical record.

6. Do not indicate in the record that an "incident" or "management" report has been filed or completed. These reports are designed to drive peer review, loss control, and quality management programs. Their mention in the hospital records can result in their loss of protection from discovery.

Appendix 7-E

Communications and Defamation

The objective of this presentation is to provide the audience with an understanding of the legal issues associated with physician–patient privilege. It also provides information about various legal complaints that can be brought against physicians who use communication in a way that is considered violative of a patient's legal rights.

Note: Prior to providing this educational program, the presenter should consult the state statute governing privilege and determine if it contains any special provisions. A copy of the statute should be provided to each participant.

PRIVILEGED COMMUNICATIONS

Privilege can be created only by state statute. The state statute should be reviewed to determine the extent of protection afforded both parties as a result of privilege. Generally speaking, the mere fact that a communication has been made to a physician is not enough to bring it within the scope of a privileged communication.

Conditions

There must be a relationship between the physician and the patient. This relationship exists if treatment of the patient is being contemplated or is actually in progress. As defined in the Uniform Rules of Evidence, patient means a person who, for the sole purpose of securing preventive, palliative, or curative treatment, or a diagnosis preliminary to such treatment, of his or her physical or mental condition, consults a physician or submits to an examination by a physician. Privilege would not exist, therefore, if the physician examined the person for the sole purpose of determining his or her eligibility for a pension or fitness for work.

The information in question must be the type that the statute covers. Nonconfidential information is not privileged (such as the date and time of treatment). Jurisdictions are split as to whether information acquired with a third party present is privileged.

Waiver

A patient may renounce the protection of the statute governing privileged communications.

CONFIDENTIAL COMMUNICATIONS

Ethical Duty

Hippocrates said, "Whatever, in connection with my professional practice, or not in connection with it, I may see or hear in the lives of the men which ought not to be spoken abroad I will not divulge as reckoning that all should be kept secret."

The American Medical Association's *Principles of Medical Ethics* states, "A physician may not reveal the confidence entrusted to him in the course of medical attendance, or the deficiencies he may observe in the character of the patients, unless he is required to do so by law or unless it becomes necessary in order to protect the welfare of the individual or the community."

Unauthorized Disclosure

A physician may face the loss of his or her license to practice medicine or an action for damages as the result of unauthorized disclosure of confidential information. A recent study found that 51 percent of doctors and 70 percent of medical students discuss confidential information at parties.

A patient may sue a physician for unauthorized disclosure on the following grounds:

- breach of a confidential relationship
- invasion of privacy
- breach of contract

DUTY TO PROTECT THIRD PARTIES

Obligations of health professionals have traditionally extended only to those patients with whom they have a legal relationship. Physicians and other health professionals now have an affirmative obligation in some jurisdictions to protect third parties against hazards created by their patients.

In a landmark case, *Tarasoff v. Regents of the University of California*, 551 P.2d 334 (Cal. 1976), a patient told his psychotherapist at the university hospital that he was going to kill Tatiana Tarasoff. The doctor had the patient detained by the police, but he was later released because he "seemed rational." The psychotherapist's superior at the hospital informed him that he should take no further action to detain the patient. No one informed Tarasoff of the threats against her life. The patient went on to kill Tarasoff. The parents of the deceased sued the university regents, the psychotherapist, and the campus police for failure to detain the patient and for failure to warn their daughter. The court held that the plaintiffs had a cause of action against the patient's psychotherapist for failing to warn Tarasoff. As a general rule, the third party is not liable for the actions of the tortfeasor, unless the third party has a special relationship with the tortfeasor. The court found that the psychotherapist and the patient had this special relationship. Additionally, the fact that the psychotherapist was working for the state did not relieve him from liability because governmental immunity covers only basic policy questions.

In another case, *Welke v. Kuzilla*, 375 N.W.2d 403 (Mich. App. 1985), the plaintiff's wife was killed in a car collision with defendant Sharlyn Kuzilla. Kuzilla was a patient of Dr. Capper who had prescribed medications for her, including an unknown substance on the evening prior to the accident. The court held that Dr. Capper owed a duty to plaintiff's decedent, an innocent driver, within the scope of foreseeable risk by virtue of his special relationship with Kuzilla.

DEFAMATION

"A communication is defamatory if it tends so to harm the reputation of another as to lower him in the estimation of the community or to deter third persons from associating or dealing with him" (Restatement of Torts [Second] Sec. 559). Defamation can take the form of libel, a written statement, or slander, a spoken statement.

Elements

Publication of the defamation must occur. This means that the statement must be spoken in the presence of a third person or must be seen by a third person. For example, if a nurse or physician makes a derogatory remark to a patient without the presence of a third person, this is not slander (there was no publication), but if the nurse or physician makes a statement about the patient to another nurse or physician, this is slander (information was published to a third person).

A statement is defamatory only if it prejudices the plaintiff in the eyes of a substantial and respectable minority of the members of the community. However, a statement is not defamatory if it offends some individual or individuals whose views are sufficiently peculiar to cause them to regard as derogatory what the vast majority of persons regard as innocent.

Some actions are *per se* defamation—no special damages must be proven. In slander cases these include statements that affect individuals in their professions and businesses or their involvement in crimes. Also, in some jurisdictions imputing the lack of chastity to a woman is considered to be in this category. All libel cases are regarded as *per se* defamation; no special damages must be shown.

Defense

There are two types of defense against defamation: privilege and truth. Absolute privilege extends only to judicial privilege. Qualified privilege extends to public or private duty to communicate whether legal or moral, or communication warranted by any reasonable occasion or exigency. Truth is an absolute defense. The burden of proving truth rests on the plaintiff's ability to establish with convincing clarity the falsity of the defendant's statements.

Informed Consent

The objective of this session is to familiarize the hospital staff with the procedures in place that relate to the doctrine of informed consent. Additional information is provided concerning the various legal issues surrounding informed consent.

In reviewing the informed consent procedures of the hospital, the presenter should also discuss any special policies written for unusual circumstances. Copies of the hospital's consent policy and forms should be distributed to the attendees.

ORIGIN OF THE DOCTRINE

The doctrine of informed consent developed out of a strong judicial deference toward individual autonomy that reflected the belief of an individual's right to be free from nonconsensual interferences with his or her own person, in conjunction with the basic moral principle that it is wrong to force another person to act against his or her will.

Long ago, the court held that a person has a legal right to consent to treatment. In *Schoendorf v. Society of New York Hospital*, 105 N.E. 92 (1914), the court held: "Every human being of adult years and sound mind has a right to determine what shall be done with his own body. . . ."

PURPOSES

Informed consent sets the boundaries of the physician–patient relationship. Physicians need to be reminded that the process, not the paper, constitutes informed consent. The article "Informed Consent in Catastrophic Disease Research and Treatment," found in 123 Penn. L.Rev. 340, 365–376 (1974), identifies six functions served by informed consent:

1. protects individual autonomy
2. protects the patient's status as a human being
3. avoids allegations of fraud and duress

4. encourages physicians to consider their decisions more carefully
5. fosters rational decision making by the patient
6. involves the public generally in medicine

STANDARDS

State codes and statutes define various elements of the doctrine of informed consent. Prior to this presentation, the risk manager should review any related jurisdictional material.

Reasonable Practitioner

The standard of reasonable practitioner measures the duty to disclose against that of a similarly situated reasonable medical practitioner. An expert medical standard must establish (1) whether a reasonable medical practitioner in the same or similar situation would make this disclosure, and (2) whether the defendant complied with this standard.

Reasonable Patient (modern trend)

The standard of reasonable patient is a modern trend. It must establish whether the physician disclosed risks that a reasonable person would find material in making a decision to undergo or not to undergo a procedure. The physician must consider disclosure of the following factors:

- diagnosis, including the medical steps preceding diagnosis
- nature and purpose of the proposed treatment
- risks of the treatment (omitting risks that are extremely remote; the disclosure threshold varies with the product of probability and severity of risk)
- probability of success
- treatment alternatives
- prognosis if treatment is not given

This doctrine is often interpreted more liberally in emergency situations. When the patient is incompetent, the physician must obtain informed consent from the person legally responsible for the patient.

OBTAINING INFORMED CONSENT

The duty of securing informed consent rests with the physician. The nurse may deliver the consent form to the patient for his or her signature, but the nurse is not authorized to explain the surgery or the critical procedure in lieu of the physician. To do so would be beyond the scope of nursing practice.

If the patient tells the nurse that he or she does not understand the nature of the impending procedure, has additional questions about the procedure, or has had second thoughts about consenting to the procedure, the nurse must not request the patient to sign the consent form. Instead, the nurse should notify the physician that the patient needs additional information or further explanation about the procedure.

In obtaining the patient's signature, the nurse is witnessing only that the signature is the patient's, not that the patient has been fully informed and understands the impending procedure. If the patient begins to verbalize second thoughts about the procedure after signing the consent form, the nurse should immediately advise the physician. A patient who changes his or her mind in effect nullifies the informed consent, and it is the responsibility of the physician, not the nurse, to discuss the procedure with the patient.

SPECIAL CIRCUMSTANCES

Hospital policies and procedures and jurisdictional precedent often govern issues related to informed consent in special circumstances, such as those involving Jehovah's Witnesses or emancipated minors. The staff should be advised to call the risk management office in these cases.

Appendix 7-G

Risk Management in the Emergency Department

This program is intended for the medical and nursing staffs of the emergency department. The program identifies the "high-risk" aspects of emergency medicine and nursing that most frequently give rise to litigation. It can assist participants in developing a proactive risk identification and management program that parallels the recommendations of the American College of Emergency Physicians (ACEP).

ORGANIZATION AND STAFF

The emergency department administrative structure includes the designation of individuals responsible for directing the emergency medical and nursing activities within the hospital. They are also responsible for facilitating the appropriate interface with other hospital departments that work closely with the emergency department.

Medical Director and Staff

The physician director of the emergency department should be board certified in emergency medicine and be a voting member of the hospital medical staff.

The following should be observed in the organization of the medical staff:

- The physician director shall have the responsibility of evaluating the performance of all physicians who staff the emergency department, including those who provide services through independent contractual or *locum tenens* arrangements.
- The physician director or designee shall be responsible for identifying and monitoring pertinent clinical indicators as part of the department-specific quality assurance and risk management program.
- All physicians working in the emergency department (regardless of board certification of eligibility) shall show proof of annual advanced cardiac life support (ACLS) certification. If the hospital is a regional

trauma center, advanced trauma life support (ATLS) also may be required.
- All physicians working in the emergency department (whether members of the medical staff or contract physicians) shall comply with the credentialing process of the general medical staff at the hospital. Delineation of privileges shall be consistent with the training and experience of the physicians in accordance with the hospital's standard credentialing process.

Nursing Staff

A nurse administrator should be designated for the emergency department, with responsibilities to include, but not limited to, the following:

- the hiring and firing of nursing staff
- the administration and coordination of all patient care services
- the identification of quality of nursing care issues that affect emergency department patients

All nursing staff working in the emergency department should show proof of annual cardiopulmonary resuscitation (CPR) recertification and, where possible, ACLS and trauma nurse specialist certification.

PROVISION OF PATIENT CARE

The following procedures are essential to quality care of emergency department patients:

- Every patient presenting to the emergency department for treatment is seen by a physician prior to discharge. The physician's examination is clearly documented in the patient's medical record.
- A documented triage process is in place that describes prompt evaluation of a patient's complaints and appropriate intervention.

- A medical record is generated for each patient who presents to the emergency department for treatment. A daily log also should track patient visits, admissions, deaths, AMAs, and other data.
- The patient's medical record reflects the initial assessment (including a complete set of vital signs and a pediatric patient's weight), brief medical and medication history, and periodic monitoring and re-evaluation if a patient has an extended stay in the department. The record is signed by the attending physician and the nurse responsible for the care provided.
- Laboratory reports and electrocardiogram (ECG) results, including those that were part of prehospital care, become a part of the permanent medical record.
- The medical record also includes a section documenting discharge instructions and follow-up care recommended to the patient.
- The emergency department has a policy and procedure in place for notifying patients of misinterpretations or misreadings of diagnostic testing performed in the department (such as ECGs, x-rays, laboratory results). Final interpretation of diagnostic tests is made by a qualified radiologist, cardiologist, or other appropriate specialist.
- Policies and procedures are in place that address the appropriateness of transferring specific patients to outlying facilities. The transfer protocols, contact persons at receiving facilities, and transfer forms to be completed are included as part of this policy.

The Importance of Understanding COBRA

In 1986 the Emergency Medical Treatment and Active Labor Act of 1986 (EMTALA)[1] was added to the Social Security Act as section 1867. This act was actually section 9121 of the Consolidated Omnibus Budget Reconciliation Act of 1986 and has most commonly been referred to as COBRA. COBRA was drafted to prevent hospitals from refusing, limiting, or terminating patient care for financial reasons.

The act requires that the hospital evaluate all patients presenting to the hospital with emergency conditions and determine (and document) the appropriateness of treating the patient until stabilized or transferring the patient elsewhere. The patient (or responsible person if the patient is a minor or an incompetent) always maintains the right to refuse to consent to the proposed transfer or treatment. In accordance with these provisions, the act requires the hospital to obtain the patient's written informed consent to refuse the offered treatment or transfer.

Although enacted in August of 1986, COBRA has recently undergone some important revisions—which became effective in 1990. The requirements of the COBRA amendments broaden who is subject to the law and now includes all participating physicians and any other physician responsible for examination, treatment, or transfer of an individual in a participating hospital.

Penalties for hospitals that violate COBRA provisions can be as high as $50,000 if it negligently violates the law. (This amount decreases to $25,000 if hospitals have less than 100 beds.) Because the interpretation of the law seems unclear, emergency department and hospital administration should carefully follow COBRA-related decisions in their jurisdiction and provide education to staff regarding the best method to ensure compliance.

SCREENING AND REVIEW PROCEDURES

The emergency department staff shall identify areas of high-risk exposure within the department and periodically review the care rendered to high-risk patients. According to a 1984 ACEP study of closed claims,[2] the following four most frequently give rise to costly litigation:

1. abdominal pain misdiagnosis relating primarily to:
   - missed appendicitis
   - missed ectopics
2. misdiagnosis of chest pain relating primarily to myocardial infarction
3. misdiagnosis of meningitis
4. mismanagement of traumatic injury relating to the following:
   - retained foreign bodies
   - tendon, nerve, or vessel injury
   - infection

Another study performed by the St. Paul Fire and Marine Insurance Company in 1986[3] identifies the same types of treatment problems.

Documentation is also a problem area in the defense of emergency department claims. The same criteria for documentation described in Appendix 7-D should be covered in this presentation.

RISK REDUCTION STRATEGIES

The emergency department should adopt the following eight strategies to reduce risk:

1. Have a policy in place for quick triage performed by a qualified staff member of the emergency department.
2. *Always* include the following information as part of the initial triage process:
   - a complete set of vital signs, including temperature, pulse, respirations, and blood pressure

- weight (of a child)
- tetanus status (if the patient presents with penetrating trauma)
- date of last menstrual period (if the patient is a woman of childbearing age)

3. Repeat any vital signs that are initially abnormal. Document medical and nursing intervention taken to correct any abnormality and the response to this intervention.

4. If the emergency department is used as a holding area for patients awaiting beds, maintain flow sheets or policies that govern the monitoring of these patients. A lack of available beds is never justification for inadequate patient monitoring.

5. Maintain good communication with patients and their families. Often delays in treatment and in obtaining laboratory results are unavoidable in the emergency department, but when delays are explained they are generally better accepted. In large urban hospitals with extremely busy departments, using volunteers who spend time with patients waiting for additional treatment is very beneficial.

6. Document all aspects of care provided, including the use of consultants. Any care that is provided and documented on hospital flow sheets, admission histories and physicals, or progress notes always should be copied and retained as part of the permanent emergency department record. Evidence of prehospital care provided by local ambulance services and paramedics, if available, also should be retained as part of the record. This enables the reviewer to get a total picture of the care provided to the patient.

7. Have in place a mechanism to address actual and potential problems in interdisciplinary communication.

8. Provide printed discharge instructions to patients or their family members prior to discharge. These instructions should complement the verbal instructions also provided to the patient. A copy of the instructions should be included as part of the permanent emergency department record. There should be a place on the discharge instructions or the face sheet of the medical record where the patient signs to verify receipt and understanding of these instructions.

NOTES

1. Emergency Medical Treatment and Active Labor Act, 42 U.S.C.A. §139 5dd (1991).

2. J.T. Rogers, *Risk Management in Emergency Medicine* (Dallas: American College of Emergency Physicians, 1985), 4.

3. M. Wood (Data collected at St. Paul Fire and Marine Insurance Company, St. Paul, 1986).

Appendix 7-H

HIV Testing and Disclosure

The objective of this program is to provide information about the legality of human immunodeficiency virus (HIV) testing and the confidentiality issues associated with these tests. The intended audience for this program includes physicians, nurses, and other hospital personnel who may have the responsibility for ordering the test, carrying out the test, or advising patients and their families about HIV testing guidelines. A copy of the state law that governs the hospital's practice should be provided as a handout during this program.

TESTING

Mandatory testing is prohibited unless *required* by law. Voluntary testing can take place if it is indicated as a diagnostic workup on a selective case-by-case basis and if appropriate informed consent is obtained by the attending physician or by an authorized clinic or health center.

The patient has the right to refuse testing unless it is *required* by law.

Confidentiality issues are generally covered by individual state statutes. Historically, a number of cases have addressed the issues of confidentiality in association with the diagnosis and treatment of various diseases.

PHYSICIAN'S DUTIES

In some states physicians are required by law to report communicable diseases to state or local health authorities; this includes cases of HIV positivity. Historically, the privilege of physician–patient confidentiality never has been absolute. Courts have repeatedly held that a physician's duty of nondisclosure is outweighed in certain circumstances by the need for public safety. Examples of these cases include *Earle v. Kuklo*, 98 A.2d 107 (N.J. Super. 1953), involving a landlord who exposed tenants to tuberculosis; *Davis v. Rodman*, 227 S.W. 612 (Ark. 1921) regarding typhoid fever; *Skillings v. Allen*, 173 N.W. 663 (Minn. 1919), scarlet fever; *Fosgate v. Corona*, 330 A.2d 355 (N.J. 1974), tuberculosis.

The physician also may have a duty to third parties that overrides the patient's right of confidentiality. Although one could argue that complying with the state reporting statute should relieve a physician from any further duty, the physician may be found liable to foreseeable third-party victims. Under *Tarasoff v. Regents of the University of California*, 551 P.2d 334 (Cal. 1976), the court held that the treating psychotherapist had a duty to warn a foreseeable victim that he was aware of threats being made by his patient. This type of reasoning could extend to a physician's duty to inform a patient's known sexual partners of the risk of transmission of the HIV virus if the patient had tested positive. Further disclosure to protect the public could be found under *Lipari v. Sears Roebuck and Company*, 497 F.2d 185 (D. Neb. 1980). In this case the patient was receiving outpatient psychiatric care at a Veterans Administration (VA) hospital. He stopped treatment against the advice of his physicians. Five weeks later, in a department store, he shot two people, killing one person and wounding another. The court, in finding the VA liable, held that the duty to third parties requires the therapist to initiate whatever precautions are reasonably necessary to protect potential victims from the therapist's patients. Although the victims were not identifiable in the cited case, the harm was foreseeable.

NEGLIGENT EXPOSURE OF OTHERS

Courts have applied to venereal disease the general principle that a person is civilly liable if he or she negligently exposes another person to an infectious disease and that person subsequently contracts the disease. See, for example, *Duke v. Housen*, 589 P.2d 334 (Wyo. 1979).

In another case, *Kathleen K. v. Robert B.*, 198 Cal. Rptr. 273 (Cal. App. 2 Dist. 1984), the court found the defendant liable on the grounds that he misrepresented that he was "disease-free" and that this constituted intentional tortious conduct causing serious injury to the plaintiff. Under the finding in this case, the act of a person with HIV positivity who exposed another person without disclosing this information may be considered an intentional, harmful, or even violent act, and thus invoke the physician's or therapist's duty (as defined by *Tarasoff*) to protect foreseeable victims.

Cases against Disclosure

In *South Florida Blood Service Inc. v. Rasmussen*, 467 So.2d 798 (Fla. App. 1985), the administrator of an estate requested that the names of blood donors be disclosed to enable him to seek damages on behalf of the decedent who had died of acquired immunodeficiency syndrome (AIDS), allegedly contracted through a blood transfusion. The court,

in refusing to order disclosure, held that the individuals' right to privacy and the state's interest in promoting the free distribution of blood outweighed the plaintiff's right to know the names of the donors.

In another case, *In Re District 27 Community School Board v. Board of Education of the City of New York*, 502 N.Y.S.2d 325 (Sup. Ct. 1986), a New York court relied on the New York Health Code, which protects the confidentiality of reports gathered for epidemiological studies. The court held that the New York commissioner of health could not use such reports to identify children with AIDS in the school system.

chapter 8

Computerizing Risk Management

Matthew Camden

INTRODUCTION

The personal computer became accepted as a legitimate business tool when International Business Machines (IBM) introduced the IBM-PC in 1981. Less than a decade later, business regards the personal computer as an essential tool to assist in analysis (as with calculators in the 1970s) and production (as with typewriters since the 1950s).

Computers greatly enhance the risk managers' ability to track and trend losses and to organize and recall vast amounts of information that is necessary for the performance of their jobs. The purpose of this chapter is to provide risk managers with a basic understanding of the development of the computer industry and to understand what must be evaluated prior to purchasing a system that will provide maximal support to the risk management process. Checklists are provided that delineate specific guidelines for purchase and vendor selection for a risk management department.

COMPUTER FEATURES

A number of features distinguish the personal computer from other computers. The fundamental distinguishing characteristic is the microprocessor, the "intelligence" and logic of the machine that interprets and processes all instructions. A personal computer has one processor; a mainframe or minicomputer has multiple processors. Each personal computer is capable of processing instructions independently. A terminal (the screen and keyboard assembly), on the other hand, is simply a link to a larger system of a mainframe or minicomputer. Without that connection, a terminal is incapable of any independent function. A personal computer also has the capacity to store information, or data, locally. All data are stored centrally on the mainframe or minicomputer; the terminal has no storage capacity.

The Apple computer, introduced in 1980, also has the ability to process information independently and store data locally. There are three primary differences, however, between the Apple computer and the IBM-PC. The first is strategy: Apple originally marketed its product as an educational tool; IBM's personal computer was intended as a business tool. Recently, each company has sought to expand its influence in the other's field, but in the beginning the line of demarcation was clear. Second, Apple computers use a processor technology fundamentally different from IBM's. Software that runs on an Apple is incompatible with IBM software. Finally, the IBM has licensed the use of its hardware technology to other companies, thus creating personal computer competitors, or clones. Apple has not licensed its technology. Therefore, in today's personal computer market, many players crowd the field. There is a general consensus of standards that developers can support, however, and prospective buyers have many choices. This is not the case with Apple. There are no alternative hardware choices and few competitive software selections. Surprisingly, this has not seemed to hurt Apple. The total market share (education, home, and business) is fairly evenly divided between Apple and personal computers (IBM and clones).

The growth in popularity and sophistication of personal computers has been stunning and unprecedented. Compaq Corporation, IBM's chief competitor in high-powered desktop computers, grew from a start-up venture in 1982 to a *billion* dollar multinational organization in only five years. Once seen as high-end calculators for the business elite, microcomputers are the most common devices for designing and engineering highways, buildings, and entire cities. One industry publication (*Computerworld*) has distributed an advertising poster that states:

> The evolution of the personal computer has been so impressive that if a Rolls Royce had been a computer, it would cost $0.98 and get one million miles per gallon.

A glance at the past decade is necessary to understand the growth of personal computers. In summary, it is directly attributable to rapid increases in technology in direct response to the buying public's business needs.

ORIGINAL APPLICATIONS

The original IBM personal computer could store data on diskettes, plastic-coated 5.25" platters that operate on the same principle as vinyl records. Data are stored in sectors, one groove on a record. Originally, a diskette could store 180,000 bytes. (A byte is composed of eight bits; consider a bit the equivalent of a letter in the alphabet.) However, each file of data created could only be 64,000 bytes long. In practice, this meant that a 75-page double-spaced document could be stored in one file. About three of these documents would fit on one diskette.

The personal computer was developed to service three common office tasks: report writing, numeric analysis, and office accounting. However, the machine itself does not include the machinery, or hardware (described above), to perform these tasks. The brute machine must follow prescribed logic to function. The logic, or software, to perform the three basic office tasks did not come from IBM, but from disparate sources. The marriage of hardware and software functionality is a major reason for the success of personal computers as business machines. Finally, it is necessary to note that with the introduction of personal computers came the introduction of personal computer printers. Risk managers should be aware of the wide variance of programs available from vendors and should evaluate them before attempting to "self design" programs.

Report Writing

The function of the typewriter was ported directly to the personal computer. The computer screen was simply a metaphor for the written page. The screen, or monitor, could display 80 letters on a line and 25 lines per screen, roughly the same measurements as double spacing would be on a sheet of looseleaf paper. Although screens can now display up to 10 times the amount of information than originally, the 80-column by 25-row measurements remain the overwhelming standard today.

The computer keyboard is an enhanced version of the typewriter keyboard. It is QWERTY in format, as a typewriter, but has additional function keys that simplify repetitive tasks. Tab keys remain the same in name and functionality, the return key has been renamed the enter key, and the margin key has disappeared. The function of typing documents was rechristened *word processing*.

The great advantage of word processing over typewriting is *memory*. Simply put, anything that is typed remains available for editing. The PC provided electronic white-out. The user (another computer-generation term) can change the middle paragraph on a page without retyping the entire page. The increase in productivity was incalculable, certainly enough to justify a purchase price that averaged about $5,000 (by comparison, today a computer with that price tag is about 20 times more powerful than the original PC).

The biggest selling word processor in 1981 was WordStar, from MicroPro Corporation. WordStar is still a big seller, but the industry leaders now are Word from Microsoft Corporation and WordPerfect from WordPerfect Corporation. Fate has not been kind to the early word processing software packages. Overwhelmed by growth and subsequent competition, many companies that helped fuel the PC revolution have long since disappeared. In fact, to illustrate how much word processing has changed, documents are no longer measured by rows and columns, rather by inches. (Under the heading of "the more things change, the more they stay the same," it should be noted that publishers have always measured print graphically.)

Numeric Analysis

As with the typewriter, the original personal computer sought to mimic the calculator. By 1981, calculators had finally miniaturized from desktop size to pocketbook size. Calculators with scientific and log functions reached offices and classrooms. Computer keyboards introduced true arithmetic keys: $+$, $-$, $*$, and $/$. The row-by-column screen metaphor is inherently mathematic. While advanced calculators could store the last view results in memory, the 64 kilobytes (K) memory of computers could store thousands of numbers and hundreds of results. Another term for the numeric analysis work pad, the *spreadsheet*, was coined.

Industry analysts agree that the spreadsheet was the "killer application," the tool that transformed PCs from boardroom novelties to middle management *workstations*.

The spreadsheet that helped launch the PC boom was Visicalc by Dan Bricklin. As the name suggests, spreadsheets are simply visible calculators.

The great boon to numeric analysis was the ability to see all previous calculations and to modify the factors determining outcomes (as indicated by the phrase, "play what-if games"). As with word processing, a machine with memory gives one the ability to edit mathematical information. The personal computer industry has made large strides since its inception, but these strides have been composed of small, significant steps.

Visicalc is no longer sold. The industry leader is Lotus 123 from Lotus Development Corporation. It has maintained the lion's share of the market since its introduction in 1983. The immediate predecessor to Lotus 123 was MultiPlan, which is still marketed. Today's major competitor to Lotus 123 is Excel from Microsoft Corporation.

Office Accounting

Prior to the introduction of the personal computer, office accounting was done with a paper-based ledger system or contracted out to specialty firms that used large computers, mainframes, and punched cards to tally accounts receivable, accounts payable, and the general ledger.

All software packages are based on a language of logic the hardware can interpret, translate into binary (based on zeros and ones—zeros representing off and one representing on) machine code, and process. Early word processing and spreadsheet software was written in the common languages of Cobol or Assembler. The user did not have to know these languages; they were presented with an *interface* that summarized processes into command sequences that were easy to use and remember (such as /FS to invoke the file save process).

Early office accounting packages were almost universally written in BASIC (Business and Scientific Instruction Code). Because most accounting routines could be anticipated and standardized, the programs written were magnitudes more complex than the other early applications. Computerized office accounting packages fundamentally impacted business. Inventory turns could be increased, cash flow could be managed, and payroll could be completed in a day, rather than a week, all due to better information management.

Although smaller companies adapted spreadsheets to serve as general ledgers, larger companies invested in full-blown accounting software packages. There were, and are, many competitors in this field.

What is compelling from a historical standpoint about the accounting packages written in BASIC is the progenitor of the PC-based BASIC program, Bill Gates. While an undergraduate at Harvard University, Gates developed a version of BASIC capable of running on computers equipped with microprocessors (the intelligence of the machine) that would evolve in the kind used in the PC. Transporting a language such as BASIC to the personal computer almost guaranteed success. Software developers, or "hackers," in college and in business now had access to affordable technology upon which to develop their talents. Without a software program like BASIC, the original IBM-PC would be like a car without an engine, a great idea that goes nowhere.

Bill Gates is now a household name. After dropping out of Harvard, he formed a software company, Microsoft Corporation. He is the first industry billionaire and a tycoon of considerable influence. Microsoft, still the largest software company in the industry, is the acknowledged leader in product development. The number two software company is Computer Associates, Inc.; it achieved this status primarily through product acquisition.

PRINTERS

The most elementary computer technology borrowed from typewriters is the ability to print. In fact, initial personal computer printers were nothing more than modified typewriters. However, as the three giant applications (word processing, spreadsheets, and office accounting) developed, it became clear that printers should become more intelligent. Users required the ability to *batch print*, meaning that a print request can be issued anytime during the computer session and the user can control the amount and presentation of the information printed.

Early PC printers were closely matched to the companion computer. In fact, IBM developed, and still retains, a major printer language standard. As the computer software communicates with the computer hardware, so the computer hardware communicates with the computer printer. The printer is connected to the computer via a communications port, and the computer transmits information to the printer via *parallel* or *serial* communications. Put simply, parallel communications are almost exclusively reserved for printer communications. This transmission medium can send eight bits (characters) at one time. It is significantly faster than serial communications, also used in all computer-to-computer communication. Serial communications transmit data one bit at a time. Early printers were either parallel or serial printers. Today, almost all printers can support either communication method.

Although all early computer and printer technology seems outmoded, inefficient, and almost ill-equipped, printers embodied first-generation technology with all its inherent flaws. The original dot matrix printers (in which a square space is allocated to each letter and the print head fills in the square with dots to create letters) were expensive and slow, and they produced unacceptable, draft-quality output. Daisy wheel printers, with heads that emulated typewriter print heads, were then introduced. They afforded near-letter-quality (NLQ) output but were even slower than dot matrix printers.

As is true with the rest of the computer industry, quality increased when competition entered the printer market. Epson America, Inc., which had been the manufacturer of IBM printers, entered the market with a new standard (the Epson printer language standard remains today) and a new product. A user could now buy a wide-carriage printer, capable of printing up to 176 characters across a wide page of green bar paper. (Previously, the printers, strictly emulating the typewritten page, afforded only 80 characters per line.) Epson increased the speed of the printers, but the quality was still only "draft," best suited for internal use. However, those users with spreadsheet and office accounting applications welcomed the ability to print one year of months and beyond on one page without cutting and pasting.

A third company, Hewlett Packard, Inc., solved the printing quandary for the other major application, word processing. Although corporations had made the move to computers, it was not uncommon to see secretaries retyping final drafts on typewriters—the print quality was just not acceptable for publication. Hewlett Packard (HP) introduced the LaserJet, a high-speed, high-quality printer that emulated the typeface and fonts produced by office typewriters. The LaserJet was up to five times more expensive than its dot matrix and daisy wheel competitors, but it was at least five times faster (printing six pages per minute in comparison to the one-page-per-minute and lesser output of other printers). However, users marvelled at the quality; this was a turning point. The ability to produce professional-looking documents was a primary reason for accepting personal computers into the workplace. Today, the Hewlett Packard Graphics Language (HPGL) remains the dominant and most emulated (meaning that competitors' products use the same logic) high-end printer control language in the personal computer industry.

NEW TECHNOLOGY AND APPLICATIONS

The personal computer of the 1990s is capable of functions not even imagined in 1981. Software applications and hardware capabilities have achieved such a level of sophistication and simplicity that many organizations have placed a PC on every desk. Trying to decide whether the hardware advances influence the software advances or vice versa is like trying to solve the chicken and egg riddle. Certainly, software functionality is limited to the real world of existing hardware. However, hardware engineers could develop the 98-cent Rolls Royce, but if there were no software applications to drive it, what would be the point? Separate examinations of technology advances in hardware and software applications amply demonstrate how the industry has progressed in leaps and bounds since 1981.

Hardware Advances

One way to demonstrate the advances in personal computer hardware is to consider what $5,000 would buy a typical consumer in 1981. The buyer would receive a monitor that was capable of displaying green text on a black background, 80 characters across and 25 rows down. The computer came with two 180K floppy drives; one drive ran the application software and one stored the data. Files could be built up to 64K in size, the amount of memory the computer came equipped with. The computer was powered by an 8088 microprocessor; this means that the machine could translate and process instructions 8 bits at a time (compare a bit to a letter in the alphabet). The speed at which the computer could process instructions was 4.77 MHz; this means that the computer could digest eight bits of data every 150 nanoseconds or so. The best way to understand these numbers is to think in terms of a real-life benchmark. Let's say that it took the original personal computer two minutes to load a 20-page document.

Now, after a decade's worth of innovation, competition, and inflation, let's look at what $5,000 buys. The monitor is capable of displaying text and *graphics* in 256 different colors. The screen can display 132 characters across and 43 lines down, corresponding more directly with a year's worth of months in a general ledger. The computer comes standard with a floppy drive that accommodates 1.44 megabytes (MB) (1,400K) of data on one 3.5" (down from 5.25") diskette. A fixed, nonremovable disk drive, called a hard disk, is also included and stores 40MB of application programs and data files. In addition to increased storage capacity, the hard disk can store and retrieve data nearly 10 times faster than a floppy disk. Data storage files are now at least 640K in size (10 times larger). On this particular computer, though, 1MB of memory can be accessed for file storage. The computer is powered by an 80386 processor that can execute instructions 32 bits at a time (four times more *throughput* than before). What's more, the processor runs at 33 MHz, which means that the computer can digest 32 bits of data every 18 nanoseconds or so. The new computer processes 4 times more data than before and 10 times faster than before. It now takes only five seconds to load a 20-page document.

Software Advances

The industry's giant applications described above, word processing, spreadsheets, and accounting, also have improved over time. The size of a file is almost unlimited; software is now smart enough to load only portions of the file into memory. The size of the portion is dependent upon the size of the system's memory. For example, if a 1,000-page report takes up 5 megabytes of disk space and the computer has 640K of main system memory, the application will access the file in 640K chunks.

Perhaps the largest advance in software is the development of graphics applications. The ability to display charts, pictures, and symbols has created a new giant application, graphics and *desktop publishing*. Corporations can produce newsletters, annual reports, overhead transparencies, and color desktop presentations with personal computers. Users can now insert company logos onto memorandums; business form creation can be completed without the help of outside service agencies; and numeric analyses can be accompanied by bar, pie, or area charts without combining software products or cutting and pasting.

Computer-aided design and manufacturing (CAD/CAM) products introduce the ability to model equipment or simulate environments in three dimensions.

Where To Begin

All this information, the jargon, and rapid changes in technology are daunting even to the experienced computer professional and certainly bewildering to the novice buying a first computer. Risk managers should be aware of the wide variance of programs available from vendors and should evaluate them before attempting to "self design" programs. Since the majority of word processing in the risk management department is done by support staff, their input in software selection is essential. The next section focuses on how to evaluate needs and select hardware and software and also covers ancillary issues such as security, support, and enhancements to existing equipment.

PURCHASING A COMPUTER

When To Buy

With advances in the personal computer field becoming regular sections of magazines and newspapers, even those who consider themselves "computer illiterate" have been exposed to increases in functionality coupled with price decreases. Now that full-featured, complete computer systems can be purchased from reliable vendors for under $1,000, many users feel comfortable in testing the market. But a good price should not be the primary reason for investing in a personal computer. It is necessary to evaluate the purposes of the machine. Risk managers who work with insurance and finance may need spreadsheet capabilities, while risk managers who concentrate on clinical and lawsuit management need other applications.

Another good rule of thumb for investment is time. How much time will the computer be used for typing, budgets, office accounting, and other applications? If additional clerical staff must be hired in reaction to increased workload, perhaps now is the time to automate some functions. A computer can help when excessive time is spent in record keeping rather than in more productive efforts. However, many beginning and growing small businesses believe that acquiring a personal computer will increase profits by somehow attracting business. A computer may increase profits by its proper use in the *management* of the business. The machine does not do the job, but it can be an important tool in accomplishing the job.

What To Buy

Software advances have developed different levels of personal computers. Similar to decisions made when buying a car, a computer user must decide what performance is required and what price is acceptable. Exhibit 8-1 identifies specific needs or concerns of the health care risk manager. If the user requires only word processing, an XT-compatible computer should be purchased. "XT" refers to an early IBM

Exhibit 8-1
RISK MANAGEMENT INFORMATION SYSTEM CHECKLIST

The following questions should be answered prior to purchasing a risk management information system:

1. Is pre-existing hardware capable of accommodating the department's current system?
2. How "user friendly" is the software?
3. Are appropriate modules available for upgrading the system as appropriate?
4. How readable are reports generated by the system?
5. Can reports be customized to meet the needs of the various audiences who will be using data? (For example, is the system capable of generating graphic and comparative/cumulative data?)
6. Can the system be customized to incorporate pre-existing risk management or other types of hospital forms?
7. Does the system have data sorting and analysis capabilities?
8. How available, useful, and costly are training and update sessions?
9. How *secure* is the system?
10. Is isolated data field information-sharing a possibility? (This is especially important when integrated departments share some of the same information.)
11. What is the projected *total* cost of the system?
12. How *flexible* is the system?
13. Can the system easily accommodate new data?
14. Are automatic updates or enhancements included in the purchase price? If not, are the prices of these aspects of the system clearly itemized?

standard and translates to *extended*. Early extended computers featured hard disks. Therefore, today's XT features a monochrome monitor, a 20MB hard disk, and a floppy disk. This unit displays only text, not graphics, and costs about $1,000.

If the user requires word processing and number-crunching, an AT-compatible system is required. "AT" refers to the IBM *advanced technology* standard. The AT features an 80286 processor that delivers 16 bits of information at a time and is generally about eight times faster than an XT. The AT might contain a 40MB hard disk, a disk drive, a color screen, and an adapter card to display graphics. This system can comfortably handle word processing, spreadsheet, and smaller data base operations. A system of this size costs about $2,000.

Finally, for larger data base, accounting, or CAD/CAM operations, a 386 system is recommended. "386" refers to the *80386 microprocessor* that delivers 32 bits of information at a time. This system sports high-quality color graphics capability, coprocessors to speed mathematical functions, large hard drives, and full-page displays to accommodate desktop publishing operations. This system is meant for the "power user," the person who spends all day at the computer in direct support of his or her job. This type of system is in the $5,000 range.

It is important to fit the hardware to software needs. As explained above, in development and in everyday use the software drives the hardware. The applications required must be decided first, then hardware selected that is best suited for the application—no more and no less. Remember that technology is advancing so rapidly that what is fastest today may not be fastest tomorrow. As well, what is bought today probably will be less expensive soon. So purchase what is needed, and plan for future growth.

From Whom To Buy

Again using the analogy of the automobile, several reasons are important in selecting a particular car dealer. Price is most likely the biggest reason, but warranty, service terms, location, and recommendations also influence the decision (see Exhibit 8-2). These are also sound arguments in selecting a computer dealer. A novice requires guidance in selecting the proper computer; a computer retail chain has salespeople trained to help in analyzing the buyer's needs. If the buyer knows exactly what hardware and software are required, he or she can save money by selecting the equipment through a mail-order firm. All the caveats of mail-order firms apply here. The buyer should research return and service policies, as well as the company itself. Research tools include computer journals and the Better Business Bureau.

Exhibit 8-2
RISK MANAGEMENT INFORMATION SYSTEM VENDOR SELECTION CHECKLIST

1. Does the vendor have prior experience in health care settings? (This is especially important if clinical monitoring, tracking, and trending functions are required.)
2. Does the vendor have experience in the insurance industry? (This is especially important if claims services are to be a function of the system.)
3. Is the vendor cost competitive? What is the vendor's general reputation in the industry for service?
4. Is the vendor ambiguous about hidden or future projected costs for training or updating and customizing the program?
5. Are the vendor's trainers experienced in hospital information systems and the many unique needs of the users of these systems?
6. Can services be unbundled if bought through the vendor or must the user buy the entire package in order to get the needed service?

The used computer market is like the used car market. It is not always possible to know exactly what is being purchased. It is a good way to save money, but orphaned, unsupported technology may not be completely compatible with today's software and hardware technology.

Finally, well-known hardware and software should be purchased. It is not necessary to buy from IBM or Compaq, but equipment should be selected from reputable manufacturers who provide warranties, telephone support, and well-written manuals. Many buyers are tempted to get the deal of the week, but a computer is a depreciable asset that is expected to last for at least three to five years. With the amortization of the equipment investment over that time period, a savings of perhaps $500 becomes less significant. In the computer industry, paying a little extra for the security blanket of quality and service is a wise decision.

SECURITY AND MAINTENANCE

Acquiring new technology means acquiring new concerns and developing safeguards to protect the institution and the investment. Storing data in electronic form brings security issues to bear. The significant investment that is made in a computer system requires basic maintenance techniques to protect the data and the system. The sensitivity of the data collected by the risk management department makes this an area of heightened concern.

Just as file cabinets containing confidential documents are locked, data stored on diskettes should be locked away. Access to programs that house the data should be password-protected. Printouts should be securely stored and discarded output ripped or shredded if confidentiality is an issue. The system itself should be housed in a room with a lock and limited access. As with any other investment, the insurance carrier must be notified of the purchase. A portable computer should have adequate insurance coverage if it is taken out of the office.

Another security issue is vulnerability to a computer-generated *virus*. A computer virus is simply a program meant to access other programs for the purpose of gathering or destroying information. The best way to avoid computer virus is to limit the software used on the computer. Only new software that is still shrink-wrapped should be purchased. Software from unknown sources should not be loaded on the system. Standards are required for software usage so that an employee or friend is not allowed to load software with an unknown origin. In short, control should be maintained over hardware and software access to minimize exposure to these risks.

It is easy to take care of the computer system. There are not many moving parts, so components are very reliable. Some computers are not meant to be moved, especially when they are turned on. Dropping the computer is always a bad idea, as well as spilling liquids on the screen or keyboard or leaving the computer in a very warm or very cold room. Although newer computers generate much less heat than their older counterparts, it is still a good idea to turn the system off at night or when it is not in use. When activating the system, the monitor should be turned on first and then the base unit. A power strip that conditions the electricity affords additional outlets and protects against spikes or surges. The unit should be kept dust-free. Screen cleaning pads are available in any computer store. Computer covers are not sold as widely as before, but if the computer is in a harsh environment covers are useful. Generally, common sense is the best guide to computer maintenance.

KEEPING UP WITH ENHANCEMENTS

It is very easy to fall into the trap of buying the latest and greatest technology. The hardware and software manufacturers try hard to convince consumers that they need the latest word processing upgrade, the latest video graphics enhancement, or a faster communications device.

Before purchasing new equipment, the computer owner should first evaluate what the present computer is doing. What applications does it support, and how are things going? If there are no complaints, the system does not require upgrading. If, however, there is a need to generate graphics to supplement reports, additional hardware may be necessary. Some types of publications may require the capabilities of desktop-publishing packages. Again, the best sources for information are industry journals, computer retail chains, user groups, and associates who share common interests and experiences. But remember, no one else can make the actual decision. The final rule of thumb: "if you can wait, wait." Something more powerful and less expensive is sure to be introduced in the near future.

CONCLUSION

The personal computer has grown from a hobbyist's kit to a boardroom decoration to an essential business tool, all in the space of a decade. The huge growth has prompted significant competition and advances. Analysts project that the next decade will be as fast-paced as the first, with a few companies dominating the market plus many quality niche players. We have already seen some developments of the future: laptop computers the size of notebooks, desktop computers with the processing power of minicomputers and mainframes, and video displays that simulate three-dimensional modeling at the speed of videotape.

All of these promises are not sufficient reasons to invest in a personal computer for the risk management department. The computer is a tool to meet a need. The need must be self-evident, a given. When the need is demonstrated, then the computer's resources will be best used. The computer can be a time manager and the user can play chess against it, but it is a very expensive way to manage time and play games. The bulk of the time spent with the computer must be in administering the three office functions discussed in this chapter: word processing, numeric analysis, and office accounting. From this base, all other applications are derived and all other uses of the computer are justified.

chapter 9

Facilitating Physician Participation: An Integrated Approach

Jay L. Goldstein and Tina L. Spector

INTRODUCTION

As the central figure in the delivery of health care, the physician must assume a leadership role in programs that examine clinical quality, cost-effectiveness and efficiency of care, risk reduction, and ultimately patient and consumer satisfaction. This role requires the physician to furnish active support and participation at all levels of these activities, including the design, implementation, and interpretation of quality assurance and risk management data. Moreover, the level of success and productivity of any quality assurance and risk management endeavor can be correlated directly to the degree of physician input in planning and executing changes that lead toward quality improvement.

An ideal quality assurance and risk management program assesses the timeliness, efficacy, and appropriateness of health care delivery in an inpatient or outpatient setting. This evaluation should be clinically relevant and therefore, by definition, must be a peer review process. The efficacy of such a program is measured not merely by the identification of global or physician-specific problems, but also by the evaluation of the problems and the changes implemented to rectify them. A significant improvement in patient care can be realized only through the actions generated by a quality assurance and risk management program, but without physician support, the credibility and support of the program cannot exist.

Because effective quality improvement is coupled with the surmounting pressures of external agencies that judge and compile information on physician practice, competence, and professional behavior, the importance of and critical need for physician support and participation of quality assurance and risk management systems is clear. This does not, of course, negate the pivotal roles of the quality assurance and risk management professionals. In addition to providing guidance, these individuals must help to establish the framework and determine the goals of the program. Encouraging education and aiding in the evaluation of physician performance, in fact, constitute one of the greatest challenges facing quality assurance and risk management professionals. Therefore, in order to ensure that a quality assurance program actually achieves optimal levels of improved patient care and reduction of risk, quality assurance and risk management professionals must be able to interact effectively with the physicians who are at the center of health care delivery.

RESISTANCE OF THE MEDICAL COMMUNITY TO FORMAL PROGRAMS

Traditionally, there has been a great deal of resistance in the medical community in relation to formalizing internal and external review processes. Despite government legislation, policies set by national and local medical societies, and bylaw requirements of hospitals, individual physicians have been slow to respond to or participate in quality assurance activities. This resistance is multifactorial but appears to center on four major factors:

1. infringement on personal choice
2. punitive nature of existing systems
3. cost and time requirements
4. lack of demonstrable impact on patient care

Infringement on Personal Choice

The first of these primary factors involves an innate resistance related to the belief that such programs will lead to an "algorithmic" practice of medicine and loss of physician autonomy. This argument may have validity if quality assurance programs are designed independently of true peer review processes and do not recognize that there is a spectrum of acceptable standards. For example, designing monitors or implementing programs without allowing for appropriate variability in practice leads to reinforcement of this belief. On the other hand, liberalizing the standards of practice based on clinically sound physician/practitioner input, as well as requiring peer review for problems that appear to extend beyond these standards, results in better participation. Monitors or quality assurance activities need not be dictatorial; rather, they should reflect rational and realistic variabilities in medical practice. Extending this idea, even with the best of intentions, "fallout" from standards actually may be clinically correct. As such, the evaluation and fine-tuning of any quality assurance activity require nonpunitive, objective peer review. This review must be fair and clinically based; it should not be a rehashing of the initial process or the dogmatic beliefs held by an individual.

Punitive Nature of Existing Systems

As noted above, the quality assurance process should be constructive, not punitive or destructive. A quality assurance program should focus on improvement of overall patient care by individuals or by the system that supports them; it is not a vehicle to undermine any given practitioner. If the program is designed or perceived initially to be vindictive or punitive, physician participation will be lost. This premise also extends into the peer review process. The physicians involved in peer reviews should be just that—peers. They should not be participating or acting as the singular "gold standard" but rather as open-minded individuals (or groups) who are fair and nonjudgmental. Although they may act in an educational capacity, their primary focus should be on evaluation and integration of the clinical aspects of the perceived individual problem. The peer review process must be a fact-finding mission, not a trial, and it is important that physicians who participate in designing, evaluating, and implementing quality assurance programs be chosen carefully.

Cost and Time Requirements

The third major concern focuses on how a quality assurance program should be constructed and the extent of time related to physician participation. The time required for the process of monitoring and evaluation should not overwhelm the physician. One way of streamlining this process is to be specific in questions that are asked. Clear-cut end points that can be evaluated objectively by nonphysicians translate into a more successful process because they lead to selected fallout with easier and more directed evaluation at the level of peer review. It must be remembered that physicians are not usually compensated for the time they spend in quality assurance activities. Therefore, the time set aside for these activities should be maximally used.

Lack of Demonstrable Impact on Patient Care

Failure of physicians to engage or participate in quality assurance and risk management may be the result of ineffective interventions or outcomes. If there has been a track record of ineffective or nonexistent corrective actions, the entire process will be negated, whereas effective interventions that have resulted in demonstrable changes will facilitate future endeavors. Therefore, it would be most beneficial to begin with or redirect monitors where corrective actions can be anticipated to impact on patient care in a positive way. This will demonstrate to participating physicians that they are involved in a meaningful and constructive program.

KEY ELEMENTS OF A SUCCESSFUL PROGRAM

Even when they understand traditional resistance and the guidelines for circumventing problems, quality assurance and risk management professionals may still be uncertain about how to overcome these problems and how best to engage the support and commitment of the medical staff. A successful program includes a number of key elements.

Organization

The quality assurance and risk management program of a health care institution must have a solid organizational framework. It should be outlined in a written plan that has been developed in part by the medical staff and approved by the executive body of the institution. Their support in achieving the goals of the plan should also be clear.

Physicians must understand their roles and responsibilities within the quality assurance and risk management organization, as well as the roles and responsibilities of other participants. The peer review process and the lines of communication must be defined in the plan and be an accurate reflection of actual practice.

The plan should discuss the integration of quality assurance and risk management activities with other evaluative activities, such as utilization review, infection control, and safety. The roles and responsibilities of clinical departments, hospital administration, hospital departments, and hospital/medical staff committees that assist in the operations and governance of the programs should be clearly defined. The role of the governing body as the ultimate authority and responsible body for the quality of patient care must be evident.

Physician Needs

The quality assurance and risk management professional must understand the multiple needs, preferences, expectations, and requirements of physicians and be willing to alter programs to fit their needs. Physicians must be addressed as "priority customers."[1] Appropriate efforts are required to respond to their unmet requirements; however, this must be done within the overall framework of the program design. The expectations and goals of a quality assurance and risk management program should not be undermined.

Value and Benefits

The challenge undertaken by quality assurance and risk management professionals is demonstrating that value can be derived from their programs. Minimally, these professionals must possess the ability to prove such value by providing evidence of clear-cut tangible and quantifiable benefits and results. Additionally, the use of financial or other incentives may be considered to reimburse physicians who assume leadership responsibilities. In some instances, physicians may receive direct benefit through publication of quality assurance and risk management data.

Responsibility/Accountability

The quality assurance and risk management professional must work with the medical staff to outline its responsibilities within quality assurance and risk management programs and define the lines of accountability. Physicians clearly accept responsibility for the care of individual patients they treat but often experience difficulty in accepting and understanding their responsibility for the aggregate monitoring of patient care.[2] Equally important, physicians accept the responsibility for setting standards for their own care and treatment of patients and therefore should accept the task of directing, or at least participating in, the efforts to accomplish the same for the entire health care team.

When examining systems of care that require improvement or alteration, quality assurance and risk management professionals should help to define the roles and responsibilities of physicians as leaders and be quick to demonstrate what can be effectively accomplished. Physicians must be made aware that they not only have a stake in the health care system but also have the responsibility and ability to make and execute recommendations that will have a positive impact on the delivery of care.

Based on the quality assurance and risk management plan as described above, specific individuals on the medical staff are automatically responsible and accountable for participation in the program.

Department Chairperson

The role of a department head has changed dramatically during recent years.[3] It has been transformed from that of a figurehead to one of responsibility and accountability for the establishment of monitoring and evaluation activities. Further, it is expected that the results of these activities will be used by the chairperson to appraise staff members' performance in the recredentialing process. In large departments, the chairperson may feel that this responsibility is more effectively met by delegating it to other key members within the department.

Physician Liaisons

Involving physicians who have been delegated the authority and responsibility of quality assurance and risk management activities for their departments or for the health care institution as a whole may be the key to the success of an effective program. These individuals may have more time and greater interest in developing and implementing productive and innovative changes. Quality assurance and risk management professionals can identify the physicians on the hospital's medical staff who have demonstrated the greatest participation in these activities and can begin an educational process with them on a one-on-one basis. Eventually, these physician liaisons will become "natural ambassadors" to the rest of the medical community.[4] Through their exposure to and communication with other physicians serving in this capacity, they may exchange information about the quality assurance and risk management program and begin to collaborate in an additive or even, at times, a synergistic manner.

The Role of Physician Leaders in the Planning Process

It is important to integrate physician leaders in the program planning process as new concepts are introduced or existing processes are modified. The expertise and insight of these individuals will be invaluable as the quality assurance and risk management professional helps the medical staff and health care institution to implement new strategies, promote new activities, and report accomplishments.

The most effective means of ensuring this assistance is to involve physicians in direct leadership roles at the level of a quality assurance and risk management council or as members of a committee.[5] Physicians are then not only participants but share in the success of the program. This success will help to maintain their pivotal roles in communication of the program's results to the medical staff. (For a sample job description describing the role of a physician director, see Exhibit 9-1.)

Time Commitments

When involving the medical staff, the quality assurance and risk management professional must carefully consider the cost of physician participation. With the exception of those who hold financially supported administrative positions, physicians are paid for taking care of patients. Their time constraints must be recognized and respected. For the most productive use of their time, meetings should be well organized and focused and the material presented or discussed at a level that requires the attention of the physicians.

Education

Quality begins with education and ends with education.[6] The greater the physicians' understanding of quality assurance and risk management processes and benefits, the greater their contributions and commitments will be. Throughout their training, physicians receive little or no formal education in quality assurance or risk management; therefore, the quality assurance and risk management professional is obligated to develop educational programs that address the application of these concepts. Physicians must be taught that quality assurance and risk management programs are not intended to limit their freedom in decision making but to assist in preventing significant quality issues being raised by external and governmental reviews and in lawsuits.

The educational programs that best illustrate the principles of quality assurance and risk management are those using actual clinical examples. Open discussion of case presentations tend to be easier to understand and are more relevant to the practicing physician. In conjunction with quality assurance and risk management professionals, physicians trained in these concepts should also play active roles in this educational process.

Support of Hospital Administration

Proactive support by hospital administration of quality assurance and risk management programs must be evident throughout all levels of the health care organization. This support must include adequate funding for these programs, as well as ongoing written and verbal reinforcements. The administration must also demonstrate recognition of the importance of the physician's role in the overall process of quality assurance and risk management.

Peer Review Process

A true peer review process is at the heart of all quality assurance and risk management programs. Physicians are best evaluated by other physicians, and peer review is not a new concept to most physicians. For years, physicians have evaluated their performances informally through morbidity and mortality conferences, case presentations, and other similar means. This informal mechanism, however, fails to be constructive because there is great variability in the review process and it fails to lead to formal conclusions and effective corrective action plans.

The peer review process in a well-managed quality assurance and risk management program must be ongoing and constructive, and involve the use of standards, criteria, or key benchmarks developed by physicians. The purpose of peer review is to provide a means to evaluate the care provided and identify acceptable and unacceptable variations in practice. Overall, physicians inherently want to provide the best quality patient care. Establishment of a structure that is impartial and open to participation by all staff members facilitates ample opportunities to identify and resolve problems in overall patient care. The process must be completed with action and follow-up plans where appropriate. Positive reinforcement of the process must be continuous.

Staff Support

Quality assurance and risk management programs must be staffed adequately by qualified individuals who are viewed by the medical staff as credible, reliable, knowledgeable, and honest. These staff members must possess excellent attitudes and superior communication and organizational skills that will enable them to maintain ongoing positive interactions with the medical staff as they carry out the goals and objectives of the programs. Additionally, the staff must be provided with adequate funding and resources to maintain an appropriate level of functioning for the programs.

Exhibit 9-1
SAMPLE JOB DESCRIPTION FOR PHYSICIAN DIRECTOR—QUALITY IMPROVEMENT

SUMMARY OF POSITION

The physician in this position reports to the Chief of Staff and the Chief Executive Officer or President of the hospital with responsibility for providing medical direction and leadership support to quality improvement and risk management activities. As part of this responsibility, the physician works toward coordination and communication among the administration, clinical departments, risk management, quality assurance, and other ancillary departments. The person in this position serves as chairperson of the hospital-wide quality assurance and improvement committee and as primary adviser to the utilization management and patient care evaluation committee.

POSITION DUTIES AND RESPONSIBILITIES

Serves as chairperson of the quality improvement committee, directs the work of the patient care evaluation committee, and has responsibility for ensuring that the following charge from the Medical Staff and hospital management is met:

- ongoing development, support, and coordination of quality improvement activities designed to ensure that
  - the highest possible quality of care is rendered at departmental and institutional levels
  - use and delivery of manpower, facilities, and services are effective and efficient
  - requirements for utilization review and quality assurance are met in accordance with negotiated hospital agreements and with external licensing, accrediting, and reimbursement organizations
  - marketing activities take into consideration the physician provider as consumer and the patient and/or the public as the final consumer and evaluator of the service provided
- provision of physician input into the activities of the quality improvement and risk management departments
- coordination of quality improvement and utilization activities of the quality assurance and risk management departments with other departments and committees within the hospital
- promotion of liaisons with or between:
  - the hospital director, CEO, or President
  - designated representatives from each clinical service who establish and maintain ongoing quality improvement activities in accordance with external review organizations and internal marketing efforts

  - external review agencies, the quality assurance and risk management departments, and the Medical Staff
  - appropriate medical staff committees
  - persons responsible for providing data through hospital information systems
- review of all proposals and studies related to quality of patient care on an annual basis and other quality initiatives completed under the auspices of the Quality of Care Committee
- development of agendas for monthly meetings of the Quality of Care Committee
- monitoring and education of medical staff on new techniques related to quality improvement, including models for evaluating clinical efficiency and effectiveness within the health care setting
- with the assistance of the quality assurance and risk management departments, physicians, nurses, and ancillary personnel, coordination of the development of treatment protocols for specific diagnosis-related groups that maintain a balance between cost containment and quality patient care
- presentation of annual reports and interim reports, as appropriate, to the hospital governing board or executive committee that detail progress of ongoing quality initiatives
- supervision of graduate students and other staff assigned to the quality improvement/quality assurance program for research experience
- member of the medical records committee

POSITION SPECIFICATIONS

Position Title: Physician Director—Quality Improvement
Reports to: Chief of Staff and Hospital Director
Education: Graduation from medical school and minimum of three years' postgraduate training; MPH, MBA, or equivalent training highly desirable
Special Skills: Ability to motivate and effect change in a complex environment. Knowledge of patient care appraisal techniques and methods of conducting audits of care. Knowledge of epidemiology, statistics, and data handling techniques as applied to patient care. Adaptability to varying workloads and tasks resulting from changing program priorities and deadlines. Good judgment and excellent interpersonal and communicative skills.

Data

The quality assurance and risk management programs must be capable of producing objective data that provide physicians with specific information about their performances. The data should be well organized and at a level that provides sufficient detail to allow for the analysis of specific factors affecting health care delivery. These data should not indicate only negative findings; positive feedback adds credibility and demonstrates fairness of the process.

The quality assurance and risk management professional should work closely with the medical staff to identify appropriate, respected organizations from which comparative standards and norms can be derived. Data should be profiled over time and compared with these standards not only to identify areas for improvement but to demonstrate levels of excellence.

At no time should the quality assurance and risk management program use data of questionable integrity. Computer systems provide an expanded ability to produce data that can be trended and efficiently analyzed.

Communication and Marketing

The quality assurance and risk management professional must capitalize on all encounters with physicians to increase their knowledge base, heighten their overall awareness, influence their attitudes, and communicate the positive results of the programs.

Department meetings are excellent arenas for presentations, not only for offering specific results of peer review activities but also for sharing hospital-wide trends and information. In these and other settings, physicians should be encouraged to discuss their needs, frustrations, and expectations regarding both the internal and external systems.[7] "Success stories" that involved other members of the medical staff offer great potential for selling the program to disinterested physicians.

Quality assurance and risk management professionals must be consistently visible and available. Regular written and visual communications, such as newsletters, handbooks, and posters, should be available to all staff members. Educating and communicating with all hospital personnel should not be overlooked; many individuals may serve as driving forces in the overall communication network. Computer systems available on an institution-wide basis can be useful in publishing the results of quality assurance and risk management activities.

FROM QUALITY ASSURANCE AND RISK MANAGEMENT TO CONTINUOUS QUALITY IMPROVEMENT

As health care institutions begin to evolve from the traditional concepts of quality assurance and risk management programs to the philosophy of total quality management and continuous quality improvement, the need for heightened physician awareness and support becomes increasingly apparent.

Similar to the pressures that U.S. manufacturers have faced, health care delivery systems need to concern themselves with problems related to competition, quality, cost, and public image.[8] Continuous quality improvement should be the natural extension of existing quality assurance and risk management programs. (See Chapter 12 for a more detailed discussion of this subject.)

Quality improvement principles focus on outcome through the examination of processes of care. The implementation of quality improvement philosophies thus should be intertwined with the health care institution's quality assurance and risk management program goals and objectives. As noted in the above discussions, physicians will remain the key to success of quality improvement efforts. As both providers and consumers of services, physicians are in a unique position to identify and prioritize areas for improvement. Because physicians are an integral part of the clinical process, they must be equally motivated to participate in the institution's quality improvement initiatives. As quality improvement philosophies become ingrained in health care institutions, quality will begin to drive decision making.

CONCLUSION

The physician remains an essential figure in any combined quality assurance, risk management, and continuous quality improvement program that is effective. In the past, traditional physician resistance to participation in these programs has been significant and has required quality assurance and risk management professionals to "undo" this resistance by initiating new incentives to incorporate physicians into this process. With such efforts as described in this chapter, this type of program can effectively lead to improvement of health care delivery.

NOTES

1. O.J. Kravolec and J. Brent, Obtaining Physician Commitment and Medical Results in the Quality Improvement Process. *Quest for Quality and Productivity in Health Care Services* (Conference Proceedings of the Society for Health Systems and American Hospital Association Health Care Information and Management Systems Society, Chicago, 1990), 196.

2. D.R. Longo, et al., *Integrated Quality Assessment, a Model for Concurrent Review* (Chicago: American Hospital Publishing Inc., 1989), 58.

3. Longo, et al., *Integrated Quality Assessment*, 59.

4. J. Schlosser, Quality Improvement in Healthcare: Why It Will Work and How to Involve Physicians, *The Quality Letter for Health Care Leaders* (September 1989): 12.

5. Kravolec and Brent, Obtaining Physician Commitment, 196.

6. Schlosser, Quality Improvement in Healthcare, 12.

7. M.B. Guthrie, Gaining Physician Support for Risk Management, *Perspectives in Healthcare Risk Management* 7, no. 3 (Summer 1987): 3.

8. S.L. Andrews, QA vs QI: The Changing Role of Quality in Health Care, *Journal of Quality Assurance* 13, no. 1 (January/February 1991): 14.

BIBLIOGRAPHY

Andrews, S.L. January/February 1991. QA vs. QI: The Changing Role of Quality in Health Care. *Journal of Quality Assurance* 13, no. 1: 14–15, 38.

Bader, B.S., and R. Veatch. December 1989–January 1990. Internal and External Peer Review in Medical Staff Reappointment. *The Quality Letter Health Care Leaders*: 1–8.

Fainter, J. January/February 1991. Quality Assurance/Quality Improvement. *Journal of Quality Assurance* 13, no. 1: 8–9, 36.

Guthrie, M.B. Summer 1987. Gaining Physician Support for Risk Management. *Perspectives in Healthcare Risk Management* 7 no. 3: 1–3.

Kravolec, O.J., and J. Brent. Obtaining Physician Commitment and Medical Results in the Quality Improvement Process. *Quest for Quality and Productivity in Health Care Services* (Conference Proceedings of the Society for Health Systems and American Hospital Association Health Care Information and Management Systems Society, Chicago, 1990), 195–199.

Longo, D.R., et al 1989. *Integrated Quality Assessment, a Model for Concurrent Review.* Chicago: American Hospital Publishing Inc.

Schlosser, J. September 1989. Quality Improvement in Healthcare: Why It Will Work and How to Involve Physicians. *The Quality Letter for Health Care Leaders:* 10–12.

Youngberg, B.J. 1990. *Quality and Risk Management in Health Care: An Information Service.* Gaithersburg, Md.: Aspen Publishers, Inc., 3:6–3:8.

chapter 10

Integrating Patient Support Services with Risk Management

Barbara J. Youngberg

INTRODUCTION

Hospitals and health care facilities are now recognized as important business operations. Traditionally, the many aspects of a hospital's operation were viewed as separate and varying in importance, with the physician as the focal point of the organization. Today, however, the goal of hospital management is to give the patient-consumer a sense of total organizational quality and commitment. This requires the education of the entire staff (professional and ancillary) on the importance of each person within the organization and recognition of his or her role in making the patient and family feel that they are dealing, at every juncture, with persons who are caring, concerned, and interested in their well-being.

It is easy to forget the importance of making a positive first impression. In a hospital, a patient may encounter many support persons before seeing a nurse or a physician. These people may believe that they play a very minor role in overall patient satisfaction when, in fact, they greatly affect a patient's first impression of the hospital. For example, many hospitals have parking facilities, valet services for same-day surgery, information desks, and patient transport programs. These ancillary patient support departments can set the tone for the patient's hospitalization through courtesy, friendliness, and helpfulness. Support personnel can also observe patients and families and recognize those who might benefit from their assistance. Like the health care professionals, they must learn the importance of recognizing that many people who come into a hospital are under

stress and often react to the circumstances in unexpected ways. Assisting the hospital staff to understand the positive impact of quality service and the importance of an atmosphere that is perceived by patients as caring and compassionate goes a long way in presenting an overall favorable impression of the organization.

These staff members are also important in helping to identify patients who seem to be functioning at a high level of stress and who may benefit from available services, such as the social service, patient relations, and financial services departments. All patient support personnel should be advised of the method for identifying these patients and families to the appropriate professionals who can give them assistance.

In addition, these professional support departments must be linked with the departments of risk management and quality assurance to discuss and recognize the importance of early intervention for patients under stress and to recognize their roles in providing service to patients and families throughout the hospitalization. Only when such a coordinated and integrated approach to patient care is developed will the risk management and quality assurance programs reach maximum effectiveness.

THE IMPORTANCE OF PATIENT RELATIONS IN HOSPITAL QUALITY MANAGEMENT PROGRAMS

The need perceived by the public for protection of their rights as patients has become a major public issue, in part because of public perceptions as to the actual or potential effects of many recent developments in health care. First, federal and state cost-cutting measures have been widely faulted for causing premature discharge and clinical mismanagement of patients due to financial considerations unrelated to the individual's health needs. Second, increasing commercial competition in the health and medical marketplace, such as the increasing privatization of hospitals and health care facilities and the burgeoning of health maintenance organizations (HMOs) and competitive medical plans, has caused much concern as to whether health care is a callous, commercial, profit-motivated enterprise rather than a caring, professional human service. Third, unprecedented federal budget deficits are seen as forcing cost containment and retrenchment in the federal government's commitment to high-quality health care.

In addition, concerns about the quality of health care have arisen as a result of the increased innovations of modern technology. In the face of "modern medicine," many health care consumers believe that

- in the face of increased technology, the "human side" of health care is reduced
- in the face of time pressures, due in part to inadequate staffing, the amount of time that health care workers actually spend with patients is reduced
- with the increased specialization, the opportunity to develop a long-term relationship with a treating physician is lessened

All of these problems come at a time when patients' expectations of information and involvement in their plan of care have been given substantial attention and support from the media.

Joint Commission Position on Patient Relations

Perhaps in response to these changes in health care, the Joint Commission on the Accreditation of Healthcare Organizations (Joint Commission) has developed standards that will require formalized methods of dealing with patient complaints that relate to quality of care. The new standards mandate that hospitals have mechanisms in place to

- make the right to file a complaint and the process by which to do so known to the patient, to the patient's family, or to the person responsible for the care of the patient
- address the issues raised by the complaint
- respond to the complaint in a timely fashion
- take appropriate corrective action when such action is deemed necessary

- reassure the person filing the complaint that future care will not be compromised

State Grievance Procedures

Many states have grievance procedures that define how patient complaints are to be handled. Maryland has one of the most detailed descriptions of the requirements for a patient's complaint program. It specifies that

- the hospital's risk management program must include a formal written program for addressing hospital complaints
- the hospital must give patients certain information about the program, including the name and phone number or address of a hospital representative that the patient may contact to make a complaint
- the hospital's representative must treat the complaining patient with dignity and courtesy and due regard for privacy and must provide the patient with certain information about the complaint handling process
- the hospital's representative must document the complaint and any action taken as a result of it

Other states' requirements range from having all patients receive written notice of their rights within 24 hours of admission and be informed as to how they may file complaints (Massachusetts) to a general requirement that the hospital have a procedure to investigate, analyze, and respond to patient grievances related to patient care (Alaska).[1]

Developing a Hospital Policy

Many hospitals have long-standing policies that address the procedures to follow when patients are dissatisfied with the quality of the care they receive. Separate departments often exist in hospitals to identify these problems and develop problem-solving techniques. These departments are usually visible within the hospital and often are very effective. However, many of them neglect to share the information they gain from patients with other departments, such as quality assurance and risk management. By failing to do so, they overlook an important step in averting potential future problems.

The patient relations department logically interfaces with a number of other hospital departments, and a mechanism should be in place to ensure that information generated through the patient relations process is shared with the appropriate persons (Figure 10-1). Departments that should work closely with patient relations include finance or patient billing, risk management, quality assurance, discharge planning, social work, and administration. All of

Figure 10-1
INFORMATION FLOW CHART—ACTION DIAGRAM

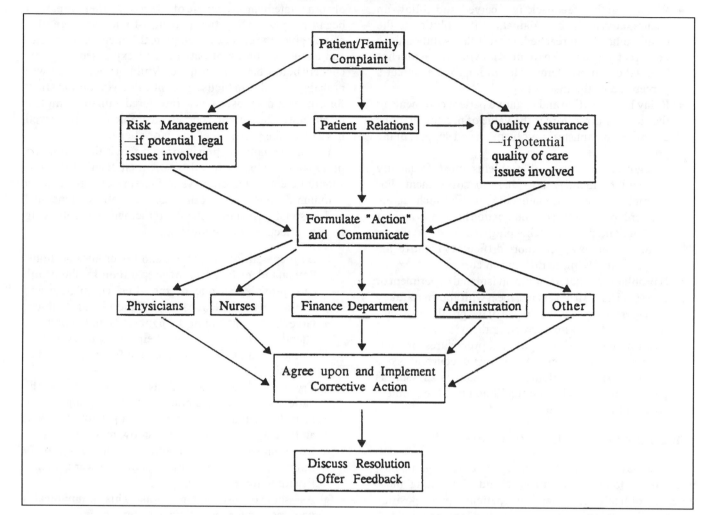

these departments should participate in the process that addresses patient relations functions and problem resolution. Patient complaints and negative patient survey results should be reviewed monthly by a quality of care committee (regular committee meetings should be attended by persons from the departments cited above). A timetable should be established for follow-up and problem resolution, with individual or department responsibilities appropriately assigned. If the patient remains in the hospital, attempts should be made to resolve any problems prior to discharge.

A number of mechanisms can be implemented to assure hospital staff that appropriate feedback is being received and that patients and their families have easy access to the process. Examples of these mechanisms follow.

- Draft a "Patient Bill of Rights" and make copies of this document available to all patients (and their families)

on admission to the hospital's inpatient or outpatient services (see Appendix 10-A).

- Install a patient "hot line" or place a card by the patient's telephone that identifies a 24-hour number for use in registering complaints or making suggestions. This number can be serviced by an answering machine during off-shift hours with a message that a response will be made the following day.
- Designate representatives from social work, patient relations, or administration to make daily rounds and inquire as to patients' and families' satisfaction with care received. Obviously, this may not be feasible if the hospital is very large or staffing is a problem.
- Review all responses to patient satisfaction surveys and follow up on all negative comments. If response to written surveys is minimal, request that individual departments make follow-up telephone calls to in-

quire about the patients' perceptions of care they receive.

- When negative feedback is received and follow-up occurs, advise the complainant that a solution to the problem has been reached, even if that solution does not directly affect the patient. Knowing that action has been taken on problems helps to improve a patient's perception of the institution.
- Relay both positive and negative patient comments to the staff. This reinforces the value of patient relations and helps to gain staff involvement and support of the program.
- Categorize the types of problems most frequently received to identify how best to solve them. For example, are most problems the result of such factors as interdepartmental communication breakdown, short staffing, and poor housekeeping and food service, or do the problems appear more difficult to identify and thus potentially more difficult to correct?
- If problems are noted within an isolated department or on a specific shift or service, meet with appropriate key managers to discuss resolution of the problems. Establish a time frame for correcting them.
- Determine if changes in policies, procedures, or internal processes are required to alleviate recurrences of a problem. If so, implement the changes as soon as possible to minimize the likelihood that the problem will continue to occur.

The Importance of Communication

To maintain a successful patient relations program, hospitals must focus on identifying and eliminating those elements of health care that fuel a patient's predisposition to sue or dissatisfaction with the care that is being provided. In using this proactive approach, health care professionals must become increasingly sensitized to the stresses associated with illness and hospitalization and must learn the importance of good listening and effective communication to avoid future patient problems and complaints.

Ongoing communication with a patient and the patient's family greatly increases the likelihood that complaints associated with patient care will not arise. The quality of the interaction between the health care provider and the patient or family is often directly equated to the quality of the health care provided; thus the need to maintain open and active communication is critical.

A risk management series published by St. Paul Insurance Companies states: "Physician communication styles have been shown to affect the quality and quantity of information obtained from patient interviews as well as the extent to which patients follow physicians' instructions. Patients express more dissatisfaction with communication than with any other aspect of health care."[2]

In one study of inteviewing styles cited by the St. Paul series, physicians were found to interrupt the patient's opening statement an average of 18 seconds after the patient began to speak. Only two percent of patients were ultimately given the chance to complete the opening statement, and about two thirds of patients had expressed only one concern before being interrupted. While an interruption was probably intended to focus a patient's description and allow for a quicker diagnosis, it also interfered with the complete disclosure of the patient's perceived problems and may well have made the patient feel angry or alienated.

Because communication is so important in the health care process and so closely linked to patient satisfaction, the staff should be counseled on ways to increase effectiveness in communications. The risk manager, as well as all medical and hospital personnel, should remember the following keys to effective communication:

- Be prepared for the patient and his or her questions. Patients identify a lack of preparation by the health care provider as one of the chief complaints and interpret it as a lack of caring and individual attention.
- Give the patient and/or the patient's family complete attention when you greet them. This takes only a moment and establishes a positive first impression of the visit.
- Try to minimize interruptions, especially during the patient's opening statement. If interrupting, do so tactfully, perhaps by referring to a patient statement and saying you would like to know more about that.
- Communicate attention and respect non-verbally through periodic eye contact, leaning forward, intense listening, tone of voice, etc.
- Ask some open-ended questions. This communicates your respect for the patient's ability and increases the opportunity to discover something that otherwise might have been missed.
- Share information with the patient throughout the visit rather than waiting until the end. This reduces patient anxiety and increases trust.
- Use simple language and repetition as appropriate and to make sure the patient understands. Use "check in" questions, such as: "Was that clear to you?" or "Do you feel comfortable with what you need to do?"
- Be genuine with the patient. Don't force small talk or familiarity if it is not comfortable for you. However, be sure to communicate interest and concern for the patient.
- Recognize that from the patient's point of view, he or she has made a special effort to see you.
- Recognize that a patient's non-compliance or disagreement with you may be due to reasons he or she feels are legitimate. Ask the patient about these reasons and discuss them jointly.

- Don't assume that a patient who doesn't ask questions doesn't want to be fully informed. The patient almost certainly does.
- Encourage patients to learn more about their health and health problems, to ask questions, and to share responsibility regarding treatment and health practices. This will improve compliance and satisfaction.[3]

Communicating Serious Incidents

Good communication skills are always important when dealing with patients and their families and become even more important when having to inform a patient (or the family of a patient) about a serious or adverse incident involving his or her care. The stress of such events often makes communication very difficult, but the importance of it cannot be overestimated. If something has gone wrong, compensation might be appropriate. It should be based on equitable damages, not on the fact that the patient or family becomes angry, frustrated, and vindicative due to a communications breakdown or a perception of details being covered up by the hospital. It is likely that the risk manager, hospital counsel, or administration will be able to negotiate a favorable settlement and disposition, even in catastrophic circumstances, when the staff has demonstrated care and concern and when communications among all parties has been kept open through frank and honest discussions of the facts and issues. This is definitely not the time to let the patient-health care provider relationship deteriorate.

The risk manager and all health care providers have pivotal roles immediately following an adverse incident. Prior to divulging any information about the incident to the patient and family, the risk manager or physician should verify that all of the facts are correct and complete. The team dealing with adverse incidents within the hospital should decide on the appropriate person to talk with the patient. It is often advisable to have the person spearhead the discussion who is best known to the patient or who has the most positive relationship with the patient. If the attending or treating physician is not the person with the most positive relationship with the patient, it may still be advisable to have the treating physician present also (or readily available) to answer technical questions. In general, the actual communication with the patient or the family regarding a serious incident is the responsibility of the physician, but at times it may be otherwise.

The person who tells the patient about the adverse incident may wish to have family members or a significant other present during the disclosure. The meeting should take place in privacy, such as an office, conference room, or other quiet area away from the center of hospital activity. If the facts are known, such as a medication error or cardiac arrest due to malfunction of the oxygen system in the operating room, the discussion should take place as soon as possible after the incident. The explanation should be honest, direct, and without finger pointing or an attempt to implicate other clinicians and health care professionals. When the result of the incident is very serious, it may be wise to encourage the patient and family members to discuss the facts of the incident at a later date after they have had the opportunity to deal with the initial shock and to formulate questions that may come to mind.

If the health care professional acknowledges the error from the onset and extends a willingness to answer questions, the patient and family may retain a healthy respect for that individual and not feel abandoned in the situation. The best response when all of the facts are not known is an explanation that focuses on outcome only. It should be accompanied by an explanation of any further tests or procedures that can be performed to help find answers not readily available. As the physician or risk manager gets additional facts or information, he or she should keep communication open and arrange for follow-up meetings with the patient and/or family members to share the findings. Using words that admit to negligence or malpractice should be avoided. A frank description of the events without either accepting or placing blame and a sincere acknowledgment of regret for the unfortunate nature of the event probably serve the situation best. It is important to control the situation by providing only factual information and not speculating on what could have happened or what might have happened!

Summary

A patient relations program serves a vital role in guaranteeing the quality of service provided. However, the staff should continually be reminded that the best formal patient relations program will not take the place of good communications and a caring, sympathetic attitude demonstrated by all persons who deal with patients and their families.

THE IMPORTANCE OF SOCIAL SERVICES IN A HOSPITAL'S QUALITY MANAGEMENT PROGRAM

The social services department has a vital role in many health care institutions and often can assist the risk management and quality assurance departments in troubleshooting patient problems and intervening in time to prevent patient injuries and complaints. Many functions of social workers have direct legal implications. Thus, social workers should always be included in the risk management educational process and the ongoing risk management and quality assurance evaluation process.

Hospital social workers should be advised of the importance of supporting and interfacing with the hospitals' quality assurance and risk management systems. They should be committed to monitoring, evaluating, identifying, and resolving problems related to the quality and appropriateness of patient care services provided by the social services department in particular, and the hospital in general. At a minimum, the department should engage in the following quality-related activities:

- The social workers' responsibilities should be defined and performed in a systematic, planned, and ongoing manner within the designated scope of service.
- The scope of service should include all major clinical functions for both inpatients and outpatients.
- The quality of service should be continually monitored and objectively compared with pre-established criteria.
- Potential problems and opportunities to improve the quality of care should be identified and reported on an ongoing basis.
- Social workers should take appropriate action to correct any problems that fall within the scope of their designated duties.
- A follow-up assessment of the effectiveness of corrective action should be performed and documented.
- All relevant information and activities should be reported to the hospital's risk management and quality assurance departments on a regular basis.
- A quality assurance/risk management manual should be shared with all members of the social services department.
- The social services department should have an identifiable mechanism for interdisciplinary review of all cases where its input has been requested or is required by law.

Hospital social workers perform a variety of professional services for patients. Like other support personnel, they must be advised of their responsibilities as discussed below.

Importance of Maintaining Confidentiality

Information received by the social services department about any individual, client, or patient may not be shared with any other person or agency without that individual's express informed consent. Much of the information that a social worker obtains from a patient may be extremely sensitive and must be carefully protected. In order to preserve a client's right to confidentiality, social workers should always abide by the following rules:

- Never discuss cases or patients where the conversations may be overheard by others. This is especially

important to remember when sensitive or patient-specific information is involved. (Avoid discussing patient cases while in the cafeteria, hallways, and other hospital common areas.)
- Never leave case files, consulting reports, or any other written material in areas where other people may inadvertently see them.
- Never allow social services department records and case files to leave the hospital.
- Instruct secretaries and other social services support personnel about the need to keep all patient information confidential.

Releases of Information

Medical and social information cannot be released without the patient or guardian's consent. If the patient desires to have information released to a government or community agency, he or she, or the legally appointed guardian, must sign an appropriate "release of information" form. This form should specify the following:

- the person or agency to whom the disclosure is to be made
- the purpose for which disclosure is to be made
- the nature of the information to be disclosed
- the date on which the consent expires
- the right to revoke the consent at any time

The release of information form must be signed by the person authorized to give consent, and the signature should be witnessed by a person who can attest to the identity of the signatory. The medical records department typically handles requests for releases of information. Social workers should be advised to refer all requests for information to this department.

Privileged and Nonprivileged Information

Social workers and their staff should be familiar with state law and hospital policies and procedures that define the difference between privileged and nonprivileged information. For example, information that usually can be shared with callers includes dates of admission and discharge and verification of hospitalization. However, this information also may be privileged if the patient requires his or her identity and/or whereabouts protected for security reasons. The following information is generally available to callers who can document a valid reason for obtaining the information:

- patient's name
- address in admission

- age
- sex
- name of attending physician
- next of kin
- occupation of employer
- general condition on discharge

This type of information may not be available if requested by the press. A hospital policy should be drafted to handle the release of information in this specific circumstance.

The following information is typically classified as confidential and requires a valid authorization prior to its release:

- all medical information
- the hospital unit in charge of the patient's care
- address or disposition upon discharge
- physician's specialty
- all social and family information
- date of birth
- social security number
- birth of baby

Confidential information generally can be released without authorization only to another health care facility (for purposes of continuing care) during an emergency. In all other cases, an authorization must be obtained.

Maintenance of Social Service Records

Initial Assessment

All referrals made to the social services department should be answered promptly. The department may have a policy that dictates how referrals are made and how they are classified to ensure a timely response. (For example, emergency department referrals for suspected abuse must be responded to immediately; in discharge planning, response could be within 24 hours.) The social worker may also wish to identify professionals with specific types of expertise to handle certain types of cases. Responses to referrals should be documented in the patient's hospital medical record, even if a social services file is also generated by the visit.

An initial assessment for each referred patient should include at least the following information:

- reason for referral
- description of the client and the relevant environment
- psychosocial history
- assessment of the situation
- proposed plan of action and/or follow-up

Treatment and Follow-up

All follow-up visits and referrals should occur on a regular basis (as defined by the social services department's internal policies) and should be documented in the hospital record. This documentation should include continued assessment of the patient's progress and ongoing social services intervention. As appropriate, the social worker should document all new information that affects the initial plan of intervention; changes in the patient's emotional, social, or physical condition; and resolution of the problem. When legal documents or state-required forms and documents are completed and filed, copies of the documents should become part of the permanent hospital record.

Closing/Transfer or Discharge Summary

A final summary of impressions and recommendations should be made at the time of the patient's discharge or transfer or at termination of services. The summary should state the reason for closing, a description of the patient's situation at closure, a list of services delivered, and an evaluation of the impact of services provided. The social worker should also include an analysis of the factors that may enhance or impede goal achievement.

Discharge Planning

Social workers typically participate in the coordinated discharge planning process to ensure (1) the continuity of quality patient care and (2) the best possible utilization of the hospital's, community's, and patient's resources. Social workers must coordinate the discharge plans with all team members, including physicians, nurses, the patient and family, and appropriate community facilities. A timely and effective discharge can help to reduce the length of hospital stay and ensure that the needs of the patient are met in an appropriate manner. The following eight steps should be encouraged to guarantee the success of this process:

1. All departments who have been involved in the patient's care during inpatient hospitalization should participate in the initial discharge planning conference.
2. The patient's and family's needs should be accurately identified and shared with all persons who will assist in the actual discharge process.
3. Any patient with potential discharge problems (e.g., the elderly requiring long-term skilled care, the homeless, the abused) should be identified as soon as possible and seen by the discharge planning team to begin early planning for discharge.
4. Social workers should meet on a regular basis with the utilization review team to discuss the patient's anticipated length of stay and aftercare needs.
5. Risk managers should discuss with social workers any patient who sustained injuries during the hospital stay

and assist in planning a discharge that will minimize the injuries.

6. Where appropriate and dictated by hospital policy, social workers should meet with family members or significant others to discuss their needs, concerns, and their part in the aftercare of the patient.

7. Social workers should always inform the treating physician of any potential problems associated with discharge.

8. Social workers should utilize all information gathered in the psychosocial assessment and follow-up sessions to determine the full range of the patient's needs at discharge and to prepare family members for the posthospital stage of care. This information includes:

- evaluation of the patient's strengths and weaknesses
- the patient's physical condition at time of discharge
- an understanding of the illness, treatment, and, as appropriate, prognosis
- assessment of the patient's and family's capacities to adapt to change
- discharge plans that can continually be adapted and modified to meet the patient's changing condition
- a formal discharge plan, complete with long-term and short-range goals, in writing and part of the hospital's permanent record (to be shared with all appropriate hospital and aftercare staff)
- all clinical services related to the discharge plan (accurately recorded in the permanent record)

Social workers should always be mindful of the fact that a hospital's care and patients' perception of the quality of that care do not necessarily end at time of discharge. For many patients, what happens to them after they leave the hospital is as important as what occurred while in the hospital.

Other Responsibilities of Social Services

Social workers in a hospital setting may have many other responsibilities as designated by the hospital. These might include handling all matters related to patient abuse (child, spouse, and elderly abuse cases), working with patients involved in criminal cases (victims and the alleged perpetrators of crimes), and dealing with suicidal patients who require involuntary commitment. Social workers should assist the hospital risk management or legal department in developing policies and protocols for these special circumstances that comply fully with state and local laws and provide optimum protection to patients and the public.

NOTES

1. General Accounting Office, "Initiatives in Hospital Risk Management," GAO/HRD-89-79 (Washington, D.C.: Government Printing Office, July 1989), 25.

2. St. Paul Insurance Companies, "A Human Factors Guide for Maintaining Effective Patient Relations" (Minneapolis: St. Paul Insurance Companies, 1989), 3. Reprinted with permission.

3. St. Paul Insurance Companies, "A Human Factors Guide," 8.

Appendix 10-A

Sample Patient Bill of Rights

A successful relationship between the patient and the health care team is based on a mutual understanding of each other's expectations. As a patient and partner in important matters concerning your health you have a right

- to expect respectful and competent treatment regardless of your race, color, religion, gender, sexual preference, veteran status, handicap, national origin, or ability to pay for current or future care
- to wear appropriate personal clothing and religious or other symbolic items as long as they do not interfere with diagnostic procedures and treatment
- to have access to persons outside the hospital by means of visitors and verbal and written communications, provided that such visitors and communications are not in violation of hospital policy and do not serve to jeopardize the safety and/or well-being of other patients and visitors
- to receive assistance in the understanding and use of these rights. If for any reason you do not understand them or you need help, the hospital must provide assistance, including an interpreter.
- to be allowed reasonable, informed participation in decisions concerning your health care; to know who is responsible for authorizing and performing procedures and treatment; and to have knowledge of, and to accept or refuse participation in, research and educational projects affecting your care and treatment
- to obtain from your physician, in terms that you can understand, complete and current information concerning your diagnosis, treatment, and prognosis. (If it is not medically advisable to give a patient this information, it will be given to that person who has been legally authorized to act on the patient's behalf.)
- to expect reasonable safety as related to hospital practices and hospital environment
- to be placed in a protective environment when it is determined necessary for your personal safety
- to know the identity and professional status of all persons who provide services to you
- to expect that emergency services and treatment, if needed, will be provided to you without delay
- to expect that your rights of privacy will be recognized. These rights extend to personal conversation, examinations, communications, and records generated as a result of the care you receive.
- to know the contents and receive a copy of your medical record, unless specifically restricted by law
- to refuse treatment to the extent permitted by law and to be informed of the medical consequences of such refusal
- to know hospital rules and regulations and how they may apply to your behavior
- to expect that within its capacity, a hospital must make reasonable response to the request of a patient for services. The hospital must make services available that are related to evaluation, service, and referral as indicated by the independent facts of the case. When medically permissible, a patient may be transferred to another facility only after he or she has received complete information and explanation concerning the need for such a transfer. The institution to which the patient is to be transferred must first have accepted the patient for transfer.
- to request and receive an explanation of your bill, regardless of your ability to pay that bill. You also have the right to counseling related to the financial resources available to assist you in the payment of your bill.
- to expect reasonable continuity of care upon discharge. You have the right to know, in advance, the appointment times and physicians that are available.

As a patient and partner on the health care team, you have the responsibility to

- provide health care practitioners with accurate and complete information related to past illnesses, hospitalizations, medication, and any other matters related to your health. If you have had previous hospitalizations under a different name, you have the responsibility to inform the hospital admissions office of this information.
- cooperate with all hospital personnel and to ask questions if directions and/or procedures are not clearly understood
- keep your appointments for follow-up care and to notify the hospital or your physician when it is impossible to keep them
- accept responsibility for your actions if refusal of treatment or failure to comply with or follow up physicians' recommendations results in worsening of your condition
- be considerate of hospital personnel and other patients and to assist in the control of noise, smoking, and the number of visitors in your room at any given time. You are also expected to be respectful of the property belonging to other patients and the hospital.
- ensure that the financial obligations of your health care are fulfilled as promptly as possible
- designate a person who can speak on your behalf and authorize treatment for you in the event of incapacity

chapter 11

Integrating Administrative Support Services with Risk Management

Barbara J. Youngberg

INTRODUCTION

Health care has become big business. To make a hospital or other health care facility a success, many departments not directly involved with actual patient care must handle and promote the administrative functions of the business. Excellent personnel and well thought out business plans in these departments can contribute to the overall success of the operation, as well as the public's perception of the facility. However, failure to recognize the potential for negative impact on the organization by the administrative departments can result in multiple problems, including lawsuits against the hospital and individual professionals.

THE RISK MANAGER'S ROLE

The risk manager has the responsibility to recognize the relationships among the various departments and the administration and the direct and indirect effects they have on patient care or on the public's perception of the institution. By analyzing the organizational structure of the hospital, the risk manager can become more familiar with the administrative departments and understand how they interface with the patient care areas. The risk manager should periodically meet with key personnel within each department to analyze current and future business plans. Areas should be identified where possible legal situations can occur. Careful development of a risk management strategy must include input from physicians, hospital administrators, legal counsel, and the risk management staff. Along with the many

departments that provide direct patient care and support, the administrative departments also must integrate their functions into the quality-related endeavors endorsed by the organization and maintain their responsibilities parallel to its overall objectives.

MARKETING AND ADVERTISING: RECOGNIZING THE RISK MANAGEMENT ISSUES

The increase in competition among hospitals and other health care entities has resulted in a recognition of the importance of marketing and advertising to the public. When this marketing is done correctly, it can bring great benefits to the organization. However, if it is inappropriate or misleading, legal battles can cost a hospital, its physicians, and other professionals not only dollars but potential damage to their reputations.

What Is Marketing?

Marketing is defined as:

> . . . the analysis, planning, implementation, and control of carefully formulated programs designed to bring about voluntary exchanges of values with target markets for the purpose of achieving organizational objectives. It relies heavily on designing the organization's offering in terms of the target market's needs and desires, and on using

effective pricing, communication, and distribution to inform, motivate, and service the markets.[1]

Hospital marketing departments are often called upon to assist in informing the public about new services, special pre-existing services offered by a hospital of which the general public may be unaware, or special strengths that differentiate one hospital from another. The marketing staff may also be asked to help in creating and presenting an image of the hospital and/or its staff to the public that will inspire confidence in the facility and increase the likelihood that the public will choose the facility over others when medical services are needed.

Defining the Marketing Process

Kotler and Clarke define the scope of marketing well:

- Marketing is defined as a managerial process that involves analysis, planning, implementation, and control.
- Marketing manifests itself in carefully formulated programs, not just random actions to achieve desired responses.
- Marketing seeks to bring about voluntary exchanges in values.
- Marketing means the selection of target markets rather than a quixotic attempt to serve every market and be all things to all people. Since the mission statements of most health care facilities forbid the refusal of service to any persons requesting it, marketing departments may wish to avoid targeting only those markets that represent a certain social or educational strata of society.
- The purpose of marketing is to help organizations ensure survival, continued health, and the flexibility necessary to operate in a regulated environment through serving their markets more effectively.
- Marketing for health care relies on designing the organization's offerings in terms of the target market's needs and desires, rather than in terms of the seller's personal tastes.
- Marketing utilizes and blends a set of tools called the marketing mix—product/service design, pricing, communication, and distribution.[2]

Understanding the marketing process and the goals and objectives of marketing can assist the risk manager in identifying potential problem areas and establishing appropriate relationships among the marketing, administration, risk management, and legal departments to ensure that negative repercussions are not the result of a hospital's marketing campaign.

Recognizing Potential Liability

With increasing competition, many hospitals feel the need to develop aggressive marketing and advertising campaigns to assist the public in recognizing the value they bring to the community in comparison with that provided by the competition. This need to sell oneself to the public has led to a number of lawsuits that relate directly to advertising campaigns and support the belief that there is clearly "liability for what you say."

To date, a large body of cases relating specifically to health care and advertising does not exist, but many attorneys believe that such litigation is just on the horizon. Attorneys cite state and federal laws prohibiting "false advertising" and "unfair methods of competition" as the ground rules that govern litigation related to the advertising practices of hospitals and health care organizations. The two most significant federal statutes outlawing false advertising and regulating the content of advertisements are the Federal Trade Commission Act (FTC Act)[3] and the Lanham Act.[4]

Historically, the states have attempted to legislate against false advertising practices. Although state laws were initially ineffective in controlling false advertising practices, many new laws based on the FTC Act and individual consumer protection statutes appear to have sharper teeth to ensure enforcement. Some of these newly enacted state statutes contain specific regulations that govern medical advertising.

The first major false advertising suit brought under the Lanham Act by the health care industry was filed in November 1986 by U.S. Healthcare, Inc., a health maintenance organization, against Blue Cross of Greater Philadelphia. This suit claimed, among other things, that statements made as part of an aggressive marketing campaign were false and in violation of the Lanham Act, and also amounted to defamation, commercial disparagement, a false portrayal, interference in contractual relations, and a violation of the New Jersey Consumer Fraud Act. Although the case was dismissed after six weeks of trial (citing First Amendment protection), arguments raised in the case have fueled similar claims. Many of these cases are currently awaiting trial. The cost of this type of litigation is substantial and obviously should be avoided when possible.

Risk managers, however, must be aware of how false or misleading marketing and advertising can be alleged in attempts to "boot-strap" allegations of negligence. In effect, attorneys may say that a hospital or individual practitioner should be held to a higher standard of care than his or her peers, because marketing and advertising campaigns have created perceptions in the minds of the public that they were better (e.g., more skilled, more highly educated, or more compassionate).

Exhibit 11-1
SUGGESTIONS FOR RISK MANAGEMENT'S ROLE IN MARKETING

- Develop a positive relationship with the marketing department and stress your desire in getting involved early in new marketing and advertising campaigns. When marketing plans or advertising campaigns relate to individual professionals or special services, involve those professionals in the marketing plans as well. If legal counsel is not included in the front-end planning, request that it review all final materials prior to distribution.

- Avoid the use of "puffery" to make it appear that available services are more sophisticated or comprehensive than they actually are. All advertising should relate closely to the exact services provided.

- Capitalize on the actual strengths of the services being marketed. Do not try to entice the public by describing what they may want rather than what the facility is capable of offering.

- Avoid the use of words that may create confusion among the general public. Recognize that many words can take on special meaning when used to describe medical services. For example, in the early 1980s "EmergiCenters" and "Urgicenters" were popular terms for freestanding clinics and gave many people the impression that such centers were capable of providing urgent care and treating patients with severe and acute emergency conditions. This was not the case, and the use of these words resulted in a number of lawsuits.

- Always be certain that assertions or impressions created by an advertising or marketing campaign do not create unrealistic expectations. Ask yourself if pictures or words in the advertisement can mislead the person reading it. For example, pictures of perfectly sculpted bodies and "model perfect" faces are frequently used in advertisements for plastic/reconstructive surgeons and plastic surgery clinics. Do they mislead the public in any way to expect the same type of results? (Incidentally, you might ask a nonlayperson this same question.)

- Avoid making statements that represent your hospital or health care facility as having higher standards than others or providing better care. These seemingly innocent words can be used against a hospital by a plaintiff's attorney in a malpractice case who seeks to prove that a particular hospital or physician actually held themselves to a higher standard than is ordinarily used to measure performance and behavior. Since the word "standard" has such a precise legal meaning, hospitals may elect to eliminate this word from all marketing and advertising programs.

- Determine if *all* promises made in the advertisement can be fulfilled under *all* circumstances. If not, you could be setting up the hospital for false advertising claims.

- Determine if any of the advertising or marketing campaigns *guarantee* results. The practice of medicine is both an art and a science that predicates its success on a number of uncontrollable variables, and guarantees in most cases are impossible. Usually, it is even risky to guarantee service, for example: "Maximum 10-minute wait in our outpatient facility." All you need is one day of staff shortage due to illness or one patient who changes from a routine visit to an emergency to negate that promise.

- Avoid making statements in advertisements that delineate divisions of responsibility among health care providers. This is especially important if the staff includes a number of independent practitioners.

- Recognize the problems associated with the inclusion of prices in any advertising or marketing campaigns. The unique characteristics of pricing for health care services (for example, the addition of fees for laboratory services, consultants, and various ancillary services) could lead to charges of deception in advertising.

- Avoid supporting your claims of superior quality through the use of comparative statistical data that can be deceptive if not adjusted for case mix, time of year, or payment source.

Integrating Quality Management into Marketing Functions

The risk management, administrative, and marketing staffs may wish to consider the possibility of involving laypersons in the review process. They often see and interpret information quite differently than health care professionals and executives. Since members of the public are most likely to bring lawsuits against an organization or individual practitioner for false advertising, their insight early in the process could assist in minimizing this type of risk.

Risk management and marketing personnel also must recognize the damage that has already been done to the health care profession by the lay media and to attempt whenever possible to correct some of the misconceptions that have been created by the press. With substantial focus being placed on the incredible success achieved through new technology (e.g., survival of a patient who has had five organ transplants, biological engineering that has resulted in dramatic lifesaving drugs and technology, and the ability of medicine to cultivate life in a test tube), the public is often given the impression that there is nothing that a hospital and its staff cannot do. Conversely, negative attention given by the press to health care in general or to a particular institution through reports of one untoward event or an interview with one disgruntled patient can create other unfair and unrealistic public impressions of health care. In these cases, it may be necessary for the marketing department, in conjunction with administration and risk management, to provide information that helps the public to view health care or a certain facility in a more reasonable and realistic framework.

Risk managers should review the literature and various court reporter periodicals to determine the types of marketing and advertising strategies that have caused their colleagues problems. They should develop their marketing plans with a number of suggestions in mind, as listed in Exhibit 11-1.

NOTES

1. P. Kotler and R.N. Clarke, *Marketing for Health Care Organizations* (Englewood Cliffs, N.J.: Prentice-Hall, Inc., 1987), 5.

2. Ibid., 4–7.

3. The Federal Trade Commission Act. 15 U.S.C. §§41–58 (1973 and Supp. 1988).

4. The Lanham Act. 15 U.S.C. §§1051–1127 (1982).

chapter 12

Incorporating Quality Improvement into Existing Quality Assurance and Risk Management Programs

Barbara J. Youngberg

INTRODUCTION

Few persons working in health care today have not heard of the new philosophies borrowed from industry that purport to be able to solve many of the quality problems inherent in today's health care system. Acronyms such as TQI (total quality improvement), CQI (continuous quality improvement), and TQM (total quality management) have become commonplace. References to the philosophies associated with these letters can be found in almost any health publication. Although the usefulness of these management techniques has been confirmed in a number of anecdotal incidents, health care professionals and managers should proceed with caution. The methodology developed in industry (initially the Japanese automobile industry) is not a "quick fix." The programs require time, resources, and a strong commitment from senior level management in order to be successful. The strategies also require *careful* modification to the health care setting, with consideration given to the nature of the product to be delivered (quite unlike an automobile) and the multiple needs, perceptions, and expectations of the internal and external customers.

Senior level administration also must recognize that although the TQI methodology focuses on *management* process, it must include traditional quality assessment and risk management techniques. Separating TQI from traditional quality assessment and risk management functions and failing to gain initial support and assistance from health care clinicians will surely doom the process. To get to the root of the problems of delivering high quality care (the

"product" that is provided), the process must incorporate and address the needs and concerns, strengths and weaknesses of these persons most intimately involved with delivering it.

As a final caution, health care professionals and managers must ensure that they do not retreat into the technical methodology, such as gathering statistics, diagramming flow patterns, and developing Pareto and "fishbone" diagrams, and forget why this new strategy is being developed. Correcting all of the systems and problems and still having a dissatisfied patient and internal customer renders the time and effort spent on quality improvement initiatives of questionable value. Historically, when a crisis hit in health care, the industry retreated from the real issues at hand and looked to novel techniques and approaches and scientific methodology as a way of solving the problems. This retreat into the academic/scientific/statistical arena often served only to move caregivers farther away from patients (and each other) and to exaggerate, rather than correct, fundamental problems associated with poor communication, unsympathetic and overburdened care providers, and frightened and often unforgiving patients.

The health care profession must begin to incorporate these new strategies by asking customers what they want, learning from them about what works well, and prioritizing quality improvement projects to promote high-quality and cost-efficient care. The professional's definition of quality may be quite different from the customer's and what is high-quality health care today may not be that one year from now. Thus, the need for constant, ongoing evaluation from the patient and the provider becomes critical to the overall continued success of the program.

Senior administration should be cautioned about the inappropriateness of identifying projects based on cost or of making quality improvement initiatives cost-driven only. Stating that reduction of costs is the singular primary motivation for incorporating quality improvement into health care will only make the processes less likely to be accepted. Managers should be advised, however, that high-quality care is *always* more cost-efficient and that maximizing quality should result in minimizing risk and the financial outlay associated with risk. Correcting system problems also assists in decreasing nonproductive "process errors" that cost an organization considerable amounts of money and time.

The Joint Commission on Accreditation of Healthcare Organizations has published draft standards requiring hospitals to implement quality improvement methodology within their current programs. These standards became effective in 1992. A hospital's desire to involve this methodology should *not* be driven by such regulatory considerations. History supports the premise that a hospital doing something it is mandated to do is less enthusiastic than one adopting certain strategies or techniques because it is convinced that they will have a direct, measurable positive impact on the quality of care provided. In quality improvement, the process and ongoing evaluation of that process and its impact on the care provided are the factors critical to success, not the file folder filled with flowcharts and diagrams evidencing a staff's knowledge of the techniques.

Quality improvement costs money and takes time and hard work. Staff members who engage in it must be excited and challenged by the opportunities it presents. Making quality improvement another "hoop to jump through" on the way to accreditation can relegate it to the long list of failed strategies in the attempt to improve health care and the way it is delivered.

UNDERSTANDING THE METHODS

The quality improvement process in health care is based on the same principles that an increasing number of successful companies are incorporating into their current management models. The fundamental goal of these strategies involves the initiation of effective strategies to raise quality and productivity while, at the same time, reducing the total cost of the service or the product. The customer is pivotal in making this process work, and customers include both the interim users and the final product users. An example in health care is the surgeon (internal customer) who receives reports from the radiology department to help provide a high-quality service to the ultimate recipient of the service, the patient (external customer).

The new techniques focus primarily on the way the system functions. In most cases, the patient care delivery system requires coordination and communication among a number of health care providers, departments, and external agencies. For this process to work smoothly, there must be frictionless interaction among all members of the team. In addition, feedback and suggestions from the customer must be sought to guarantee that the product meets desired specifications. These philosophies, when applied to health care, will increase the amount of accountability currently available in the health care delivery system, not only to the ultimate customer—the patient—but also to the internal customers and external regulators.

Before the 1920s, when many products were made in small shops and family-operated businesses, the quality of work was monitored by the persons running the production lines or by product inspectors. As the industrial revolution spread and assembly lines and mass production became more prevalent, the ability to monitor quality became increasingly difficult. Alternatives were developed to decrease the frequency of monitoring or to allow for statistical sampling of products being produced. Little time or effort was devoted to evaluating the systems that had been developed to produce the product—the focus was on the product itself.

After World War II, American occupation forces in Japan expressed a willingness to assist the Japanese economy by providing them with mechanisms for making their industrial firms more competitive with foreign suppliers. The Japanese recognized that the American public was a major potential customer and understood the importance of developing products that ultimately would be sold in the United States. As a result of this cooperative interest, a number of American experts were sent to Japan to teach their manufacturers and industrial leaders statistical applications to production and manufacturing processes. One of these experts, W. Edwards Deming, was a pioneer in statistical process control. His theories were embraced by the Japanese and incorporated into their growing industries, but Dr. Deming failed to generate the same enthusiasm in the United States.

With the well-documented growth in Japanese industry and the acknowledgment of Japanese product superiority, American industry began to look at the processes that supported and created Japan's success. Dr. Deming's philosophy began the foundation for that analysis and became the new management philosophy for many large companies in the United States that were quick to expound on its benefits. The health care industry, in an effort to model itself on the successful U.S. companies using these quality improvement techniques, began to hire consultant industrial experts for advice about incorporating these strategies into its everyday operations.

Dr. Deming has summarized his philosophy about quality improvement techniques into a set of principles that have become known as the "14 points." The summary of this philosophy is reduction of variability in the product being produced, and the 14 points basically address the ways in which management can reduce variation:

1. Create a constancy of purpose. An environment that places quality above all other considerations is one that customers (internal and external) will choose to interact with.
2. Adopt a new philosophy. This may include building on pre-existing strategies that have proved effective and are enhanced by the total quality management process and philosophy.
3. Cease dependence on inspection. Quality should become the goal of every worker in the environment. Persons within the organization should be motivated to improve in order to satisfy themselves and their customers, not a third-party reviewer.
4. Cease awarding business on the basis of price alone. If a supplier recognizes that customers will be involved in long-term relationships, it can develop ways to make the product increasingly appealing that have limited association with cost.
5. Improve continuously and forever. The total quality improvement process is ongoing and requires constant reevaluation and improvement to remain successful.
6. Institute training and retraining on the job. Persons within the organization cannot be expected to embrace the philosophy until they become knowledgeable about it. Obtaining this knowledge on the job is evidence of management's commitment to the process and the value it places on learning the necessary skills.
7. Adopt and institute leadership. The process works best when persons who have already gained the respect of colleagues endorse it. Identify the persons who are leaders at each level of the organization and train them first.
8. Drive out fear. If employees believe that the new philosophy will somehow make their jobs less important, they will not embrace it. If they believe the new system will serve a punitive function, they also will be reluctant to get involved. Both of these beliefs must be erased before the philosophy will be accepted.
9. Break down barriers among staff members. Success of the total quality improvement process is dependent on all levels of the organization working collaboratively to solve problems. If turf issues or egos do not allow for this, the system will fail.
10. Eliminate slogans, exhortations, and targets for the work force. Solid information is needed to make workers see that their work is valued. Trivializing work by reducing it to slogans does nothing to further quality.
11. Eliminate numerical quotas for both workers and managers. Although statistics and analyses are important aspects of total quality management techniques, they should never be used as a basis for reward. When everyone in the organization is committed to quality improvement, numbers can become powerful, but they should never be used to reward or punish individuals.
12. Remove barriers that rob people of pride in workmanship. No financial reward can exceed the sense of pride that is gained with the assurance of a job well done and work that is valued. Allowing persons at all levels of the organization to participate in the quality improvement process and acknowledging that their input is important can further enhance quality improvement initiatives. People tend to respond more favorably when they are considered part of the solution rather than part of the problem.
13. Institute a vigorous program of education and self-improvement. An informed and educated staff is more likely to contribute in a meaningful way to the quality improvement process.
14. Put everybody in the organization to work on the transformation. Regardless of the final product, it can generally be said that each process involves contributions from persons at many levels and with many responsibilities. Incorporate that belief into the total quality management initiative.

MODIFYING THE MODELS FOR HEALTH CARE

To begin total quality initiatives, it may be necessary to develop a better way to identify what customers (internal and external) expect. This may require that more sensitive marketing tools be created and also that the health care entity institute a mechanism for more systematically identifying the needs of the internal customers. Until now, most evaluations have been designed to identify patients' needs and perceptions. This process may require expansion to include identifying the needs of physicians, nurses, other professional personnel, and support services within the organization. Guidelines for accomplishing this can include

- carefully analyzing the "product"
- addressing the issues of efficiency and efficacy when developing strategies to improve quality
- incorporating appropriateness criteria into the analysis of the product
- developing tools to evaluate outcome as well as process issues

Asking patients for feedback goes beyond temperature of the meals and cleanliness of the floors. To gain an understanding of the service being provided, the following factors must be considered when developing quality improvement programs in the health care setting:

- Ensure that the system is *not* punitive. Stress that total quality improvement looks to process failures, not to people failures. Emphasize that the ability of someone to do a job effectively and with the highest quality is enhanced if the system works to support, rather than impede, that person. Emphasize by example to persons working within the hospital how interdependent each department is on guaranteeing the success of another. Recognize that questionable behavior of an individual sometimes may be identified but that quality improvement is not designed to address it. Hospital peer review processes, traditional risk management and quality assurance programs, and other administrative functions should address individual evidence of disquality and discipline.

- Ensure that approach is multidisciplinary and includes professionals from all levels of the organization (see Exhibit 12-1).

- Empower project teams with the ability to effect change. Quality circles that were used in the past to

address problems and identify possible solutions are not effective. The people who brainstorm about the problem and think of potential solutions should be allowed to "sell" change to the organization. Forcing this process into the hands of senior administrators, who may not understand the problem fully, can result in inaction or delayed action. Choose teams carefully to avoid persons who wish to control the process or who are viewed as divisive in the organization.

- Address problems that can be fixed. Many organizations waste considerable time mulling over issues beyond their scope to change. Failure to effect change can lead to frustration of the process and limit the likelihood that future interest can be sustained.

- Require top level commitment and support. This support can be evidenced in writing to the entire staff at the outset of the adoption of quality improvement initiatives (see Exhibit 12-2 for a sample quality improvement charge) but should also be evidenced continually as the initiative progresses. Recognize that this support may sometimes take the form of financial support, endorsement of the importance of the necessary time required for discussion of problems, or assistance

---

Exhibit 12-1
EXAMPLE OF QUALITY IMPROVEMENT PROJECT TEAM

The hospital has decided to utilize the quality improvement process to analyze problems associated with the delay in laboratory results necessary to guide treatment in the outpatient area. Using the methodology developed to further quality improvement, the following persons are asked to participate on the project team:

- a *physician internist* who identified the problem as being one that prevented the timely treatment of patients in the outpatient area
- the *registered nurse* who is in charge of the outpatient area and who processes laboratory requests and interacts with all patients seen in the department
- a *phlebotomist* who draws all of the blood samples on outpatients in the hospital
- a *representative of the hospital transport program* who either escorts the patient to the laboratory or carries the sample to the laboratory if it is drawn in the outpatient setting
- a *hematology-oncology nurse* whose chemotherapy treatments are often delayed pending laboratory results
- a *representative of hospital administration* who has responsibility for the outpatient services
- a *representative from patient relations* who reviews satisfaction surveys completed by patients

---

Exhibit 12-2
DRAFT QUALITY IMPROVEMENT CHARGE

Providing quality service is the business of each person within this organization. With health care dollars decreasing and the public's perception of what we are capable of delivering increasing, all persons working in health care are confronted with an exciting challenge—placing the patient at the center of all that we do and supporting each other to ensure that the job done is done as efficiently as possible.

We must recognize and believe that no one person in this organization is unimportant. The person who delivers the meals or transports a patient from one department to another is no less or more important than the nurse administering a medication or a physician performing open-heart surgery. Each person in this organization provides a valuable service and supports a process that guarantees a favorable outcome and satisfied customer. One person doing less than his or her best can impact a patient's entire hospitalization.

This organization and its leadership will provide you with the time to engage in quality initiatives and the tools to perform your job effectively. We will continue to learn new methods and strategies for incorporating this philosophy into our day to day activities. Your participation and support is vital to help us meet our goal of providing the best possible service to our customers.

when needed to effectuate change. The senior administration should be at least as knowledgeable of the process as the staff. Failure of the senior administration to learn the techniques could suggest that they are considered unimportant.

- Re-evaluate continually the process to ensure its usefulness and appropriateness. A greater percentage of time spent on process and not patient care indicates a problem, and it may be difficult to justify quality improvement activities.
- Reward persons who participate in the process. Rewards should evidence appreciation for their hard work and recognition of their commitment to providing quality care. Rewards need not be financial, and indeed the Deming method supports their not being financial.
- Build on systems already in place that have demonstrated effectiveness. Do not eliminate things that work. Many hospitals have developed separate quality improvement departments that, in essence, reinvent the wheel and often work to the exclusion of other departments already committed to evaluating and improving quality. Spend the time evaluating current organization strengths and weaknesses and current systems that evaluate quality in a traditional manner. Determine ways to dovetail these functions into the new techniques.
- Assess continually ways to make the system more capable of evaluating clinical quality as opposed to process-only issues. Since the direction of health care seems to be moving toward clinical outcome and appropriateness evaluation, the institution may be challenged to develop assessment techniques that address those areas. "Process-only" evaluation may not give all the answers.

- Enhance information systems to support the program. If computer support is required to effect or evaluate change, persons responsible for developing the support should be part of the quality improvement team.

There is much yet to be learned about applying industrial techniques to the health care setting. It is important to recognize and admit early in the process that the technique may not always be appropriate. Selling it as the universal answer to a problem and having it fall short can lead health care professionals to discredit the entire process. It also should be recognized that changes do not occur overnight. Improvement is incremental and continuous, and it may require modification of the process prior to becoming effective.

BIBLIOGRAPHY

Berwick, D.M. 1989. Continuous improvement as an ideal in health care. *New England Journal of Medicine* 320:53–56.

Berwick, D.M. 1989. Health services research and quality of care assignments for the 1990s. *Medical Care* 27:763–771.

Berwick, D.M. July 1990. Peer review and quality management: Are they compatible? *Quality Review Bulletin* 246–251.

Brook, R., et al. August 1990. Assessing Quality of Care: Three Different Approaches. *Business & Health* 27–42.

Deming, W.E. 1986. *Out of the Crisis.* Cambridge, Mass.: MIT Press.

July 1990. Is it worth all the trouble to convert from QA to QI and how do QI and QA differ? *Hospital Peer Review* 15:97–101.

Juran, J.M. 1989. *Juran on Leadership for Quality.* New York: The Free Press.

Schoenbaum, S.C., and G.R. Plotkin. 1989. Making the Transition from Quality Assurance to Quality Improvement. *HMO Practice* 3:161–163.

Walton, M. 1986. *The Deming Management Method.* New York: Putnam Publishing Group.

chapter 13

A Quality Assurance Program for Credentialing, Reappointment, and Privilege Delineation of Health Care Professionals

Diane Runberg and Barbara J. Youngberg

INTRODUCTION

Medical Staff Leader[1] asked its physician executive and chief of staff readers to identify the major concerns in their jobs. Physician executives identified internal peer review and credentialing issues as their top priorities (tie vote), and chiefs of staff selected credentialing issues as their single greatest concern. Both peer review and credentialing (interrelated issues) represent areas where physicians come into conflict with organizational structure and where institutions (and often external regulatory agencies) exert pressure on individual practitioners to demonstrate their capabilities.

Credentialing and reappointment processes and privilege delineation also are of great concern and present significant challenges to quality assurance and risk management personnel. Persons responsible for credentialing and reappointment recognize that strong and sensitive programs can greatly reduce the risk of incompetent or otherwise unqualified health care providers becoming or remaining part of the medical staff. Historically, these procedures have related only to physician providers. Many hospitals now recognize the importance of credentialing, reappointment, and privilege delineation for a broad spectrum of caregivers. In the past, these programs have been little more than "rubber stamp" procedures. Hospitals and other health care institutions now realize the necessity of developing meaningful processes to ensure that competent and caring professionals are hired and retained. The strength of the team of providers enhances the overall ability of the facility to ensure high quality of care.

The Joint Commission on Accreditation of Healthcare Organizations (Joint Commission) focuses on how the granting of delineated clinical privileges occurs. Licensure, specific training, experience, and current competence are among the factors considered in this process. Joint Commission surveyors look for backup documentation to support decisions of department heads or the executive committee to recommend physicians for staff privileges and for permission to perform specific procedures within the hospital. This documentation can be supported by evidence of proper training and education, queries to the National Practitioner Data Bank (see Chapter 21 for reporting requirements of the National Practitioner Data Bank), peer review processes, or quality assurance activities.

ROLE OF THE NATIONAL PRACTITIONER DATA BANK

The impact of the legislation prompting the establishment of the National Practitioner Data Bank (the Bank) is discussed in detail in Chapter 21. Although the Bank was established primarily to track malpractice payments of health care practitioners and to prevent the practitioners from moving from state to state because of a new state's lack of knowledge relative to these activities, it also serves as a repository for information related to the loss or reduction of clinical privileges. The reporting of such circumstances is mandated under the provisions of the legislation that governs the operation of the Bank. Part of the credentialing and reappointment process now includes a mandatory query to the Bank to determine if a physician has correctly reported information relative to his or her practice that might influence an institution's decision to grant the physician staff privileges.

SETTING UP THE PROCESSES

Processes for the purpose of ensuring professional staff competency can be divided into three specific areas: (1) credentialing, (2) reappointment, (3) and privilege delineation.

Initial Staff Credentialing

The initial credentialing process addresses the health care professional's prior education, experience, and expertise, and his or her ability to function in the institutional setting. Detailed applications should be developed by the institution that request information related to professional education and training, prior employment, and personal and professional references. Letters should be sent to persons identified as references to gain additional information about the applicant. Each letter should always be followed up with a telephone call. A person is more likely to be honest and forthright over the telephone, where the applicant does not have access to the conversation, than in a letter that might ultimately be seen by the applicant. Letters of verification also should be sent to the state licensure authority and to the school that issued the professional's diploma to verify the date of graduation and the completion of all course requirements. These letters should be retained as part of the permanent personnel file if the applicant is employed.

Although many health care facilities currently are following these procedures for physician staff only, some institutions are enhancing current application processes for other professionals, such as registered nurses, certified registered nurse anesthetists, physician extenders, and midwives. The processes obviously can be modified as appropriate for each of these groups.

Another important aspect of the initial credentialing process relates to the applicant's professional liability experience. Although questions are included in most current applications for employment, health care facilities should be aware of the need to word such questions carefully so as to capture complete information about lawsuits, verdicts, settlements (in and out of court), and dollar amounts paid by hospital trust funds on behalf of professional staff, as well as money paid by liability insurance carriers. In the past, many hospitals asked only for information related to jury verdicts or final judgments. This information is insufficient for a clear understanding of the professional's potential to become involved in claims or lawsuits related to negligent practice. As a means of further substantiation, the person responsible for gathering the

information also should send letters to any insurance companies that have provided professional liability insurance to the health care professional; they often are willing to furnish claims-related information. In the future, the last step may be eliminated because insurance carriers are now expected to report this type of information to the Bank. Thus, a query to the Bank eventually will be sufficient to obtain the necessary information.

Many staff members express concern about the potential for legal ramifications related to the credentialing process, especially in light of the numerous antitrust suits filed in this area. The staff should be advised of the need to enforce employment regulations uniformly in all potential hirings and to adhere strictly to the respective state antidiscriminatory employment regulations and statutes. Generally, legal issues arise when one applicant is treated in a manner inconsistent with the way others are treated.

A checklist should be developed by the medical staff office (or the office with the responsibility of collecting credentialing information to be used by the executive committee) for final approval. The person who collects the data should forward the file only when all of the information has been returned and when final action is required. This prevents fragmentation of the process and the possibility that vital pieces of the application form will be lost or never received. All of the material in the file should be kept confidential.

The checklist for the collection of credentialing information should include the following items:

- fully completed and signed application form
- copy of Drug Enforcement Administration (DEA) Certificate
- copy of certificate from the appropriate medical specialty board (if the applicant is board certified)
- copy of certificate of current medical malpractice insurance
- copy of current license
- copies of medical licenses in any other states where the physician may be licensed
- copies of premedical college degrees
- copy of valid medical school degree
- certified copy of an exchange certificate for foreign medical graduate certificate, if the applicant is a foreign medical graduate
- a full detailed description if the applicant answered yes to any questions within the application related to prior disciplinary actions, professional liability, or loss of licensure
- names of three physicians for medical references, along with their completed reference forms
- evidence that follow-up telephone calls have been made to physician references and the results of those conversations (if a telephone conversation differed in

any way from a written reference, the difference should be explained)
- completed privilege delineation form
- response from inquiry to the Bank or evidence that the Bank has been queried

After all of the information had been received and reviewed, a final decision about the applicant can be made. The hospital department chairman also may wish to complete a checklist to verify that all appropriate information has been reviewed and acted on. This checklist can become a part of the permanent file.

Drafting a Policy To Protect Credentialing Information

An internal hospital policy should be drafted to describe how credential files are to be maintained and accessed. Objectives of this policy should be clearly stated and should address the need to include only the following:

- information that is relevant and material to the credentialing/reappointment process
- information that ensures the protection of the health professional's rights
- information that provides assurance to patients and regulatory agencies that professionals delivering care are well qualified

Depending on state law, the hospital may wish to maintain two separate files for each health care professional. The first file contains only that information necessary for privileges and appointments/reappointments. This file would be accessible to those persons who discharge official medical staff duties as they relate to the appointment/reappointment and privilege delineation of professional staff. The second file contains information protected (or protectable) under state law that relates to quality assurance, risk management, or peer review activities. Written references, including the department chairman's review form, should be included in this file. (See Exhibit 13–1 for a more complete list of material to be maintained in each file.) The policy should clearly dictate who has access to each type of file and under what circumstances. The circumstances under which a professional can review his or her own file also should be addressed.

The policy also should clearly state that the file is never to leave the office where it is housed, that it should be reviewed in the presence of a representative from the medical staff or professional office, and that at no time should copies of the file be made or alterations made to the original file.

The Reappointment Process

The reappointment process differs in many ways from the initial credentialing process. The information related to the professional's education and training presumably is unchanged. Rather than focusing on the professional's behavior prior to obtaining staff privileges or a position at the institution, the reappointment process focuses on the issues of behavior and quality of care during the period of the professional's work within the facility. Other persons within the institution, including peers, quality assurance professionals, medical records staff, and risk management and legal staff may be asked to provide information relative to the professional's performance since his or her last reappointment (or initial appointment). Pursuant to the statute governing the Bank, individuals on staff also are the subject of repeated queries to the Bank every two years.

The person responsible for collecting information for the reappointment process should be knowledgeable about the

---

Exhibit 13–1
INFORMATION CONTAINED IN SEPARATE CREDENTIAL FILES

Discoverable credentials file	Nondiscoverable items for second file
<ul><li>letter appointing the professional to the staff</li><li>application processing checklist</li><li>application</li><li>privilege delineation form</li><li>proof of insurance</li><li>copy of license(s)</li><li>American Medical Association form</li><li>curriculum value</li><li>miscellaneous items</li></ul>	<ul><li>quality assurance review forms</li><li>department chair review form</li><li>professional reference questionnaires</li><li>all information regarding legal involvement</li><li>faculty reappointment form (if one is used)</li><li>National Practitioner Data Bank information</li><li>professional liability insurance experience questionnaire</li><li>all information regarding disciplinary action</li><li>any type of negative information about the professional</li></ul>

many systems in place within the hospital that identify quality problems and that track and trend this information for a variety of purposes and uses. Some of this information may include

- attendance at medical staff and quality of care committee meetings
- claim and lawsuit information from the risk management department
- evidence of frequent medical record delinquencies from the medical record department
- evidence of professional review organizations or other third-party payment denial
- evidence of "quality sanctions" resulting from internal peer review processes
- any other internally generated reports that either positively or negatively address the professional's performance, competence, or demeanor (such as infection rate information, abnormal or questionable surgical pathology reports, high rate of return to the operating room, and adverse results of outpatient management)
- information from the department chairperson concerning issues related to the professional's behavior while on staff

Privilege Delineation

The process of privilege delineation focuses more specifically on the types of procedures or activities in which the professional can engage when he or she becomes part of the medical or professional staff. Historically, hospitals have placed little emphasis on developing specific criteria for types of physicians and sophisticated procedures, but many now realize the wisdom in addressing, with a high degree of specificity, the types of activities in which their professionals engage. Some require the professional not only to complete a detailed form that can establish a baseline of performance (see Appendixes 13-A and 13-B) but also to work with a proctor or preceptor prior to performing certain procedures (particularly those deemed high risk) independently. The continued ability to perform various tasks also should be periodically evaluated and may be dependent on continued training, the number of procedures performed, changes in health, and other factors.

CONCLUSION

Only by combining vigorous credentialing of health care professionals with a comprehensive privilege delineation program and with information gained by quality assurance and risk management personnel can the patient and the hospital be confident that the most qualified persons are providing care.

NOTE

1. American Hospital Association, MD Execs. and Chiefs of Staff See Eye-to-Eye, *Medical Staff Leader* 20, no. 2 (February 1991):1.

Nursing Privilege Delineation Checklist

COMPETENCY CHECKLIST

MEDICAL/SURGICAL NURSING

NAME: _____

SIGNATURE: _____

DATE: _____

Please check the appropriate column indicating your level of competency for each skill. Add additional comments, if needed, in the space provided, and return with your application.

Level of Competency

0—no experience
1—minimal experience, need review and supervision

2—can perform without supervision
3—perform well and can act as a resource person

Skills

Care of the patient with NEUROLOGICAL disorders:	0	1	2	3	Comments
Neurological assessment					
Understanding of Glasgow Coma Scale					
Intracranial pressure monitoring					
Seizure precautions					
Use of:					
Crutchfield tongs					
Halo traction					
Circo-Electric bed					
Stryker frame					
Care of patient with:					
CVA					
Spinal cord injury					
Seizures					
Neuromuscular disease					

Care of the patient with CARDIOVASCULAR disorders:	0	1	2	3	Comments
Cardiopulmonary resuscitation					
Obtaining ECG—12 lead					
Obtaining ECG—rhythm strip					
Cardiac monitors					
Interpretation of arrhythmias					
Telemetry					
Defibrillation					
Cardioversion					
Pacemaker—permanent					
Pacemaker—temporary					
Ultrasonic Doppler					
Peripheral pulses					
Rotating tourniquets					
CVP reading					
Drawing arterial blood sample					
Drawing venous blood sample					

Care of the patient with RESPIRATORY disorders:	0	1	2	3	Comments
Establishment of airway					
Lung assessment					
Oropharyngeal suctioning					
Trach care					
Tracheostomy tubes					
Ventilator					
Oxygen equipment					
Ambuing technique					
Incentive spirometry					
Chest tubes					

Care of the patient with RENAL/GENITOURINARY disorders:	0	1	2	3	Comments
Catheter care					
Insertion of female catheter					
Insertion of male catheter					
G-U irrigations					
Suprapubic tube					
Nephrostomy tube					
Shunts and fistulas					
Care of patient on peritoneal dialysis					
Care of patient on hemodialysis					
Renal transplant					

Care of the patient with ORTHOPEDIC disorders:	0	1	2	3	Comments
Cast care					
Halo traction					
Skeletal traction					
Skin traction					
Circo-Electric bed					
Crutch walking					

Care of the patient with GASTROINTESTINAL disorders:	0	1	2	3	Comments
Nasogastric tubes					
Nasointestinal tubes					
Feeding tubes					
Care of patient with:					
GI bleed					
Dehiscence					
Multiple abdominal wounds and drains					
Colostomy					

MISCELLANEOUS NURSING PROCEDURES:	0	1	2	3	Comments
Starting IV angiocaths					
Knowledge and administration of hyperalimentation					
Isolation techniques					
Care of burn patients					
Care of Hickman catheters and triple lumen catheters					
Knowledge and administration of IV chemotherapy drugs					
Silastic catheter care:					
Dressing					
Blood draw					
Cap change					
Heparen lock					
Central line:					
Dressing change					
Tubing change					
Dressing—sterile, wet to dry					
AccuCheck II					
Glucometer II					
IV equipment/infusion flanges					

Physician Privilege Delineation Checklist— Gynecological Privileges

Candidate: _____

Level I: Gynecological Privileges—Routine Care

Requested: Approved:

_____   Privileges include diagnosis, management, and consultation for patients with routine   Yes   No
gynecological conditions/illness, including gynecological surgery. This level *does not*
include radical oncology procedures, reproductive endocrinology, or microsurgery.
Physicians granted this level are eligible to request the following procedures:

Procedures

Requested:		Approved:		Requested:		Approved:	
Ovaries				_____ Salpingo—uterostomy		Yes	No
				_____ Insufflation of fallopian tube		Yes	No
_____ Diagnostic procedures on ovaries		Yes	No	_____ Other operations on fallopian tubes		Yes	No
_____ Excision or destruction of ovarian lesion/tissue		Yes	No	*Vulva and perineum*			
_____ Oophorectomy (unilateral or bilateral)		Yes	No	_____ Diagnostic procedures on vulva		Yes	No
_____ Salpingo-oophorectomy (unilateral or bilateral)		Yes	No	_____ Incision on vulva and perineum		Yes	No
				_____ Repair of vulva and perineum		Yes	No
_____ Repair of ovary		Yes	No	_____ Operations on Bartholin's gland		Yes	No
_____ Lysis of adhesions		Yes	No	_____ Excision or destruction of vulva and perineum		Yes	No
_____ Other operations on ovary		Yes	No	_____ Operations on clitoris		Yes	No
Fallopian tubes				_____ Simple vulvectomy (unilateral or bilateral)		Yes	No
_____ Repair of fallopian tube(s)		Yes	No				
_____ Diagnostic procedures on fallopian tubes		Yes	No	*Cervix*			
_____ Salpingostomy		Yes	No	_____ Diagnostic procedures		Yes	No
_____ Endoscopic destruction or occlusion of fallopian tubes (unilateral or bilateral)		Yes	No	_____ Conization		Yes	No
				Destruction of lesion or tissue			
				_____ —via cauterization		Yes	No
_____ Other endoscopic procedures of fallopian tubes		Yes	No	_____ —via cryosurgery		Yes	No
				_____ Amputation of cervix		Yes	No
_____ Other bilateral destruction or occlusion of fallopian tubes		Yes	No	_____ Repair/incision of cervix		Yes	No
				_____ Other operations on cervix		Yes	No
_____ Salpingectomy (unilateral or bilateral)		Yes	No	_____ Remove cervical cerclage material		Yes	No
_____ —with removal of tubal pregnancy		Yes	No	_____ Placement of cervical cerclage material		Yes	No
_____ Excision or destruction of lesions of fallopian tubes		Yes	No	*Uterus*			
_____ Salpingo-oophorostomy		Yes	No	_____ Diagnostic hysteroscopy with biopsy		Yes	No
_____ Salpingo-salpingostomy		Yes	No	_____ Hysterotomy		Yes	No

Source: Courtesy of University Hospitals of Cleveland, Cleveland, OH.

Procedures

Requested:		Approved:		Requested:		Approved:	

uterus continued

_____	Diagnostic procedures on uterus and supporting structures	Yes	No
_____	Excision or destruction of lesion or tissue of uterus and supporting structures	Yes	No
_____	Subtotal abdominal hysterectomy	Yes	No
_____	Total abdominal hysterectomy	Yes	No
_____	Vaginal hysterectomy	Yes	No
_____	Dilatation and curettage of uterus	Yes	No
	Dilatation and curettage— pregnancy		
_____	—for termination of pregnancy	Yes	No
_____	—postdelivery	Yes	No
_____	—postabortion	Yes	No
_____	Repair of uterine-supporting structures	Yes	No
_____	Uterine repair	Yes	No
	Aspiration curettage of uterus for termination of pregnancy		
_____	a. < 12 weeks	Yes	No
_____	b. 12–16 weeks, D&E	Yes	No
_____	c. > 16 weeks, D&E, induction procedure	Yes	No
_____	—postdelivery	Yes	No
_____	—postabortion	Yes	No
_____	—evacuation—GTN	Yes	No
_____	Insertion of IUD	Yes	No
_____	Other _____	Yes	No
	_____	Yes	No

Vagina and cul-de-sac

_____	Vaginal tubal ligation	Yes	No
_____	Culdocentesis	Yes	No
_____	Incision of vagina and cul-de-sac	Yes	No
_____	Diagnostic procedures on vagina and cul-de-sac	Yes	No
_____	Excision or destruction of vagina and cul-de-sac	Yes	No
_____	Repair of cystocele and rectocele	Yes	No
_____	Enterocele repair	Yes	No
_____	Other repairs of vagina	Yes	No
_____	Repair of rectovaginal fistula	Yes	No
_____	Vaginal suspension and fixation	Yes	No
_____	Hymenorrhaphy	Yes	No
_____	Obliteration of vaginal vault	Yes	No

Abdominal region

_____	Incidental appendectomy	Yes	No
_____	Laparotomy	Yes	No

_____	Laparoscopy	Yes	No
_____	Exploratory laparotomy	Yes	No
_____	Other diagnostic procedures of abdominal region	Yes	No
_____	Excision or destruction of lesion or tissue of abdominal wall or umbilicus	Yes	No
_____	Excision or destruction of peritoneal tissue	Yes	No
_____	Lysis of peritoneal adhesions	Yes	No
_____	Suture/repair of abdominal wall and peritoneum	Yes	No
_____	Other operations of abdominal region	Yes	No
_____	Umbilical hernia repair in conjunction with other necessary procedures	Yes	No
_____	Abdominal paracentesis	Yes	No
_____	Peritoneal biopsy	Yes	No
_____	Abdominal cerclage	Yes	No

Urogynecological

_____	Repair of fistulas (vesicovaginal)	Yes	No
_____	Repair of suburethral diverticulum	Yes	No
_____	Cystoscopy/urethroscopy	Yes	No
_____	Suture of laceration of bladder	Yes	No
_____	Retropubic urethral suspension	Yes	No
_____	Paraurethral suspension	Yes	No
_____	Ureteral catheterization	Yes	No
_____	Urinary incontinence repair	Yes	No

Miscellaneous

_____	Anoscopy	Yes	No
	Sigmoidoscopy		
_____	—rigid	Yes	No
_____	—flexible	Yes	No
_____	*Needle aspiration biopsy of breast mass	Yes	No
	†Laser surgery		
_____	Level 1—lower genital tract disease (CO_2)	Yes	No
_____	Level 2—abdominal laser surgery (CO_2)	Yes	No
_____	Level 3—laser laparoscopic surgery (CO_2)	Yes	No
_____	Non-CO_2 privileges	Yes	No
_____	Other _____	Yes	No
_____	_____	Yes	No
_____	_____	Yes	No

*Requires signature on departmental policy statement.
†Requires documentation of training and current competence as defined by departmental policy.

Candidate: _____

Level II: Gynecological Privileges—Advanced

Requested: Approved:

_____ Privileges include diagnosis, management, and consultation for patients with more complicated   Yes   No
gynecological conditions requiring additional subspecialty training as defined in the minimum
requirement section of this form.

Requested: **Gynecological Oncology Privileges**   Approved:
_____   Yes   No

Procedures

Requested: Approved: Requested: Approved:

*Bowel and pelvic radical
procedures*   *Urinary procedures*

_____ Simple excision of lymphatic   Yes   No   _____ Formation of cutaneous   Yes   No
        structure   ureteroileostomy
_____ Excision of inguinal lymph nodes Yes   No   _____ Urinary diversion to intestine   Yes   No
_____ Excision of regional lymph nodes Yes   No   _____ Cystotomy   Yes   No
_____ Radical excision of iliac lymph   Yes   No   _____ Cystoscopy   Yes   No
        nodes   _____ Ureteroneocystostomy   Yes   No
_____ Radical groin dissection   Yes   No   _____ Transurethral bladder biopsy   Yes   No
_____ Radical node dissection   Yes   No   _____ Other bladder biopsy   Yes   No
_____ Gastrotomy and gastrostomy   Yes   No
_____ Large bowel incision   Yes   No   *Miscellaneous*
_____ Large bowel biopsy   Yes   No
_____ Local excision of large bowel   Yes   No   _____ Percutaneous liver biopsy   Yes   No
_____ Partial resection of small intestine Yes No _____ Radical vulvectomy   Yes   No
_____ Hemicolectomy   Yes   No   _____ Radical abdominal hysterectomy   Yes   No
_____ Small to small intestinal   Yes   No   _____ Radical vaginal hysterectomy   Yes   No
        anastomosis   _____ Radical vaginectomy   Yes   No
_____ Small to large intestinal anastomosis Yes No _____ Vaginal reconstruction   Yes   No
_____ Exteriorization of large intestine Yes No _____ Obliteration and total excision of Yes No
_____ Colostomy   Yes   No   vagina
_____ Suture of laceration of small or Yes   No   _____ Brachytherapy implantation   Yes   No
        large bowel
_____ Revision of stoma of intestine   Yes   No
_____ Rigid proctosigmoidoscopy   Yes   No
_____ Pelvic exenteration   Yes   No
_____ Intraperitoneal chemotherapy   Yes   No

Requested: **Reproductive Endocrinology and Infertility Privileges**   Approved:
_____   Yes   No

Procedures

Requested: Approved:

_____ ‡In vitro fertilization   Yes   No
_____ Operative hysteroscopy   Yes   No
_____ ‡Microsurgery   Yes   No

_____
‡Requires documentation of training and current competence as defined by departmental policy.

Level I: Obstetric Care Privileges—Routine Care

Requested: Approved:

_____ Privileges include diagnosis, management, and consultation for patients with obstetric conditions,   Yes   No
including surgery and deliveries, not requiring high-risk treatment/management. This level includes
management of prenatal, intrapartum, and postpartum patients, including management of complications.

Procedures

Requested:		Approved:		Requested:		Approved:	
Maternal-fetal monitoring				_____ Manual rotations		Yes	No
_____ —BSST		Yes	No	_____ Episiotomy and repair		Yes	No
_____ —NST		Yes	No	_____ Manual removal of placenta		Yes	No
_____ —OCT		Yes	No	_____ Postpartum uterine exploration		Yes	No
_____ —Scalp gases		Yes	No	_____ Repair of vaginal, cervical, and		Yes	No
_____ Biophysical profile		Yes	No	perineal lacerations			
_____ Diagnostic amniocentesis		Yes	No	_____ Induction and augmentation of labor		Yes	No
> 15 weeks				_____ Management of postpartum		Yes	No
_____ Amniotomy		Yes	No	hemorrhagic problems, including			
_____ All spontaneous vaginal deliveries—		Yes	No	evacuation of vaginal/vulvar			
single and twin				hematoma			
Operative vaginal deliveries				_____ Repair of obstetric laceration of		Yes	No
_____ —vacuum		Yes	No	uterus			
_____ —low forceps		Yes	No	_____ Other repair of obstetric laceration		Yes	No
_____ —mid forceps		Yes	No	_____ Correction of inverted uterus		Yes	No
_____ **Multiple births (greater than 2)		Yes	No	_____ Circumcision of newborn		Yes	No
_____ **Breech deliveries		Yes	No	_____ External cephalic version		Yes	No
_____ All cesarean (abdominal) deliveries		Yes	No	_____ Other _____		Yes	No
_____ Postpartum hysterectomy		Yes	No	_____ _____		Yes	No
_____ Administration of local and		Yes	No	_____ _____		Yes	No
pudendal anesthesia (excluding				_____ _____		Yes	No
paracervical)							

Level II: Obstetric Care—Advanced

Requested: Approved:

_____ Privileges including diagnosis, management, and consultation on complex, high-risk obstetric   Yes   No
patients, requiring subspecialty training in Maternal-Fetal Medicine.

Procedures

Requested:		Approved:		Requested:		Approved:	
_____ Early amniocentesis		Yes	No	_____ Intrauterine operations on fetus and		Yes	No
_____ CV sampling		Yes	No	amnion			
_____ Percutaneous umbilical blood		Yes	No	_____ Diagnostic procedures on fetus and		Ycs	No
sampling				amnion			
_____ Ultrasound—Level 2		Yes	No	_____ Intrauterine transfusion		Yes	No
_____ Fetal echocardiography/Doppler		Yes	No				

_____	_____
Candidate	Date
_____	_____
Department Director	Date

_____
**Requires signature on departmental policy statement.

chapter *14*

Ethical Issues in Risk Management

Carole Runyan Price

THE POPULARITY OF ETHICS

Ethics is enjoying a resurgence of popularity. One can hardly pick up a newspaper or magazine without finding an article about ethics in business, the political arena, or health care. For example, Edwin Meese, former U.S. attorney general, was a prominent legal figure who fell victim to allegations of unethical behavior. James Wright, former U.S. Senate majority leader, resigned from office amid a furor of ethical controversy. John Tower's unsuccessful bid for secretary of defense was a clear message that certain personal activities are generally viewed as unethical behavior and are no longer tolerated by the public. When ethical ammunition was leveled against Tony Coelho, a former California congressman, he resigned with surprising swiftness even before the gun was fired. In fact it has been rumored that both political parties have considered pushing for a moratorium on "ethics bashing" in order to regain political stability. In a society still not fully recovered from "Watergate," in which political self-interest is so prevalent, such a political maneuver is perhaps not surprising, but it does not lack irony.

ETHICAL ISSUES IN HEALTH CARE

Ethical issues in health care were not particularly prevalent or newsworthy 15 to 20 years ago. The number of such issues was small, and national attention was minimal. However, times have changed. Medical technology has advanced at lightning speed during these 20 years. There seems to be a confluence of factors causing national attention to focus on ethics in health care. They include advancing medical technology, decreasing economic resources, changing legal definitions of individual and societal rights, and an increasing reliance on ethical precepts in an attempt to balance the first three factors. Perhaps a fifth factor is that we are in a time of peace. In times of war, military, technological, and economic forces seem to dominate all other factors.

The sheer number of ethical issues has multiplied at a staggering rate. What was once almost unthinkable is now commonplace. Moral quandaries in medicine and the life sciences are rapidly evolving. An illustrative, but by no means exhaustive, list includes the following:

- abortion
- in vitro fertilization
- ownership or "rights" of fertilized eggs
- surrogate motherhood
- the use of fetal tissue in medical research
- sterilization
- organ and tissue transplantation
- acquired immunodeficiency syndrome (AIDS) treatment and research
- failure to obtain informed consent for treatment
- the right to receive treatment
- the right to refuse treatment when refusal is intended to result in the patient's death
- do not resuscitate orders

- mandatory medical treatment for pregnant women who endanger the lives of their fetuses
- elder abuse
- animal research
- legislation dealing with "anti-dumping" of patients

Even such a short list as this points up the fact that few of these issues have sharp, clear edges; rather, they frequently involve concurrent entanglement in a combination of legal, ethical, and economic principles.

GENERAL PRINCIPLES OF ETHICS

This section is not a scholarly treatise on ethics, but rather its purpose is to provide the essence of major ethical principles in terms that the average layperson (in this case risk manager or physician) can understand. Rev. Ernlé W.D. Young, Ph.D., has written one of the more succinct and coherent discussions of ethical principles in his recent book *Alpha and Omega, Ethics at the Frontiers of Life and Death.* With his kind permission, I draw liberally from his work.

Traditionally medicine has been deontological in its approach to moral problems. The deontological approach holds that "certain actions are right or wrong and are thus required or prohibited regardless of the consequences."[1] This is in contrast to a teleological or consequentialist approach to ethics in which the decision maker weighs the immediate and long-range benefits and harms of each alternative and selects a course of action either to maximize the benefits or minimize the harms for the greatest number.[2]

Under the deontological approach, Rev. Young cites four broad principles: (1) beneficence, (2) nonmaleficence, (3) justice, and (4) autonomy.[3] Beneficence refers to benefiting the patient and is frequently associated with attempting to save the patient's life.[4] Nonmaleficence, on the other hand, refers to the precept to do no harm.[5] Medical interventions most often result in minimal or no harm to the patient. However, certain situations raise the ethical question of whether to continue a treatment or to prolong a patient's life when this may in fact be of considerable "harm" to the patient.

Justice is the basic principle of fairness. Fairness requires that we not do for some what we are unwilling to do for all. The concept of justice raises the extremely complex questions of who shall have access to health care, how much, and who shall decide.[6] Access to health care is also closely intertwined with allocation of health care resources. Is health care a right, a privilege, or both? Should everyone be entitled to polio vaccine or penicillin? How about a hip transplant or a heart and lung transplant? The ethical and economic waters become murky indeed.

Autonomy is a more recently accepted principle; it "requires that, as far as possible patients be respected as

Figure 14-1
FOUR BROAD PRINCIPLES UNDER THE DEONTOLOGICAL APPROACH TO MORAL PROBLEMS

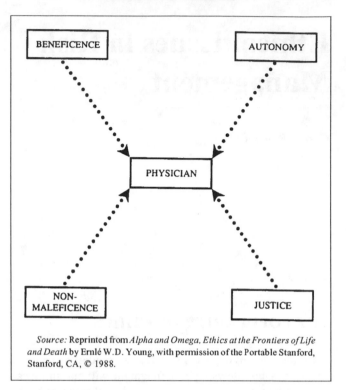

Source: Reprinted from *Alpha and Omega, Ethics at the Frontiers of Life and Death* by Ernlé W.D. Young, with permission of the Portable Stanford, Stanford, CA, © 1988.

equal partners in arriving at decisions affecting their own lives."[7] To be effective, autonomy also means that the patient fulfill his or her responsibilities in the decision-making process (e.g., to comply with the agreed-upon treatment plan, to ask questions if something is not understood). Rev. Young has illustrated the balances of the four principles in Figure 14-1.

The difficulty, of course, comes in balancing these principles. No one principle is absolute. The alternatives must be carefully weighed against one another in order to achieve a rational balance.

HOSPITAL ETHICS COMMITTEE

History

Perhaps the seminal case to raise ethical issues of national magnitude was *In re Quinlan*, which exploded on the legal and ethical arena in 1976. The New Jersey Supreme Court stated in *Quinlan* that "[T]he evidence in this case convinces us that the focal point of the decision should be the prognosis as to the possibility of return to a cognitive and sapient life, as distinguished from the forced continuance of that biological vegetative existence to which Karen seems doomed."[8] The concept of quality of life was then legally identified as a factor that could be considered in matters involving decisions on whether to withdraw life support. *Quinlan* went on to link such decisions to the existence of hospital ethics committees that had to concur in the decisions. It is worth noting that after life support was withdrawn Karen Quinlan survived for some ten years. The long interval before her death may have been a major reason that the *Quinlan* decision did not create an immediate proliferation of ethics committees. One may speculate that interest gradually abated precisely because she survived for such a long period, coupled with the fact that her father accepted the legal decision and remained devoted to his daughter until her death.

The next major litigation involving ethical events was an Indiana case that came to be known as "Infant Doe." In 1982 the Indiana Supreme Court let stand a trial court decision permitting the parents of a child with Down syndrome to withhold surgery that would have corrected an intestinal blockage. This case shocked the conscience of the nation. The federal government acted swiftly by issuing directives and regulations. A new legal theory was invoked. Section 504 of the 1973 Rehabilitation Act was broadened to permit the investigation of alleged wrongful withholding of life-sustaining treatment to children born with handicaps.[9] Investigative groups dubbed "Baby Doe Squads" could descend on hospitals on the basis of anonymous complaints called in on a 24-hour hotline.[10] In addition to legal sanctions and notoriety, the regulations provided that if a hospital were found to be in violation of the act, its federal funding could be withheld. Since many hospitals were dependent on federal funding, the possibility of sanction could not be taken lightly.

During the ensuing legal battles, the "Baby Jane Doe" case surfaced in Long Island in 1983. In that case the U.S. Court of Appeals held that the federal government was not entitled to access to Baby Jane Doe's medical records on the grounds that this type of request went beyond the scope of the 1973 Rehabilitation Act.[11] The U.S. Department of Health and Human Services (HHS) in 1984 reissued a revised set of regulations leaving more discretion to state governments to deal with such matters under state child abuse and neglect legislation. HHS also recommended that hospitals appoint infant review committees.[12] As it turned out, recommending the creation of ethics committees was a strategic decision. In its 1983 report, *Deciding to Forego Life-Sustaining Treatment: A Report on the Ethical, Medical, and Legal Issues in Treatment Decisions*, the President's Commission for the Study of Ethical Problems in Medicine and Biomedical and Behavioral Research estimated the frequency of ethics committees ranged from 41 percent of Catholic hospitals to only 1 percent of other U.S. hospitals.[13]

Since then ethics committees slowly but steadily have been gaining ground.

Role

Although the formation of ethics committees has been encouraged by case law, the report of the President's Commission, and HHS regulations, there is no legal requirement for a hospital to establish an ethics committee. Judging from the numbers of articles and the requests for information, however, there appears to be a trend toward the proliferation of such committees.

The three primary functions of hospital ethics committees, according to Alexander Capron, tend to include education, writing guidelines, and case review.[14] A committee should clarify early what it perceives as its functions. A charge to the committee that outlines its general nature should be promulgated and provide enough flexibility so that the committee's role and interests may evolve over time without rewriting the charge. A statement explaining the purpose of the Stanford University Hospital Ethics Committee provides an example of one approach (see Appendixes 14-A and 14-B).

Capron suggests the following six factors that should be considered when establishing an ethics committee:

1. membership
2. appointment and removal of members
3. powers of the committee
4. timing of committee action
5. responsibility and liability
6. record keeping[15]

An institution may have different ethics committees for specific purposes. For example, the purpose of the Stanford University Medical Center Ethics Committee, formed in 1986, is primarily concerned with education, including publication of guidelines and position papers. Three of these have appeared in the *New England Journal of Medicine*.[16] The committee's more than 40 members represent many campus groups, as well as the community. The Stanford University Hospital Ethics Committee, on the other hand, focuses its attention on education but also does consultative case review on an advisory basis upon request; it has only 8 members (see Appendix 14-C).

Yet a third model is the Stanford University Hospital Infant Review Committee that functions informally under the leadership of a neonatalogist. The committee, established more than ten years ago, engages in philosophical discussions of the family/physician decision-making process and case review on an advisory basis. The membership is voluntary and includes members of the infant health care team, faculty and community physicians, housestaff, nurses, social workers, representatives of patient and community relations and the administration, a community ethicist, and a medical center ethicist.

There is no one model for an ethics committee. The type of committee and the primary functions of each committee are best decided by individual health care institutions or units within the institutions.

In setting up a new ethics committee or in re-examining an existing one, consideration should be given to potential liability. If the risk manager is an attorney, that person can research relevant case law and applicable legislation in order to take advantage of any legal protections available. The risk manager who is not an attorney should consult the hospital attorney if there is one or engage an attorney knowledgeable in the subject matter and relevant legal requirements, decisions, and practices. A risk/benefit analysis clearly favors making a relatively low financial investment in legal fees in order to obtain greater protection for members of the ethics committee individually and severally as well as for any actions taken by the committee.

One possible way to obtain confidentiality over the minutes and activities of the ethics committee is to have it appointed as an organized medical staff committee engaged in quality assurance or peer review matters. Clearly, the amount of legal protection that will be needed depends on the nature and scope of the committee and applicable state laws. A committee engaged only in education or discussing and distributing position papers is less likely to need protection than a committee engaged in timely case review. There is also less risk legally and politically if committees engaged in case review do so on an advisory basis as a resource, or "sounding board," for the attending physician or health care team rather than as a decision-making body. Advisory committees also tend in the long run to be more effective, provided that someone who is politically influential in the organization stipulates that the work of these committees is important.

The most effective committee members are those who either possess the requisite medical and ethical knowledge or who are willing to acquire such expertise. The study of ethical decision making in health care is a complex and time-consuming task, and members must be willing to commit their time and effort. It is well to note that an ethics committee whose primary purpose is dealing with wide-ranging ethical issues can tolerate, indeed benefit, from a diversity of personalities and positions. An advisory case review committee, however, usually needs people with considerable interpersonal skills and may be too fragile, especially at first, to tolerate dogmatic and controversial personalities who are more interested in making "political statements" than in seeking satisfactory resolution of the issues. One of the considerations for membership should be interpersonal skills that are likely to enhance the committee's chance for success.

PATIENTS' HEALTH CARE DECISIONS

The act of making an ethical decision in health care is often agonizing and complex. It becomes even more confounding when there is no identified decision maker to represent the patient. A competent patient, who is able and willing to make health care decisions, should exercise this right. However, there are frequent occasions where the patient is either temporarily or permanently unable to make health care decisions. In these situations a surrogate who is legally empowered to make such decisions is immensely helpful.

In California, for example, there are generally three well-recognized methods by which individuals can indicate their preferences in health care decisions to be carried out should they become incompetent: (1) a physician's directive in accordance with the California Natural Death Act[17] enacted in 1976; (2) a living will; and (3) a durable power of attorney for health care,[18] available in California since January 1985.

THE PATIENT SELF-DETERMINATION ACT AND WHAT THE EXPERTS ARE SAYING ABOUT IT*

The "Patient Self-Determination Act" requires hospitals, nursing homes, home health agencies, hospices and other institutional Medicare and Medicaid providers to give patients, at the time of admission, written information concerning their rights under state laws to accept or refuse medical care and to formulate advance directives. Under the Act, the health care provider must develop policies and procedures that specify that the provider will:

- provide all patients/residents, at the time of admission, written information about their right to execute advance directives, which include such documents as living wills and durable power of attorney forms. The provider will also have to inform patients/residents in writing of the policies regarding the implementation of medical directives. The law requires that *states* will develop the information that will go to patients; *providers* will only have to distribute it.
- document in the medical record whether an advance directive has been signed.
- not condition the provision of care or discriminate against the patient based on whether the individual has executed an advance directive.
- ensure that all of the policies and procedures enacted by the provider are in compliance with the state law.

*Source: Reprinted from Quality and Risk Management in Health Care, Vol. 1, No. 4, June 1991, © Aspen Publishers, Inc.

- provide education to staff and the community regarding advance directives and patients' right to refuse treatment. To achieve this, the law requires an institutional ethics committee (in all states in health care institutions that qualify for Medicare or Medicaid funding) to initiate educational programs on ethical issues in health care, to advise on particular cases, and to serve as a forum for such issues.

This law also requires that the department of Health and Human Services develop and implement a comprehensive education program to provide the public an opportunity to learn about end-of-life choices and the option to sign an advance directive and durable power of attorney in case of incapacity. In addition, the bill requires the remaining states that have not enacted Natural Death Acts to do so.

Controversy surrounds several aspects of the Act. Many hospital executives, advocates for the elderly, and other health care professionals support the goal of the law—to encourage the use of advance directives. But some experts have many questions about the burden of responsibility for advance directives education being placed on hospitals (and especially on admitting clerks) when it may be more appropriate for physicians.

The Positive Aspects of the Act*

Those who support the Act cite recent studies showing that patients want to discuss future decisions regarding life-sustaining therapy and that the majority of patients do not have adverse emotional reactions to these discussions. After years of voluntary education about living wills, only nine percent of Americans have such documents. Opportunities to learn about advance directives have been few. Those supporting it say the "Patient Self-Determination Act" represents an effort to provide more opportunities for learning in institutions where eighty percent of Americans die.

Advocates note that the Act does not preclude physicians from educating their patients, although surveys have revealed that physicians discuss these issues with the minority of their patients. From the few studies reported, physicians seem to be in favor of advance directives for medical care, but they seem reluctant to initiate discussions about them. Some supporters of the Act go one step further and suggest that the federal government should fund programs to disseminate advance directive documents and engage the public in discussion, and it should reward physicians and other providers who encourage advance planning as a type of "preventative medicine for difficult decisions."

Any stimulus to increasing communication of advance directives is considered good by experts who have spoken in favor of the law. After the media coverage of the Missouri trial that addressed the parents' request for withdrawal of a feeding tube from Nancy Cruzan, the Society for the Right to Die/Concern for the Dying, a New York-based advocacy organization, sent out 750,000 forms for living wills (over a period of six months). This was a 500 percent increase in demand for the documents and the Society is now averaging 150,000 new requests per month.

John C. Fletcher, director of the Center for Biomedical Ethics at the University of Virginia, views the intent of the requirement for institutional ethics committees as encouragement of the local development of ethics programs, which provide a system of checks and balances against domination of any one sector in ethical decision making. Many experts see the requirement for all states to develop Natural Death Acts as assurance that what the Constitution affords every person—the right to refuse treatment, including life-sustaining treatment—will be further protected and extended.

The Negatives of the Act*

Those in opposition to the law feel uneasy about the potential for abuse of implementing the requirements of the Act. They are concerned that information will be given to people as they are wheeled into a hospital (and mixed in with a large number of standard hospital admission forms) or have rushed consultations about directives in the emergency department.

Most experts recognize that it would be more appropriate for physicians (or other appropriate professionals such as social workers) to give out the information and discuss the issues with patients, but, they say, physicians just don't do that and other professionals often are not provided with the opportunity. Alexander Morgan Capron, Professor of Law and Medicine at the University of Southern California in Los Angeles, says the net effect of the Act is to let physicians off the hook, since the federal government is telling hospitals it is their job to inform patients of living wills and durable powers of attorney. Instead, Professor Capron says, physicians should be encouraged to make a discussion about advance directives part of routine patient care.

Physicians who have an opposing view say their major concern is that patients could change their minds about heroic treatment after becoming terminally ill. They are familiar with such indecision in the face of suffering. Whether patients can make reliable value decisions or truly informed decisions about something they have never experienced is frequently questioned.

Added to the ethical positions of opposition are the health care professionals who object to the potential "tons of paperwork" and regulatory burden that will be involved in implementing the law. Michael Bromberg, executive director of the Federation of American Health Systems, Washington, D.C., said the task of disseminating advance directive information should be handled by the Health Care Financing Administration, which administers Medicare and Medicaid, and the Social Security Administration. It's "one more thing the hospital has to do," he said.

Proposed Exceptions to the Act*

Rep. Brian J. Donnelly (D-MA) has introduced a bill that would alter several provisions on advance directives in the "Patient Self-Determination Act." First, the Donnelly proposal would allow an exemption for providers from the law's requirements based upon moral, ethical, or religious beliefs. A hospital or other provider would be allowed to exempt itself from the law by certifying to the HHS Secretary that its board of directors had voted to be exempt based upon moral, ethical, or religious beliefs. The proposal would exempt skilled nursing facilities from the law's requirements entirely.

Second, the Donnelly proposal also would extend the requirements to physicians who accept funds under the Social Security Act. Like hospitals, physicians would be required to make available to adult patients written information concerning their rights regarding advance directives. Physicians also would be permitted to exempt themselves based upon moral, ethical, or religious beliefs.

Third, the proposal would prohibit certain persons from witnessing the execution of advance directives. Employees of a provider could not serve as witness for a Medicare or Medicaid beneficiary while the individual was an inpatient. Physicians could not witness the advance directives of individuals under their care.

Finally, the proposal would also repeal the provision of the Act which requires state Medicaid plans (or other assistance programs) to include advance directive requirements, and thus compliance with the law's requirements would not be a condition of participating in Medicaid.

The act at this point fails to address issues related to decision making for terminally ill children or incompetents. It also makes no mention of a perspective of parents' rights in making decisions about an unborn child who is known to be severely deformed or otherwise handicapped. It is not anticipated that these decision-making issues will ever become part of the Act.

Where the Act Came From*

Recent landmark court cases have set medicolegal and bioethical precedents. The "Patient Self-Determination Act"

was created as a result of a number of important points reflected in these cases:

- A competent person may, under most circumstances, refuse a specific medical treatment. Controversies over this fundamental right of individual autonomy arise when one or more "state interests" are jeopardized, these being the preservation of life, the protection of third parties, the prevention of suicide, and the maintenance of the ethical integrity of the medical community.
- An incompetent patient must be afforded the same fundamental rights as a competent person. Legally, family members may generally express the will of an incompetent relative.
- A decision to withdraw a medical treatment is tantamount to withholding the initiation of a medical treatment.
- When a patient, the patient's family, and the patient's physicians are in accord about a decision to withhold or withdraw life-sustaining measures, a specific court order is usually not required, as ample legal precedents have been established.
- Generally, artificially supplied nutrition and hydration through physician-placed tubes may be considered medical treatments, and they may be withheld or withdrawn as are other medical treatments. At the present time, specific state laws govern this principle.
- The contemporary concept of "brain death" is widely held and rarely challenged.
- The concept of "Do Not Resuscitate" orders is widely accepted and does not require specific prior judicial consent. The hesitancy of many physicians to write these orders, however, often becomes an issue in the care of the terminally ill.
- The concept of a living will is being increasingly accepted and only rarely challenged. Many states are now adopting legislation that describes the conditions under which a valid living will can be executed.

A number of other points are less firmly established and less clearly identified by the courts:

- The rights of a parent to express the will of a child, particularly when at odds with recommendations made by the minor's physicians, may not always take priority.
- An incompetent patient's right to suspend therapy (when not previously specifically expressed and when a chronic but nonterminal condition exists) may be exercised.
- When the underlying condition results from other than an end-stage neurologic insult and when the prognosis is uncertain, the same inferences may not always be

*Source: Reprinted from *Quality and Risk Management in Health Care*, Vol. 1, No. 4, June 1991, © Aspen Publishers, Inc.

drawn as when an end-stage neurologic condition exists.

- When there is a fundamental disagreement among a patient, his or her family, and his or her physicians, the courts may become the final arbiters.
- Whenever there is doubt about the possibility of future improvement in a patient's condition, treatment must continue.
- The role of third parties and surrogates in instigating legal actions may increase in the future.

Physician's Directive

The physician's directive is the least effective method of the patient's three health care decisions. The intent of the Natural Death Act was laudable, but so many restrictions apply before the instrument is legally binding that, practically speaking, it is of minimal benefit. The most difficult hurdle to overcome is the prerequisite that the patient must be in a terminal condition and have been so informed at least 14 days prior to signing the directive.

Living Will

The second most effective instrument is a living will, but it may not be legally binding in some states. However, it does provide the opportunity for a person to make known his or her wishes about health care decisions, particularly those affecting the prolongation of life. The living will is recognized as an important step in the movement advocating "death with dignity." A living will can be personally written, signed, and dated as an expression of preference, but forms are also available through organizations.

Durable Power of Attorney for Health Care

The most effective method of ensuring that health care decisions are consistent with one's wishes is to execute a durable power of attorney for health care. At Stanford Medical Center, patients, families, and physicians are encouraged to become familiar with this option. It is described, along with the two others listed above, in a letter prepared by the center's ethics committee and available to patients and members of the community through the Office of Community and Patient Relations (see Appendix 14-D). From risk management and legal perspectives, the more informed that patients, families, and physicians are about the available medical choices and the mechanisms to document patients' decisions, the less the risk of legal liability. Equally important from an ethical perspective is the desire to effectuate clear channels of communication and respect for the wishes of patients.

It is obvious that the durable power of attorney is particularly helpful in dealing with the elderly and adult children of the elderly. Less well appreciated, however, is the usefulness of the document for any age group. For example, trauma victims who may be temporarily or permanently incompetent are often young adult males in their 20s. Single parents also find the document valuable.

RISK MANAGER'S ROLE: A BALANCING ACT

Ethical, economic, and legal issues are often simultaneously involved in health care decisions. The task of risk managers is to understand fully the significance of each of these pressures and to try to achieve resolutions acceptable to the constituents and principles involved. This is no small feat. It means that risk managers must educate themselves in all of these disciplines at least to the extent that they know when other resources are imperative or would be helpful. It entails being able to identify readily and accurately the important issues in a given situation and to facilitate the discussion and assessment of alternative solutions. A keystone of the author's philosophy always has been that good ethics makes for good economics. If patients believe that a risk manager cares and his or her actions demonstrate a caring attitude, they are much less apt to go for the "pound of flesh" along with every dollar they can wring out of the institution. A risk manager who "fakes" it may survive in the short term, but in the long run his or her professional career may suffer irreparable damage.

Judgment, intuition, a sixth sense, or whatever one calls it, enters into the equation. Some of this can be learned by experience. Some of it, however, relates to an innate talent that one either has or does not have, and no amount of experience will create it. For example, some years ago (the statute of limitations is long past) a female patient in her 50s was scheduled for open heart surgery. After the medical team had opened the chest, they discovered that water leaking onto the instruments had destroyed the sterile field. They quickly closed the patient and called me. I learned that a groundskeeper had left a hose running on the rooftop patio, and it had leaked into the operating suite. I was present shortly after the patient came out of anesthesia. She had difficulty understanding what had happened. She said, "They tell me that I didn't have the operation, yet I'm all bandaged up and I hurt. Can you tell me what happened?" I told her the truth, and I told her that I cared about her. I visited her regularly during the next three days.

I also told the patient that I was prepared to write off the costs of this hospitalization and those of the second hospitalization. I told her that the best thing her surgeons could have done was to close her up until we discovered what had happened. The day before she was to go home, she told me that her friends had advised her to sue the hospital. I smiled and responded that it was clearly an option, but that her decision whether or not to sue would have no bearing on my offer to waive the costs of this hospitalization and the future surgery. She was quiet a long time and then said, "I really just want to get well." She was verbalizing something that I had sensed from the very beginning. I told her that she need not make a decision then, explained the statute of limitations, and said that if she did sue, I would understand. She came back for surgery in three weeks and did beautifully. I was there from admitting to discharge to make certain that matters went smoothly. A suit was not filed.

In a second example, a woman was pregnant with twins, and the fetal monitoring strip showed fetal distress. An immediate cesarean section was ordered. The anesthesiologist was not entirely familiar with the anesthesia machine and in his haste did not complete its checklist. The incision was made, and the woman screamed in pain for several minutes until the malfunction could be corrected and the anesthetic took effect. I was called by the community obstetrician and the anesthesia department. The strategy decided on was that I would work with the patient's physician and deal with the patient. I made frequent contacts with the patient while she was in the hospital and followed up after she went home. She often broke into tears when recalling the incident. I waived the hospital bill and also took my cue from the patient that she really did appreciate my concern, but that she preferred not to discuss it further. A suit was filed. It was settled for $30,000, a decidedly low amount. It is clear that the nature of the interaction between the patient and the risk manager played a significant part in the low settlement figure.

Both of these cases underscore the philosophy that good ethics makes for good economics. The patients were told the truth. They knew someone cared, and they were satisfied with the outcome. Certainly with some patients these approaches could be disastrous. That is where the indefinable quality of judgment is so important. Each matter needs to be assessed on a case-by-case basis, together with a risk/benefit analysis of the available options. The delicate balance is to weigh all the relevant factors and reach a conclusion that preserves the integrity of the patient, the hospital, and the risk manager. The responsibilities of the risk manager and the effective implementation of these responsibilities are critically important on both micro and macro levels. A skilled risk manager can save a health care institution and society thousands, or even million, of dollars and can be a role model in ensuring that ethical principles are maintained among the parties involved and for the benefit of society as well. This makes a risk manager's role both challenging and satisfying.

Hospital risk managers need to be aware of the importance of making staff familiar with ethical issues and problems in the health care setting. Drafting manuals or policies that discuss these issues is essential for avoiding problems associated with ethics.

NOTES

1. E.W.D. Young, *Alpha and Omega, Ethics at the Frontiers of Life and Death* (Stanford, Calif.: The Portable Stanford, 1988), 21.

2. Ibid., 20.

3. Ibid., 21.

4. Ibid.

5. Ibid., 22.

6. Ibid.

7. Ibid., 23.

8. *In the Matter of Karen Quinlan*, 355 A.2d 647, 669 (N.J. 1976). See also A.M. Capron, Legal Perspectives on Institutional Ethics Committees, in *Making Choices: Ethical Issues for Health Care Professionals*, ed. E. Friedman (Chicago: American Hospital Publishing, Inc., 1986), 178.

9. Capron, Legal Perspectives, 178.

10. Ibid., 178.

11. Ibid., 179.

12. Ibid.

13. R.A. McCormick, Ethics Committees: Promise or Peril? in *Making Choices: Ethical Issues for Health Care Professionals*, ed. E. Friedman (Chicago: American Hospital Publishing, Inc., 1986), 185.

14. Capron, Legal Perspectives, 179.

15. Ibid.

16. J.A. Thomas, et al., Animal Research at Stanford University: Principles, Policies, and Practices, *New England Journal of Medicine* 318, no. 24 (1988), 1630; J. Ruark and T. Raffin, Initiating and Withdrawing Life Support, *New England Journal of Medicine* 318, no. 1 (1988), 25; H.T. Greeley, et al., The Ethical Use of Human Fetal Tissue in Medicine, *New England Journal of Medicine* 320, no. 16 (1989), 1093.

17. The Natural Death Act. CAL. HEALTH & SAFETY CODE §7185 et seq.

18. Durable Power of Attorney for Health Care. CAL. CIV. CODE §§2410 to 2443.

Appendix 14-A

Sample Statement of Purpose for Ethics Committee

STANFORD UNIVERSITY HOSPITAL ETHICS COMMITTEE

STATEMENT OF PURPOSE

This Committee shall consult and advise on ethical issues of a clinical nature, both generally and in specific cases, and provide education on such issues in collaboration with the Stanford University Medical Center Committee on Ethics. The duties of the committee shall include:

1. Providing timely consultative services on request to facilitate the examination and where possible the resolution of specific clinical ethical issues by the principals involved (who might include the medical and nursing staff as well as the patient, family members or their representatives).
2. Making recommendations concerning the resolution of any chronic, persistent, or recurring clinical ethical issues of a systemic nature.
3. Developing expertise on selected units of the Hospital in identification of and consultation about clinical ethical issues; such regional experts could serve on the Committee, work on unit-specific and more general issues, and initially screen in consultation with the clinical nursing coordinator and/or Medical Director requests for consultation to the Committee.
4. Conducting educational efforts within the Committee, the Hospital, and the wider community concerning clinical ethical issues in medicine (which could include in-service presentations, ethical rounds, grand rounds, open lectures, seminars, and workshops).
5. Coordinating with the Stanford University Medical Center Committee on Ethics in carrying out its duties.

The ex-officio members of the Committee shall include the Chief of Staff, the chair of the Stanford University Medical Center Committee on Ethics, a representative from Hospital administration, and a representative from the general counsel's office. The general members of the committee may include physician representatives from internal medicine, neurology, pediatrics, psychiatry, and surgery; representatives (nurses, etc.) from EIA, CCU, and WIB, NICU, the medical and surgical ICUs, the intensive care nursery, pediatrics, emergency department, clinical research unit, the compromised host/bone marrow transplant unit, nursing stress management, the alcohol and drug treatment center, the chaplaincy, social service, community and patient relations; a resident representative; and a medical student representative. The Committee shall meet in regular session approximately once a month.

Each month four to five members of the Committee shall assume "on call" duties. Part or all of this subcommittee will respond within 24 hours to requests from individuals or units for a consultation. If necessary, after an evaluation by the subcommittee, a special meeting of the full Committee shall be called. The consensus of the subcommittee or Committee, and the reasons for its conclusions, shall be made available to the referring party.

Source: Courtesy of Stanford University Medical Center, Stanford, CA.

Appendix 14-B

Sample Administrative Charge to Ethics Committee

To: SUMC Committee on Ethics

From: _____, President, Stanford University Hospital
        _____, Vice President and Dean, School of Medicine

Subject: Administrative Charge to Ethics Committee

In view of the recent reorganization of the Medical Center, it is timely to confirm the original charge to the SUMC Ethics Committee and to acknowledge its important role.

In doing so, we have an opportunity to reinforce the Committee's identity and missions and to highlight objectives and goals for the future. We emphasize that this Committee has been an important body in an environment where many ethical issues arise on a regular basis. The Committee has been successful in identifying and examining many of these issues—issues that health care professionals confront every day but for which answers are not always straightforward, obvious or easy. Because of the Committee's efforts to promote the understanding and education of medical ethics at many levels, a series of ethics seminars is now part of the Preparation for Clinical Medicine course, a requirement for the M.D. degree at Stanford Medical School. Additionally, the Ethics Committee has sensitively educated the medical and lay community about patients' rights, particularly in the context of withdrawing life support.

For these reasons, the SUMC Ethics Committee should continue its work, and we endorse the initial charge as follows:

The Committee's purpose is to:

1. Aid in identification of the Medical Center's ethical issues.
2. Increase awareness and understanding of the Medical Center's ethical issues.
3. Suggest policies and practices aimed to ensure sound decision making with respect to the Center's ethical issues.
4. Assist in the incorporation of teaching of ethical issues into the Center's educational programs.

In addition, it will be important for the SUMC Ethics Committee to develop a close relationship with the newly formed Hospital Ethics Committee. We hope the Centerwide Committee will work closely with the new hospital committee and will assist in developing educational programs, policies and practices as needed.

Source: Courtesy of Stanford University Medical Center, Stanford, CA.

Appendix 14-C

Sample Ethics Committee Role As Consultant

STANFORD UNIVERSITY HOSPITAL ETHICS COMMITTEE

The Chief of Staff has recently appointed a Hospital Ethics Committee, which is now one of the committees of the medical staff. The Committee is to be available for clinical ethical consultations. It is not intended to usurp the decision-making prerogative of attending physicians and their patients. The eight members of the Committee are:

Co-Director, Center for Bioethics (Chair)
Professor of Medicine
Assistant Professor of Neurology
Community Surgeon
Staff Counsel
Director of Physician Services and Risk Management
Clinical Nursing Coordinator, ICU
Nurse Consultant, Stress Management Dispute Resolution
A representative of Patient and Community Relations will be appointed as a consultant to the Committee.

Referrals to the Committee may be made by patients, family members, staff nurses, medical students, house officers, attending physicians, or other health care personnel. However, both as a matter of courtesy and to screen (in preliminary fashion) the calls to the Committee, the following protocol is recommended by the Committee:

Before initiating a referral to the Committee:

a. The relevant ethical issues should be identified and discussed on the unit by the various health care providers and the family; and
b. both the attending physician and the Clinical Nursing Coordinator should be advised that a consultation is being invited from the Hospital Ethics Committee.

Referrals to the Committee should go directly to the chair, Ernlé W.D. Young (Office #3-5101). Young (or an available member of the Committee) will respond in timely fashion, making a preliminary assessment of the situation. As is necessary and appropriate, other members of the Committee as well as consultants not on the Committee may be called in to meet with the principals on the unit. If the attending requests this, the Committee's recommendations will be recorded in the patient's chart. This will not happen unless it is expressly invited.

The Committee will meet regularly to review recent referrals; to identify and discuss issues of a recurring nature, making recommendations about their resolution to the Chief of Staff, or the Stanford Medical Center Ethics Committee, or both; and to educate its members and the hospital community about the role, responsibilities, limitations, and opportunities of clinical ethical consultations.

Orig. Date: 4/1/88

Source: Courtesy of Stanford University Medical Center, Stanford, CA.

Appendix 14-D

Sample Ethical Statement

Office of Community and Patient Relations

MAKING MEDICAL DECISIONS . . . Guidance for Community Members, Patients and Families

Patients sometimes lose the ability to make sound judgments, for reasons that may range from confusion caused by medication to coma following a major accident. When patients cannot make decisions about their medical care, others, such as family members and physicians, must take responsibility for these decisions. Often, it is difficult for them to know what the patient would want. Their deliberations in these complex situations are made easier when patients have previously expressed their wishes about their medical care, including the withholding or withdrawal of extraordinary life support.

The ability to prolong the lives of seriously ill patients by extraordinary technology raises numerous ethical questions. There have been attempts to resolve some of these issues by legislative, judicial and other means. One result has been the creation of documents to express one's wishes about medical treatment at a time when one is no longer able to make those decisions or communicate those wishes directly.

A California law effective January 1, 1985, created the *Durable Power of Attorney for Health Care*. The Durable Power of Attorney allows competent adults to name others as their "attorneys in fact." Those named are empowered to make almost all medical decisions if the person appointing them becomes incapable of doing so. This document is probably the most effective way of ensuring that a person's wishes are carried out. Two other documents are sometimes used. However, they have serious drawbacks that make them less effective than the Durable Power of Attorney:

*The Living Will states a person's desire to avoid extraordinary medical measures in the event of a terminal illness. Although the Living Will can guide the family and medical team, it is not legally binding in California. Families and physicians are under no legal obligation to honor it.

*The California Natural Death Act Directive provides that in certain limited circumstances, life-sustaining procedures may be withheld or withdrawn from a terminally ill patient. However, a number of impractical requirements must be met. The document cannot be signed until two weeks after two physicians have certified that the patient is terminally ill. If it is signed before this time, it is not legally enforceable. Because of these restrictions, the Directive is rarely useful in guiding decisions made by others on behalf of the patient.

You may have a copy of your completed Durable Power of Attorney placed in your medical record at Stanford University Hospital. Please call Medical Records, 723-6262, or Patient Relations, 723-7167, for instructions. For information or forms, please contact Community and Patient Relations, Room H-1352, or phone (415) 723-7167.

Source: Courtesy of Stanford University Medical Center, Stanford, CA.

chapter 15

AIDS—A New Risk Management Challenge

Barbara J. Youngberg

INTRODUCTION

Acquired immunodeficiency syndrome (AIDS) poses numerous threats and challenges for health care workers in the 1990s. It has been estimated that in 1989 there were between 1 million and 1.5 million persons infected with the human immunodeficiency virus (HIV) in the United States and that a majority of these persons will become seriously ill with HIV-related illnesses within eight to ten years after infection. The gravity of these statistics and the demands that caring for these patients will place on the health care system are enormous. Issues that evolve during the care of these patients mandate risk managers to consider methods of dealing with what already has become a crisis in many urban areas. Legal, ethical, and standard of care issues must be considered in identifying the risk management implications related to the "AIDS crisis."

As in many programs involving risk management, the first step in developing a program to address AIDS-related issues is to identify some of these issues. This chapter begins that process as well as provides more detailed information and assists the risk manager in developing specific risk modification programs in those areas.

Effective risk management response to the problems associated with AIDS must be based on an understanding of the disease itself. Although the disease is relatively new and there is significant knowledge yet to be learned, there is sufficient current information to assist in the development of policies and protocols. Critical to program and policy development is the goal of protecting health care workers, patients, and their families by preventing the transmission of the virus while also recognizing the legal and ethical considerations associated with this protection. Based on what is now known about the transmission of the disease, protection of others should not include the isolation or ostracism of the HIV-positive person, whether a patient or a health care worker.

POTENTIAL RISK MANAGEMENT ISSUES

Many complex issues are associated with the prevention of AIDS transmission. Four of these issues are discussed in the list below:

1. HIV testing.
   - Is testing of high-risk patients mandatory? If not, should it be?
   - Does the hospital or other health care setting have the right to perform routine testing of all patients or of patients believed to pose a threat of risk for health care workers?
   - Does the hospital or health care setting have the right to mandate testing of its employees who frequently perform invasive procedures? Does it have the right to mandate testing as a means of negating future workers' compensation claims by employees or former employees who allege the virus was contracted during the course of employment (with the test as part of the pre-employment screening process)?

- If testing is performed on a person (with or without consent), what issues, related to confidentiality must be addressed?
- Can state regulatory compliance supersede the patient's right to privacy?
- What type of educational program has the hospital developed to assist health care workers in providing information to persons being tested or persons receiving results of HIV positivity? (See sample consent forms, Appendixes 15-A and 15-B.)
- Can a hospital be held liable for battery if consent is not properly obtained? (Examples of proper consent are included as Appendixes 15-A and 15-B.)

2. Consequences of HIV positivity in a health care worker. What can or must a hospital do?
- Do antidiscrimination statutes of the state prevent the hospital from terminating an employee who tests positive for the HIV virus?
- Does the hospital have a duty to notify patients being cared for by the HIV-positive health care worker of his or her HIV status?
- Under the Vocational Rehabilitation Act, must the hospital or health care facility make reasonable accommodations to enable the HIV-positive health care worker to continue his or her employment?
- Is HIV-positive status of a health care worker sufficient grounds for limiting duties or privileges? Can direct patient contact be prohibited? Again, if an HIV-positive health care worker is allowed to care for patients, does the hospital or the employee have an obligation to inform the patient of the employee's HIV status?
- Does the patient's right to know supersede the health care worker's right to privacy?

3. Potential risk management issues related to HIV testing.
- What Centers for Disease Control (CDC) guidelines relate to testing? Do any professional organizations or state regulatory agencies have standards that differ from those promulgated by the CDC?
- What are some of the liability issues of concern to hospitals and health care facilities who are testing patients for the HIV virus?
  — improper test interpretation or mixup with another patient's test results
  — improper notification; for example, notifying family member of another's test result or providing incorrect information to a patient
  — failure to notify of test results
  — ailure to provide the appropriate and recommended counseling and support. Liability may be imposed in this case if the patient develops depression or commits suicide (see Exhib-

it 15-1, which describes appropriate aspects for counseling patients testing for HIV).

4. Potential risk management issues associated with reporting HIV test results to third parties.
- Does the hospital have a duty to protect third parties if it has knowledge they are at risk for exposure to HIV from a person who has tested positive? This type of duty might be imposed under logic, such as was presented in *Tarasoff v. Board of Regents of the University of California*, 551 P.2d 334 (Cal. 1976).
- Does the health care facility have a duty to report HIV positivity to the state health department or to the CDC?

PROVIDING CARE TO AIDS PATIENTS

Duty of the Hospital

A hospital has a responsibility to provide care for all members of the community and to not refuse care to any person presenting at the facility regardless of that person's ability to pay. The validity of this statement has been debated many times by hospitals faced with shrinking reimbursement and an increased number of patients unable to pay for care. They feel forced to identify a way to balance the services they offer and the clientele they serve.

AIDS often strikes the poor, the unemployed, and those without health care benefits. It is a disease with an enormous financial impact on the health care system, because cost of treatment is expensive and lengths of hospital stay are often long. Legal precedent and public policy stress the obligation of hospitals (especially those that have emergency departments) to accept all patients presenting for care. When a patient's condition has stabilized, the hospital may transfer the patient to an alternate facility. The hospital must be careful not to violate the "anti-dumping" statutes. These statutes require that the patient's condition be stabilized prior to transfer.

Duty of Health Care Workers

Case law suggests that physicians and nurses have a legal duty to provide care to AIDS patients who are admitted to their place of employment for treatment. Other professional standards and state laws mandate that health care workers not refuse to care for any patient.

Obviously, the refusal of health care workers to care for AIDS patients is often based on a lack of understanding of how the disease is transmitted or the fear that they may be exposed to the disease. For these reasons, the hospital or health care setting should have an educational program in

Exhibit 15-1
APPROPRIATE ASPECTS OF COUNSELING FOR HIV TESTING

It is widely agreed that all HIV testing should be accompanied by counseling. Pre-test and post-test counseling should be mandatory for all persons wishing to be tested and should focus on a number of different aspects. Counseling can help to allay the anxieties of individuals testing negative who may be confused about the virus, its transmissibility, and about the test itself. It can also greatly benefit those who test positive: providing them information that can prevent further transmission, help to maintain their own health to prevent serious and often life-threatening conditions, and provide psychological support or referrals to assist the HIV positive individual and family and friends with coping with a positive result.

Pre-test counseling should be provided to all persons requesting HIV testing and should include information in the following areas:

- Details about the test itself. This includes a description of the ELISA (enzyme-linked immunosorbent assay) test and the Western Blot test (currently the test used to confirm HIV positivity).
- Included in the description of the test should be a brief discussion of the incidence of "false positive" or equivocal results.
- The counselor should also make it known that the test is not an AIDS test—rather the test is a test for exposure to the HIV virus. A positive result does not necessarily mean that a person has AIDS or that he or she will ever develop AIDS.
- A description of AIDS, ARC (AIDS-related complex), and HIV infection.
- A description of the risk factors (and risk groups) that predispose a person to becoming exposed to the HIV virus.
- A list of the cofactors that may be important in determining the conditions under which exposure to the virus results in disease.
- The importance of informed consent and confidentiality related to HIV testing.
- A discussion of the potential social and psychological implications of testing.

Post-test counseling should include reinforcement of the information provided at the pre-test counseling session. This session should stress to the negative individual the behaviors that limit the likelihood of future exposure to the virus. The counselor should also stress the possible need for a retest in the event unsafe behavior was engaged in within three months prior to this test being done. If a person's test results are positive, additional counseling should be provided and should include the following:

- A description of the early clinical manifestations of HIV infection, AIDS, and the AIDS-related conditions. These persons should be advised to seek immediate medical attention if any of these symptoms occur.
- A brief description of the status of research related to HIV positivity and AIDS and a brief description of current treatment methodologies.
- The continued risk of infecting others through unprotected sexual intercourse or sharing of hypodermic needles.
- The fact that blood, plasma, body organs, other tissue, or sperm should not be donated.
- If children have been born to women since 1979 who have subsequently tested positive, they should be taken to a physician or clinic and evaluated.
- Women with positive HIV antibody test results should be advised that they have a high risk of transmitting HIV to their fetus or newborn child and that the child may develop AIDS or another HIV-related condition.
- The importance of informing their sexual contact(s) or needle-sharing partner(s) of the test results and the recommendation that they receive medical evaluation, counseling, and HIV antibody testing.
- The need to inform medical practitioners such as physicians and dentists of their HIV positive status.
- Precautions to take in the event they are injured and the injury results in bleeding (the current recommendation is to clean contaminated surfaces with a solution of household bleach that has been diluted to a 1:10 strength in water).
- Local resources that have programs for persons who are HIV positive, or who go on to develop ARC or AIDS. If resources are available for friends and families, these should also be described.

place that provides the necessary information to assist all health care workers in understanding how the disease is transmitted and how transmission can be avoided. The education program should consist of information related to the following:

- the most current guidelines published by the CDC regarding AIDS transmission

- description of the universal precautions that should be in force in all areas of the hospital or health care setting
- identification of other specialty-proposed guidelines and the determination if these are more appropriate for the health care setting
- an aggressive safety and infection control program that offers continual in-service education to staff about all new theories related to HIV transmission

- support of risk management in providing the hospital staff with information about the infrequency of HIV transmission to health care workers (if specific cases do suggest that transmission occurred, the staff should be provided with an appropriate analysis of the circumstances surrounding the transmission in an attempt to "tighten up" the hospital's program to decrease the likelihood of this type of transmission)

ETHICAL ISSUES

Risk management may be asked to become part of the hospital team that examines the ethical implications of caring for patients who have contracted an "incurable disease." Obviously, these types of issues are best raised in the framework of an interinstitutional ethics committee, but the risk manager should be prepared to present the types of ethical issues that have given rise to litigation in the past. An increasing number of patients are considering the possibility of living wills that are allowable in a number of states. The risk manager should be able to identify the hospital's position on this type of document. Obviously, this position must be made clear to the medical and nursing staff. (See Chapter 14 for additional information on this subject.)

DEVELOPING A POLICY FOR ADMINISTRATION OF ZIDOVUDINE TO HEALTH CARE WORKERS FOLLOWING OCCUPATIONAL HIV EXPOSURE

The issue of providing zidovudine (AZT) to health care workers following occupational exposure to the HIV virus has recently received considerable attention. Following a CDC position statement and confirmation by medical researchers of the possible benefits of early AZT administration, hospitals are now addressing (1) the appropriateness of making AZT available to health care workers and (2) policies and procedures required to govern and control its use.

Evaluating the Risk of Exposure

The risks of occupationally acquired HIV infection for most health care workers are minimal. Several studies place the chances of becoming infected from a needle that is known to be HIV-contaminated at less than 0.4 percent. The risk cannot be taken lightly, however, due to the lethal and contagious features of the HIV infection. In a recent study performed at the University of California at San Francisco, investigators determined that surgical teams face a risk ranging from one infection every 80 years in health care facilities where HIV infection is less than 3 percent of the total local population to one infection every 8 years at San Francisco General Hospital, whose patient population has a much higher incidence of infection.[1]

The CDC has identified 34 U.S. health care workers who have become infected after accidental exposure to the AIDS virus on the job—a number that many believe is deceptively small because of under-reporting. This low element of risk should not allow hospitals to ignore the potential problem and risk to their employees. Accidents and health care worker exposure will continue to occur at some rate, and hospitals must develop effective postexposure prophylactic regimens to address the actual and potential problems created by the exposure.

The Need for Education

The first step in limiting exposure of health care workers to HIV is education about the methods required to protect themselves from exposure. Certain guidelines have been developed by the CDC that establish universal precautions for health care workers to use in caring for all patients. By following these guidelines, health care workers minimize the risk of exposure to HIV and other infections. Staff education should include the information contained in the guidelines.

Hospital staff must also receive education about the AZT program itself. This should include

- the need for reporting occupational exposure to HIV immediately following exposure
- the person to contact in the event of a probable exposure to HIV
- entry criteria for the chemoprophylaxis program
- the risks of HIV infection associated with various types of occupational exposure
- information regarding counseling services available to health care workers exposed to HIV
- state-of-the-art information about the safety and efficacy of AZT and/or any other drugs available or being tested for the treatment of HIV infection
- legal issues associated with informed consent, particularly as they relate to confidentiality and disclosure (see Appendix 15-C)

Identifying the Health Care Worker at Risk

Hospitals have started to develop policies on establishing programs to minimize the risk of HIV infection to health care workers. Some have chosen a liberal approach of offering AZT to almost all workers in whom HIV transmission is even conceivable and paying for the total cost of

Exhibit 15-2
HIV EXPOSURES: DEFINITIONS AND ZIDOVUDINE ELIGIBILITY AND RISKS

DEFINITIONS

Massive parenteral exposure

- transfusion of blood
- injection of large volume of blood of body fluids (>1 ml)
- parenteral exposure to laboratory specimens containing high titer of virus

Definite parenteral exposure

- deep or intramuscular injury with a blood or body fluid–contaminated sharp
- laceration or similar wound produced by an instrument visibly contaminated with blood or body fluid that causes bleeding in a health care worker
- any inoculation with HIV or hepatitis B virus (usually in research settings)

Possible parenteral exposure

- subcutaneous injury with blood or body fluid–contaminated sharp
- wound produced by an instrument contaminated with blood or body fluid that does not cause visible bleeding
- prior wound or skin lesion contaminated with blood or body fluid
- mucous membrane inoculation with blood or body fluid

Doubtful parenteral exposure

- subcutaneous injury with nonbloody or body fluid–contaminated sharp
- superficial wound produced by nonbody fluid–contaminated instrument that does not cause visible bleeding
- prior wound or skin lesion contaminated with nonbloody body fluid
- mucous membrane inoculation with nonbloody fluid

Nonparenteral exposure

- intact skin visibly contaminated with blood or body fluid

Body fluids deemed potentially infectious for HIV

Blood products; bloody fluids; semen; cerebrospinal fluid; amniotic fluid; menstrual discharge; pleural, peritoneal, and pericardial fluid; inflammatory exudates; and any fluid or tissue contaminated with blood (other fluids are generally regarded as noninfectious).

EXPOSURES ELIGIBLE FOR ZIDOVUDINE

When defined exposures have been identified, the hospital must establish a policy as to who should receive zidovudine (AZT). Obviously, the positive and negative aspects of AZT treatment must be discussed with the health care worker who is considering the treatment. Sample parameters for administering AZT are listed below.

Massive parenteral exposure

AZT is definitely encouraged. Counseling services are also offered and encouraged.

Definite parenteral exposure

AZT is offered. Counseling services are also offered and encouraged.

Possible parenteral exposure

AZT is not routinely recommended but may be indicated for select cases. It is discussed with each exposed health care worker, and the treatment is then offered if the health care worker chooses it. Counseling services are also offered.

Doubtful parenteral exposure

AZT is never recommended but can be prescribed in select cases. The health care worker would be advised of the extremely small risk of infection associated with this type of exposure. Counseling services are offered.

Nonparenteral exposure

AZT is not prescribed. Counseling is offered.

EVALUATING THE RISKS OF TREATMENT

Health care workers must be given adequate information about proposed treatments in order to render proper informed consents. They should be advised that AZT is not currently indicated during pregnancy and should not be administered to pregnant females. The workers should also be informed about the possible teratogenicity of AZT. Information related to the safety of orally administered AZT comes primarily from animal studies and from studies of HIV-infected patients treated with AZT. In these studies, AZT has been reasonably well tolerated; however, some studies have demonstrated toxicities, particularly those evaluating AZT treatment of patients with AIDS. These toxicities usually have been hematologic and dose-related, but toxicities related to other organ systems have also been identified. Rarely, severe anemia, neutropenia, and thrombocytopenia occurred during the first four weeks of therapy. Additional adverse effects associated with AZT administration include headache, fatigue, myalgias, insomnia, nausea, myositis, paresthesias, and hepatitis.*

When the health care worker has been evaluated and treatment has started, periodic evaluations should be performed to determine his or her physical and psychological condition. A program that is responsive to all of the needs and concerns of health care workers may help to minimize the fear of occupational exposure to HIV.

Source: D.K. Henderson and J. Gerberding, "Prophylactic Zidovudine after Occupational Exposure to the Human Immunodeficiency Virus: An Interim Analysis," *Journal of Infectious Diseases* 160, no. 2 (August 1989): 323.

treatment. Many of these hospitals have considered changing their hiring policies to mandate that a Western Blot test and enzyme-linked immunosorbent assay (ELISA) become part of the pre-employment screening process. This minimizes the possibility that a health care worker would begin employment already infected and seek to receive AZT therapy at no cost. Obviously, state laws must be consulted when planning mandatory testing programs.

Other hospitals have taken a more systematic approach by evaluating both the type of contact and the likelihood of infection secondary to that contact. Based on this information, a decision is made related to the various treatment options.

Defining the Exposure

Since only a small minority of exposed persons seroconvert to HIV after needle-stick or mucous membrane exposure, prophylaxis should be judiciously targeted toward those at greatest risk. The health care worker who is perceived to be at greatest risk is the one suffering inadvertent injection of blood or gross contamination of an open or inflammatory skin lesion or mucous membrane. Deep needle stick with a hollow bore needle (e.g., needles used in phlebotomy or intravascular access) may also be considered.

Scratch or puncture wounds from a nonhollow needle or a needle used for intramuscular injection; a low-grade contamination of mucous membranes (for example, a light blood spattering on the face); and exposure to saliva, including bites by HIV-infected persons, are less hazardous and generally do not warrant prophylaxis. Exposure to nonsanguinous body fluids, including mucus, ascites, tears, cerebrospinal fluid, amniotic fluid, and feces, also does not generally require prophylaxis; the primary exception might be an injection injury with fluids known to contain white blood cells.

Such information as provided in Exhibit 15-2 should be placed on all hospital units and should be readily available in areas where potential exposure is greatest (e.g., operating room and emergency departments).

MANDATORY TESTING ISSUES: A CHALLENGE FOR HEALTH PROFESSIONALS

A Bill Aimed at Punishing HIV-Infected Providers

Many issues relate to HIV and AIDS in this country. Recent headlines announced that the U.S. Senate, bowing to the public's fear of AIDS, voted to impose a 10-year prison sentence on HIV-positive health care workers who perform high-risk procedures on their patients without informing the patients of the possible risks associated with the infection. In addition, many state legislatures and professional health organizations are debating about the appropriateness of mandating HIV testing for all health care workers and imposing limitations or restrictions on their practices should they test positive.

An 81–18 vote for the Senate bill came after discussion of the proposal drafted by Sen. Jesse Helms (R-N.C.). The bill cited the case of Kimberly Bergalis of Florida, who allegedly contracted AIDS from her HIV-infected dentist. The rhetoric, following the introduction of this proposal, relied heavily on perpetuating fear of the AIDS virus, rather than on promoting an understanding of methods of transmission and practicing safeguards required to minimize the risks. Although the bill later failed in the Senate-House negotiations, the Senate hearings surrounding its introduction should alert health care professionals of the crucial need to consider all issues associated with HIV and to develop comprehensive policies relating to the risk of transmission and infection in order to educate and protect both patients and providers. These policies must be sensitive to patients and providers and must be respectful of their rights. Similar punitive bills may be introduced again. Providers should position themselves now to respond to such proposals and to assist in the development of more appropriate alternatives.

A Compromise Bill

With a 99–0 vote, the Senate later passed a compromise bill that would require health care workers who perform risky procedures to be tested for HIV and to stop performing those procedures if they test positive. Disciplinary action under this bill would be left to state licensing boards.

Understanding the Controversy

The HIV controversy has been fueled by recent cases in which physicians have notified hospital administration of their HIV-positive status. As a result, hospitals have been required to address the many risk and quality issues associated with the potential for transmission of the virus from provider to patient. Lawsuits are already being filed by both patients and providers who are trying to substantiate actual or threatened injuries that such disclosures could cause.

Legislators must recognize the impact that punitive legislation could have on a provider's willingness to undergo testing or to advise the hospital administration of his or her HIV status. Thus, the punitive legislation may exacerbate the problem, rather than correct it.

HIV Testing and Disclosure

The numerous issues related to HIV testing and disclosure must be considered and understood prior to implementation of hospital policies or protocols to address these issues. Among the policies and procedures a hospital may require are the following:

- Patient notification procedures are required for notification of patients whose physician tests HIV positive and when a record search for potential HIV-positive patients indicates that transfused blood has been found to carry the virus. Drafting of a policy and procedure may include a sample notification letter (see Exhibit 15-3) and decisions as to whether notification is made in person, by mail, or by telephone. The most appropriate staff member to notify patients can also be addressed.

- Offers to test patients for HIV should be made if transmission of the virus could possibly have occurred. The cost of testing, the inclusion of specific counseling programs, and recommendation for or availability of retesting might be addressed in this policy (see Exhibit 15-1).

- Policies related to the administration of AZT to those testing positive should include both employees and patients exposed to the virus and those who test positive.

- Employment policies should govern the type of precautions to be observed and the type of limitations to be imposed on HIV-positive employees in order to minimize the risk of transmission of the virus. Pursuant to these guidelines, hospitals should ensure that HIV-positive caregivers do not perform "exposure-prone" procedures. These procedures should be identified by the medical staff and other representatives of the medical center (see Appendix 15-D for CDC recommendations).

Recent response to HIV positivity in health care workers has often resulted in poorly conceived policies that often seek to calm the hysteria, rather than to correct the problem.

Exhibit 15-3
SAMPLE PATIENT NOTIFICATION LETTER

Patient's Name
Address
City, State Zip

Dear (Insert Patient's full name)

You are receiving this letter because you were a patient at our hospital between (insert dates). One of the physicians who may have participated in your care at the hospital has since died of acquired immunodeficiency syndrome (AIDS). Although he did not have AIDS at the time he cared for you, he may have been carrying the virus that causes the disease.

At the time that this physician practiced at our hospital, we had no reason to believe that there was any risk of transmission of the human immunodeficiency virus (HIV) from health care worker to patient. Even now we are unsure as to what, if any, risk is possible regarding such transmission.

We do not believe that you were infected through any contact with this physician. However, because it was recently shown that a dentist may have transmitted the AIDS virus to several of his patients, we are notifying you of this physician's illness. Although the possibility that physicians can infect their patients is still considered to be remote by the best authorities in the country, the risk cannot be entirely ruled out.

We are offering free confidential counseling and testing to all patients who received care from this physician. We will also provide you with educational information about HIV and how the disease is transmitted.

We recommend that you call us at 555-5555 to set up a time for counseling and testing that is convenient for you. Out-of-town patients may call us collect or use our toll free number (800 555-1111). We have knowledgeable staff available to respond to your questions and to schedule your appointment for counseling and testing. All inquiries, counseling, and testing will be confidential.

Sincerely,

Hospital Administrator

Exhibit 15-4
SAMPLE MEMORANDUM FOR PUBLIC EDUCATION

FACT SHEET

During the past few months, the hospital has received many calls from current and former patients concerning possible exposure to the human immunodeficiency virus (HIV) from health care professionals who work within our facility. We feel it prudent to notify all of our customers through this memorandum of the known facts about transmission of HIV and to provide answers to the most frequently asked questions.

What Is AIDS and How Might I Become Infected?

AIDS stands for acquired immunodeficiency syndrome, a viral disease in which the body's immune system weakens. A healthy immune system fights off infections and certain other disease. When a person contracts AIDS, he or she develops a variety of life-threatening illnesses. HIV is the virus that causes AIDS. A simple blood test can detect exposure to HIV.

Why All of the Attention Now about HIV Infection and Doctors?

Recent newspaper articles have reported that a young woman in Florida contracted HIV after being exposed to it through her dentist. News about this exposure has led to a public response based on fear, rather than factual information. We are now attempting to correct any misinformation.

The Dentist Was Diagnosed with HIV in 1987 and Died in 1989. Why Were Patients Not Notified Earlier?

Until it was learned that the dentist had AIDS, no health care worker has ever been known to infect a patient with HIV, so it was believed that patients did not need to be notified of the possibility. The information about this case in which an HIV-infected dentist appears to have transmitted the virus to at least one of his patients has prompted us to notify our patients about the facts concerning HIV transmission.

How Did the Hospital Select Patients To Be Notified?

The hospital has searched its records in an attempt to identify patients who *possibly* may have been exposed to the virus. If you are concerned about possible exposure and if you have not received a notification letter from us, you may call and provide us with your name and dates of hospitalization. We will then review your records.

What Are the Chances That a Patient Will Contract AIDS from His or Her Physician?

No one has ever shown that a surgeon with AIDS has infected his or her patient. We believe the chances of your being infected are close to zero.

Who Will Pay for My Medical Expenses Should the Test Prove That I Contracted the AIDS Virus from My Physician?

Initial testing for the presence of HIV is provided by the hospital at no charge. If additional testing or more specific genotyping is necessary, that cost also will be borne by the hospital. The administration of zidovudine (AZT) and other drugs that are commonly used to strengthen the body's immune system or to fight the AIDS virus will be considered on a case-by-case basis. When the administration of specific drugs or treatments is deemed appropriate, the hospital will assume the cost.

If a Person Tests Negative Now, Does the Test Completely Rule Out Infection from a Particular Physician?

An HIV test will generally register positive 4 to 6 weeks following exposure to HIV. Many physicians believe, and research suggests, that a person will take no longer than 6 months to test positive following exposure. If your potential exposure to the virus was more than 6 months ago and you now test negative, chances are very likely that you will remain negative unless you are subsequently exposed to the virus.

continues

Exhibit 15-4 continued

Is There Any Way To Find Out Who May Have Been Exposed to the Virus and Who Has Been Tested?

No. All such information is held in the strictest confidence. Similarly, any information regarding your possible exposure, testing, and results of the test will remain confidential.

What Is the Hospital's Policy Regarding the HIV-Infected Health Care Worker?

At this hospital, we believe that persons who are infected should notify the hospital administration of their HIV positivity. We adhere to the guidelines of the Centers for Disease Control (CDC) and the recommendations of the American Medical Association, which state that persons who are HIV positive should not engage in "exposure-prone" procedures. Further, we educate all of our staff members on the importance of protecting their patients and themselves from possible transmission of HIV and other viruses through the wearing of gloves and other appropriate barriers—also in compliance with CDC recommendations. We will continue our efforts to provide education to patients and hospital staff regarding ways to minimize and hopefully eliminate the spread of this virus.

Offering the public the panacea of mandatory provider testing and the imposition of jail terms for HIV-positive health care professioals who continue to practice can cause more problems than cures.

If the public is led to believe that a document hanging on a physician's wall that announces his or her negative HIV status negates any potential risk, it must be advised that a person's HIV status can change. A negative result today does not guarantee a negative result tomorrow. If the most vocal advocates for mandatory testing would understand that monthly, annual, or other incremental testing of a provider does not guarantee the patient's freedom from risk of HIV exposure, perhaps they would recognize that, over the long term, education is a more effective method of minimizing transmission.

Further, the type of law proposed by Senator Helms would stipulate that persons who perform invasive procedures with knowledge of their HIV positivity can be subject to imprisonment. Might some providers elect not to have the test performed so that they have no such knowledge?

Politicians and health care providers often seek the easy way out of these tough issues. The public has a right to be concerned about AIDS, given the lethality of the disease and the growing number of infected Americans who are transmitting the virus to others. The imposition of vigilante techniques, however, rather than the education of patients and providers about the mechanisms for transmission, seems a far inferior method of handling this burgeoning health care crisis.

Clinicians, risk managers, quality administrators, and health care attorneys must recognize that the challenge of the complex issues associated with HIV transmission first requires understanding and education. The development of a program should begin with the education of providers and patients. The program should stress the continued importance of wearing gloves for all invasive procedures, proper sterilization of instruments, and advice to patients of the right to challenge practitioners who are not adhering to these standards (see Exhibit 15-4 for a sample education memorandum).

Professionals who are involved in the issues associated with controlling HIV transmission should begin their work by consulting with CDC and the many professional organizations that have drafted policy statements or guidelines. Such documents can provide a framework for addressing specific situations (see Appendixes 15-D and 15-E).

NEW POLICIES FOR HIV INFECTION/AIDS*

The American Hospital Association (AHA) recently revised its recommendations on AIDS and HIV infection to reflect what has transpired since it formulated its initial policy in 1988. Topics covered in the new regulations include issues related to patient testing and issues associated with infected health care workers.

In relation to issues surrounding look-back programs, the AHA recommends against *routine* retrospective notification of patients who have been treated by an infected health care worker. The AHA believes that rather than alarming patients unnecessarily the hospital should carefully evaluate each patient situation in an attempt to determine whether or not there was a heightened risk of transmission or if the patient did have the type of contact with the caregiver where transmission could have occurred. Contrary to the position advanced by the Centers for Disease Control (CDC), the AHA does not advise HIV-infected practitioners to disclose their HIV status to their patients.

---

*Source: *Quality & Risk Management in Health Care*, No. 11, March 1992, © Aspen Publishers, Inc.

In addition, in the area of health care providers it is recommended that the hospital do more to ensure that universal precautions are followed by all providers and that the hospital develop strict enforcement procedures related to universal precautions.

On the subject of patient testing, the AHA now urges hospitals to incorporate in the standard procedure for taking a patient's medical history a risk evaluation that would help to identify those persons who might be at high risk for HIV. It is then recommended that voluntary HIV testing should be offered to those persons who admit to one or more risk factors. In those hospitals where there is a high HIV seroprevalence, practitioners may wish to routinely offer testing and educational information, and encourage patients to be voluntarily tested unless they are part of the population deemed to be low risk.

The recommendations cited in this new report seem to focus more on the proactive approach for handling HIV/AIDS-related issues. In part they were drafted in response to changes that have occurred in the legislative arena and to the better information that is now available concerning the transmission of the virus. New policies and recommendations such as those developed by the AHA should be reviewed as hospitals seek to ensure that their own policies and procedures reflect current thinking, legislative changes, and legal climate.

CONCLUSION

Like many other risk management efforts, the initial focus of a risk management program based on potential AIDS-related exposure lies in the education of health care workers. Fears and anxieties surrounding the potential transmission of the AIDS virus often can be allayed through appropriate education. However, even when this hurdle has been overcome, many risk management challenges remain.

NOTE

1. S. Taravella, Researchers Urge AZT Programs for Hospital Workers, *Modern Healthcare* 20, no. 27 (July 9, 1990): 34.

Appendix 15-A

Sample Patient Consent Form

I hereby authorize Dr._____
to order the performance of blood tests to determine the presence of antibodies to the human immunodeficiency virus (HIV) in my blood or the presence of HIV viral antigen. I understand that infection with HIV may produce no symptoms, may be associated with mild illness, or may sometimes progress to the acquired immunodeficiency syndrome (AIDS).

I have discussed with my doctor the reason for performance of these tests. I understand that false-positive and false-negative test results can occur. That is, a positive test result may not necessarily accurately predict the presence of HIV infection and, conversely, that HIV infection can still be present even if some or all test results are negative.

I understand that the results of these tests, whether positive or negative, will become a permanent part of my hospital or outpatient medical record. I understand that information in my medical record can be obtained by my health insurance carrier, if I have one, by any person or entity to whom I give written permission for access to my medical record and, under certain circumstances, by subpoena or by court order.

I certify that I have read and fully understand the above consent statement which has been preceded by an explanation by my doctor and was understood by me.

_____

Signature of Patient (or person authorized to consent for patient and relationship of such person)

_____

Signature of Witness

_____   _____

Attending Physician Signature   Date

Appendix 15-B

Recommended Consent Form for HIV Antibody Testing

The human immunodeficiency virus (HIV) has been recognized by most experts to be closely associated with acquired immunodeficiency syndrome (AIDS).

Tests are now available to determine the presence of antibodies to HIV in the blood. Antibodies are substances made by the body to fight infection. After the virus gets into the body, it takes time to produce antibodies. A person may be infected with the virus, but more time may be needed for the body to make antibodies. For this reason, the antibody test result may show that a person is "negative" (does not have antibody), but actually that person may carry the virus in his or her body or body fluids.

A positive HIV antibody test indicates a previous exposure to the virus and the body's immune response to it. A positive antibody test does not mean a person has AIDS or will necessarily come down with AIDS.

If your HIV antibody test results are known, it may help your doctor decide how best to treat you for some illnesses or exposures such as tuberculosis. It may also help you to make personal decisions if you know that you are at risk of getting the virus or giving it to someone else.

If your blood test is positive and the test result is known by others, they may think you have AIDS. This may not be true, but you might be discriminated against by friends, family, employers, landlords, insurance companies, and others. Therefore, you should be extremely careful in disclosing your test results. Your state or municipal division of human rights may be available to investigate and prosecute instances of illegal discrimination against HIV-infected persons.

Your state has laws and regulations that protect the confidentiality of medical records and laboratory test results. Nevertheless, as with any sensitive information, there is the potential for unauthorized disclosure or release of the information. Should this occur, contact the department of health for assistance.

I have read (or have had read to me) the above description of the HIV antibody test and understand the limitations and possible consequences of this test. I also have had explained to me the blood drawing procedures and the risks, if any. I agree to testing for HIV antibodies.

Signature of patient (or person legally authorized to consent on patient's behalf and relationship)   Date

160

HUMAN IMMUNODEFICIENCY VIRUS TEST RESULTS

The HIV antibody test result on this sample was:
    (   ) Nonreactive by EIA procedure
    (   ) Reactive by EIA procedure
EIA test value for this sample: _____ O.D. Units
Minimum cutoff for reactive samples: _____ O.D. Units

Western Bolt result was:
    (   ) Separate report   (   ) Nonreactive
    (   ) Reactive   (   ) Indeterminate

The HIV antigen test result was:
    (   ) Nonreactive by EIA procedure
    (   ) Reactive by EIA procedure
EIA test value for this sample: _____ O.D. Units
Minimum cutoff for reactive samples: _____ O.D. Units

Note: The natural history of HIV antigenemia and antibody development is not completely known. Also, in any immunological test, false-positive and false-negative reactions can occur. If your patient is reactive in the HIV antibody or antigen EIA test, there should be a retest using a second fasting blood sample. If the repeat antibody test is reactive, a Western Blot test should be ordered. To save time, you can order the HIV antibody EIA test and a Western Blot test at the same time, with instructions to only do the Western Blot test if the EIA test for antibody is reactive.

Sample Consent Form for Prophylactic Zidovudine Following HIV Exposure

You are being offered a treatment that in recent medical studies has been shown to reduce the symptoms of human immunodeficiency virus (HIV) infection and possibly to prevent (or delay) acquisition of HIV following a possibly hazardous exposure. It is important to understand that the efficacy of zidovudine (AZT) therapy in preventing infection from this virus is unknown at this time (although multiple studies have demonstrated encouraging results). AZT is not approved for this usage by the Food and Drug Administration (FDA); therefore, the final decision to take the drug in this "experimental" capacity rests with you. We hope the information that we have provided will assist you in making a truly informed decision.

AZT has been chosen for this purpose because it is a readily available drug that inhibits the reproduction of the acquired immunodeficiency syndrome (AIDS) virus. When administered early, it has prevented infection in animals exposed to a virus that is similar in some respects to HIV. The first dose of AZT should be taken within the first four hours following exposure, although some studies have suggested that prophylaxis may begin as late as four days following exposure.

Multiple studies related to the risk of infection following occupational exposure have been performed. These studies suggest that there is a relatively low risk of becoming infected with HIV; however, this risk increases when major exposures occur.

The toxicity of AZT may be significant. Cancer-causing activity has been shown with lifelong administration to rodents, although it did not appear to be a very potent carcinogen. The cancer-causing potential in humans is unknown at this time. Clearly, the most important side effect is the suppression of white and red blood cells that could put you at risk for infection or anemia. We will monitor you for evidence of this adverse condition while you are receiving AZT and we may be forced to terminate your treatment if it occurs. Other possible side effects are nausea, vomiting, headache, insomnia, and muscle aches or muscle weakness. Less common side effects include diarrhea, fever, rash, agitation, confusion, and altered liver function. Any changes noted in your health while you are on this drug should be reported to your physician. They may result in a revised treatment plan.

AZT should not be taken if you are pregnant. The likelihood of injury to the fetus is not known, but it remains a significant concern. If you elect to begin treatment with AZT, a diaphragm or condom with spermicide should be used to prevent pregnancy and to prevent possible transmission of the infection to a sexual partner. Since the possibility of your acquiring the infection is sufficient to warrant your treatment, you should make serious efforts to prevent its potential transmission to other persons.

We ask that you give permission for an HIV antibody test before beginning therapy and 3, 6, and 12 months after therapy starts. We will use all reasonable efforts to maintain the confidentiality of the results of these tests. As medical record information, this test will be regarded as confidential and will not be disclosed to unauthorized third parties without your consent. We ask further that you recognize that any waiver of the privilege of confidentiality and privacy that you may sign or will sign for insurance benefits or third-party payment of your care means that the result of your test may be disclosed to third-party payers and insurance companies.

We ask that you further consent to other blood and urine tests throughout the course of treatment that may be necessary to monitor your body's response to treatment. All possible tests and the results of those tests will be explained to you in detail by your physician.

The dosage of AZT is 200 mg every four hours around the clock. The drug may be taken with water. We ask that you call your physician immediately if you feel you are experiencing any adverse reaction to the drug. If your physician is unavailable, we ask that you call the physician in the emergency department of this hospital for advice.

I have read the above and have had all of my questions related to the above material explained to me. My signature indicates that I wish to take AZT under professional guidance and agree to cooperate with my physician regarding appropriate follow-up tests.

Patient signature _____

Name of treating physician _____

Witness signature _____

Date _____

Appendix 15-D

Statement of the American Medical Association
on HIV-Infected Physicians

FOR IMMEDIATE RELEASE   January 17, 1991

AMA STATEMENT ON HIV-INFECTED PHYSICIANS

Physicians who are HIV positive have an ethical obligation not to engage in any professional activity which has an identifiable risk of transmission of the infection to the patient. Many patients have been treated by HIV-infected physicians and there have been no documented cases of transmission from physician to patient.

However, the recent cases of possible dentist-to-patient transmission have caused some uncertainty about the risk of transmission from physicians to patients under certain circumstances. In cases of uncertainty about the risks to patient health, the medical profession, as a matter of medical ethics, should err on the side of protecting patients.

The health of patients must always be the paramount concern of physicians. Consequently, until the uncertainty about transmission is resolved, the American Medical Association believes that HIV-infected physicians should either abstain from performing invasive procedures which pose an identifiable risk of transmission or disclose their seropositive status prior to performing a procedure and proceed only if there is informed consent.

As a corollary, physicians who are at risk of acquiring HIV infection, and who perform invasive procedures, should determine their HIV status.

Some invasive procedures pose no identifiable risk of transmission, e.g., a bronchoscopy. Others, such as surgical procedures, cannot, with the same conclusiveness, be said at this time to pose no identifiable risk of transmission given the current analysis of the Centers for Disease Control regarding three patients of a Florida dentist.

The American Medical Association further believes that physicians who are HIV positive and who must restrict their normal professional activities have a right to continue their career in medicine in a capacity that poses no identifiable risk to their patients. The American Medical Association pledges its support and protection of these physicians and believes the profession and the public have a need and an obligation to ensure that they continue to be productive as long as they practice medicine safely and responsibly.

Source: Courtesy of the American Medical Association, Department of Public Information, Chicago, IL.

Statement of the American Medical Association to the Centers for Disease Control Regarding HIV Transmission during Invasive Procedures

My name is Nancy W. Dickey, M.D. I am a family physician practicing in Richmond, Texas and I am a member of the American Medical Association's Board of Trustees. With me is M. Roy Schwarz, M.D., the AMA's Senior Vice President for Medical Education and Science. We appreciate this opportunity to comment on the Centers for Disease Control (CDC) risk assessment data on HIV-infected health care workers and to offer the AMA's assessment of these risks.

The AMA appreciates how difficult it is at present to estimate the risk of infection to patients by HIV- and HBV-infected health care workers. Unfortunately, there are enough data to alert us that transmission of HIV from an infected health care worker has occurred, but not enough data to describe with confidence how extensive the problem is.

BASIC PRINCIPLES

The problem of the HIV-infected physician is a difficult one. There are no perfect solutions. However, the AMA believes certain basic principles should guide the CDC and the medical profession.

First, a physician who has a transmissible and fatal disease should not place his or her patients at risk. That has been the view of the AMA's Council on Ethical and Judicial Affairs, which maintains the Code of Ethics that is generally regarded as the medical profession's code, for a long time.

It has also long been the view of AMA's Ethics Council—confirmed by common sense and now by the CDC's recent report regarding the Florida dentist who appears to have infected three patients—that the risk of transmission from an HIV-infected physician during certain invasive procedures is very low but real. So some restraint on invasive procedures is necessary as a matter of the oldest precept of medical ethics—that *the physician shall do no harm.*

This is not a new or reactive position of the profession, and it is really the only acceptable position. Attached is the Ethics Council's opinion on the issue dated December 1987. Moreover, taking this position we are acutely aware of the rights—as well as the duties—of physicians and other health care workers infected with AIDS.

Some four years ago the American Medical Association challenged the view of the Department of Justice that the Rehabilitation Act did not protect people with AIDS from irrational discrimination. The AMA filed a brief *amicus curiae* in the Supreme Court in the landmark case *School Board of Nassau County v. Arline*, 480 U.S. 273 (1987), arguing that persons with infectious diseases, including AIDS, were "handicapped" within the meaning of the Rehabilitation Act, and we offered a four-part analysis for determining when such individuals were fully protected under the Act. The Supreme Court disagreed with the Justice Department and said "we agree with amicus the American Medical Association" and then quoted the key test as presented in our brief (480 U.S. 273, at 288). AMA then filed medical/legal briefs supporting the rights of persons with AIDS to be free from arbitrary discrimination in the leading cases in the courts at the time, including *Ray v. School District of DeSoto County*, 666 F. Supp. 1524 (M.D. Fla. 1987) and *Chalk (Doe) v. Orange County Department of Education* (9th Cir. 1987).

Secondly, the chief complication of this position cited by certain groups involves a policy that *the AMA opposes—mandatory testing of physicians.* When the very low probability of a surgeon acquiring AIDS from an infected patient is multiplied by the even lower probability that the same physician would then transmit the infection to patients, the risk to patients of becoming infected is virtually immeasurable, much lower than the risk that an *already* infected surgeon would transmit the disease.

Physicians who are at some measurable risk of acquiring AIDS—because they do significant invasive procedures on many HIV-infected patients or for other well-known reasons—do have an obligation to determine their seropositive status—to protect their loved ones as well as their pa-

Source: Statement presented by Nancy W. Dickey, M.D., February 21, 1991. Courtesy of the American Medical Association, Department of Public Information, Chicago, IL.

tients—but this is by no means all surgeons or all physicians who do any invasive procedures.

Physicians who are HIV positive have an ethical obligation to avoid any professional activity which has an identifiable risk of transmission of the infection to a patient. Or, they may proceed with the patient's informed consent. We believe that AMA's longstanding policy continues to be the best for physicians and patients. It will work because it reflects a fundamental tenet of professional ethics by which the vast majority of physicians abide. Indeed, many infected physicians have voluntarily restricted their practices. It will work because the liability risk to physicians and the improved treatment techniques for HIV infection will cause those at significant risk to be tested and seek help. It will work because AMA pledges to stand by and help the small number of physicians whose practices must be restricted.

Even if the policy is not universally effective, it is better than any of the alternatives. And patients are certainly better off knowing that the profession has publicly reaffirmed that their interests will always come first.

CDC RISK MODEL

You have asked also for our comments on the CDC's risk model. The CDC's attempt to assess the risk and calculate the number of patients infected by physicians is based on a series of assumptions as the CDC correctly concedes. Although these assumptions are well-reasoned, different but equally reasonable assumptions would have a significant effect on the CDC estimates and alter the risk estimates for patients.

For example, the CDC's risk model is based on an infected health care worker receiving a needlestick during an invasive procedure and the contaminated needle coming into contact with the patient's wound. The model does not take into account other mechanisms of patient exposure such as bleeding into a patient's wound, skin and mucous membrane exposure, or contaminated instruments.

Another factor limiting the accuracy of the CDC's estimates is the uncertainty over how many surgeons and dental workers are HIV positive. The CDC's method for estimating the number of surgeons with HIV infection relies on other imprecise estimates such as the number of people in the U.S. infected with HIV. This multiplies the chance of error.

Other limitations of the risk model and the estimates are spelled out in the CDC's draft document. Therefore, it would be appropriate for the CDC to conclude that at this time it is not possible to calculate an accurate estimate of the risk of transmission of HIV from health care worker to patient.

Let me again emphasize that the Association's policy is based on the principle of medical ethics that the health of patients must always be the paramount concern of physicians. Therefore, because of the uncertainty about the risks to patient health, physicians should err on the side of protecting patients.

In reaffirming this policy, the AMA gave thoughtful consideration to the consequences or "ripple effects" of our position. For example, some say that our policy will lead to mandatory HIV testing for those who perform invasive procedures or that, because of the economic consequences, fewer physicians will be willing to risk infection by performing invasive procedures on HIV-positive patients. We strongly disagree. Mandatory HIV testing for health care workers would be no more successful or cost-effective than mandatory testing for marriage license applicants. Two states tried mandatory testing for marriage license applicants but the low incidence of HIV infection in this population led to repeal in both states. In addition, testing of health care workers would need to be done periodically and even then there would be infected health care workers who would test negative because they had not yet seroconverted.

We also reject the suggestion that surgeons would violate our ethical obligation to treat HIV-infected patients out of fear of the economic consequences of becoming infected. Physicians treating HIV-infected patients have already accepted the small but real risk of life-threatening health consequences and will not be deterred by economic consequences to their medical practice.

AMA/YALE TASK FORCE

We know there are no easy answers for HIV-infected physicians. We would like, however, to reassure HIV-positive physicians that the AMA's pledge of support is serious and not limited to AMA members. We have organized a Task Force on Personal and Educational Needs of HIV-Infected Physicians. Working with a group at Yale, this Task Force will address current resources available, new resources needed, specific projects appropriate for the AMA, and potential roles for organized medicine and others.

We have focused these comments on HIV and not HBV. This is because the risk of transmission of HBV between surgeon and patient has been identified for some time. Existing CDC guidelines already call for exclusion of HBV-infected health care workers under certain circumstances. Aggressive efforts by the AMA and other health organizations toward the vaccination of health care workers against HBV can eliminate the problem of HBV transmission to patients in the future. In the meantime, hepatitis B immune globulin is available to treat those exposed to HBV. On the other hand, there is no comparable vaccine or treatment for HIV, so we believe that the number of HIV-infected individuals and health care workers will grow and the risk of transmission will remain.

CONCLUSION

The AMA commends the CDC for drafting a carefully considered model for calculating the risk of HIV transmission to patients during invasive procedures. Unfortunately, the AMA finds that there is simply insufficient data to allow this model to yield useful estimates. This being the case, we recommend that the CDC acknowledge the limits of current knowledge and emphasize patient protection as the foremost consideration of CDC guidelines.

chapter 16

A Basic Insurance Primer

Vickey Masta-Gornic

INTRODUCTION

Insurance procurement at one time was the primary function of the industrial risk manager. With the development and increasing popularity of the risk management process today utilized by hospital risk managers this function has come to be known as the last step in the risk management process. When should insurance be purchased? What type of risk is amenable to insurance? How much insurance should be purchased? Should an organization self-insure, form or join a risk-retention group, start a captive insurance company?

UNDERSTANDING RISK

In order to answer the above questions, first it is necessary to understand the definition of risk. Textbooks define risk in various ways. One definition is that pure risk involves only financial loss, for example, the risk of fire. Should this risk not occur there would be no effect on the institution. However, if the risk does occur the institution incurs a financial loss. Another textbook defines risk as the possibility that loss will occur. Loss is categorized as being either sudden and accidental or an occurrence that is neither intended nor expected. A blending of these definitions provides all of the information an organization needs to decide what type of risk to retain and what type of risk to transfer.

Measuring Risk

Measurement of the institution's risk also assists in making a decision about risk transfer versus risk retention. Risk can be measured by analyzing the frequency and severity of losses and operations.

Frequency of Risk

In analyzing the frequency of risk or the probability that an event might occur, start with the losses. Does the institution have several small-dollar losses in a particular category, for example, patient falls? The nature of the health care business may result in patients falling out of bed. This example may reflect the operational risk that patients will fall out of bed but most likely will not be seriously injured. These are classified as high-frequency, low-severity occurrences.

Occasionally, a patient will fall out of bed and sustain a fracture. This is an example of a high-frequency event that has a high-severity consequence.

Severity of Risk

The second step in the analysis is to look at the severity of losses and at the severity risk of operations. Most institutions experience a low-frequency, high-severity loss occasionally. An example is a patient who suffers a catastrophic outcome such as brain damage.

An institution with a high-frequency/high-severity trend of losses will find that it is almost impossible to transfer its risk. Insurance carriers analyze frequency and severity of losses in order to determine whether or not to accept a risk.

Dealing with Risk

After the loss and operation analysis has been completed, the institution must decide how to deal with the risk. It has four primary options:

1. Risk may be *eliminated* by no longer offering a particular service.
2. Risk may be *avoided* by providing education to alter practices within the institution.
3. Risk may be *retained* because the analysis indicates low-frequency/low-severity types of losses (for example, lost patient dentures).
4. Risk may be *transferred*, such as fire insurance on the facility. The probability of a facility being damaged through fire is quite low; however, the cost of repairs following a fire is likely to be more of a financial burden than the institution could handle.

Risks that are avoided or eliminated are dealt with first in the risk management process. This chapter is concerned with the risks that are transferred or retained.

The institution must determine its insurance, or transfer, options. What is the definition of insurance? The *Handbook of Health Care Risk Management*[1] defines insurance as "a mechanism permitting the individual to substitute the certainty of a small defined loss (the insurance premium) for the risk of a large gratuitous loss that is predictable neither as to size or as to the time of occurrence." In other words, it may be better for the organization to pay a small premium of a known amount rather than to have an unexpected financial loss in the middle of a fiscal year that has been neither predicted nor budgeted. It is important to remember, however, that a health care organization always pays for its losses. In the definition of insurance, note that premiums are defined as a loss. Should the organization have a large loss or many small losses, the insurance company will recover those dollars paid out through increases in premiums during future years.

TYPES OF INSURANCE

Property Insurance

Property insurance provides protection to an organization in case of damage to the insured buildings or an interruption in services that results in loss of revenue. Commonly referred to as fire insurance, property coverage can be written in one of two ways. The first is a named peril coverage that provides payments for loss where there are specific events such as fire, windstorm, sprinkler leakage, explosion, hail, or lightning. It provides coverage for the building structure as well as the contents. The second type of coverage is a comprehensive all-risk policy. It converts the standard named peril policy to include coverage for any event unless it is specifically excluded from the policy. This is completely opposite of the way most insurance contracts are written.

A comprehensive all-risk policy can also cover other business operation risks in addition to the value of the actual buildings and their contents. These coverages are added by endorsements to the basic policy and may include sub-limits where appropriate. Endorsements may include the following:

- *Business interruption* insurance provides coverage for any loss of revenue experienced by an institution following a loss, for example, damage to computerized tomography (CT) scanning equipment that results in closing the CT unit for a long period of time. Any revenues lost as a result of the closure would be covered under the business interruption section of the comprehensive all-risk policy.
- *Extra expenses* coverage reimburses the institution for expenses incurred in either attempting to minimize damages or in reducing the length of time it takes to make the operation whole again. This could include, for example, shipping replacement equipment by air. The additional cost for air freight would be reimbursed as an extraordinary expense under this section of the policy.
- *Boiler and machinery* provides coverage for the pressure vessels and boilers within the institution. Included in this coverage are air conditioning and refrigeration units housed within the institution, as well as extra expense and business interruption coverage if failure of a unit creates an interruption in services at the institution.
- *Differences in conditions* acknowledges that certain geographical conditions may produce a loss. Examples of coverage provided under this endorsement are earthquake and flood insurance. Generally, they carry significant deductibles and lower limits or sub-limits of liability.
- *Electronic data processing* (EDP) insurance provides coverage for computer equipment housed in the institution and includes risks such as exposure to fire, lightning, windstorm, and other named perils. It also provides coverage for EDP storage media. Extra expense and business interruption insurance also can be purchased in conjunction with EDP coverage.

There are many benefits associated with combining coverages in a comprehensive all-risk policy. They include:

- a reduction in premium due to economies of scale
- better management by both the insured and the insurer because all insurance information is in one policy
- more efficiency in budget preparation and estimation of any premium increases with one policy
- more effective administration of insurance program

Liability Insurance

Liability insurance provides coverage for any obligation of the insured to pay money to a third party as a result of negligence of the insured or an employee or agent acting on behalf of the named insured. Examples include professional liability, comprehensive general liability, directors' and officers' liability, automobile liability, or any other liability coverage that indemnifies a third party.

It is important to understand what triggers coverage under a liability policy. There are two types of liability insurance coverages in use today: occurrence policies and claims-made policies.

An occurrence policy provides coverage to an insured from the inception date of the policy. All incidents that occur during the policy period are covered under this policy regardless of when claims are asserted. For example, the statute of limitations on infants may not expire for 21 years. Very few organizations maintain an insurance policy for 21 years; however, if a claim is asserted within that period, that claim will be covered under the occurrence policy that was in force when the loss occurred.

The advantage of occurrence-based coverage is that insurance is always available for a premium that was paid, even though the premium period was many years ago. Disadvantages relate to policy limits eroded by inflation or time factors with the result that available funds are insufficient to cover a loss that occurred 10 or 20 years ago.

A claims-made policy covers events from the policy inception date to the policy termination date. In order for an event to be covered, the claim must be reported during the time that the policy is in effect. For example, a claim that occurred in 1975 but was not reported until 1985 would not be covered under a claims-made policy in effect in 1975. Claims-made coverage may be modified, however, through the purchase of a reporting endorsement that extends the amount of time an insured has to report a claim. This is commonly known as "tail" coverage.

There may be a cash flow advantage to the insured with claims-made coverage, because insurance carriers recognize that a liability claim generally is not paid until several years after the incident. Carriers allow for this eventuality in the premiums they charge. For professional liability policies, generally up to a 60 percent reduction in premium is offered in the first year, a 40 percent discount in the second year, and 20 percent in the third.

By reviewing claims-made coverage there is no need to purchase a tail. However, claims will be covered under the policy year in which they are reported. It is important to remember that no claim will be covered that occurred before the retroactive date on the policy. The retroactive date is normally the original policy inception date, but it may be negotiated with the insurance carrier.

Claims-made coverage has two primary advantages: (1) the cash flow advantage, which is especially helpful to physicians or other professionals who are starting out in practice; and (2) the coverage of claims in the policy year in which they are reported with no inflationary effect on the limits. There are several possible disadvantages: (1) a gap in coverage if an extended reporting endorsement (tail) is not purchased or cannot be purchased; (2) the price of the tail coverage; and (3) after termination of a policy, the insurer's lack of incentive to offer coverage at a reasonable price.

It is advisable to check the insurance contract for endorsements that specify the tail premium calculation and offer waivers for insureds who become disabled or who retire. It is also important for a hospital to have an endorsement or letters of intent between the insured and the carrier so that it does not have to purchase a tail for every covered physician who terminates employment with the health care organization.

Professional Liability

The most well-known type of liability insurance within health care institutions is professional liability coverage. Also known as medical malpractice insurance, it covers the rendering or failure to render professional services. Professional liability coverage is necessary for physicians, nurses, technicians, and all other allied professional hospital staff.

Comprehensive General Liability

Comprehensive general liability coverage provides insurance for risks arising out of the public use of the institution's property. An example of a loss in this category is a visitor who slips and falls in the hospital corridor and goes to the emergency room for treatment.

Other areas of the institution protected under the general liability policy include the hospital gift and coffee shops and any contractual relationship the institution may have where it assumes the liability of others.

Comprehensive general liability also includes the following coverages:

- advertisers' liability
- host liquor liability
- invasion of privacy
- personal injury coverages, such as libel and slander
- products liability

Directors' and Officers' Liability

This type of insurance provides coverage for the board of directors and officers of the health care organization. The policy covers any claims resulting from activities of the board, such as the following:

- approval of medical staff appointments
- day-to-day decisions made by the board
- development of standards of care within the organization
- the board's mission to act in the best interests of the institution and the community

Although many states have enacted legislation to protect governing boards of not-for-profit organizations, directors' and officers' insurance is still important because a board may be sued for an event that is not addressed in the legislation, or, more frequently, defense costs are incurred because suits must be defended.

Blanket Crime

More commonly known as employee bonding, this insurance is sometimes purchased in conjunction with directors' and officers' coverage. It provides protection for employee dishonesty, including the theft of money and other institutional assets.

Kidnap and ransom insurance is often purchased along with blanket crime coverage. It provides protection if the institution is obligated to pay a ransom for any employee or patient who is kidnapped.

Automobile Liability

Automobile insurance offers two types of coverage. The first provides for any physical damage to a vehicle, much the same as that purchased for personal automobile protection. If an automobile is damaged in an accident, this policy pays for repairs or replacement. It is important to remember that the coverage should be extended to include leased vehicles on an automatic basis if the institution maintains a fleet.

The second part of this policy provides automobile liability coverage. This refers to claims that the institution is obligated to pay as a result of an automobile accident in which a third party is injured. It also provides for property damage liability should a vehicle damage the property of others.

Excess Liability

Excess liability coverage provides additional limits above the primary medical malpractice insurance. It expands the limits of liability for an institution in case of a high-severity loss.

This type of insurance may be modified to become *umbrella coverage*. It then provides limits not only above medical malpractice insurance, but it also provides additional limits for other liability coverages that are specifically named on the policy, such as automobile liability and directors' and officers' liability.

Other specialty coverages are available. An assessment of the risks in each institution must be made in order to determine the needs of the organization.

INSURANCE FINANCING OPTIONS

Insurance companies provide several options for paying premiums. Some options involve risk assumptions and the necessity of a strong risk management program within the health care institution; others simply transfer the risk.

Guaranteed Cost Program

This is the most common method of paying premiums. It involves the assessment and payment of a single premium for an insurance policy. For example, in return for a premium of $20,000, an insurance company will provide automobile coverage for the hospital's automobiles. No adjustments to the premium will take place during the policy year.

Dividend Program

A dividend program provides a return premium if a predetermined ratio of premium to losses is met. This type of program is generally written for a group of institutions based on the experience of the group; however, it may be written for a single hospital. An individual premium is assessed for each member of the group at the beginning of the policy year. On a specific date, the insurance carrier reviews the expenses of the institutions in the program. If the losses are better than expected (based on predetermined criteria) a dividend is returned to the policyholder. The dividend may be a percentage of the premium paid or the savings realized. The advantage of this plan is the influence it provides for loss prevention.

Other Financing Options

The following insurance financing options differ from those above in that they combine risk transfer with risk financing. In other words, the institution accepts a portion of the financial risk. The programs discussed above also can be modified to provide for the inclusion of some financial risk through deductibles or retentions.

Loss Deductible

A *deductible* is the dollar amount that is subtracted from any payment made by an insurance carrier. Deductible amounts are set by the carrier with a corresponding reduction in premium. When a loss occurs the insurance company pays the claim minus the deductible amount. The institution must analyze its losses to make sure that the reduction in premium is not offset by the dollar amount of the losses below the deductible.

Self-Insured Retention

A dollar amount is selected by an organization to self-insure below an insured level of coverage. It is commonly called a self-insured retention or SIR level. Some carriers do not handle losses within the SIR layer and only want to be updated on their status; others handle every loss as if it were a deductible program. In order to manage this type of program properly, a strong risk management department with claims handling capabilities is necessary.

Incurred Loss Retrospectively Rated Program

This is a relatively new insurance financing option. At predetermined periods reserves on losses are valued and compared with premium amounts and insurance company expenses. This comparison results in either a return premium or an additional premium payment. The interval of comparisons varies according to the type of policy. For example, workers' compensation losses are reported and paid rapidly and the calculations are made monthly. Medical malpractice losses and reserves develop over a long period; comparisons may be made annually or semiannually.

As an additional incentive for this type of program, an insurer may offer a cash flow advantage by reducing the initial premium payment and allowing the insured to make additional payments based on the calculations. Because of the cash flow features the valuations generally result in additional premiums.

The program offers advantages for both parties. Minimum and maximum premium factors are specified in the insurance contract. The minimum premium provides for a guaranteed premium for the insurer, and the maximum provides a cap on the amount payable by the insured.

Paid Loss Retrospectively Rated Program

This program is essentially the same as the incurred loss program with the exception of the comparison base. Rather than reserves on losses, which may be overstated or understated, actual paid losses are the basis for the calculation. Cash flow benefits also may be built into this program and caps applied for the protection of both parties.

SELF-INSURANCE

The most commonly utilized alternative to insurance is the self-insurance program. Many hospitals elected to utilize self-insurance during the malpractice crisis of the 1970s and again during the most recent malpractice crises in the mid-1980s. Self-insurance simply means that a hospital no longer purchases an insurance policy but elects to pay claim losses either out of operating funds or through a trust fund set up at a financial institution.

In most cases, an insurance statement is drafted by the institution to establish the conditions under which the self-insurance program will pay a loss. These conditions are usually the same as those found under the former insurance contract. For example, a medical malpractice self-insurance trust fund would pay for the rendering of or failure to render professional services.

Before establishing a self-insurance program, the organization should examine three important factors:

1. A review of the organization and its risk-taking philosophy to determine if the organization is not adverse to taking risk through self-insurance and the amount of risk that it is willing to accept. This can be accomplished by looking at the financial implications of self-insurance, including the following:
   - hiring an actuary to analyze the loss history
   - analyzing trends and patterns of occurrences and losses
   - utilizing these data to project future losses
   - determining the cost of funding projected losses through a net present-value analysis
   - comparing the cost of funding a self-insurance trust with the cost of any available commercial insurance
2. A loss prevention program that is designed to control the risk the organization is assuming.
3. The availability and affordability of excess coverage. Insurance is usually purchased in an effort to avoid catastrophic loss or other losses that are high-severity and low-frequency in nature. Does the organization allow for the possibility that this excess insurance may be unavailable? Many excess carriers are wary of self-insured institutions during the first few years of a self-insurance program. A careful market analysis is required to determine the availability of excess coverage before a final decision is made to self-insure.

Advantages and Disadvantages

The true advantage of self-insurance is the control that an organization gains over its insurance program. Additional advantages of a self-insurance program include the following:

- The organization maintains control of its claims handling, including claims settlements and loss adjustment expenses.
- Self-insurance offers a unified defense for physicians and the institution when the employed physicians and members of the housestaff are included in the program. This may eliminate any adversarial relationships during a trial or settlement negotiations and also reduce defense costs if one attorney is utilized by all the parties named in a suit.
- The program eliminates insurance company profit from funding requirements.
- Loss control services are designed for an individual institution or by the institution itself.
- Investment income accrues to the institution and offsets some of the funding requirements for the self-insurance trust.
- The self-insurance program may provide a bond among the hospital-based physicians and other staff and act as an incentive to reduce losses.

The primary disadvantages of a self-insurance program are the following:

- A catastrophic loss could greatly reduce the available funds of an institution.
- Excess insurance may not be available; therefore, the institution will assume the entire risk exposure.

Risk Management Services

When a health care provider self-insures, it must replace the services currently provided by the insurance company. The institution may accomplish this by one of three methods: (1) hire a company to provide these services on its behalf, (2) handle the services through the institution's risk management program, or (3) use a combination of these two methods.

Services that the institution will require for a self-insurance program include the following:

- *Incident reporting system.* A modification of the system utilized by the present insurance carrier may be used, or a new reporting format may be developed.
- *Information systems.* For a small institution, a manual information system may be sufficient. A large institution should design a computerized system to provide information to its various departments and the medical staff.
- *Trending and analysis of occurrences.* These data are necessary in order to monitor the self-insurance program effectively. A computerized information system is helpful for this function.

- *Actuarial services.* These are required to project losses and determine funding levels in the trust. Hiring an outside actuary may increase the program's credibility with excess insurance carriers.
- *Claims management services.* In addition to processing claims, these services include legal representation and claims investigation.
- *Periodic surveys and inspections.* These are important functions of an insurance carrier. The inspection process should not be neglected by a self-insured institution, but become an integral part of its program.
- *Educational programs for physicians, nursing staff, and other hospital personnel.* Education is a vital self-insurance tool that must be provided in a consistent manner.

Forms of Self-Insurance

Several methods are used to conduct self-insurance programs. Some institutions pay claims directly from operating funds, while others specifically set aside monies for this purpose.

Disbursement from Operating Funds

"Going bare" means that the organization chooses not to transfer any risk, nor put aside monies to pay for potential losses. If a loss occurs, the organization must pay that claim out of operating funds.

Self-Insurance Fund

A self-insurance fund is a vehicle utilized by an organization to set aside monies to pay for losses. Often, an institution will establish a trust fund, a formal mechanism used to monitor the funds that have been put aside. A less formal system may take the form of a bank account, under the control of the institution into which funds are deposited and disbursed only for professional liability purposes.

Trust Fund

In an irrevocable trust fund limitations are placed on the usage of the money, including disbursements and investments, and the health care organization's ability to close the account. These limitations are spelled out in a document called a trust agreement between the health care organization and the financial institution that will manage the trust. There are several standard sections of an agreement:

Purpose. This explains the rationale for the trust and generally describes the program and its participants. Most trusts are set up as separate entities under Regulation 501(c)(3) of the Internal Revenue Code, which exempts the monies from income tax.

Trust Assets. This section defines the assets of the trust, such as premium payments, and indicates the basis for payments, for instance, if they are actuarially determined. This section also may mandate that the organization fund the amount recommended by the actuary or require approval of the organization's board of directors. Trust assets should include interest earned on investments.

Duties of Trustee. The trustee performs the following duties in the management of a trust fund:

- receives and invests payments made by the organization into the fund
- prepares and maintains records of fund investments, receipts, and disbursements
- receives a fee for management of the trust

Powers of the Trustee. The trustee may have authority to:

- make investment decisions
- monitor expenditures
- verify the adequacy of the insurance
- ensure the adequacy of the budget system

Payments. This section describes the purposes for which monies can be expended from the account. For example, these may include:

- settlement of claims
- administrative expenses
- insurance and reinsurance premiums
- actuarial fees

Removal or Resignation of Trustee. The organization should have the right to remove the trustee within a specified number of days, or the trustee may resign without notice. In either case, all records must be up-to-date and given to the organization or the new trustee.

Termination. The organization may terminate the trust without notice; however, an account must remain open to pay for any outstanding claims (tail). Some trusts require that an actuary determine the incurred but not reported (IBNR) claims.

Channeling

Channeling is an option available with a self-insurance program that is not readily available through commercial insurance. By definition, channeling is the voluntary inclusion of attending physicians in the insurance program or the insurance trust established by the health care organization. The advantages of a channeling program may include the following:

- *Economies of scale.* By bringing the medical staff into the insurance program, the institution can establish a greater risk pool that increases the monies available and spreads the risk of the self-insurance trust.
- *Reduction in legal fees, investigative fees, and loss adjustment expenses.* In many cases the physicians, nursing staff, and hospital are named in the same suit and one attorney may be hired to handle the investigation and defense.
- *Incentive for physicians to participate in the institution's risk management program.* If the physician's defense is provided by the institution, the physician is much more likely to participate in the risk management program or incident reporting system.
- *Enhancement of peer review.* Physicians have the opportunity to control premium costs through the reduction of losses.

The channeling concept is still a new one; therefore, there is no documented evidence that the benefits listed above can be realized. The theory of channeling makes sense, and it may be within the best interest of the institution at least to attempt a channeling program.

As a precautionary measure, channeling should not be attempted until the institution's self-insurance program is running effectively so that the organization does not take on too much administrative or financial risk at one time.

SELECTING A BROKER OR AN AGENT

A broker is an individual or organization hired by the hospital to represent the hospital's interests in the insurance marketplace.

An agent is an individual or an organization hired by the insurance carrier to sell its products and represent its interests to the health care organization.

The distinction between a broker and an agent has become blurred in today's insurance marketplace. Whether the health care organization utilizes a broker or an agent, the establishment of a good working relationship with the broker or agent is extremely important. The insurance buyer in the hospital depends on this individual or organization for information regarding the marketplace, new products, new concepts in insurance or self-insurance, and other alternative methods of funding for losses.

Broker Relationship

For the above reasons, selection of a broker is an important process that should be undertaken in a highly structured manner. The first rule of thumb is not to disrupt a broker relationship without just cause. Once a broker is selected it is important that the relationship be maintained. The broker should understand that as long as good service is provided the institution will not change brokers. However, when a change in broker is necessary, there are three steps that should be followed in making a new selection. The first step is to poll professional peers through associations and compile a list of broker candidates for consideration.

In the second step, a list of questions should be compiled for submission to the broker candidates. Written responses should be requested to such questions as the following:

- How does the brokerage firm assist a health care organization in identifying risks, analyzing risks, and designing a plan for treatment of the risks associated with that organization?
- Does the brokerage have any affiliations with insurance carriers?
- Who are the staff members and what are their qualifications?
- How much time will the brokerage staff spend on the health care organization's account?
- What are the national and international affiliations that can be utilized by the hospital? For example, what is the broker's entrée into the marketplace and how does the firm access markets for excess or surplus lines?
- What types of loss analyses and actuarial services does the brokerage provide?
- Can the firm provide models for self-insurance and captive insurance programs? If so, has the firm established these programs before? Please provide a list of clients for whom these services have been provided.
- Can the firm provide a conceptual model for insurance alternatives for the health care organization?

After the completed questionnaires are received, the selection process is the third step. Risk managers should not attempt to make this determination on their own. Following analysis of the materials provided, obvious eliminations can be made. Each of the remaining candidates should be interviewed personally in order to assess the possibilities of an effective broker/client working relationship. The hospital's financial officer or administrator should also participate in the interviews.

Ideally, one firm should be selected to handle the hospital's insurance needs. However, sometimes circumstances require that two brokers be hired. In this case, make sure that both brokers understand their respective roles.

Underwriter Relationship

A good relationship should be developed with the underwriter of the insurance company. The risk manager should meet with the underwriter at least once a year. During this meeting, the underwriter should be provided with the following information:

- job descriptions or resumes relevant to loss control services
- internal policies and procedures
- changes in hospital services
- other information that will be useful to the underwriter at policy renewal

Renewal applications should be neat, legible, very well organized, and easy for the underwriter to use. The more the underwriter knows about the risk, the better service he or she can provide in adjusting premiums favorably. It is usually helpful to invite the underwriter and other staff from the insurance company to visit the health care organization. The risk manager can arrange tours, introduce the underwriters to the risk management and administrative staffs, and be prepared with answers to questions about the institution and its mission.

These meetings offer a good opportunity to negotiate coverage changes through endorsements to the institution's insurance policy. The endorsements can either limit or increase coverage. When negotiating insurance premiums, it is important to remember that coverages also can be negotiated. Generally, these negotiations are more successful when the insurance buyer is involved in them. Before asking for an enhancement in coverage, the risk manager should understand exactly why the enhancement is desired and how it will benefit the organization and determine the best way to present this information to the insurer.

For example, to remove the peer review exclusion on a directors' and officers' policy, it is important to prove that the exposure in the institution is limited, or controlled, so that the underwriter is willing to consider the request. By inviting the underwriter to the institution, introducing him or her to the people involved in the peer review process, and sharing the policies and procedures of the organization, it is easier to prove the limited exposure.

COMPETITIVE BIDDING PROCESS

A health care organization may decide, from time to time, to obtain competitive quotes for its insurance coverages. This will enable them to compare products, prices, and services from competing markets. There are many reasons for seeking these quotations. They include:

- premium costs for a specific line or all lines of insurance
- an exploration of the marketplace and available terms and conditions

- a special project or joint venture
- a change in the risk-taking philosophy of the organization
- unavailability of the required type of coverage from the current insurer

Methodology

An organization can handle competitive bidding for insurance carriers in one of two ways: (1) by retaining the current broker; or (2) by allowing several brokerage firms, including the incumbent, to compete in the process.

If the current broker will maintain the account, the procedure is simple. The health care organization will:

- provide the broker with, or allow the firm to prepare, the bid specification
- provide the broker with, or allow the firm to choose, the various insurance markets to be approached
- provide a return date for all proposals
- utilize the broker's expertise and, in accordance with the hospital's risk-taking philosophy, choose a market

If the competition is to include the broker, the process can be more complicated. It is important to note that in today's insurance marketplace competitive bidding is not the best method of selecting a broker. The available carriers and the lines of coverage they write have become so specialized that often there are not enough markets for assignment to all of the brokers participating in the process.

The initial procedure for including brokers in the competitive bidding process consists of two primary steps:

1. The process described in the previous section of this chapter about selecting a broker should be followed to determine who will participate with the insurers.
2. Specifications must be prepared for distribution. They should include the following:
   - the organization, its purpose, and the appropriate contact person for the organization
   - due date of the proposal and the form for submission
   - any special requests from the organization
   - request for any unusual endorsements extending or limiting coverage
   - request for the A.M. Best rating of the carrier (This rating firm analyzes insurance carriers as to financial strength and management skills. Ratings for stability range from A+ (the highest) to C and several unrated categories. The rating also includes financial size categories measured by roman numerals and underwriting information, such as number of employees, property values, square footage, and payroll information.)
   - loss experience for each line in the market with an attached explanation of any significant loss payment, reserve, or trend

After the specifications have been finalized, the broker should submit a list of market preferences to the risk manager. These market requests must be reviewed and assigned to the brokers. The incumbent broker should receive the organization's current insurance carrier. All other markets should be assigned as requested unless there is a conflict, in which case assignments should be made randomly.

It is very important that not more than one broker approach an insurer. Broker of record letters, stating that a specific broker has access to a specific insurance market, should be used. Each broker has a sample letter for this purpose. Confusion in assignments could lead an insurer to back out of the bidding process. It is also important to screen out insurance carriers with the same parent company, as many times the companies may block one another from quoting on a risk.

Insurers must be allowed ample time to prepare the quotations. During this time it is not uncommon for questions to be directed to the risk manager. The same information should be given to all carriers. For example, if one carrier asks a question and receives information that was not provided in the original specifications, this information must be sent to the other participants.

Finally, the organization must analyze the information received from the insurers. Brokers should have the opportunity to present the proposals and bring representatives of the insurers. The proposals should be converted to the same format; any financial information should be analyzed and stated in common terms.

After the proposals are analyzed, a decision should be based on the needs of the health care organization. In making this decision, the following should be considered:

- The purpose of purchasing insurance is to transfer a specific type of risk. Therefore, the coverage provided should be the main focus of the review.
- If the institution does not have a strong risk management program, the services provided by an insurer may be of great value to the organization. These services should be closely analyzed.
- The cost of the coverage, including any cash flow advantage, must be examined. Also, the cost of completing any requirements of coverage made by the insurer should be carefully considered. A proposal

may look appealing until all of the hidden costs are analyzed.

When a choice has been made, it is wise to allow a broker and an insurer to stay on the account for several years. This provides an opportunity for all parties to interact and a cooperative environment for premium reduction and coverage enhancement.

In today's marketplace, it is extremely important that risk managers utilize the described process to ensure the best use of the available resources.

NOTE

1. G.T. Troyer and S.L. Salman, *Handbook of Health Care Risk Management* (Gaithersburg, MD: Aspen Publishers, Inc., 1986), 183.

BIBLIOGRAPHY

Levick, D.E. 1988. *Risk Management and Insurance Audit Techniques.* Boston: Shelby Publishing Corporation.

Risk Management Foundation of the Harvard Medical Institutions, Inc. August 1989. *Forum.* Detroit: Tillinghast, A Towers Perrin Company.

chapter 17

Risk Financing: An Important Risk Management Function

Barbara J. Youngberg

INTRODUCTION

The basic concepts behind risk financing seek to ensure that a hospital can meet all of its financial obligations that arise out of known and unknown risks and perils. A variety of methods can be adopted to ensure that all risks can be paid when they arise. The most common methods used by health care facilities include the purchase of commercial insurance that transfers the risk to a third party, the self-funding of all risk through a variety of mechanisms that allows for the hospital to fund for its risk, and a combination of the two methods. Organizational structure, expertise of staff, size of the risk management department, state law, and prior relationships with financial institutions and markets may influence the decision of the hospital to select one method of risk financing over another.

Over the past 10 years the responsibilities of risk managers have increased, and the addition of financing the risks identified in a particular hospital or health care institution's program have been added. Although the mechanics of these types of financing can vary greatly among entities or institutions, risk managers have become aware of the increasing need to broaden their backgrounds to include areas of managerial accounting, insurance program administration, actuarial science, and financial planning. Risk managers working in more sophisticated settings have even been asked to become included in the investment of funds allocated to cover the identified risks of the institution. When this occurs, risk managers find the need to add investment theory to their portfolio of knowledge. This chapter discusses many aspects of basic and technical risk financing and is supplemented to provide risk managers with information related to the growing areas in finance for which risk managers will have responsibility.

As with any other risk management activity, the responsibility for the financing of risk should involve many departments within the hospital. When attempting to estimate accurately the risk and the financial implications of that risk, risk managers will want to include representatives from hospital administration, finance, planning and development, and any other departments that could add to or mitigate the actual or potential losses within the institution.

ASSESSING THE CURRENT PROGRAM

The group involved in risk financing decisions may want to discuss the following areas and questions as they attempt to place a dollar value on the amount of risk they will be asked to finance and the type of program they will develop.

- What type of insurance coverage is currently *purchased* to cover exposures within the hospital? The coverage could include professional liability insurance, directors' and officers' coverage, workers' compensation, property and casualty coverage, and other types of business-related insurance coverage (accounts receivable coverage, business interruption coverage, and "boutique coverage" such as underground storage tank and asbestos exposure coverage).

When analyzing the responses to this question, the risk manager will obviously want to ask questions about the cost of each of these coverages, the limits of protection that each coverage provides, the point at which the coverage attaches, and the solvency and special services offered by the carrier providing the coverage.

The process of purchasing insurance and analyzing its appropriateness is a technically complicated one and requires either the sophistication of a professional risk manager or the assistance of an insurance broker or consultant. If you feel that outside brokerage or consultant support is needed, care should be taken to hire a professional who has expertise in health care entities. The uniqueness of the many risks associated with the operation of a health care facility requires the expertise of a person or company who has this specialized experience. The broker selected should have knowledge of state laws governing special insurance programs and should be able to show the hospital staff how they might benefit from choosing one type of program over another.

- What are the current self-insurance obligations of the hospital or health care entity, and how much of that self-insurance must be allocated annually to cover all present and future expenses? How will these funds be invested?

  In the area of self-insurance, the risk manager may learn that the level of self-insurance varies considerably with each line of coverage. The analysis of self-insurance should include a discussion of the amount of cash needed to cover excess insurance or catastrophic coverage. This would have to be considered if there are losses in excess of the policies purchased. In determining the financing for this type of exposure, the risk manager and the risk financing team will want to determine what form of financing provides the most opportunity for the institution and allows for the greatest operational cash flow. In making this decision, the risk manager may want to consider securing lines or letters of credit, cash deposits, or purchasing bonds, stocks, or other financial instruments.

- The cost of the current operation of a risk management and loss financing program and additional costs necessary should a more sophisticated program be proposed.

  Many risk managers go to great lengths to calculate the costs of risk transfer and loss financing but forget to include the costs associated with running a loss-control program. These costs include both the administrative costs and the programmatic ones. In the discussion that follows on premium allocation, some

of the elements and additional costs of a loss-control program are discussed.

Often, the responsibilities of a risk manager involved in finance do not end with the determination of what a loss-control program will cost the institution but continue with how costs will be allocated among all people who receive benefit from the program. Although it has been reduced to a science by many actuaries and insurance carriers, the allocation of premium generally requires the consideration of several intangible variables.

- Are there any advantages in having the hospital "go bare?"

  A hospital that chooses to go bare places itself at tremendous risk as it operates (for all intents and purposes) on a pay-as-you-go philosophy. If the hospital incurs no losses, it has saved the money it may have otherwise paid to an insurance carrier. The hospital also has avoided having cash tied up in funds and not available to cover ongoing operating expenses. However, if the institution incurs a loss, particularly a catastrophic one, a financial hardship might result that could have a profound impact on the continued vitality of the organization.

  Some hospitals elect this option fearing that, if they fund for risk or purchase commercial insurance, they may jeopardize pre-existing state or federal immunity. Others are forced into this option because of their dire financial operating margin. This option should be considered only after carefully weighing its risks and benefits for the institution and only if strong loss-control programs are in place.

EVALUATING THE OPTIONS

Self-insurance (either total or partial) presumes the hospital chooses to place a predetermined sum of money into a fund, which it controls, to pay for future losses. Obviously, the more accurately the risk manager can quantify the potential risks, the more likely that funds set aside will be adequate to pay for these risks. The advantage of this system is that, if the risks prove to be less costly than anticipated, dollars can be returned to the general operating budget of the hospital.

The potential disadvantage of this type of risk financing program is that it requires a sound risk management and loss-control program and a commitment from administration to hire appropriate staff and to provide appropriate administrative support to ensure the program functions appropriately. In addition, there is always the possibility that the amount of risk financed is less than the ultimate cost of the risk. In this case, the hospital will have to fund the additional cost.

Many hospitals structure their programs to include both layers of purchased commercial insurance and self-insurance. In these types of programs, a layer of risk commonly known as the self-insured retention (SIR) is financed by the hospital; commercial insurance is purchased to finance the risks above the level of the SIR; and the hospital may then self-fund any potential for catastrophic losses. Attempting to calculate accurately the risk presents the initial challenge for the risk manager.

BASIC ELEMENTS OF RISK

Initially, it is recommended that hospital risk managers begin assessing their level of risk in a manner comparable with that of an insurance company. This process should always occur independent of whether a hospital chooses to purchase insurance, partially self-fund, totally self-fund, or go bare. This analysis would include:

- number of licensed beds and occupied beds. You should make certain that you plan for expansion and for occupancy trends. The licensed beds should also be broken down into acute care beds, long-term care beds, and bassinets. When calculating acute care beds, you also may want to place greater risk value on intensive care beds, such as surgical, medical, neonatal, pediatric, burn, and transplant.
- number of outpatient visits, clinic visits, and emergency department visits. If your facility is a designated trauma center, you also may want to calculate the percentage of emergency department visits that are trauma cases that can pose an increased risk to the institution because of their complexity.
- number of hospital staff that will be protected by the hospital program, with analyses of type of service staff provides, their direct contact with patients, and level of their interaction. You should always calculate these numbers in relation to full-time equivalents (FTEs) rather than merely a count of persons on the payroll because a person who only works two days a week poses less of a risk than one who works five days a week. Usually, a full-time equivalent is equal to a person who works 40 hours a week. It is essential in this analysis that you determine if contract employees, such as agency nurses and contract physicians working in the emergency department, radiology, pathology, and anesthesia, have coverage through their contracting agency or if they expect the hospital to cover them.
- analysis of the types of clinical services offered by your facility and the risks attached to those services. This might include number of surgical procedures performed under general anesthesia versus local anesthesia, number of deliveries including those termed high-risk deliveries, and number of transplants.
- if available, an analysis of historical loss information for your institution. This analysis should be done to determine the average cost per year of claims and lawsuits within your institution. If this information is not available, you may be able to request such information from insurance carriers, but be certain that you are looking at losses sustained by a similar facility located in the same or similar locale.

After you have gathered this information, you will begin to develop a sense of the amount of risk present in your institution. Although calculating risk with *absolute* accuracy is probably impossible, this type of data will assist and enable you to develop a risk picture of your institution. In turn, this will help you get valid comparative data.

If expertise is not available within your institution in the areas of law, portfolio investment, claims administration, and information systems, you may want to consult with individuals outside the institution for assistance. In particular, you may seek specific assistance from:

- attorneys. You will need to speak both with attorneys who specialize in administrative matters and those who specialize in the defense of hospital professional liability claims. These attorneys can provide information on how claims should be handled in your program, the cost of defending claims, the types of claims that have the greatest historical value in your jurisdiction, and information related to state laws that govern how hospitals administratively must set up self-insured or partially insured programs.
- insurance brokers or consultants. These people may be able to provide information for the best plan given your hospital's risk profile. You should ask that they be prepared to provide you with information that includes establishing total commercially insured or total self-insured programs as well as those programs that have excess coverage sitting over varying levels of insurance. Also, these professionals may provide you with advice on the availability and appropriateness of hiring third-party administrators, consultants, or investigators to provide support for your program. You should ask them for a cost analysis for these services so you can determine the appropriateness and feasibility of training in-house staff to provide these functions.
- actuaries. These professionals will help predict your risk based on the exposure information you have collected. Many of the large actuarial firms have comprehensive data bases that help them predict your levels of future loss per type of exposure. If you elect

to pursue some type of self-insurance, you may be required by state auditors or insurance underwriters to have actuarial assistance in establishing and funding your program.

- information specialists. Maintaining a strong risk management and risk financing program will require computer support. Many commercial programs have been developed to perform the functions required for sophisticated risk management and risk financing. Some of these commercial programs can be customized to meet your individual needs. You also may want to consult with your hospital information officer about the possibility of developing your own internally programmed information system, which interfaces with other hospital programs.

If you choose to fund a portion of your institution's risk, you will need to consider additional factors. The self-funding portions of this type of program can occur using several different mechanisms. Each mechanism has both risks and benefits, and each requires a different level of sophistication. A careful analysis should be performed before choosing the best mechanism for your institution.

DETERMINING THE RISK OF YOUR INSTITUTION

Before deciding about the limits of commercial insurance to be purchased, the risk manager will need to quantify the risk inherent in the operation of the facility. Determining the level of risk of an institution can be a complicated process that must take into consideration several variables. Although some of the elements involved in the calculation of risk are obvious, the process and analysis, at least initially, require the skills of a trained actuary or someone knowledgeable in actuarial science. Failing to assess accurately the risk and finance for an institution can have catastrophic future financial implications if unanticipated losses occur and require payment. Generally, the application provided to you by the insurance company will ask the appropriate questions to calculate risk. However, you may want to perform your own assessment to help determine the limits of coverage you purchase and the types of special coverage you might need.

PURCHASING COMMERCIAL INSURANCE

Although the purchase of commercial insurance from the first dollar up is the preferred method of some hospitals for transferring risk, it is by far the most costly. Except in unique circumstances, premiums are paid to a company for potential losses. After these premiums are paid, they are never refunded although no losses occur. Though costly, this method provides the least amount of risk to the hospital and also generally requires the least amount of staff, additional administrative time, and expense. If you have correctly evaluated your risk, purchased the appropriate types and levels of coverage, and if the carrier remains solvent, you can assume that injuries or occurrences arising within your institution will be covered.

Some hospitals, however, believe that this type of fully insured program represents a disincentive for persons within the institution from adhering to stringent risk management protocols. Some hospitals also believe that commercial insurance possibly prevents the development of and participation in a strong institutional quality management program because losses are not felt directly by the individual or institution. Despite the likelihood that premiums will increase if losses are not controlled, practitioners and administrators see the increase after the fact and, therefore, do not necessarily correlate the increase in premiums to a particular lawsuit or a series of claims or lawsuits.

MECHANISMS FOR SELF-FUNDING

Simple Trust

The most common vehicle for the funding of a self-insured obligation is the simple trust. Under a trust agreement, a specified level of funds is set aside to pay for losses as they occur. In most cases, annual or periodic contributions to the trust are made based on an actuarial determination of the expected value of actual losses, losses incurred but not reported (IBNR), and future losses. In most situations, persons determining the amount of funding necessary to ensure the trust will indeed cover losses first analyze the time required for cases arising in their jurisdiction to actually come to trial or otherwise be resolved. This allows for a discounting of the ultimate value of the final resolution of a claim due to the amount of investment return that will be gained over a period before resolution of the claim.

Setting up a simple trust for financing hospital losses requires less administrative overhead than many of the other models to be discussed later in this chapter. In most cases, using a simple trust eliminates the need to budget for premium taxes, brokerage fees, acquisition costs, or sophisticated management fees. Also, in most cases the establishment of a simple trust does not require state approval, which must be obtained when establishing other types of insuring vehicles. There may be exceptions to this in those states where there are legislatively established patient's compensation funds or specific professional liability insurance requirements.

Risk managers setting up a simple trust will want to determine with their hospital finance department the impact this type of self-insurance program may have on bond indenture requirements and the need to produce certificates of insurance for any capital funding programs. Generally, these issues can be clarified in the trusts documents.

Captive Insurance Company

A more sophisticated form of self-insurance involves the setting up of a captive insurance company. By definition, a captive insurance program is a limited purpose licensed insurance company whose predominate business is insuring the risks of its owners. Captives can be set up "onshore" (within the contiguous United States) or "offshore" (outside the contiguous United States) and can be either for profit or not-for-profit. The selection of forum and captive type determines the laws governing its operation and may also dictate funding requirements, capitalization, and tax status.

Setting up a captive insurance company necessitates a high level of staff sophistication. It also requires administrative commitment that this will be a long-term initiative that may, for the first few years, cost more than a basic program.

There are many reasons why hospitals elect to form a captive. Some of them are appropriate; some are not. One most appropriate reason is the desire to encourage cooperation among those persons and entities insured but to enable them to develop and implement jointly a program based on sound risk management, quality improvement, and loss-control initiatives. The fact that there is a common financial interest shared by all participants in the captive helps ensure that such principles are taken seriously.

In addition, a hospital that supports establishing a captive insurance company to provide coverage for physicians and staff as well as the hospital entity can plan defense strategies that coalesce to support all members of the health care team involved (or named) in a litigation. Such a structure also allows for representation from one attorney and thereby can greatly reduce the costs of investigation and defense. Such strategies prevent individually named defendants from working with individual counsel to focus blame on other named defendants.

Because the operation of a captive is a labor intensive process requiring varying levels of commitment and expertise, many hospitals also believe that the mere presence of the captive helps build stronger ties among the hospital, risk management department, and medical staff. Furthermore, this group's ability to control the captive insurance program and the services it provides helps foster a team spirit and a greater appreciation and understanding of the needs of each professional group and the group as a whole.

A captive should not be considered a short-term solution to ride out the high cost of malpractice premiums or as a method to save money paid in insurance taxes or fees. Also, it is inappropriate to think of a captive as a shelter for money not subject to taxation that will never be called up to pay for losses. This is unlikely to materialize and should not be presented as a reason for establishing this type of self-insurance program.

Setting up a Captive

Much work must be done before setting up a captive insurance company. Initial feasibility studies should be performed that address issues such as loss development trends within the institution including those of individual caregivers, current policy and premium information, and the goals that hospital administration, risk management staff, and medical staff seek to accomplish by establishing the captive. When the feasibility study has been completed, the risk manager and persons involved in choosing this risk financing option should evaluate the various state and offshore statutes that govern the operation of a captive. Issues such as capitalization, minimum premium, investment restrictions, location of principal office and selection of officers, underwriting criteria, and reporting and auditing requirements should be analyzed. This ensures the correct site is chosen for the captive. A corporate attorney who specializes in the formation of captives should be consulted at the beginning of the process to provide guidance on the legal and regulatory formalities associated with such a decision.

Some structural issues that must be considered at this juncture are the form of the organization, the effects of the form chosen on the organization, issues related to capitalization, and management issues that include who will be covered, what the limits and exclusions of coverage will be, and who will comprise the captive management team.

The form of the captive chosen can vary greatly and will impact the future operation of the captive. Although domicile of the captive is generally the first decision made, you also may want to decide initially whether you want to establish a new captive or purchase or rent an existing one. Also, before choosing the site of the captive, you should determine whether you want to provide policies through the captive or serve as a front. The answers to these decisions will help you choose an appropriate site. Although many captive insurance companies are established offshore, many hospitals feel that the repercussions from the hospital board of trustees, stemming from frequent trips "to the islands," makes the selection of an offshore site less appealing. These issues will need to be discussed with senior management and the hospital board of trustees.

In consideration of the issue of location, a meeting with senior hospital administration and the board of trustees should include a discussion of the impact of the location, taxes, state regulation, the Securities Exchange Commission (SEC), and other hospital legal matters. Decision makers should recognize that each site chosen has positive and negative aspects of its operation, and care should be taken to choose a site that will mitigate the likelihood of long-term problems.

The issue of capitalization is the greatest hurdle to overcome and is often the single reason a particular site is chosen. Although the amount of initial capitalization is important, other issues such as withdrawal of capital should also be discussed. Persons addressing capitalization issues also should address whether funds must be held in escrow until minimal capitalization requirements have been met and what happens if capitalization requirements are not met or if levels of funding fall below required amounts, for example, in the event of a catastrophic loss.

Management issues also should be discussed with particular attention paid to how the hospital and physicians want to share or delegate the operational responsibilities associated with captive management. The decision to hire a captive manager (especially if the captive is offshore) should be discussed, and a decision should be made whether the hospital wants to establish a "paper captive" with no employees and an independent contractor serving as a managing general agent (MGA) or a fully staffed captive. Delegation of duties among the management staff is important, especially as they relate to the setting of premium, the allocation of premium, and the administration and handling of claims and lawsuits.

Regulatory Issues Associated with the Formation of a Captive

There are many regulatory issues associated with the formation and operation of a captive insurance company, which should be handled by a professional with special expertise in this area. Regulatory issues vary, depending on whether the captive issues stock or whether it is set up as a mutual company or reciprocal. Other regulatory issues will be impacted based on the type(s) of coverage provided by the captive—some states have specific statutes regarding specific types of coverage—and on the governance structure selected by the risk financing committee.

Jurisdictional Issues Impacting Captive Management

When selecting a site for the captive and when operating the captive after it has been established, the risk manager or captive manager should keep apprised of rate filings and approvals, whether there is a mandate to participate in guaranty or insolvency funds, and whether certificates of authority must be obtained from other states where business is being transacted. In states with special captive statutes, it is important to review all provisions of the statute to ensure your captive is operating in full compliance.

After the risk financing mechanism has been established, the risk manager should address how the appropriate levels of financing will be achieved. This establishment of premium and the allocation of premium among program members are more difficult functions the risk manager may be asked to perform. Inherent in this difficulty is the fact that there is no clear formula by which to establish appropriate levels of premium. The following discussion includes factors that should be considered before developing an allocation scheme. Many of them will have been completed during the process of calculating risk, which was discussed earlier.

DEVELOPING A FORMULA FOR THE ALLOCATION OF PREMIUM

In attempting to allocate equitably the cost of a hospital's professional liability insurance program among all insured entities, the risk manager often must balance several factors—many of which change from year to year. A literature search related to risk management, insurance, and finance reveals little information that directly deals with how this process is most successfully accomplished.

Although there is probably no single *best* method for equitable premium allocation, some factors do remain constant and thus should be considered when developing a formula. The following discussion explains some of the constant factors, as well as the elements that become part of the analysis and some problems often associated with attempting to standardize a formula.

Historical data is most helpful in developing the program's projected cost. If such information is available, it can be used to develop a benchmark for the various factors that follow.

Cost

Before developing an individual allocation formula, the **total** cost of the annual program should be calculated. Elements of **total** cost for a hospital's professional liability insurance program might include:

- actuarially determined prospective funding requirements of all self-assumed risk (typically referred to as SIR)
- cost of any applicable excess insurance
- allocated loss adjustment expenses (referred to as ALAE) that generally include all costs per claim exclusive of indemnity payments. These calculations are generally estimated based on historical data, adjusted by an appropriate inflation factor. These costs include:
  - attorney's fees
  - adjuster's fees
  - expert witness/review fees
  - all other costs related to the defense/settlement of claims
- any administrative costs associated with the operation of the insurance program. These costs might include:
  - consultant studies (actuaries, brokers, accountants)
  - corporate attorneys' fees associated with the insurance program management, which may be significant if the insurance program involves a trust, captive, or other form of hybrid insurance arrangement
  - salaries paid to staff (risk managers and claims managers) to administer the insurance program
  - costs of equipment, supplies, office space, and so forth as appropriate (amortized over years of program operation)
- any costs carried over from prior years (retrospective funding) in case additional funding of the program's SIR is required, which is most often the result of unexpected verdicts or excessive settlements or any problems with impairment of the aggregate

The risk manager must then determine how to best split the cost between the hospital program and the physicians' program. This determination can be left for the underwriter or can be delegated to a broker if one is involved in the program design.

Rate Setting

After the cost of each program is determined, the next step in developing a formula is a part of the process termed **rate setting** in the insurance market. In a hospital-controlled insurance program, this process often becomes difficult due to the many political and individual considerations the hospital administration chooses that affect the allocation of individual or specialty group premiums charged.

The simplest part of this allocation (premium setting) process is to tally the number of entities that will be insured under the program. You will then need to classify these entities as individual exposure units (a single faculty physician) or as complex multi-exposure units (the hospital entity or the OB/GYN practice plan), based on the risk they pose to the financial integrity of the program. Classification of the entities is based on the conceptual risk threat they pose to the institution.

At this point, the process becomes increasingly difficult. The following are some reasons for this difficulty.

- Evaluation of prior claims historical data is essential as it provides the risk manager with an indication of dollars paid by each entity *in the past*.

  Unfortunately, the data are not always indicative of future trends. To gain more accurate and valuable data related to losses, the risk manager also should evaluate recent verdicts and settlements in the jurisdiction where the hospital is located and determine if any recent tort reform is likely to affect future settlements/verdicts.
- Political pressure within the institution may seek to influence the price paid by certain groups. For example, physicians with high admissions patterns ("high admitters") or prestigious practice plans may attempt to negotiate their premiums downward in exchange for continued loyal support of the hospital.
- Hospital administration might feel that it has a firm control on the faculty physicians and elect to "price as the market will bear." In this case, the hospital passes back to the faculty the cost of the losses.
- Physicians may have great influence and power on the institution's operations and may leverage the bulk of the cost against the hospital, especially if the hospital has a history of being profitable.
- It is very difficult to sell "retro-funding" (collecting funds to pay for loss *after* it occurs).

Despite these factors, there are some aids that can help the risk manager in making some logical determinations about premium setting in a group program.

Individual Physician or Practice Plan Rate Setting

An analysis of the loss history is the characteristic first step in establishing an exposure unit. Historically, those specialties associated with a high degree of risk of harm were charged the highest premium. Losses (both numbers of losses and dollars spent on losses) supported the fact that obstetricians, anesthesiologists, emergency department physicians, and neurosurgeons were indeed associated with the highest degree of risk. In your individual analysis, you may find that a particular high-risk department within your hospital has an exemplary claims history directly related to the quality control programs supported by the discipline. In this case, credits can be used to offset premiums.

In setting rates for individuals and practice plans, the following data should be collected and analyzed:

- numbers of physicians in group (should be calculated in FTEs based on the number of hours spent in clinical practice), with determination that each physician is primarily engaged in clinical practice or clinical research and not laboratory, or nonclinical, activity
- historical loss trend analysis, considering
  — number of claims filed
  — dollars paid per claim and in the aggregate
  — individual physicians named in claims to determine if an individual physician is the source of the problem or if the problem can be traced to the entire department
  — any operational changes in the department that may have a positive or negative effect on future losses (for example, new high-risk procedures being performed, or certain procedures being abandoned by the hospital)
  — any new programs implemented in response to loss history, especially those related to quality assurance and risk management
  — recent tort reform that might affect future outcomes
  — any increase or decrease in department size
  — history of premiums paid by group and/or individual

Hospital Rate Determination

In determining what percentage of the premium should be paid by the hospital, the risk manager also must evaluate several other factors. Many of these factors parallel those previously discussed in the determination of physicians' rates. The following list includes some considerations that must be evaluated when analyzing the hospital's exposure.

- Obtain the raw numbers of employees, including nurses (RNs, LPNs, and certified registered nurse anesthetists [CRNAs]), interns, residents, technicians, and any other personnel who have direct contact with patients and who participate in the rendering of patient care.
- Analyze the exposure of residents through available rating tables that provide relative "exposure units."
- Ascertain whether any hospital personnel are contract employees and, if so, find out if they have the responsibility of carrying their own coverage. This is often the case of CRNAs and certified nurse midwives (CNMs) who work for and are covered under the physician group policy.

- Evaluate loss history to determine the number of claims against the hospital and covered residents and interns.
- Determine if any immunity exists protecting or limiting the exposure of the hospital entity or its employees.
- Evaluate claims based on the same data and questions previously discussed in dealing with individual physician or practice plan rate setting.
- Determine if individual staff members, residents, or interns repeatedly appear in claims or lawsuits. Verify that they are no longer employed by the institution.
- Determine if the hospital has any plans for expansion that could add risk to the hospital entity. At the same time, determine if the hospital plans to cut any high-risk programs.
- Identify all off-premises exposures and evaluate them as you would the individual hospital exposures.
- Evaluate historical data dealing with the cost and amount of coverage purchased.

After you have analyzed both the physician programs and the hospital entity and assigned units to each, you can begin the process of equitably allocating premiums to offset the total cost of the program.

Risk Classification

The risk manager now can look at several available resources to obtain baseline information about how rates are set by commercial carriers. The following list provides some of these resources:

- Various individual state insurance tables provide information related to the *maximum* rates that various classes of physicians can be charged. Naturally, these rates are inflated to reflect various commissions paid to brokers and other intermediaries. However, they can be used in the calculation of percentages among various physician groups. Obviously, these rates would not reflect the savings that can be gained through a group purchase effort, although these savings can be easily factored into the rate calculation later.
- National Association of Insurance Commissioners (NAIC) rating table and Insurance Services Office (ISO) data can be used to allocate cost. Sample copies of this data are available from either of these organizations.
- Independent actuaries also may be able to provide an institution with tables that have been developed to assist in segregating hospital/physician exposures. This will be helpful as the hospital prepares its funding analysis.

All of the above-mentioned data can be helpful in assisting risk managers in getting a sense of proportion as they begin the rate setting process for a group program.

chapter 18

The Risk Manager's Responsibility for Off-Premises Locations

Harold L. Anderson, Josephine Goode-Johnson, Vickey Masta-Gornic, and Mark Schneider

INTRODUCTION

Off-premises business operations, whether they be a solely owned satellite facility, a joint venture, or an acquired separate business, present an important opportunity and challenge for the health care risk manager. At the time the business is being planned or considered for purchase, the risk manager should become involved in weighing the pros and cons of the business decision. Optimism of top executives is the customary starting point for business expansions or joint ventures. The risk manager's job is to temper that optimism with careful scrutiny of the proposal for downside risks. Next to financial performance criteria, risk management issues tend to be the largest area for caution for new operations and often are the ones given the least consideration.

The risk manager should take advantage of this period of high visibility and high corporate utility by using a risk management review of off-premises activities and new business agreements to evaluate exposures and to establish from the start solid risk management guidelines.

Risk management programs traditionally focus on the development and monitoring of departments and clinical services within the organization. Consequently, an often overlooked area of potential liability exposure arises from the relationships and agreements among and between other health care providers and health care facilities known as off-premises exposures. These exposures result from services provided at other locations by hospital staff as well as when persons other than hospital employees provide service within or on behalf of the home institution. To gain control of these actual and potential exposures, the risk manager must begin by identifying the nature of the exposures. Following this identification process, the risk manager should develop strategies for best controlling the risks of the exposures.

IDENTIFICATION OF THE EXPOSURES

Many hospitals have recognized the need to expand their services away from the primary hospital site. This might occur because persons within the hospital (faculty and students primarily) need to broaden their clinical experience or because patients during their illnesses require services not offered by the primary hospital. Most recently these types of exposures have begun to develop as hospitals seek to expand their scope of business.

An additional type of exposure discussed in this chapter is that exposure created when a hospital brings professionals from agencies or contracting groups (off-premises staff) to supplement their staff. Although this type of exposure does not neatly fit the definition of off-premises, discussion is included because many of the same contractual and supervisory issues arise with this exposure as with the other exposures more appropriately included.

In each type of exposure, quality issues may arise that expose the hospital to liability that has not been anticipated, funded, or insured. Identifying the potential for liability and exploring ways to control the environment to lessen the likelihood of liability should be part of every risk manager's job. Some of the specific areas where off-premises liability may arise are:

- contractual liability when services not available at the primary hospital are contracted elsewhere
- management agreements that allow hospital personnel to contract their administrative and management skills to other outside agencies
- joint venture agreements that allow hospitals to consolidate some of their services or to expand their business opportunities
- affiliation agreements that allow education and training of medical students, nursing students, and faculty away from the primary teaching site
- use of agency or contractual employees at the primary site

CONTRACTUAL LIABILITY EXPOSURE

A proactive risk manager must develop strong, interactive relationships with senior management and other operational professionals within the organization to ensure advance awareness of potential contractual relationships. This advance notice offers an opportunity for the risk manager to provide assistance in the identification of potential risks being assumed and, more importantly, affords the risk manager the opportunity to develop guidelines or protocols of reducing the inherent risks. In all instances, the risk manager should work with in-house legal counsel and the quality assurance/improvement staff to plan for the most effective system for controlling the inherent risk arising from this exposure. The overall risk and quality management review should seek to determine the scope of pre-existing institutional policies, evidence of compliance with regulatory mandates, and compliance with the insurance contracts the hospital has in place. The team performing the initial evaluation should identify potential risks associated with the contract terms and recommend mechanisms to minimize the hospital's potential exposure.

General Conditions

While contracts are customized to the facility, certain basic provisions should always be included in the risk manager's assessment to provide maximum protection. These include:

- intent of the agreement, which should clearly define the general reason for the agreement

- duties and responsibilities of each party bound by the contract
- actual length of time during which the agreement will be in force and any specific conditions that could void the contract
- how each party will determine if the agreement should continue and, if it does continue, how the duration of the agreement will be determined. Automatic renewal provisions should not be contemplated without stated criteria for the evaluation of the contracted services or providers.
- termination clause that should state the conditions under which each party may end the contract before and/or on the stated contract period
- indemnification clauses, which are a risk transfer mechanism in which each party attempts to transfer liability of agents to the other party. These should be carefully reviewed and compared with the hospital's professional liability insurance contract to ensure no potential gaps in coverage exist.
- insurance provisions in the contract, which should specifically state the type and limits of the coverages expected and provided by each party

The intent of the agreement should be strictly observed. Often, the original intent of the contract is obscured by an extension of the services without a subsequent amendment to the contract. This ambiguity can pose a significant disadvantage in determining future liabilities and increase the difficulty in resolving contractual disputes.

The length of time the contract is in effect (term of the contract) and determination dates should be clearly detailed and followed. Systems such as tickler files may assist the risk manager in ensuring all contracts up for renewal are reviewed promptly and renegotiated appropriately. If a contract is allowed to renew automatically, the risk manager loses control over the terms and conditions and also loses the opportunity to periodically review whether the contract on its face is sufficiently clear to describe accurately the nature of the services contracted. If inaccuracies are identified, they can and should be addressed at the time of renewal.

Legal counsel should review all indemnification agreements in all contracts. A poorly worded or unfavorable indemnification clause could expose the institution to unnecessary liability. This is particularly important when hospital employees are offsite, or agent/employees of another institution or agency are working in the home institution. A review of the hospital's professional liability insurance policy should occur when the contract is reviewed to ensure the language is consistent and that no gaps in coverage occur. Usually, it will not be possible to transfer all risk, but the liability should be equalized through the indemnification clause.

The insurance provision should be specific in any contract. Specific insurance types and specific coverage limits should be required. If the other institution has agreed to provide insurance, a certificate of insurance should be requested, and the receiving institution should be named as an additional insured. When the off-premises institution provides coverage, the following should be reviewed:

- solvency of the insurance company providing coverage (company should be A-rated or better)
- adequacy of the limits of coverage provided
- type of coverage (occurrence versus claims made)
- policy period (does it extend through the contract period?)
- existence of an extended reporting period
- existence of any conditions and restrictions of the coverage provided
- contractual liability exclusions
- a 30-days'-notice requirement for cancellation, reduction, or material change in the terms and conditions of the contract
- waiver of subrogation

Last, a clause should be written into the contract requiring that the insurer of the off-premises site be reasonably acceptable to both parties to the contract.

Regardless of whether the activity specified in the agreement appears limited, risk managers should review other types of coverage for applicability. Examples of coverage types that should be reviewed are property coverage, comprehensive liability coverage, auto coverage, crime coverage, workers' compensation, and directors' and officers' liability coverage.

In recent years the solvency of commercial insurance carriers has become a major issue. However, the solvency of self-insured programs, both formal such as trusts, captives, risk-allocated trust funds, and expensing and unfunded liabilities (going bare) must be considered. As previously mentioned, insurance rating organizations can provide valuable information about judging the solvency of insurance carriers and programs. Additional sources of information about financial stability may be gleaned from annual audit reports, financial statements, and trust fund balance reviews. Also, a program description including exposure units (beds, visits, FTEs) should be reviewed to determine the adequacy of the funding given the hospital's potential for risk.

In evaluating the delineation of duties and responsibilities of each party, the risk manager should ensure that employment status of each party to the contract is defined. In instances where this is unclear, a potential corporate exposure may be hidden. Some institutions will send residents and staff on rotations while some institutions will only receive rotations, but usually both types of arrangement will occur. Insurance coverage must be considered for the rotating staff, for the supervising staff, and for the vicarious liability that could arise about the employer of the rotating agent. Additionally, if the contract requires administrative responsibilities while at the other institution (e.g., medical or unit director), coverage for these risks also should be explored.

In reviewing the contract for duties and responsibilities of the contracting parties, the following questions should be explored and answered.

- Are the appropriate personnel, equipment, facilities, and resources available to fulfill the contractual obligations?
- Is the responsibility for coverage of particular units or for the handling of particular problems clearly defined?
- Is there a mechanism in place to verify the appropriateness of training and preparing staff who will be providing or supporting care?
- Are supervisory responsibilities clearly delineated?
- Are administrative responsibilities defined?
- Are reporting relationships delineated?
- Are documentation requirements defined, and is there a mechanism to ensure they are followed?
- Are applicable policies that define and govern the contractual relationship available, and are they followed?
- What are the health care requirements and immunization requirements, and are they followed?
- Are there health and injury policies and procedures, and are they strictly enforced?
- Is there documented evidence the off-premises site is in full compliance with licensure and regulatory agencies?
- Is there a policy within the organization that addresses the confidentiality of information?
- Is there a formal facility education/orientation program?

Many contracts will not contain specifics in the operational clauses. If they do not, the risk manager should arrange a meeting before signing the contract to discuss issues related to incident reporting, notice and documentation requirements, claims investigation, joint defense and cooperation, consent to settle provisions, and access to medical records. Agreeing on these protocols before a problem develops will allow for a smoother resolution of that problem should it occur.

It is important for both parties to know the parameters of each facility risk management and quality assurance program so adequate protection of the information is provided and assured. Specific reporting requirements of each institution and the dissemination of this information should be evaluated to determine the contractual and insurance requirements. Often this will be driven by the institution providing the insurance coverage. Even in instances where the home institution is providing coverage, the off-premises institution may require incident notification; therefore, any rotating employee or agent should be advised of the appropriate protocol for reporting all adverse events. The risk manager should guide the rotating employee or agent through all phases of the investigation. However, the information also should be shared with the risk management staff at the off-premises site so problems identified as a result of the investigation can be corrected.

As you can see from this discussion, the review of contracts is a risk management function that should be taken seriously. Many aspects of a contract—even those typically reduced to boilerplate—can cause unanticipated problems and financial loss to the primary institution. Many of these problems can be avoided by doing a careful review of the contract and drafting acceptable terms before the enforcement of the contract.

MANAGED FACILITIES AND MANAGEMENT CONTRACTS

Many contracts and relationships now developed by health care institutions relate to the management of facilities. Several issues related to these types of agreements should be addressed by the risk manager. When management experience and expertise are desired and contracted, the risk manager should review the management agreement to verify that a clear delineation of administrative duties and coverage exists. It is important to note who will be specifically responsible for each aspect of the service provided. The information describing this could include a position description and/or curriculum vitae of key individuals serving in an administrative capacity.

Also, the delineation of the medical director's duties and coverage should be contained in the management agreement. This should specify the clinical aspects of such coverage. Again, a position description and/or curriculum vitae should be included. In addition, verification that the facilities credentialing process was completed and that a current appointment letter is on file should occur.

Individual organizations' ethical philosophies can sometimes conflict. When this occurs, management decisions can further fuel the conflict. When management relations are being developed, the risk manager should verify that all parties are aware of the potential conflict and have thoroughly addressed how specific ethical situations will be handled. Some of the ethical/management issues that may arise relate to do-not-resuscitate (DNR) orders, specific

religious issues that may dictate how or if care is provided, and how the institution addresses cultural and ethnic differences of both patients and staff.

The management agreement between the two facilities should provide certain protective requirements. Programs or policies affording protection should be reviewed and maintained on file. Some items might include:

- quality assurance and risk management plans and management's role in both developing and maintaining them
- occurrence/incident reporting protocols and a description of how management becomes aware of hospital events that could become problematic
- Joint Commission on Accreditation of Healthcare Organizations (Joint Commission) survey results and how the hospital is addressing contingencies (if some were identified in the survey process)
- peer review and due process procedures
- Equal Employment Opportunity Commission (EEOC) compliance and personnel management issues that will be the responsibility of management
- medical staff bylaws and the expectations that the medical staff has of hospital management
- general hospital policy and procedures manual, especially as they relate to the operational issues of the hospital

By maintaining both current and historical documentation of these requirements and by putting the managing organization in a proactive role to ensure quality management will be fostered, risk managers can be more confident that these types of arrangements will not pose additional risks to their organizations.

EVALUATING JOINT VENTURES AND OTHER NEW BUSINESS EXPOSURES

Due Diligence

As a result of corporate mergers and acquisitions and health care expansions during the last decade, due diligence procedures have become an accepted necessity. Also, they have become standardized, with the risk manager playing the role of evaluating hazards and insurable exposures. The premises exposures include:

- fire hazards
- asbestos
- underground storage tanks
- delayed maintenance
- code violations

Another area of exposure requiring evaluation is the litigation history and claims history of the business to be managed. In addition, the risk manager should assemble a picture about prior coverage to determine if there are pending losses that could exceed coverage limits and to determine if there are noticeable gaps in coverage. These gaps could have arisen from unavailability of coverage or from negative decisions by underwriters about the exposure. The other area of exposure requiring evaluation is the potential for inheriting personnel problems from workers' compensation losses, EEOC litigation, or Occupational Safety and Health Administration (OSHA) violations.

Looking at projections for the use of the new entity and gathering jurisdictional or industry data to project future liabilities also are useful parts of the preliminary analysis. One increasingly difficult problem for not-for-profit corporations arises when property is donated. The risk manager should work with the development office to establish precautions and guidelines about offers of property and premises. Due diligence procedures need to be used before ownership is transferred to the not-for-profit cooperation.

Coverage

For a separate off-premises operation, whether a satellite, subsidiary business, or joint venture, the standard insurance coverages need to be reviewed independently. Insurable exposures may be different, or there may be important reasons to maintain separate policies for these operations. The standard lines of coverage to verify are:

- general liability, including products and completed operations
- auto liability
- workers' compensation
- professional liability
- property coverage, including business interruption and extra expense
- directors' and officers' coverage

Three coverage lines requiring careful attention for these situations are directors' and officers' coverage, property insurance, and products liability. Particularly in the case of a joint venture, directors' and officers' liability coverage will be a pressing concern to the board of trustees. The board of trustees should be cautioned that this may be a difficult or exceedingly expensive coverage to obtain for a new joint venture corporation. The risk manager needs to be as well informed as possible on the corporate structure, operations, and anticipated financial transactions to have the best chance of obtaining good coverage quotations. If the coverage appears difficult to obtain, an alternative should be explored, such as endorsing coverage for joint venture

activities onto the directors' and officers' policies of the parent corporations. For solely owned subsidiaries, the parent corporation's current directors' and officers' carrier should be advised of the formation of the subsidiary corporation, emphasizing the interrelatedness of the corporate structure.

Further, to the additional values of buildings and contents, a new off-premises business operation poses business interruption risk. The risk manager needs to evaluate the likely extent of revenue and income loss if damage is caused by fire or extended perils. Some thought should be given to the cost required to maintain these operations at a temporary location with leased equipment. Considering the scarcity of health care professionals, any business interruption projections involving health care operations should assume the perpetuation of payroll for health care professionals as a continuing expense.

Some off-premises business operations involve the sale of products. The relationship to the product (whether manufacturer, wholesaler, supplier, or adviser) should be analyzed about the products' liability provisions of the general liability policy. Risk managers' extensive knowledge of the product flow and its liability implications will enable them to propose endorsements to further delineate proper coverage.

One major decision about coverage of an off-premises business operation is whether to blend the coverage into the existing corporate insurance program or to establish a separate set of policies. The first consideration is the preservation of the tax-exempt status of self-insurance funding for not-for-profit operations. Other considerations will be whether the operations are closely controlled by the parent and whether these operations provide interconnected services.

The entire profit versus not-for-profit question deserves risk management attention from other perspectives as well. It is important to recognize that the difference in status produces significantly different business goals. Risk managers can see the differences appear in several ways. For example:

- Different public perception of a profit corporation increases the potential size of liability verdicts.
- Fast pace, high pressure, and undercapitalization lead to operational shortcuts that produce losses.
- Parent corporation managers may not be familiar with new fields of operation that can produce losses through poor service choices or miscommunication.

Exposure History

For off-premises business operations being bought out or newly managed by the health care corporation, there are some additional areas for obtaining a history of prior exposures. The risk manager can use these to pinpoint immediate areas of concern or to suggest improvements that reduce long-term risk. The first source of historical exposure is from financial statements. The assets give some indication of insurable interests to be covered. The liability discussion may give some indication of litigation exposures. Equally important, the cash flow will give some indication of the financial stability of this operation. Here the risk management implication is that a stable, profitable operation has the finances available to spend for management quality and for safety precautions. Safety is one of the first activities to suffer reduction when an operation is losing money. Auditor's letters of recommendations should be scrutinized for significant problem areas. Additional information can come from regulatory filings. If it is a health care organization, the Joint Commission survey should provide important information. Also, any state license applications or regulatory hearings will give some indication of potential weak spots.

An important but often unnoticed part of disaster planning is for the risk manager to obtain all of the business operations' prior insurance policies. In particular, property, general liability, and umbrella policies would be useful if latent defects in the property, such as the discovery of asbestos or in-ground pollution, prompted a search for available coverage.

Management Relations

If the parent health care corporation purchases or takes over the management of an off-premises business operation, one of the more difficult technical feats is to merge two existing insurance programs into one. Consideration needs to be given to the variations in the following coverage conditions:

- coverage triggers (specific kinds of events that can cause a claim under each policy)
- coverage forms, especially between claims made and occurrence forms
- retroactive dates (canceling the policy with the shorter retroactive date creates a retrospective gap in coverage)
- limits and self-insured retentions, especially about aggregate underlying retentions

Taking control of an established operation provides a useful opportunity to establish a schedule for verification of coverages provided to the business entity by contractual agreement. In organizations with numerous departments letting contracts, the certificates of insurance and other coverage verifications are likely to be decentralized. Centralizing this activity in the risk manager's office not only

verifies third-party indemnification, but establishes the risk manager in the chain of communications regarding future contracts.

Operational Assessments

Risk management guidelines should be expanded to include the additional off-premises business operations. At a minimum, clear lines of communication should be established for matters that have liability potential. One useful way to enhance communications and clarify risk management services and expectations with offsite operations is to provide managers of that operation with the results of the exposure surveys and with summaries of any site reviews.

Any safety protocols for the parent corporation should be expanded to include the off-premises operations. OSHA requirements, particularly in the area of employee right-to-know rules, should be verified or established. Managers of the offsite premises should be alerted to additional exposures in the following areas:

- environmental impairment, including underground storage tanks and asbestos
- business's obligations for leased property or equipment
- business interruption bottlenecks within the operation. Remember that most health care procedures are interdependent. If one particular activity is interrupted, for example radiology, this may significantly interrupt the entire operation.
- business interruption caused by external sources. Consideration needs to be given to access utilities, especially electricity and telephone service. In addition, the impact of the loss of critical suppliers should be examined. Where there are no useful alternatives to these external sources, including these as sources of business interruption under the terms of the property insurance policy should be explored.

For off-premises operations involving the sale or distribution of products, a different liability atmosphere exists. The important risk management concerns are:

- strict liability exposures for inherently dangerous products
- warranties
- quality control
- contractual agreements with manufacturers

Product liability litigation average tends to be more expensive for defense costs and tends to have a longer duration.

It would be useful to check for unusual items owned by the offsite premises to see if any special liability policies are appropriate. Examples are aircraft (owned or leased), helicopters (owned or leased), and boat and/or docks.

Medical waste is becoming a significant long-term liability consideration. If the offsite operation involves health care services for medical products, a review of its procedures for disposing of medical or hazardous waste becomes important. These procedures should be closely coordinated with that of the parent organization.

As a final point of assessment, the risk manager should become familiar with the administrative organization chart and lines of communication for the off-premises operation. This should apply not only to the internal organization of that operation but also to its relationship and lines of communication with the parent organization. Of importance to the risk manager is knowing how to obtain urgently needed information about the business operation, particularly if that need arises late at night or on weekends.

AFFILIATION AGREEMENTS

The development of affiliations between the primary teaching site and other satellite sites requires risk managers to incorporate much of the same information as has been described in the contract and new business section of this chapter. In many instances, affiliation agreements are entered into by hospitals that have an educational or teaching focus to their operation. In those types of institutions, risk managers may find that students (nursing and medical), interns, residents, and fellows rotate to locations away from the primary facility to broaden their clinical experience. Risk managers also may find that faculty or nurse managers rotate to these sites to provide education and/or supervision to another hospital's personnel. Although these types of arrangements can be mutually beneficial, risk managers must assure that issues associated with this affiliation do not pose risk management problems for the primary teaching hospital.

The problem that most frequently arises in these instances is one related to supervision. A risk manager at the primary teaching facility is generally aware of how supervision occurs within the primary teaching hospital and also is able to determine who has the ultimate authority and accountability for patient care. This determination may be more difficult in smaller institutions or in institutions where backup is provided on-call and may not be readily available.

Other issues related to the handling and investigation of injury, the defense of personnel if litigation arises, and the determination of the appropriateness of support for those persons rotating to the affiliate site should be discussed and agreed upon before the onset of the relationship.

A risk manager also may want to develop a tracking system that provides a thumbnail sketch of issues related to all of the sites where students or staff are working

(see Exhibit 18-1). This will allow the risk manager to ascertain quickly how affiliation issues have been addressed.

USE OF AGENCY OR CONTRACT EMPLOYEES AT THE PRIMARY SITE

Agency Exposures

Health care institutions always have had an exposure due to the utilization of private duty nurses. Given the current shortage of numerous health care workers, especially nurses, the use of agency personnel to meet the staffing needs of institutions has expanded greatly. A well-structured approach to controlling this liability is essential in this climate. The following discussion focuses on the use of agency nurses and nursing assistants; however, the theory can be applied to any health care specialty.

Agency personnel may be used for several purposes including supplemental staffing, private duty nursing, or companion personnel. Each of these has slightly different standards and will be addressed individually. However, the starting point is the same for each.

Before accepting personnel, the agency itself should be investigated. A key individual must assess the agency to ensure that its hiring practices, policies and procedures, and liability insurance are acceptable to the hospital. To ensure this is done, the number of agencies can be limited. This also prevents individuals who have not been oriented to the institutional policies and procedures from working there.

The first step in the process is for the agency to furnish the institution with specific information about the business. The following information should be collected and analyzed:

- proof of licensure or certification for the operation
- professional liability insurance with limits of liability and underwritten by a company acceptable to the health care institution
- all policies and procedures of the agency, including license verification of agency personnel
- job descriptions
- rates
- employee applications
- skills assessment profiles
- physical examination
- evaluation form for the agency
- dress code

All of this information will be reviewed by the nursing department to ensure that it meets the standards set by the health care organization. The nursing department or other involved department should share the information with the

Exhibit 18-1
SUMMARY OF AFFILIATE CONTRACTS

	UNIVERSITY FACILITY	AFFILIATED HOSPITAL	NONAFFILIATED HOSPITAL CLINIC	OUT OF STATE	MOONLIGHTING
FACULTY					
Wear University Name Tag	Yes	Yes	Yes	Yes	NA
Assume Payroll Expense	University	University	University	University	NA
Provide Indemnification	University	University	University	University	NA
Covered by Governmental Immunity	Yes	Yes	Yes	Yes	NA
FACULTY ON DUAL PAYROLL					
Wear University Name Tag	Yes	Yes	Yes	Yes	NA
Assume Payroll Expense	University	Affiliated Hospital	University	University	NA
Provide Indemnification	University	Affiliated Hospital	University	University	NA
Covered by Governmental Immunity	Yes	Yes	Yes	No	NA
RESIDENTS/STUDENTS					
Wear University Name Tag	Yes	No	Yes	No	No
Assume Payroll Expense	Yes	Affiliated Hospital	University	Not University	Not University
Provide Indemnification	University	Affiliated Hospital	University	Not University	Not University
Covered by Governmental Immunity	Yes	No	Yes	No	No

risk management department to ensure that all necessary material has been documented and that the insurance is in order. This is particularly important when an agency is self-insured. In this case, the risk manager should ask the company for specific verification of the self-insurance program, including financial statements if necessary. Also, make sure that any contracts include specifics about responsibilities should the self-insurance program have financial difficulties.

Some hospitals have chosen to limit the number of agencies with whom they work. This allows for closer control over the operational procedures outlined with the agency.

The procedure followed by the hospital will vary depending on that role the agency personnel will be filling. Due to the current shortage of nursing personnel, many hospitals are using agency personnel as supplemental staff. The following guidelines should be followed when personnel are acting as staff.

The organization should have a policy for internal notification of the need for supplemental staff. This allows for control in a central location of the numbers and types of people from agencies within the institution. Each institution must set its own guidelines for determining when agency personnel are to be used.

Once the internal mechanism is in place, the nursing department must verify specific information about the personnel before it starts work. For example:

- licensure verification
  - Proof of licensure must be presented by each nurse.
  - A copy will be maintained by the hospital.
- proof of insurance
  - Certificate of insurance, acceptable to the hospital, must be presented by the nurse or agency.
  - This certificate will be kept on file and must be renewed for services to continue.
- verification of satisfactory health assessment
  - This must be in accordance with the state's department of health or other regulatory requirements.
- orientation to hospital policies and procedures
  - The RN schedule includes CPR certification, emergency care, IV therapy, documentation, medicine, body mechanics, fire and electrical safety, infection control including universal precautions, and occurrence/incident reporting procedures.
- evaluations
  - Evaluations of supplemental staff will be completed on a regular basis. Evaluations will be completed after the first assignment and quarterly thereafter. The nurse manager of the unit will be responsible for completion of the evaluation.

- Evaluation will include the three components of the nursing process: assessment, planning, implementation.

Private duty nurses or nursing assistants may be requested by the patient or family. The cost of this service is the responsibility of the patient or family. The patient or family also is responsible for making arrangements with an agency approved by the nursing division. A list of such agencies is available upon request. Private duty nurses must meet the same standards as listed above for supplemental staff. Private duty nurses must attend the same orientation as supplemental staff.

The responsibilities of the hospital's nursing staff for patients with a private duty nurse include but are not limited to:

- ensuring that the private duty nurse has clearance from nursing administration
- orienting the private duty nurse to the policies and procedures of the unit
- using the skills assessment (credentialing) information provided by the nurse
- instructing the private duty nurse in the use of occurrence/incident reporting forms

The responsibilities of the private duty nurse include but are not limited to:

- keeping the staff informed of patients' status and treatments
- maintaining documentation of patients' care
- completing the occurrence/incident reporting form, if necessary. This form is to be given to the nurse manager or supervisor for appropriate follow-up and then sent to the risk management office.

The contractual agreements between the agencies and the health care institution are the most important part of any agreement. See Appendix 18-A for a sample nursing agency agreement. In case of dispute or litigation, they will determine the involvement of the hospital.

CONCLUSION

Because of the scope of the risk managers' organizational knowledge and because of risk managers' ability to spot dangerous or extremely expensive problems, incorporating an off-premises business operation into the management plan of the parent organization showcases risk managers' talents and usefulness. Risk managers should take advantage of these opportunities to demonstrate their usefulness and to establish procedures at the new facilities and in the new business ventures that provide long-term benefits.

Sample Nursing Agreement

This Agreement is made on the _____ by and between _____, a nonprofit corporation organized under the laws of _____ (hereinafter referred to as "the Hospital") and _____ (hereinafter referred to as "the Agency"). Both the Hospital and the Agency are hereinafter referred to as "Parties" to this Agreement. The initial contract period under this Agreement will be from _____ to _____. It is understood and agreed that this contract may be renewed from year to year upon mutual agreement of the parties hereto evidenced by a statement to that effect executed within thirty (30) days prior to the initial termination and each termination date thereafter.

RECITALS

WHEREAS, the Hospital is a health care institution dedicated to providing quality health care to patients who enter the institution for such purposes; and

WHEREAS, the Agency is a corporation that supplies health care professionals such as registered nurses and licensed practical nurses ("nurses") to health care institutions;

WHEREAS, the Hospital seeks to engage the services of such registered and licensed practical nurses through the Agency;

NOW THEREFORE, in consideration of the recitals and mutual covenants, agreements, and inducements contained herein, the Parties hereby agree as follows:

CLAUSE 1: DEFINITIONS

1.1 <u>Agreement</u>. As used herein, Agreement means this written contract entered into between the Hospital and the Agency and any amendment(s) thereto as may be in the future adopted as hereinafter provided.

1.2 <u>Hospital Policies</u>. The term "Hospital Policies" shall mean and include the Articles of Incorporation, bylaws and rules of the Hospital, the procedures and policies adopted by the medical staff and nursing department, Nursing Department rules and regulations, and other policies, practices, and procedures of the Hospital.

CLAUSE 2: DUTIES OF THE AGENCY

2.1 Agency will provide to Hospital Registered Nurses and Licensed Practical Nurses from time to time in a quantity specified by the Hospital and with qualifications as specified by the Hospital.

2.2 Agency will provide only nurses with a professional nursing license that is valid at the time he/she is assigned to work at the Hospital. Agency shall keep on file a copy of the license for each nurse supplied to the Hospital. Such license shall be made available to the Hospital upon request.

2.3 Agency shall ensure that all nurses provided to the Hospital by this contract will follow all Hospital procedures and policies.

2.4 If at any time the Hospital is dissatisfied with the service of any nurse supplied by the Agency, the Hospital in its sole discretion may dismiss the nurse and upon notice from the Hospital, the Agency will make reasonable efforts to provide a replacement.

CLAUSE 3: DUTIES OF THE HOSPITAL

3.1 Hospital shall explain the Hospital policies that the nurses working under this contract will be required to follow.

3.2 Upon commencement of a contracted service period, the Hospital agrees to give the Agency either notice initially or at least forty-eight (48) hours' notice prior to completion of said service period.

CLAUSE 4: COMPENSATION

4.1 Hospital agrees to pay the Agency for the services of nurses provided under this Agreement at the rate of

_____ per hour for weekdays up to 4 P.M.; _____ per hour for weekdays after 4 P.M.; and _____ per hour for weekends.

4.2 Agency shall provide written notice of changes in hourly rates at least seven (7) days before the rate change is to become effective.

4.3 Payment shall be made by the Hospital within _____ days of receipt of an invoice specifying the nurse's name and the hours worked.

CLAUSE 5: STATUS OF THE PARTIES

5.1 It is expressly understood and agreed that, in the performance of services under this Agreement, all nurses supplied by the Agency shall be independent contractors with respect to the Hospital and not as employees or agents of the Hospital. Further, it is expressly understood and agreed by the parties that nothing contained in this Agreement shall be construed to create a joint venture, partnership, association or other affiliation or like relationship between the Parties, it being specifically agreed that their relationship is and shall remain that of independent Parties to a contractual relationship as set forth in this Agreement.

5.2 No nurse shall have any claim under this Agreement or otherwise against the Hospital for vacation pay, paid sick leave, retirement benefits, social security, workers' compensation, health, disability, professional malpractice, or unemployment insurance benefits or other employee benefits of any kind. The Agency will indemnify and hold the Hospital harmless from any and all liability arising from claims relating to the failure to make such payments, withholdings, and benefits of any kind. This duty of the Agency shall survive the termination of this Agreement.

5.3 The Hospital will not withhold on behalf of such independent contractor/nurse any sums for income tax, unemployment insurance, social security, or any other withholding pursuant to any law or requirement of any governmental body. The Agency will indemnify and hold the Hospital harmless from any and all liability arising from claims relating to the failure to make such payments, withholdings, and benefits of any kind. This duty of the Agency shall survive the termination of this Agreement.

CLAUSE 6: PROFESSIONAL LIABILITY INSURANCE

6.1 Agency will provide to the Hospital only nurses with proof of professional liability insurance with minimum limits of $1,000,000 per occurrence and $3,000,000 aggregate. The duty to maintain such coverage for the period the nurse is assigned to the Hospital shall survive the termination of this Agreement. In the event that the form of insurance is in a claims made form, the Agency warrants and represents that it will at all times in the future maintain appropriate tail coverage for claims, demands, or actions reported in future years for past acts or omissions.

6.2 Such insurance policies shall be issued by insurance companies reasonably acceptable to the Hospital and licensed to conduct business in _____ and shall be written as primary coverage and not contributing with or in excess of any coverage that the Hospital may carry. The Agency shall furnish to the Hospital's Office of Risk Management, at least thirty (30) days before the date when the Agency first provides health care professionals to the Hospital and at least thirty (30) days before the expiration of any certificate previously furnished, a certificate of insurance for the above-mentioned policies, together with evidence of payment of all applicable premiums. Each insurance policy required to be carried hereunder shall provide (and any certificate evidencing the existence of each such insurance policy shall certify) that such insurance policy shall not be cancelled unless the Hospital shall have received twenty (20) days' prior written notice of cancellation. The Agency shall provide immediate notice to the Hospital's Office of Risk Management of any significant change in the aforementioned coverage or limits. Neither the issuance of any insurance policy required under this Agreement, nor the minimum limits specified herein with respect to insurance coverage, shall be deemed to limit or restrict in any way the Agency's liability arising from this Agreement.

6.3 The Hospital shall not be required to provide such insurance nor shall the Hospital be liable for the payment of any premiums on such insurance.

CLAUSE 7: APPORTIONMENT OF LIABILITY AND DAMAGES/ INDEMNIFICATION

7.1 Nurses referred to in this Agreement are deemed to be employees of the Agency.

7.2 It is hereby stipulated and agreed between the Hospital and the Agency that with respect to any claim or action arising out of any services performed under or pursuant to this Agreement, each entity shall only be liable for payment of that portion of any and all liability, costs, expenses, demands, settlements, or judgments resulting from the negligence, actions, or omissions of its own agents, officers, and employees.

7.3   In any case in which liability and damages are not judicially apportioned between the Hospital and the Agency, the Parties hereby agree that their respective pro rata shares of any liability, costs, expenses, demands, settlements, or judgments will be decided in accordance with the procedures set forth in Paragraph 8 of this Clause.

7.4   The Agency hereby agrees to indemnify, protect, and save harmless the Hospital, its agents, officers, and employees from any and all claims, demands, actions, or judgments for which the Hospital may become liable based upon or arising from services provided by a nurse pursuant to this Agreement and resulting from the negligence, actions, or omissions of the Agency or any of its officers, agents, or employees. This duty of the Agency shall survive termination of this Agreement.

7.5   In any action or claim arising out of any services performed under or pursuant to this agreement, the Hospital shall assume the defense of itself, its own officers, agents, or employees in accordance with the usual provisions of its malpractice insurance and its own agreements with its officers, agents, or employees.

7.6   In any action or claim arising out of any services performed by a nurse under or pursuant to this Agreement, the Agency shall assume the defense of itself, its officers, agents, or employees, in accordance with the usual provision of its malpractice insurance and its own agreement with said officers, agents, or employees.

7.7   The Agency warrants in accordance with Clause 6, Paragraph 1 of this Agreement that nurses supplied to the Hospital by the Agency are insured under the Agency's malpractice insurance or through malpractice insurance coverage procured by the Agency for nurses in their employ or by the nurses on their own behalf.

7.8   In any case in which liability and/or damages are not judicially apportioned between the Hospital and the Agency, each of said entities hereby agrees to contribute its share of any damages or settlements of claims, the amount of which shall correspond to the percentage of casual negligence attributable to their respective institutions, agents, employees, and officers. The Hospital and the Agency further agree to make a good faith effort to achieve a mutually agreed

upon apportionment of the liability of their respective institutions, agents, employees, and officers.

7.9   It is hereby stipulated and agreed between the Hospital and the Agency that in any case in which Paragraph 8 of this Clause applies and in which the Parties are unable to reach a mutual agreement with respect to the apportionment of liability and damages between the two entities, that the Hospital and the Agency shall, with the consent of their respective insurance carriers, submit their dispute to a panel of three arbitrators whose decision with regard to the apportionment of liability and damages between the two entities shall be final and binding on both entities. Each entity shall select one arbitrator and the third arbitrator shall be appointed by agreement of the two arbitrators so selected.

CLAUSE 8: TERMINATION

8.1   This Agreement, and each renewal term hereunder, may be terminated and cancelled with or without cause without penalty, at any time, by the following methods:

a.   *Termination by Agreement.* In the event the Hospital and the Agency shall mutually agree in writing, this Agreement may be terminated on the terms and date stipulated therein.

b.   *Termination for Specific Breaches.* In the event the Agency shall fail by omission or commission in any substantial manner to provide the services as specified in Clause 2 hereof, this Agreement may be terminated at the discretion of the Hospital by notice.

c.   *Optional Termination.* In the event either party to this agreement shall, with or without cause, at any time give to the other the following advance written notice, this Agreement shall terminate on the future date specified in such notice:

1) Hospital must provide at least 90 days' written notice.

2) Agency must provide at least 90 days' written notice.

8.2   Upon termination of this Agreement, as hereinabove provided, neither party shall have any further obligation hereunder except for (i) obligations accruing prior to the date of termination and (ii) obligations, promises, or covenants contained herein that are expressly made to extend beyond the terms of this Agreement.

CLAUSE 9: OTHER TERMS AND CONDITIONS

9.1   This Agreement evidences the entire Agreement between the Parties hereto and may not be changed, altered, or modified in any manner unless such change is agreed to in writing by both the Hospital and the Agency.

9.2   This Agreement has been executed and delivered in, and shall be interpreted, construed, and enforced pursuant to and in accordance with, the laws of _____.

9.3   The waiver by either party of a breach or violation of any provision of this Agreement shall not operate as, or be construed to be, a waiver of any subsequent breach of the same or other provisions hereof.

9.4   Neither party shall be held responsible for any delay or failure in performance hereunder arising out of causes beyond its control or without its fault or negligence. Such causes may include, but are not limited to, fires, strikes, acts of God, or national disasters.

9.5   If any term or provision of this Agreement shall to any extent be held invalid or unenforceable, the remaining terms and provisions of the Agreement shall not be affected, but each term and provision of the Agreement shall be valid and enforced to the fullest extent permitted by law.

9.6   This Agreement is for the provision of personal, professional services and may not be assigned or transferred by either party without the prior written consent of the other.

9.7   This Agreement supersedes all previous contracts and constitutes the entire Agreement between the Parties. Oral statements or prior written material not specifically incorporated herein shall be of no force and effect and no changes in or additions to this Agreement shall be recognized unless incorporated herein by amendment as provided herein, such amendment(s) to become effective on the date stipulated therein. The Agency specifically acknowledges that in entering into and executing this Agreement, the Agency relies solely upon the representations and agreements contained in this Agreement and no others.

9.8   Until the expiration of four years after furnishing the services called for by this Agreement, the Agency, upon request, shall make available to the Secretary, U.S. Department of Health and Human Services, the U.S. Comptroller General, and their representatives, this Agreement and all other books, documents, and records as are necessary to certify the nature and extent of the costs incurred by the Hospital in purchasing services under this Agreement.

IN WITNESS THEREOF, the Parties have caused this Agreement to be executed in and governed by and administered in accordance with the laws of _____.

HOSPITAL

By: _____

Title: _____

Date: _____

AGENCY

By: _____

Title: _____

Date: _____

chapter 19

Guidelines for In-House Claims Management

Josephine Goode-Johnson

INTRODUCTION

Early identification, investigation, and resolution of potentially compensable events are the major objectives of an effective claims management program. Successful achievement of these objectives depends on strong commitment and support from all participants and an effective risk management program maximizing the four basic components of identification, analysis, treatment, and evaluation. Because these components become the foundation of the claims management process, the first step toward program development is an overall assessment.

ASSESSING THE ENVIRONMENT

The risk or claims manager should first assess the environment in which the program is to be established. This assessment should include the following actions:

- ensure top-level commitment and support of the system
- review existing risk identification systems to ensure protection of information
- evaluate the scope of the proposed program as it relates to the requirements of insurance companies and other risk-financing vehicles
- determine management informational system needs
- survey existing resources and establish goals and objectives

Top Level Commitment

It is imperative that senior administration and the institution's governing board understand the scope of responsibility and accountability necessary to develop and maintain an in-house claims management system. The risk or claims manager, as applicable, should ensure that those ultimately responsible for its success and support understand, at minimum, the following aspects of the proposed program:

- structure of the program, including its relationships and reporting requirements
- procedures for obtaining and protecting required information
- limitation of informational access (procedures and reasons)
- investigational policies and procedures
- requirements of participants (insured or covered persons)
- basic risk financing as it relates to financial stability of the program
- types of coverage, restrictions, and exclusions

This list is not meant to be all-inclusive, but to suggest basic guidelines toward developing the governing board's education and interest in order to increase its support of the program.

Risk Identification Systems

Most institutions already have mechanisms in place to identify untoward patient occurrences ranging from basic incident reporting to elaborate networks involving receipt of information from other in-house systems. The incident report remains one of the oldest methods of communicating information of adverse occurrences. Participants in the program should be encouraged to report information freely and objectively; they should be assured that reports are nonpunitive. Depending on the program's structure and methods for protecting the confidentiality of the information, other methods such as telephone reports and anonymous telephone lines may be explored to supplement written reports.

Additionally, the risk or claims manager should educate nonclinical departments in the importance of providing information regarding potentially compensable events. Through this method, managers can extend beyond traditional sources to ensure prompt identification of these incidents. The following departments are often able to provide early warning indicators:

- *Medical records* can advise the claims management office of requests for records by plaintiffs' attorneys.
- *Quality assurance* can provide information from generic screening criteria and other medical staff sources, as applicable.
- *Billing offices* can notify the claims office of serious medical care complaints when following up on delinquent bills.
- *Volunteer services* can relay complaints about patient care. Volunteers are often the first to hear from disgruntled patients, because they are viewed by the patients as neutral.

Prior to implementing any risk identification techniques, it is imperative to take measures to protect program information from discoverability. Legal counsel should be consulted to ensure that all program identification methods, guidelines, structures, and documentation are appropriate and effective for the institution's particular circumstances.

In self-insured programs it is also helpful, if possible, to advise covered participants of their obligation to report adverse outcomes as a condition of their coverage.

Scope of the Program

The in-house program will be significantly impacted by the institution's method of risk financing. For example, if the institution is self-insured, the risk or claims manager must ascertain whether excess or umbrella coverage will be purchased. If so, many of the program reporting requirements both internally and externally will be affected by the excess policy. If the program will purchase first dollar commercial insurance, the program requirements, structure, data collection, and other features will be somewhat defined by this primary policy. Consequently, a full review of the type of risk-financing mechanism should be conducted with an eye toward determining the scope of in-house responsibility that can and should be assumed in accordance with internal and external constraints.

Management Informational System

Whether the institution will have first-dollar commercial insurance coverage or utilize alternative risk-funding mechanisms will also impact the claims management informational system. If utilizing commercial insurance coverage, the manager must ascertain the type of information the company provides and the regularity of the reports. At a minimum, it is recommended that the insurance company provide a loss experience and case status update on a regular basis (see Exhibit 19-1 for a sample checklist). For those institutions using risk-financing alternatives, detailed information regarding development of an in-house claims management information system is discussed in a later section of this chapter.

GOALS AND OBJECTIVES

The success of the program is directly related to the manager's ability to formulate achievable, realistic, and measurable goals utilizing available resources. After the scope of the program is determined and it is clear where the in-house claims program responsibilities begin and end, objectives should be established and clearly stated. The objectives must be consistent with the institution's goals and with the corporate culture.

Planning at this stage should consider internal, external, and vertical communication; protocols; policies and procedures; and claims management requirements.

PROGRAM DEVELOPMENT

When the manager has completed the overall assessment to determine the appropriate scope and structure of the program, a claims management philosophy statement should be developed, setting forth the philosophy of claims handling for the institution. The statement and subsequent policies should guide the staff in routine handling of claims and should also be in line with other relevant primary or excess coverage.

An efficient and effective risk identification mechanism is the foundation for development of the claims management system. Guidelines must be developed to determine

Exhibit 19-1
SAMPLE CHECKLIST FOR A COMMERCIALLY INSURED INSTITUTION

I. Read the complete insurance policy and pay particular attention to the following sections:
  A. Insuring agreements—defines the coverage granted by the policy.
  B. Exclusions—specific acts or events that the insurer eliminates from the coverage of the policy.
  C. Conditions—defines the rights, privileges, duties, and obligations of the insured and the insurer.
  D. Definitions—defines special meanings assigned to words or phrases in the contract.
  E. Declarations—contains fundamental information of the contract (e.g., name and address of insured, policy period, limits of liability).
II. Review specific reporting requirements of the policy, inclusive of:
  A. What constitutes a reportable claim.
  B. Who is to report to the company.
  C. How often and in what manner reports are made.
  D. Who is to conduct an investigation in the event of a claim.
III. Develop a system of classifications for incidents.
IV. Determine which incidents are to be reported to insurers and how often.
V. Request acknowledgment of receipt of incidents from insurer.

VI. Discuss with insurer reports to be received:
  A. Status report on open claims at least quarterly, inclusive of whether suit has been filed, attorney assignments, liability exposure, and other relevant factors.
  B. Quarterly loss experience—details all reserved matters and should also include:
    1. Claimant name.
    2. Claimant number.
    3. Expense reserved.
    4. Indemnity reserved.
    5. Paid-to-date expense.
    6. Date of loss.
    7. Paid-to-date indemnity.
    8. Total incurred.
    9. Brief synopsis of claim.
VII. Review loss experience quarterly to determine:
  A. Encroachment on aggregate policy limits.
  B. Patterns of frequency and severity.
  C. Areas for risk prevention and loss control.
  D. Meaningful reports to governing board.
  E. Departmental manager's involvement.
  F. Time frames for action.
  G. Performance criteria and monitors.
  H. Control mechanisms.

how the information is to be collected, trended, logged in, classified, and shared or transferred, as applicable, depending upon the program's scope. Information received from all sources should be logged into the system (computerized or manual) upon receipt. The information log should include:

- date of receipt
- date of the incident
- patient's name
- patient's identification number
- location of the incident

Within 24 hours of receipt, each incident should be reviewed and classified for further activity. A simple classification system establishing definitions for each classification in accordance with applicable primary or excess insurance definitions is needed. For example, the claims or risk manager may choose to use the following classifications and definitions (see Appendix 19-A):

1. *incident:* adverse occurrence having no loss potential; to be evaluated for loss prevention, education, statistical analysis, and trending purposes, as applicable
2. *investigative incident:* adverse occurrence appearing to have some potential loss exposure by description:

- will need further investigation to make risk prevention or loss control referrals, or liability determination
- if questionable exposure, will be suspended for future review
- if no exposure, will be referred to the quality assurance department, physician peer review, etc., or used to develop loss prevention programs
- if exposure exists, will establish file as potential claim

3. *potential claim:* adverse occurrence having definite loss, potential and exposure; needs complete internal investigation; possible referral for educational purposes, statistical analysis, and loss prevention
4. *claim:* defined as a written demand for monetary reimbursement; could develop into formal legal action

These simple risk management definitions may be helpful in identifying and classifying information; however, for claims management purposes, they should be further refined. Insurance companies and self-insured programs generally use three major definitions: incidents, claims, and suits. Consequently, the incident classification system for claims management purposes may merge incidents, investigative incidents, and potential claims into a category called incidents. When the manager receives a written demand for compensation, the incident then becomes a claim. If resolution is not achieved and formal legal action is pursued in the judicial system, the claim then becomes a suit.

ESTABLISHING THE CLAIMS FILE

A claims file should be established when it is determined that the possibility of financial loss, liability, or exposure exists. In the event that the institution is procuring primary coverage, this file may be established by the insurance company and the claims manager's file may be only a monitoring file. The insurance company may require complete investigation by its own investigators but may rely on the claims manager for coordination of the insured's activities, such as locating and scheduling, and obtaining copies of relevant policies, procedures, and other data. It is important that the claims manager ensure that information in the files is protected from discoverability, whether monitoring files or complete in-house investigative files.

Usually the file jacket or folder contains basic identification information on the claim (e.g., claimant's name, claim number). Inside the file a simple form (see Exhibit 19-2) can be developed manually or run from the computerized claims management information system (see Appendix 19-B) to provide pertinent information at a glance. The form should contain the following data:

- date of incident
- date of claim
- allegation
- claim number
- date file opened
- date file closed
- current status
- changes in reserves (indemnity and expense)
- plaintiff's name
- defendant's name
- name of plaintiff's attorney
- name of defense attorney
- department
- location
- diary date
- disposition of case

The body of the file should be organized and filed in chronological order. The following information should be included:

- incident report or other source of information
- date the incident occurred
- date the incident was reported to the claims management department

- date reported to insurer (as applicable)
- date reported to attorney (as applicable)
- how the information was reported

This information is useful in evaluating the effectiveness of the identification program at a later date. If a significant amount of time elapsed between the incident and when it was reported to the claims management department, it may indicate a need to educate program participants in the necessity of early reporting and the advantages of prompt investigation and negotiation. The date the incident is reported to the insurer must be noted for proof of compliance with the insurer's reporting requirements. If the information was reported by someone other than the individual involved, education again may be necessary.

Documentation of the investigation findings and any internal expert physician reviews or evaluations should be contained in the file. Many hospitals, particularly teaching programs, take advantage of the wide variety of faculty specialties and use this expertise to help screen incidents for deviations from standards of care and resultant exposures (Exhibit 19-3). If a hospital employs this method, it is strongly suggested that education programs for all experts are conducted to discuss confidentiality and objective assessment.

A review of the medical record surrounding the events of the incident should be conducted in detail. The review should not only examine the clinical components of the record but also assess the following:

- whether the incident is documented in the medical record
- whether the information is recorded in an objective, factual manner
- whether there are disparaging or other undesirable comments in the record regarding the patient or among services, consultants, and providers

A summary of the record highlights should be dictated and placed in the file for reference. All correspondence related in any manner to the incident should be included in chronological order in the file. Extremely sensitive information that causes concern to the risk or claims manager should be removed from the file and transferred immediately to the attorney if there is any question of protection of the information. Insureds should be strongly cautioned against keeping copies of sensitive information in their patient files. Plaintiffs' attorneys can legally obtain any information that is considered part of the routine hospital operation.

When it is determined that the file should be transferred to defense counsel for handling, a copy of the assignment letter should accompany copies of relevant information. All notices of claims, assignment of counsel, health claim arbitration, and other relevant judicial proceedings should

Exhibit 19-2
SAMPLE BASIC IDENTIFICATION FORM FOR CLAIM FILE

UNIVERSITY OF COLORADO HEALTH SCIENCES CENTER

Date of Incident	Date of Report	Claimant Identification
Date Claim Filed	Date Suit Filed	
Policy Period	Other Insurance	

RESERVES				PAYMENTS				
Indemnity	Expense	Initial	Date	Indemnity	Legal	Expense	Date	Check No.

Risk Management Committee Review

Legal Counsel Assigned for Defense

Plaintiff Legal Counsel

Date of Pretrial	Date of Settlement Conference

Date of Trial

FINAL PAYMENTS

Indemnity	Legal	Expense	Total
$	$	$	$

FINAL WRITE-OFFS

Hospital	Physicians	Others
$	$	$

DISPOSITION:
☐ Claim Without Payment
☐ Claim Settled
☐ Settled Before Trial
☐ Dismissed
☐ Non-suit
☐ Settled During Trial
☐ Judgment for Defense
☐ Judgment for Plaintiff
☐ No Claim Settlement
☐ Statute Ran Out
☐ Other: _____

continues

Exhibit 19-2 continued

RISK MANAGEMENT FILE		DIARY	
DATE	Contents	Date	Contents

Hospital Records Received	
Date	Record

Other Reports Received	
Date	Report

Records to Defense Attorney	
Date	Record

Records to Plaintiff Attorney	
Date	Record

Depositions Received	
Date	From

Appeal of Verdict

Filed by: ☐ Defense ☐ Plaintiff

Date: _____ Court: _____

Grounds: _____

Appeal Defense Attorney: _____

Hearing Date: _____

Decision: _____

Source: Courtesy of University of Colorado Health Sciences Center, Denver, CO.

Exhibit 19-3
GUIDELINES FOR IN-HOUSE EXPERT EVALUATIONS

Request review by chief of department or designee where incident occurred, including but not limited to:

1. Expert opinion of patient care, management, and treatment prior to incident or complication, surrounding the incident or complication, and following the incident and throughout discharge.
2. Whether there is exposure or deviation from standard of care.
3. Whether reasonable steps were taken to avoid incident or complication.
4. Opinion of injury and prognosis; whether permanent or temporary.
5. Whether complication or injury should have been anticipated.
6. Whether policies, procedures, and protocols were observed.
7. Whether informed consent was adequate.
8. Whether laboratory tests, studies, and consultations were timely and appropriate.
9. Whether initial history and physical examination were adequate to make diagnosis.
10. Whether there are contradictions, inconsistencies, unnecessary time delays, and possible alterations.
11. Whether the incident caused injury or an adverse outcome.

Exhibit 19-4
CHECKLIST FOR EQUIPMENT INCIDENTS

1. Sequester the equipment involved in the incident under lock and key immediately.
2. Do not test or alter the equipment except under controlled circumstances.
3. Take pictures, if possible, under attorney supervision.
4. Obtain copies of maintenance contract and service records.
5. Review contracts for hold-harmless language from the manufacturer.
6. Determine responsibility for service and maintenance (internal and external).
7. Obtain independent testing, if necessary.
8. Obtain name of manufacturer, serial number, and purchase records.
9. Determine if alerts issued by manufacturer were known and observed.
10. Make determination in cooperation with the defense attorney whether equipment should be returned to service, be repaired, or other action taken.

be maintained in the file. Copies of status reports from defense counsel and insurers should be reviewed, handled appropriately, and placed in the file, along with documentation of expense payments, medical bills, and other items.

The manager should request that the medical record, original x-ray films, pathology specimens, and other clinical evidence are sequestered in their respective departments. This ensures that the originals are available and have not been tampered with as legal proceedings progress. All equipment involved in injury should be evaluated and sequestered (see Exhibit 19-4). Sequestering can be as simplified as requiring that the items in question be placed in a locked area with limited, monitored access within the specific department. Requests for sequestering by the claims office can be refined to standard format, with copies of the requests placed in the file. Written notification should be requested from the departments if the information is not available, so the manager can begin an early and extensive search, if necessary. Lost or misplaced information may create difficulty in negotiating a claim.

At the conclusion of the initial investigation, a claim summary or brief of not more than three pages should be placed in the file. A checklist detailing elements of the initial investigation should include:

- Claimant information: Name, date of birth, sex, address, telephone number, marital status, occupation, employer, income, dependents, and other relevant social factors.
- Insured defendant information: Name, address, telephone number, medical staff or employment status, specialty, involvement in case, and insurance information (policy number, policy period, limits).
- Codefendant information: Name, address, telephone number, medical staff or employment status, specialty, involvement in case, and insurance information (insurance carrier, policy number, policy period, limits).
- Claimant's allegations of improper treatment.
- Claimant's injuries: Nature of injury, extent of injury (temporary or permanent, partial or total), additional treatment required as a result of the injury, medical examination results, and prognosis.
- Medical record review: Medical record number, dates of admission and discharge, admitting history, admitting and discharge diagnoses, chronology of treatment, review of physician and nursing notes, laboratory reports, consent forms, and other relevant documents.
- Interviews of physicians, hospital staff, and other witnesses to the incident.
- Copies of relevant hospital policies, procedures, and protocols.

- Results of any expert review, peer review, or other administrative review of the incident.
- Equipment incidents: Name and address of equipment manufacturer, copies of purchase information and warranties, copies of equipment maintenance contracts and equipment maintenance reports, reports from clinical engineering department subsequent to incident, reports of similar problems with type of equipment in question [from within the institution or from outside sources such as the Food and Drug Administration and the Emergency Care Research Institute (ECRI)].
- Evaluation of the damages claimed.
- Evaluation of liability: Applicable standard of care; responsibility of involved parties, including assessment of codefendant's liability.
- Settlement value and strategy.

The summary saves lengthy reviews of the entire file by providing a brief synopsis of the following items:

- pertinent points from the record of the clinical course
- claimants
- possible defendants
- allegations
- legal status
- deviations from standard of care
- plaintiff's counsel
- defense counsel
- witness testimony
- demand
- comments
- future activity

The initial investigation should be completed within 30 days of notification of the incident and the file updated as additional information is received. Ongoing evaluation dates are necessary to ensure appropriate monitoring and evaluation. Monitoring of ongoing events (such as testimony of experts and witnesses) and regular updates of the patient's clinical status are necessary to keep abreast of significant factors that may influence liability and exposure (see Appendixes 19-C and 19-D). A status report checklist should include:

- Current status of patient
- Autopsy report
- Medical record deficiencies
- Follow-up activities conducted to date
- Documentation and status of all persons involved
- Medical bills or charges
- Patient profile including: family history, employment status, insurance coverage, dependents, etc.

- Patient and family response to incident
- Expert review
- Record review
- Sequester medical records, x-ray, pathology specimens

Source of Incident

_____

_____

_____

INVESTIGATIVE TECHNIQUES

Legal counsel should be consulted when the scope of the program is first determined to ensure protection from discoverability of data and to review pertinent policies and the extent of the risk or claim manager's responsibility. It is necessary to decide, for example, whether the manager will take witness statements, discuss the case in detail with involved providers, make referrals, and gather specific information for in-house files. The attorney should aid in establishing these basic ground rules in accordance with legal and insurance restraints.

If it is determined that the above activities are indeed within the scope of the manager's responsibility, he or she will discuss the facts of each incident with the physician and other involved staff members, after a review of the medical record. Interviews should be concise, timely, and factual. For the sake of objectivity, it is important that the interviewer not lead the interviewee. All information should be verified and substantiated as far as possible without compromising the integrity of the investigation. Personnel with direct or indirect knowledge of the matter should be noted regardless of whether they are to be interviewed. Interview statements must become a part of the permanent claim file. It is recommended that the interviewer take detailed notes of a meeting rather than obtain a long written and signed statement. A summary of the meeting should be written and placed in the body of the claim file.

The investigation should identify all personnel involved in the care of the patient at the time of the occurrence. The current name, address, and telephone number of each person should be obtained. It is also useful to include his or her work status (e.g., full time, part time, contractual) and work location.

An objective report of the actual interview must be documented. The manager should determine how the patient and the family were advised of the incident. It is important to record the patient's and family's reactions to the incident; their support system, interactions, and social factors; and their reactions to the staff before and after the incident. The staff should keep the manager aware of the patient's status, attitudes, and other significant information throughout the hospitalization. The manager should also determine the economic history of the patient, whether there are any dependents, the source of payment for clinical care, and whether there were any witnesses to the incident. Witnesses' names, addresses, and telephone numbers must be recorded. (See Exhibit 19-5.)

EVALUATION OF MEDICAL RECORD

The medical record should be reviewed, if possible, while the patient is still in the hospital. State statutes determine whether negotiations with the patient can take place during the hospitalization, but it is important to review the incident and effect risk control and loss prevention measures as quickly as possible.

If a formal complaint has been lodged, a meticulous review of all related medical records from the viewpoint of the allegations as presented in the complaint is necessary. If an early warning identification system is in place, evaluation of the record may occur prior to presentation of any formal action. In these circumstances, the manager must assess the potential areas of liability and exposure. The record review should include any emergency and outpatient clinic records. It is helpful to find out exactly what is considered part of the patient's medical record (such as electrocardiogram tracings, fetal monitoring strips), because hospitals are held increasingly accountable for the loss of this type of documentation.

When reviewing the medical record, the entire record should be assessed, not just those facts surrounding the particular incident. There is always the possibility that the cause of an alleged claim is a result of a previously unidentified incident. Consequently, the review should be focused on all potential areas of liability, as well as those in the claim. The review should be accomplished by someone knowledgeable in acceptable standards of medical care appropriate to the case and should be supplemented by findings from interviews with providers directly involved in the patient's care.

Exhibits 19-6 and 19-7 provide general guidelines to follow when reviewing medical records.

BILL ABATEMENTS

Often the issue of medical bill abatement surfaces in an adverse patient incident. Whether to abate a hospital bill is a matter of philosophy in many instances. Some hospital administrators feel that abatement of a bill acknowledges guilt, while others believe that it mitigates damages and establishes a sense of good will.

In hospitals where bill abatement is evaluated on a case-by-case basis, general guidelines and criteria should be established to ensure uniform evaluation. Among these are the following:

- a review of the bill for adjustment
- a complete review of the medical record surrounding the alleged injury

---

Exhibit 19-5
CHECKLIST FOR CONDUCTING STAFF INTERVIEWS

1. Obtain objective report of the incident.
2. Determine if, how, and by whom the patient was advised of the incident.
3. Determine patient's reaction to the incident.
4. Determine family's reaction to the incident.
5. Evaluate family's support system and interaction.
6. Evaluate social factors of patient.
7. Determine the patient's and family's interactions with and attitudes toward the staff before the incident and after the incident.
8. Advise the staff to keep the manager informed of the patient's status and attitude and other significant factors throughout the hospitalization.
9. Ascertain economic history of patient, any dependents, and the source of bill payment.
10. Determine if there were any witnesses to the incident; document names, addresses, and telephone numbers.

Exhibit 19-6
GUIDELINES TO MEDICAL RECORD REVIEW

1. Always attempt to review the medical record while the patient is in the hospital.
2. Note documentation of the incident in the medical record.
3. Note any mention of an incident report being filed in the medical record.
4. Document any reference that the family and patient were advised of the incident, as well as any documented descriptive comments of the patient or family.
5. Check to see if an attorney has requested the record.
6. Observe whether there is any criticism of the treatment, management, or staff in the record.
7. Note any negative or unsubstantiated comments that have been written by the staff regarding the patient or family.
8. Note whether the record appears to follow a defined rationale or if it has loose ends.
9. Note legibility of documentation.
10. Note any area that could be construed as altered documentation.

Exhibit 19-7
MEDICAL RECORD REVIEW CHECKLIST

1. Date of admission (note prolonged stay).
2. Reason for admission.
3. Mention of previous incidents, complications, allergy reactions, and complaints regarding quality of care.
4. Admitting history.
5. Compare admitting diagnosis with treatment, appropriate tests, consultations, and other clinical actions.
6. If a change in diagnosis or condition warranted transfer to another area, was it accomplished in a timely manner?
7. When did physician first see and examine patient?
8. Is there appropriate correlation among doctors' orders, laboratory reports, nurses' notes, and progress notes?
9. Was original surgery or admission necessary?
10. Was consent form signed by a physician?
11. What risks are specifically mentioned?
12. Does consent form conform to performed surgery?
13. Were additional procedures done?
14. Do progress notes conform to procedure and consent form?
15. What does operative note state? Is it standard?
16. Dates when operative notes were dictated and transcribed.
17. Is there a written progress note of the operation and does it describe the incident? If so, how?
18. Does the anesthesia note collaborate with the progress notes?
19. Does the anesthesia note indicate any difficulty in intubation, excessive anesthesia time, or other problems?
20. Were preoperative electrocardiogram and chest x-ray evaluations included in the anesthesia preoperative note?
21. How long was the patient in the recovery room?
22. Note nurses' notes on patient's arrival in unit, general status, and condition.
23. Are there long gaps in nursing observation notes?
24. Compare the time of surgery to the first indication of complication or incident discovery.
25. Was patient appropriately monitored and observed by all involved staff?
26. Note any inconsistencies between physician's and nurses' notes.
27. Note any delays in diagnosis, prescription for appropriate treatment, and implementation of treatment.
28. Were consultants used appropriately, and was there a timely referral?
29. Does the record reflect the patient's complaints or lack thereof at each visit?
30. Do the examination and disposition reflect attention to the complaint?
31. Is there follow-up documentation that test results were reviewed?

- independent evaluation of the treatment to determine specific deviations from the standard of care
- consultation with and recommendations of the direct providers related to the alleged injury
- objective assessment of the outcome of the incident or complication (e.g., prolonged hospital stay, damages, injury, additional procedures, additional incurred costs)
- assessment of patient's and family's attitudes toward staff before the incident
- assessment of patient's and family's attitudes toward the incident
- availability of third-party coverage
- liability and other negative exposures

The manager should consider whether abatement can make amends to the patient or family to the extent that it can stop costly litigation and promote an environment conducive to further negotiation. A signed release form from the patient should be considered, unless it would jeopardize an already fragile resolution.

EFFECTIVE COMMUNICATION

Communication is essential to effective claims control. In addition to notifying insurance carriers and defense counsel as applicable, claims management must keep appropriate senior administration aware of necessary information. The manager should identify circumstances in which the administration requires notification of routine claim matters.

Other issues should be brought immediately to the senior administrator's attention. They include the following:

- potential adverse publicity
- cross claims and third-party actions
- excessive difficulty with particular program participant
- possibility of a significant adverse verdict
- notification of trial dates

SETTLEMENT NEGOTIATIONS

Many institutions with in-house programs choose to spread responsibility and authority for settlements between the claims manager and an advisory committee often called a claims management or review committee. The committee reviews the outcomes of the claims management process and provides ongoing internal review of active claims and settlements, whether handled by defense counsel or the claims manager.

Responsibilities of the committee may include the following:

- provides expert evaluation in claims and suits as requested
- aids in the development of claim management philosophy, policy, and procedure
- reviews and approves claim strategies and settlements to the extent of approved reserves
- evaluates the appropriateness of a structured settlement as a means for resolving a case involving serious injury (see Exhibit 19-8)

When the committee reviews a claim, it is often helpful to have the chief of service of the department in which it occurred at the meeting, in addition to the physicians assigned to the committee. The chief of service can assist in refining the clinical aspects of the claim, identify potential experts, and offer information about departmental claim activity that can be useful in quality and risk management assessments.

Whether claim reserving is conducted in house or provided by an insurance company adjuster or a contractual service, it is necessary to determine whether the claims manager, the review committee, or both have authority to authorize payment of funds for settlement purposes. Many factors must be considered when claims are negotiated in house. It is imperative that an objective and factual evaluation of the incident, damages, treatment, and prognosis is completed for each claim.

The risk or claims manager should specifically analyze the claims allegations and evaluate special damages (costs outside of clinical treatment, physical therapy, x-rays, and other hospital services). It is important to keep these damages under control. When possible, the institution's resources can be used for follow-up care.

The institution's liability through its employees and the exposure in relation to the verification and extent of injuries must be evaluated. It is necessary to verify coverage of the persons involved in the incident and identify any factors that may influence the plaintiff's posture. The manager should also consider other factors that may have a significant

---

Exhibit 19-8
WHEN TO USE STRUCTURED SETTLEMENTS

Utilizing structured settlements for the payment of large or catastrophic claims can benefit both the plaintiff and the defendant. Some states now mandate the acceptance of structured settlements or periodic payments in cases where a large portion of the award relates to future medical costs. This form of award enables the hospital (or other defendant) to purchase an annuity or similar program that provides for future payouts at scheduled increments. Types of structured settlements include the following:

- annuity contracts
- trusts funded with U.S. Treasury bonds
- funds for rehabilitation
- lump sum payments of cash to compensate for lost income, medical expenses, and attorney's fees (generally these payments include past expenses and out-of-pocket losses)
- reversionary medical trust to pay for ongoing or future medical care
- educational fund for the benefit of the victim's dependent children
- term insurance to pay for funeral expenses

Many cases are well suited for the use of structured settlements. The most common types include the following:

- wrongful death, especially when there are surviving dependents
- serious personal injury cases in which substantial future medical expenses are anticipated, such as

  — serious irreversible brain damage
  — quadriplegia or paraplegia
  — injuries resulting in permanent disabilities that limit or prevent the injured from future gainful employment
  — injuries where it is anticipated that the injured party will require lifetime physical therapy

- all cases involving minors
- all cases involving incompetents
- all cases where the injured party would be unable to pay for future education for himself or herself or for dependents' education
- cases involving substantial judgments and large attorney's fees, especially if the fees represent a third or more of a judgment
- cases in which an attempt is made to bridge the gap between high cash demands and realistic evaluations, especially in those where liability may be difficult to ascertain (including claims where issues related to liability become overshadowed by the emotional impact of significant injury, for example, a severely damaged infant)

impact on the case, such as medical coverage and public attitudes.

State statutes should be reviewed to determine if any reform measures could impact the claim (such as a cap on noneconomic damages).

It is important that the claims manager remain in control during discussions with the plaintiff's counsel. The manager should evaluate the plaintiff's position objectively, state his or her position, consider the attorney's response, and evaluate the demand. The manager should not feel pressured into any commitment before re-evaluation and should be very careful not to educate the plaintiff's counsel.

When all aspects of the claim have been fully evaluated and the manager needs further guidance, defense counsel should be utilized whether or not it has been officially retained (see Appendix 19-E).

Following this thorough investigative process, the claims risk manager and hospital administration may elect to notify the plaintiff and/or his/her attorney of their desire to settle or deny the claim. They may also elect to continue their investigation until further evidence of fault or injury can be established. Form letters can be developed to be used at this phase of the investigation process (see Appendix 19-F).

LITIGATION MANAGEMENT

Litigation management is an often neglected area of claims administration. Specific guidelines for managing defense counsel should be established and discussed with counsel prior to retention. At minimum, the following seven factors should be considered in developing guidelines and objectives for sound litigation management:

1. Criteria to be used in the selection and assignment of counsel:
   - history of prior success in the area of medical malpractice, especially in trial of complex injury cases (request a list of claims that were settled by the firm and those resolved via a defense verdict)
   - evidence of technical expertise of the firm's staff (such as a registered nurse/attorney or physician/attorney)
   - evidence that senior partners with the most trial experience and expertise will be directly involved in handling appropriate cases (less experienced, and hopefully, less costly counsel should be available for routine motions and initial discovery)
   - evidence that the firm has access to quality medical experts and the respect of local physicians
2. Preliminary evaluation from counsel, completed within two weeks from the date of case assignment, to

include the following reports:
   - an analysis of each element of negligence
   - an identification of all potentially culpable defendants
   - an identification of the various potential defenses that might be successful
   - a list of the types of experts that would be most appropriate and the names of persons who could be engaged as experts
   - an analysis of the skill and expertise of opposing counsel, if that person has been identified
   - a timetable for the development of the case in anticipation of trial or settlement
3. Timetables for reporting actions. The risk or claims manager and defense counsel should share their timetables to allow them both to remain continually apprised of significant developments of the case. The manager should ask that defense counsel agree to abide by the timetables.
4. Motions that must be approved by the institution prior to defense counsel's instigation include:
   - any motion that might serve to affect the material elements of a case
   - any motion that might serve to add additional parties to the litigation
   - any motion that might seek to bring about an outcome not anticipated by parties to the litigation
5. Copies of the following documents should be furnished the risk or claims manager:
   - original summons and complaints and any amendments thereto
   - summary of all expert depositions that are material to the successful defense of malpractice claims
   - any offers of settlement or dismissal, including offers to dismiss a single defendant where there are multiple parties involved in the litigation
   - evaluation of an injured plaintiff performed by a damage expert or by an economist
   - any other documents that the initial investigation and evaluation identify as being potentially material to the complete evaluation of the discovery process
6. Legal fee and expense guidelines
7. Methods to evaluate counsel's performance

CONCLUSION

Development of an effective claims management system requires top level commitment, establishment of clear goals and objectives, and an accurate assessment of resources, requirements, structure, corporate culture, and scope of responsibility. Managers should meet with legal counsel prior to development of the system so that it will be effective in maintaining confidentiality and protection from discoverability of collected data. Clear policies and procedures regarding the process must be developed and communicated to all participants. Full support of legal counsel, the administration, the professional staff, and the governing board is absolutely necessary. Their commitment serves as the foundation of the program.

Appendix 19-A

Procedures for Classification of Information

1. *Policy*

   It is the policy of the Office of Risk Management that all information relating to potential loss, regardless of the source, will be reviewed and evaluated by an assigned coordinator within 24 hours of receipt.

2. *Purpose*

   This procedure has been developed to establish general guidelines to be considered in evaluating and classifying information with loss potential and liability exposure.

3. *Responsibility*

   It is the responsibility of the Risk Management Coordinators to collate and categorize incoming data. It may be necessary, at times, to clarify an item with the Director of Risk Management or the Claims Manager.

4. *Procedure*

   4.1 Definition of an Incident—any known therapeutic or diagnostic complication, unexpected outcome, or untoward event affecting the routine care of a patient.

   4.2 Sources of Information—may be formally or informally presented to the office on a daily basis, including but not limited to, written incident reports, departmental telephone calls, occurrence screens, and medical records.

   4.3 Identification Criteria—the following information should be considered when identifying loss potential and assessing liability exposure.

       4.3.1 the probable frequency of the occurrence of the loss
       4.3.2 the probable severity of the loss
       4.3.3 the possible severity of the loss
       4.3.4 the effect the potential loss would have on the organization

   4.4 Categories of Information

       4.4.1 Non-Incidents—information that is received but does not have any risk or loss potential (e.g., planned return to OR, anticipated death, etc.). This information will be discarded without further action or investigation after verification.

       4.4.2 Incidents—information meeting the definition of an incident as defined in section 4.1. This information will be evaluated, investigated, and trended as applicable.

           4.4.2.1 Those items that, after evaluation, are found not to have a poor outcome (e.g., falls, medication errors).
           4.4.2.2 Suspense
               4.4.2.2.1 Information that may be placed in the suspense file, at the direction of the Claims Manager, following sufficient investigation to determine that a deviation from the standard of care does not exist, regardless of outcome. This information will not be presented at the monthly Claims Conference.

           EXAMPLE: A screen states that a patient may have suffered because of a questionable failure of equipment. After investigation, it is found that the equipment was functioning properly and the patient's condition deteriorated because of the course of the disease.

4.4.2.2.2 Incidents that require additional workup and may or may not be potential claims. These items are placed in the Suspense File after discussion at the monthly Claims Conference.

EXAMPLE: An incident in which a patient's family is not satisfied with the care the patient has received. After investigation it is determined that there is no deviation from the standard of care, but the family continues to complain.

4.4.2.3 Potential Claims—information that, following a complete investigation, reveals potential loss or liability exposure. This information will be transferred to the Claims Manager for final evaluation and disposition at the monthly Claims Conference.

Appendix 19-B

Computerized Claims Information Data Entry Sheet

* 1. Division: _____

2. Claim type: _____

* 3. Date of loss: _____

4. Date of claim: _____

* 5. Location: _____
_____

* 6. Status/action taken: _____
_____

* 7. Description/patient present status: _____
_____

* 8. Diagnosis: _____

* 9. Service: _____

10. Date closed: _____

11. Insurer: _____

12. Indemnity reserve: _____

13. Expense reserve: _____

* 14. Last name: _____

* 15. First name: _____

16. Address: _____

17. City: _____

18. State: _____

19. Zip code: _____

20. Telephone: _____

* 21. D.O.B./age: _____

22. Attorney: _____

23. Patient insurance: _____

CODEFENDANT

24. Last name: _____

25. First name: _____

26. Address: _____

27. City: _____

28. State: _____

29. Zip code: _____

30. Telephone: _____

31. Comment: _____

SUPPLEMENTAL FIELDS

1. Assigned to: _____

2. Date received by Risk Management: _____

_____

*This information should be available on a master claim run.

3. Synopsis: _____
   _____
   _____

4. Date notified excess insurance carrier 1 & 2: _____
5. Notice of circumstance (serious injury) date: _____
* 6. History no.: _____
* 7. Trust insureds/staff involved: _____
   _____
   _____
   _____

8. Diary date: _____
9. Excess code: _____
10. Trust defendants: _____
   _____
   _____
   _____

11. Defense counsel: _____
   _____

12. Marital status: _____
13. Defendants: _____
14. Occupation: _____
15. Excess report due: _____
16. Date of indemnity payment: _____
* 17. Source/date of admission: _____
18. Reporting method: _____
   _____
   _____

19. Reporting source: _____

20. Date reported: _____
21. Date completed: _____
22. Policy/procedure variation: _____
23. Policy/procedure clear: _____
   _____

24. Documentation problems: _____
   _____

25. Resident supervision: _____
   _____

26. Contractual R.N.: _____
   _____

27. Per diem R.N.: _____
   _____

* 28. Type of incident: _____
   _____
   _____

29. Deviation from standard care: _____
   _____

30. Damages: _____
   _____
   _____

_____

*This information should be available on a master claim run.

31. Issues: _____
    _____
    _____

* 32. Unit: _____
* 33. Equipment: _____
34. Area: _____
35. Date: _____
36. Time: _____
37. Category: _____
38. Injury: _____
39. Witnesses: _____
    _____
    _____

---

*This information should be available on a master claim run.

Claims Review Memorandum

(Date)

TO: Claims Manager
FROM: Risk Management Coordinator
RE: Claims Review Conference

The following cases are to be set up as claims:

_____

_____

_____

_____

The following cases are to be placed in the suspense file:

_____

_____

_____

_____

Appendix 19-D

Claims Investigation Process and File

1. Claim referred to Risk Management by Legal Office   _____
2. Legal Office notifies named physicians and chairperson of Department re: claim/suit   _____
3. Claim/suit file set up by way of the following:
   A. Set up file   _____
   B. UH medical record requested   _____
   C. Notice to Radiology and Medical Records   _____
   D. Billing information requested   _____
   E. Bills on hold and/or change guarantor   _____
   F. Medical records requested from other facilities   _____
   G. Check for existing Incident Report and/or heads-up file   _____
   H. Enter incident into data base   _____
4. Reviewed by Director of Risk Management and assigned to _____   _____
5. Reported to carrier if appropriate   _____
6. Investigator notifies department and, if appropriate, involves chairperson, physician, and nursing administration in process   _____
7. Referred for expert review to: _____   _____
   _____
8. Reviewed with Director of Risk Management   _____
9. Risk Management Investigative Summary to University Counsel   _____
10. A. Denial
    —Letter to plaintiff/plaintiff's counsel   _____
    —Letter to attending physician and chairperson   _____
    —Billing follow-up   _____
    —Remove Risk Management as guarantor   _____
    —Notify Medical Records/Radiology   _____
    —Update claim data   _____
    —Close out file   _____
    B. Settlement
    —Settlement/release agreement   _____
    —Letter to attending physicians and chairperson   _____
    —Copy of letter to Medical Staff Office   _____
    —Write off appropriate bills   _____
    —Letter to bank authorizing trust payment   _____
    —Remove Risk Management as guarantor   _____
    —Notify Medical Records/Radiology   _____
    —Update claim/suit data   _____
    —Close out file   _____
11. Suits
    A. Change to suit file   _____

Appendix 19-E

Case Assessment and Evaluation

Date of Presentation: _____

1. Description of incident (include date of incident, location, reporting source, and brief description of problem):

2. Chronology of treatment (brief outline of pertinent events during hospitalization that impacted incident; include relevant surgical and therapeutic procedures and patient disposition):

3. Summary of peer review or expert evaluation (brief summary of pertinent factors impacting incident gathered from interviews with experts and others):

4. Identified deviations from standards of care/problems and issues (brief summary of risk, quality of care, standards, or other issues arising from care and status):

5. Damages (summary of alleged damages resulting from incident; additional treatment required, etc.; present condition):

6. Assessment/evaluation (analyze all obtained information; provide information on liability exposure; additional significant information to be obtained; recommendation of status):

Sample Form Letters for Litigation Management

SETTLEMENT LETTER

To:
From: Risk Management Committee or Director of Risk Management
Date:
Case Name:

   The above-referenced claim is being settled in the name of the Hospital for $_____. Thank you for your cooperation in dealing with this claim. If you would like additional details regarding this settlement, please feel free to contact the risk management office.

_____
(Department Chair)

cc: Medical Staff Office

DENIAL OF CLAIM LETTER

(Date)

To:
Law Firm:
Address:

Re: _____
Claim No.: _____

Dear _____:

    Your letter of _____, 19___, has been received and referred to our office for review. Upon investigation of this claim, we find no factual basis to support the alleged liability of this hospital or its staff. If you wish to submit additional information to substantiate your claim, we will review it and respond to you at that time. In the absence of such additional information, you should consider your claim to be denied.

                Sincerely,

                Risk Manager

cc: Hospital Attorney
        Hospital Administrator

DENIAL OF CLAIM

To: [Plaintiff Counsel or plaintiff (if representing self)]
From: Risk Management Committee or Director of Risk Management
Date:
Claim Name:

    The claim filed by _____ has been denied. In accordance with the state statute, section _____, the claimant now has _____ years from the Notice of Claim to file a lawsuit. This time period is the maximum amount of time the law provides in which to file a lawsuit. If you have any questions or information that you could share to prepare for the potential defense of this claim, please do not hesitate to call the risk management office.
    Thank you.

                _____
                (Department Chairman)

cc:

REQUEST FOR EXPERT REVIEW

To: [Name of expert reviewer]
From: Director of Risk Management
Date:
Subject:
Case Name:

Attached please find a copy of the Notice of Claim and the medical records for the above-captioned patient. In my role as risk manager, I am requesting that you review this record in an attempt to determine if the hospital or any members of its staff are at risk for any care provided to this patient. Specifically, I ask that you address whether or not you believe the appropriate "standard of care" was met in the care rendered to this patient.

Upon completion of your review, please notify me so that we might arrange a time to discuss your impressions and, if appropriate, to dictate them.

Since you are examining the medical record and not the patient, your impressions should be shared with our office only and therefore will remain protected from discovery. The medical record and any written material containing your impressions should be returned to the risk management office.

Your understanding of the importance of this process, as well as your willingness to maintain the confidentiality of any information gained from this record, is appreciated.

Thank you in advance for your assistance.

INCIDENT NOTICE TO PHYSICIAN

(Date)

To: [Physician]
Address:

Dear Dr. _____:

                RE: History No. _____
                       Name of Patient: _____

This is to advise you that the above patient experienced complications during (his/her) recent hospitalization. I would like to discuss this matter in more detail with you and would appreciate your contacting me immediately upon receipt of this letter so we may establish a mutually convenient time to do so. I have included the patient's history number so you may review the medical record prior to our meeting.

Attached for your information is a copy of our general guidelines regarding occurrences of this type. Please review them carefully and feel free to contact me if you have any questions prior to our scheduled meeting.

Thank you for your cooperation and support.

                                        Sincerely,

                                        Claims Manager

NOTICE OF PATIENT REPRESENTATION

(Date)

To: [Physician or nurse]
Address:

Dear Dr. _____:

          RE: History No. _____
                      Name of Patient _____

This is to advise you that we have received a letter of representation from an attorney on behalf of the above-named patient. I would like to discuss this matter in more detail with you and would appreciate your contacting me immediately upon receipt of this letter. I have included the patient's history number so you may review the medical record prior to our conversation.

Attached for your information is a copy of our general guidelines regarding occurrences of this type. Please review them carefully and feel free to contact me if you have any questions prior to our discussion.

Thank you for your cooperation and support.

                           Sincerely,

                           Claims Manager

NOTICE OF ARBITRATION FILING

(Date)

To: [Physician]
Address:

Dear Dr. _____:

          RE: History No. _____
                      Name of Patient _____

This is to advise you that a claim has been filed in the Health Claim Arbitration Office regarding the above-captioned matter in which you have been named as a defendant.

When you are served with the claim (by certified mail, in person, or by other means), please contact me directly to advise me of the exact date of your service so that I may begin appropriate insurance notification and defense coordination. You will not need to take any further action other than immediate notification to me at this time.

In the interim period, we ask that you not discuss this matter with anyone. If you would like verification of any person contacting you to discuss the matter, we will be happy to do so.

If I may be of any assistance to you, or if you would like to further discuss this matter, please do not hesitate to contact me directly.

                           Sincerely,

                           Claims Manager

CLAIMS HANDLING MEMORANDUM

(Date)

TO: Risk Management Coordinators
FROM:
RE: Claims Handling

The following procedures should be followed in preparing all files for the Claims Review Conference:

1. Arrange each file in chronological order, with the earliest piece of information on the bottom, working up to the most recent. Your checklist should go on top, with the outline underneath.
2. Transfer all notes (such as telephone messages) from scraps of paper to sheets of yellow lined paper. The Claims Status Report format will continue to be used for all subsequent investigation.
3. Dictation must be completed and submitted for typing by the last week of each month. This gives you one month within which you are working up cases. The conference is scheduled during the first 7 to 10 days of the following month to allow time for your dictation to be transcribed while you are completing outlines, etc.

With regard to your memorandum after the CRC, please proceed as follows:

1. Separate claims from suspense and list all cases by patient's name in a column.
2. Include HX numbers.
3. Submit two copies of your memorandum, along with the files, within two days of the conference.

chapter 20

Post-Litigation Stress Management

Barbara J. Youngberg

INTRODUCTION

As growing numbers of physicians and hospital staff find themselves defending the care they are providing patients in the hospital, the emotional and physical impact of this process has been identified. There is no question that the litigation process, particularly when it involves death or serious injury to a patient along with alleged professional misconduct or negligence, can damage the personal and professional integrity of a health care practitioner. It can also result in psychological manifestations of depression, anxiety, hostility, and anger. If these symptoms go unrecognized and untreated, the practitioner may well go on to outward expressions of anger, frustration, and other negative emotions and become involved in even a greater number of suits.

The risk manager is often in a key position to assist hospital staff in recognizing and dealing with these feelings. Generally, the risk manager is involved in the litigation process, and this firsthand knowledge of what has transpired can provide a basis for developing support services for the staff.

LITIGATION STRESS SYNDROME

No matter what the eventual outcome of the litigation process, the preceding events can create substantial stress for those involved. Now commonly referred to as "litigation stress syndrome," it must be addressed so that staff members can return to their duties and their lives. Special programs should be developed by risk management and the administration of the hospital to assist these individuals in gaining an understanding of the syndrome and working their way through it. Establishing the following programs may be helpful in this process:

- Education on the common and healthy reactions to malpractice suits that are felt by the practitioner and his or her family. This session might be presented by the hospital social worker or a psychologist. Clearly, its focus should be to assure the practitioner and the family that when one's integrity is challenged, normal feelings of anger, frustration, and depression are appropriate. Describing various coping mechanisms can help the practitioner and the family understand that they are not reacting "abnormally."

- Ongoing group or individual therapy throughout the litigation process to assist the practitioner and the family to deal with the feelings evoked by the process. The therapy could continue after resolution of the litigation until the problems and issues associated with it have been settled and the practitioner and family members feel that their lives are back to normal. Practitioners who have "survived the process" can be valuable additions to the group.

- Encouragement of peer counseling. This provides reaffirmation to the practitioner that he or she was not negligent and colleagues still consider the practitioner to be a caring and skilled professional.

- Education related to the litigation process itself. The risk manager or hospital legal counsel should conduct the session to describe the elements of the litigation process. In addition, the practitioner should be informed of the likelihood that the plaintiff's counsel will attempt to discredit the practitioner and to make him or her angry as part of courtroom strategy. Allowing the practitioner to witness trials or to go through a mock deposition can greatly assist in understanding the psychology of the process and developing the knowledge that these "attacks" are often nothing more than the plaintiff's attempt to sway the opinion of the jury. The practitioner can be advised that maintaining a professional demeanor and representing oneself as a caring, concerned professional can be an effective way to convince the jury of the practitioner's innocence.

UNDERSTANDING THE LITIGATION PROCESS

Education aimed at the staff's understanding of the mechanics of the legal system and litigation process should be part of every hospital's risk management program. At a minimum, this information should include the following:

- A basic explanation of the elements of negligence (e.g., breach of duty, injury, proximate cause, and damages). It could be pointed out in this discussion that these elements are often difficult for juries to understand. In an ideal world they would be the basis of finding fault, but in the real world juries often react to the emotional aspects of the process.
- The role of the expert in a malpractice case and how a defendant can assist in procuring the best expert. Allowing defendant practitioners to assist in their own defense also helps them to have a greater understanding of the process and may reduce their feelings of powerlessness.
- The role of a jury and the problems associated with a jury trial. The jury often consists of the peers of the plaintiff, rather than peers of the physician. Jurors often feel obligated to award money to a severely injured person, especially if they feel that person "needs the money more than the physician or the hospital." Because technical issues associated with malpractice cases may be difficult to understand, jurors often rely more on their feelings instead of the facts.
- The impact of the legal process on a practitioner. It should not be the final word on the competence of a physician.

Assisting the physician to understand these aspects of the litigation process prior to his or her actual involvement in the suit can relieve much of the tension, frustration, and anger. A physician who can control these feelings will make a better witness on his or her own behalf and will appear less defensive or aggressive to the jury.

STRESS MANAGEMENT

During the litigation process, support should be provided to help the practitioner identify and deal with the feelings and issues as they arise. Gregory K. Gable, in his report titled *Litigation Stress*, offers the following ten personal suggestions to professionals involved in liability litigation:[1]

1. It is very important to discuss ways of coping with stress of professional liability litigation. The first coping strategy that I suggest is to accept what is. There are no easy solutions. The suit is likely to occur even though you acted competently, even though you may have maintained good relations with the patient, and even though you keep up to date in your field. Becoming more aware that suits are likely to happen can lay the groundwork for coping successfully later on, if and when a lawsuit occurs.
2. Learn more about the litigation process. Learn how the system works and why. We need to educate physicians about how to work more closely with the defense attorney and with the malpractice carrier to increase the chances of a successful defense—regardless of the professional technical merits of the case in the physician's opinion.
3. Discuss the emotional responses to the suit and disruptions to your life with your family and with supportive colleagues if possible. A local support network or support group would be invaluable. Professional malpractice is a major stressor. Talking about the emotional reactions that one experiences with family and colleagues is the single best coping strategy that a physician can employ.
4. Recognize that the resolution of this problem will be slow. This process will drag on for a period of months and probably years. Physicians tend to develop survival skills in medical school that serve them well throughout their medical careers. One such skill is to separate oneself rapidly from the emotional response to a medical crisis. When blood is spurting from an artery, the physician quickly suppresses the anxiety/fear reaction—then he or she quickly goes to work on dealing with the source of the anxiety—something which usually can be accomplished rapidly. All in all—a very effective coping mechanism. This is a good coping mechanism to use in the physician role. The mechanism works horribly in coping with professional liability litigation stress. Part 1—separating from the feelings—can be accomplished fairly

easily. The physician can learn to suppress the anxiety from the suit; part 2 is impossible. Surgical procedures cannot be applied to the problem of a lawsuit. It goes on and on. It takes a lot of energy to maintain this suppression of feelings over a long period of time. And when some activity on the case surfaces, feelings come flooding back—probably more intense for having been suppressed. When six months or more go by between case actions, this becomes a recurrent cycle. It is important to talk over these feeling thoroughly—and enter the race for the long haul.

5. For the family, it is important to know that the physician can become very preoccupied, angry, withdrawn, and may neglect feelings or needs of family members due to his or her own pain. The April 27, 1987, issue of *Medical Economics* contained an article titled "Malpractice Suits Are a Family Affair" that was written by Howard Eisenberg, a senior editor of that publication.[2] He quotes the spouse of a physician faced with a large malpractice suit: "The suit crept into every corner of our lives." He goes on to note that the worst thing a doctor defendant can do is to try to protect the family by keeping his feelings to himself. The very best thing a spouse can do is to encourage frequent open discussions about the suit and the emotional responses to it. A husband and wife can get through it best by expressing their feelings, discussing their options, worrying together about their future, and sharing their pain. Both gain strength from the knowledge that the other understands and cares.

6. The children need to be included in many of the discussions and encouraged to discuss their feelings about the suit. Much better to get their fears out in the open where they can be dispelled.

7. Most spouses faced with the reality of a lawsuit complain that they do not know what to say to help. The truth is, there aren't any major magic words, but it is very important to convey three basic messages. (1) "I believe in you, you are a good physician regardless of the outcome of the case or of the suit." This is a very important message to state clearly multiple times. Don't take for granted that the physician knows this already. He or she may in fact be experiencing shaken self-esteem and may need to hear this. (2) "No matter what happens, I'll stand by you. We will weather the storm together." Many physicians report secret fantasies about losing spouse and family, along with house, car, and self-respect in the throes of litigation stress. (3) It is very important to touch the physician physically, emphasizing supportive statements by touching, massaging, or hugging. It adds to the value of the message.

8. Take time out—no matter how busy or upset—to do some focused nonwork, nonmedical family, or couple activity. This is essential as often as possible whether you feel like it or not.

9. The family also needs to be informed about the legal system.

10. Develop and build on joint activities or hobbies to provide a relief from medicine and from everyday stresses.

REFERRAL RESOURCES

The risk manager can also offer additional support through a variety of referral programs that have been developed by state medical associations, specialty organizations, the American Medical Association, and physician insurance companies. State medical associations and societies with particularly well-developed programs focusing on liability stress include the Illinois State Medical Society, Medical Society of New Jersey, Medical Association of Georgia, Pennsylvania Medical Society, and the Texas Medical Association. These programs offer various services, such as society-sponsored educational programs and resources, support groups for the practitioner and his or her family, and a number of risk management resources.

CONCLUSION

Risk managers must become increasingly aware of the significance of the litigation stress syndrome and its effects on health care practitioners. It is necessary for risk management and other health care professionals to develop programs that recognize and deal with the problems of this syndrome.

NOTES

1. G.K. Gable, Litigation Stress, *ACMS Bulletin* (February 25, 1989): 108.
2. H. Eisenberg, Malpractice Suits Are a Family Affair, *Medical Economics* (April 27, 1987).

BIBLIOGRAPHY

Anderson, C.T. March 24/31, 1989. The scarlet lawsuit. *American Medical News*: 45.

Anonymous. March 1985. Being sued for malpractice: A personal account. *Malpractice Digest*: 24.

Brown, S. June 22, 1987. The doctor who chose death over a malpractice trial. *Medical Economics*.

Chapman, S. November 1986. Physician's support groups take sting out of malpractice. *Physicians Management*.

Charles, S.C. 1987. Malpractice suits: Their effects on doctors, patients, and families. *Journal of the Medical Association of Georgia* 76: 171–172.

Charles, S.C., et al. 1987. Sued and nonsued physicians—satisfactions, dissatisfactions and sources of stress. *Psychosomatics* 28: 462–468.

Charles, S.C., et al. April 1985. Sued and nonsued physicians—self reported reactions to malpractice litigation. *American Journal of Psychiatry* 142: 4.

Crane, M. December 5, 1988. How lawyers stack juries against doctors. *Medical Economics*: 40.

Hurwitz, R.M. May 25, 1987. Nothing is so lonely as being sued for malpractice. *Medical Economics*.

Meyer, L. May 11, 1987. A juror confirms your worst fears about malpractice trials. *Medical Economics*.

Reading, E.G. March 1987. Malpractice stress syndrome: A new diagnosis? *New Jersey Medicine* 36: 256.

Reading, E.G. 1986. The malpractice stress syndrome. *Journal of the Medical Society of New Jersey* 83: 289–290.

Ross, S.M. April 1987. Eight who survived. *Virginia Medical* 114: 218.

Samkoff, J.S., and G. Gable. July 1988. PMS program addresses litigation stress. *Pennsylvania Medicine*: 28–31.

Samples, P. August 12, 1988. A place to go to talk about the pain. *American Medical News*: 27.

Snider, H.C. 1989. *Jury of My Peers: A Surgeon's Encounter with the Malpractice Crisis*. Greenwood, Fla.: Penkevill Publishing Co.

Wilbert, J.R., et al. January 1987. Coping with the stress of malpractice litigation. *Illinois Medical Journal* 171: 1.

chapter 21

Legislative and Regulatory Issues

Paul T. Napolski, Mark S. Rubin, and Lei Ann Marshall-Cohen

HEALTH CARE QUALITY IMPROVEMENT ACT

Several well-publicized lawsuits during the past few years, brought mainly by physicians whose clinical privileges were denied or revoked, have made many physicians and hospital trustees hesitant to participate in the peer review process. Fortunately, federal legislation (see Appendix 21-A) and the Health Care Quality Improvement Act of 1986 (the Act) (P.L. 99–660; 42 U.S.C. Secs. 11101–11152) provide some protection from the adverse precedent-setting decisions in many of those cases.

Impetus for Legislation

The significance of the changes brought about by the Act insofar as it relates to potential antitrust liability for those participating in the peer review process can be appreciated only by considering the decision of the U.S. Supreme Court in *Patrick v. Burget,* 108 S. Ct. 1658 (1988). The trial court had found that physicians who were involved in the peer review process at an Oregon hospital were liable for damages for antitrust violations in connection with the termination of clinical privileges of a colleague. Under the antitrust laws, the $650,000 damage award was trebled by the district court. The verdict was reversed on appeal, with the Ninth Circuit Court of Appeals holding that, since peer review was

required under Oregon state law, the actions of the participants were immune from claims of antitrust violations because of the "state action" exemption as set forth in the Supreme Court decision in *Parker v. Brown,* 63 S. Ct. 307 (1943). On appeal to the Supreme Court, however, this argument was rejected, since the state did not actively review the peer review process in private hospitals, an absolute requirement for qualification of exemption under the Sherman Act. The court of appeals decision was reversed.

Antitrust Exemption

While the *Patrick* case was making its way through the federal court system, Congress was considering the legislation that would have an impact on fact situations similar to that set forth in the case. Although *Patrick* was not decided by the Supreme Court until 1988, the changes made by the Act were inapplicable to the case, since it involved actions taken during the late 1970s and early 1980s. The federal antitrust protections afforded by the Act apply only to peer review actions taken on or after November 14, 1986. Application to state antitrust laws automatically took effect on October 14, 1989, unless a state had "opted in" for application to actions that occurred before that date or had "opted out" prior to October 14, 1989, in which case the provisions of the Act are inapplicable to claims under state antitrust laws.

Information Clearinghouse

In addition to the protection from claims of antitrust violations afforded by the Act, it also establishes a federal clearinghouse for peer review and malpractice information, administered by the Department of Health and Human Services through a contract with UNISYS. The law requires the creation of a National Practitioner Data Bank containing information dealing with malpractice awards and settlements, adverse clinical privilege data, and adverse membership data from professional societies. See the next section of this chapter for a more detailed explanation of the information required to be reported to the data bank and accessing the data.

Antitrust Immunity for Peer Review Participants

The immunity provided by the Act is actually twofold. The first deals with the actions of professional review bodies, members and staffs of those bodies, persons under contract or agreement with the bodies, and persons who participate with or assist the bodies. The second involves immunity for those providing *true and correct* information to professional review bodies, including the health care entity itself and any governing body or committee of the entity that conducts professional review activity.

The immunity provisions will provide a complete defense, within limits, to a lawsuit brought by a physician who has been denied hospital privileges or whose privileges have been curtailed or revoked. The Act relieves a hospital only of a monetary liability antitrust claim. It does not bar a physician from obtaining an injunction to block the implementation of a peer review decision. The immunity from liability for damages does not apply to any claim for damages under any federal or state law relating to the civil rights of any person, nor to suits brought by the United States or a state attorney general alleging other civil or criminal violations, including actions under Section 4C of the Clayton Act.

Proper Peer Review Procedure

To qualify for immunity, the professional review action must meet the following four requirements:

1. reasonable belief that the action furthers the quality of health care
2. exertion of reasonable effort to obtain all the facts
3. due process procedures, including adequate notice and hearing, as set forth in the Act, or other procedures that are fair to the physician under the circumstances
4. continued reasonable belief that the action is warranted after obtaining the facts and meeting the due process requirement

There is an exception to the immunity provided that ties into the reporting requirements set forth in Part B of the Act. This exception applies even if the four requirements listed above have been fully met. If there is reason to believe that a health care entity did not report the information required in Part B (i.e., malpractice awards and settlements, licensure disciplinary actions, and adverse clinical privilege or membership data), and after investigation such is proven to be the case, immunity for an entity would not apply to peer review actions for a three-year period. In order for the immunity to be lost and due process requirements to be met, the health care entity must be provided with a notice of noncompliance with the reporting procedure and be given an opportunity to correct the noncompliance, as well as be provided with an opportunity for a hearing. If, after providing for such remedial measures, it is determined that the entity has "failed substantially" to meet the reporting requirements, its name will be published in the *Federal Register* and 30 days after date of publication the three-year nonimmune period commences to run.

The National Practitioner Data Bank became operational in April 15, 1990. Care must be taken to comply with all the reporting provisions so as not to lose the immunity afforded by Part A of the Act. It should also be noted that if, in fact, immunity is lost because of substantial noncompliance, the period for bringing a successful action alleging antitrust violations does not end after three years. Individual state and federal statutes of limitation provide extended periods for filing suits involving peer review actions occurring during the nonimmunity period, and potential liability can extend far beyond the three years.

Costs and Attorneys' Fees

If a hospital is successful in defending a suit challenging a peer review action, it could be entitled to recover its costs, including attorneys' fees, from the plaintiff. To do so, however, the claim or the conduct of the claimant during litigation must be shown to have been (1) frivolous, (2) unreasonable, (3) without foundation, or (4) in bad faith. The key operative words in this section of the Act require the defendant to be the "substantially prevailing party" in order to be awarded such costs. The phrase in and of itself leaves broad latitude for interpretation by the courts in deciding these awards. In addition, it is extremely difficult to prove that a particular claim is totally without merit, thus further limiting the likelihood of a fee award under the provisions of the Act.

Conclusion

Because of the relative newness of this legislation, no cases have been reported that uphold its validity or interpret any of its provisions. There have been references to the Act in several recent cases, but only to point out that the peer review actions that were the subjects of those cases took place before the effective date of the Act.

NATIONAL PRACTITIONER DATA BANK

The Act, as previously noted, sets forth requirements for the creation of a federal data bank. This part of the Act relates to congressional findings of an alleged increase in the occurrence of medical malpractice and the need to restrict the ability of incompetent physicians to move from state to state without disclosure to licensing authorities of prior negligence or incompetent performance. A degree of control over the latter problem is to be obtained through the creation and use of the National Practitioner Data Bank (NPDB). (See Appendix 21-B for Department of Health and Human Services regulations that will govern operation of the NPDB.)

Reporting Requirements

Any entity, including an insurance company or a self-insured hospital, that makes a malpractice payment on behalf of a physician or other licensed health care practitioner as the result of a judgment in a medical malpractice action, or in settlement or partial settlement thereof, must report the requisite data to the NPDB, as well as to the appropriate state licensing board. The data that must be reported include the name of the physician or licensed health care practitioner; the amount of the payment; the name of the hospital with which the physician or practitioner is affiliated or associated; a description of the acts, omissions, injuries, or illnesses upon which the action or claim was based; and other information that may be required from time to time as determined by the Secretary of Health and Human Services.

A state medical or dental board must report the revocation or suspension of a license or actions in which a physician is censured, reprimanded, or placed on probation by reason of his or her professional competence or conduct. The surrendering of a physician's license also must be reported. (Note: The statutory definition of a "physician" includes a doctor of medicine or osteopathy and a doctor of dental surgery or medical dentistry.) The information to be reported is basically the same as that required in connection with the payment of a malpractice settlement or judgment.

Any health care entity (this term includes hospitals, health maintenance organizations, group medical practices, and professional societies) that follows a formal peer review process must report any adverse action it takes against a physician's clinical privileges when such action affects those privileges for a period of longer than 30 days. The entity must also report if it accepts the surrender of clinical privileges by a physician while the physician is under investigation by the entity or in return for not conducting such an investigation or proceeding (see Figure 21-1). An entity may, if it chooses, report any actions taken against other licensed health care practitioners who are not physicians, if the entity would be required to report such information were the practitioners physicians.

A professional society must report an adverse action taken against the membership of a physician when the action has been reached through a peer review proceeding that affords due process to the member. Professional societies of other health fields may, if they choose, report adverse membership actions, but only when the actions have been reached through peer review proceedings with due process.

All reports relating to clinical privileges and peer review actions required under this section of the Act are made to the appropriate state board of medical examiners or board of dental examiners. In turn, each board transmits the information to the NPDB. A health care entity that fails to comply with the reporting requirements loses its antitrust immunity protection under Part A of the Act. If a state board fails to comply with reporting requirements, the Secretary of Health and Human Services can designate another qualified agency for the reporting of the requisite information.

Querying the Data Bank

All hospitals must request information from the NPDB when a physician or other licensed health care practitioner applies for a medical staff position or requests clinical privileges (see Figure 21-2). Hospitals must also request information every two years regarding members of their medical staffs or physicians with clinical privileges. Requests for information may be made at any time in addition to those times mandated by the Act and can include inquiries regarding health care practitioners other than physicians and dentists.

State licensing boards and other health care entities may make inquiries of the data bank when they feel it is required in view of their stated purposes and programs during negotiations with individuals for staff membership.

If a medical malpractice action is filed against a hospital and one of its physicians or practitioners, and that hospital has not made the requisite inquiries mandated by the Act, the hospital will be presumed to have knowledge of any information reported to the data bank about that physician or practitioner. The plaintiff's attorney, upon proving that the hospital did not make the requisite inquiries, may access the data bank and obtain the information contained therein regarding the individual physician or practitioner.

Figure 21-1
REPORTING INFORMATION TO THE NATIONAL PRACTITIONER DATA BANK

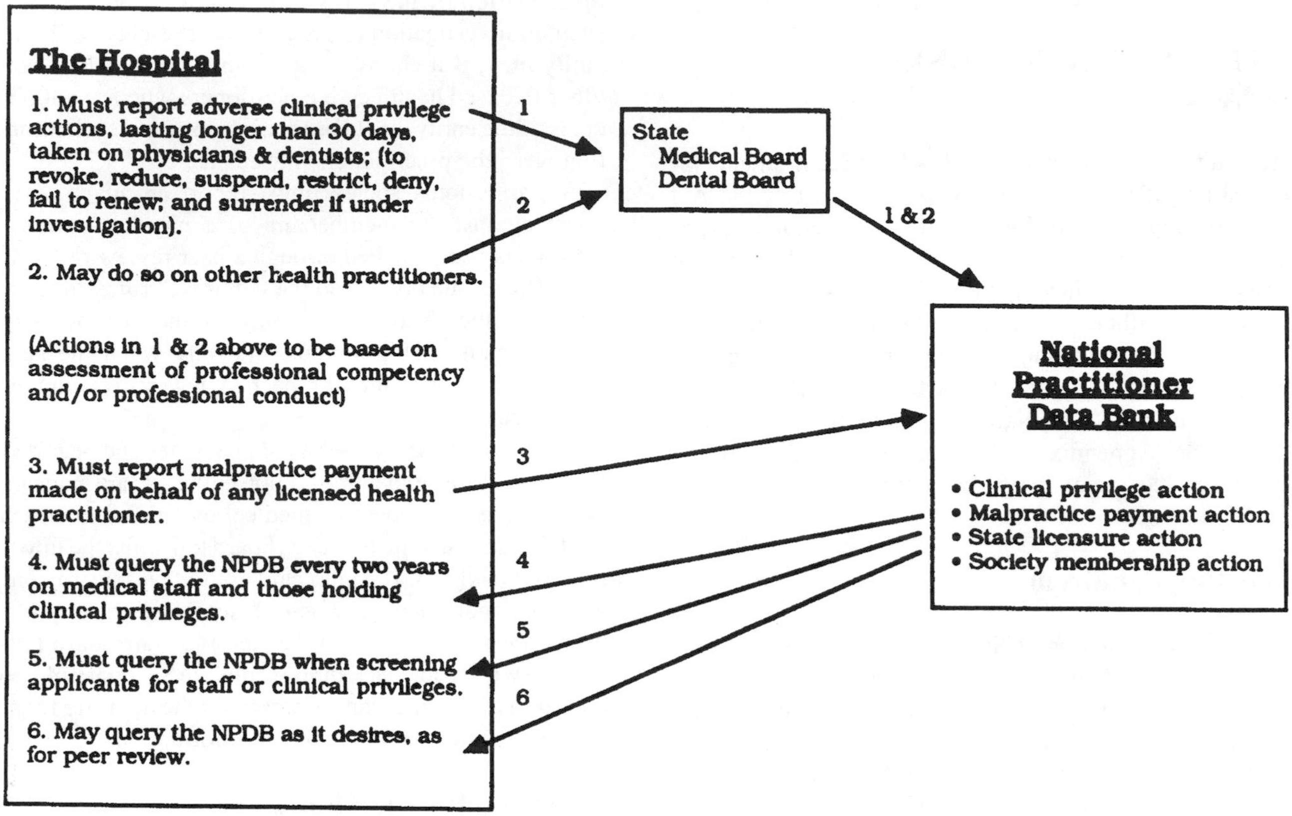

Source: Reprinted from *QRC Advisor,* Vol. 5, No. 12, p. 8, by Margaret A. Wilson, p. 6, Aspen Publishers, Inc., © 1989.

An individual physician or practitioner may obtain his or her records from the data bank. In addition, that individual will receive a copy of all data entered into the data bank regarding the individual each time information is reported to the NPDB. Regulations are to be promulgated setting forth procedures for challenging the disputed accuracy of any information in the data bank.

Immunity for Reporting

Any person or entity reporting information that is required to be reported under the Act receives a degree of immunity from liability in a civil action, unless, at the time of reporting, the information was known to be false.

A SUMMARY OF TORT REFORM

Elimination of Joint and Several Liability

Joint and several liability is a concept created under common law that allows a plaintiff to recover the total damage awarded to the plaintiff from any single defendant in a multidefendant lawsuit, regardless of fault in the action. For example, the defendant could be found only 5 percent at fault, yet still be liable for 100 percent of the damages. Naturally, the plaintiff would look to the defendant with the greatest amount of assets or the largest insurance policy to cover the damage award.

Some states currently retain this doctrine, but many have abolished it completely, eliminated it for noneconomic damages, or passed partial modifications. Elimination or modification of the concept could reduce damage awards and settlements, especially in cases where fault is tenuous but the injury itself is substantial.

The following states have passed legislation eliminating or modifying the concept of joint and several liability: Alaska, Arizona, California, Colorado, Connecticut, Florida, Georgia, Hawaii, Idaho, Illinois, Kansas, Kentucky, Louisiana, Michigan, Minnesota, Missouri, Montana, Nevada, New Hampshire, New Jersey, New Mexico, New York, North Dakota, Ohio, Oklahoma, Oregon, South Carolina, South Dakota, Texas, Utah, Washington, West Virginia, and Wyoming.

Figure 21-2
TWO-WAY REPORTING FOR USERS OF THE NATIONAL PRACTITIONER DATA BANK

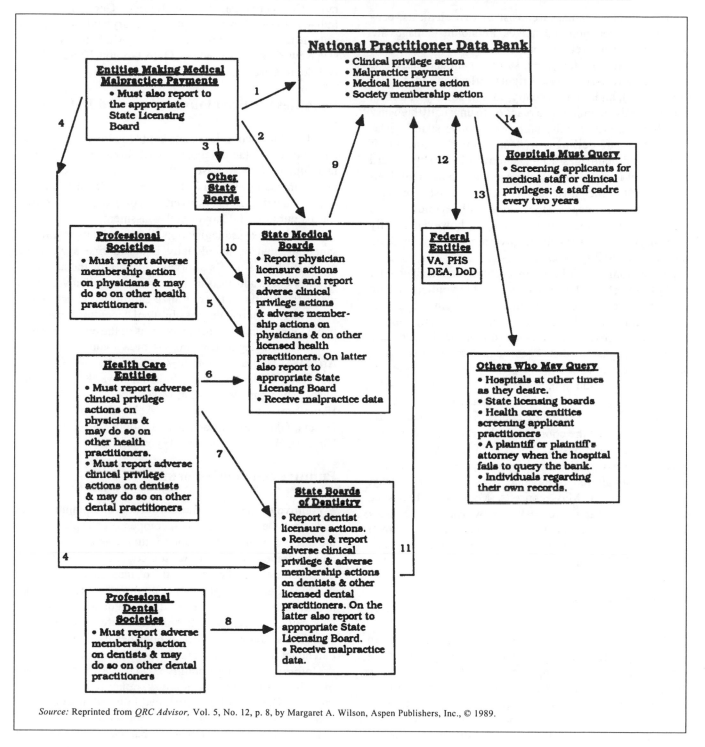

Adoption of Damage Award Caps

Compensatory damages consist of two elements, economic and noneconomic damages. Economic damages are actual "out-of-pocket" expenses or losses. Noneconomic damages relate to intangibles, such as pain and suffering, loss of consortium (a spouse's right to affection and services of the other), and, more recently, loss of society of a child or other family member. In a reaction to unusually high jury awards for noneconomic damages, various state legislatures have put ceilings or "caps" on the amount of noneconomic damages a jury can award. Damage award caps do not normally affect the economic portion of damages, except in such instances where state legislatures have capped total damages (including both economic and noneconomic). Caps on total damages, however, usually relate only to actions involving government entities or dram shop/liquor liability cases.

Noneconomic award caps are currently the most popular kind of tort reform, because they result in verdicts that are more predictable and less influenced by sympathy. State and federal courts have also recently set limits on the amounts of recoverable damages and, in certain instances, have reduced jury verdicts because they felt that excessive damages were awarded.

A word of caution in this area is necessary. Several state statutes setting caps on damages have been declared unconstitutional, with the reviewing courts focusing primarily on rights of access to the court set forth in state constitutions.

States that have passed this type of legislation include Alabama, Alaska, Arkansas, Colorado, Delaware, Florida, Georgia, Hawaii, Idaho, Indiana, Iowa, Kansas, Kentucky, Maine, Maryland, Massachusetts, Michigan, Minnesota, Missouri, Montana, Nebraska, New Hampshire, New Mexico, North Dakota, Oregon, South Carolina, South Dakota, Utah, Virginia, Washington, West Virginia, Wisconsin, and Wyoming.

Collateral Source Rule Change

The collateral source rule prohibits a defendant from introducing, during trial, any evidence of an injured plaintiff's receipt of any type of compensation for damages from any other source, such as workers' compensation or private disability insurance, that duplicates compensation being sought in the lawsuit. It also prohibits the reduction of any damage award because of the receipt of such compensation.

The most common type of reform in this area is an offset or reduction of a jury award equal to the amount of the compensation already received. These offsets and reductions have reduced settlements and jury awards where receipt of such amounts can be introduced into evidence.

States that have passed legislation modifying the collateral source rule include Alabama, Alaska, California, Colorado, Connecticut, Delaware, Florida, Georgia, Illinois, Indiana, Iowa, Kansas, Kentucky, Maryland, Massachusetts, Michigan, Minnesota, Missouri, Montana, New Jersey, New York, North Dakota, Ohio, Oregon, Rhode Island, and South Carolina.

Penalties for Frivolous Actions and Defenses

A frivolous action is a suit that (1) is brought to either harass or injure the defendant(s), (2) involves insufficient facts upon which to base a claim, or (3) is based on an unrecognized legal theory of recovery. A defense is frivolous when it does not controvert the complaint and is raised for the purpose of delay or embarrassment.

States have passed legislation allowing the imposition of sanctions, that is, a judicially imposed fine against the plaintiff, the plaintiff's attorney, or both, or the award of attorneys' fees and costs to the innocent party. This requires plaintiffs' attorneys to scrutinize carefully any action before filing suit or risk the possibility of becoming personally liable for payment of penalties or costs of the opposing party.

States with legislation in this area include Alabama, Arizona, Arkansas, Colorado, Connecticut, Florida, Georgia, Hawaii, Idaho, Illinois, Indiana, Iowa, Kansas, Kentucky, Michigan, Minnesota, Mississippi, Nebraska, New Hampshire, New Jersey, New York, North Carolina, North Dakota, Oklahoma, Rhode Island, South Carolina, Texas, Virginia, West Virginia, and Wyoming.

Punitive Damage Reforms

Punitive damages are those awarded to a plaintiff over and above the amount that will compensate the plaintiff for the alleged injury, where such injury was aggravated by malice, fraud, willful and wanton conduct of a defendant, or, in some cases, the "bad faith" of insurance companies. The award gives the plaintiff restitution for the additional aggravation suffered because of the conduct of the defendant and as a means of punishing the defendant for unacceptable behavior. In effect, it punishes the insurer of the defendant in most instances.

Unfortunately, large punitive damage awards are more often based on sympathy of a jury, rather than the facts of the case. They are often demanded in pleadings where, in fact, no malice, fraud, or willful conduct exists.

Legislation has been passed that eliminates punitive damages or, in certain instances, limits their application to only the most flagrant actions. The U.S. Supreme Court recently held that the Eighth Amendment's excessive fines clause was not violated by the awarding of punitive damages in civil lawsuits between private parties. However, the

Court did leave open the possibility that punitive damages might be challenged under a Fourteenth Amendment due process claim.

States that have passed legislation limiting punitive damages in some form include Alabama, Alaska, California, Colorado, Delaware, Florida, Georgia, Hawaii, Idaho, Illinois, Iowa, Kansas, Kentucky, Maryland, Minnesota, Missouri, Montana, New Hampshire, New Jersey, North Dakota, Oklahoma, Oregon, South Carolina, South Dakota, Texas, Virginia, and West Virginia.

Immunity of Public Entities

The common law doctrine of sovereign immunity holds that a public entity is exempt from tort liability while it is engaged in a governmental function. At one time, this doctrine also applied to charitable institutions. The doctrine, in all its applications, has been severely eroded over the years by court decisions.

States have attempted to impose ceilings on the amount of damages plaintiffs can recover in efforts to regain some protection under this doctrine. A number of these statutes attempting to limit recovery have been successfully challenged on constitutional grounds, so the efficacy of the protection afforded under the sovereign immunity doctrine is questionable.

States attempting to limit recovery under statutes of this nature include California, Colorado, Georgia, Idaho, Illinois, Indiana, Kansas, Maryland, Michigan, Mississippi, Nevada, North Carolina, South Carolina, Tennessee, Texas, Utah, Virginia, West Virginia, and Wyoming.

Mandatory Periodic Payments

Reforms in this area relate to the legal allowance or requirement of the defendant, who is ordered to pay a large damage award for future losses, to make payment in several smaller amounts spread out over the period of the plaintiff's disability or lifetime in lieu of one lump sum payment. These reforms target the damage awards for their intended purpose, which is the compensation of the injured party. They also attempt to eliminate the windfall to the beneficiaries of an injured party in the event of his or her death.

Some state statutes require that parties to a lawsuit elect to have the case tried so as to result in periodic payments of any judgment. Others allow periodic payments of a judgment only at the court's discretion and where a certain threshold dollar amount has been met.

States legislating in this area include Alabama, Alaska, Connecticut, Florida, Hawaii, Idaho, Iowa, Kansas, Maine, Maryland, Michigan, Minnesota, Missouri, Montana, New York, North Dakota, Ohio, Rhode Island, South Dakota, Utah, and Washington.

PROPOSED REFORMS

In addition to the reforms listed in the section above, several other types have been discussed and proposed but not largely acted upon by state legislatures.

Pretrial Screening and Mandatory Arbitration

States have instituted panels that review medical malpractice cases prior to the time of trial. Some have gone so far as to require screening by these panels prior to a lawsuit being filed. These panels normally consist of representatives from both the medical and legal communities. A preliminary examination of the plaintiff's allegations is made to determine whether or not the case is frivolous. Normally, the plaintiff retains the right to file the suit even if the panel determines that a valid claim has not been presented. However, in a case that has been termed frivolous by the review panel, it usually is required to contain an expense and fee reversal clause if the plaintiff continues the action and loses.

Some panels have the power to refer the case to an arbitrator who attempts to resolve the claim without the necessity and delay involved in a full trial of the issues. Referral to an arbitrator can result in early settlement, reduce the costs associated with litigation, and help to unclog some of the backlog plaguing court systems in major metropolitan areas. In one of the most recent cases dealing with statutes of this type, the Illinois Supreme Court is expected to rule on the constitutionality of a state statute requiring physicians to certify that malpractice cases are meritorious. The challenge is based on the allegation that the statute unconstitutionally delegates judicial authority to physicians and deprives medical malpractice victims access to the courts.

Limitations on Attorneys' Fees

Attorneys' fees in a liability action are most often determined on a contingent fee basis, that is, the fee is a percentage of the award. Proposed limits to these fees have included provisions that (1) institute a sliding scale to reduce the percentage as the amount of the award or settlement increases; (2) specify in the statute the percentage amount recoverable as fees; and (3) allow the court to set the fee by using a standard of "reasonableness."

While limitation of attorneys' fees may reduce the overall damage award in any given case, these statutory provisions might be successfully challenged on the basis of an unlawful interference with the right to contract.

Expert Witness Laws

Reforms in this area require that a person called as an expert witness be required to meet certain specified standards before he or she can testify. These standards could include state licensing, board certification in the same specialty as the defendant, and minimum training and practical experience in the same area. Expert witness reforms are attempts to limit the use of "professional" expert witnesses who testify in any number of cases, whether or not the cases involve their particular areas of expertise.

Limitations to *Ad Damnum* Clause

The *ad damnum* clause, usually the last paragraph in a count of a plaintiff's complaint, states the amount of damages being sought for the alleged injury or loss. In some instances, the amount of damages sought bears absolutely no logical relationship to the actual loss or injury, but is merely inserted as a starting point for settlement negotiations.

Reforms have included statutes prohibiting any specific monetary amount of damages in the allegations or prayer for relief, other than as required to establish the jurisdiction of the court, the right to a jury trial, or other stated purposes. Usually a general allegation that the amount of the claim exceeds the statutory jurisdictional amount is sufficient. Some states require that the pleadings be only for such damages "as are reasonable."

Conclusion

All forms of tort reform have been, and will continue to be, challenged by the plaintiff's bar. Some challenges have been successful, others have not, and still others are pending. This area of the law is constantly changing and must be periodically reviewed for current status to determine current risk.

HOW CAN A HOSPITAL RISK MANAGER COPE WITH COBRA?

In response to increased public concern about the care being rendered to indigent patients, the federal government in 1985 attempted to establish criteria that would govern how hospitals and physicians transfer and discharge patients. This "anti-dumping" statute was titled the Consolidated Omnibus Budget Reconciliation Act of 1985 (COBRA), 42 U.S.C.A. Sec. 1395dd—P.L. 99–272, Sec. 9121, as amended by P.L. 101–239, Sec. 6211, enacted December 19, 1989, effective July 1, 1990. (See Appendix 21-C.) The potential impact of this law was the subject of considerable discussion by health care administrators, risk managers, and

legal counsel, who felt that the law created a litigation time bomb just waiting to explode and believed that its attempt to legislate the practice of medicine set a dangerous precedent for future legislators. As legal and enforcement activities increase relative to this Act, the number of lawsuits filed may also begin to rise.

To make matters worse, Congress recently decided to add significant amendments to medical COBRA. These amendments became effective on July 1, 1990. Rather than addressing the many problems created by the 1985 COBRA, the amendments further confuse the original Act and, in some cases, actually exacerbate the problems initially created. It is also anticipated that changes in the law will allow an increase in the number of monetary penalties imposed by the Health and Human Services (HHS) office of the inspector general.

Requirements of COBRA

This Act currently applies to all participating physicians and any physician who is responsible for the examination, treatment, or transfer of an individual in a participating hospital, including a physician on call for the care of such individual. The Act requires that the hospital evaluate all patients who present with an "emergency medical condition" and determines the appropriateness of treating the patient until stabilized or transferring the patient to another medical facility. A patient maintains the right to refuse to consent to the proposed transfer or treatment. An amendment to the Act also requires the hospital to obtain the patient's "written informed consent to refuse" the offered treatment or transfer if the patient does indeed reject the treatment or transfer plan proposed.

At first glance, the requirements of the Act do not appear too onerous. The definitions of the terms included in the Act, however, are so ambiguous that health care attorneys and hospital administrators are fearful that compliance will prove to be impossible and that no opportunity for challenge will be available.

Penalties

Amendments to COBRA expand on the issue of compliance with the Act. It now states that a hospital can be liable for civil penalties as high as $50,000 if it negligently violates the law. (This amount is decreased to $25,000 for hospitals with fewer than 100 beds.) Of even greater significance is a hospital's exclusion from Medicare participation if it fails to meet the requirements of COBRA.

On the positive side, according to the House Ways and Means Committee, hospitals have obtained a partial victory because it was agreed that the enforcement efforts by the HHS inspector general's office and the Health Care Financing Administration (HCFA) "should be focused on violations that directly affect the health or welfare of patients and not on violations that are merely paperwork or procedural violations."

The American College of Emergency Physicians (ACEP) also believes that it scored some victories through its congressional lobbying efforts on some of the important amendments related to patient transfer, including the following:

- If an emergency physician contacts an on-call physician who fails or refuses to respond, the emergency physician is not liable for an illegal transfer if he or she certifies that the benefits of transfer outweighed the risk because the on-call physician was unavailable.
- "Whistle-blower" protection is provided for physicians who report illegal transfers, thereby preventing retaliation by hospitals.
- Hospitals are required to provide a list of on-call physicians who will respond to requests from emergency physicians for follow-up care.
- A provision was deleted that would have allowed individuals to bring suit against physicians who illegally transfer a patient and to recover $25,000 plus attorneys' fees.
- A provision was deleted that would have imposed a new standard of strict liability for any allegations of patient dumping by removal of the existing "knowingly" standard for civil monetary penalties. This provision could have resulted in a major increase in the number of cases brought by the inspector general.

Summary of Requirements for Emergency Departments

COBRA requirements specify that every individual who comes into a hospital's emergency department and requests an examination and treatment for a medical condition must be provided with an appropriate screening examination within the capabilities of the hospital. ACEP has developed standards for the appropriate evaluation and transfer of emergency department patients to comply with COBRA and to guarantee the quality of emergency department care (Exhibit 21-1).

The COBRA legislation focuses on a number of other quality-related issues, some of which relate to patient notice and record keeping. By July 1, each hospital was required to post a sign in the emergency department area that indicates its participation in the Medicaid program and describes patients' rights as they relate to treatment and transfer. Additionally, hospitals receiving Medicaid funds are required to keep records of all incoming and outgoing transfers. These records may be reviewed by HCFA at some time in the future.

Clinical record keeping also must be improved. The law now requires ongoing documentation of evidence of patient stability. This could be interpreted to mean all patients within the department as well as those waiting in the triage area. Obviously, the intent of the act is not to promote the unproductive use of staff who perform vital sign checks of patients in the area but rather to verify that unstable patients are being appropriately monitored.

Also related to the area of clinical record keeping is the requirement to obtain a written consent from each patient who is transferred. This consent constitutes evidence that the patient received and understood information explaining the risks and benefits associated with the transfer.

Another important change in COBRA relates to pregnant women and their care, treatment, and potential transfer. Pregnant women cannot be transferred if they are having contractions and there is inadequate time for transfer prior to delivery. Transfer is possible only if it does not pose a threat to the woman or her unborn child. The physician authorizing the transfer must document in the record that no deterioration is likely to result from or during the transfer.

The new on-call requirements are perceived to have both positive and negative impacts on the hospital's emergency department. The law now requires that the emergency department physician file a written report citing evidence that an on-call physician failed to respond for evaluation of a patient or did not respond within a reasonable period of time.

The Risk Manager's Role

The risk manager plays a critical role in assisting emergency department and administrative staff to understand and comply with the mandates of COBRA. Not only will a comprehensive approach to this new legislation limit the number of lawsuits that are related to violations, but hopefully it will also help in ensuring that the highest quality of patient care is provided.

Timothy D. Krugh, in an article in *The Journal of Health and Hospital Law*, suggests the following steps that risk managers should follow to avoid COBRA violations:[1]

- Organize a COBRA task force or team to study the problem, formulate a master plan for compliance, and mobilize widespread awareness of COBRA's implications and support for the joint effort to maximize compliance. Representatives from the administration, legal staff or hospital counsel, risk management, emergency department, outpatient services, and medical and nursing staffs should be consulted, as well as an outside expert on COBRA.
- Develop specific policies and procedures to ensure compliance with all aspects of COBRA. These proce-

Exhibit 21-1
ACEP POLICY: PRINCIPLES OF APPROPRIATE PATIENT TRANSFER

The American College of Emergency Physicians believes that quality emergency care should be available to all who seek it. For that care to be provided, patients sometimes are transferred to another health care facility from the emergency facility where they sought care. To ensure access to emergency care and patient safety when transfers occur, ACEP endorses the following principles regarding patient transfer:*

- The health and well-being of the patient must be the overriding concern when any patient transfer is considered.
- Emergency physicians and hospital personnel should comply with applicable state and federal regulations regarding patient transfer. A "medical screening examination," mandated by federal law, should be performed by a physician. In the event a physician is not physically present in the emergency department 24 hours a day, the screening examination may be performed by properly trained ancillary personnel according to written policies and procedures.
- The patient should be transferred to another facility only after medical evaluation and, when possible, stabilization. Stabilization includes evaluation and initiation of treatment to ensure, within reasonable medical probability, that transfer of the patient will not result in death or in loss or serious impairment of bodily functions, parts, or organs.
- The physician should inform the patient or responsible party of the reasons for and the risks and likely benefits of transfer and document this in the medical record. The competence of the patient to agree or refuse to be transferred should be assessed prior to obtaining his or her consent. If the patient is incompetent to make this decision, a person legally responsi-

ble for the patient should accept or refuse the transfer on behalf of the patient.

- The hospital and medical staffs should identify individuals responsible for transfer decisions and clearly delineate their duties regarding the patient transfer process.
- The patient should be transferred to a facility appropriate to the medical needs of the patient, with adequate space and personnel available.
- A physician or other responsible person at the receiving hospital must agree to accept the patient prior to the transfer.
- The patient transfer should not be refused by the receiving hospital when the transfer is medically indicated and the receiving hospital has the capability and/or responsibility to provide care for the patient. Economic reasons should not be the basis for transferring or refusing to accept a medically unstable patient.
- Communication to exchange clinical information between responsible persons at the transferring and receiving hospitals must occur prior to transfer.
- An appropriate medical summary and other pertinent records should accompany the patient to the receiving institution.
- The patient should be transferred in a vehicle that is staffed by qualified personnel and that contains appropriate equipment.
- When transfer of patients is part of a regional plan to provide optimal care for patients at specialized medical facilities, written transfer protocols and interfacility agreements should be in place.

(Adopted September 1989.)

*Source: Courtesy of the American College of Emergency Physicians, Irving, TX.

---

dures will be primarily in the areas of emergency department care, all transfers, and all discharges, but there may be other areas to consider, such as outpatient testing.

- Develop a paper trail to fully document compliance in all of the areas affected by COBRA. This may be the most practical and effective way to maximize compliance. Simple and appropriate forms, checklists, and record formats that both remind and require documentation should be developed. Perhaps a "patient transfer-discharge" form, containing a checklist of COBRA's requirements, could be completed for every patient visit to the emergency department, hospital, and outpatient department.
- Develop and provide in-house or in-service COBRA awareness, education, and training programs for the administration, emergency department, outpatient serv-

ices, and medical and nursing staffs. This is not a simple law, and many misconceptions exist.

- Prepare and use a list of preapproved hospitals that have agreed to accept your transfers.
- Develop and implement an in-house COBRA compliance review system.
- Conduct a simulated response to a hypothetical HCFA notice of termination.

THE PATIENT SELF-DETERMINATION ACT OF 1990

The Patient Self-Determination Act (P.L. 101–508, 42 U.S.C. Secs. 4206 and 4751) became effective in November 1991. This Act was part of the Omnibus Budget Reconciliation Act of 1990 (OBRA), which was drafted, in part, as a response to heightened media attention given to a patient's right to accept or refuse medical treatment (see Appendix 21-D). This attention was prompted by the U.S. Supreme Court decision in the *Cruzan* case, an attempt to set forth criteria under which a patient's wishes should be upheld even if those wishes would result in the patient's death. The Patient Self-Determination Act (PSDA) is intended to enhance "self-determination" by making the public, in general, and patients of health care facilities, in particular, aware of their options and their respective state laws related to their participation in decision making in life and death matters.

Summary of the Law

As of November 1991, the PSDA requires all health care providers and other organizations, defined in the Act as hospitals, skilled nursing facilities, home health agencies, providers of home health or personal care services, hospice programs, and health maintenance organizations, that participate in Medicare and Medicaid programs to:

- draft and maintain written policies and procedures to ensure that they will be in compliance with the PSDA
- provide all adults who receive medical care at the facility with written information describing their rights under existing state laws as related to the care they receive; this includes the right to accept or refuse treatment, as well as the right to formulate advanced directives
- describe to these adults the provider's or organization's policy regarding the implementation of these rights
- document in each person's medical record whether an advanced directive has been signed
- participate in community education related to issues concerning advanced directives
- comply with applicable state and statutory law respecting advanced directives

The law clearly states that providers must not condition care or discriminate against persons who have elected to execute advanced directives. In addition, the PSDA requires the Secretary of Health and Human Services to develop and implement a national education campaign to inform the public about advanced directives and the patient's rights concerning health care decisions. The development and dissemination of written materials are also included in this charge.

Penalties for Noncompliance

Compliance with the PSDA is required as part of each covered provider's Medicare and Medicaid obligations.

Violations of the provisions of the statute can result in termination of those programs and loss of federal funding. In addition, failure to comply with the provisions of the Act can expose the hospital to litigation.

Potential Quality Problems Associated with Enforcement

Although this Act, in theory, will help to ensure that patients become integrally involved in decisions related to their health and that they become knowledgeable regarding their options, many observers fear that compliance with the Act will take place in the hospital's admitting department where the written material provided to patients will get lost in the morass of paperwork accompanying a routine hospital admission. Others fear that the persons who are in the best position to educate patients (physicians, nurses, clergy, and social workers) will not recognize the benefits to the health care system and to the patient of having accurate information provided at an appropriate time and of allowing for patient-provider interaction when questions arise.

Ensuring Effective Compliance

Health care professionals should take the time to ensure that information provided to patients is appropriate and that relevant issues are covered thoroughly. Specific professionals in the health care setting should be given responsibility for patient education, and a process should be developed to ensure that the patient understands the information provided and knows how to utilize it. The various types of legal forms should be explained and be readily available if the patient wishes to execute them (see Chapter 14 on ethical issues and sample forms).

Some hospitals may wish to develop a questionnaire that attempts to evaluate a patient's values about death and dying. This document can then be used as the basis for a discussion of these very sensitive and personal matters. An excellent example is the values history form developed by the Ethics Committee at Southern Chester County Medical Center in West Grove, Pennsylvania (see Appendix 21-E). This type of questionnaire can identify the patient's motivations that may affect his or her decisions. The form asks personal "quality of life" questions in a nonthreatening manner and readily elicits the patient's responses.

After this dialogue with the patient and family has taken place, the appropriate staff member should discuss the options allowed under state law. Hospital policies should clearly delineate how the hospital complies with the law, and available forms for the patient to complete should provide evidence of such compliance.

The hospital administration may wish to provide education to the staff related to the Patient Self-Determination

Act and issues involved in ethical decision making. This type of course may be helpful for all physicians and nurses who feel uncomfortable when discussing such information with patients or their families. The sessions can be led by social workers, chaplains, or other professionals who frequently deal with the subjects of death and dying.

SAFE MEDICAL DEVICES ACT*

On November 28, 1990, President Bush signed into law the "Safe Medical Devices Act of 1990" (Public Law 101-629), which imposes new reporting requirements on "device user facilities." The reporting requirements (which became effective at the end of 1991) could increase the number of device-related lawsuits filed against hospitals or health care professionals using the devices and have increased the amount of paper work associated with device-related incidents. Risk managers should take the time to become familiar with the requirements and develop an internal system that enables them to identify situations where reporting is mandated.

They can also begin developing a system to streamline the process for collecting the required information. This might include providing in-service training for staff on the new law, and assessing the current incident reporting system to assure that device-related injuries are consistently reported and that questions asked in the incident report will yield the type of information requested under the new law. The risk manager can also begin working with the biomedical engineering department or the hospital's product safety committee to explain how this new law might affect their activities.

History of the Safe Medical Devices Act

The Safe Medical Devices Act of 1990 seeks to make mandatory what has in the past been voluntary. The purpose of the 1976 law (The Medical Device Amendments of 1976—21 U.S.C. section 301 et seq.) was to develop a mechanism that would allow for the regulation of medical devices and ensure that they were safe and effective. Although the mechanism for achieving this was clearly spelled out, the original Act allowed for voluntary reporting by hospitals of device-related incidents, making it difficult and at times impossible to track device-related problems or even to become aware that they occurred. Manufacturers and importers of medical devices were required under this Act to submit reports of device-related deaths and serious injuries as they became aware of them. They were also required to report device malfunctions, but only if the

malfunction was likely to cause death or serious injury. In an effort to tighten up the reporting, thereby ensuring that the FDA would learn of all device-related incidents and be able to take the necessary action with the device manufacturers, the 1990 Act made the prior voluntary report by hospitals and other health care facilities (medical device user facilities) mandatory.

The Act has significant implications for health care entities in that it grants the Food and Drug Administration regulatory authority over them. The additional burden of reporting device-related incidents and using a separate form and criteria could add to an already stressed risk management/quality assurance program. Gathering all the data that will be required in a report will require coordination and communication between a number of hospital departments. Compiling the information for the semiannual summary reports will require additional work by risk management.

SUMMARY OF THE SAFE MEDICAL DEVICES ACT OF 1990

Legislative History

The Act was signed into law November 28, 1990 with an effective date of November 28, 1991.

Who Must File the Report?

Hospitals, ambulatory surgical facilities, nursing homes and any facilities (other than a physician's office) wherein health care is provided will be required to file reports to the FDA.

Specifics of Reporting

These reports must be completed within 10 working days after the facility becomes aware of any information that suggests that a medical device was involved in the death, illness, or injury of a patient. (In the 1986 law, manufacturers and importers were required to submit reports even though they may have believed that the incident in question was related to user error, improper equipment service or maintenance, or other "user-related" problems. This expansion on reporting requirements is not clearly stated in the 1990 Act.) In addition, summaries of user reports must be submitted on January 1st and July 1st of each year. Once the report is completed, it is to be forwarded to the manufacturer of the device, or to the FDA if the manufacturer is not known.

The Role of the Manufacturer

Once the manufacturer has received a copy of the report from the device-user facility, it is required to comply with

*Source: Reprinted from *Quality and Risk Management in Health Care*, Vol. 1, No. 3, March 1991, © Aspen Publishers, Inc.

existing medical device reporting regulations and investigate the incident further. When appropriate, the manufacturer will also be required to file a report with the FDA.

THE AMERICANS WITH DISABILITIES ACT

Enacted on July 26, 1990, the Americans with Disabilities Act (ADA) (42 U.S.C. 12101 et seq.) is the most important piece of civil rights legislation since the mid-1960s. With its twin thrusts concerning employment opportunities and accessibility, the ADA levels the playing field for people with disabilities. Health care providers who meet the challenge of the ADA will be practicing sound risk management and, in addition, promoting their business objectives.

When signing the ADA, President Bush observed that the law provides a "powerful expansion of protections" for people with disabilities and is intended to "remove the physical barriers we have created and the social barriers we have accepted." In addition to expanding civil rights, the ADA thus serves an important educative function for the estimated 43 million people with disabilities it protects and the general population that must learn more about the rights of people with disabilities.

A key factor that greatly aided the passage of the ADA was projected cost savings: the estimated $200 billion spent annually to support Americans with disabilities while keeping them dependent. As noted by President Bush, people with disabilities, when given the opportunity to become independent via the ADA, "will move proudly into the economic mainstream of American life, and that's what this legislation is all about." The ADA represents a response to the federal Workforce 2000 report, which noted that traditional sources of labor are shrinking, and that minority populations—including people with disabilities—are an underused labor source.

As increasing numbers of people with disabilities move into the mainstream of economic life, health care providers, many of whom have good records of hiring persons with disabilities and making their facilities accessible, will have new opportunities to attract able employees and new clients. The ADA is thus truly a means to do well by doing good. However, since the health care industry is likely to be a testing ground for the ADA, sound risk management becomes especially important.

Source: Reprinted from *Quality and Risk Management in Health Care,* Vol. 1, No. 6, December 1991, © Aspen Publishers, Inc.

THE ADA: A SUMMARY

Who Is Protected?

The starting point for dealing with the ADA is identifying who is covered by determining who is a person with a disability. With respect to an individual, the ADA defines "disability" to mean one of three things:

- *a physical or mental impairment that substantially limits one or more of a person's major life activities,* as in the case of someone who uses a wheelchair, has multiple sclerosis or AIDS, or is visually or hearing impaired
- *a record of such an impairment,* such as a history of cancer or heart disease
- *being regarded as having such an impairment,* such as a person who is badly scarred as a result of burns, or has tested HIV positive but is otherwise healthy

The ADA's three-part definition parallels the definition of disability used in other federal statutes, such as the Rehabilitation Act of 1973. However, the ADA also identifies individuals in certain categories or having particular behavioral conditions as being *excluded* from the definition: current users of illegal drugs, persons with temporary conditions such as pregnancy, homosexuals, and persons with certain behavior disorders such as kleptomania and pyromania are excluded.

In addition to expanding protections for people with disabilities, the ADA provides powerful new protections against discrimination for individuals who have *associations* or relationships with people with disabilities.

Legal and Practical Parameters

The ADA codifies many of the cases that have been decided under the Rehabilitation Act and expands the rights of people with disabilities.

The ADA's major protections for people with disabilities are contained in three sections: Title I, Employment; Title II, Public Services; and Title III, Public Accommodations and Services Operated by Private Entities. As set forth in the tables on pages 245–246, summarizing the ADA's requirements (which appear in a total of five titles) and the schedule for their implementation, *effective dates* vary for different portions of the ADA. The first effective date has already passed; the ADA becomes fully effective on July 26, 1994.

Regulations to implement the law were developed by numerous federal agencies and issued on July 26, 1991. Those agencies promulgated proposed rules in January and

February of 1991 and held public hearings. Various health care providers and associations commented on those rules.

The ADA sets out straightforward *enforcement* mechanisms: the statute tracks other federal laws (including Titles II and VII of the Civil Rights Act of 1964) and allows for administrative remedies, civil penalties and actions for injunctive relief, back and front pay, and attorney's fees—but not, at present, punitive damages. As with the Civil Rights Act, charges of discrimination in violation of the ADA's employment section (Title I) will first be filed with the Equal Employment Opportunity Commission. Under Titles II and III, individuals can choose an administrative remedy or file directly in court. The Civil Rights Act of 1991 includes additional types of damages to Title VII and, correspondingly, to the ADA, adding a potent remedy for plaintiffs before the Act has even become fully effective.

As for the statute's relationship to other laws, the ADA *preempts* weaker federal and state laws, but not equivalent or stronger federal or state laws. Thus, more potent federal and state law *remedies* remain in force. The ADA and corresponding regulations adopt many of the principles and language of the Rehabilitation Act of 1973 (and related cases); the ADA extends the Rehabilitation Act beyond its original scope, and amends that act by deleting coverage for alcoholism that prevents the performance of the job and by providing protection for former (but not current) drug abusers. *Some health care providers will need to comply with the provisions of both the Rehabilitation Act and the ADA if they are recipients of federal financial assistance or parties to federal contracts.* Although the employment provisions basically overlap, reporting requirements and, in the case of Section 503, affirmative action guidelines differ.

The ADA provides no *additional funding* for health care providers to meet their new statutory obligations. However, the financial impact of ADA compliance can be offset through the use of certain *tax benefits.* A tax deduction of up to $15,000 per year is available for the costs associated with removing structural or transportation barriers. A tax credit, called the Disabled Access Credit, is also available to smaller entities: those with gross revenues of a million dollars or less and thirty or fewer employees can receive a credit of up to $5,000 for both structural changes and costs associated with providing reasonable accommodations to employees, such as interpreter services or the purchase of adaptive equipment.

Finally, it should be noted that the ADA prohibits covered entities from circumventing the law by "contracting out" services to vendors—such as employment agencies, food services, and cleaning services—who in turn act in discriminatory ways with respect to the covered entity's (as opposed to the vendor's) employees or the people that the entity serves. Covered entities thus cannot do indirectly what the ADA prohibits them from doing directly.

The ADA and Health Care

The first and most obvious health care aspect of the ADA is that the statute gives protections to people with disabilities, which by definition means people with physical or mental impairments—the very population group that health care providers serve! What, then, will the principal impact of the ADA be on health care providers as they serve people with disabilities? Let's look, *title, by title,* at the primary effects of the ADA.

Title I prohibits employers with fifteen or more employees from discriminating against people with disabilities in all aspects of the employment relationship. The prohibition against discrimination extends to job application procedures, the hiring, advancement or discharge of employees, employee compensation and benefits, job training, and other terms, conditions, and privileges of employment.

To qualify for Title I protections, the person must be a "qualified individual with a disability," able to perform the "essential functions of the job" with or without a reasonable accommodation. Essential job functions are job tasks that are fundamental rather than marginal to the execution of the job. In determining what are essential functions, such factors as work experience of incumbents in the job, terms of a collective bargaining agreement, written job descriptions, and the employer's judgment as to what tasks are essential will be considered. For example, lifting may be an essential function for a floor nurse in a hospital, but not for a nurse in a doctor's office.

Employers are required to provide "reasonable accommodations" for qualified applicants or employees with disabilities. Reasonable accommodation is defined as "modifications or adjustments to a job application process, work environment or the manner in which a job is performed that enable a qualified individual with a disability to be considered for or able to perform the job." Examples include removal of structural barriers in the workplace or at the worksite, modified work schedules (such as flex-time), provision of auxiliary aids such as interpreters, readers or adaptive devices, job restructuring, or job reassignment. The applicant or employee has the responsibility of requesting the accommodation. In contrast, the selection of any particular accommodation rests with the employer, who need not select the "best" accommodation, provided that the chosen one is effective. For example, an employer need not buy a custom-designed desk for a person who uses a wheelchair, if raising a standard desk with blocks would be an equally effective but less expensive accommodation. Creative management to encourage successful job performance, as is the case with all employees, is the key: toward this end, the regulations contemplate an interactive "process" between applicant/employee and em-

Table 21–1
AMERICANS WITH DISABILITIES ACT: A SUMMARY

Title	Law's Effective Date	Regulations by Federal Agency	Enforcement Jurisdiction
Title I—Employment	July 26, 1992 for employers with twenty-five (25) or more employees; July 26, 1994 for employers with fifteen (15) or more employees	July 26, 1991, all regulations from Equal Employment Opportunity Commission (EEOC).	Remedies identical to those under Title VII of the Civil Rights Act of 1964 (private right of action, injunctive relief, i.e., job reinstatement, back pay, and EEOC enforcement).
Title II—Public Services All activities of local and state governments	January 26, 1991	July 26, 1991, all regulations from Attorney General.	Remedies identical to those under the Rehabilitation Act of 1973 Section 505 (private right of action, injunctive relief, and some damages).
(Part I) Public transportation (buses, light and rapid rail including fixed-route systems, paratransit, demand response systems, and transportation facilities).	August 26, 1990, all orders for purchases or leases of new vehicles must be for accessible vehicles; one-car-per-train must be accessible as soon as practicable, but no later than July 26, 1995; paratransit services must be provided after January 26, 1992; new stations built after January 26, 1992 must be accessible. Key stations must be retrofitted by July 26, 1993, with some extensions allowed up to July 26, 2020.	July 26, 1991, all regulations from Secretary of Transportation.	Same as above.
(Part II) Public transportation by intercity Amtrak and commuter rail (including transportation facilities).	By July 26, 2000, Amtrak passenger coaches must have same number of accessible seats as would have been available if every car were built accessible; half of such seats must be available by July 26, 1995. Same one-car-per-train rule and new stations rule as above. All existing Amtrak stations must be retrofitted by July 26, 2010; key commuter stations must be retrofitted by July 26, 1993, with some extensions allowed up to 20 years.	July 26, 1991, all regulations from Secretary of Transportation.	Same as above.

ployer to identify the accommodation appropriate to the circumstances.

Where an employer can establish that providing a requested accommodation would cause an "undue hardship" on its business, the employer is not required to make that accommodation. Undue hardship is defined as an action requiring significant difficulty or expense. The determination of undue hardship is made considering a variety of factors, including the size and financial resources of the employer or its parent company, the nature and cost of the accommodation sought, and the type of the business. Accordingly, a large hospital system might be required to make an accommodation that would not be required of a small,

independent hospital. It is important to note that the impact of making an accommodation on employee morale is *not* enough, by itself, to establish undue hardship.

In addition to its prohibitions of discrimination against people with disabilities, the ADA adds a new and important prohibition of "associational discrimination": employers will violate the ADA if they exclude or deny equal jobs or benefits to qualified individuals who have known relationships or associations with individuals with known disabilities. This provision provides able-bodied individuals the right to file charges of discrimination (although they do not have the right to reasonable accommodation) based on relationships or associations including family, friends, or

Table 21–2
AMERICANS WITH DISABILITIES ACT: A SUMMARY

Title	Law's Effective Date	Regulations by Federal Agency	Enforcement Jurisdiction
Title III—Public accommodations operated by private entities.			
A. Public accommodations (all business and service providers).	In general, January 26, 1992, except no lawsuits may be filed before July 26, 1992 against businesses with twenty-five (25) or fewer employees and revenues of $1 million or less, or before January 26, 1993 for businesses with ten (10) or fewer employees and revenues of $500,000 or less.	July 26, 1991, regulations from Attorney General. Standards must be consistent with the Architectural and Transportation Barriers Compliance Board (ATBCB) guidelines.	For individuals, remedies identical to Title II of the Civil Rights Act of 1964 (private right of action, injunctive relief: For Attorney General enforcement in pattern or practice cases or cases of general importance with civil penalties and compensatory damages).
B. New construction/alteration to public accommodations and commercial facilities.	January 26, 1992, for alterations. January 26, 1993 for new construction.	Same as above.	Same as above.
C. Public transportation provided by private entities.	In general, January 26, 1992, but by August 26, 1990 all orders for purchases or leases of new vehicles must be for accessible vehicles. Calls for a three (3) year study of over-the-road buses to determine access needs with requirements effective July 26, 1996 to July 26, 1997.	July 26, 1991, regulations from Secretary of Transportation. Regulations will be based on standards issued by the Architectural Transportation Barriers Compliance Board (ATBCB).	Same as above.
Title IV—Telecommunications	July 26, 1993, telecommunications relay services to operate twenty-four (24) hours per day.	July 26, 1991, all regulations by the Federal Communications Commission.	Private right of action and Federal Communications Commission.
Title V—Miscellaneous	Effective dates of Title V are those determined by most of the analogous sections in Titles I through IV.	In general this title depicts the ADA's relationship to other laws, explains insurance issues, prohibits state immunity, provides congressional inclusion, sets regulations by ATBCB, explains implementation of each title and notes amendments to the Rehabilitation Act of 1973.	

business. For example, an employer cannot deny a promotion to an able-bodied worker because her child has cerebral palsy and the employer has a hypothetical concern about absenteeism in the new position. Similarly, if an employee is living with a person with AIDS, the employee cannot be terminated based on that relationship.

An employer can inquire whether an individual can perform the essential functions of the job and what accommodations would be necessary for a person with an obvious disability to perform those functions, and even (at the appropriate time) invite individuals to identify themselves as persons with disabilities to satisfy data collection requirements of the Rehabilitation Act. *However, the ADA sets specific standards pertaining to what can be asked and/ or examined about a person's disabilities. NO* pre-offer inquiries regarding medical history or pre-offer medical

examinations are permitted. Job application forms should thus be reviewed to ensure that impermissible questions are removed. Medical information or examinations are permissible after a conditional offer of employment has been extended but only if *all* employees in that job category are subject to such review. All medical information obtained about an applicant or employee must be kept confidential and maintained in a file separate from the individual's general employment record.

Drug testing is not restricted by the ADA as long as all employees or all employees in a particular job category are subject to testing. Employers cannot single out individuals with disabilities for testing.

It is important to note that the above restrictions do not prevent employers from utilizing "qualification standards," provided that the standards relate to the essential functions of the job in question and are consistent with business necessity. Similarly, nonmedical job tests are permissible, so long as persons with disabilities are not singled out, the tests are job-related, and reasonable accommodations to the testing process are made where appropriate.

Employers can terminate or refuse to hire a person with a disability if that individual poses a "direct threat" to the health and safety of themselves or others that cannot be eliminated or reduced to an acceptable level through reasonable accommodation. The direct threat standard sets a very high threshold: an employer must show objective evidence of behavior or overt acts or threats relating to the individual; fear or speculation about what might happen is not enough. Obviously, the concept of "direct threat," which was the AIDS battleground during the ADA's legislative life, raises significant concerns in the health care arena, and should be studied closely by providers. Suffice it to say that the high standard established by the ADA may reshape cases concerning AIDS (and other) discrimination that have arisen under the Rehabilitation Act and, in addition, may affect the debate concerning mandatory AIDS/HIV testing.

The ADA does not prohibit health care providers that are controlled by religious entities from giving preference in employment decisions to persons of a particular religion or denomination, provided that the provider does not discriminate against members of that religion or denomination who have disabilities. Such employers can also require that employee observe certain tenets of the religion at the workplace, such as restrictions on smoking or dietary restrictions. Note that this is an exemption that may be specifically limited by state law, if state law prohibits discrimination on the basis of religion. Also, health care providers that are religious entities that also are subject to the Rehabilitation Act will need to comply with its prohibition of discrimination on the basis of disability as well.

Finally, health care providers must post notices in a format accessible to applicants, employees, and their members describing the applicable provisions of the ADA.

Title II prevents public entities—including units of state and local government, such as state hospitals—from discriminating against people with disabilities. Generally, public entities that are employers are subject to all of the requirements of Title I, with respect to applicants and employees who are "qualified individuals with disabilities."

All services, programs, or activities offered by public entities must be nondiscriminatory. New construction and alterations must meet specific accessibility requirements. Existing facilities must be reviewed to ensure complete program accessibility either through facility access or alternative delivery of services or programs. Specific accessibility requirements are imposed on transportation facilities or vehicles utilized by those providers, including hospital shuttle vans.

Public entities are also required to undertake a self-evaluation to determine areas of noncompliance and identify appropriate changes. Entities with fifty or more employees must maintain the self-evaluation on file, available for public inspection.

Title III prevents private health care providers—including hospitals and professional offices that are *not* state or locally funded (and thus not public entities subject to Title II) from discriminating against people with disabilities. This prohibition extends to the goods, services, facilities, privileges, advantages, and accommodations of those providers, which must generally be offered "in the most integrated setting appropriate to the needs of the individual." The scope of the prohibition also includes equal participation in activities, integrated activities, and utilization of nondiscriminatory administrative methods, eligibility criteria, and contracts. Where accessible features are provided, adequate maintenance and prompt repair are required.

Health care providers will need to supply "auxiliary aids and services," such as interpreters or readers, unless doing so would cause an "undue burden." This provision specifically requires that when hospitals offer telephone and television as a benefit to patients, Telecommunication Devices for the Deaf (TDDs) and television decoders (permitting closed caption viewing) must be made available to patients who are deaf or hearing impaired.

The ADA requires health care providers to ensure that eligibility criteria for services do not screen out people with disabilities, unless there is a legitimate and neutral safety concern. Policies that discriminate, such as a refusal to permit service animals to accompany owners, must be revised; e.g., the health care facility must be modified (if necessary) to permit the use of service animals, unless doing so would fundamentally alter the public accommodation or pose a threat to safety.

New construction and alterations are required to be accessible. The ADA contains specific accessibility standards that must be incorporated into all new construction intended for first occupancy after January 26, 1993 and any alteration that affects the useability of a space by January 26, 1992. In addition to the general requirements for accessible design, *the regulations have specific criteria applicable to medical care facilities relating to patient rooms and other areas.* This is another area where state law may include design code requirements for accessibility, and an analysis must be undertaken to determine which standards are stricter to ensure that both state and federal design requirements are being met.

A major requirement of Title III is that barriers in existing facilities must be removed where such changes are "readily achievable." That term is defined as changes that are "easily accomplishable, without much difficulty or expense." The size and resources of a business will be considered in determining whether this standard has been met. Obviously, the larger and more profitable the facility, the higher the level of modification that will be required. The readily achievable standard is an ongoing responsibility. Changes may be made over time in order to keep within the law's dictate of being low-cost. Examples of readily achievable changes include installation of grab bars in a toilet stall, addition of raised letter or Braille signage for bathrooms and other directional signage, or ramping of a few steps.

The readily achievable standard does not require that existing facilities be totally retrofitted to meet the accessibility requirements of new construction, but that barriers be removed in a phased-in manner. Four priorities have been established to assist entities in planning for readily achievable barrier removal: (1) entrances; (2) access to goods and services; (3) access to bathrooms; (4) all other areas or facilities such as telephones, drinking fountains, and other public spaces. If barrier removal is not readily achievable, entities must find alternative methods of supplying services if the alternatives are readily achievable. Neither barrier removal nor such alternative methods need be undertaken if making the change would fundamentally alter the nature of the service being offered.

Title III also contains requirements that privately owned public transportation, such as hospital shuttle vans if over a certain size, be accessible. Related transportation facilities must also meet certain requirements.

The prohibition against associational discrimination also protects able-bodied individuals from discrimination in a Title III context. For example, a landlord could not refuse to lease space to a physician who specializes in infectious disease because his or her patient population included people with AIDS.

The ADA prohibits the modification of policies, practices, or procedures to limit access to the public service or accommodation in question. Accordingly, a doctor cannot refuse to treat an individual that he or she was competent to treat, simply because that individual has a disability, and a drug treatment clinic cannot refuse to treat HIV positive individuals. Of course, health care providers need not treat persons with conditions outside of the provider's area of expertise, even if the patient has a disability.

Private entities or places of public accommodation, including health care providers, do not have to serve a person with a disability where such service would pose a "direct threat" to the health and safety of themselves or others that cannot be eliminated or reduced to an acceptable level through policy modification or the provision of auxiliary aids. As with Title I, the "direct threat" provision of Title III is intended to encompass an extremely narrow set of circumstances and such actions must be based on objective individual data.

"Special" Treatment for Health Care Providers?

Health care providers may be subject to stricter scrutiny and/or be held to higher standards of what constitutes a "reasonable accommodation" or is "readily achievable" than other entities covered by the ADA. There are two reasons that providers may be subjected to special (tougher) treatment. First, health care providers regularly serve and thus should be especially sensitive to the needs of people protected by the ADA (i.e., people with health impairments). Second, accommodating a need in the health care setting (e.g., an emergency room) may be more critical than serving the same person's needs in other contexts (e.g., a fast food restaurant).

Obligations and Opportunities: Risk Management and the ADA

While the ADA imposes obligations on health care providers without any provision for reimbursement, the statute can also be viewed as creating many opportunities for providers to meet their employment needs by hiring able employees and to advance their business and professional purposes by attracting additional clients. However, because the health care industry serves the vital societal need of caring for health—i.e., treating *disability*—the industry is likely to be a testing ground for ADA compliance. Accordingly, it is essential to meet the challenge of the ADA utilizing principles of sound *risk management*. The following checklist will assist you.

ADA CHECKLIST

- Develop policies and procedures to ensure ADA compliance, which at a minimum should include the Practice Pointers below.
- Implement in-service programs for professional and other staff, incorporating training on both employment and accessibility (general public services), to educate them about these new policies and procedures.
- With respect to both employment and accessibility, institute measures to protect against "associational" discrimination—a new form of discrimination prohibited by the ADA.
- Review all job descriptions to include the delineation of essential versus marginal functions. If no written job descriptions exist, consider developing them, utilizing "qualification standards" where appropriate.

- Review the steps of the job application process, including the application form. Consider developing standardized questions for interviewers to ensure that staff are not asking impermissible questions.
- Coordinate all recruitment, retention, and other human resource activities, keeping in mind that they are not conducted in a vacuum; e.g., a determination of what constitutes an "essential function" for an employee who becomes disabled may shape what is "essential" for applicants, and vice versa.
- Ensure that employee records segregate confidential medical data from general personnel information.
- Emphasize that identifying the appropriate accommodation calls for an interactive process between employer and applicant/employee. Having mechanisms in place to facilitate this process will often result in the identification of effective yet inexpensive accommodations.
- Identify resource groups in your community to utilize as a reasonable accommodation bank. For example, if an applicant indicates a need for a sign language interpreter for an interview, you should know what the appropriate referral agency is in your community so that you can quickly make such arrangements. Also, keep a list of useful (and sometimes free) resources outside of your community, e.g., the federal Job Accommodation Network (1-800-526-7234), an information, consulting and referral service that provides useful ideas about accommodations.
- Conduct an access audit of your facility under both federal and state or local requirements. Preferably, this should be a "zero-based" audit, reviewing your facility from the full range of perspectives: patients, visitors, employees, volunteers, vendors, etc. Identify necessary changes and determine whether the cost of modification is readily achievable. Develop a long-range plan for readily achievable barrier removal.
- Review all of your policies and procedures for delivery of service to the public, including community services

that may be offered by the provider, such as educational programs. Identify areas of noncompliance and implement the appropriate changes.
- Identify all materials that are distributed to the public and arrange for such material to be available in alternative formats, such as large print, Braille, or cassette. In addition to leading to compliance, this will attract new patients.
- Do not "contract out" services to vendors—such as employment agencies, food services, and cleaning services—without assurances (and/or indemnities) that the vendors will not discriminate against your applicants/employees and the people that you serve. Remember, it's against the law to do indirectly what the law prohibits you from doing directly!
- Document all efforts you undertake to bring yourself into compliance with the ADA. This should include documenting all actions you take to accommodate a person's disability (including the reasons for selecting anything but the "best" accommodation), and the basis for all decisions you make not to do so, e.g., undue hardship, undue burden, would fundamentally alter the service, etc.).
- Choose and use your defenses wisely. Remember that "direct threat" has a high threshold and will be difficult to establish except in the narrowest of circumstances, and that you must be able to back up claims of "undue hardship" and "undue burden." Abuse of these defenses is not likely to be tolerated, especially by health care providers, who by definition serve the people the ADA was enacted to protect.

NOTE

1. T.D. Krugh, Is COBRA Poised to Strike? A Critical Analysis of Medical COBRA, *The Journal of Health and Hospital Law,* 23, no. 6:171.

Appendix 21-A

Congressional Statute: Peer Review

CHAPTER 117—ENCOURAGING GOOD FAITH PROFESSIONAL REVIEW ACTIVITIES

Sec.
11101. Findings.

SUBCHAPTER I—PROMOTION OF PROFESSIONAL REVIEW ACTIVITIES

11111. Professional review.
  (a) In general.
  (b) Exception.
  (c) Treatment under State laws.
11112. Standards for professional review actions.
  (a) In general.
  (b) Adequate notice and hearing.
  (c) Adequate procedures in investigations or health emergencies.
11113. Payment of reasonable attorneys' fees and costs in defense of suit.
11114. Guidelines of the Secretary.
11115. Construction.
  (a) In general.
  (b) Scope of clinical privileges.
  (c) Treatment of nurses and other practitioners.
  (d) Trcatment of patient malpractice claims.

SUBCHAPTER II—REPORTING OF INFORMATION

11131. Requiring reports on medical malpractice payments.
  (a) In general.
  (b) Information to be reported.
  (c) Sanctions for failure to report.
  (d) Report on treatment of small payments.

Sec.
11132. Reporting of sanctions taken by boards of medical examiners.
  (a) In general.
  (b) Failure to report.
11133. Reporting of certain professional review actions taken by health care entities.
  (a) Reporting by health care entities.
  (b) Reporting by Board of Medical Examiners.
  (c) Sanctions.
  (d) References to Board of Medical Examiners.
11134. Form of reporting.
  (a) Timing and form.
  (b) To whom reported.
  (c) Reporting to State licensing boards.
11135. Duty of hospitals to obtain information.
  (a) In general.
  (b) Failure to obtain information.
  (c) Reliance on information provided.
11136. Disclosure and correction of information.
11137. Miscellaneous provisions.
  (a) Providing licensing boards and other health care entities with access to information.
  (b) Confidentiality of information.
  (c) Relief from liability for reporting.
  (d) Interpretation of information.

SUBCHAPTER III—DEFINITIONS AND REPORTS

11151. Definitions.
11152. Reports and memoranda of understanding.
  (a) Annual reports to Congress.
  (b) Memoranda of understanding.
  (c) Memorandum of understanding with drug enforcement administration.

Source: Reprinted from the Health Care Quality Improvement Act of 1986 (P.L. 99–660; 42 U.S.C. Secs. 11101–11152).

§ 11101. Findings

The Congress finds the following:

(1) The increasing occurrence of medical malpractice and the need to improve the quality of medical care have become nationwide problems that warrant greater efforts than those that can be undertaken by any individual State.

(2) There is a national need to restrict the ability of incompetent physicians to move from State to State without disclosure or discovery of the physician's previous damaging or incompetent performance.

(3) This nationwide problem can be remedied through effective professional peer review.

(4) The threat of private money damage liability under Federal laws, including treble damage liability under Federal antitrust law, unreasonably discourages physicians from participating in effective professional peer review.

(5) There is an overriding national need to provide incentive and protection for physicians engaging in effective professional peer review.

(Pub.L. 99–660, Title IV, § 402, Nov. 14, 1986, 100 Stat. 3784.)

References in Text. Federal antitrust law, referred to in par. (4), probably means the antitrust laws as defined in section 12 of Title 15, Commerce and Trade.

Short Title. Section 401 of Pub.L. 99–660 provided that: "This title [enacting this chapter] may be cited as the 'Health Care Quality Improvement Act of 1986'."

Legislative History. For legislative history and purpose of Pub.L. 99–660, see 1986 U.S. Code Cong. and Adm. News, p. 6287.

Library References

Physicians and Surgeons ⟜ 17.5.

C.J.S. Physicians, Surgeons, and Other Health-Care Providers § 97 et seq.

SUBCHAPTER I—PROMOTION OF PROFESSIONAL REVIEW ACTIVITIES

§ 11111. Professional review

(a) In general

(1) Limitation on damages for professional review actions

If a professional review action (as defined in section 11151(9) of this title) of a professional review body meets all the standards specified in section 11112(a) of this title, except as provided in subsection (b) of this section—
(A) the professional review body,
(B) any person acting as a member or staff to the body,
(C) any person under a contract or other formal agreement with the body, and
(D) any person who participates with or assists the body with respect to the action,

shall not be liable in damages under any law of the United States or of any State (or political subdivision thereof) with respect to the action. The preceding sentence shall not apply to damages under any law of the United States or any State relating to the civil rights of any person or persons, including the Civil Rights Act of 1964, 42 U.S.C. 2000e et seq. and the Civil Rights Acts, 42 U.S.C. 1981 et seq. Nothing in this paragraph shall prevent the United States or any Attorney General of a State from bringing an action, including an action under section 4C of the Clayton Act, 15 U.S.C. § 15C [15 U.S.C.A. § 15c], where such an action is otherwise authorized.

(2) Protection for those providing information to professional review bodies

Notwithstanding any other provision of law, no person (whether as a witness or otherwise) providing information to a professional review body regarding the competence or professional conduct of a physician shall be held, by reason of having provided such information, to be liable in damages under any law of the United States or of any State (or political subdivision thereof) unless such information is false and the person providing it knew that such information was false.

(b) Exception

If the Secretary has reason to believe that a health care entity has failed to report information in accordance with section 11133(a) of this title, the Secretary shall conduct an investigation. If, after providing notice of noncompliance, an opportunity to correct the noncompliance, and an opportunity for a hearing, the Secretary determines that a health care entity has failed substantially to report information in accordance with section 11133(a) of this title, the Secretary shall publish the name of the entity in the Federal Register. The protections of subsection (a)(1) of this section shall not apply to an entity the name of which is published in the Federal Register under the previous sentence with respect to professional review actions of the entity commenced during the 3-year period beginning 30 days after the date of publication of the name.

(c) Treatment under State laws

(1) Professional review actions taken on or after October 14, 1989

Except as provided in paragraph (2), subsection (a) of this section shall apply to State laws in a State only for professional review actions commenced on or after October 14, 1989.

(2) Exceptions

(A) State early opt-in

Subsection (a) of this section shall apply to State laws in a State for actions commenced before October 14, 1989, if the State by legislation elects such treatment.

(B) State opt-out

Subsection (a) of this section shall not apply to State laws in a State for actions commenced on or after October 14, 1989, if the State by legislation elects such treatment.

(C) Effective date of election

An election under State law is not effective, for purposes of subparagraphs (A) and (B), for actions commenced before the effective date of the State law, which may not be earlier than the date of the enactment of that law.

(Pub.L. 99–660, Title IV, § 411, Nov. 14, 1986, 100 Stat. 3784.)

References in Text.   The Civil Rights Act of 1964, 42 U.S.C. 2000e, et seq., referred to in subsec. (a)(1) probably means Pub.L. 88–352, Title VII, July 2, 1964, 78 Stat. 253, which is classified generally to subchapter VI (section 2000e et seq.) of chapter 21 of this title.

The Civil Rights Acts, 42 U.S.C. 1981, et seq., referred to in subsec. (a)(1), probably means the provisions contained in chapter 21 (section 1981 et seq.) of this title.

Effective Date.   Section 416 of Pub.L. 99–660 provided that: "This part [subchapter] shall apply to professional review actions commenced on or after the date of the enactment of this Act [Nov. 14, 1986]."

Legislative History.   For legislative history and purpose of Pub.L. 99–660, see 1986 U.S. Code Cong. and Adm. News, p. 6287.

Library References
Physicians and Surgeons . ⌨ 17.5
C.J.S. Physicians, Surgeons, and Other Health-Care Providers § 97 et seq.

§ 11112.   Standards for professional review actions

(a) In general

For purposes of the protection set forth in section 11111(a) of this title, a professional review action must be taken
   (1) in the reasonable belief that the action was in the furtherance of quality health care,
   (2) after a reasonable effort to obtain the facts of the matter,
   (3) after adequate notice and hearing procedures are afforded to the physician involved or after such other procedures as are fair to the physician under the circumstances, and
   (4) in the reasonable belief that the action was warranted by the facts known after such reasonable effort to obtain facts and after meeting the requirement of paragraph (3).

A professional review action shall be presumed to have met the preceding standards necessary for the protection set out in section 11111(a) of this title unless the presumption is rebutted by a preponderance of the evidence.

(b) Adequate notice and hearing

A health care entity is deemed to have met the adequate notice and hearing requirement of subsection (a)(3) of this section with respect to a physician if the following conditions are met (or are waived voluntarily by the physician):

(1) Notice of proposed action

The physician has been given notice stating—

(A)(i) that a professional review action has been proposed to be taken against the physician,

(ii) reasons for the proposed action,

(B)(i) that the physician has the right to request a hearing on the proposed action,

(ii) any time limit (of not less than 30 days) within which to request such a hearing, and

(C) a summary of the rights in the hearing under paragraph (3).

(2) Notice of hearing

If a hearing is requested on a timely basis under paragraph (1)(B), the physician involved must be given notice stating—

(A) the place, time, and date of the hearing, which date shall not be less than 30 days after the date of the notice, and

(B) a list of the witnesses (if any) expected to testify at the hearing on behalf of the professional review body.

(3) Conduct of hearing and notice

If a hearing is requested on a timely basis under paragraph (1)(B)—

(A) subject to subparagraph (B), the hearing shall be held (as determined by the health care entity)—

(i) before an arbitrator mutually acceptable to the physician and the health care entity,

(ii) before a hearing officer who is appointed by the entity and who is not in direct economic competition with the physician involved, or

(iii) before a panel of individuals who are appointed by the entity and are not in direct economic competition with the physician involved;

(B) the right to the hearing may be forfeited if the physician fails, without good cause, to appear;

(C) in the hearing the physician involved has the right—

(i) to representation by an attorney or other person of the physician's choice,

(ii) to have a record made of the proceedings, copies of which may be obtained by the physician upon payment of any reasonable charges associated with the preparation thereof,

(iii) to call, examine, and cross-examine witnesses,

(iv) to present evidence determined to be relevant by the hearing officer, regardless of its admissibility in a court of law, and

(v) to submit a written statement at the close of the hearing; and

(D) upon completion of the hearing, the physician involved has the right—

(i) to receive the written recommendation of the arbitrator, officer, or panel, including a statement of the basis for the recommendations, and

(ii) to receive a written decision of the health care entity, including a statement of the basis for the decision.

A professional review body's failure to meet the conditions described in this subsection shall not, in itself, constitute failure to meet the standards of subsection (a)(3) of this section.

(c) Adequate procedures in investigations or health emergencies

For purposes of section 11111(a) of this title, nothing in this section shall be construed as—

(1) requiring the procedures referred to in subsection (a)(3) of this section—

(A) where there is no adverse professional review action taken, or

(B) in the case of a suspension or restriction of clinical privileges, for a period of not longer than 14 days, during which an investigation is being conducted to determine the need for a professional review action; or

(2) precluding an immediate suspension or restriction of clinical privileges, subject to subsequent notice and hearing or other adequate procedures, where the failure to take such an action may result in an imminent danger to the health of any individual.

(Pub.L. 99–660, Title IV, § 412, Nov. 14, 1986, 100 Stat. 3785.)

Effective Date. Section to apply to professional review actions commenced on or after Nov. 14, 1986, see section 416 of Pub.L. 99–660, set out as a note under section 12011 of this title.

Legislative History. For legislative history and purpose of Pub.L. 99–660, see 1986 U.S. Code Cong. and Adm. News, p. 6287.

Law Review Commentaries

Physician staff privilege cases: Antitrust liability and the Health Care Quality Improvement Act. Note, 29 W & M L.Rev. 625 (1988).

Library References

Physicians and Surgeons ⟶ 18.1

C.J.S. Physicians, Surgeons, and Other Health-Care Providers § 97 et seq.

§ 11113.   Payment of reasonable attorneys' fees and costs in defense of suit

In any suit brought against a defendant, to the extent that a defendant has met the standards set forth under section 11112(a) of this title and the defendant substantially prevails, the court shall, at the conclusion of the action, award to a substantially prevailing party defending against any such claim the cost of the suit attributable to such claim, including a reasonable attorney's fee, if the claim or the claimant's conduct during the litigation of the claim, was frivolous, unreasonable, without foundation, or in bad faith. For the purposes of this section, a defendant shall not be considered to have substantially prevailed when the plaintiff obtains an award for damages or permanent injunctive or declaratory relief.

(Pub.L. 99–660, Title IV, § 413, Nov. 14, 1986, 100 Stat. 3787.)

Effective Date. Section to apply to professional review actions commenced on or after Nov. 14, 1986, see section 416 of Pub.L. 99–660, set out as a note under section 12011 of this title.

Legislative History. For legislative history and purpose of Pub.L. 99–660, see 1986 U.S. Code Cong. and Adm. News, p. 6287.

Library References

Physicians and Surgeons ⟶ 18.110.

C.J.S. Physicians, Surgeons, and Other Health-Care Providers § 97 et seq.

§ 11114.   Guidelines of the Secretary

The Secretary may establish, after notice and opportunity for comment, such voluntary guidelines as may assist the professional review bodies in meeting the standards described in section 11112(a) of this title.

(Pub.L. 99–660, Title IV, § 414, Nov. 14, 1986, 100 Stat. 3787.)

Effective Date. Section to apply to professional review actions commenced on or after Nov. 14, 1986, see section 416 of Pub.L. 99–660, set out as a note under section 12011 of this title.

Legislative History. For legislative history and purpose of Pub.L. 99–660, see 1986 U.S. Code Cong. and Adm. News, p. 6287.

§ 11115.   Construction

(a) In general

Except as specifically provided in this subchapter, nothing in this subchapter shall be construed as changing the liabilities or immunities under law.

(b) Scope of clinical privileges

Nothing in this subchapter shall be construed as requiring health care entities to provide clinical privileges to any or all classes or types of physicians or other licensed health care practitioners.

(c) Treatment of nurses and other practitioners

Nothing in this subchapter shall be construed as affecting, or modifying any provision of Federal or State law, with respect to activities of professional review bodies regarding nurses, other licensed health care practitioners, or other health professionals who are not physicians.

(d) Treatment of patient malpractice claims

Nothing in this chapter shall be construed as affecting in any manner the rights and remedies afforded patients under any provision of Federal or State law to seek redress for any harm or injury suffered as a result of negligent treatment or care by any physician, health care practitioner, or health care entity, or as limiting any defenses or immunities available to any physician, health care practitioner, or health care entity.

(Pub.L. 99–660, Title IV, § 415, Nov. 14, 1986, 100 Stat. 3787.)

Effective Date. Section to apply to professional review actions commenced on or after Nov. 14, 1986, see section 416 of Pub.L. 99–660, set out as a note under section 11111 of this title.

Legislative History. For legislative history and purpose of Pub.L. 99–660, see 1986 U.S. Code Cong. and Adm. News, p. 6287.

SUBCHAPTER II—REPORTING OF INFORMATION

§ 11131. Requiring reports on medical malpractice payments

(a) In general

Each entity (including an insurance company) which makes payment under a policy of insurance, self-insurance, or otherwise in settlement (or partial settlement) of, or in satisfaction of a judgment in, a medical malpractice action or claim shall report, in accordance with section 11134 of this title, information respecting the payment and circumstances thereof.

(b) Information to be reported

The information to be reported under subsection (a) of this section includes—

(1) the name of any physician or licensed health care practitioner for whose benefit the payment is made,

(2) the amount of the payment,

(3) the name (if known) of any hospital with which the physician or practitioner is affiliated or associated,

(4) a description of the acts or omissions and injuries or illnesses upon which the action or claim was based, and

(5) such other information as the Secretary determines is required for appropriate interpretation of information reported under this section.

(c) Sanctions for failure to report

Any entity that fails to report information on a payment required to be reported under this section shall be subject to a civil money penalty of not more than $10,000 for each such payment involved. Such penalty shall be imposed and collected in the same manner as civil money penalties under subsection (a) of section 1320a–7a of this title are imposed and collected under that section.

(d) Report on treatment of small payments

The Secretary shall study and report to Congress, not later than two years after November 14, 1986, on whether information respecting small payments should continue to be required to be reported under subsection (a) of this section and whether information respecting all claims made concerning a medical malpractice action should be required to be reported under such subsection.

(Pub.L. 99–660, Title IV, § 421, Nov. 14, 1986, 100 Stat. 3788.)

Legislative History. For legislative history and purpose of Pub.L. 99–660, see 1986 U.S. Code Cong. and Adm. News, p. 6287.

Library References

Physicians and Surgeons ⟸ 16.
C.J.S. Physicians, Surgeons, and Other Health-Care Providers § 70 et seq.

§ 11132.   Reporting of sanctions taken by boards of medical examiners

(a) In general

(1) Actions subject to reporting

Each Board of Medical Examiners—

(A) which revokes or suspends (or otherwise restricts) a physician's license or censures, reprimands, or places on probation a physician, for reasons relating to the physician's professional competence or professional conduct, or

(B) to which a physician's license is surrendered,

shall report, in accordance with section 11134 of this title, the information described in paragraph (2).

(2) Information to be reported

The information to be reported under paragraph (1) is—

(A) the name of the physician involved,

(B) a description of the Acts or omissions or other reasons (if known) for the revocation, suspension, or surrender of license, and

(C) such other information respecting the circumstances of the action or surrender as the Secretary deems appropriate.

(b) Failure to report

If, after notice of noncompliance and providing opportunity to correct noncompliance, the Secretary determines that a Board of Medical Examiners has failed to report information in accordance with subsection (a) of this section, the Secretary shall designate another qualified entity for the reporting of information under section 11133 of this title.

(Pub.L. 99–660, Title IV, § 422, Nov. 14, 1986, 100 Stat. 3789.)

Legislative History. For legislative history and purpose of Pub.L. 99–660, see 1986 U.S. Code Cong. and Adm. News, p. 6287.

Library References

Physicians and Surgeons ⟸ 9, 17.5.
C.J.S. Physicians, Surgeons, and Other Health-Care Providers §§ 9 et seq., 97 et seq.

§ 11133.   Reporting of certain professional review actions taken by health care entities

(a) Reporting by health care entities

(1) On physicians

Each health care entity which—

(A) takes a professional review action that adversely affects the clinical privileges of a physician for a period longer than 30 days;

(B) accepts the surrender of clinical privileges of a physician—

(i) while the physician is under an investigation by the entity relating to possible incompetence or improper professional conduct, or

(ii) in return for not conducting such an investigation or proceeding; or

(C) in the case of such an entity which is a professional society, takes a professional review action which adversely affects the membership of a physician in the society, shall report to the Board of Medical Examiners, in accordance with section 11134(a) of this title, the information described in paragraph (3).

(2) Permissive reporting on other licensed health care practitioners

A health care entity may report to the Board of Medical Examiners, in accordance with section 11134(a) of this title, the information described in paragraph (3) in the case of a licensed health care practitioner who is not a physician, if the entity would be required to report such information under paragraph (1) with respect to the practitioner if the practitioner were a physician.

(3) Information to be reported

The information to be reported under this subsection is—

(A) the name of the physician or practitioner involved,

(B) a description of the acts or omissions or other reasons for the action or, if known, for the surrender, and

(C) such other information respecting the circumstances of the action or surrender as the Secretary deems appropriate.

(b) Reporting by Board of Medical Examiners

Each Board of Medical Examiners shall report, in accordance with section 11134 of this title, the information reported to it under subsection (a) of this section and known instances of a health care entity's failure to report information under subsection (a)(1) of this section.

(c) Sanctions

(1) Health care entities

A health care entity that fails substantially to meet the requirement of subsection (a)(1) of this section shall lose the protections of section 11111(a)(1) of this title if the Secretary publishes the name of the entity under section 11111(b) of this title.

(2) Board of Medical Examiners

If, after notice of noncompliance and providing an opportunity to correct noncompliance, the Secretary determines that a Board of Medical Examiners has failed to report information in accordance with subsection (b) of this section, the Secretary shall designate another qualified entity for the reporting of information under subsection (b) of this section.

(d) References to Board of Medical Examiners

Any reference in this subchapter to a Board of Medical Examiners includes, in the case of a Board in a State that fails to meet the reporting requirements of section 11132(a) of this title or subsection (b) of this section, a reference to such other qualified entity as the Secretary designates.

(Pub.L. 99–660, Title IV, § 423, Nov. 14, 1986, 100 Stat. 3789.)

Legislative History. For legislative history and purpose of Pub.L. 99–660, see 1986 U.S. Code Cong. and Adm. News, p. 6287.

Library References
Physicians and Surgeons 9, ⋘17.5.
C.J.S. Physicians, Surgeons, and Other Health-Care Providers §§ 9 et seq., 97 et seq.

§ 11134.   Form of reporting

(a) Timing and form

The information required to be reported under sections 11131, 11132(a), and 11133 of this title shall be reported regularly (but not less often than monthly) and in such form and manner as the Secretary prescribes. Such information shall first be required to be reported on a date (not later than one year after November 14, 1986) specified by the Secretary.

(b) To whom reported

The information required to be reported under sections 11131, 11132(a), and 11133(b) of this title shall be reported to the Secretary, or, in the Secretary's discretion, to an appropriate private or public agency which has made suitable arrangements with the Secretary with respect to receipt, storage, protection of confidentiality, and dissemination of the information under this subchapter.

(c) Reporting to State licensing boards

(1) Malpractice payments

Information required to be reported under section 11131 of this title shall also be reported to the appropriate State licensing board (or boards) in the State in which the medical malpractice claim arose.

(2) Reporting to other licensing boards

Information required to be reported under section 11132(b) of this title shall also be reported to the appropriate State licensing board in the State in which the health care entity is located if it is not otherwise reported to such board under subsection (b) of this section.

(Pub.L. 99–660, Title IV, § 424, Nov. 14, 1986, 100 Stat. 3790.)

Legislative History.   For legislative history and purpose of Pub.L. 99–660, see 1986 U.S. Code Cong. and Adm. News, p. 6287.

§ 11135.   Duty of hospitals to obtain information

(a) In general

It is the duty of each hospital to request from the Secretary (or the agency designated under section 11134(b) of this title), on and after the date information is first required to be reported under section 11134(a) of this title—

(1) at the time a physician or licensed health care practitioner applies to be on the medical staff (courtesy or otherwise) of, or for clinical privileges at, the hospital, information reported under this subchapter concerning the physician or practitioner, and

(2) once every 2 years information reported under this subchapter concerning any physician or such practitioner who is on the medical staff (courtesy or otherwise) of, or has been granted clinical privileges at, the hospital.

A hospital may request such information at other times.

(b) Failure to obtain information

With respect to a medical malpractice action, a hospital which does not request information respecting a physician or practitioner as required under subsection (a) of this section is presumed to have knowledge of any information reported under this subchapter to the Secretary with respect to the physician or practitioner.

(c) Reliance on information provided

Each hospital may rely upon information provided to the hospital under this chapter and shall not be held liable for such reliance in the absence of the hospital's knowledge that the information provided was false.

(Pub.L. 99–660, Title IV, § 425, Nov. 14, 1986, 100 Stat. 3790.)

Legislative History.   For legislative history and purpose of Pub.L. 99–660, see 1986 U.S. Code Cong. and Adm. News, p. 6287.

Library References
Hospitals. ⟳ 6.
C.J.S. Hospital § 5 et seq.

§ 11136.   Disclosure and correction of information

With respect to the information reported to the Secretary (or the agency designated under section 11134(b) of this title) under this subchapter respecting a physician or other licensed health care practitioner, the Secretary shall, by regulation, provide for

(1) disclosure of the information, upon request, to the physician or practitioner, and

(2) procedures in the case of disputed accuracy of the information.

(Pub.L. 99–660, Title IV, § 426, Nov. 14, 1986, 100 Stat. 3791.)

Legislative History.   For legislative history and purpose of Pub.L. 99–660, see 1986 U.S. Code Cong. and Adm. News, p. 6287.

§ 11137.   Miscellaneous provisions

(a) Providing licensing boards and other health care entities with access to information

The Secretary (or the agency designated under section 11134(b) of this title shall, upon request, provide information reported under this subchapter with respect to a physician or other licensed health care practitioner to State licensing boards, to hospitals, and to other health care entities (including health maintenance organizations) that have entered (or may be entering) into an employment or affiliation relationship with the physician or practitioner or to which the physician or practitioner has applied for clinical privileges or appointment to the medical staff.

(b) Confidentiality of information

(1) In general

Information reported under this subchapter is considered confidential and shall not be disclosed (other than to the physician or practitioner involved) except with respect to professional review activity, as necessary to carry out subsections (b) and (c) of section 11135 of this title (as specified in regulations by the Secretary), or in accordance with regulations of the Secretary promulgated pursuant to subsection (a) of this section. Nothing in this subsection shall prevent the disclosure of such information by a party which is otherwise authorized, under applicable State law, to make such disclosure. Information reported under this part that is in a form that does not permit the identification of any particular health care entity, physician, other health care practitioner, or patient shall not be considered confidential. The Secretary (or the agency designated under section 11134(b) of this title), on application by any person, shall prepare such information in such form and shall disclose such information in such form.

(2) Penalty for violations

Any person who violates paragraph (1) shall be subject to a civil money penalty of not more than $10,000 for each such violation involved. Such penalty shall be imposed and collected in the same manner as civil money penalties under subsection (a) of section 1320a–7a of this title are imposed and collected under that section.

(3) Use of information

Subject to paragraph (1), information provided under section 11135 of this title and subsection (a) of this section is intended to be used solely with respect to activities in the furtherance of the quality of health care.

(4) Fees

The Secretary may establish or approve reasonable fees for the disclosure of information under this section or section 11136 of this title. The amount of such a fee may not exceed the costs of processing the requests for disclosure and of providing such information. Such fees shall be available to the Secretary (or, in the Secretary's discretion, to the agency designated under section 11134(b) of this title) to cover such costs.

(c) Relief from liability for reporting

No person or entity (including the agency designated under section 11134(b) of this title) shall be held liable in any civil action with respect to any report made under this subchapter (including information provided under subsection (a) of this section* without knowledge of the falsity of the information contained in the report.

(d) Interpretation of information

In interpreting information reported under this subchapter, a payment in settlement of a medical malpractice action or claim shall not be construed as creating a presumption that medical malpractice has occurred.

(Pub.L. 99–660, Title IV, § 427, Nov. 14, 1986, 100 Stat. 3791, amended Pub.L. 100–177, Title IV, § 402(a), (b), Dec. 1, 1987, 101 Stat. 1007.)

*So in original. Amendment by section 402(a)(2)(B) of Pub.L. 100–177 failed to include a closing parenthesis.

1987 Amendment. Subsec. (b)(1). Pub.L. 100–177, § 402(a)(1)(A), substituted "as necessary to carry out subsections (b) and (c) of section 11135 of this title (as specified in regulations by the Secretary)" for "with respect to medical malpractice actions."

Pub.L. 100–177, § 402(a)(1)(B), added provisions that information reported under this part that is in a form that does not permit the identification of any particular health care entity, physician, other health care practitioner, or patient shall not be considered confidential, and that the Secretary (or the agency designated under section 11134(b) of this title), on application by any person, shall prepare such information in such form and shall disclose such information in such form.

Subsec. (b)(4). Pub.L. 100–177, § 402(b), added par. (4).

Subsec. (c). Pub.L. 100–177, § 402(a)(2), substituted "No person or entity (including the agency designated under section 11134(b) of this title) shall be held liable in any civil action with respect to any report made under this subchapter (including information provided under subsection (a) of this section without knowledge of the falsity of the information contained in the report" for "No person or entity shall be held liable in any civil action with respect to any report made under this subchapter without knowledge of the falsity of the information contained in the report."

Effective Date of 1987 Amendment. Section 402(c) of Pub.L. 100–177 provided that:

"(1) In general.—The amendments made by subsection (a) [amending subsecs. (b)(1) and (c) of this section] shall become effective on November 14, 1986."

"(2) Fees.—The amendment made by subsection (b) [enacting subsec. (b)(4) of this section] shall become effective on the date of enactment of this Act [Dec. 1, 1987]."

Legislative History. For legislative history and purpose of Pub.L. 99–660, see 1986 U.S. Code Cong. and Adm. News, p. 6287. See also, Pub.L. 100–177, see 1987 U.S. Code Cong. and Adm. News, p. 960.

SUBCHAPTER III—DEFINITIONS AND REPORTS

§ 11151. Definitions

In this title:

(1) The term "adversely affecting" includes reducing, restricting, suspending, revoking, denying, or failing to renew clinical privileges or membership in a health care entity.

(2) The term "Board of Medical Examiners" includes a body comparable to such a Board (as determined by the State) with responsibility for the licensing of physicians and also includes a subdivision of such a Board or body.

(3) The term "clinical privileges" includes privileges, membership on the medical staff, and the other circumstances pertaining to the furnishing of medical care under which a physician or other licensed health care practitioner is permitted to furnish such care by a health care entity.

(4)(A) The term "health care entity" means—

(i) a hospital that is licensed to provide health care services by the State in which it is located,

(ii) an entity (including a health maintenance organization or group medical practice) that provides health care services and that follows a formal peer review process for the purpose of furthering quality health care (as determined under regulations of the Secretary), and

(iii) subject to subparagraph (B), a professional society (or committee thereof) of physicians or other licensed health care practitioners that follows a formal peer review process for the purpose of furthering quality health care (as determined under regulations of the Secretary).

(B) The term "health care entity" does not include a professional society (or committee thereof) if, within the previous 5 years, the society has been found by the Federal Trade Commission or any court to have engaged in any anti-competitive practice which had the effect of restricting the practice of licensed health care practitioners.

(5) The term "hospital" means an entity described in paragraphs (1) and (7) of section 1395x(e) of this title.

(6) The terms "licensed health care practitioner" and "practitioner" mean, with respect to a State, an individual (other than a physician) who is licensed or otherwise authorized by the State to provide health care services.

(7) The term "medical malpractice action or claim" means a written claim or demand for payment based on a health care provider's furnishing (or failure to furnish) health care services, and includes the filing of a cause of action, based on the law of tort, brought in any court of any State or the United States seeking monetary damages.

(8) The term "physician" means a doctor of medicine or osteopathy or a doctor of dental surgery or medical dentistry legally authorized to practice medicine and surgery or dentistry by a State (or any individual who, without authority holds himself or herself out to be so authorized).

(9) The term "professional review action" means an action or recommendation of a professional review body which is taken or made in the conduct of professional review activity, which is based on the competence or professional conduct of an individual physician (which conduct affects or could affect adversely the health or welfare of a patient or patients), and which affects (or may affect) adversely the clinical privileges, or membership in a professional society, of the physician. Such term includes a formal decision of a professional review body not to take an action or make a recommendation described in the previous sentence and also includes professional review activities relating to a professional review action. In this chapter, an action is not considered to be based on the competence or professional conduct of a physician if the action is primarily based on—

(A) the physician's association, or lack of association, with a professional society or association,

(B) the physician's fees or the physician's advertising or engaging in other competitive acts intended to solicit or retain business,

(C) the physician's participation in prepaid group health plans, salaried employment, or any other manner of delivering health services, whether on a fee-for-service or other basis,

(D) a physician's association with, supervision of, delegation of authority to, support for, training of, or participation in a private group practice with, a member or members of a particular class of health care practitioner or professional, or

(E) any other matter that does not relate to the competence or professional conduct of a physician.

(10) The term "professional review activity" means an activity of a health care entity with respect to an individual physician—

(A) to determine whether the physician may have clinical privileges with respect to, or membership in, the entity,

(B) to determine the scope or conditions of such privileges or membership, or

(C) to change or modify such privileges or membership.

(11) The term "professional review body" means a health care entity and the governing body or any committee of a health care entity which conducts professional review activity, and includes any committee of the medical staff of such an entity when assisting the governing body in a professional review activity.

(12) The term "Secretary" means the Secretary of Health and Human Services.

(13) The term "State" means the 50 States, the District of Columbia, Puerto Rico, the Virgin Islands, Guam, American Samoa, and the Northern Mariana Islands.

(14) The term "State licensing board" means, with respect to a physician or health care provider in a State, the agency of the State which is primarily responsible for the licensing of the physician or provider to furnish health care services.

(Pub.L. 99–660, Title IV, § 431, Nov. 14, 1986, 100 Stat. 3792.)

Legislative History. For legislative history and purpose of Pub.L. 99–660, see 1986 U.S. Code Cong. and Adm. News, p. 6287.

§ 11152.   Reports and memoranda of understanding

(a) Annual reports to Congress

The Secretary shall report to Congress, annually during the three years after November 14, 1986, on the implementation of this chapter.

(b) Memoranda of understanding

The Secretary of Health and Human Services shall seek to enter into memoranda of understanding with the Secretary of Defense and the Administrator of Veterans' Affairs to apply the provisions of subchapter II of this chapter to hospitals and other facilities and health care providers under the jurisdiction of the Secretary or Administrator, respectively. The Secretary shall report to Congress, not later than two years after November 14, 1986, on any such memoranda and on the cooperation among such officials in establishing such memoranda.

(c) Memorandum of understanding with drug enforcement administration

The Secretary of Health and Human Services shall seek to enter into a memorandum of understanding with the Administrator of Drug Enforcement relating to providing for the reporting by the Administrator to the Secretary of information respecting physicians and other practitioners whose registration to dispense controlled substances has been suspended or revoked under section 824 of Title 21. The Secretary shall report to Congress, not later than two years after November 14, 1986, on any such memorandum and on the cooperation between the Secretary and the Administrator in establishing such a memorandum.

(Pub.L. 99–660, Title IV, § 432, Nov. 14, 1986, 100 Stat. 3794.)

Legislative History. For legislative history and purpose of Pub.L. 99–660, see 1986 U.S. Code Cong. and Adm. News, p. 6287.

Appendix 21-B

National Practitioner Data Bank Regulations

Dated: September 7, 1989.

James O. Mason,

Assistant Secretary for Health.

Approved October 11, 1989.

Louis W. Sullivan,

Secretary.

PART 60—NATIONAL PRACTITIONER DATA BANK FOR ADVERSE INFORMATION ON PHYSICIANS AND OTHER HEALTH CARE PRACTITIONERS

Subpart A—General Provisions

Sec.

60.1 The National Practitioner Data Bank.
60.2 Applicability of these regulations.
60.3 Definitions.

Subpart B—Reporting of Information

60.4 How information must be reported.
60.5 When information must be reported.
60.6 Reporting errors, omissions, and revisions.
60.7 Reporting medical malpractice payments.
60.8 Reporting licensure actions taken by Boards of Medical Examiners.
60.9 Reporting adverse actions on clinical privileges.

Subpart C—Disclosure of Information by the National Practitioner Data Bank

60.10 Information which hospitals must request from the National Practitioner Data Bank.
60.11 Requesting information from the National Practitioner Data Bank.
60.12 Fees applicable to requests for information.
60.13 Confidentiality of National Practitioner Data Bank information.
60.14 How to dispute the accuracy of National Practitioner Data Bank information.

Authority : Secs. 401–432 of the Health Care Quality Improvement Act of 1986, Pub. L. 99–660, 100 Stat. 3784–3794, as amended by section 402 of Pub. L. 100–177, 101 Stat. 1007–1008 (42 U.S.C. 11101–11152).

Subpart A—General Provisions

§ 60.1   The National Practitioner Data Bank.

The Health Care Quality Improvement Act of 1986 (the Act), title IV of Pub. L. 99–660, as amended, authorizes the Secretary to establish (either directly or by contract) a National Practitioner Data Bank to collect and release certain information relating to the professional competence and conduct of physicians, dentists and other health care practitioners. These regulations set forth the reporting and disclosure requirements for the National Practitioner Data Bank.

§ 60.2   Applicability of these regulations.

These regulations establish reporting requirements applicable to hospitals; health care entities; Boards of Medical Examiners; professional societies of physicians, dentists or other health care practitioners which take adverse licensure or professional review actions; and individuals and entities (including insurance companies) making payments as a result of medical malpractice actions or claims. They also establish procedures to enable individuals or entities to obtain information from the National Practitioner Data Bank or to dispute the accuracy of National Practitioner Data Bank information.

§ 60.3   Definitions.

Act means the Health Care Quality Improvement Act of 1986, title IV of Pub. L. 99–660, as amended.

Adversely affecting means reducing, restricting, suspending, revoking, or denying clinical privileges or membership in a health care entity.

Board of Medical Examiners, or "Board," means a body or subdivision of such body which is designated by a State for the purpose of licensing, monitoring and disciplining physicians or dentists. This term includes a Board of Osteopathic Examiners or its subdivision, a Board of Dentistry or its subdivision, or an equivalent body as determined by the State. Where the Secretary, pursuant to section 423(c)(2) of the Act, has designated an alternate entity to carry out the reporting activities of § 60.9 due to a Board's failure to comply with § 60.8, the term "Board of Medical Examiners" or "Board" refers to this alternate entity.

Clinical privileges means the authorization by a health care entity to a physician, dentist or other health care practitioner for the provision of health care services, including privileges and membership on the medical staff.

Dentist means a doctor of dental surgery, doctor of dental medicine, or the equivalent who is legally authorized to practice dentistry by a State (or who, without authority, holds himself or herself out to be so authorized).

Formal peer review process means the conduct of professional review activities through formally adopted written procedures which provide for adequate notice and an opportunity for a hearing.

Health care entity means:

(a) A hospital;

(b) An entity that provides health care services, and engages in professional review activity through a formal peer review process for the purpose of furthering quality health care, or a committee of that entity; or

(c) A professional society or a committee or agent thereof, including those at the national, State, or local level, of physicians, dentists, or other health care practitioners that engages in professional review activity through a formal peer review process, for the purpose of furthering quality health care.

Source: Reprinted from the *Federal Register,* Vol. 54, No. 199, pp. 42722–42734, October 17, 1989.

For purposes of paragraph (b) of this definition, an entity includes: a health maintenance organization which is licensed by a State or determined to be qualified as such by the Department of Health and Human Services; and any group or prepaid medical or dental practice which meets the criteria of paragraph (b).

Health care practitioners means an individual other than a physician or dentist, who is licensed or otherwise authorized by a State to provide health care services.

Hospital means an entity described in paragraphs (1) and (7) of section 1861(e) of the Social Security Act.

Medical malpractice action or claim means a written complaint or claim demanding payment based on a physician's, dentist's or other health care practitioner's provision of or failure to provide health care services, and includes the filing of a cause of action based on the law of tort, brought in any State or Federal Court or other adjudicative body.

Physician means a doctor of medicine or osteopathy legally authorized to practice medicine or surgery by a State (or who, without authority, holds himself or herself out to be so authorized).

Professional review action means an action or recommendation of a health care entity:

(a) Taken in the course of professional review activity;

(b) Based on the professional competence or professional conduct of an individual physician, dentist or other health care practitioner which affects or could affect adversely the health or welfare of a patient or patients; and

(c) Which adversely affects or may adversely affect the clinical privileges or membership in a professional society of the physician, dentist or other health care practitioner.

(d) This term excludes actions which are primarily based on:

(1) The physician's, dentist's or other health care practitioner's association, or lack of association, with a professional society or association;

(2) The physician's, dentist's or other health care practitioner's fees or the physician's, dentist's or other health care practitioner's advertising or engaging in other competitive acts intended to solicit or retain business;

(3) The physician's, dentist's or other health care practitioner's participation in prepaid group health plans, salaried employment, or any other manner of delivering health services whether on a fee-for-service or other basis;

(4) A physician's, dentist's or other health care practitioner's association with, supervision of, delegation of authority to, support for, training of, or participation in a private group practice with, a member or members of a particular class of health care practitioner or professional; or

(5) Any other matter that does not relate to the competence or professional conduct of a physician, dentist or other health care practitioner.

Professional review activity means an activity of a health care entity with respect to an individual physician, dentist or other health care practitioner:

(a) To determine whether the physician, dentist or other health care practitioner may have clinical privileges with respect to, or membership in, the entity;

(b) To determine the scope or conditions of such privileges or membership; or

(c) To change or modify such privileges or membership.

Secretary means the Secretary of Health and Human Services and any other officer or employee of the Department of Health and Human Services to whom the authority involved has been delegated.

State means the fifty States, the District of Columbia, Puerto Rico, the Virgin Islands, Guam, American Samoa, and the Northern Mariana Islands.

Subpart B—Reporting of Information

§ 60.4   How information must be reported.

Information must be reported to the Data Bank or to a Board of Medical Examiners as required under §§ 60.7, 60.8, and 60.9 in such form and manner as the Secretary may prescribe.

§ 60.5   When information must be reported.

Information required under §§ 60.7, 60.8, and 60.9 must be submitted to the Data Bank within 30 days following the action to be reported, beginning with actions occurring on or after the effective date of these regulations or the date of the establishment of the Data Bank, whichever is later, as follows:

(a) *Malpractice Payments (§ 60.7)*. Persons or entities must submit information to the Data Bank within 30 days from the date that a payment, as described in § 60.7, is made. If required under § 60.7, this information must be submitted simultaneously to the appropriate State licensing board.

(b) *Licensure Actions (§ 60.8)*. The Board must submit information within 30 days from the date the licensure action was taken.

(c) *Adverse Actions (§ 60.9)*. A health care entity must report an adverse action to the Board within 15 days from the date the adverse action was taken. The Board must submit the information received from a health care entity within 15 days from the date on which it received this information. If required under § 60.9, this information must be submitted by the Board simultaneously to the appropriate State licensing board in the State in which the health care entity is located, if the Board is not such licensing Board.

§ 60.6   Reporting errors, omissions, and revisions.

(a) Persons and entities are responsible for the accuracy of information which they report to the Data Bank. If errors or omissions are found after information has been reported, the person or entity which reported it must send an addition or correction to the Data Bank or, in the case of reports made under § 60.9, to the Board of Medical Examiners, as soon as possible.

(b) An individual or entity which reports information on licensure or clinical privileges under §§ 60.8 or 60.9 must also report any revision of the action originally reported. Revisions include reversal of a professional review action or reinstatement of a license. Revisions are subject to the same time constraints and procedures of §§ 60.5, 60.8, and 60.9, as applicable to the original action which was reported.

(Section 60.6(a) approved by the Office of Management and Budget under control number 0915–0126)

§ 60.7   Reporting medical malpractice payments.

(a) *Who must report*. Each person or entity, including an insurance company, which makes a payment under an insurance policy, self-insurance, or otherwise, for the benefit of a physician, dentist or other health care practitioner in settlement of or in satisfaction in whole or in part of a claim or a judgment against such physician, dentist, or other health care practitioner for medical malpractice, must report information as set forth in paragraph (b) to the Data Bank and to the appropriate State licensing board(s) in the State in which the act or omission upon which the medical malpractice claim was based. For purposes of this section, the waiver of an outstanding debt is not construed as a "payment" and is not required to be reported.

(b) *What information must be reported*. Persons or entities described in paragraph (a) must report the following information:

(1) With respect to the physician, dentist or other health care practitioner for whose benefit the payment is made—

(i) Name,

(ii) Work address,

(iii) Home address, if known,

(iv) Social Security number, if known, and if obtained in accordance with section 7 of the Privacy Act of 1974,

(v) Date of birth,

(vi) Name of each professional school attended and year of graduation,

(vii) For each professional license: the license number, the field of licensure, and the name of the State or Territory in which the license is held,

(viii) Drug Enforcement Administration registration number, if known,

(ix) Name of each hospital with which he or she is affiliated, if known;

(2) With respect to the reporting person or entity—

(i) Name and address of the person or entity making the payment,

(ii) Name, title, and telephone number of the responsible official submitting the report on behalf of the entity, and

(iii) Relationship of the reporting person or entity to the physician, dentist, or other health care practitioner for whose benefit the payment is made;

(3) With respect to the judgment or settlement resulting in the payment—

(i) Where an action or claim has been filed with an adjudicative body, identification of the adjudicative body and the case number,

(ii) Date or dates on which the act(s) or omission(s) which gave rise to the action or claim occurred,

(iii) Date of judgment or settlement,

(iv) Amount paid, date of payment, and whether payment is for a judgment or a settlement,

(v) Description and amount of judgment or settlement and any conditions attached thereto, including terms of payment,

(vi) A description of the acts or omissions and injuries or illnesses upon which the action or claim was based,

(vii) Classification of the acts or omissions in accordance with a reporting code adopted by the Secretary, and

(viii) Other information as required by the Secretary from time to time after publication in the **Federal Register** and after an opportunity for public comment.

(c) *Sanctions.* Any person or entity that fails to report information on a payment required to be reported under this section is subject to a civil money penalty of up to $10,000 for each such payment involved. This penalty will be imposed pursuant to procedures at 42 CFR part 1003.

(d) *Interpretation of information.* A payment in settlement of a medical malpractice action or claim shall not be construed as creating a presumption that medical malpractice has occurred.

(Approved by the Office of Management and Budget under control number 0915–0126)

§ 60.8 **Reporting licensure actions taken by Boards of Medical Examiners.**

(a) *What actions must be reported.* Each Board of Medical Examiners must report to the Data Bank any action based on reasons relating to a physician's or dentist's professional competence or professional conduct—

(1) Which revokes or suspends (or otherwise restricts) a physician's or dentist's license,

(2) Which censures, reprimands, or places on probation a physician or dentist, or

(3) Under which a physician's or dentist's license is surrendered.

(b) *Information that must be reported.* The Board must report the following information for each action:

(1) The physician's or dentist's name,

(2) The physician's or dentist's work address,

(3) The physician's or dentist's home address, if known,

(4) The physician's or dentist's Social Security number, if known, and if obtained in accordance with section 7 of the Privacy Act of 1974,

(5) The physician's or dentist's date of birth,

(6) Name of each professional school attended by the physician or dentist and year of graduation,

(7) For each professional license, the physician's or dentist's license number, the field of licensure and the name of the State or Territory in which the license is held,

(8) The physician's or dentist's Drug Enforcement Administration registration number, if known,

(9) A description of the acts or omissions or other reasons for the action taken,

(10) A description of the Board action, the date the action was taken, and its effective date,

(11) Classification of the action in accordance with a reporting code adopted by the Secretary, and

(12) Other information as required by the Secretary from time to time after publication in the **Federal Register** and after an opportunity for public comment.

(c) *Sanctions.* If, after notice of noncompliance and providing opportunity to correct noncompliance, the Secretary determines that a Board has failed to submit a report as required by this section, the Secretary will designate another qualified entity for the reporting of information under § 60.9.

(Approved by the Office of Management and Budget under control number 0915–0126)

§ 60.9 **Reporting adverse actions on clinical privileges.**

(a) *Reporting to the Board of Medical Examiners.*—(1) *Actions that must be reported and to whom the report must be made.* Each health care entity must report to the Board of Medical Examiners in the State in which the health care entity is located the following actions:

(i) Any professional review action that adversely affects the clinical privileges of a physician or dentist for a period longer than 30 days;

(ii) Acceptance of the surrender of clinical privileges or any restriction of such privileges by a physician or dentist—

(A) While the physician or dentist is under investigation by the health care entity relating to possible incompetence or improper professional conduct, or

(B) In return for not conducting such an investigation or proceeding; or

(iii) In the case of a health care entity which is a professional society, when it takes a professional review action.

(2) *Voluntary reporting on other health care practitioners.* A health care entity may report to the Board of Medical Examiners information as described in paragraph (a)(3) of this section concerning actions described in paragraph (a)(1) in this section with respect to other health care practitioners.

(3) *What information must be reported.* The health care entity must report the following information concerning actions described in paragraph (a)(1) of this section with respect to the physician or dentist:

(i) Name,

(ii) Work address,

(iii) Home address, if known,

(iv) Social Security number, if known, and if obtained in accordance with section 7 of the Privacy Act of 1974,

(v) Date of birth,

(vi) Name of each professional school attended and year of graduation,

(vii) For each professional license: the license number, the field of licensure, and the name of the State or Territory in which the license is held,

(viii) Drug Enforcement Administration registration number, if known,

(ix) A description of the acts or omissions or other reasons for privilege loss, or, if known, for surrender,

(x) Action taken, date the action was taken, and effective date of the action, and

(xi) Other information as required by the Secretary from time to time after publication in the **Federal Register** and after an opportunity for public comment.

(b) *Reporting by the Board of Medical Examiners to the National Practitioner Data Bank.* Each Board must report, in accordance with §§ 60.4 and 60.5, the information reported to it by a health care entity and any known instances of a health care entity's failure to report information as required under paragraph (a)(1) of this section. In addition, each Board must simultaneously report this information to the appropriate State licensing board in the State in which the health care entity is located, if the Board is not such licensing board.

(c) *Sanctions*—(1) *Health care entities.* If the Secretary has reason to believe that a health care entity has substantially failed to report information in accordance with § 60.9, the Secretary will conduct an investigation. If the investigation shows that the health care entity has not complied with § 60.9, the Secretary will provide the entity with a written notice describing the noncompliance, giving the health care entity an opportunity to correct the noncompliance, and stating that the entity may request, within 30 days after receipt of such notice, a hearing with respect to the noncompliance. The request for a hearing must contain a statement of the material factual issues in dispute to demonstrate that there is cause for a hearing. These issues must be both substantive and relevant. The hearing will be held in the Washington, DC, metropolitan area. The Secretary will deny a hearing if:

(i) The request for a hearing is untimely,

(ii) The health care entity does not provide a statement of material factual issues in dispute, or

(iii) The statement of factual issues in dispute is frivolous or inconsequential.

In the event that the Secretary denies a hearing, the Secretary will send a written denial to the health care entity setting forth the reasons for denial. If a hearing is denied, or if as a result of the hearing the entity is found to be in noncompliance, the Secretary will publish the name of the health care entity in the Federal Register. In such case, the immunity protections provided under section 411(a) of the Act will not apply to the health care entity for professional review activities that occur during the 3-year period beginning 30 days after the date of publication of the entity's name in the Federal Register.

(2) *Board of Medical Examiners.* If, after notice of noncompliance and providing opportunity to correct noncompliance, the Secretary determines that a Board has failed to report information in accordance with paragraph (b) of this section, the Secretary will designate another qualified entity for the reporting of this information.

(Approved by the Office of Management and Budget under control number 0915–0126)

Subpart C—Disclosure of Information by the National Practitioner Data Bank

§ 60.10   Information which hospitals must request from the National Practitioner Data Bank.

(a) *When information must be requested.* Each hospital, either directly or through an authorized agent, must request information from the Data Bank concerning a physician, dentist or other health care practitioner as follows:

(1) At the time a physician, dentist or other health care practitioner applies for a position on its medical staff (courtesy or otherwise), or for clinical privileges at the hospital; and

(2) Every 2 years concerning any physician, dentist, or other health care practitioner who is on its medical staff (courtesy or otherwise), or has clinical privileges at the hospital.

(b) *Failure to request information.* Any hospital which does not request the information as required in paragraph (a) of this section is presumed to have knowledge of any information reported to the Data Bank concerning this physician, dentist or other health care practitioner.

(c) *Reliance on the obtained information.* Each hospital may rely upon the information provided by the Data Bank to the hospital. A hospital shall not be held liable for this reliance unless the hospital has knowledge that the information provided was false.

(Approved by the Office of Management and Budget under control number 0915–0126)

§ 60.11   Requesting information from the National Practitioner Data Bank.

(a) *Who may request information and what information may be available.* Information in the Data Bank will be available, upon request, to the persons or entities, or their authorized agents, as described below:

(1) A hospital that requests information concerning a physician, dentist or other health care practitioner who is on its medical staff (courtesy or otherwise) or has clinical privileges at the hospital,

(2) A physician, dentist, or other health care practitioner who requests information concerning himself or herself,

(3) Boards of Medical Examiners or other State licensing boards,

(4) Health care entities which have entered or may be entering employment or affiliation relationships with a physician, dentist or other health care practitioner has applied for clinical privileges or appointment to the medical staff,

(5) An attorney, or individual representing himself or herself, who has filed a medical malpractice action or claim in a State or Federal court or other adjudicative body against a hospital, and who requests information regarding a specific physician, dentist, or other health care practitioner who is also named in the action or claim. Provided, that this information will be disclosed only upon the submission of evidence that the hospital failed to request information from the Data Bank as required by § 60.10(a), and may be used solely with respect to litigation resulting from the action or claim against the hospital.

(6) A health care entity with respect to professional review activity, and

(7) A person or entity who requests information in a form which does not permit the identification of any particular health care entity, physician, dentist, or other health care practitioner.

(b) *Procedures for obtaining National Practitioner Data Bank information.* Persons and entities may obtain information from the Data Bank by submitting a request in such form and manner as the Secretary may prescribe. These requests are subject to fees as described in § 60.12

§ 60.12   Fees applicable to requests for information.

(a) *Policy on Fees.* The fees described in this section apply to all requests for information from the Data Bank, other than those of individuals for information concerning themselves. These fees are authorized by section 427(b)(4) of the Health Care Quality Improvement Act of 1986 (42 U.S.C. 11137). They reflect the costs of processing requests for disclosure and of providing such information. The actual fees will be announced by the Secretary in periodic notices in the Federal Register.

(b) *Criteria for determining the fee.* The amount of each fee will be determined based on the following criteria:

(1) Use of electronic data processing equipment to obtain information—the actual cost for the service, including computer search time, runs, printouts, and time of computer programmers and operators, or other employees.

(2) Photocopying or other forms of reproduction, such as magnetic tapes—actual cost of the operator's time, plus the cost of the machine time and the materials used,

(3) Postage—actual cost, and

(4) Sending information by special methods requested by the applicant, such as express mail or electronic transfer—the actual cost of the special service.

(c) *Assessing and collecting fees.* (1) A request for information from the Data Bank will be regarded as also an agreement to pay the associated fee.

(2) Normally, a bill will be sent along with or following the delivery of the requested information. However, in order to avoid sending numerous small bills to frequent requesters, the charges may be aggregated for certain periods. For example, such a requester may receive a bill monthly or quarterly.

(3) In the event that a requester has failed to pay previous bills, the requester will be required to pay the fee before a request for information is processed.

(4) Fees must be paid by check or money order made payable to "U.S. Department of Health and Human Services" or to the unit stated in the billing and must be sent to the billing unit. Payment must be received within 30 days of the billing date or the applicant will be charged interest and a late fee on the amount overdue.

§ 60.13   Confidentiality of National Practitioner Data Bank information.

(a) *Limitations on disclosure.* Information reported to the Data Bank is considered confidential and shall not be disclosed outside the Department of Health and Human Services, except as specified in § 60.10, § 60.11 and § 60.14. Persons and entities which receive information from the Data Bank either directly or from another party must use it solely with respect to the purpose for which it was provided. Nothing in this paragraph shall prevent the disclosure of information by a party which is authorized under applicable State law to make such disclosure.

(b) *Penalty for violations.* Any person who violates paragraph (a) shall be subject to a civil money penalty of up to $10,000 for each violation. This penalty will be imposed pursuant to procedures at 42 CFR part 1003.

§ 60.14 How to dispute the accuracy of National Practitioner Data Bank Information.

(1) *Who may dispute National Practitioner Data Bank information.* Any physician, dentist or other health care practitioner may dispute the accuracy of information in the Data Bank concerning himself or herself. The Secretary will routinely mail a copy of any report filed in the Data Bank to the subject individual.

(b) *Procedures for filing a dispute.* A physician, dentist or other health care practitioner has 60 days from the date on which the Secretary mails the report in question to him or her in which to dispute the accuracy of the report. The procedures for disputing a report are:

(1) Informing the Secretary and the reporting entity, in writing, of the disagreement, and the basis for it.

(2) Requesting simultaneously that the disputed information be entered into a "disputed" status and be reported to inquirers as being in a "disputed" status, and

(3) Attempting to enter into discussion with the reporting entity to resolve the dispute.

(c) *Procedures for revising disputed information.* (1) If the reporting entity revises the information originally submitted to the Data Bank, the Secretary will notify all entities to whom reports have been sent that the original information has been revised.

(2) If the reporting entity does not revise the reported information, the Secretary will, upon request, review the written information submitted by both parties (the physician, dentist or other health care practitioner), and the reporting entity. After review, the Secretary will either—

(i) If the Secretary concludes that the information is accurate, include a brief statement by the physician, dentist or other health care practitioner describing the disagreement concerning the information, and an explanation of the basis for the decision that it is accurate, or

(ii) If the Secretary concludes that the information was incorrect, send corrected information to previous inquirers.

(Approved by the Office of Management and Budget under control number 0915–0126)
[FR Doc. 89–24425 Filed 10–16–89; 8:45 am]
BILLING CODE 4140–16–M

Appendix 21-C

COBRA—Congressional Statute and Amendments

COBRA STATUTE

Subpart B—Technical and Miscellaneous Provisions

SEC. 6211. MEDICARE HOSPITAL PATIENT PROTECTION AMENDMENTS.

(a) SCOPE OF HOSPITAL RESPONSIBILITY FOR SCREENING.—Subsection (a) of section 1867 of the Social Security Act (42 U.S.C. 1395dd) is amended by striking "department" the third place it appears and inserting the following: "department, including ancillary services routinely available to the emergency department,".

(b) INFORMED REFUSALS OF TREATMENT OR TRANSFERS.—Subsection (b) of such section is amended—

    (1) in paragraph (2)—

        (A) by inserting "and informs the individual (or a person acting on the individual's behalf) of the risks and benefits to the individual of such examination and treatment," after "in that paragraph",

        (B) by striking "or treatment" and inserting "and treatment", and

        (C) by adding at the end the following new sentence: "The hospital shall take all reasonable steps to secure the individual's (or person's) written informed consent to refuse such examination and treatment."; and

    (2) in paragraph (3)—

        (A) by inserting "and informs the individual (or a person acting on the individual's behalf) of the risks and benefits to the individual of such transfer," after "with subsection (c)", and

        (B) by adding at the end the following new sentence: "The hospital shall take all reasonable steps to secure the individual's (or person's) written informed consent to refuse such transfer.".

(c) AUTHORIZATION FOR TRANSFERS.—

    (1) INFORMED CONSENT FOR TRANSFERS AT INDIVIDUAL REQUEST.—Subsection (c)(1)(A)(i) of such section is amended by striking "requests that the transfer be effected" and inserting "after being informed of the hospital's obligations under this section and of the risk of transfer, in writing requests transfer to another medical facility".

    (2) CLARIFYING PHYSICIAN AUTHORIZATION FOR TRANSFERS.—Subsection (c)(1)(A) of such section is amended—

        (A) by striking "or" at the end of clause (i);

        (B) in clause (ii)—

            (i) by striking ", or other qualified medical personnel when a physician is not readily available in the emergency department,", and

Source: Reprinted from *U.S. Code Congressional and Administrative News,* P.L. 101-239, Sec. 6211, December 1989.

(ii) by inserting "of transfer" after "information available at the time";

(C) by striking "; and" at the end of clause (ii) and inserting ", or", and

(D) by adding at the end the following new clause:

"(iii) if a physician is not physically present in the emergency department at the time an individual is transferred, a qualified medical person (as defined by the Secretary in regulations) has signed a certification described in clause (ii) after a physician (as defined in section 1861(r)(1)), in consultation with the person, has made the determination described in such clause, and subsequently countersigns the certification; and".

(3) STANDARD FOR AUTHORIZING TRANSFER.—Subsection (c)(1)(A)(ii) of such section is amended—

(A) by striking ", based upon the reasonable risks and benefits to the patient, and", and

(B) by striking "individual's medical condition" and inserting "individual and, in the case of labor, to the unborn child".

(4) INCLUSION OF SUMMARY OF RISKS AND BENEFITS IN CERTIFICATE OF TRANSFER.—Subsection (c)(1) of such section is amended by adding at the end the following:

"A certification described in clause (ii) or (iii) of subparagraph (A) shall include a summary of the risks and benefits upon which the certification is based.".

(5) PROVISION OF SERVICES PENDING TRANSFER.—Subsection (c)(2) of such section is amended—

(A) by redesignating subparagraphs (A) through (D) as subparagraphs (B) through (E), respectively, and

(B) by inserting before subparagraph (B), as so redesignated, the following new subparagraph:

"(A) in which the transferring hospital provides the medical treatment within its capacity which minimizes the risks to the individual's health and, in the case of a woman in labor, the health of the unborn child;"

(d) REQUIRING MAINTENANCE OF RECORDS OF TRANSFERS.—Subsection (c)(2)(C) of such section, as redesignated by subsection (c)(5)(A) of this section, is amended—

(1) by striking "provides" and inserting "sends to" and

(2) by striking "with appropriate medical records" and all that follows through "transferring hospital" and inserting "all medical records (or copies thereof), related to the emergency condition for which the individual has presented, available at the time of the transfer, including records related to the individual's emergency medical condition, observations of signs or symptoms, preliminary diagnosis, treatment provided, results of any tests and the informed written consent or certification (or copy thereof) provided under paragraph (1)(A), and the name and address of any on-call physician (described in subsection (d)(2)(C)) who has refused or failed to appear within a reasonable time to provide necessary stabilizing treatment".

(e) PHYSICIAN LIABILITY.—Subsection (d)(2) of such subsection is amended—

(1) by amending subparagraph (B) to read as follows:

"(B) Subject to subparagraph (C), any physician who is responsible for the examination, treatment, or transfer of an individual in a participating hospital, including a physician on-call for the care of such an individual, and who knowingly violates a requirement of this section, including a physician who—

"(i) signs a certification under subsection (c)(1)(A) that the medical benefits reasonably to be expected from a transfer to another facility outweigh the risks associated with the transfer, if the physician knew or should have known that the benefits did not outweigh the risks, or

"(ii) misrepresents an individual's condition or other information, including a hospital's obligations under this section, is subject to a civil money penalty of not more than $50,000 for each such violation and, if the violation is knowing and willful or negligent, to exclusion from participation in this title and State health care programs. The provisions of section 1128A (other than the first and second sentences of subsection (a) and subsection (b)) shall apply to a civil money penalty and exclusion under this subparagraph in the same manner as such provisions apply with respect to a penalty, exclusion, or proceeding under section 1128A(a)."; and

(2) by striking subparagraph (C) and inserting the following:

"(C) If, after an initial examination, a physician determines that the individual requires the services of a physician listed by the hospital on its list of on-call physicians (required to be maintained under section 1866(a)(1)(I)) and notifies the on-call physician and the on-call physician fails or refuses to appear within a reasonable period of time, and the physician orders the transfer of the individual because the physician determines that without the services of the on-call physician the benefits of transfer outweigh the risks of transfer, the physician authorizing the transfer shall not be subject to a penalty under subparagraph (B). However, the previous sentence shall not apply to the hospital or to the on-call physician who failed or refused to appear.".

(f) ADDITIONAL OBLIGATIONS.—Such section is amended by adding at the end the following new subsections:

"(g) NONDISCRIMINATION.—A participating hospital that has specialized capabilities or facilities (such as burn units, shock-trauma units, neonatal intensive care units, or (with respect to rural areas) regional referral centers as identified by the Secretary in regulation) shall not refuse to accept an appropriate transfer of an individual who requires such specialized capabilities or facilities if the hospital has the capacity to treat the individual.

"(h) NO DELAY IN EXAMINATION OR TREATMENT.—A participating hospital may not delay provision of an appropriate medical screening examination required under subsection (a) or further medical examination and treatment required under subsection (b) in order to inquire about the individual's method of payment or insurance status.

"(i) WHISTLEBLOWER PROTECTIONS.—A participating hospital may not penalize or take adverse action against a physician because the physician refuses to authorize the transfer of an individual with an emergency medical condition that has not been stabilized.".

(g) CHANGE IN "PATIENT" TERMINOLOGY.—

(1) Subsection (c) of such section is amended—

(A) by striking "PATIENT" and inserting "INDIVIDUAL", and

(B) by striking "a patient" "the patient", "patient's", and "patients" each place each appears and inserting "an individual", "the individual", "individual's", and "individuals", respectively.

(2) Subsection (e)(5) of such section is amended by striking "a patient" each place it appears and inserting "an individual".

(h) CLARIFICATION OF "EMERGENCY MEDICAL CONDITION" DEFINITION.—

(1) IN GENERAL.—Subsection (e) of such section (as amended by section 6003(g)(3)(D)(xiv)) is amended—

(A) in paragraph (1), by striking "means" and all that follows and inserting the following:

"means—

"(A) a medical condition manifesting itself by acute symptoms of sufficient severity (including severe pain) such that the absence of immediate medical attention could reasonably be expected to result in—

"(i) placing the health of the individual (or, with respect to a pregnant woman, the health of the woman or her unborn child) in serious jeopardy, "(ii) serious impairment to bodily functions, or

"(iii) serious dysfunction of any bodily organ or part;"

"(B) with respect to a pregnant women who is having contractions—

"(i) that there is inadequate time to effect a safe transfer to another hospital before delivery, or

"(ii) that transfer may pose a threat to the health or safety of the woman or the unborn child."

(B) by striking paragraph (2);

(C) in paragraph (4)(A)—

(i) by inserting "described in paragraph (1)(A)" after "emergency medical condition",

(ii) by inserting "or occur during" after "likely to result from",

(iii) by inserting before the period at the end the following: ", or, with respect to an emergency medical condition described in paragraph (1)(B), to deliver (including the placenta)";

(D) in paragraph (4)(B)—

(i) by inserting "described in paragraph (1)(A)" after "emergency medical condition",

(ii) by inserting "or occur during" after "to result from", and

(iii) by inserting before the period at the end the following: ", or, with respect to an emergency medical condition described in paragraph (1)(B), that the woman has delivered (including the placenta)"; and

(E) by redesignating paragraphs (3) through (6) as paragraphs (2) through (5), respectively.

(2) CONFORMING AMENDMENTS.—Such section is further amended—

(A) in the heading, by striking "ACTIVE";

(B) in subsection (a), by striking "or to determine if the individual is in active labor (within the meaning of section (e)(2))";

(C) in the heading of subsection (b), by striking "ACTIVE";

(D) in subsection (b)(1)—

(i) by striking "or is in active labor", and

(ii) in subparagraph (A), by striking "or to provide for treatment of the labor"; and

(E) in subsection (c)(1), by striking "(e)(4)(B)) or is in active labor" and inserting "(e)(3)(B))".

(i) EFFECTIVE DATE.—The amendments made by this section shall take effect on the first day of the first month that begins more than 180 days after the date of the enactment of this Act, without regard to whether regulations to carry out such amendments have been promulgated by such date.

42 USC 1395dd note.

AMENDMENTS

§ 1395dd. Examination and treatment for emergency medical conditions and women in active labor

(a) Medical screening requirement

In the case of a hospital that has a hospital emergency department, if any individual (whether or not eligible for benefits under this subchapter) comes to the emergency department and a request is made on the individual's behalf for examination or treatment for a medical condition, the hospital must provide for an appropriate medical screening examination within the capability of the hospital's emergency department to determine whether or not an emergency medical condition (within the meaning of subsection (e)(1) of this section) exists or to determine if the individual is in active labor (within the meaning of subsection (e)(2) of this section).

(b) Necessary stabilizing treatment for emergency medical conditions and active labor

(1) In general

If any individual (whether or not eligible for benefits under this subchapter) comes to a hospital and the hospital determines that the individual has an emergency medical condition or is in active labor, the hospital must provide either—

> (A) within the staff and facilities available at the hospital, for such further medical examination and such treatment as may be required to stabilize the medical condition or to provide for treatment of the labor, or

> (B) for transfer of the individual to another medical facility in accordance with subsection (c) of this section.

(2) Refusal to consent to treatment

A hospital is deemed to meet the requirement of paragraph (1)(A) with respect to an individual if the hospital offers the individual the further medical examination and treatment described in that paragraph but the individual (or a person acting on the individual's behalf) refuses to consent to the examination or treatment.

(3) Refusal to consent to transfer

A hospital is deemed to meet the requirement of paragraph (1) with respect to an individual if the hospital offers to transfer the individual to another medical facility in accordance with subsection (c) of this section but the individual (or a person acting on the individual's behalf) refuses to consent to the transfer.

(c) Restricting transfers until patient stabilized

(1) Rule

If a patient at a hospital has an emergency medical condition which has not been stabilized (within the meaning of subsection (e)(4)(B) of this section) or is in active labor, the hospital may not transfer the patient unless—

> (A)(i) the patient (or a legally responsible person acting on the patient's behalf) requests that the transfer be effected, or

> (ii) a physician (within the meaning of section 1395x(r)(1) of this title), or other qualified medical personnel when a physician is not readily available in the emergency department, has signed a certification that, based upon the reasonable risks and benefits to the patient, and based upon the information available at the time, the medical benefits reasonably expected from the provision of appropriate medical treatment at another medical facility outweigh the increased risks to the individual's medical condition from effecting the transfer; and

> (B) the transfer is an appropriate transfer (within the meaning of paragraph (2)) to that facility.

(2) Appropriate transfer

An appropriate transfer to a medical facility is a transfer—

> (A) in which the receiving facility—

> > (i) has available space and qualified personnel for the treatment of the patient, and

---

Source: Reprinted from USCA 42 § 1395dd—42 § 1395ff, April 1990.

(ii) has agreed to accept transfer of the patient and to provide appropriate medical treatment;

(B) in which the transferring hospital provides the receiving facility with appropriate medical records (or copies thereof) of the examination and treatment effected at the transferring hospital;

(C) in which the transfer is effected through qualified personnel and transportation equipment, as required including the use of necessary and medically appropriate life support measures during the transfer; and

(D) which meets such other requirements as the Secretary may find necessary in the interest of the health and safety of patients transferred.

(d) Enforcement

(1) As requirement of Medicare provider agreement

If a hospital knowingly and willfully, or negligently, fails to meet the requirements of this section, such hospital is subject to—

(A) termination of its provider agreement under this title in accordance with section 1395cc(b) of this title, or

(B) at the option of the Secretary, suspension of such agreement for such period of time as the Secretary determines to be appropriate, upon reasonable notice to the hospital and to the public.

If a civil money penalty is imposed on a responsible physician under paragraph (2), the Secretary may impose the sanction described in section 1395u(j)(2)(A) of this title (relating to barring from participation in the medicare program) in the same manner as it is imposed under section 1395u(j) of this title.

(2) Civil monetary penalties

(A) A participating hospital that knowingly violates a requirement of this section is subject to a civil money penalty of not more than $50,000 for each such violation. The provisions of section 1320a–7a of this title (other than subsections (a) and (b)) shall apply to a civil money penalty under this subparagraph in the same manner as such provisions apply with respect to a penalty or proceeding under section 1320a–7a(a) of this title.

(B) The responsible physician in a participating hospital with respect to the hospital's violation of a requirement of this subsection is subject to the sanctions described in section 1395u(j)(2) of this title, except that, for purposes of this subparagraph, the civil money penalty with respect to each violation may not exceed $50,000, rather than $2,000.

(C) As used in the this [1] paragraph the term "responsible physician" means, with respect to a hospital's violation of a requirement of this section, a physician who—

(i) is employed by, or under contract with, the participating hospital, and

(ii) acting as such an employee or under such a contract, has professional responsibility for the provision of examinations or treatments for the individual, or transfers of the individual, with respect to which the violation occurred.

(3) Civil enforcement

(A) Personal harm

Any individual who suffers personal harm as a direct result of a participating hospital's violation of a requirement of this section may, in a civil action against the participating hospital, obtain those damages available for personal injury under the law of the State in which the hospital is located, and such equitable relief as is appropriate.

(B) Financial loss to other medical facility

Any medical facility that suffers a financial loss as a direct result of a participating hospital's violation of a requirement of this section may, in a civil action against the participating hospital, obtain those damages available for financial loss, under the law of the State in which the hospital is located, and such equitable relief as is appropriate.

(C) Limitations on actions

No action may be brought under this paragraph more than two years after the date of the violation with respect to which the action is brought.

(e) Definitions

In this section:

(1) The term "emergency medical condition" means a medical condition manifesting itself by acute symptoms of sufficient severity (including severe pain) such that the absence of immediate medical attention could reasonably be expected to result in—

(A) placing the patient's health in serious jeopardy,

(B) serious impairment to bodily functions, or

(C) serious dysfunction of any bodily organ or part.

(2) The term "active labor" means labor at a time at which—

(A) delivery is imminent,

(B) there is inadequate time to effect safe transfer to another hospital prior to delivery, or

(C) a transfer may pose a threat of the health and safety of the patient or the unborn child.

(3) The term "participating hospital" means hospital that has entered into a provider agreement under section 1395cc of this title.

(4)(A) The term "to stabilize" means, with respect to an emergency medical condition, to provide such medical treatment of the condition as may be necessary to assure, within reasonable medical probability, that no material deterioration of the condition is likely to result from the transfer of the individual from a facility.

(B) The term "stabilized" means, with respect to an emergency medical condition, that no material deterioration of the condition is likely, within reasonable medical probability, to result from the transfer of the individual from a facility.

(5) The term "transfer" means the movement (including the discharge) of a patient outside a hospital's facilities at the direction of any person employed by (or affiliated or associated, directly or indirectly, with) the hospital, but does not include such a movement of a patient who (A) has been declared dead, or (B) leaves the facility without the permission of any such person.

(6) The term "hospital" includes a rural primary care hospital (as defined in section 1861(mm)(1)).

(f) Preemption

The provisions of this section do not preempt any State or local law requirement, except to the extent that the requirement directly conflicts with a requirement of this section.

(Aug. 14, 1935, c. 531, Title XVIII, § 1867, as added Apr. 7, 1986, Pub.L. 99–272, Title IX, § 9121(b), 100 Stat. 164, and amended Oct. 21, 1986, Pub.L. 99–509, Title IX, § 9307(c)(4), 100 Stat. 1996; Oct. 22, 1986, Pub.L. 99–514, Title XVIII, § 1895(b)(4), 100 Stat. 2933; Dec. 22, 1987, Pub.L. 100–203, Title IV, § 4009(a), 101 Stat. 1330–56, 1330–57; Dec. 22, 1987, Pub.L. 100–203, Title IV, § 4009(a)(1), formerly § 4009(a)(1), (2), 101 Stat. 1330–56, 1330–57, amended and renumbered July 1, 1988, Pub.L. 100–360, Title IV, § 411(b)(8)(A)(i), 102 Stat. 771, as amended Oct. 13, 1988, Pub.L. 100–485, Title VI, § 608(d)(18)(E), 102 Stat. 2419; Dec. 19, 1989, Pub.L. 101–239, Title VI, § 6003(g)(3)(D)(XIV), 103 Stat. 2154.)

1 So in original.

Amendments of Section

Pub.L. 101–239, Title VI, § 6211(i), Dec. 19, 1989, 103 Stat. 2249, provided that:

"The amendments made by this section [amending this section as set out hereunder] shall take effect on the first day of the first month that begins more than 180 days after the date of the enactment of this Act [Dec. 19, 1989], without regard to whether regulations to carry out such amendments have been promulgated by such date."

Pub.L. 101–239, Title VI, § 6211(h)(2)(A), Dec. 19, 1989, 103 Stat. 2249, effective as provided above, substituted in the heading "women in labor" for "women in active labor".

Amendment of Subsec. (a)

Pub.L. 101–239, Title VI, § 6211(a), (h)(2)(B), Dec. 19, 1989, 103 Stat. 2245, 2249, effective as provided above, substituted "emergency department, including ancillary services routinely available to the emergency

*department" for "emergency department" and struck out "or to deter-
mine if the individual is in active labor (within the meaning of subsection (e)(2) of this section)" enacted as "within the meaning of section
(e)(2)".*

Amendment of Subsec. (b)

*Pub.L. 101-239, Title VI, § 6211(h)(2)(C), (D)(i), (ii), Dec. 19, 1989, 103
Stat. 2249, effective as provided above, substituted in: subsec. (b) heading,
"labor" for "active labor"; subsec. (b)(1), "medical condition" for "medical condition or is in active labor"; and subsec. (b)(1)(A), "medical
condition" for "medical condition or to provide for treatment of the
labor", respectively.*

*Pub.L. 101-239, Title VI, § 6211(b)(1)(A)-(C), Dec. 19, 1989, 103 Stat.
2245, effective as provided above, amended subsec. (b)(2)*

*(A) by inserting "and informs the individual (or person acting on the
individual's behalf) of the risks and benefits to the individual of such
examination and treatment," after "in that paragraph",*

(B) by striking "or treatment" and inserting "and treatment", and

*(C) by adding at the end the following new sentence: "The hospital
shall take all reasonable steps to secure the individual's (or person's)
written informed consent to refuse such examination and treatment."*

Amendment of Subsec. (b)

*Pub.L. 101-239, Title VI, § 6211(b)(2)(A), (B), Dec. 19, 1989, 103 Stat.
2245, effective as provided above, amended subsec. (b)(3)*

*(A) by inserting "and informs the individual (or a person acting on
the individual's behalf) of the risks and benefits to the individual of such
transfer," after "with subsection (c) of this section", and*

*(B) by adding at the end the following new sentence: "The hospital
shall take all reasonable steps to secure the individual's (or person's)
written informed consent to refuse such transfer."*

Amendment of Subsec. (c)

*Pub.L. 101-239, Title VI, § 6211(g)(1), Dec. 19, 1989, 103 Stat. 2248,
effective as provided above, substituted in subsec. (c) heading "individual" for "patient".*

Amendment of Subsec. (c)

*Pub.L. 101-239, Title VI, § 6211(g)(1), (h)(2)(E), Dec. 19, 1989, 103 Stat.
2248, 2249, effective as provided above, substituted in subsec. (c), introductory text, "individual" for "patient" and "subsection (e)(3)(B) of this
section)" for "subsection (e)(4)(B) of this section) or is in active labor".*

*Pub.L. 101-239, Title VI, § 6211(c)(1), (2)(A), (g)(1)(B), Dec. 19, 1989, 103
Stat. 2246, 2248, effective as provided above, amended subsec. (c)(1)(A), cl.
(i), by striking "requests that the transfer be effected" and inserting
"after being informed of the hospital's obligations under this section and
of the risk of transfer, in writing requests transfer to another medical
facility"; by striking "or" at the end of clause (i); and by substituting
"individual" and "individual's" for "patient" and "patient's", respectively.*

*Pub.L. 101-239, Title VI, § 6211(c)(2)(B)(i), (ii), (C), (3)(A), (B), (g)(1)(B),
Dec. 19, 1989, 103 Stat. 2246, 2248, amended subsec. (c)(1)(A), cl. (ii),
effective as provided above,*

*(c)(2)(B)(i) by striking ", or other qualified medical personnel when a
physician is not readily available in the emergency department,", and*

*(ii) by inserting "of transfer" after "information available at the
time";*

(C) by striking "; and" at the end of clause (ii) and inserting ". or";

*(3)(A) by striking ", based upon the reasonable risks and benefits to
the patient, and", and*

*(B) by striking "individual's medical condition" and inserting "indi-
vidual and, in the case of labor, to the unborn child"; and*

(g)(1)(B) by substituting "individual" for "patient", respectively.

Pub.L. 101–239, Title VI, § 6211(c)(2)(D), Dec. 19, 1989, 103 Stat. 2246, effective as provided above, enacted subsec. (c)(1)(A)(iii), reading as follows:

"(iii) if a physician is not physically present in the emergency department at the time an individual is transferred, a qualified medical person (as defined by the Secretary in regulations) has signed a certification described in clause (ii) after a physician (as defined in section 1395x(r)(1) of this title), in consultation with the person, has made the determination described in such clause, and subsequently countersigns the certification; and".

Pub.L. 101–239, Title VI, § 6211(c)(4), Dec. 19, 1989, 103 Stat. 2246, effective as provided above, amended subsec. (c)(1) by adding at the end the following:

"A certification described in clause (ii) or (iii) of subparagraph (A) shall include a summary of the risks and benefits upon which the certification is based."

Pub.L. 101–239, Title VI, § 6211(c)(5)(B), Dec. 19, 1989, 103 Stat. 2246, effective as provided above, added the following new subpar. (c)(2)(A):

"(A) in which the transferring hospital provides the medical treatment within its capacity which minimizes the risks to the individual's health and, in the case of a woman in labor, the health of the unborn child;"

Pub.L. 101–239, Title VI, § 6211(c)(5)(A), (g)(1)(B), Dec. 19, 1989, 103 Stat. 2246, 2248, effective as provided above, redesignated as subsec. (c)(2)(B) former subsec. (c)(2)(A) and substituted in subsec. (c)(2)(B)(i), (ii), "individual" for "patient".

Pub.L. 101–239, Title VI, § 6211(c)(5)(A), (d)(1), (2), Dec. 19, 1989, 103 Stat. 2246, effective as provided above, redesignated as subsec. (c)(2)(C) former subsec. (c)(2)(B) and amended subsec. (c)(2)(C)

(1) by striking "provides" and inserting "sends to", and

(2) by striking "with appropriate medical records" and all that follows through "transferring hospital" and inserting "all medical records (or copies thereof), related to the emergency condition for which the individual has presented, available at the time of the transfer, including records related to the individual's emergency medical condition, observations of signs or symptoms, preliminary diagnosis, treatment provided, results of any tests and the informed written consent or certification (or copy thereof) provided under paragraph (1)(A), and the name and address of any on-call physician (described in subsection (d)(2)(C) of this section) who has refused or failed to appear within a reasonable time to provide necessary stabilizing treatment".

Pub.L. 101–239, Title VI, § 6211(c)(5)(A), (g)(1)(B), Dec. 19, 1989, 103 Stat. 2246, 2248, redesignated as subsec. (c)(2)(D), (E) former subsec. (c)(2)(C), (D) and substituted in subsec. (c)(2)(E) "individuals" for "patients".

Amendment of Subsec. (d)(2)

Pub.L. 101–239, Title VI, § 6211(e)(1), (2), Dec. 19, 1989, 103 Stat. 2247, effective as provided above, amended subpar. (B) and struck out subpar. (C) and inserted subpar. (C), the subpars. (B) and (C) to read as follows:

(B) Subject to subparagraph (C), any physician who is responsible for the examination, treatment, or transfer of an individual in a participating hospital, including a physician on-call for the care of such an individual, and who knowingly violates a requirement of this section, including a physician who—

(i) signs a certification under subsection (c)(1)(A) of this section that the medical benefits reasonably to be expected from a transfer to another facility outweigh the risks associated with the transfer, if the physician knew or should have known that the benefits did not outweigh the risks, or

(ii) misrepresents an individual's condition or other information, including a hospital's obligations under this section,

is subject to a civil money penalty of not more than $50,000 for each such violation and, if the violation is knowing and willful or negligent, to exclusion from participation in this subchapter and State health care programs. The provisions of section 1320a–7a of this title (other than *the first and second sentences of subsection (a) and subsection (b)) shall apply to a civil money penalty and exclusion under this subparagraph in the same manner as such provisions apply with respect to a penalty, exclusion, or proceeding under section 1320a-7a(a) of this title.*

(C) If, after an initial examination, a physician determines that the individual requires the services of a physician listed by the hospital on its list of on-call physicians (required to be maintained under section 1395cc(a)(1)(I) of this title) and notifies the on-call physician and the on-call physician fails or refuses to appear within a reasonable period of time, and the physician orders the transfer of the individual because the physician determines that without the services of the on-call physician the benefits of transfer outweigh the risks of transfer, the physician authorizing the transfer shall not be subject to a penalty under subparagraph (B). However, the previous sentence shall not apply to the hospital or to the on-call physician who failed or refused to appear.

Amendment of Subsec. (e)

Pub.L. 101-239, Title VI, § 6211(h)(1)(A), Dec. 19, 1989, 103 Stat. 2248, effective as provided above, amended subsec. (e), as amended by Pub.L. 101-239, § 6003(g)(3)(D)(xiv), in par. (1), by striking "means" and all that follows and inserting the following:

"means—

"(A) a medical condition manifesting itself by acute symptoms of sufficient severity (including severe pain) such that the absence of immediate medical attention could reasonably be expected to result in—

"(i) placing the health of the individual (or, with respect to a pregnant woman, the health of the woman or her unborn child) in serious jeopardy,

"(ii) serious impairment to bodily functions, or

"(iii) serious dysfunction of any bodily organ or part; or

"(B) with respect to a pregnant women who is having contractions—

"(i) that there is inadequate time to effect a safe transfer to another hospital before delivery, or

"(ii) that transfer may pose a threat to the health or safety of the woman or the unborn child."

Pub.L. 101-239, Title VI, § 6211(h)(1)(B), (E), Dec. 19, 1989, 103 Stat. 2248, 2249, effective as provided above, struck out subsec. (e)(2) and redesignated as subsec. (e)(2) former subsec. (e)(3).

Amendment of Subsec. (e)

Pub.L. 101-239, Title VI, § 6211(h)(1)(C)(i)-(iii), (D)(i)-(iii), (E), Dec. 19, 1989, 103 Stat. 2248, 2249, amended subsec. (e), effective as provided above,

(C) in subsec. (e)(4)(A)—

(i) by inserting "described in paragraph (1)(A)" after "emergency medical condition",

(ii) by inserting "or occur during" after "likely to result from",

(iii) by inserting before the period at the end the following: ", or, with respect to an emergency medical condition described in paragraph (1)(B), to deliver (including the placenta)";

(D) in subsec. (e)(4)(B)—

(i) by inserting "described in paragraph (1)(A)" after "emergency medical condition",

(ii) by inserting "or occur during" after "to result from", and

(iii) by inserting before the period at the end the following: ", or, with respect to an emergency medical condition described in paragraph (1)(B), that the woman has delivered (including the placenta)"; and

(E) by redesignating subsec. (e)(4) as subsec. (e)(3).

Amendment of Subsec. (e)

Pub.L. 101–239, Title VI, § 6211(g)(2), (h)(1)(E), Dec. 19, 1989, 103 Stat. 2248, 2249, effective as provided above, substituted in subsec. (e)(5) "an individual" for "a patient" in two places and redesignated subsec. (e)(5) as subsec. (e)(4).

Amendment of Subsec. (e)

Pub.L. 101–239, Title VI, § 6211(h)(1)(E), Dec. 19, 1989, 103 Stat. 2249, effective as provided above, redesignated subsec. (e)(6) as subsec. (e)(5).

Enactment of Subsecs. (g) to (i)

Pub.L. 101–239, Title VI, § 6211(f), Dec. 19, 1969, 103 Stat. 2247, effective as provided above, added subsecs. (g) to (i) as follows:

(g) Nondiscrimination

A participating hospital that has specialized capabilities or facilities (such as burn units, shock-trauma units, neonatal intensive care units, or (with respect to rural areas) regional referral centers as identified by the Secretary in regulation) shall not refuse to accept an appropriate transfer of an individual who requires such specialized capabilities or facilities if the hospital has the capacity to treat the individual.

(h) No delay in examination or treatment

A participating hospital may not delay provision of an appropriate medical screening examination required under subsection (a) of this section or further medical examination and treatment required under subsection (b) of this section in order to inquire about the individual's method of payment or insurance status.

(i) Whistleblower protections

A participating hospital may not penalize or take adverse action against a physician because the physician refuses to authorize the transfer of an individual with an emergency medical condition that has not been stabilized.

Historical and Statutory Notes

Prior Provisions. A prior section 1395dd, Act Aug. 14, 1935, c. 531, Title XVIII, § 1867, as added July 30, 1965, Pub.L. 89–97, Title I, § 102(a), 79 Stat. 329, and amended Jan. 2, 1968, Pub.L. 90–248, Title I, § 164(a), 81 Stat. 873; Oct. 30, 1972, Pub.L. 92–603, Title II, § 288, 86 Stat. 1457, which related to the creation, composition, meetings and functions of the Health Insurance Benefits Advisory Council and the appointment of a Chairman and members thereto, and qualifications, terms of office, compensation, and reimbursement of travel expenses of those members, was repealed by Pub.L. 98–369, Title III, § 2349(a), July 18, 1984, 98 Stat. 1097.

1988 Amendment. Subsec. (d)(2). Pub.L. 100–360, § 411(b)(8)(A)(i), amended Pub.L. 100–203, § 4009(a)(1), to add subpars. (A) and (B), designate provision defining the term "responsible physician" as subpar. (C) and, in subpar. (C) as so designated, substitute "this paragraph" for "previous sentence" and redesignated former subpars. (A) and (B) as cls. (i) and (ii), respectively, and strike out provision that in addition to the other grounds for imposition of a civil money penalty under section 1320a–7a(a) of this title, a participating hospital that knowingly violates a requirement of this section and the responsible physician in the hospital with respect to such a violation are each subject, under that section, to a civil money penalty of not more than $50,000 for each such violation.

1987 Amendments. Subsec. (d)(1). Pub.L. 100–203, § 4009(d)(2), added provisions which permitted Secretary to impose sanction described in section 1395u(j) of this title, relating to barring from participation in medicare program, in same manner as imposed under section 1395u(j)(2)(A) of this title, if civil money penalty is imposed on responsible physician under par. (2).

Subsec. (d)(2). Pub.L. 100–203, § 4009(a)(1), formerly § 4009(a), redesignated § 4009(a)(1) and amended Pub.L. 100–360, § 411(b)(8)(A)(i), as amended Pub.L. 100–485, § 608(d)(18)(E), added subpars. (A) and (B), designated provision defining term "responsible physician" as subpar. (C) and, in subpar. (C) as so designated, substituted "this paragraph" for "the previous sentence" and redesignated former subpars. (A) and (B) as cls. (i) and (ii), respectively, and struck out provision that in addition to the other grounds for imposition of a civil money penalty under section 1320a–7a(a) of this title, a participating hospital that knowingly violated a requirement of this section and the responsible physician in the hospital with respect to such a violation were each subject, under that section, to a civil money penalty of not more than $50,000 for each such violation.

Subsec. (d)(2). Pub.L. 100–203, § 4009(a)(1), substituted "$50,000" for "$25,000".

1986 Amendment. Subsec. (b)(2), (3). Pub.L. 99–509, § 9307(c)(4), struck out "legally responsible" following "individual (or a".

Effective Date of 1988 Amendment. Amendment to this section by section 608(d) of Pub.L. 100–485 effective as if included in the enactment of Pub.L. 100–360, see section 608(g)(1) of Pub.L. 100–485, set out as a note under section 704 of this title.

Except as specifically provided in section 411 of Pub.L. 100–360, amendment by section 411 of Pub.L. 100–360, as it relates to a provision in the Omnibus Budget Reconciliation Act of 1987, Pub.L. 100–203, effective as if included in the enactment of that provision of Pub.L. 100–203, see section 411(a)(2) of Pub.L. 100–360, set out as a note under section 106 of Title 1, General Provisions.

Effective Date of 1987 Amendment. Section 4009(a)(2), formerly 4009(a)(3) of Pub.L. 100–203, as renumbered by Pub.L. 100–360, Title IV, § 411(b)(8)(A)(ii), July 1, 1988, 102 Stat. 772, provided that: "The amendments made by this subsection [amending subsec. (d)(2), of this section] shall apply to actions occurring on or after the date of the enactment of this Act [Dec. 22, 1987]."

Effective Date of 1986 Amendment. Amendment to this section by section 1895 of Pub.L. 99–514 to be effective, unless otherwise provided, as if included in the enactment of the Consolidated Omnibus Budget Reconciliation Act of 1985, Pub.L. 99–272, which was approved Apr. 7, 1986, see section 1895(e) of Pub.L. 99–514, set out as a note under section 162 of Title 26, Internal Revenue Code.

Effective Date. Section 9121(c) of Pub.L. 99–272 provided that: "The amendments made by this section [enacting this section and section 1395cc(a)(1)(I) of this title] shall take effect on the first day of the first month that begins at least 90 days after the date of the enactment of this Act [Apr. 7, 1986]."

Legislative History. For legislative history and purpose of Pub.L. 99–272, see 1986 U.S.Code Cong. and Adm.News, p. 42. See, also, Pub.L. 99–509, 1986 U.S.Code Cong. and Adm.News, p. 3607; Pub.L. 99–514, 1986 U.S.Code Cong. and Adm.News, p. 4075; Pub.L. 100–203, 1987 U.S. Code Cong. and Adm. News, p. 2313–1; Pub.L. 100–360, 1988 U.S.Code Cong. and Adm.News, p. 803; Pub.L. 100–485, 1988 U.S.Code Cong. and Adm.News, p. 2776; Pub.L. 101–239, 1989 U.S. Code Cong. and Adm.News, p. 1906.

Law Review Commentaries

COBRA: Straightening out the serpentine law regarding "patient dumping". Susan F. Krieser Bienick, 14 Minn.T.Law, 10 (Winter 1989).

Preventing patient dumping: Sharpening the COBRA's fangs. Note, 61 N.Y.U.L.Rev. 1186 (1986).

Notes of Decisions

Damages, state regulation or control   3
Jurisdiction   1
State regulation or control
    Generally   2
    Damages   3

---

1. Jurisdiction

Indigent patient stated cause of action for alleged denial of stabilizing treatment under subsec. (6)(1)(A) of this section against county hospital physicians and county hospital to which she was transferred after she reported to emergency room of private hospital with complaints of premature labor pains. Thompson v. St. Anne's Hosp., N.D. Ill.1989, 716 F.Supp. 8.

Federal district court had jurisdiction over patient's action against hospital for violation of Emergency Medical Treatment and Active Labor Act, in which patient alleged that she was discharged by hospital before her condition had been stabilized. Bryant v. Riddle Memorial Hosp., E.D.Pa.1988, 689 F.Supp. 490.

2. State regulation or control—Generally

Federal statute authorizing private cause of action against hospital for improper transfer of patient did not incorporate state procedural limitations. Reid v. Indianapolis Osteopathic Medical Hosp., Inc., S.D.Ind.1989, 709 F.Supp. 853.

3. —— Damages

Federal statute authorizing private cause of action against hospital for improperly transferring patient incorporated Indiana's substantive limitation on maximum amount recoverable for personal injury from health care provider. Reid v. Indianapolis Osteopathic Medical Hosp., Inc., S.D.Ind.1989, 709 F.Supp. 853.

The Patient Self-Determination Act

SEC. 4206. MEDICARE PROVIDER AGREEMENTS ASSURING THE IMPLEMENTATION OF A PATIENT'S RIGHT TO PARTICIPATE IN AND DIRECT HEALTH CARE DECISIONS AFFECTING THE PATIENT.

(a) IN GENERAL.—Section 1866(a)(1) (42 U.S.C. 1395cc(a)(1)) is amended—

    (1) in subsection (a)(1)—

        (A) by striking "and" at the end of subparagraph (O),

        (B) by striking the period at the end of subparagraph (P) and inserting ", and", and

        (C) by inserting after subparagraph (P) the following new subparagraph:

"(Q) in the case of hospitals, skilled nursing facilities, home health agencies, and hospice programs, to comply with the requirement of subsection (f) (relating to maintaining written policies and procedures respecting advance directives)."; and

    (2) by inserting after subsection (e) the following new subsection:

"(f)(1) For purposes of subsection (a)(1)(Q) and sections 1819(c)(2)(E), 1833(r), 1876(c)(8), and 1891(a)(6), the requirement of this subsection is that a provider of services or prepaid or eligible organization (as the case may be) maintain written policies and procedures with respect to all adult individuals receiving medical care by or through the provider or organization—

    "(A) to provide written information to each such individual concerning—

        "(i) an individual's rights under State law (whether statutory or as recognized by the courts of the State) to make decisions concerning such medical care, including the right to accept or refuse medical or surgical treatment and the right to formulate advance directives (as defined in paragraph (3)), and

        "(ii) the written policies of the provider or organization respecting the implementation of such rights;

    "(B) to document in the individual's medical record whether or not the individual has executed an advance directive;

    "(C) not to condition the provision of care or otherwise discriminate against an individual based on whether or not the individual has executed an advance directive;

    "(D) to ensure compliance with requirements of State law (whether statutory or as recognized by the courts of the State) respecting advance directives at facilities of the provider or organization; and

    "(E) to provide (individually or with others) for education for staff and the community on issues concerning advance directives.

Subparagraph (C) shall not be construed as requiring the provision of care which conflicts with an advance directive.

"(2) The written information described in paragraph (1)(A) shall be provided to an adult individual—

    "(A) in the case of a hospital, at the time of the individual's admission as an inpatient,

    "(B) in the case of a skilled nursing facility, at the time of the individual's admission as a resident.

Source: Reprinted from the Patient Self-Determination Act of 1990 (P.L. 101-508; U.S.C. Sec. 4206).

"(C) in the case of a home health agency, in advance of the individual coming under the care of the agency,

"(D) in the case of a hospice program, at the time of initial receipt of hospice care by the individual from the program, and

"(E) in the case of an eligible organization (as defined in section 1876(b)) or an organization provided payments under section 1833(a)(1)(A), at the time of enrollment of the individual with the organization.

"(3) In this subsection, the term 'advance directive' means a written instruction, such as a living will or durable power of attorney for health care, recognized under State law (whether statutory or as recognized by the courts of the State) and relating to the provision of such care when the individual is incapacitated.".

(b) APPLICATION TO PREPAID ORGANIZATIONS.—

(1) ELIGIBLE ORGANIZATIONS.—Section 1876(c) of such Act (42 U.S.C. 1395mm(c)) is amended by adding at the end the following new paragraph:

"(8) A contract under this section shall provide that the eligible organization shall meet the requirement of section 1866(f) (relating to maintaining written policies and procedures respecting advance directives).".

(2) OTHER PREPAID ORGANIZATIONS.—Section 1833 of such Act (42 U.S.C. 1395l) is amended by adding at the end the following new subsection:

"(r) The Secretary may not provide for payment under subsection (a)(1)(A) with respect to an organization unless the organization provides assurances satisfactory to the Secretary that the organization meets the requirement of section 1866(f) (relating to maintaining written policies and procedures respecting advance directives).".

42 USC 1395cc
note.

(c) EFFECT ON STATE LAW.—Nothing in subsections (a) and (b) shall be construed to prohibit the application of a State law which allows for an objection on the basis of conscience for any health care provider or any agent of such provider which, as a matter of conscience, cannot implement an advance directive.

(d) CONFORMING AMENDMENTS.—

(1) Section 1819(c)(1) of such Act (42 U.S.C. 1395i–3(c)(1)) is amended by adding at the end the following new subparagraph:

"(E) INFORMATION RESPECTING ADVANCE DIRECTIVES.—A skilled nursing facility must comply with the requirement of section 1866(f) (relating to maintaining written policies and procedures respecting advance directives).".

(2) Section 1891(a) of such Act (42 U.S.C. 1395bbb(a)) is amended by adding at the end the following:

"(6) The agency complies with the requirement of section 1866(f) (relating to maintaining written policies and procedures respecting advance directives).".

(e) EFFECTIVE DATES.—

(1) The amendments made by subsections (a) and (d) shall apply with respect to services furnished on or after the first day of the first month beginning more than 1 year after the date of the enactment of this Act. 42 USC 1395i–3
note.

(2) The amendments made by subsection (b) shall apply to contracts under section 1876 of the Social Security Act and payments under section 1833(a)(1)(A) of such Act as of first day of the first month beginning more than 1 year after the date of the enactment of this Act. 42 USC 1395l
note.

Appendix 21-E

Patient Values History Form

SOUTHERN CHESTER COUNTY MEDICAL CENTER
1015 West Baltimore Pike
West Grove, PA 19390-9499

VALUES HISTORY FORM
Prepared for the residents of southern Chester County by the
Ethics Committee at Southern Chester County Medical Center,
based on material prepared by Doukas, Lipson, and McCullough
Value History, Section 1, and The School of Law,
University of New Mexico—Sections 2 and 3

NAME: _____

DATE: _____

If someone assisted you in completing this form please fill in his or her name, address, and relationship to you.

NAME: _____

ADDRESS: _____

_____

_____

TELEPHONE: _____

RELATIONSHIP: _____

The purpose of this form is to assist you in thinking about and writing down what is important to you about your health. If you should at some time become unable to make health care decisions for yourself, your thoughts as expressed on this form may help others make a decision for you in accordance with what you would have chosen. This is not a legal document. It can be changed, updated, or rescinded at any time. It is hoped that this form will encourage a discussion between you and your family/loved ones about your values regarding life, health care, wishes, etc.

If you need more space than is provided, write on the back of the page so that you can express yourself fully. Feel free to omit topics on which your views are not formed and topics which do not appeal to you. Also, feel free to add value statements that are important to you but not listed.

The first section provides a list of common values about the Quality of Life. Please review the list. Some of these will help you define the Quality of Life that you would like to live if you are ever in a nursing home or hospital.

Source: Courtesy of Southern Chester County Medical Center, West Grove, PA.

The second section of this form asks whether you have already expressed your wishes concerning medical treatment through either written or oral communications and if not, whether you would like to do so now.

The third section of this form provides an opportunity for you to discuss your values, wishes, and preferences in a number of different areas, such as your personal relationships, your overall attitude toward life, and your thoughts about illness. You may wish to think carefully before stating your wishes.

SECTION 1

VALUES RELEVANT TO YOUR VIEWS ON THE QUALITY OF LIFE

Please think about these, and circle the number by those you think are very important to you.

1. I want to maintain my capacity to think clearly.

2. I want to feel safe and secure.

3. I want to avoid unnecessary pain and suffering.

4. I want to be treated with respect.

5. I want to be treated with dignity when I can no longer speak for myself.

6. I do not want to be an unnecessary burden on my family.

7. I want to maintain a good relationship with my family.

8. I want to be able to be with my loved ones before I die.

9. I want to be able to make my own decisions.

10. I want to experience a comfortable dying process.

11. I want to leave good memories of myself to my loved ones.

12. I want to be treated in accord with my religious beliefs and traditions.

13. I want respect shown for my body after I die.

14. I want to help others by making a contribution to medical education and research.

15. Other values important to me are:

_____

_____

_____

SECTION 2

A.   WRITTEN LEGAL DOCUMENTS

Have you written any of the following legal documents? If so, please complete the requested information.

Living Will

Date written: _____

Document location: _____

Comments: (e.g., whom have you named to be your decision maker?)

_____

_____

B.   WISHES CONCERNING SPECIFIC MEDICAL PROCEDURES

If you have ever expressed your wishes either written or orally, concerning any of the following medical procedures, please complete the requested information. If you have not previously indicated your wishes on these procedures and would like to do so now, please complete this information.

Organ Donation

To whom expressed: _____

If oral, when? _____

If written, when? _____

Document location: _____

Comments: _____

_____

_____

Cardiopulmonary Resuscitation (CPR)

To whom expressed? _____

If oral, when? _____

If written, when? _____

Document location: _____

Comments: _____

_____

_____

Respiratory ("Breathing Machines")

To whom expressed: _____

If oral, when? _____

If written, when? _____

Document location: _____

Comments: _____

_____

_____

Artificial Nutrition (feeding through a tube in the stomach)

To whom expressed: _____

If oral, when? _____

If written, when? _____

Document location: _____

Comments: _____

_____

_____

C. **GENERAL COMMENTS**

Do you wish to make any general comments about the information you provided in this section?

_____

_____

SECTION 3

A. **YOUR OVERALL ATTITUDE TOWARD YOUR HEALTH**

1. How would you describe your current health status?

   Excellent ___   Good ___   Fair ___   Poor ___

2. If you have current medical problems, how do they affect your ability to function?

   _____

   _____

3. How do you feel about your current health status?

   Pleased ___ Satisfactory ___   Troublesome ___   Worried ___

4. How well are you able to take care of yourself on a daily basis?

   Very Well ___   Satisfactory ___   Not Very Well ___

5. What are your current medications?

   _____

   _____

6. Do you wish to make any general comments about your overall health?

   _____

   _____

B. YOUR PERCEPTION OF THE ROLE OF YOUR DOCTOR AND OTHER HEALTH CAREGIVERS

1. Do you think your doctors should make the final decision concerning any treatment you might need?

   Yes ___   No___

2. How do you relate to your caregivers such as nurses, therapists, doctors, chaplains, social workers, etc.?

   _____

   _____

3. Do you wish to make any general comments about your doctor and other health caregivers or give them advice about how to treat you?

   _____

   _____

C. YOUR THOUGHTS ABOUT INDEPENDENCE AND CONTROL

1. How important are independence and self-sufficiency in your life?

   _____

   _____

2. If you were to experience decreased physical and mental abilities, how would that affect your attitude toward independence and self-sufficiency?

   _____

   _____

3. Do you wish to make any general comments about the value of independence and control in your life?

   _____

   _____

D.   YOUR PERSONAL RELATIONSHIPS

1.   Do you expect that your friends, family and/or others will support your decisions regarding medical treatment you may need now or in the future?

_____

_____

2.   Have you made any arrangements for your family or friends to make medical treatment decisions on your behalf? If so, who has agreed to make decisions for you and in what circumstances? If not, who do you wish to make decisions?

_____

_____

3.   What, if any, unfinished business from the past are you concerned about (e.g., personal and family relationships, business and legal matters)?

_____

_____

4.   What role do your friends and family play in your life?

_____

_____

5.   Do you wish to make any general comments about the personal relationships in your life?

_____

_____

E.   YOUR OVERALL ATTITUDE TOWARD LIFE

1.   What activities do you enjoy (e.g., hobbies, watching TV, etc.)?

_____

_____

2.   Are you happy to be alive?   _____

3.   Do you feel that life is worth living?   _____

4.   How satisfied are you with what you have achieved in your life?

_____

_____

5.   What makes you laugh/cry?

_____

_____

6.   What do you fear most? What frightens or upsets you?

_____

_____

7.   What goals do you have for the future?

_____

_____

8.   Do you wish to make any general comments about your attitude toward life?

_____

_____

F.   YOUR ATTITUDE TOWARD ILLNESS, DYING, AND DEATH

1.   What will be important to you when you are dying (e.g., physical comfort, no pain, family members present, etc.)?

_____

_____

2.   Where would you prefer to die?

_____

_____

3.   What is your attitude toward death?

_____

_____

4.   How do you feel about the use of life-sustaining measures in the face of:

Terminal Illness?   _____

Permanent Coma?   _____

Irreversible Chronic Illness (e.g., Alzheimer's disease)?   _____

5.   Do you wish to make any general comments about your attitude toward illness, dying, and death?

_____

_____

G.   YOUR RELIGIOUS BACKGROUND AND BELIEFS

1.   What is your religious background?

_____

2.   How do your religious beliefs affect your attitude toward serious or terminal illness?

_____

_____

3.   How does your church or synagogue view the role of prayer or religious sacraments in an illness?

_____

_____

4.   Do you wish to make any general comments about your religious background and beliefs?

_____

_____

H.   YOUR LIVING ENVIRONMENT

1.   What has been your living situation over the last ten years (e.g., lived alone, lived with others, etc.)?

_____

_____

2.   How difficult is it for you to maintain the kind of environment for yourself that you find comfortable? Does any illness or medical problem you have now mean that it will be harder in the future?

_____

_____

3.   Would you consider a change in your living environment? If so, what changes and under what conditions?

_____

_____

4.   Do you wish to make any general comments about your living environment?

_____

_____

I.   YOUR ATTITUDE CONCERNING FINANCES

1.   How much do you worry about having enough money to provide for your care?

_____

_____

2.   Do you wish to make any general comments concerning your finances and the cost of health care?

_____

_____

J.   YOUR WISHES CONCERNING YOUR FUNERAL

1.   What are your wishes concerning your funeral and burial or cremation?

_____

_____

2.   Have you made your funeral arrangements? If so, with whom?

_____

_____

3.   Do you wish to make any general comments about how you would like your funeral and burial or cremation to be arranged or conducted?

_____

_____

4.   Have you discussed your comments on the above questions with your family and clergy person?

_____

_____

SUGGESTIONS FOR USE

After you have completed this form, you may wish to provide copies to your nearest family member, clergy person, attorney, physician, and other people interested in you. If you have a Living Will or Durable Power of Attorney for Health Care Decisions, you may wish to attach a copy of this form to those documents.

Keep a list of those to whom you gave copies. If you make any changes, date it and send them a copy.

chapter 22

Complying with the Mandates of OSHA

Barbara J. Youngberg and Kristi Kelsey

INTRODUCTION

The Occupational Safety and Health Administration (OSHA) has enacted new legislation addressing the responsibility of employers to inform all employees at risk of contact with blood and bloody body fluids of their rights and responsibilities regarding the spread of blood-borne pathogens. Phase-in for implementation occurred over a period of four months. (See Exhibit 22-1.)

Exhibit 22-1
COMPLIANCE CALENDAR[1]

ITEM	EFFECTIVE DATE	60 DAYS	90 DAYS	120 DAYS
Standard	3/6/92			
Exposure Control Plan		5/5/92		
Information and Training			6/4/92	
Recordkeeping			6/4/92	
Engineer and Work Practice Controls				7/6/92
Personal Protective Equipment				7/6/92
Housekeeping				7/6/92
HBV Vaccination Postexposure Follow-up				7/6/92
Labels and Signs				7/6/92

[1]OSHA Instruction CPL 2–2.44B shall remain in effect for complaint inspections until the effective dates of the requirements of 29 CFR 1910.1030.
Implementation table from U.S. Government Printing Office: 1992–312–410/64773.

SUMMARY OF THE SPECIFICS OF THE REGULATION

The regulations state that it is every employer's obligation to:

- educate staff about hepatitis B virus (HBV) and human immunodeficiency virus (HIV) infections
- provide, after education, the opportunity for staff to receive HBV vaccination at the employer's expense
- maintain appropriate documentation demonstrating compliance with the OSHA regulations

This new legislation is in response to the significant number of health care workers who have been infected with HBV as well as to the large numbers of people in the United States who are believed to be carriers of the virus. More than one million people carry HBV in their bloodstream. Another 300,000—most of them young adults—are infected each year through contact with the blood or body fluids of an HBV carrier.[1]

Through exposure at work, at least 12,000 U.S. health care workers are infected each year. Approximately 250 of those exposed die.[2] (See Exhibit 22-2 for specific details regarding hepatitis.)

Although recent attention has focused on the risks of health care workers exposed to HIV, hospital workers should be aware that HBV transmission is much more common. Equally important, HBV can be controlled with a vaccine. In fact, studies performed by the Centers for Disease Control (CDC) confirm that the hepatitis B vaccine is 80 to 95 percent effective in preventing hepatitis B viral infection and clinical hepatitis B. If, after vaccination recipients develop a protective antibody response, then they are 100 percent protected. The vaccination's protection lasts for at least nine years—this is as long as the vaccine has been available so protection could be significantly longer.

The U.S. Department of Labor has developed instructions detailing employer compliance requirements with the Occupational Exposure to Bloodborne Pathogen Final Rule. The instructions, released on March 6, 1992, not only describe how the new standard differs from the previous one, it also provides specific instructions for enforcing the standard.

Due to the standard's significance to health care institutions and their workers, hospital risk managers, administrators, infection control departments, and employee health personnel should be familiar with the standard and should develop implementation strategies to ensure compliance with all provisions of the Act. Implementation of the mandates of this rule allow for the completion of the Exposure Control Plan by May 5, 1992. The information and training section of the rule and the recordkeeping section took effect on June 4, 1992. The sections dealing with methods of compliance, HBV vaccination postexposure follow-up, and labels and signs took effect on July 6, 1992.

Exhibit 22-2

TYPES OF HEPATITIS AND TRANSMISSION

Type	Incubation Period	Usual Onset	Mode of Transmission	Signs and Symptoms	Prognosis Carrier State	Chronic Hepatitis	Mortality
Hepatitis A (HAV)	15–50 days, avg. 28	Acute	Fecal-oral route (often food- or water-borne)	Fever, malaise, anorexia, nausea, abdominal discomfort followed by jaundice Symptoms usually last 1–2 weeks, increasing in severity with age. Often no symptoms, especially in children	None, self-limiting	Does not develop	0.6%
Hepatitis B (HBV)	45–180 days, avg. 60–90	Insidious	Percutaneous/permucosal exposure to blood or blood products Sexual contact Perinatal contact	Anorexia, abdominal discomfort, nausea and vomiting, occasionally arthralgias and rash progressing to jaundice Symptoms usually last 1–4 weeks; may be 6 months before patient recovers totally	6–10% of adults become carriers	Develops in 50% of carriers	0.5–2.0%
Hepatitis C (HCV; Non-A, Non-B)	14–180 days, avg. 56	Insidious	Percutaneous/permucosal exposure to blood or blood products Risk through sexual contact suspected	Similar to HBV, but usually less severe	40–60% become carriers	Develops in 50% of infected patients	1–2%
Hepatitis D (HDV; Delta Hepatitis)	30–160 days	Acute	Similar to HBV; HBV infection a precondition Risk through sexual contact less than for HBV	Occurs as superinfection or coinfection with HBV, intensifies HBV symptoms	Self-limiting, or patient may progress to carrier	Develops most often when HDV is a superinfection	As high as 30% in chronic patients
Hepatitis E (HEV; Non-A, Non-B)	21–42 days	Acute	Fecal-oral route; usually seen in developing countries		Not known	No cases reported	1–2%, 10–20% in pregnant women

Source: Published in *RN*, April 1992. Copyright © 1992 Medical Economics Publishing, Montvale, New Jersey. Reprinted with permission.

WHO MUST COMPLY WITH THE ACT

This Act applies to all employees who are likely to be exposed to blood or other potentially infectious materials, including certain human body fluids. This situation—termed occupational exposure—is defined as reasonably anticipated skin, eye, mucous membrane, or parenteral contact with potentially infectious materials that may result from the performance of an employee's duties. Thus, the potential for on-the-job exposure is crucial to the Act's application. The definition excludes incidental exposure that may take place on the job (e.g., one employee assisting another who has cut a finger while opening a packing box with a sharp instrument).

OSHA identifies 24 industry sectors in which employees are in contact with or handle blood or other potentially infectious materials. These sectors include the following:

- hospitals
- physician offices
- medical labs
- dental labs
- nursing homes
- dialysis centers
- hospices
- home health care
- residential care facilities
- drug treatment centers
- government outpatient facilities
- blood collections and processing centers
- health clinics in industrial facilities
- personnel services
- funeral homes and crematories
- research laboratories
- linen services
- medical and dental equipment repair
- law enforcement
- fire and rescue services
- correctional institutions
- schools
- lifesaving services such as private ambulance companies
- regulated waste management and disposal service

All employees in these sectors are subject to the new OSHA rules. This recent ruling also contains specific provisions relating to research laboratories (laboratories producing or using research scale amounts of HIV or HBV) and production facilities (facilities engaged in industrial scale, large volume, or high concentration production of HIV or HBV).

FOCUS ON EXPOSURE CONTROL

OSHA wants to prevent exposure incidents whenever possible since individuals may become infected from a single exposure incident. Exposure control (previously termed "infection control" in the proposed rulings) includes two elements:

1. exposure determination
2. an exposure control plan

Exposure Determination

All personnel who hold positions determined to involve occupational exposure are entitled to the protection of OSHA's rule. People within the identified sectors having responsibility for employee health and regulatory compliance must therefore identify all job classifications in which occupational exposure may occur. These regulations require that job classifications be listed when all employees in those classifications have occupational exposure. In the event the employer determines that listing a particular job classification is not sufficiently specific to identify exposed employees, the employer may list the job classifications in which some, but not all, employees in those classifications have occupational exposure. The employer may then clarify the tasks and/or procedures associated with exposure in those classifications. The determination of whether a position involves a risk of exposure must be made without regard to the use of personal protective equipment.

The U.S. Department of Labor (DOL) has developed detailed instructions to aid employers in complying with the new OSHA regulations. It provides a specific list of job classifications that may be associated with tasks that have occupational exposure to blood and other potentially infectious material. The DOL instructions identify the following groups; however these groups are not automatically covered unless they have occupational exposure:

- physicians, physician assistants, nurses, nurse practitioners, and other health care employees in clinics and physicians' offices
- employees of clinical and diagnostic laboratories
- housekeepers in health care facilities
- personnel in hospital laundries or commercial laundries that service health care or public safety institutions
- tissue bank personnel
- employees in blood banks and plasma centers who collect, transport, and test blood
- freestanding clinic employees (e.g., hemodialysis clinics, urgent care clinics, health maintenance organization (HMO) clinics, and family planning clinics)

- employees in clinics in industrial, educational, and correctional facilities (e.g., those who collect blood and clean and dress wounds)
- employees assigned to provide emergency first aid
- dentists, dental hygienists, dental assistants, and dental laboratory technicians
- staff of institutions for the developmentally disabled
- hospice employees
- home health care workers
- staff of nursing homes and long-term care facilities
- employees of funeral homes and mortuaries
- HIV and HBV research laboratory and production facility workers
- employees handling regulated waste
- medical equipment service and repair personnel
- emergency medical technicians, paramedics, and other emergency medical service providers
- firefighters, law enforcement personnel, and correctional officers (employees in the private sector, the federal government, or a state or local government in a state that has an OSHA-approved state plan).

Exposure Control Plan

A written exposure control plan must be developed by each employer having one or more employees with occupational exposure. The plan must identify the individuals who will receive training, protective equipment, vaccination, and comply with OSHA's other requirements. At a minimum, the exposure control plan must include the following:

- the determination of which employee positions involve the risk of exposure
- a schedule and procedures for implementing compliance methodologies
- an evaluation procedure for circumstances surrounding exposure incidents

Each employer must make a copy of its plan accessible to employees and, on request, to the Assistant Secretary of Labor and/or the Director of the National Institute for Occupational Safety and Health for examination and copying. The plan must be reviewed at least annually and as necessary to reflect new or modified tasks and procedures that affect occupational exposure; it should also be updated to reflect new or revised employee positions with such exposure.

METHODS OF COMPLIANCE

The OSHA rule establishes four compliance methodologies: (1) general; (2) engineering and work practice; (3) personal protective equipment; and (4) housekeeping. Again, the DOL has provided detailed instructions for compliance.

General Compliance

OSHA has adopted the universal precautions previously recommended by the CDC. The previous exemption to the use of universal precautions contained in the proposed rule has been limited to the requirements for personal protective equipment. OSHA has further modified the rule to require that where differentiation between body fluids is difficult or impossible, all body fluids should be considered potentially infectious.

Engineering and Work Practice Controls

Engineering and work practice controls are viewed as the primary means of eliminating or minimizing employee exposure. These measures either remove the hazard and eliminate or reduce the risk of employee exposure or alter the manner in which a task is performed. The rule contains specific procedures—handwashing, recapping needles, and reusable sharps—for such practices.

Handwashing

The employer must provide readily accessible handwashing facilities to employees. When such arrangements are not feasible, the employer must provide an alternative antiseptic hand cleanser together with clean cloth/paper towels. In addition, the employer must ensure that employees wash their hands as soon as feasible after removal of gloves or other personal protective equipment. The employer must also ensure that employees wash their hands or other skin with soap and water or flush mucous membranes with water as soon as possible following contact with blood or other potentially infectious materials.

Recapping Needles

Recapping needles will only be allowed where the employer can demonstrate that there is no feasible alternative or that such action is required by a specific medical procedure. In these instances, a mechanical device or a one-handed technique must be used to recap or remove the needle. Shearing or breaking of contaminated needles is prohibited. Contaminated needles may not be recapped, bent, or resheathed except as specifically provided. The rule reflects OSHA's belief that the immediate discarding of used needles into a readily accessible sharps container is the best way of minimizing employee exposure.

Reusable Sharps

Reusable sharps must be placed in puncture resistant containers, labeled, or color coded in accordance with OSHA's rule. The container must be leak proof on the sides and bottom.

Personal Protective Equipment

Where occupational exposure still remains after the institution of engineering and work practice controls, personal protective equipment must be used. The employer must provide appropriate equipment in appropriate sizes at no cost to the employee. Equipment is considered appropriate only if it does not permit blood or other potentially infectious materials to pass through or reach the employee's work clothes, street clothes, undergarments, skin, eyes, mouth, or other mucous membranes under normal conditions of use and for the duration of time for which the equipment will be used. Such equipment may include gloves, gowns, lab coats, face shields or masks, protective eyewear, mouth pieces, resuscitation bags, pocket masks, or other ventilation devices. The rule requires the employer to clean, launder, and dispose of, or repair and replace, personal protective equipment at no cost to the employee. The rule further requires that all personal protective equipment be removed prior to leaving the work area. Employers are not obligated to provide general work clothes, only protective equipment. Whether an employer is obligated to provide a particular item depends on whether the item functions as protection against contamination with blood or other potentially infectious materials.

There is a limited exemption from the use of personal protective equipment when, in the employee's professional judgment, such use would prevent the delivery of health care services or impose an increased hazard to the employee's safety. Each such exemption must be documented and investigated to determine whether prevention of similar circumstances in the future is possible.

Housekeeping

The rule requires employers to follow certain housekeeping procedures in order to maintain work sites in a clean and sanitary condition. Accordingly, all equipment and surfaces must be cleaned and disinfected after contact with blood or other potentially infectious materials; broken glass that may be contaminated must not be picked up with the hands, but by mechanical means; specimens of blood or other potentially infectious materials must be placed in closable, leakproof containers that are labeled or color coded. The housekeeping provisions also regulate the manner in which employers treat laundry that is contaminated with blood or other potentially infectious materials.

MISCELLANEOUS REQUIREMENTS

HBV Vaccination and Postexposure Follow-up

The rule requires employers to offer HBV vaccine to all employees who have occupational exposure, and to provide postexposure evaluation and follow-up for all employees who have had an exposure incident. Postexposure evaluation and follow-up include collecting and testing the source patient's blood to determine the presence of HBV or HIV infection (if permission can be obtained from the patient), collecting and testing the exposed employee's blood, counseling, illness reporting, and postexposure prophylaxis. (See Chapter 15 for an example of a postexposure program for potential HIV-infected employees.)

Vaccination, evaluation, and follow-up services must be provided at no cost to the employee, at a reasonable time and place, and under the supervision of a licensed physician or other appropriately trained and licensed health care professional. These services must be provided according to U.S. Department of Public Health Service current recommendations.

The HBV vaccine must be made available after the employee has received the training mandated by the rule and within ten days of initial assignment to all employees who have occupational exposure. If an employee initially declines the vaccine but later decides to accept it, employers then must provide the vaccine. Moreover, employers are obligated to provide a booster dose if an employee later needs one. Employers must ensure that employees who decline HBV vaccination sign a statement to that effect. (See example of such statement in Exhibit 22-3.)

Employers must provide employees who have had an exposure incident with specific information, including:

- a copy of the final rule
- a description of the exposed employee's duties as they relate to the exposure incident
- documentation of the route(s) of exposure and circumstances under which exposure occurred
- results of the source individual's blood testing
- all medical records relevant to the appropriate treatment of the employee
- a written copy of the evaluating professional's opinion within 15 days of the completion of the evaluation

Labels and Signs

The rule requires that employers affix warning labels on containers of regulated waste, refrigerators and freezers

Exhibit 22-3
EMPLOYEE HEPATITIS B VIRUS (HBV)
STATUS FORM

Please complete the following form, checking those responses that apply to your situation. Sign and date the form and return to employee health services.

[　] I have received the HBV vaccination series—please enclose documentation.
Date of vaccination _____

[　] I will need to have the HBV vaccination.

[　] I understand that, due to my occupational exposure to blood or other potentially infectious materials, I may be at risk of acquiring hepatitis B virus (HBV) infection. I have been given the opportunity to be vaccinated with the hepatitis B vaccine, at no charge to myself. However, I decline hepatitis B vaccine at this time. I understand that by declining this vaccine, I continue to be at risk for acquiring hepatitis B, a serious disease. If in the future I continue to be at risk for occupational exposure to blood or other infectious materials and I want to be vaccinated with the hepatitis B vaccine, I can receive the vaccination series at no charge.

Signature: _____ Date _____

Exhibit 22-4
LABELING REQUIREMENT

Item	No Label Required	Biohazard Label		Red Color-Coded Container
Regulated waste container		X	or	X
Reusable contaminated sharps		X	or	X
Refrigerator/freezer holding blood or other potentially infectious material (OPIM)		X		
Containers used for storage, transport, or shipping of blood or OPIM		X	or	X
Blood products released for clinical use	X			
Individual specimen containers of blood or OPIM remaining in facility	X[1]	or X	or	X
Specimens shipped from the primary facility to another facility		X	or	X
Individual containers of blood or OPIM placed in labeled container during storage, transport, shipment, or disposal	X			
Contaminated equipment needing servicing or shipping		X[2]		
Contaminated laundry	X[3]	or X	or	X
Laundry sent to another facility that does not use universal precautions		X	or	X

[1] Labels are not required if universal precautions are used in handling all specimens and containers are recognizable as containing specimens.
[2] Label must specify, in addition, the location of the contamination.
[3] Alternative label or color code must be used when facility uses universal precautions in handling all soiled laundry and employees can recognize containers as requiring compliance with universal precautions.

Exhibit 22-5
SAMPLE HOSPITAL POLICY FOLLOWING EXPOSURE

Subject: BODY FLUID EXPOSURE
Policy: All body fluid/needlestick exposures are to be evaluated and monitored for infectious disease. Patient and employee education will include appropriate testing and counseling.
Purpose: This document establishes a policy to define guidelines for management of the employee who sustains a body fluid exposure. Such a policy is developed in compliance with OSHA.

PROCEDURES

When an employee sustains a body fluid exposure, the following ten procedures will be instituted:

1. All wounds must be cleansed with Betadine®. Mucous membranes must be irrigated with normal saline or water.
2. The supervisor in charge of the unit must be notified. If the supervisor is not on duty, the house supervisor should be notified.
3. The employee must report to the employee health service immediately. If the employee health service is closed, the employee must report to the emergency department.
4. At the employee health service (or the emergency department), the employee exposure will be evaluated. The body secretion/employee injury form will be completed.

5. A serum specimen from the source will be tested for the presence of the following:
   - hepatitis B surface antigen
   - human immunodeficiency virus (HIV) infection (Accidental Exposure Form)
   - liver functions if indicated
6. Serum from the employee will be tested for the presence of the following:
   - hepatitis antibody
   - HIV infection (if desired, consent must be signed)
   - liver function tests as a baseline
7. The source is evaluated and the employee determines the initial treatment. The HIV patient exposure algorithm guides the initial treatment plan in the event of a known or suspected exposure to HIV-infected body fluids. Final treatment plans are the decision of the employee's health care provider in conjunction with the employee.
8. HIV post-test counseling will be provided for each individual based on the guidelines established by the CDC.
9. Referrals may be made to the sexually transmitted disease clinic or the public health department. The employee may have the option of choosing to be tested by the hospital or may be referred to the public health department.
10. If the exposure is high risk or from a known HIV source, immediate counseling is recommended to decrease the stress related to the exposure.

containing blood or other potentially infectious materials, and other containers used to store or transport potentially infectious materials. When a facility uses universal precautions in handling all specimens, labeling in accordance with this rule is not necessary if containers are recognizable as containing specimens. This exemption applies only while such specimens/containers remain within the facility. Containers of blood or blood components that are labeled as to their contents and have been released for distribution are exempt from the labeling requirement. Exhibit 22-4 summarizes labeling requirements.

Information and Training

Employers must provide training to employees at the time of initial assignment to tasks where occupational exposure may occur (within 90 days after the effective date of the rule) and annually thereafter. (See Appendix 22-A for an example of an educational fact sheet for employees.) Training must include the following:

- access to a copy of the OSHA regulation and an explanation of its content
- a general explanation of the modes of transmission, epidemiology, and symptoms of blood-borne disease
- an explanation of the practices that will prevent or reduce exposure
- information on the types, proper use, location, removal, and disposal of personal protective equipment
- an explanation of the employment procedure to follow if an exposure incident occurs (see Exhibit 22-5)

Recordkeeping

Employers are required to maintain certain records for each employee, including the employee's HBV vaccination records and relevant medical records, as well as a copy of the results of examinations, medical testing, and follow-up procedures relating to any postexposure evaluation. All medical records must be kept confidential and retained for at least the duration of the employee's employment plus

30 years. Training session records, including the content, attendance, dates, and instructor names, must be maintained for a three-year period.

NOTES

1. Centers for Disease Control, Hepatitis B Virus: A Comprehensive Strategy for Eliminating Transmission in the United States through Universal Childhood Vaccination, *MMWR* 40(1991):RR-3.

2. Centers for Disease Control, Protection against Viral Hepatitis. Recommendations for the Immunization Practices Advisory Committee, *MMWR* 39(1990):RR-2.

SUGGESTED READING

McDermott, Will & Emery, *Health Law Update* 8, No. 26 (December 30, 1991).

Appendix 22-A

Sample Educational Fact Sheet for Employees

Safety Tips about Hepatitis B and the Human Immunodeficiency Virus *(excerpted from information provided by the Centers for Disease Control—Public Health Service Statement on the Management of Occupational Exposure to the human immunodeficiency virus and hepatitis B virus)*

- Consider all patients as potentially infected with blood-borne pathogens.
- Use Universal Precautions when working with blood, tissues, and fluids containing visible blood, semen, and vaginal secretions.
- Use Universal Precautions with CSF, synovial fluid, pleural fluid, peritoneal fluid, pericardial fluid, and amniotic fluid.
- Feces, nasal secretions, sputum, sweat, tears, urine, and vomitus do not require Universal Precautions unless they contain visible blood.
- Wear gloves where exposures to breast milk are frequent (e.g., breast milk banking).
- Use gloves when touching blood, body fluids requiring Universal Precautions, mucous membranes, or nonintact skin of all patients.
- Use gloves when handling items/surfaces soiled with blood or body fluids requiring Universal Precautions.
- Change gloves and wash hands between patients.
- Sterile gloves are used for contact with normally sterile areas of the body.
- Examination gloves are used for procedures not requiring sterile gloves.
- Do not wash/disinfect/reuse surgical or examination gloves.
- Use general purpose utility gloves for housekeeping, instrument cleaning, or decontamination.
- Wash hands and other skin surfaces immediately and thoroughly if contaminated with blood or other body fluids requiring Universal Precautions.
- Wash hands immediately after gloves are removed.
- When involved with invasive procedures, routinely use appropriate barrier precautions to prevent skin and mucous membrane contact with blood and other body fluids requiring Universal Precautions.
- Wear gloves and surgical masks for all invasive procedures.
- Wear protective eyewear/face shields during procedures likely to generate droplets of blood, other body fluids requiring Universal Precautions, or bone chips.
- Wear gowns or aprons during procedures likely to generate splashes of blood or other body fluids requiring Universal Precautions.
- Minimize mouth-to-mouth resuscitation. Mouthpieces, resuscitation bags, or other ventilation devices should be available for use in areas in which the need for resuscitation is predictable.
- Needles should not be recapped by hand, purposely bent or broken by hand, removed from disposable syringes, or otherwise manipulated by hand.
- After use, disposable needles and syringes, scalpel blades, and other sharps should be placed in a puncture-resistant container, located as close as practical to the use area.
- Large-bore reusable needles should be transported to reprocessing areas in puncture-resistant containers.
- Wear gloves and gown when handling placenta or infant until blood and amniotic fluid are removed from the infant's skin.
- Wear gloves when performing umbilical cord care.
- When cleaning spills of blood or other body fluids, use tuberculocidal hospital disinfectants.
- When cleaning inpatient areas, remove visible material, then decontaminate.
- Always wear gloves while cleaning or decontaminating.

- Occupational exposure is defined as:
  "An exposure that occurs during the performance of job duties that may place a worker at risk of HIV or HBV infection is defined as a percutaneous injury (e.g., a needlestick or cut with a sharp object), contact with mucous membrane, or contact with skin (especially when the exposed skin is chapped, abraded, or afflicted with dermatitis or the contact is prolonged or involving an extensive area) with blood, tissues, or other body fluids to which Universal Precautions apply, and laboratory specimens that contain HIV/HBV (e.g., suspensions of concentrated virus)."

chapter 23

Infectious and Hazardous Waste Management

James D. Knight

INTRODUCTION

As generators of infectious and hazardous waste products, hospitals are responsible for the safe and effective disposal of these products within the law. Probably few things can give a risk manager more cause for nightmares than the thought of some of the hospital's waste showing up in a public water supply or alongside a highway. This chapter is intended to offer the basic facts regarding waste products and their disposal in a manner that will keep both the risk manager and the hospital out of the courts and off the six o'clock news. Handling of waste products may not be a part of a risk manager's normal duties, but he or she should pay special attention to how it is being done. Risk management will get its share of the blame if things go wrong.

DEFINITION OF TERMS

The federal Environmental Protection Agency (EPA) provides specific definitions for various categories of waste products, including solid waste, medical waste, and infectious waste.

Solid Waste

Solid waste is defined by EPA as "discarded solid, liquid, semisolid, or contained gaseous material, among other materials."

Medical Waste

Medical waste is a subset of solid waste and is defined by EPA as "any solid waste which is generated in the diagnosis, treatment, or immunization of human beings or animals, in research pertaining thereto, or in the production or testing of biologicals. The term does not include any hazardous waste identified or listed under Subtitle C of the Resource Conservation and Recovery Act (P.L. 42 U.S.C. 3251), or any household waste as defined in regulations under Subtitle C."

Infectious Waste

Infectious waste is a subset of medical waste and generally falls into one of seven classes of waste as listed below:

1. *Cultures and stocks of infectious agents.* These include specimens from medical and pathology laboratories, discarded live and attenuated vaccines, wastes from the production of biologicals, and other laboratory wastes.
2. *Isolation wastes.* These include all waste coming from the room of a patient isolated to prevent the spread of a communicable disease, as defined by the Centers for Disease Control (CDC).
3. *Human blood and blood products.* All waste human blood and blood products, such as serum, plasma, and other blood components.
4. *Pathological wastes.* Tissues, organs, body parts, and body fluids. All pathological wastes should be considered infectious.

5. *Contaminated sharps.* All discarded sharps that have come into contact with infectious agents during use in patient care or in medical research should be considered infectious.
6. *Contaminated animal carcasses, body parts, and bedding.*
7. *Miscellaneous contaminated wastes.* Some waste products are not designated by EPA as infectious. Because of the potential hazards associated with these wastes, however, a determination to manage them as infectious should be made by a responsible party at the institution. This usually is the infection control committee. Miscellaneous wastes include:

- wastes from surgery and autopsy
- contaminated laboratory wastes
- dialysis unit wastes
- contaminated equipment

HISTORY OF LEGISLATION

In the United States, approximately 15 percent of the total waste stream of hospitals can be considered hazardous. It is estimated that approximately two pounds of hazardous or infectious waste are generated per day per patient. Increased legislation during recent years has forced hospitals to take more responsibility for the proper disposal of these wastes.

Congress enacted the Resource Conservation and Recovery Act (RCRA) in 1976. This was designed to control the flow of hazardous wastes from "cradle to grave."

In 1978 the EPA proposed comprehensive regulations under the Solid Waste Disposal Act, as amended by RCRA, for hazardous waste management. In this proposal, EPA proposed to classify certain infectious wastes as hazardous waste. This did not occur; however, in 1986 these regulations were published as a guidance document entitled *EPA Guide for Infectious Waste Management.*

In 1988 Congress enacted the Medical Waste Tracking Act (MWTA). This act amends the Solid Waste Disposal Act to require the administrator of the EPA to promulgate regulations on the management of infectious waste; it was signed into law on November 1, 1988.

As a result of this act, the EPA developed interim final rules that were published in the *Federal Register* on March 24, 1989. Although the MWTA affects only eight states as a pilot project, the rule developed by EPA took into consideration information acquired at public hearings on earlier proposed regulations. Therefore, it is considered by a number of experts to be indicative of future regulations.

As of this writing, Congress is planning future hearings on a national standard for the management of medical waste products.

INFECTIOUS WASTE

The possibility exists that infectious waste, as defined above, will create the most headaches for the new (or even experienced) risk manager. Because infectious waste, in the final analysis, is defined by each hospital within EPA and CDC guidelines, it varies from hospital to hospital. With the advent of "universal precautions" (Occupational Safety and Health Administration Enforcement Directive CPL 2.2.44), there will be a temptation to overclassify infectious waste.

The best option is to work closely with the hospital's infection control practitioner to establish a definition prior to going to the infection control committee. The costs of disposing infectious waste increase every year. New and creative ways of disposal must be found.

Infectious waste may be disposed of in any one of several ways that render it incapable of transmitting disease. The acceptable methods are:

- incineration
- steam sterilization
- irradiation

Although some states still allow landfill as a method of disposal, it is generally believed that this method will not be allowed much longer. During the past few years, incineration has been the most popular method of disposal. With most states adopting more stringent air quality laws, it is becoming more difficult to obtain permits for new incinerator facilities. If the hospital now operates its own incinerator, this is probably the best option to use.

Steam sterilization has become more popular recently. Several companies are marketing commercial-sized autoclaves, some in conjunction with roll-off containers. In this way, infectious waste can be sterilized and taken out with the regular waste stream to a landfill.

Transportation

If infectious waste is disposed of away from the hospital site, the risk manager must be aware of specific requirements for transportation. The federal government and most states have strict procedures for the packaging and transportation of infectious waste products. Most states require waste to be packaged in double plastic bags and then in puncture-resistant cartons. A check with the state regulatory agency is necessary to learn of any special requirements for handling the waste. The hospital's responsibility for the waste does not end when the transporter picks it up. Waste must be manifested and copies retained permanently. See Figure 23-1 for a view of the proper distribution of mani-

Figure 23-1
MANIFEST GENERATION AND DISTRIBUTION FOR USE IN TRANSPORTATION OF INFECTIOUS WASTE

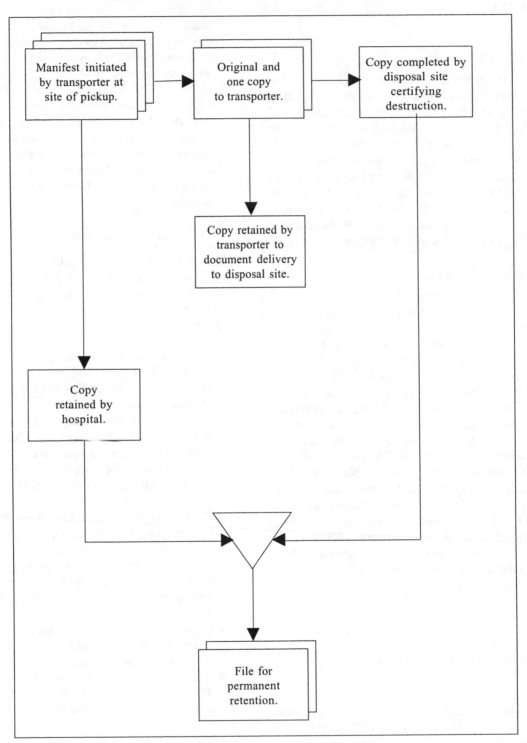

fests. A copy of a manifest that meets the requirements of the MWTA is attached as Appendix 23-A. Sample specifications for a transportation and disposal contract are attached as Appendix 23-B.

Collection

The collection process for infectious waste sets the tone for the entire waste management program. Waste should be collected on the department/unit level in distinctive containers marked with the universal biohazard symbol. The containers can range from red plastic bags to specially constructed waste cans with plastic inserts. Whatever the method of collection, the staff must be educated as to what goes into the containers. Otherwise, pizza boxes, birthday party leftovers, and many other items will be treated as infectious waste. At a disposal cost of 20 to 40 cents per pound, such items could become very expensive trash.

HAZARDOUS WASTE

Under RCRA, a material is a solid waste (whether it is in a solid, liquid, semisolid, or contained gaseous state) if it is no longer fit for its original intended use and must be disposed of or treated before it can be used again. A material is a hazardous waste if it meets the definition of a solid waste and is either RCRA-listed by source or by chemical name or demonstrates one or more of the following four characteristics: (1) ignitability, (2) corrosivity, (3) reactivity, or (4) extraction procedure (EP) toxicity. Some wastes are considered to be "acutely hazardous." These are wastes that the EPA has determined to be so dangerous in small amounts that they are regulated in the same manner as large amounts of other hazardous wastes. If the hospital generates more than 1 kg (2.2 pounds) of acutely hazardous waste in a calendar month or stores more than that amount for any period of time, it is subject to all of the regulations applying to generators that produce more than 1,000 kg of hazardous waste per calendar month.

Generator Categories

Conditionally Exempt Small-Quantity Generators

A conditionally exempt small-quantity generator (CE-SQG) produces less than 100 kg (220 pounds or 25 gallons) of hazardous waste or no more than 1 kg (2.2 pounds) of acutely hazardous waste per calendar month. This category of generator, as required by law, must conform to the following:

- Identify all hazardous waste generated each month.
- Never, at any time, accumulate more than 1,000 kg of hazardous waste or no more than 1 kg of acutely hazardous waste. The institution may accumulate hazardous waste on site until these levels are reached; at that time a 90-day disposal deadline begins.
- Dispose of its hazardous or acutely hazardous waste at an approved municipal landfill or toxic site dump facility (TSD). A CE-SQG is not required to obtain an EPA identification number or to use a manifest to track its disposed waste. However, it is highly recommended that the institution use the manifest system for its own liability protection and recordkeeping. A CE-SQG also has the option of treating or disposing of its hazardous waste on site without having to obtain a TSD facility permit.

Small-Quantity Generators

A small-quantity generator (SQG) produces 100 to 1,000 kg (220 to 2,200 pounds or 25 gallons to 300 gallons) of hazardous waste or no more than 1 kg of acutely hazardous waste per calendar month. The law requires an SQG to conform to the following:

- Identify all hazardous waste generated each month.
- Obtain an EPA identification number.
- Store no more than 6,000 kg of hazardous waste or 1 kg of acutely hazardous waste on site for up to 180 days, or for up to 270 days if the waste must be shipped to a TSD facility that is located over 200 miles away. If these time or quantity limits are exceeded, the SQG will be considered a storage facility. It must then obtain an RCRA storage permit and meet all the necessary storage requirements.
- Store hazardous wastes in 55-gallon metal drums, tanks, or other containers suitable for the storage and transport of the type of waste generated.
- Label, mark, or placard each package, drum, or other container in accordance with applicable Department of Transportation (DOT) regulations under 49 CFR Part 172.
- Prepare a manifest before transporting, or offering for transportation, any hazardous waste for off-site treatment, storage, or disposal.
- Retain a copy of each manifest signed by the designated TSD facility for at least three years from the date the waste was accepted by the initial transporter.

Generators

An institution that generates more than 1,000 kg of hazardous waste or more than 1 kg of acutely hazardous waste in any calendar month is required to conform to the following:

- Identify all hazardous waste generated each month.
- Obtain an EPA identification number.
- Accumulate hazardous waste on site for no more than 90 days, unless the institution is granted an extension to the 90-day period. A generator who accumulates hazardous waste for more than 90 days is considered an operator of a storage facility and is subject to the requirements of 40 CFR Parts 264, 265, and 270.
- Store hazardous wastes in 55-gallon metal drums, tanks, or other containers suitable for the storage and transport of the type of waste generated.
- Label, mark, or placard each package, drum, or other container in accordance with applicable DOT regulations under 49 CFR Part 172.
- Prepare a manifest before transporting, or offering for transportation, any hazardous waste for off-site treatment, storage, or disposal.
- Retain a copy of each manifest signed by the designated TSD facility for at least three years from the date the waste was accepted by the initial waste transporter.
- Prepare and submit a biennial report covering the generator's hazardous waste activities for the two previous calendar years, including the following information:

  - the generator's EPA identification number, name, and address
  - the calendar years covered by the report
  - the EPA identification number, name, and address of each off-site TSD facility used during the report year
  - the name and EPA identification number of each transporter used during the report years
  - a description of each hazardous waste shipment to an off-site facility that includes the EPA hazardous waste number, the DOT hazard class, and the quantity of each hazardous waste shipped
  - the EPA Form 8700–13A certification signed by the generator or authorized representative

Planning for Emergencies

When an institution generates hazardous waste and accumulates it on site, it must take necessary precautions and steps to prevent any sudden or accidental release of the waste to the environment. Careful operation and maintenance of the responsible department are imperative to reduce the possibility of fire, explosion, or release of hazardous waste, including infectious waste. Appropriate types of emergency equipment are required for the kinds of hazardous waste handled at the site. Arrangements should be made with local officials to ensure that they can respond to any potential emergency. To accomplish these tasks effectively, the institution must develop and practice a contingency plan that attempts to foresee and prepare for any accidents that could possibly occur.

Good Housekeeping

Effective hazardous and infectious waste management can be thought of simply as "good housekeeping." The following practices are recommended:

- using and reusing materials as much as possible
- recycling and reclaiming wastes
- treating waste to reduce its hazards
- reducing the amount of waste generated (this practice also means savings in raw material costs and capital expenditures for management and disposal of hazardous waste)

SOURCES OF WASTE

Virtually every clinical area of a hospital produces a waste product that is either hazardous or infectious or both. In constructing a waste management plan, it is necessary to survey each of these areas to see what it contains. Generally, the largest generators of infectious waste are the operating rooms and labor and delivery areas. The primary generators of hazardous materials are the laboratories, but the maintenance shops and research areas should not be overlooked.

CONCLUSION

A final word about disposal is in order. Whatever the method of disposal, on site or off, it should be checked periodically to ensure that waste is disposed of in a manner appropriate for its type. The risk manager should inspect incinerator sites and off-site areas such as landfills to determine if the waste is being handled correctly.

"Gotchas"

Three "gotchas" should be remembered by the risk manager who wants to be successful in this field:

1. Waste management in the medical field is becoming big business. Each day a new company starts up to get a "piece of the action." Many of these companies are reputable and efficient, but many are not. It should be

kept in mind that many pitfalls exist for the unwary. Violation of federal and state laws and regulations carry civil and monetary penalties that are consistently applied. References and background of any company that wants to do business in this field should be carefully investigated.

2. Ignorance of the law, as they say, is no excuse. Become familiar with RCRA, MWTA, and all other applicable laws, rules, and guidelines. Most of these are a guaranteed cure for insomnia, but they can keep the institution and risk manager out of trouble.

3. An effective waste management plan requires continuous monitoring. The risk manager may become known as a pest, but that is often needed to keep ahead of the problems that can crop up periodically without notice. Before contracting with a disposal company, it is a good idea to inspect visually every phase of its operation. The same applies to transportation companies. If possible, the risk manager should ride along with them to see how waste is handled. If anything appears to be wrong, it should be checked by the local regulatory agency.

Appendix 23-A

Medical Waste Tracking Form

American Medical Transport

Medical Waste Manifest

1. Manifest Number

INSTRUCTIONS FOR COMPLETING MEDICAL WASTE TRACKING FORM

Copy 1 — GENERATOR COPY:	WHITE
Copy 2 — DESTINATION FACILITY COPY:	CANARY
Copy 3 — TRANSPORTER COPY:	PINK
Copy 4 — GENERATOR COPY:	GOLD

As required under 40 CFR Part 259:

1. This mulit-copy (4-Page) shipping document must accompany each shipment of regulated medical waste generated in a Covered State.

2. Items numbered 1-14, must be completed before the generator can sign the certification. Item 23 must be completed by the destination facility.

For assistance in completing this form, contact your nearest State office, Regional EPA office, or call (800) 424-9346.

GENERATOR

2. Generator's Name and Mailing Address

3. Telephone Number (   )

4. Transporter's Name and Mailing Address

5. Telephone Number (   )

7. Contact Person

6. EPA Med. Waste ID No.

8. Destination Facility Name and Address

9. Telephone Number (   )

10. State Permit or ID No.

11. US EPA Waste Description

12. Total No. Containers

13. Total Weight or Volume

14. Special Handling Instructions and Additional Information

15. Generator's Certification:

Under penalty of criminal and civil prosecution for the making or submission of false statements. representations, or omissions, I declare on behalf of the generator that the contents of this consignment are fully and accurately described above and are classified, packaged, marked and labeled in accordance with all applicable State and Federal laws and regulations, and that I have been authorized in writing to make such declarations by the person in charge of the generator's operation.

Printed/Typed Name   Signature   Date

TRANSPORTER

16. Transporter 1 (Certification of Receipt of Medical Waste as described in items 11, 12, & 13)

Printed/Typed Name   Signature   Date

17. Transporter 2 or Intermediate Handler (name and address)

18. Telephone Number (   )

19. EPA Med. Waste ID No.

20. Contact Person

21. Transporter 2 or Intermediate Handler (Certification of Receipt of Medical Waste as described in items 11, 12 & 13)

Printed/Typed Name   Signature   Date

22. New Manifest Number (for consolidated or remanifested waste)

DESTINATION

23. Destination Facility (Certification of Receipt of Medical Waste as described in items 11, 12, & 13)

☐ Received in accordance with items 11, 12, & 13

Printed/Typed Name   Signature   Date

(If other than destination facility, indicate address, phone, and permit or ID no. in box 14)

24. Discrepancy Box (Any discrepancies should be noted by item number and initials)

Source: Courtesy of American Medical Transport, Tulsa, OK.

Sample Transportation and Disposal Contract for Biomedical Waste

Contract Period: _____ through _____.

    This contract shall be in force until expiration date or until 30 days after notice has been given by the _____ of its desire to terminate the contract. After the first six months of this contract the vendor may cancel with a 30-day written notice.

    This contract is for an indefinite quantity and the _____ may, or may not, buy the quantity mentioned. Vendor must clear all shipments with agency prior to shipping any portion of the contract.

* * * * PLEASE READ THE SPECIFICATIONS VERY CAREFULLY * * * *

1. Pickup, transportation, and disposal by incineration of hospital infectious waste. Price per pound _____
    Estimated amount of waste: _____ lbs. per year
2. Shipping containers and liners for infectious waste. Price each _____
    Estimated number of containers _____

SPECIFICATIONS

    1. The contractor shall collect, remove from the _____ property, and properly incinerate all "Biomedical Waste" generated by the _____. Incineration shall be in accordance with all applicable federal, state, and municipal regulations, laws, and ordinances in an incinerator that is approved by the locality in which it is situated for the incineration of biomedical waste as defined below. Pickup shall be on a schedule mutually agreeable to both parties, but not less than three times weekly, and shall be at sites designated by the _____.

Biomedical wastes shall include those wastes:

    A. Defined by the United States Environmental Protection Agency as infectious wastes and any other waste identified as infectious or similar wastes in any other applicable federal, state, county, or municipal laws, regulations, or guidelines, and

    B. Chemotherapy waste (also known as antineoplastic or cytotoxic waste). The term chemotherapy waste means those discarded items that have been contaminated by chemotherapeutic drugs.

    2. The containers provided for the collection and transportation of biomedical waste products shall conform in all respects to all federal, state, and local requirements. Containers shall be constructed of cardboard or fiberboard of no less than 200-lb test with a "B" flute and moisture-resistant adhesive. Containers shall have minimum dimensions of $17^7/_8"$ × $14^7/_8"$ × $20^7/_8"$. Containers shall have a positive locking feature when closed and shall also have lifting handles formed as an integral part of the container. The container shall have the international biohazard symbol printed on each side in red. A liner shall be provided with each container, said liner to be red in color and be constructed of 3-mil plastic. Liners shall be of the 30-gallon size.

    3. The contractor shall assume title to all biomedical waste collected from the _____ and shall hold the _____ and the State of _____ harmless for accidental spillage once the material is picked up by the contractor.

    4. The contractor will provide all equipment and supplies necessary to provide the services described above. All equipment and supplies will conform in all respects to all applicable federal, state, county, and municipal laws and regulations pertaining to the collection and disposal of biomedical waste products. The contractor will obtain, keep current, and provide copies of all necessary licenses, permits, and other documents that may be required by any federal, state, county, or municipal jurisdiction. A copy of the permit to operate for any and all incinerators to be used must be furnished to the _____ prior to the award of the contract.

5. The contractor shall procure and maintain the following insurance coverages and limits for the duration and purpose of the agreement:

    A. Workers' compensation.

    B. Employer's liability—$100,000 each occurrence.

    C. Comprehensive general liability (including contractual liability)—$1,000,000 each occurrence.

    D. Comprehensive automobile liability—$1,000,000 each occurrence.

    E. Environmental impairment insurance—as required by applicable law or regulation. Current certificates of insurance will be provided to the _____ upon request.

6. The contractor will indemnify and hold _____ harmless from any and all loss, damages, suits, penalties, costs, liabilities, and expenses arising out of any claim for loss or damage to property including property of the _____ employees, caused by or resulting from the contractor's negligence or willful misconduct or breach of agreement.

7. The contractor will comply with all applicable laws, regulations, and rules regarding documentation of transportation and disposal of biomedical waste, and will provide the _____ with certification of incineration of all waste products accepted by the contractor within seven (7) days of date of pickup by the transporter.

8. The price bid by the contractor shall be expressed on a per-pound basis and shall include all pickup, transportation, and incineration of biomedical waste according to a schedule as defined by the _____ and all equipment and supplies (less containers and liners) necessary to accomplish same.

9. No preprinted contract will be considered. Any amendments to the above specifications may be negotiated prior to the award of contract.

10. A sample of the box and liner and a copy of the incinerator permit/license heretofore referred to shall be provided by bidder and must be received in the Risk Management Office of the _____ for approval by the _____ by noon on _____, a date which is four (4) working days prior to the closing date of the bid.

chapter 24

Preparing for the Risks of Tomorrow's Technology

Frank Dodero

INTRODUCTION

Although most health professionals use modern technological devices in their everyday lives, very few of them may understand how the devices actually work. The relationship is based on a combination of faith and familiarity. The user has faith in the ability of a device to perform if it is used and maintained properly and is familiar with the purpose and expected outcome.

This being the case, one can imagine the loss of control experienced by a person entering the health care arena where unbelievable and unfamiliar technological devices and tests are used by others to diagnose and treat patients and, often, to save lives. In addition to the fear generated by this loss of control, the ever-increasing use of high-tech devices and tests may have a tendency to erode the already fragile health care provider–patient relationship by reducing the amount of time spent in delivering "hands-on" care and building personal trust—an element most risk managers would agree is essential to reducing liability exposure in the event of an adverse outcome.

Given this set of circumstances and the inherent risks associated with the use of modern medical technology, it is vitally important that all health care entities carefully evaluate their current risk management and quality assurance protocols to determine whether they will be effective in preventing potential losses while managing those that do occur.

This chapter examines the liability exposure associated with the use of modern medical technology and discusses various types of advancing technology and how to keep pace with the risks. It also focuses on how institutions involved in clinical research may protect and progress at the same time and offers a brief look at current governmental reporting requirements.

LIABILITY EXPOSURE ASSOCIATED WITH THE USE OF MODERN MEDICAL TECHNOLOGY

Modern medical technology, for the purpose of this chapter, is defined as all medical devices and tests used in the diagnosis, monitoring, and treatment of disease.

Liability for modern medical technology-related occurrences may arise in a number of ways. The causes of potential liability in the following list differ, but almost all of them are based on the theory of negligence:

- misdiagnosis or failure to diagnose[1]
- provision of defective equipment
- misuse of equipment
- absence of appropriate equipment
- improper selection of equipment or test
- improper inspection, maintenance, or repair of equipment
- lack of informed consent

Negligence-Related Liability

To be successful in a negligence suit, the plaintiff must prove four essential elements: (1) that a duty was owed, (2) that a duty owed was breached, (3) that an injury occurred, and (4) that the duty breached was the proximate cause of the injury that occurred.

In proving that a duty was owed, the plaintiff must first establish that the use of certain technology to diagnose, monitor, or treat a specific medical condition was or should have been applied in accordance with the required standard of care. Second, the plaintiff must prove that the defendant committed a breach of the duty owed by deviating from the applicable standard of care through either commission (i.e., the technology used was appropriate but defective or misused, or the results were misinterpreted) or omission (i.e., the appropriate technology was never used). Third, the plaintiff must show that actual harm was suffered or an injury occurred. Finally, the plaintiff must prove that the defendant's breach was the proximate cause of the harm or injury.

A health care entity can be held liable for negligence based on one of two legal theories: (1) respondeat superior, which states that an employer is held legally responsible for the acts of an employee while working within the scope of his or her employment, or (2) corporate liability, which states that a health care entity owes an independent legal duty of care directly to the patient.

Respondeat Superior

Prior to the loss of charitable immunity, nonprofit health care entities, such as hospitals, invoked the "borrowed servant" legal doctrine. This doctrine states that when an employee of one employer is loaned to another employer, that special employer becomes liable for the employee's actions under the theory of respondeat superior. The same is true with the "captain of the ship" doctrine, an outgrowth of the borrowed servant doctrine, that is generally applied to surgeons. It is based on the rationale that the surgeon has the power to supervise and control the work of the operating room team. However, now that charitable immunity has been eliminated in most jurisdictions, the health care entity is almost always held liable when nurses, pharmacists, technicians, and technologists are responsible, or, in some cases, just involved in a technology-related adverse occurrence.

Corporate Liability

Under the corporate liability doctrine, the health care entity has a legal duty to observe certain standards. In the past, corporate liability was limited to such activities as providing appropriate supplies, equipment, and facilities. Today, however, a health care entity can be held negligent for improperly selecting, credentialing, reviewing, and evaluating the competency of its physicians. In other words, if the misdiagnosis of a patient is based on the results of an ultrasound, the patient may claim that the health care entity was negligent in granting clinical privileges related to the use of such equipment without adequate evidence of the physician's competency.[2]

Products Liability

In addition to negligence-related liability, health care entities in the business of supplying medical products or inventing new diagnostic or therapeutic technology must be concerned with products liability. An allegation invoking a strict liability most often relates to injuries that result from defective products. There are three bases on which a patient can maintain a product liability action. The first pertains to the product's design as unreasonably dangerous. The second is a manufacturing claim, in which the patient may allege that the material used to produce the product was faulty or that an error took place in the manufacturing process. Third, a patient may claim that he or she did not receive adequate warnings (i.e., informed consent) or instructions regarding the dangers or proper use of the product.[3]

ADVANCING TECHNOLOGY—KEEPING PACE WITH THE RISKS

A report in *Hospitals* listed several key clinical services that will be dramatically changed by new technology. These include cardiology, women's health, oncology, orthopedics, and neurology (see Exhibit 24-1).[4]

Because this chapter could not possibly focus on the individual risks associated with each of these technological advances, general risks related to all therapeutic and diagnostic technology are discussed, with specific devices and tests cited as examples.

Therapeutic medical technology is used to alter a patient's physiological functions from a state of illness to one of wellness. Diagnostic medical technology is used to obtain patient data through monitoring, gathering information, manipulating, and displaying. Despite these differences, both types of technologies have potential risks associated with their use.

Occurrences Related to Direct Injury

All technological devices and tests, although varying in degree, present the risk of direct injury through side effects. Injury suffered in this fashion can be caused by mechanical energy, thermal energy, electrical energy, electromagnetic energy, or the material used.[5] For example, a patient undergoes radiation treatment with a linear accelerator and receives a radiation overdose (electromagnetic energy via x-rays) attributed to a software flaw; he later dies of his

Exhibit 24-1
NEW DEVELOPMENTS IN KEY CLINICAL SERVICES

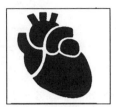

More developments in cardiology

- A larger array of sophisticated drugs to manage hypertension is becoming available.
- Pacemakers that allow wearers to exercise will become more common.
- Heart-lung transplants will become less risky and more common.
- Magnetic resonance imaging (MRI) of the heart will be developed in three years at the latest. 3-D coronary MRI will achieve the resolution to allow noninvasive angiography in the next three to five years.
- Stents—little springs—will be left in an artery to keep plaque pushed against the vessel wall. About 30 percent of balloon angioplasties fail because plaque falls back into the artery from the artery wall.

More developments in women's health

- Vaginal ultrasound may replace abdominal ultrasound in early pregnancy and gynecology exams because the uterus, fallopian tubes, and ovaries are more clearly visualized.
- More accurate, earlier birth-defect tests will enable women over the high-risk age of 35 to have children.
- At least one new intrauterine device (IUD) will be introduced. Physicians now believe that the reason IUDs failed was because of sexually transmitted diseases, not poor product design.
- Female birth control will be administered through injections every three months.
- Embryo freezing and thawing techniques, which should increase in use, will allow more attempts at pregnancy per IVF cycle and perhaps reduce labor costs.

More developments in oncology

- Tests to screen for some malignancies or premalignancies in an individual will be possible in three to five years.
- Though not a revolutionary advance, scientists are continuing to learn how to better pinpoint radiation therapy on a cancer. Proton beam radiation, a $10 million technology being attempted at Loma Linda (CA) University Medical Center, will remain a major strategic investment by only a few academic institutions unless it shows a major benefit.
- Magnetic resonance imaging will become more important in cancer imaging because of its ability to show biochemical changes in tumors and to show whether particular agents are affecting tumors.

- The trend to implantable therapeutic devices is shown in three areas: implantable infusion pumps for chemotherapy, interstitial placement of radium implants directly into tumors, and surgical insertion of hyperthermia needles to apply heat therapy more precisely.
- Patient-controlled analgesia devices will grow in use, allowing cancer patients to self-administer pain killers as needed, within limits programmed into the pump.
- Another underlying opportunity as cancer patients survive longer is rehabilitation services to meet the needs of those with long-term disabilities as a result of aggressive therapies.

continues

Exhibit 24–1 continued

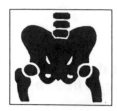

More developments in orthopedics

- Concerning the continuing debate on cemented versus cementless attachment of hip prostheses, experts predict that the long-term trend will be away from use of cement in all cases where it is not imperative.
- Expect developments in bone lengthening. The Ilizeroff technique invented in Russia, using external fixater pins, may have a "tremendous role" in filling in the spaces left after bone cancer surgery and in correcting deformities that would otherwise require amputation. Also, artificial bones and drugs for stimulating bone growth will be used in face reconstruction and elsewhere.

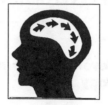

More developments in neurology

- There will be a greater interest in neurologic and neurovascular rehabilitation as the number of head-trauma survivors rises and as the number of neurological infirmities increases with the aging population.
- Because of malpractice concerns, the United States will continue to convert to nonionic, low-osmolar contrast agents used in brain and spine imaging, even though they are 6 to 18 times more expensive than ionic agents, according to BBI. As a side note, Blue Cross of California has recently begun to reimburse for the use of nonionic agents in high-risk patients and the elderly. A new and less expensive generation of nonionic agents will probably not be available for at least two years, according to the AHA's *Technology Scanner* periodical.

Source: Reprinted from *Hospitals*, Vol. 62, No. 10, pp. 56–61, with permission of American Hospital Publishing Company, © 1988.

---

injuries.[6] Another example is the patient with World War II shrapnel, a ferromagnetic object, imbedded in his thigh who undergoes a magnetic resonance imaging scan and suffers an injury from the projectile effect that involves the forceful attraction of ferromagnetic and mechanical energy.[7]

In the case of injury related to the materials used, a current discussion pertains to the use of conventional versus low-osmolality radiopaque contrast media and the results of a report recently concluded by the University Hospital Consortium's Technology Advancement Center (Exhibit 24-2).

Occurrences Related to the Misinterpretation of Data

Misinterpretation of data can occur even when suitable diagnostic or monitoring technology has been appropriately applied and the information obtained or displayed correctly. In such cases, the clinician's actions, education, training, and conscientiousness will be evaluated and compared with those of other medical professionals.[8]

To illustrate, all high-risk mothers in labor are monitored by electronic fetal monitors, yet how well trained are the personnel responsible for interpreting the tracings? The

same may be true for the patient in an intensive cardiac care unit whose life depends on the accurate interpretation of numerous high-tech monitoring devices (e.g., cardiac telemetry, Swan-Ganz catheter readings). Another consideration involves the risk and potential liability of misinterpretation in genetic testing.

Occurrences Related to the Malperformance of Technology

The malperformance of diagnostic, and in some cases therapeutic, technology can be divided into two types. The first is technology that is obviously nonfunctional—the data or results are nonexistent or unbelievable. The second type of malperformance occurs when the diagnostic output is believable but incorrect with respect to the patient's true condition.

Obviously Nonfunctional Technology

Three categories of adverse patient outcomes can occur from this type of malperformance. First, therapeutic results that are nonexistent because of a nonfunctioning device or treatment may be first attributed to nonresponsiveness,

Exhibit 24-2
CONCLUSIONS OF REPORT ON CONVENTIONAL
VERSUS LOW-OSMOLALITY RADIOPAQUE CONTRAST MEDIA

The report concludes that:

- Any preference for either conventional or low-osmolality agent must be based on considerations of safety, rather than efficacy.
- Randomized, controlled studies in small numbers of patients have demonstrated low-osmolality agents to be better tolerated by patients (i.e., less pain and heat sensation) but have *not* established meaningful differences in the incidence of other common and important adverse effects.
- Large-scale, well-controlled, randomized clinical trials have not been performed to assess adequately the relative safety of conventional and low-osmolality agents with regard to severe or life-threatening adverse reactions.
- Large-scale surveillance studies performed in several countries suggest that the adverse effects with the use of low-osmolality agents are approximately five times less likely than adverse effects with the use of conventional agents. The absolute difference in the percentage of patients with severe

side effects in these studies, however, is very small. Conclusions drawn from all these studies are controversial because of the manner in which they were conducted, and thus their significant potential for bias.

- More work needs to be done to identify true "high-risk" patients and to discover whether use of low-osmolality agents in these patients is, indeed, safer than use of conventional agents.
- With the exception of myelography, where use of selected low-osmolality contrast media is the accepted standard of practice, the data available to date do not allow a definitive assessment of the relative or absolute risks of conventional or low-osmolality media based either on the route or injection (intra-arterial versus intravenous) or on the type of procedure performed.
- With increased utilization of the low-osmolality media, adverse effects (e.g., delayed rashes, thromboembolic complications) with the nonionic low-osmolality agents have been identified that occur at a higher frequency with these agents than observed previously with use of the conventional media.

Source: Courtesy of University Hospital Consortium, Oak Brook, IL.

---

thereby delaying effective care. Second, to the degree that a physician would have acted on the basis of the desired diagnostic information, a technological failure to provide that information represents a breakdown in the overall quality of care. Third, the nonfunctioning of emergency or on-line monitoring devices may divert attention away from the patient to the equipment and thus directly interfere with and delay necessary intervention.

Believable but Incorrect Diagnostic Output

This particular type of malperformance can result from the equipment itself, the technique with which it is applied, or a combination of the two. Any action that is taken or not taken on the basis of incorrect information may result in an adverse patient outcome.[9]

Occurrences Related to Inappropriate Usage

All therapeutic and diagnostic devices and tests have limitations. When a device or test is used for a purpose for which it has not been sufficiently proved or is otherwise inappropriate or inadequate, adverse outcomes may occur.[10]

Occurrences Related to In Vitro Fertilization and Genetic Manipulation

The age of technology can now assist humans in shaping their own biological futures. Such technological advancements, however, are not without risks.[11-13] Many of these risks are probably still unknown, but some are readily apparent or at least predictable.

Diagnosis through genetic testing poses a minimum of two predictable risks. First, with the ability to prenatally diagnose many disorders, is a health care entity obligated to offer each and every test? Second, the health care entity must consider the liability it would incur if a patient's confidentiality concerning genetic test results is breached. If this occurs, certain individuals may be found unemployable or uninsurable and, as a result, hold the health care entity responsible.

In vitro fertilization, in particular involving surrogate parenting, presents a different set of risks. In some cases, in vitro fertilization results in the destruction of early embryos. This is a sensitive issue for right-to-life advocates that may lead to future litigation. Surrogate parenting usually is arranged through a legal agreement, which should be well thought out and expertly devised beforehand. If it is not, subsequent legal action may result.

Keeping Pace with the Risks

Although the risks and resultant occurrences may differ among various settings, implementation of the following ten recommendations can reduce and control a health care entity's liability associated with advanced technology:

1. Establish a multidisciplinary committee to evaluate the purchase and use of all biomedical equipment and other biotechnology.
2. Review thoroughly all contracts with both manufacturers and independent contractors. The health care entity should assume responsibility only for the misuse of a product or for using it in a way not intended by the manufacturer. Any contract that limits the manufacturer's liability or includes a hold harmless clause should be examined carefully.[14]
3. Educate and train all personnel appropriately in the purposes and use of biomedical equipment. In addition to primary orientation, periodic in-service education is necessary.
4. Develop specific written policies on all biomedical equipment that govern when and how it is used and who should be involved in its use (see Appendix 24–A for a sample protocol).
5. Develop a comprehensive biomedical preventive maintenance program that includes
   - equipment utilization in-service training for all employees and, when necessary, patients and family members
   - a documented maintenance and repair tracking system
   - written procedures for recalling equipment in the event of failure or malperformance (this policy should include a statement directing those involved not to notify the manufacturer)
6. Establish a control point through which all information, including both external and internal risk data, must flow. External sources of information include medical and technical literature, manufacturers, the FDA/USP Device Experience Network and Medical Device Reporting Regulations, and insurance company reports (see Exhibit 24-3). Internal sources of information include occurrence reporting and investigation and quality assurance reports.[15]
7. Develop a comprehensive and meaningful informed consent policy that should be invoked prior to the use of all diagnostic and therapeutic devices or tests with potentially hazardous side effects. While not yet a common practice, it has been suggested that all consent forms be written in plain and simple language.[16]
8. Evaluate the processes used in granting physician privileges. Specific requirements for each type of technology should be developed and adhered to.
9. Remind physicians, nurses, and other front-line users that the interpretation of diagnostic data or therapeutic results must always be considered in the context of the overall patient situation. Corroborating information, when obtainable, is also important.
10. Develop guidelines that address how malperforming technology should be documented in the medical record.

Documentation of Malperforming Technology

Considerable controversy exists over whether an equipment or product malperformance should be documented in the medical record. As always, there are two schools of thought. The first, favoring medical record documentation, states that documenting an injury caused by equipment or product malperformance may help to protect the health care professional from liability for negligence and preserves evidence of the professional person's observations made at the time of the injury. In some cases, it also may be necessary to document the malperformance because it relates to patient care. For example, if a respirator is not functioning properly, it is medically important to distinguish between the effects of the malperformance versus patient pathology when interpreting the resultant abnormality in the blood gases.

The second school of thought, discouraging medical record documentation, states that by documenting an equipment or product malperformance the record may support a product liability action against the manufacturer. If this action proceeds, the health care professional is likely to be drawn into the litigation by the manufacturer in an attempt to prove that the injury was caused by negligence rather than an equipment or product malperformance. The manufacturer may attempt to establish negligence by showing that the health care professional failed to inspect or maintain the equipment or product or to follow the manufacturer's instructions when using the equipment or product.

This author recommends that a malperformance related to patient care be documented in the patient's record. However, the health care professional should not describe the *cause* of a malperformance or *allege* that a defect exists. Such information is outside the health care professional's expertise and is better left to a qualified engineer or biomedical expert. Objective documentation of what has been perceived or observed should be included in the record and nothing else.

Exhibit 24-3
SOURCES FOR MEDICAL EQUIPMENT INFORMATION

American Society of Hospital Engineering (Membership: $75/year with institutional membership in American Hospital Association, $105/year without AHA membership)
Clinical Engineering Section
875 North Michigan Ave.
Chicago, IL 60611
(312) 280-6101

Association for the Advancement of Medical Instrumentation (Membership: $110/year)
3330 Washington Blvd., 4th Floor
Arlington, VA 22201
(800) 332-2264

Accreditation Manual for Hospitals ($60)
BTSM Series ($30 each; $125 initial subscription; $85/year renewal)
Joint Commission on Accreditation of Healthcare Organizations
875 North Michigan Ave.
Chicago, IL 60611
(312) 642-6061

Biomedical Safety & Standards (Newsletter, $124/year)
The Guide to Biomedical Standards ($24)
Quest Publishing
1351 Titan Way
Brea, CA 92621
(714) 738-6400

Device Experience Network Monthly Report ($150/year for paper copy)
National Technical Information Service
Springfield, VA 22161
(703) 487-4630
(To report an equipment problem, call the USP's Problem Reporting Program at (800) 638-6725; in Maryland, call (301) 881-0256 collect.)

FDA Enforcement Report ($44/year)
Superintendent of Documents
U.S. Government Printing Office
Washington, DC 20402

"Health Device System" including *Health Devices* and *Health Devices Alerts* ($1350/year), BMEDSS ($35/hour, plus $10/hour for selected databases for Health Device System members, $25/hour for nonmembers)
ECRI (Emergency Care Research Institute)
5200 Butler Pike
Plymouth Meeting, PA 19462
(215) 825-6000

Medical Electronics ($22/year)
Measurements and Data Corp.
2994 W. Liberty Ave.
Pittsburgh, PA 15216
(412) 343-9666

Product SOS ($285—hospital discount price)
Medical Device Register, Inc.
655 Washington Blvd.
Stamford, CT 06901
(203) 348-6319

Source: Reprinted from *Journal of Clinical Engineering*, Vol. 14, No. 2, pp. 113-119, with permission of Quest Publishing Company, © 1989.

Following a patient injury from an equipment or product malfunction or defect, the risk management office is notified. In addition, a patient occurrence incident report form is completed so that appropriate quality assurance and quality improvement processes can be initiated.

It is important that the malperforming equipment or product involved in the occurrence be removed and secured for later inspection.

CLINICAL RESEARCH—HOW TO PROTECT AND PROGRESS AT THE SAME TIME

Without clinical research, the development of new technology for diagnostic and therapeutic purposes could not move forward. At the point where basic science and clinical research meet, the fear of liability often threatens innovation. A new drug or device developed in the laboratory must be clinically tested, and this means that patients must be willing to accept the risk of adverse outcomes. Although society as a whole is willing to accept a controlled level of risk to ensure continued advances in clinical practice, it has not moved to compensate patients for adverse outcomes outside of litigation. In so protecting individual patients on a case-by-case basis, the courts may unintentionally be placing society at risk by inadvertently supporting a reduced pace of innovation.[17]

Certain practices, however, can help to minimize the risk of liability to the health care entity involved in clinical research.

Consent for Innovative Therapy

A diagnostic or therapeutic procedure that deviates from an accepted approach may be recommended to a patient if the physician believes that this innovation offers advantages over the standard procedure, but the new procedure may require an informed consent more stringent than for customary therapies. When informed consent has not been properly carried out, court decisions have tended to hold medical innovators to a standard of strict liability for adverse outcomes.

It also is recommended that the use of any innovative procedure conform with the health care entity's research standards (e.g., approval by an institutional review board) and include a negotiated consent indicating that the procedure is being performed, at least in part, with research intent.[18] (See Appendix 24-B for a sample informed consent document.)

Institutional Review Board

The federal government has promulgated guidelines for the establishment of institutional review boards (IRBs) in an attempt to minimize the risk to research subjects and to ensure the quality of studies performed. An IRB must have at least five members of varying backgrounds. At least one member must be from a nonscientific area and at least one from outside the institution. Research that involves minimal risks (those ordinarily encountered in daily life or during the performance of routine physical or psychological examinations or tests) may be approved by the chairperson alone. All other research must be approved by the full IRB, which must determine that the following seven criteria will be satisfied:

1. Risks to subjects are minimized.
2. Risks to subjects are reasonable in relation to anticipated benefits, if any, to the subjects and the importance of the knowledge that may reasonably be expected to result.
3. Selection of subjects is equitable.
4. Informed consent will be sought.
5. Informed consent will be appropriately documented.
6. Where appropriate, the research plan makes adequate provision for monitoring the data collected to insure the safety of subjects.
7. Where appropriate, adequate provisions are made to protect the privacy of subjects and maintain the confidentiality of data.[19]

As stated in items 4 and 5 above, informed consent must be obtained. In obtaining informed consent, the prospective patient/subject must be provided with the following:

- a statement that the study involves research, an explanation of the purposes of the research and expected duration of the subject's participation, a description of the procedures to be followed, and identification of any procedures that are experimental
- a description of any reasonably foreseeable risk or discomforts to the subject
- a description of any benefits to the subject or to others that may be reasonably expected from the research
- a disclosure of appropriate alternative procedures or courses of treatment, if any, that might be advantageous to the subject
- a statement describing the extent, if any, to which confidentiality of records identifying the subject will be maintained
- for research involving more than minimal risk, an explanation as to whether any compensation and any medical treatments are available if injury occurs and, if so, what they consist of or where further information may be obtained
- Information about how to contact the appropriate person for answers to pertinent questions about the research and the research subject's rights and who to contact in the event of a research-related injury to the subject
- a statement that participation is voluntary, refusal to participate will involve no penalty or loss of benefits to which the subject is otherwise entitled, and the subject may discontinue participation at any time without penalty or loss of benefits to which the subject is otherwise entitled.[20]

Other Recommendations

Each health care entity should establish a policy and procedure that addresses research protocols. Those institutions involved in corporate-sponsored research should negotiate for protective clauses in their agreements.[21]

REPORTING OF DEATHS AND SERIOUS INJURIES AND ILLNESSES ASSOCIATED WITH MEDICAL DEVICES

In November 1990, the federal government enacted the Safe Medical Devices Act, which had a significant impact on health care entities. Effective November 29, 1991, the law required the reporting of all deaths or serious injuries and illnesses associated with medical devices to either the Food and Drug Administration (FDA) or to the manufacturer of the device within ten days of the incident. The purpose of reporting is to improve the

FDA's ability to identify and track medical device problems.

Health care entities should continue to report problems associated with medical devices to the manufacturers of the products through the voluntary Product Problem Reporting Program (see Appendix 24-C).

CONCLUSION

As shown throughout this chapter, the benefits derived from advanced technology are not without risks. However, if addressed appropriately by a health care entity, the risks can be manageable. The first step in the process of managing these risks must come in the form of commitments by health care administrators and the medical staff. The commitments should then be directed toward strengthening the individual health care provider–patient relationship through enhanced communication concerning the use of technology; educating society as a whole on the necessity of sustaining support for the improvement of clinical care through innovative technology and research; and providing the essential resources to develop, establish, and maintain effective risk management and quality assurance practices.

NOTES

1. W.A. Hyman, Risks Associated with Diagnostic Devices, *Journal of Clinical Engineering* 11, no. 4 (1986):273-278.

2. Medical Devices and the Law: The Hospital's Responsibilities, *Health Technology* 3, no. 3 (Fall 1989):3-12.

3. D. Boho, Products Liability: Development, Case Strategy—Blending the Technical and Legal Aspects: Comparative Fault. (Paper presented at Insurer Symposium sponsored by Hinshaw, Culbertson, Moelmann, Chicago: Hoban & Fuller, 1990).

4. R. Wilkinson, New Technology That Will Change Key Services, *Hospitals* 62, no. 10 (20 May 1988):56-61.

5. Hyman, Risks, 273-278.

6. J. Riffer, Liability Threat #5: Technology—and How To Cope with It, *Hospitals* 60, no. 22 (20 November 1986):53.

7. K. Williamson, MRI's—New Technology, New Risks, *The Continental Rx* 2, no. 2 (Spring 1990):1-2.

8. Hyman, Risks, 273-278.

9. Ibid.

10. Ibid.

11. J. Carey, et al., The Genetic Age, *Business Week* (28 May 1990): 68-83.

12. B. Youngberg, The Risks of "High Tech" Parenthood, *Quality and Risk Management in Health Care* 1, no. 2 (December 1990): 1-3.

13. R. Kotulak and P. Gorner, Babies by Design, *Chicago Tribune Magazine* (3 March 1991): 14-19.

14. D. Holthaus, Computerized Patient Care: Blessing or Curse?, *Hospitals* 162, no. 16 (August 1988):32.

15. W.A. Hyman and A. Rakshit, Information Sources for Medical Equipment Risk Management, *Journal of Clinical Engineering* 14, no. 2 (1989): 113-119.

16. G.G. Drutchas and A.T. Schierloh, Consent Forms in Plain Language, *Michigan Hospitals* (June 1985):7-13.

17. D.R. Challoner, et al., Sounding Board—Effects of the Liability Climate on the Academic Health Center, *The New England Journal of Medicine* 319, no. 24 (1988): 1603-1605.

18. T. Christoffel, *Health and the Law, a Handbook for Health Professionals* (New York: Free Press, 1982), 295.

19. Ibid., 296.

20. Ibid., 295.

21. R.Z. Cohn and W.A. Knowlton, Controlling Liability through Indemnity and Insurance Provisions in Corporate Sponsored Research Agreement, *Forum* 11, no. 1 (January/February 1990):6-7.

Appendix 24-A

Sample Protocol for Use of Laser Systems in Gynecology

PURPOSE

To provide for patient safety during surgery.
To provide for personnel safety during surgery.
To provide for the optimum usage of the laser.
To provide for the proper care of the laser.

PROCEDURE

I. Credentialing standards
   A. Selected staff members trained in laser surgery will form the committee through which permission must be obtained for the use of the laser.
   B. Staff members wishing to utilize the laser must be trained in the use, care, and physics of each type of requested laser and must have participated in a training session with hands-on experience consisting of the following:
      1. A CME course will be required indicating that the staff member has been qualified in laser physics.
      2. The staff member must have obtained hands-on experience through a laser course or training by another staff member.
      3. An official, signed letter will be kept on file to indicate that the individual has shown adequate skills in using the laser. A laser-trained registered nurse will maintain an updated list to ensure that physicians are educated as to the parts that need to be sterilized, how to protect the lens mechanism, and the necessary safety procedures.
      4. The staff member, after successfully completing the laser course, must complete the appropriate number of surgical cases for each laser application requested before attaining full laser privileges.
   5. The staff member will receive a copy of the laser policy and procedure protocol and be placed on the list as being qualified to perform laser surgery.
   6. Physicians meeting the criteria and wishing to apply for privileges should submit their credentials to the Department Chairman, who will in turn submit them to the Laser Committee Chairperson.
   C. Staff members trained in the use of the CO_2 or YAG laser *must be present* during the use of the laser by residents.

II. Scheduling procedure
   A current list of qualified physicians will be available to the scheduling coordinator at all times.

III. Patient safety
   A. The operative permit is to state that the CO_2 or YAG laser is to be used during the procedure. In instances where this is not possible (i.e., an emergency case when the use of the laser would be in the patient's best interests), the surgeon is to be informed of the lack of a specific consent, and the surgeon must accept responsibility and document such in the progress notes.
   B. Surgeons using the lasers have the responsibility to know how to use the lasers properly in order to protect the patient and the OR personnel.
   C. The surgeon will assume responsibility for selecting wattage and the appropriate lens for each procedure.
   D. To minimize the possibility of a fire hazard, all laser surgery is to be done with a standby water basin and all sponges are to be moistened prior to use.
   E. During the procedure, the patient's eyes are to be protected with safety glasses.

Source: Courtesy of University of Illinois Hospital, Chicago, IL.

F. When the unit is not in use, the circulating nurse or relief is to put the laser on standby in an effort to avoid accidental discharging of the laser toward an area not involved in the surgery or toward the OR personnel. When the laser is left unattended for a substantial period of time, the laser shall be turned off.

IV. Personnel safety

A. All employees, when working in areas in which a potential exposure to direct or reflected laser light greater than 0.005 watt (5 milliwatts) exists, shall be provided with eye protection safety glasses that will protect for the specific wavelength of the laser and be of optical density that is adequate for the energy involved. The wavelength for the CO_2 laser system is 10.6 microns. The wavelength for the YAG laser system is 1.06 microns. There are specific goggles to be used for this laser system only.

B. Areas in which lasers are used shall be posted with standard laser warning placards.

C. Beam shutters or caps shall be utilized, or the laser turned off, when laser transmission is not actually required. When the laser is left unattended for a substantial period of time, such as during lunch hour, overnight, or at a change of shifts, the laser shall be turned off and the key locked in the medication cabinet.

D. The laser beam shall not be directed at employees.

E. Laser equipment shall bear a label to indicate maximum output. Employees shall not be exposed to light intensities above:
   1. Direct staring: 1 microwatt per square centimeter
   2. Incidental observing: 1 milliwatt per square centimeter
   3. Diffuse reflected light: 2½ watts per square centimeter

F. The CO_2 and YAG lasers produce a nonionizing form of electromagnetic radiation and are not a danger to an unborn fetus.

G. The CO_2 vapor plume can be toxic. Adequate suction traps must be used at all times. Please use specified laser suction only and not standard wall suction.

V. Proper care of the laser

A. Only qualified and trained employees shall be assigned to install, adjust, and operate the laser equipment.

B. A registered nurse or surgical technician trained in the proper care and handling of the CO_2 or YAG lasers will be assigned to each case.

C. A preoperative, intraoperative, and postoperative safety checklist will be completed by the circulating nurse on each procedure and maintained in the operating room.

D. The unit manager or the laser charge nurse should be called immediately if technical difficulties arise with the laser unit.

E. If the unit manager or the laser charge nurse is unable to resolve these difficulties, he or she will inform the supervisor of the operating room and contact the laser representative, who will call the special engineer.

F. The head nurse will notify the scheduling secretary, who will inform the physicians with cases scheduled or those who desire to schedule laser procedures when the laser is not functioning.

G. The scheduling secretary will be responsible for notifying the physicians when the unit is back in operation.

H. The patient will be charged a set fee for laser usage.

CREDENTIALING

I. Basic requirements

A. Basic hands-on laboratory and didactic training in a two-day (or longer) course.

B. Training and laboratory experience with *each* type of laser application requested are required.

C. Laboratory training for each type of laser requested (CO_2 or YAG):
   1. Three sessions before the technique is first performed on a patient.
   2. Use of surgical specimens, fruits, lunch meats, or placentas to become experienced in the basic operating characteristics of the hospital equipment.

II. Provide a list of the required number of patients on whom you have performed laser surgery under supervision and name the supervising physician. Provide a letter of recommendation/competency from the physician who supervised your laser surgery cases.

III. CO_2 laser of lower genital tract

A. Experience in operation and safety of the equipment (as outlined above).

B. Demonstration of adequate competency and experience in colposcopic evaluation and diagnosis of the lower genital tract. Submit documentation of this training.

C. Requirement of prior histologic diagnosis before attempting the laser procedure on a patient.

D. Provision of a list of patients on whom you have performed supervised laser procedures
 1. Vaporization technique—five cases.
 2. Excisional technique—two cases.

IV. Intra-abdominal surgery prerequisites
 A. Hands-on course oriented toward intra-abdominal surgery.
 B. Three cases as a first assistant to an experienced laser surgeon. Three additional cases as a surgeon supervised by an experienced laser surgeon.
 C. In the beginning, restriction of the use of laser to small nodular endometriosis and filmy and easily manipulated adhesions. Complete these operations with more standard or microsurgical techniques.
 D. With increasing experience and exposure, lateral adhesions, the use of mirror techniques, and lateral wall absorption techniques can be instituted. Be intentionally slow in the progression of techniques.

V. Laser laparoscope—CO_2
 A. Prior training and experience with other CO_2 laser applications, either intra-abdominal or lower genital tract.
 B. Experience with laser laparoscopic techniques in the laboratory setting and developing familiarity with equipment and safety strategies before attempting procedure on a patient. *One to three sessions required* (at the discretion of the supervising surgeon).

C. Three cases as observer of laser laparoscopic techniques in the operating room before hands-on applications.
D. Familiarity with both single and double puncture techniques required.
 1. Lysis of adhesions—perform three cases under supervision.
 2. Vaporization of endometriosis—perform three cases under supervision.

VI. Endometrial hysteroscopic laser (YAG)
 A. Demonstration of knowledge regarding specific care and use of N-YAG laser.
 B. Requirement of operative hysteroscopic experience.
 C. Five cases under supervision of experienced laser surgeon.

VII. When a physician desires to add an additional type of approved laser wavelength to an existing type of application (i.e., adding YAG or argon laser to laparoscopic techniques), a formal request to the Credentials Committee is required that demonstrates general approval of the technique and sufficient documentation of training and competency. Since this is an evolving technology, no pre-existing criteria may exist for new applications; therefore the Laser Subcommittee will evaluate each request on an individual basis. As use of a technique evolves, credentialing criteria will be developed.

Informed Consent for Research Protocols

OBJECTIVE

All human subject research conducted at the hospital and clinics or by the staff shall be conducted ethically and in accordance with the hospital's research policies and federal and state laws.[1]

POLICY

Prior to any human subject research, the Institutional Review Board (IRB) of the hospital must approve the protocol, the informed consent document, and any written solicitation for subjects. No human subject research shall occur at the hospital without the approval of the IRB and without the research subject's voluntary written consent, except as noted below.

A principal investigator may address questions regarding research protocols and informed consent requirements to the chair of the IRB or to the hospital's Office for Protection from Research Risks. A specific policy and procedure governs the use and control of the investigational drugs.

DEFINITIONS

For purposes of this policy, *research* means a systematic investigation designed to develop or contribute to generalizable knowledge or the acquisition of data that may be used in the future to develop generalizable knowledge.

For purposes of this policy, *protocol* is any plan of an experimental nature, including plans relating to investigational drugs and investigational medical devices.

For purposes of this policy, the *principal investigator* (PI) means the hospital staff member or student who is conducting the research, any coinvestigator(s) associated with the PI on the research protocol, and any staff member who is knowledgeable of the project and has been specifically designated by the PI. A student may serve as a PI only when a faculty member has specifically agreed to serve as co-PI on the protocol.

For purposes of this policy, *research subject* means a hospital or clinic patient from whom the PI conducting research obtains (1) data through intervention or interaction with the individual or (2) identifiable private information.

PROCEDURE

A. The PI shall seek and obtain approval of the research protocol and informed consent document from the IRB prior to the collection of any data.

B. 1. The PI is responsible for obtaining written informed consent from all subjects in the research protocol, except in those cases where specific written informed consent is not required because the protocol has been exempted *in advance* by the IRB. The responsibility for obtaining written informed consent cannot be delegated.

   2. Prior to the collection of any data, the PI must discuss the research protocol with the subject. The PI must, at a minimum, provide the following information to the subject:

      a. A statement that the study involves research, an explanation of the purpose of the research and the expected duration of the subject's participation, a description of the procedures to be followed, and identification of any procedures that are experimental.

      b. A description of any reasonably foreseeable risks or discomforts to the subject.

      c. A description of the potential benefits to the subject or to others that may reasonably be expected from the research, or a statement that no benefits are expected.

      d. A disclosure of appropriate alternative procedures or courses of treatment, if any, that might be advantageous to the subject.

      e. A statement describing the extent to which the confidentiality of records identifying the subject will be maintained.

f. A statement that the subject's refusal to participate in the research study will not jeopardize the subject's receiving medical treatment at the hospital.

g. A statement that the subject's consent, once given, may be withdrawn at any time.

h. A statement noting whether compensation is available and whether any medical treatment is available if injury occurs and, if so, the person to contact in the event of a research-related injury.

i. A clarification that any costs of treatment (i.e., those entirely outside of the research protocol) are the responsibility of the subject.

j. A notice of the person to contact for answers to questions regarding the research protocol and the research subject's rights.

C. 1. The subject or the subject's legally authorized representative (or the parent if the subject is under 18 years old unless the minor subject is legally considered an adult) must sign the informed consent document in the presence of the PI. A witness who was present at the signing of the informed consent document and the PI must also sign the form. If a minor subject is age 12 or older, his or her assent should be obtained in addition to the consent of the minor subject's parents or legally authorized representative.

2. The PI shall place one copy of the signed informed consent document in the patient's medical record and shall record a statement in the progress notes that the informed consent discussion occurred and that the consent was obtained. A copy of the informed consent document shall be given to the subject. The PI shall retain the original, signed informed consent document.

3. In the extremely rare circumstance, if the informed consent discussion did not occur or if the written informed consent document was not signed, the PI must notify the IRB within five working days regarding the circumstances associated with the failure to obtain the subject's consent.

D. If any medication is to be given to or procedures performed on a subject, who is a patient at the hospital or clinic for other reasons, as part of the research protocol, the attending physician with primary responsibility for the patient's care must be informed and must consent. The responsible attending physician must write orders accordingly. These experimental medications and procedures shall be charted in the patient's medical record in a manner consistent with other medications and procedures.

NOTE

1. U.S. Department of Health and Human Services, Regulations, 21 CFR Part 50, 21 CFR Part 312, 45 CFR Part 46, as amended, April 1, 1989 edition.

Appendix 24-C

How To Report Problems with Medical Devices

Medical Device & Laboratory Product Problem Reporting Program

Don't be left with doubts about the quality of the medical devices used in your practice. Restore your confidence in their ability to work safely and efficiently by reporting to the MEDICAL DEVICE AND LABORATORY PRODUCT PROBLEM REPORTING PROGRAM (PRP).

The PRP is a nationwide reporting system for all health professionals to report their observations about the quality and safety of medical products used in their practice. The program is funded by the Food and Drug Administration (FDA), Center for Devices and Radiological Health, and is coordinated by the United States Pharmacopeia (USP)—an independent, non-governmental body composed of representatives from associations and colleges of medicine, nursing, and pharmacy.

Product problems can be reported by calling USP toll free at 1-800-638-6725 (in Maryland call collect 1-301-881-0256), where a staff of health professionals is available to assist you with your report, or by completing the enclosed reporting form. Reports are forwarded to the FDA the day they are received and reports perceived as imminent hazards are phoned immediately to the FDA's attention. USP also forwards a copy of each report to the device manufacturer so that the firm will be aware of your concerns and can follow up with you. Alternatively, you may request anonymity and USP will act as an intermediary for any future correspondence. Please remember, that the PRP does not replace your in-house reporting system.

All PRP reports are entered into the Device Experience Network (DEN), the FDA data base for analysis by product, manufacturer, and/or problem. This valuable information is utilized to identify any industry-wide problems or trends, and calls attention to specific product problems.

Guidelines for reporting to the PRP are available from USP as a separate publication. An educational videotape, which describes the Medical Device and Laboratory Product Problem Reporting Program in detail, is also available free of charge just by calling the toll-free number listed above.

Examples of products to report:

- Intravenous Pumps
- Surgical/Examination Gloves
- Cardiac and Respiratory Monitors
- Implants
- Dialysis Products
- Catheters
- Reagent Kits
- X-Ray Equipment
- Ventilators
- Sutures

Examples of product problems to report:

- Performance Failures
- Erroneous Information
- Poor Packaging
- Questionable Sterility
- Improper Labeling
- Defective Components
- Incomplete or Confusing Instructions

Source: 91-01 Published by the United States Pharmacopeial Convention, Inc., pursuant to FDA Contract 223-88-6061, 12601 Twinbrook Parkway, Rockville, MD 20852.

Know Your Options

The USP sends a copy of each report it receives to the Food and Drug Administration (FDA). The FDA may contact you for further information about your report or to discuss your observations. The identity disclosure options on the form then allow you to express your preference as to what *other* disclosure of your identity can be made (other than to FDA) on copies of the report that are distributed either to the product manufacturer by the USP or to third parties by the FDA in response to requests for information. Since the options are exclusive of one another, only one selection is necessary.

REVIEW OF DISCLOSURE OPTIONS

First option:
No Public Disclosure

The first selection, "No Public Disclosure," is the most limited option and provides that your name will not be released by the FDA or the USP. Although a copy of the report is sent to the manufacturer to inform him of your problem, by checking the "No Public Disclosure" option, your identity will not be included on that copy and the USP will act as your intermediary for any further correspondence with the firm.

Second option:
To the Manufacturer/Distributor

The USP sends a copy of your report to the manufacturer/distributor of the product. By selecting the second option, "To the manufacturer/distributor," you are giving the USP express

permission to include your name on this copy only. For those who have used the PRP in past years, it may be helpful to know that checking this option provides that your report will be handled as it has been over the years. By including your name on this copy you enable the manufacturer to directly discuss the problem with you. This discussion may include a request for a sample or follow up at your institution to inspect the device or inservice instruction where necessary.

Third option:
To the Manufacturer/Distributor and to Anyone Who Requests a Copy of the Report from the FDA

According to Federal Freedom of Information regulations, FDA records must be made uniformly available to the general public upon request. Those in the general public who may request such information could include other practitioners who are making purchase decisions, manufacturers seeking out disgruntled customers of competitors, members of the press, insurance agents, and attorneys to name a few. Checking this box allows your name to remain on any copies distributed to the general public. Depending on your perspective, this selection may or may not be desirable as it could result in many wanted or unwanted phone calls for you! The FDA will not release your name, hospital name, address, telephone number, etc. *unless you select this option!*

We hope that this brief overview will assist you in making an informed decision about your choice. If you have any questions about this procedure, please do not hesitate to call us at 1-800-638-6725 and our staff will be glad to assist you.

	Form Approved: OMB No. 0910-0143
Medical Device & Laboratory Product Problem Reporting Program	DATE RECEIVED
	ACCESS NO

---

1. PRODUCT IDENTIFICATION:

Name of Product and Type of Device
(Include sizes or other identifying characteristics and attach labeling, if available)

_____

_____

Manufacturer's Name _____

Manufacturer's City, State, Zip Code _____

_____

Is this a disposable item?   YES ☐   NO ☐

Lot Number(s) and Expiration Date(s) (if applicable)

Serial Number(s)

Manufacturer's Product Number and/or Model Number

---

2. REPORTER INFORMATION:

Your Name _____   Today's Date _____

Title and Department _____

Facility's Name _____

Street Address _____

City _____   State _____   Zip _____   Phone ( ) _____   Ext: _____

---

3. PROBLEM INFORMATION:

Date event occurred _____

Please indicate how you want your identity publicly disclosed:

No public disclosure ☐

To the manufacturer/distributor ☐

To the manufacturer/distributor and to anyone who requests a copy of the report from the FDA ☐

This event has been reported to: Manufacturer ☐ FDA ☐

Other _____

If requested, will the actual product involved in the event be available for evaluation by the manufacturer or FDA?   YES ☐   NO ☐

Problem noted or suspected (Describe the event in as much detail as necessary. Attach additional pages if required. Include how and where the product was used. Include other equipment or products that were involved. Sketches may be helpful in describing problem areas.)

RETURN TO
United States Pharmacopeia
12601 Twinbrook Parkway
Rockville, Maryland   20852
Attention: Dr Joseph G Valentino

OR

CALL TOLL FREE ANYTIME
800-638-6725*
IN THE CONTINENTAL UNITED STATES
*In Maryland, call collect (301) 881-0256
between 9:00 AM and 4:30 PM

Courtesy of U.S. Pharmacopeial Convention, Inc.

chapter 25

Managing Risks Associated with Employment

Frank Dodero and Steve Straka

INTRODUCTION

Today's health care facilities are complex businesses that employ many professional and support persons. Although employees can be a business' greatest strength, they can also be the source of risk and quality problems. Risk managers working in health care settings need to be aware of the challenges inherent in managing employees and the ways in which employee issues can give rise to legal risks and quality problems within the health care setting. This chapter identifies specific employee-related issues and provides strategies for dealing with these issues.

HOW THE EXTERNAL HEALTH CARE ENVIRONMENT IMPACTS EMPLOYEE ISSUES

The health care environment is a dynamic and stressful one. Recent changes in health care funding have greatly changed the way hospitals are reimbursed for care. In many cases, these changes have resulted in internal problems and stress due to layoffs and job restructuring. The public's increased scrutiny of the health care system has created an unfair picture of health care providers—depicting them as callous, mercenary, and poorly trained. The need to respond to these public perceptions and to continue to provide high-quality empathetic care has placed additional stress on the health care organization as well as its employees. The continued lack of tort reform limiting malpractice and legal actions against the institution further stresses the health care system and adds to the negative public image of health care professionals.

INTERNAL STRESSORS AFFECTING EMPLOYEES

Internal factors also contribute to employee stress. The physical demands associated with many hospital jobs and the high-stress/emotional component experienced by professional caregivers who often care for critically ill patients (and their families) further add to stress level and can cause additional problems. Finally, hospitals operate 24 hours a day, which requires employees to do shift work. Often this means rapidly adjusting internal clocks; at the same time employees must be properly rested for work—a situation that adds to job stress and dissatisfaction.

IDENTIFYING AND DEALING WITH THE IMPAIRED EMPLOYEE

Even though hospitals are perceived as places where care is given, at times it is the caregiver who needs care. Lawsuits have arisen when hospital staff failed to recognize coworkers at risk and that coworker has caused the patient injury or harm. Often it is at this stage that employee problems receive attention and strategies are developed to identify staff at risk and to provide appropriate assistance. A far better solution is to develop a proactive plan that enables health care workers to understand and recognize employees at risk and to encourage them to get help before an accident or injury occurs. Developing proactive policies and procedures and educating the staff allows employees to receive assistance before problems arise. (See the policy regarding the hospital's position on impaired employees in Exhibit 25-1.) Ensuring that the reporting employee will not be penalized and the report is confidential is important in reassuring the staff that there will not be negative repercussions.

Exhibit 25-1
HOSPITAL POLICY RELATED TO EMPLOYEE IMPAIRMENT

Policy for Impaired Person/Staff
Purpose: To define impaired practice.
To outline the responsibilities of the hospital administration, human resources, and the employee assistance program to the impaired person/employee.
To describe the responsibility of staff in identifying impaired persons.
To describe the responsibility of the impaired person.
Definition: The impaired person is defined as one who attempts to practice or function professionally while judgment and psychomotor skills are compromised or diminished by psychiatric, organic, or substance abuse illness, or by extenuating life-crisis situations.
Policy: It is the foremost responsibility of the hospital, through its administration, to provide safe, competent patient care. When care is compromised by impaired practice, the actions of hospital administration and the employee assistance program focus on safeguarding the patient. The hospital, through its administration, upholds that its employees shall assume the obligation of self-regulation, recognizing that action or inaction in situations of impairment affect the care and safety of its clients and the reputation and function of the organization. Hospital administration expects that all employees perform their duties in a safe, efficient, and professional manner, and encourages the impaired person to voluntarily seek confidential assistance from the employee assistance program. Hospital administration supports those who seek help; on the other hand, it will be firm in disciplining impaired persons who refuse to seek help.

The impaired person jeopardizes patient care through incompetent, unethical, or illegal practice. Every employee of the hospital is obligated to identify the impaired person (be it self or other). Thus, patient safety can be maintained and assistance can be offered to the impaired person. It is the belief of the hospital administration that in most cases treatment will allow the impaired person to resume or remain a useful employee.
Substance Abuse: Substance abuse is viewed as an illness. The employee may use available sick benefits as well as vacation and holiday entitlement during the period of absence from the job for the purpose of treatment if verified by a physician or treatment facility. Thereafter, the provisions of an unpaid leave of absence will prevail.
Emotional or Psychiatric Conditions: Case management techniques, for all referred or requested services for emotional or psychiatric conditions, will follow procedures established for substance abuse. While follow-up is considered absolutely necessary in all therapeutic regimens, the potential danger of more than one professional providing therapy in emotional or psychiatric cases is noted. Therefore, employees who seek treatment for emotional or psychiatric cases are required to continue in the established therapeutic relationship or treatment modality until that relationship is ended by the treating program, therapist, psychologist, or psychiatrist.
General Provisions: No documentation of the employee assistance program will be made in the employee's official personnel file in employee records.

If an employee will be on an unpaid leave of absence for any period of time, the Employee Benefits Section, Personnel, must be consulted and arrangements made with the employee so that insurance coverage will not lapse without the employee's knowledge.

The employee will be supported during the prescribed period of treatment and rehabilitation up to the limits of insurance coverage and benefits provided by the hospital.

Case management techniques may vary for employees covered under health maintenance insurance plans. The employee has the option of going independently to resources within the hospital, including outpatient psychiatry, social work, and the chaplaincy. However, the provisions of this policy still prevail.

It is the hospital's expectation that all employees will continue satisfactory job performance and abide by all hospital rules and regulations at all times, irrespective of the presence of substance abuse or other treatable conditions.

The disclosure of substance abuse, or emotional or psychiatric conditions will not stop an impending disciplinary action.

Any questions regarding this policy may be referred to the Employee Assistance Program Director.

IDENTIFICATION OF SIGNS OF IMPAIRMENT

The St. Paul Insurance Company has developed a system of *flags* that can be used to identify whether a physician may be working in an impaired state.[1] (Although the program specifically addresses physicians, the same flags could be used to evaluate the behavior of other hospital staff.) Behaviors identified as *red flags* include the following:

- driving while intoxicated (DWI)
- intoxication at social gatherings
- alcohol on breath while at work
- alcohol withdrawal tremors
- personality change over recent months or from day to day
- "illness" on Mondays (pattern of calling in sick on Mondays)
- neglecting medical staff (or other staff) duties
- missing appointments with patients or meetings with coworkers
- inappropriate or dangerous orders

In addition, the St. Paul Companies provide a list of *pink flags* to assist in the identification of potentially impaired employees. "A 'pink flag' by itself may not indicate a problem although a cluster of 'pink flags' or any 'red flags' certainly deserves closer scrutiny."[2] Pink flags include the following:

- a work volume that is either extremely high or very low
- solo practitioner (or a person who seems to have problems getting along with others)
- minimalist practice: cookbook style with a high reliance on consultants
- frequent malpractice suits
- drinking a lot of fluids, large gain or loss in weight
- social withdrawal
- unexplained absences from work
- physicians conducting rounds at unusual hours

- complaints about forgetfulness from colleagues or patients
- falling behind in charts

Again these pink and red flags are signs, varying in degree of seriousness, that a provider (or employee) may be impaired. **None of these signs means that a physician or other hospital employee has an alcohol or drug problem.** Rather, these indicators are among the early symptoms sometimes associated with alcohol and drug problems. The presence of a cluster of pink flags or a red flag indicates that a person with special expertise should be consulted to intervene.

DEVELOPING A SELF-IDENTIFICATION PROGRAM

It is important to foster an attitude that an employee can admit to having a problem and seek professional help. This type of program places less responsibility on other staff members, who may feel that they are not in the best position to determine if a coworker has a problem that inhibits his or her ability to provide safe care. It also avoids possible negative repercussions from reporting a fellow employee (particularly if the report turns out to be unwarranted) that could make future interaction between coworkers difficult, if not impossible.

In a self-reporting program, employees must be assured that the program's purpose is to enable the employee to receive assistance—not to provide the institution with a reason to terminate the impaired employee. The program must be carefully structured. It should explain how help will be provided to the employee; how progress and success within the program will be measured; and how to handle the situation with superiors to ensure that when appropriate the employee is able to return to the job.

All employees should be apprised of the program's existence and should be given written information explaining how the program works. Their responsibilities under the program should be clearly delineated. A sample hospital policy describing a self-identification program is included as Exhibit 25-2.

Exhibit 25-2
HOSPITAL POLICY STATEMENT ON SELF-IDENTIFICATION OF IMPAIRED EMPLOYEES

Employees Who Come Forward with Their Substance Abuse Problems

Purpose: The purpose of this policy is to encourage hospital personnel who are impaired (due to drug, emotional, or psychiatric problems) to admit their problems and to seek treatment without the fear that they will lose their jobs and prior to the impairment causing any injury to patients or other staff members. This will help to ensure safe and appropriate patient care; it will also provide a confidential system to assist employees who are experiencing temporary difficulties.

Policy: The hospital will not discriminate against employees who identify themselves as substance abusers or as persons with emotional or psychiatric problems. The hospital will actively assist self-identified employees to secure appropriate counseling and treatment and will monitor all follow-up plans and recommendations through the employee health and assistance programs.

Implementation: Implementation of this policy will be handled through the offices of employee assistance, human resources, and employee health. It will be available to all employees of the hospital who identify themselves as having a psychiatric, emotional, or substance abuse problem that could affect their ability to provide safe patient care.

Procedure: To receive services through the employee assistance program, the employee must self-identify to any one of the persons in the above-cited departments. The person hearing the self-identification shall assist the employee in completing the referral to the employee assistance program and in identifying the scope of proposed services.

Substance Abuse: Individuals must complete treatment for substance abuse because their impaired judgment could endanger the care of the patients. When employees confidentially identify themselves as substance abusers, the employee assistance team will work with the employee to develop a treatment modality. The employee will be assigned a code number to guarantee anonymity. The match of code numbers to employee is maintained only in the employee assistance office. The employee assistance specialist will act as a liaison with the employee's supervisor or department director if time away from work is required. The employee assistance specialist will assure that all necessary forms are completed. Paperwork following treatment and prior to the employee's return to work will also be coordinated by the employee assistance specialist.

STRIKE SURVIVAL: A MATTER OF PLANNING

Controlling risk and ensuring quality in the complex hospital environment are responsibilities fraught with challenges. Many risk and quality improvement managers are well-versed at developing strategies to address the common problems that impact quality and create risk; they are less familiar with issues that arise in special circumstances, which can incapacitate a facility and have a significant impact on patient care. Labor and employment issues can greatly impact how care is provided and should be evaluated carefully. When a potential for a problem exists (for example, if there are a high number of unionized employees) proactive strategies should be developed to handle all possible scenarios. Strategies should be developed with input from everyone who could be impacted by the problem. This might include the hospital administrator, chief nursing officer, medical director, risk manager, hospital attorney, personnel director, and safety and security staff.

Although the strength of today's unions appears to have diminished considerably, the possibility of a strike still exists. The basis for a strike can be founded on three major predications: recognition, unfair labor practices, or economics. Regardless of the reason, when it occurs within the health care setting the rationale is the same: a strike is designed to disrupt the institution's operations, inconvenience patients and staff, and apply pressure so that the community will compel the institution to settle the dispute by agreeing to the union's demands.

Surviving a strike cannot be accomplished without preparation. The purpose of this section is to provide information to develop a plan should a strike occur. It is not a guide to labor relations, contract negotiating, or employee communication, all of which should be an integral part of operations prior to the threat of a strike.

Hospital vs. Union

As a prologue to every strike plan there should be a section dedicated to assessment. When faced with the prospect of a strike, the hospital's management team must evaluate its strength as opposed to the strength of the union. To do this the following questions need to be answered:

- Do the union leaders control the membership?
- How many hospital employees will participate in the strike?
- Does the union have strike benefits?
- If the union does have strike benefits, how much money does it have in reserve and when will benefits begin?
- Are strikers eligible for unemployment benefits?
- Would other unions honor the strike?
- How long are the union members prepared to strike?

Assessing the Hospital's Strength

- What effect will the strike have on revenue?
- Will lost revenue be recoverable in the poststrike period?
- How long will a strike be acceptable?
- Is there a critical point at which the community pressure on the hospital will be unbearable as to affect its long-term survival?
- Will the hospital have the support to make up for the employees who are withholding their services—supervisors, nonbargaining unit employees, temporaries, bargaining unit employees who will cross the picket line?
- Can the hospital replace economic strikers with permanent new hires?
- Are health benefits for the striking employees covered under a union plan or the hospital's own plan?
- What are the outside forces that can be brought to bear on the hospital?

Organizing a Strike Control Group

All strike plans should begin with a section that defines the purpose and responsibilities of the hospital's strike control group (SCG). The purpose of the SCG, which is usually led by the chief executive officer of the hospital, is to direct and coordinate the hospital's overall operations in preparation for a strike, during a strike, and immediately after the strike has ended. It should consist of key members from administration, the medical and nursing staff, as well as representatives from safety/security and building maintenance.

The first responsibility of the SCG, prior to a strike, is to designate a strike information officer. This person is responsible for interacting with and reporting to the group the day-to-day activities of each department once the SCG begins to meet.

The second prestrike responsibility is to determine departmental readiness. Each department should have:

- employee lists indicating the following information on each employee on unit or responsible for clinical department:
  –job title and accompanying credentials, if applicable
  –normal working shift
  –mode of transportation to and from work
  –home address and telephone
  –union membership status
- one primary and one secondary person designated as the departmental strike liaison
- a list of vendors and key contacts (persons who interact with staff of unit/department on a regular basis)

Once a strike has been declared, the SCG should begin to implement each component of the strike plan as described in the succeeding sections.

Establishing a Communication Network Center

The development of a communication network center (CNC) is probably the most important element of a strike survival plan. The CNC should address communication issues related to patients, members of the bargaining unit (striking and nonstriking), nonbargaining unit employees, and the community via the media. In addition to designating a media spokesperson for the hospital, the CNC should be responsible for generating specific communiqués directed toward patients and their safety (Exhibit 25-3); the security issues and expectations of all nonstriking bargaining and nonbargaining unit employees (Exhibits 25-4 and 25-5); the expectations of all supervisors (Exhibit 25-6); and the ground rules for all striking bargaining unit employees (Exhibit 25-7).

Physically, the CNC should set up within the hospital, equipped with multiple telephone lines and staffed with an administrative member of the SCG and one clerical person on a 24-hour basis. While many of its activities will be proactive, the CNC should also be concerned with the following:

- documenting the events of the strike
- collecting, organizing, and maintaining all operational information, including but not limited to, inpatient census, percent occupancy, admissions, discharges, transfers, emergency department visits, outpatient appointments, operating room procedures, staffing levels, units open, units closed, and units consolidated (Exhibit 25-8)
- answering vendor inquiries
- responding to physician concerns
- countering union propaganda

Exhibit 25-3
ANNOUNCEMENT OF POTENTIAL EMPLOYEE STRIKE

Date

Dear Patient,

There is a possibility that the bargaining unit that represents the _____ at our hospital may call for a strike beginning at _____.

I want to assure you that we are taking every step possible to keep the hospital open, to ensure your well-being, and to maintain quality service to all our patients.

We have evaluated each individual's needs and are prepared to meet those needs.

I also want you to know that we are taking every reasonable step to settle the negotiation without a strike. As a matter of fact, a negotiation session between the two parties is being held today with a federal mediator. We will inform you of any progress in the negotiations.

I thank you for your understanding and regret any inconvenience this situation may cause you or your family.

Sincerely,

Hospital CEO

Exhibit 25-4
MEMO ON SECURITY ISSUES—NONSTRIKING EMPLOYEES

Date

To: All Nonbargaining Unit Employees
         All Nonstriking Bargaining Unit Employees
From: Hospital CEO
Re: **Security in the Event of a Strike**

To all employees who come to work in the event of a strike, let me assure you that EVERY REASONABLE EFFORT IS BEING MADE TO ENSURE YOUR SAFE PASSAGE INTO, WITHIN, AND OUT OF THE HOSPITAL BUILDING.

Members of the hospital administration and I, myself, have been in direct contact with the hospital police official and legal counsel to make all of the necessary arrangements to protect your right to work.

In addition to the security guards and police, there will be designated off-site parking and shuttle service available. Your supervisors will be made aware of this information in advance. Please contact them for necessary information.

Please remember these simple rules:

1. You have the right to come to work.
2. You do not have to reply to any comments made by picketing individuals.
3. Security will be present throughout the hospital and outside of the hospital to ensure that you are protected.

Thank you for your commitment and support. It is employees such as you who make this outstanding institution what it is.

**Exhibit 25-5
EXPECTATIONS OF NONSTRIKING
EMPLOYEES—FACT SHEET**

The following is essential information about policies and procedures to be followed in the event of a strike:

- We expect all nonbargaining employees to report to work as usual and display photo IDs at all times. However, it will be necessary to temporarily reassign some employees and/or alter work schedules during the strike to maintain the highest level of service possible.
- It also may be necessary for some employees to be assigned overtime. Normal overtime pay policy will apply.
- All vacations and scheduled leaves are cancelled until further notice. Any absences by nonbargaining employees that are not for a bona fide reason will be treated as a violation of rules and regulations and could result in discipline.
- Any use of sick leave during the strike will require documentation acceptable to the employer in order to substantiate the absence.

Safety/Security Issues

If the development of a CNC can be viewed as the central nervous system of a strike plan, it is the safety/security section that acts as its immune system. Without one, it is very likely that all operations will be impaired. Safety/security issues affect everyone and everything from personal well-being to property damage. If the hospital administration thinks that its own security personnel may not be able to maintain control during a strike, then an independent security force specializing in security during labor disputes should be contracted. Security personnel, as well as local police, should be made aware of the nature of the labor problem, the number and type of employees involved, the names and addresses of union and employer representatives, the cause of the strike, and every violent or potentially violent incident that occurs.

One of the first issues that should be addressed by the safety/security section of the hospital's plan is the picket line. Friendly, loyal employees can become aggressive during a strike. Aside from mass picketing, which can prevent employees, patients and their families, and vendors from accessing the facility, picket line violence can and usually does occur. This can include physical damage to

**Exhibit 25-6
EXPECTATIONS OF SUPERVISORS—FACT SHEET**

Due to special operational issues presented by a possible strike, the following procedures will apply:

Vacation and Personal Leave

All vacations and personal leaves are to be cancelled effective immediately and until further notice to provide the greatest flexibility in assigning staff to cover critical need areas. This applies to all departments, regardless of function.

Sick Leave

If there is a strike, an employee who calls in sick or requests the use of sick leave must be informed that documentation will be required to substantiate the absence. All sick leave absences regardless of length of time are to be reviewed prior to granting paid sick leave benefits in accordance with established policies and procedures.

Leaves of Absence

If there is a strike, employees who are already absent on preapproved leaves may continue on such leaves on the basis of normal policies governing the duration of leaves. If an employee is needed and willing to report to work, such circumstances are to be reviewed on a case-by-case basis with the hospital personnel officer.

Reassignments

Each department head has been asked to identify staff who are available for reassignment to assist units that may be short staffed. If you are asked to provide staff for reassignment, such assignments should be made first from qualified volunteers. I ask for your cooperation in being flexible when called upon, so that all units can function as fully and effectively as possible.

THANK YOU

Exhibit 25-7
GROUND RULES FOR STRIKING EMPLOYEES

To All Striking Bargaining Unit Employees

In the event of a strike, the hospital intends to enforce the following policies:

- Ingress and egress to the hospital both in person and/or by vehicle must be maintained at all times. Accordingly, while the right of employees to picket and engage in other legally protected activities will be honored, such picketing and related activity must not interfere with the ability of employees, patients, and visitors to enter and leave the hospital.
- No picketing or other strike-related activity will be permitted on streets or roads used by vehicles to enter or leave the premises of the hospital.
- No picketing or demonstrations will be permitted inside any hospital buildings, including tunnels or corridors connecting hospital buildings.

- Unless specific permission is granted by the Director of Nursing or his/her designee, no striking employees will be permitted in the patient care areas, including corridors and sitting rooms on floors of the hospital that house patients' rooms, operating rooms, or any patient care rooms.
- Unless specifically authorized, no person, including striking employees, will be permitted to enter the hospital or connected buildings before or after the normal hours such buildings are open to the public.

The hospital believes that these policies are essential for the care and well-being of patients and to protect them from disturbances due to picketing and/or strike-related activities. These policies are also necessary to protect the right of employees, patients, and members of the public to freely enter and leave the hospital buildings.

Exhibit 25-8
OPERATIONS OVERVIEW

Report date _____ Report time _____ (circle one) AM   PM

Census _____ Percent occupancy _____ Admissions _____ Discharges _____
Transfers _____ To (list hospitals) _____

No. nurses on duty: Admin. _____ Staff _____ Temp. _____
No. units closed _____ Which units (please list) _____
No. units consolidated _____ Which units (please list) _____

Operating Room status: No. of rooms in service _____ No. of rooms out of service _____
Capacity descriptor: Normal _____ Nonelectives _____ Urgent _____
Emergency Department status: No. of visits last 24 hours _____
Ambulatory care status: No. of outpatient visits _____

General description of hospital operational status:

Other comments/incidents:

people and their cars, as well as threats and recording license numbers of the cars of nonstriking members of the bargaining unit. If at all possible, picket line ground rules should be established to avoid these occurrences. For example, only two pickets at each entrance and exit, picketers must be continuously moving, and weapons or other objects that could cause harm on the picket line are prohibited. Further, instructions should be provided to employees concerning picket line safety and security. These might include the following:

- Do not drive to work alone.
- Roll up windows and lock doors before crossing lines.
- Do not force your way through the picket line; wait for an escort.
- Ignore verbal taunts and harassment.
- If physical harm, or potential physical harm occurs, report the incident immediately.
- Remember that if you are physically assaulted arrests will be made.

Another method of controlling, and in some cases preventing violence, is to publicly announce the maintenance of a strike log used to record all incidents of violence or potential violence. A report should be initiated for each incident and should include the date, time, place, person(s) involved, and a brief but comprehensive incident description.

The hospital may also want to consider the following additional precautions:

- having additional officers patrol parking lots
- escorting employees to their cars after work
- establishing overnight accommodations within the hospital for those employees wishing to remain in the hospital
- installing additional outside fence lighting
- purchasing parabolic microphones for crowd control
- videotaping the picket line
- providing officers with Polaroid cameras

Finally, the actions of the safety/security team should be conveyed to the CNC so that communication lines remain open to all strike-affected individuals.

Physician Involvement

While it may not be a comforting thought, surviving a strike with more than institutional pride may hinge on the hospital's relationship with its physicians. If hospital services are reduced and the patient census decreases appreciably, physicians who are not directly employed by the hospital will be adversely affected. Their patients may feel it is unsafe to come to the hospital for care or the profession-

als (nurses, technicians, or clerical support) may not be available to provide necessary care. The administration that has developed a strong and mutually beneficial relationship with its medical staff will be far better off than the institution with an adversarial one. Hospitals with physicians who are unsupportive should entertain thoughts of an early agreement.

Other Practical Stratagems

In addition to the major areas of the plan mentioned earlier, the SCG should consider implementing the procedures outlined below.

- Cross train staff to the best degree possible.
- Stockpile critical supplies.
- Determine the census needed to maintain an economic balance to pay salaries of hospital personnel during a strike.
- Alert all suppliers to the possibility of a strike and ascertain their positions with regard to crossing picket lines.
- Consider an outside warehouse facility to serve as a drop point for deliveries.
- If an outside warehouse is used, address the problem of transporting the supplies to the hospital by leasing trucks.
- Discharge as many patients as possible.
- Consider reducing the number of elective procedures performed.
- Decide whether to keep the Emergency Department open.
- Consolidate inpatients to a smaller number of units.

The Aftermath

The last portion of a strike plan should deal with the SCG's responsibilities once the strike ends. These should include, but are not necessarily limited to, the following:

- Determine required staffing levels and establish recall procedures for striking employees.
- Review the adequacy of the strike plan, making sure to revise if necessary.
- Evaluate the emotional climate to determine whether special programs should be developed to cope with the post-traumatic strike period.

NOTES

1. St. Paul Companies, "A Human Factors Guide—Physician Alcohol and Drug Impairment," A Risk Management Series (St. Paul: St. Paul Companies, 1989), 3.

2. Ibid.

chapter 26

Managing the Risks of
Agency Nurses

Linda Sue Barmore

INTRODUCTION

The United States is experiencing a long-term, chronic nursing shortage. This shortage has reached a crisis level several times during the twentieth century[1] and has persisted despite ongoing efforts to increase the supply of nurses to meet demand.[2] Hospitals that are consistently understaffed risk legal liability, and the quality of care they provide may be affected. Risk managers should recognize these facts and work with nursing leadership to ensure the availability of high-quality nursing personnel from various sources so that patient care is not compromised.

Statistics regarding the nursing shortage and its related problems are sobering.

- Registered nurses comprise about 67.4 percent of hospitals' full-time nursing staffs and about 68.4 percent of their part-time nursing staffs.[3]
- Hospitals have vacancies in budgeted positions for registered nurses that range from 8 to 17 percent of a hospital's total budget for these positions.[4]
- In 1987, federal estimates showed that the supply of registered nurses with bachelor's degrees would fall short of demand by about 390,000 in 1990; this figure is expected to increase to about 578,000 by the year 2000.[5]
- The rate of registered nurse turnover in most acute care hospitals is extremely high (60–200 percent in some

hospitals), a factor that generally indicates larger problems within an organization.[6]
- One of the most frequent reasons nurses give for leaving the nursing profession is understaffing.[7]
- In 1988, hospitals spent $3.1 billion to recruit and train nurses.[8]

Accordingly, a hospital should explore methods of maintaining adequate nursing staff levels as a means of (1) decreasing the nursing turnover rate and thereby decreasing the costs associated with the recruitment and training of nurses and (2) maintaining a desirable level of the quality of patient care, a factor that, in turn, decreases the hospital's exposure to legal liability. Most hospital and nursing administrators agree that a stable and competent nursing work force is crucial to the maintenance of quality patient care.[9] As statistics reveal, however, the nursing shortage has undermined the ability of hospitals to attract and maintain a stable nursing work force.

INCREASED USE OF TEMPORARY NURSING AGENCIES

Many hospitals are coping with understaffing by using temporary agency or registry nurses to fill their needs. An American Hospital Association survey of its member hospitals in 1988 indicated that 21 percent of rural hospitals, 42.4 percent of urban hospitals located in areas with a population of less than one million, and 64.6 percent of urban hospitals located in areas with a population of one million or more utilized temporary nursing service agencies as an alternative staffing mechanism (see Exhibits 26-1 and 26-2).[10] Most frequently, hospitals used temporary nursing service agency personnel to fill budgeted but vacant positions.[11] In other cases, hospitals used agency personnel to replace sick or absent registered nurses or to handle unusual workloads.[12]

Temporary nursing services have proliferated since the late 1970s.[13] These agencies hire nurses and broker them to hospitals and other health care providers. A significant number of registered nurses work for temporary agencies. Including both primary and secondary positions held by nurses, estimates indicated that about 3 percent of employed nurses were working through temporary employment services in 1980.[14] Their work through a nursing agency was the primary nursing position for about 49 percent of nurses who were employed by these agencies.[15] Consequently, temporary nursing agencies have a significant pool of supplemental registered nurses and can provide a valuable resource to hospitals that otherwise would be dangerously understaffed.

Exhibit 26-1
AHA STATISTICS ON AGENCY NURSE USE

Hospital Characteristics	Number of Hospitals	Percent of Hospitals Using Temporary Nursing Service Agency Staff
Location		
Rural	543	21.0
Urban (<1 million)	361	42.4
Urban (>1 million)	302	64.6
Type of organization		
Federal government	70	14.3
Other government	356	27.5
Investor owned	120	53.3
Nonprofit	660	43.9
Number of inpatient beds		
1–49	245	26.1
50–99	288	28.8
100–199	278	43.5
200–299	151	47.7
300–399	89	47.2
400–499	53	52.8
500 +	102	51.0
Region		
New England	77	59.7
Mid-Atlantic	128	44.5
South Atlantic	194	45.4
East North Central	201	37.3
East South Central	96	19.8
West North Central	163	13.5
West South Central	149	34.9
Mountain	67	35.8
Pacific	131	60.3
Total	1,206	38.3
		(461)

Source: 1988 Report of the Hospital Nursing Personnel Survey, copyright 1988 by the American Hospital Association.

Exhibit 26-2
RATIONALE FOR UTILIZATION OF TEMPORARY NURSING AGENCY PERSONNEL
BY HOSPITAL CHARACTERISTICS

Hospital Characteristics	Number of Hospitals	Percent of Hospitals That Used Rationale*			
		1	2	3	4
Location					
Rural	56	75.0	50.0	44.6	1.8
Urban (<1 million)	118	83.1	66.1	59.3	6.8
Urban (>1 million)	155	87.7	81.3	61.9	5.8
Type of entity					
Federal government	7	85.7	28.6	14.3	28.6
Other government	67	76.1	71.6	53.7	4.5
Investor owned	58	79.3	82.8	70.7	10.3
Nonprofit	197	87.8	68.0	57.4	3.6
Number of inpatient beds					
1–49	47	70.2	61.7	40.4	6.4
50–99	58	77.6	60.3	55.2	3.4
100–199	72	86.1	70.8	66.7	6.9
200–299	51	82.4	86.3	70.6	5.9
300–399	41	90.2	73.2	48.8	2.4
400–499	28	92.9	75.0	57.1	10.7
500 +	32	96.9	68.8	62.5	3.1
Region					
New England	29	93.1	55.2	34.5	0.0
Mid-Atlantic	50	94.0	72.0	38.0	4.0
South Atlantic	51	82.4	74.5	64.7	7.8
East North Central	38	86.8	65.8	60.5	10.5
East South Central	12	83.3	75.0	58.3	8.3
West North Central	21	66.7	61.9	81.0	0.0
West South Central	38	81.6	65.8	57.9	7.9
Mountain	27	70.4	40.7	59.3	11.1
Pacific	63	84.1	93.7	69.8	1.6
Total	329	83.4	70.5	58.1	5.5

*1 = To fill budgeted but vacant positions
 2 = To replace sick or absent registered nurses
 3 = To handle unusual workloads
 4 = To perform other functions

Source: 1988 Report of the Hospital Nursing Personnel Survey, copyright 1988 by the American Hospital Association.

NEGATIVE ASPECTS OF UTILIZING CONTRACT NURSES

Although these temporary agencies may offer nurses an attractive alternative to permanent hospital positions and may be useful to hospitals as a source of registered nurses, there can be significant drawbacks for hospitals that hire such nurses. Major disadvantages associated with tempo- rary nursing agency personnel, as identified by the Nursing Service Administrators Conference Group and the litera- ture, include the following:[16]

- time, amount, and cost required for orientation of the temporary nurse
- lack of an agency nurse's familiarity with hospital policies and procedures

- rapid escalation of agency charges
- considerable variance in the business practices of agencies regarding hiring standards
- failure of hospitals to retain performance appraisals on temporary staff nurses
- occurrence of a situation in which an agency nurse, whom the hospital had found unacceptable. is terminated by one agency but reappears at the hospital through another agency

Hospitals that use agency nurses should take the necessary action to avoid or minimize the effects of such disadvantages. An understanding of legal liability encountered by a hospital when it utilizes agency nurses must precede the search for solutions to these problems.

LEGAL LIABILITY OF THE HOSPITAL

Generally, a hospital may be held legally liable under two tort theories for its use of agency nurses: (1) *respondeat superior* and (2) corporate negligence.

Respondeat Superior

The doctrine of *respondeat superior* is a form of vicarious liability that imposes legal responsibility for the acts or omissions of one person on another person or entity because of the relationship of the negligent person to the party who is held vicariously liable. To be held legally liable for the acts or omissions of an agency nurse, a hospital must be deemed to be the employer of the agency nurse. Determination of the actual employer of an agency nurse depends on who has the right to control the agency nurse with respect to the work in question. A temporary nursing agency's policies and contracts should be carefully reviewed by the hospital before it enters into any agreement with the agency. Terms of the contract must be consistent with the policies of the hospital and the professional liability coverage that protects the hospital staff.

Courts frequently apply the borrowed servant doctrine to cases in which an agency nurse is working as a supplemental hospital staff member.[17] The borrowed servant doctrine is a principle of agency law. It holds that if an employee is in the general employ of one employer (the agency) and in the special employ of another (the hospital), the employer whose business purpose was being carried out by the loaned servant at the time that the servant was negligent is responsible for the employee's tortious act under the doctrine of *respondeat superior*.[18] Therefore, if an agency nurse acts negligently or fails to act when he or she has a duty to do so, the hospital for which the agency nurse is working at the time of the incident may be held vicariously liable for any damages that result from the nurse's negligence.

For an agency nurse to be deemed negligent depends on (1) whether the nurse had a duty to act and failed to do so or did so in a manner that deviated from the expected standard of care, and (2) whether the patient was injured as a result. All agency nurses are expected to provide the same degree of care that a reasonably prudent nurse with the same level of expertise and training would give under the same or similar circumstances. The professional standards of care for all nurses are codified in each state's legal definition of nursing.[19] Although each state has a nurse practice act that defines nursing standards of care in general terms, these standards are defined in detail by each hospital's policies and procedures. An agency nurse is expected to know and to follow the policies and procedures of the hospital in which he or she is employed.

In addition, the American Nurses' Association (ANA) has issued standards and guidelines that specify the professional responsibilities of agency nurses. The guidelines state that an agency nurse has the following six duties:

1. to maintain current licensure
2. to select reputable employers
3. to maintain proficient nursing skills
4. to observe the standards of professional practice
5. to document his or her nursing practice
6. to adhere to the policies and procedures of the agencies and clients[20]

As factor 4 indicates, the agency nurse is held to the ANA's Code of Nurses. The code provides guidance to all nurses regarding the nursing profession's expectations and requirements in ethical matters.

Corporate Negligence

Under the doctrine of corporate negligence, hospitals have been held to have a direct and independent responsibility to provide due care to hospitalized patients.[21] With regard to potential tort liability, a hospital's responsibility to exercise due care is indistinguishable from that of any other enterprise.[22] The doctrine of corporate negligence places a burden on the hospital's governance and management staff to exercise due diligence in preventing incompetent health care providers from practicing at the hospital.[23] The board's duty extends to establishing procedures by which the board can reasonably ensure that its policies are being carried out and that the hospital is meeting its responsibility for accountability.[24] This means that quality assurance and risk management are integral to the board's responsibility of assuring quality care.

The doctrine of corporate negligence requires a hospital to:[25]

- exercise ordinary care in the selection of its staff
- carefully review each staff applicant's qualifications and credentials
- monitor each staff member's performance
- take corrective action if the hospital becomes aware that a staff member is incompetent

Thus, a hospital must evaluate and choose its staff carefully to avoid legal liability. In addition, if a hospital knows (or should know) through its management or governing body that a staff member (or a supplemental staff member under contract to provide patient care) is failing to meet the minimum standards of practice, it has a duty to take appropriate action to guard against reoccurrences.[26] If the hospital fails to act, its lack of action amounts to corporate negligence.

A hospital's corporate responsibility to exercise due care is spelled out in (1) standards of the Joint Commission on Accreditation of Healthcare Organizations (Joint Commission); (2) state licensure, health department, and health planning standards; and (3) the hospital's own articles of incorporation, bylaws, and policies and procedures.[27] The development of hospital corporate liability signifies the courts' recognition of the superior position of hospitals in screening and supervising their staffs.[28]

POSITION OF THE JOINT COMMISSION

Joint Commission standards relating to nursing care require the hospital to ascertain that all members of the nursing staff are competent to carry out their assigned responsibilities. Meeting this standard requires the hospital to evaluate periodically the ability of its nurses to deliver patient care. Accordingly, the hospital must have policies and procedures that define the process to be used by its supervisory personnel in objectively evaluating competence. In addition, the hospital must have supervisory nursing personnel with the necessary education and experience to make sound staffing and evaluative decisions.

Since the advent of temporary nurse agencies, the Joint Commission has amended its standards to address concern regarding the effect that temporary nurses may have on the continuity and quality of patient care in hospitals. The amended standards state that if the hospital uses such outside sources for nursing personnel, the nurses retained through agencies must be oriented before they can provide patient care at the institution. The hospital must also document that the agency nurse is currently licensed and is competent to deliver patient care in the assigned area. The performance of an agency nurse must be evaluated in a manner defined by the hospital's policies and procedures.

The Joint Commission's amended standards also state that the nurse executive must be responsible for implementing the monitoring and evaluation process with respect to the hospital's nursing staff. Within this duty, the standards specifically include the same responsibility for implementing the process for any outside nursing personnel used by the hospital.

COMPLIANCE WITH STATE STATUTES

Many states require hospitals to meet their licensing act standards and the requirements of any regulations promulgated under that act, in addition to meeting the Joint Commission accreditation standards. The state's licensing act may require the hospital to have policies and procedures for determining staffing needs, for maintaining certain staffing levels, and for evaluating staff competence. When a hospital has instituted policies and procedures, it is expected to follow them. If the hospital breaches its duty to follow its own rules and a patient is harmed as a result, the hospital could be held legally liable under the doctrine of corporate negligence.

State statutes may also impose certain requirements on the temporary nurse agency. The statutory section pertaining to nurse agencies is generally found under the heading of employment agencies, nurses' registries, or temporary nurse agencies. (For example, California, Maine, Massachusetts, and Texas have such statutory sections; Illinois has a nurse agency licensing act.) Under these statutory provisions, a temporary nursing agency may be required to (1) ascertain and document that the nurses it hires are properly licensed, (2) evaluate the competency of the nurses that it hires, and (3) perform a thorough employment check on each nurse.

HOW TO AVOID LEGAL LIABILITY RESULTING FROM THE USE OF AGENCY NURSES

It is impossible for a hospital to avoid all risks associated with its use of agency nurses. Some risk inevitably results from the duty of the hospital to supervise and assume responsibility for its employees and the duty to deliver due care to its patients.[29] In contractual situations, however, it is possible for a hospital to avoid unnecessary risk, to apportion the risk that cannot be avoided, and to manage its share of risk.[30] Therefore, the hospital should begin the contract process with a temporary nurse agency by defining the duties and objectives of both the hospital and the agency. The hospital should then structure its contractual relationship with the agency around these duties and objectives.

If the hospital wishes to use agency nurses, it should consider contracting only with specific agencies for the supplemental staff. The hospital requires experienced legal counsel or a consulting firm to develop a basic contract. (See Appendix 26-A for a sample contract that describes the rights and responsibilities of each party to the contract).

The hospital should assess the qualifications of the available temporary nurse agencies regarding their business practices and hiring standards. Next, the hospital can approach those agencies that appear to have the ability to meet its needs and send its contract negotiator to discuss possible arrangements with the interested agencies. The negotiable factors may vary, depending on the specific needs of the hospital. Some key elements, however, include the cost of the temporary nursing services. the cost of and the responsibility for the orientation program for the agency nurses, the delineation of the parties' duties, and the term of the contract.[31]

Temporary agency nurses generally receive a higher hourly salary than hospital staff nurses. This may create indirect costs to the hospital because the salary discrepancies may cause tension between the hospital staff nurses and the agency nurses and can lead to resentment and job dissatisfaction on the part of the hospital staff nurses. Such factors tend to increase the nurse turnover rate and therefore may indirectly cost the hospital money. Also, because the hospital pays a higher dollar amount per hour for agency nurses, their use consequently creates a significant increase in direct costs to the hospital at a time when cost containment is a crucial issue. Accordingly, the high cost of temporary agency nursing staff is a key issue in the negotiation of agency contracts. The hospital should aim to keep the amount paid for agency nurses per shift comparable with the amount paid (including benefits) for staff nurses of similar training and background. In addition, the hospital should insist on committed rates for the staff covered under the contract for the entire term of the contract.

Competence of Agency Staff

Measures to control the hiring policies and standards of the contracted temporary nursing agency should be a part of the contract. The hospital must make certain that the temporary agency requires its nurse applicants to complete an application process that adequately demonstrates to the agency (and to the hospital) (1) the nurse's strengths and weaknesses with respect to his or her ability to deliver quality patient care, (2) any current or past problems that may affect the nurse's ability to function properly at work, and (3) proper licensure and other qualifications to work as a nurse in that particular state (see Appendixes 26-B through 26-F for sample forms).

The temporary nurse agency should require each applicant to complete an application for employment that provides the following information about the applicant:[32]

- any physical, mental, or medical disability that could in any way interfere with the applicant's ability to perform the job functions of the position
- any criminal convictions, except for misdemeanors or summary offenses
- specialty areas of practice and any specialized training or experience
- educational background
- professional registration (license or certification)
- completion date of the applicant's last cardiopulmonary resuscitation (CPR) course
- complete employment history

The agency must obtain employer references (see Appendix 26-G for a sample form) that require the applicant's past employers to provide the agency with an evaluation of the applicant regarding the following attributes:[33]

- quality of work
- quantity of work
- attitude and ability to work in stressful situations
- dependability
- cooperation
- interpersonal skills
- ability to accept a leadership role
- attendance
- punctuality
- personal appearance

In addition to the above, the agency should collect information concerning the applicant's competency in the areas in which he or she will function. The agency should use competency checklists for all areas of medical and surgical practice and other nursing areas.

The hospital-agency contract should require the agency to retain on file a copy of the applicant's (1) license to practice; (2) Basic Cardiac Life Support (BCLS) or Advanced Cardiac Life Support (ACLS) certification; (3) CPR certification; (4) health history form; (5) physician's statement, including the results from any required tests; (6) I-9 form for employment eligibility verification, if appropriate; and (7) tax withholding forms. (See Appendix 26-H for a checklist used by an agency to ensure that each applicant has provided all of the required information.[34])

The contract should also require the temporary agency to make available all application documents for the hospital's inspection. In addition, the hospital may wish to obtain copies of certain documents for its own files. For example, the hospital may want a copy of a nurse's competency checklist so that it can make appropriate use of the nurse's abilities. The hospital may also request a copy of each agency nurse's license to practice and BCLS or ACLS certification. These points must be thoroughly considered in advance and included in the delineation of responsibilities in the contract.

Formal Orientation

The formal orientation period is another crucial negotiation factor. The hospital must determine how long the orientation period must be to meet its concerns about quality of care. Next, both parties must determine who pays for the agency nurses' attendance at the orientation and who actually prepares and presents the orientation program. Because the hospital is ultimately responsible for having properly oriented and competently trained nurses to deliver patient care, it is logical for the hospital to control the actual content and administration of the program and to determine its length. Whether the agency or the hospital pays for the orientation program may depend on the relative bargaining position of each party, as well as other terms of the contract. For example, a hospital may negotiate a contract under which the contracted agency agrees to pay for a one-day orientation program in return for the hospital's agreement that it will contact that agency first when it requires supplemental nursing staff.[35]

In the early years of temporary nursing agency operations, the majority of agency nurses did not receive any orientation to the hospital in which they were working.[36] The majority of those who did receive orientation rated it as inadequate.[37] In light of the new Joint Commission accreditation standards, concerns about quality of care, and licensure requirements of the various states, all hospitals that use agency nurses should institute an orientation process for them. It is difficult, however, to design a program that adequately orients the agency nurse and yet remains cost-effective. Because the lengthy orientation period that most hospitals provide their permanent nursing staff is inappropriate for temporary agency nurses, a hospital should develop a program specifically for these nurses.

The hospital should begin the process of developing an agency nurse orientation by formulating a policy statement based on its mission and strategic objectives.[38] This policy statement should reflect the hospital's concern regarding the quality of patient care at its facility. It should clearly define the relationship between the agency nurse and the hospital nursing staff, and it should inform the agency nurse of his or her responsibility to follow the hospital's policies and procedures. Many such models are available (see Exhibit 26-3); however, each hospital should develop its own policy statement based on its particular needs and objectives.

The hospital should also consider the following eight factors when developing its agency nurse orientation program:[39]

Exhibit 26-3
POLICY STATEMENT ON UTILIZATION OF SUPPLEMENTAL NURSING STAFF AT THE HOSPITAL OF THE FUTURE

The Hospital of the Future has a strong commitment to providing the highest possible level of nursing care. When our own staff is insufficient to meet the needs and demands of our internal or external customer, supplemental staffing agencies will be called upon to assist in meeting our staffing needs. It is expected that the care delivered by nurses from these supplemental services will reflect the hospital's philosophy and the philosophy of the department of nursing services.

When supplemental staff nurses are used, they will be made to feel an important part of our staff. Each nurse will be provided with a designated resource person who will assist the nurse in acclimating to the new environment and ensure that he or she is meeting all needs of the patients and their families. In the event the supplemental nurse or the resource nurse believes that the unit or patient assignment is inappropriate to the supplemental nurse's ability, an attempt will be made to transfer that nurse to a more appropriate assignment. At no time will the comfort of the nurse be given precedence over the quality of care provided to the patient.

The supplemental staff nurse will be expected to comply with all routine procedures in place for regular nursing staff. Further, he or she will be expected to develop a working knowledge of procedures that have been developed by the Hospital of the Future to guarantee that the highest quality of care consistently will be provided. The following policies and procedures will be available for review and should be reviewed by the supplemental nursing staff:

- the hospital's philosophy regarding patient rights
- the hospital's mission statement
- methodology used for making patient assignments
- appropriate documentation of patient care
- infection control and safety policies
- the hospital's ethics policy
- policies for protecting the rights of patients

1. overall value of the orientation program to quality of patient care that the hospital desires to achieve
2. cost of the program
3. program acceptability to agency nurses
4. program acceptability to the hospital's permanent nursing staff
5. standardization of the program so that the hospital and its permanent nursing staff can safely assume that all agency nurses who have been through the orientation program have at least the basic capabilities required for successful completion of the orientation
6. ease of implementation
7. compliance with Joint Commission standards
8. compliance with state and federal licensing and provider requirements

With its policy statement and the above considerations in mind, the hospital should develop some agency orientation program tools. The following list identifies items to be included in an orientation packet that can convey appropriate information to agency nurses:

- hospital's policy and philosophy statement regarding the use of supplemental staff and agency nurses
- philosophy of the nursing department
- mission statement of the hospital
- staff nurse job description that coincides with the position to be assumed by the agency nurse or job description for a specific staff-level position to be filled by the agency nurse
- description of the role of the nurse who is the designated resource for the agency nurse
- procedure for agency nurse sign-in with a copy of the sign-in sheet
- evaluation form to be completed by the charge nurse
- evaluation form to be completed by the agency nurse
- procedures for evaluation and disciplinary action
- overview of charting standards and abbreviations used in the hospital
- overview of policy for administering medications
- overview of emergency and disaster protocol
- map of the hospital and list of important telephone extensions

This material can be provided on the nurse's first day at the hospital or can be part of an orientation program that includes both experiential and reading modules.[40] The hospital's staff nurses serve in a resource capacity during the experiential portion of the agency nurse's orientation. Staff nurses can also be asked to evaluate the agency nurse's performance in this phase of the program. A small handbook can also serve to reinforce the hospital's key policies and procedures.[41] Each hospital should design its own orientation program so that it provides the agency nurse with all of the essential information required in safely and efficiently providing quality nursing care to the hospital's patients. The hospital should consider the value of a program that includes some experiential modules because they allow an opportunity to determine the ability of the agency nurse to deliver patient care. The orientation program should include a feedback mechanism for evaluation of the agency nurse's performance during the orientation process. Before allowing the agency nurse to deliver patient care, the hospital must carefully document that the nurse completed the orientation and was judged competent to deliver patient care in the areas to which he or she will be assigned.

Evaluation of Performance

Following the orientation program and the initial evaluation, the hospital is required to evaluate periodically the performance of the agency nurse. The contract between the hospital and the agency should clearly delineate if the hospital, the agency, or both will maintain a record of these periodic evaluations. Ideally, the hospital should evaluate and retain documentation of the agency nurse's performance and provide the temporary agency and the agency nurse with a copy of each evaluation. To ensure that quality and other standards are met, the hospital should evaluate the agency nurse one or more times during the first year that the nurse is assigned to the hospital. When the hospital is confident that the agency nurse is competent in the areas in which he or she is assigned, it should evaluate the nurse on an annual basis unless the supervisory nurse determines that an interim evaluation is necessary (see Exhibit 26-4 for a sample evaluation tool that can be used by a contracting hospital).

The hospital may also wish to require that an agency nurse has had prior experience in nursing. Experience of at least one year should significantly decrease the amount of orientation and supervision required for an agency nurse. Demanding a minimum experience level enables the hospital to standardize an orientation program that is suitable for nurses who can function at a level higher than that of a graduate nurse. This can also decrease the frustration of hospital staff nurses because experienced agency nurses can deliver patient care more independently.

Delineation of Responsibilities

The importance of delineating responsibilities of the parties in the contract cannot be overstressed. The hospital must work with the contracting agency to define clearly each party's individual responsibilities.[42] The hospital must carefully assess its needs and the regulatory environment in which it and the agency function before negotiating a contract. It is essential that the contract specify the party to

Exhibit 26-4
SAMPLE PERFORMANCE EVALUATION

Nurse Name: _____

Name of Hospital: _____

Assignment: _____ (From) _____ (To) _____

Hospital Contact: _____

The UHC Recruitment Services maintains performance evaluations on all nursing staff in compliance with JCAHO standards. Please evaluate the above named individual and check the category (above average, satisfactory, and below average) that best describes her/his performance.

Above average or below average ratings require a comment. Please use back of form, if necessary, for additional comments. Thank you.

Position Held in Your Employ: _____

Employment Dates: From: _____ To: _____

Position: _____ Temporary _____ Regular Status _____

Reason for Leaving: _____   Eligible for Re-Hire? _____

PERSONAL EVALUATION:	ABOVE AVG.	SATISFACTORY	BELOW AVG.	COMMENTS
Quality of Work				
Quantity of Work				
Attitude				
Ability to Work in Stressful and or New Situation				
Dependability				
Cooperation				
Interpersonal Skills				
Ability to Accept Leadership Role				
Attendance and Punctuality				
Personal Appearance				

Hospital: _____   City: _____   State/Zip: _____

Signature: _____   Title: _____   Date: _____

RNEVAL 10/91

Source: Courtesy of University Hospital Consortium, Oak Brook, IL.

be responsible for meeting the duties and obligations mandated by law, as well as the standards of the Joint Commission and the nursing profession. The delineation of responsibilities allows the hospital, through its policies and procedures relating to agency nurses, to apportion and manage any risk that it is unable to avoid.

NOTES

1. New Jersey General Assembly Committee on Health and Human Resources, Public Hearing to Examine the Problem of Nursing Staff Shortages in the State (1987), 19.

2. B. Bullough, et al., *Nursing Issues and Nursing Strategies for the Eighties* (New York: Springer Publishing Co., 1983), 22. (At the time this book was published, efforts to increase the supply of nurses to meet demand had been ongoing for about 15 years.)

3. RNs: Two-Thirds of Nursing Staff, *Hospitals* 60, no. 23 (1986): 74.

4. National Commission on Nursing, Initial Report and Preliminary Recommendations. Vol. 2 (1981), cited in Nurses' Legal Dilemma: When Hospital Staffing Compromises Professional Standards, E.K. Politis, *U.S.F.L. Rev.* 18, no. 109 (1983): 119.

5. American Hospital Association, Special Report: Nurse-Liability Woes, *AHA News.*

6. F.T. Helmer and P. McKnight, Management Strategies to Minimize Nursing Turnover, *Health Care Management Review* 14, no. 73 (1989): 74–75.

7. K. Sigardson, Why Nurses Leave Nursing: A Survey of Former Nurses, *Nursing Administration Quarterly* 7, no. 1 (Fall 1982): 1.

8. C.K. Davis, cited in Pay Equity—A "Cocamamie Idea"? The Future of Health Care May Depend Upon It, L.R. Lupica, *The American Journal of Law and Medicine* 13 (1988): 597–598.

9. National Commission on Nursing, *Summary of Public Hearings,* vol. 25 (1981), cited in Pay Equity, Lupica: 597.

10. American Hospital Association Center for Nursing, *1988 Report of the Hospital Nursing Personnel Surveys.*

11. Ibid.

12. Ibid.

13. Bullough, et al., *Nursing Issues,* 31.

14. Research Summaries, *Monthly Labor Review* 33 (August 1983).

15. Ibid.

16. N.L. Chaska, et al., A Joint Effort to Mediate the "Outside Force" Staffing Dilemma, *Journal of Nursing Administration* 10, no. 12 (1980): 13–18; C.M. Boyer, The Use of Supplemental Nurses: Why, Where, How? *Journal of Nursing Administration* 9, no. 3 (1979): 56–60; T. Langfor and P.A. Prescott, Hospitals and Supplemental Nursing Agencies: An Uneasy Balance, *Journal of Nursing Administration* 9, no. 11 (1979): 16–20; D.R. Sheridan, et al., Using Registry Nurses: Coping with Cost and Quality Issues, *Journal of Nursing Administration* 12 no. 10 (1982): 26.

17. *Nurses' Legal Handbook, Legal Aspects of Nursing Practice* (Springhouse, Pa., Springhouse Corporation, 1984): 58.

18. Restatement of the Law of Agency (2d), Section 227, 500, American Law Institute (1958).

19. E.K. Politis, Nurses' Legal Dilemma: When Hospital Staffing Compromises Professional Standards, *U.S.F.L. Rev.* 18 (1983): 109.

20. *Nurses' Legal Handbook,* 56, 59.

21. *Darling v. Charleston Community Hospital,* 211 N.E.2d 53 (Ill. 1965).

22. R.E. Stromberg, The Legal Perspective, *Trustee* 30 (1977): 25.

23. E.P. Bernzweig, *The Nurse's Liability for Malpractice: A Programmed Course,* 5th ed. (St. Louis: C.V. Mosby Co., 1990), 88.

24. Stromberg, The Legal Perspective, 25.

25. J.P. Marren, Tackling the Legal Issues in Managed Care (Paper presented at The First National Managed Care Forum sponsored by the Society for Healthcare Planning and Marketing of the American Hospital Association, February 3–6, 1991, Chicago, Ill.), 5.

26. Stromberg, The Legal Perspective, 25.

27. Bernzweig, *Nurse's Liability for Malpractice,* 88.

28. Ibid.

29. Marren, Tackling the Legal Issues, 5.

30. Ibid.

31. Sheridan, et al., Using Registry Nurses, 26–27.

32. University Hospital Consortium Recruitment Network-Travel, *Application for Employment* (1990). Available through University Hospital Consortium, 2001 Spring Road, Suite 700, Oakbrook, IL 60521-1890.

33. University Hospital Consortium Recruitment Network-Travel, *Employer Reference* (1990). Available through University Hospital Consortium (see Note 32 for address).

34. University Hospital Consortium Recruitment Network-Travel, *Applicant Check List* (1990). Available through University Hospital Consortium (see Note 32 for address).

35. Sheridan, et al., Using Registry Nurses, 26–27.

36. P.A. Prescott and T.L. Langford, Supplemental Agency Nurses and Hospital Staff Nurses: What Are the Differences? *Nursing Health Care* 2, no. 4 (1981): 200, 204.

37. Ibid.

38. Sheridan, et al., Using Registry Nurses, 26, 28.

39. Ibid.

40. Ibid., 26, 29.

41. Ibid.

42. Ibid.

Appendix 26-A

Sample Nurse Agency Contract

_____

_____

_____

_____

_____

_____

Dear _____:

This letter, when accepted by _____ (the "Hospital"), will constitute an agreement (the "Agreement") between UHC Professional Resource Network ("PRN") and the Hospital under which the UHC Travel Nurse Service ("TNS"), a division of PRN, will recruit registered nurses ("nurses") for temporary placement in the Hospital upon the request of the Hospital on the terms and conditions stated herein.

1.   TERMS OF AGREEMENT

   The term of this Agreement will commence on _____ and will expire on _____, unless sooner terminated as provided in Paragraph 3.

2.   DESCRIPTION OF SERVICES

   TNS will use its best efforts to recruit nurses for temporary placement in the Hospital upon the request of the Hospital.

3.   TNS POLICIES

   The Policies and Procedures (the "Policies") attached hereto as Exhibit A are incorporated into and made a part of this Agreement. TNS and the Hospital each agree to be bound by and comply with the terms of the Policies applicable to it.

Source: Courtesy of University Hospital Consortium, Oak Brook, IL.

4.   <u>RESPONSIBILITIES OF THE PARTIES</u>

A.   In addition to the responsibilities stated in the Policies, TNS will have and fulfill the following responsibilities:

(1)   TNS will submit to the Hospital an information package on each nurse TNS refers to the Hospital. The package will include the following information:
   a.   general personnel data
   b.   completed skills list
   c.   completed reference checks
   d.   evidence of appropriate licensure/certification
   e.   completed physical examination
   f.   hospital evaluations (if any) from previous assignments.
   g.   CPR certification

(2)   Unless otherwise agreed to by the parties in writing, for each nurse accepted by the Hospital, TNS will be responsible for paying the nurse's transportation expenses to the Hospital from the nurse's place of departure at the commencement of the assignment and from the Hospital to the nurse's place of destination at the conclusion of the assignment.   TNS will pay an amount equal to twenty-seven and one-half cents (27.5 cents) per mile.   TNS's total obligation for transportation expenses will not exceed the cost of round trip airfare for the total distance or five hundred and twenty dollars ($520.00), whichever is less. Notwithstanding anything to the contrary herein, TNS will not be responsible for paying the nurse's transportation expenses if the nurse leaves the assignment before its scheduled expiration date, unless the nurse leaves the assignment for justifiable reasons as determined by TNS in its sole discretion.

(3)   Unless otherwise agreed to by the parties in writing, for each nurse accepted by the Hospital, TNS will be responsible for making arrangements for housing and for paying the nurse's housing costs during the pendency of the assignment.   Housing will consist of either a shared or a private apartment and will be near the Hospital, if available.   Notwithstanding anything to the contrary herein, TNS will not be responsible for paying the nurse's housing costs which become due after the termination of the assignment if the nurse leaves the assignment before its scheduled expiration date unless the nurse leaves the assignment for justifiable reasons as determined by TNS in its sole discretion, whereupon the payment will not exceed two (2) days following the termination of the assignment.

(4)   TNS will coordinate the execution of an assignment agreement between the Hospital and each nurse accepted by the Hospital. TNS will provide executed copies of the assignment agreement to the Hospital and the nurse.

B.   In addition to the responsibilities stated in the Policies, the Hospital will have and fulfill the following responsibilities:

(1)   The Hospital will designate a representative who will serve as the primary liaison between the Hospital and TNS.

(2)   The Hospital will verify the qualifications and skills of each nurse accepted by it, including the nurse's possession of a currently valid license issued by the state in which the Hospital is located.

(3)   The Hospital will provide to each nurse accepted by it an orientation of not less than two (2) full days. The orientation will include both a general hospital orientation and a "where practicable" unit specific orientation.

(4)   The Hospital will offer to each nurse accepted by it a minimum assignment of thirteen (13) weeks unless otherwise agreed to in writing by TNS, the Hospital and the nurse. The Hospital may renew an assignment in increments variable weekly by mutual agreement of the Hospital, TNS and the nurse. The Hospital shall, "where practicable," give TNS at least fifteen (15) days prior written notice of its intent to renew an assignment.

(5)   The Hospital will offer and provide a work week of 36-40 hours per week. (Provision can be made for part-time work as agreed upon by Hospital, Nurse, and TNS.)
Hospital will be billed for designated hours per week as put forth in the executed assignment agreement.

5.   **SUPERVISION OF NURSES**

The Hospital will have the sole and exclusive authority and responsibility to supervise the work of the nurse.

6.   **CANCELLATION OF ASSIGNMENT**

The Hospital may terminate an assignment which has not commenced either by giving written notice of the termination at least fourteen (14) days prior to the scheduled commencement date of the assignment or by paying TNS a fee in an amount equal to two (2) times the weekly TNS Service Fee.

7. TERMINATION OF AGREEMENT

a. The Hospital may terminate an assignment if it determines that the nurse is unacceptable. In terminating an assignment, the Hospital will comply with its policies and procedures, the terms of all contracts to which it is bound and all applicable laws and regulations. The Hospital will notify TNS in writing of the termination of an assignment. The Hospital will give TNS such written notification prior to the Hospital's taking action unless circumstances render such notification impossible.

b. If the Hospital terminates a nurse assignment, the Hospital will pay to TNS all fees chargeable to the Hospital under this Agreement up to and including the date of termination. In addition, the Hospital will pay to TNS a penalty if the Hospital terminates the assignment without reasonable cause which is supported by written documentation from the Hospital and the nurse submitted to TNS within ten (10) days after the date of termination. "Reasonable cause," as used herein, will not include circumstances such as reduction in work force, a strike or a work stoppage. The penalty will be an amount equal to the sum of two (2) times TNS's weekly service fee, the nurse's transportation expenses, including the nurse's transportation expenses from the Hospital to the nurse's place of destination (calculated in accordance with Paragraph 4A(3) (less any amounts previously reimbursed by the Hospital to TNS) and the nurse's housing costs, including the nurse's housing costs which are due or which become due after the termination of the assignment (calculated in accordance with Paragraph 4A(4) (less any amounts previously reimbursed by the Hospital to TNS). The penalty will be due and payable thirty (30) days after the Hospital's receipt of the penalty notice.

8. ASSIGNMENT

The Hospital may select one of two options in connection with its acceptance of UHC-TNS travel nurse staff. The Hospital may lease the nurse from TNS (Option A) or, in the alternative, it may employ the nurse (Option B).

A. Option A: Nurse Maintained on TNS Payroll

(1) If the Hospital selects Option A, TNS will maintain the nurse on its payroll and remit such compensation and other obligations to the nurse or to governmental agencies, as

appropriate and the Hospital will reimburse TNS for these expenses.

(2)   In accordance with Paragraph 8C(2), the Hospital will pay monthly to TNS an hourly fee (the "Option A Fee").

(3)   For purposes of calculating the nurse's salary, the Hospital agrees to pay TNS at a rate of:

_____/HR;   _____/HR for overtime (as required by applicable law and as calculated by the Hospital); _____/HR for holidays (as defined by the Hospital)

B.   <u>Option B: Nurse Maintained on Hospital Payroll</u>

(1)   If the Hospital selects Option B, the Hospital will maintain the nurse on its payroll, and will be responsible for the nurse's compensation, including the payment of wages, tax withholdings, social security and other obligations, including workers' compensation, imposed by federal, state, and local law.

(2)   In accordance with Paragraph 8C(2), the Hospital will pay monthly to TNS an hourly fee (the "Option B Fee").

(3)   The Hospital agrees to pay the nurse at a rate of:

_____/HR; _____/HR for overtime (as required by applicable law and as calculated by the Hospital) ;

_____/HR per hour for holidays (as defined by the Hospital)

C.   <u>Options A & B: Payment Provisions</u>

(1)   The Hospital will notify TNS weekly of all hours worked by each nurse. The Hospital may provide TNS with initial notification by means of a telephone call or a faxed report. (The Hospital shall submit to TNS written confirmation of all information sent to TNS by verbal means).

(2)   TNS will submit to the Hospital a monthly statement setting forth the Option Fee. Payment will be due within thirty (30) days after the date the Hospital receives the monthly statement.

THE HOSPITAL SELECTS THE OPTION CHECKED BELOW:

___ OPTION A   ___ OPTION B   ___ OTHER OPTION

9.   <u>HOLIDAYS</u>

Holidays are defined by the hospital as listed below:

<u>NAMES</u>	<u>HOURS</u>
1. _____	_____ TO _____
2. _____	_____ TO _____
3. _____	_____ TO _____
4. _____	_____ TO _____
5. _____	_____ TO _____
6. _____	_____ TO _____
7. _____	_____ TO _____
8. _____	_____ TO _____
9. _____	_____ TO _____
10. _____	_____ TO _____
11. _____	_____ TO _____
12. _____	_____ TO _____

10.   <u>REGULAR STATUS EMPLOYMENT</u>

The Hospital may offer a nurse a regular-status position upon completion of the nurse's assignment without incurring additional fees or a penalty. If the Hospital hires the nurse for a regular-status position prior to completion of the assignment, the Hospital will continue to pay TNS the fees due it under this Agreement until the scheduled end date of the assignment.

11. **MEDICARE ACCESS CLAUSE**

Until the expiration of four (4) years after the furnishing of the services described in this Agreement, TNS shall make available, upon written request to the Secretary of Health and Human Services, or upon request to the Controller General, or any other of their duly authorized representatives, a copy of this Agreement and such books, documents and records as are necessary to certify the nature and extent of the costs of such services.

12. **NOTICES**

Any notices required or authorized under this Agreement shall be in writing and shall be deemed "given" two (2) days after the notice is sent by certified mail, return receipt requested, addressed as follows:

HOSPITAL: _____
_____
_____
_____

TNS: UHC Professional Resource Network
UHC Travel Nurse Service
2001 Spring Road, Suite 700
Oak Brook, IL 60521-1890
1-800-326-2020 FAX: 1-708-954-5897

13. **GOVERNING LAW**

This Agreement shall be governed by the laws of the state of Illinois.

14. **NO WAIVER**

The express or implied waiver of any provision hereof shall not be construed to be a waiver of any other provision or a waiver of any similar or recurring breach.

15. **FURTHER ASSURANCES**

Each party agrees to perform any further acts and to execute and deliver any further documents which may be reasonably necessary to carry out the provisions of this Agreement.

16. **ASSIGNMENT**

PRN may assign this Agreement and its rights and duties under this Agreement to an affiliate or subsidiary of PRN.

17.   REPRESENTATIONS AND WARRANTIES

The Hospital warrants and represents that it may lawfully contract with TNS for the assignment or employment of travel nurses and that such assignment and employment are not restricted by any collective bargaining agreement or any order or judgment of any court or governmental agency and that the Hospital will be responsible for the payment of all taxes that may arise as a result of its employment of the travel nurses and any compensation paid to them by the Hospital.   The Hospital further warrants and represents that such assignment and employment will not violate any federal, state, or local law, order or decree respecting equal employment opportunity.   TNS shall defend, indemnify and hold the Hospital harmless for and against any and all claims, ("claims") demands, causes of action lawsuits and costs and expenses, including reasonable attorney's fees, incurred by Hospital arising out of or related to the performance of this Agreement by TNS, including but not limited to claims for personal injury and professional malpractice.   The Hospital shall defend, indemnify and hold TNS harmless from and against any claims, demands, causes of action, lawsuits, damages and costs and expenses, including reasonable attorney's fees incurred by TNS, as a proximate result of the acts or omissions of the Hospital employees except those arising from or related to TNS's gross negligence or willful misconduct on the part of it or its employees.

UHC has an obligation to report all claims involving TNS nurses to our insurance carriers in order to ensure coverage under the terms of our policies.   In light of this requirement, it is incumbent that institutions contracted with under the TNS program notify us within 30 days of knowledge that a TNS nurse is or may be involved in a "claim."   Failure to do so shall negate any participation by UHC in settlement of a claim.

18.   ENTIRE AGREEMENT

This Agreement, together with such other documents approved by the parties and attached to this Agreement, constitute the entire agreement between the parties and supersede all prior oral and written agreements, understandings, commitments, and practices between them. Except as otherwise provided in this Agreement, no amendments to either this Agreement or the documents attached to this Agreement may be made except by a writing signed by the parties.

IN WITNESS WHEREOF, the parties have executed this
Agreement on the date opposite their signatures below:

HOSPITAL

BY:_____

DATE:_____

ITS:_____

UHC PRN

BY:_____

DATE:_____

ITS:_____

Appendix 26-B

Sample Employment Application

An Equal Opportunity Employer

PERSONAL

Position Applied For:

☐ UHC Travel Nurse Service   Date: _____

☐ UHC Supplemental Employment Service (per diem)

Date Available For Work: _____   Social Security Number: _____

Name (Last Name First): _____

Present Address: _____
           (No. and Street)   (City)   (State)   (Zip)

Phone: (   ) _____   Daytime Phone: (   ) _____

Best Time to Contact: _____

Permanent Address: _____
           (No. and Street)   (City)   (State)   (Zip)

Permanent Phone: (   ) _____   Date of Birth: _____
                                    (Need not be completed; Age not used in employment decision)

Emergency Contact: _____   Emergency Contact Phone: (   ) _____

Are you able to perform the job functions of the position for which you have applied? ____Yes ____No
If no, what reasonable accommodation(s) will you require?

_____

Have you ever been convicted of a crime excluding misdemeanors or summary offenses? ____ Yes ____ No
If yes, please explain: _____

_____

Have you previously worked as a travel nurse? ____ Yes ____ No

Have you previously worked in a university hospital? ____ Yes ____ No

How did you become aware of the UHC Recruitment Services travel program?   ____ Journal Ad   ____ Newspaper Ad

____ Word of Mouth   ____ Minority Agency   ____ Job Fair   ____ Radio/TV

If "Word of Mouth," please provide name of individual _____

Have you worked for UHC before? ____ Yes ____ No   If yes, when: _____

Do you have any relatives employed by the UHC Recruitment Services? ____ Yes ____ No If yes, who? _____

Source: Courtesy of University Hospital Consortium, Oak Brook, IL.

362

POSITION

Specialty Areas of Practice: (for type of hospital use Univ., Teach., Comm., Rural or Veteran)

(1) _____ Yrs. of Exp. _____ Type of Hospital _____

(2) _____ Yrs. of Exp. _____ Type of Hospital _____

(3) _____ Yrs. of Exp. _____ Type of Hospital _____

(4) _____ Yrs. of Exp. _____ Type of Hospital _____

At which university hospitals are you particularly interested in practicing?   _____

_____

_____

Avail.: _____ Any   _____ Day   _____ Even.   _____ Night   _____ Week-end   _____ Holiday

Length of Shift Interested In: ___Any   ___8-Hour   ___10-Hour   ___12-Hour Other: _____
Specify

EDUCATION

SCHOOL	NAME/LOCATION	DATES ATTENDED	MAJOR	DEGREE ATTAINED
School of Nursing:				
College/University:				

PROFESSIONAL CERTIFICATIONS

STATE / TYPE	STATE / TYPE	STATE / TYPE	STATE / TYPE	STATE / TYPE

Please include BCLS/CPR documentation with your application.

Specialized training and or experience: _____

_____

_____

Responses are true and complete. I understand that falsification of information is sufficient cause for dismissal. In the event of employment, I agree that my employment with UHC Recruitment Services is at will, which means that UHC Recruitment Services has the right to discharge me for any reason whatsoever, or I have the right to terminate my own employment for any reason whatsoever.

Signature: _____   Date: _____

EMPLOYMENT HISTORY

Other names under which you've been employed: _____

I hereby give permission to UHC Recruitment Services to contact any of the references marked, "Yes".

_____
Signature

In order to expedite your file to our hospitals, please send us copies of any recent evaluations or letters of reference you may have. Also, please fill out the reference information on this application completely. Thank you.

Present or Most Recent Employer: Dates: From _____ to _____   May we contact for reference? _____ Yes____ No

Institution: _____ Phone: _____ Supervisor: _____

Full Address: _____ Salary: _____ Reason for Leaving: _____

_____   _____

Specialty Area: _____ Duties: _____

Unit Name: _____

Next Previous Employer: Dates: From ____ to _____   May we contact for reference? _____ Yes____ No

Institution: _____ Phone: _____ Supervisor: _____

Full Address: _____ Salary: _____ Reason for Leaving: _____

_____   _____

Specialty Area: _____ Duties: _____

Unit Name: _____

Next Previous Employer: Dates: From ____ to _____   May we contact for reference? _____ Yes ____ No

Institution: _____ Phone: _____ Supervisor: _____

Full Address: _____ Salary: _____ Reason for Leaving: _____

_____   _____

Specialty Area: _____ Duties: _____

Unit Name: _____

Next Previous Employer: Dates: From _____ to _____   May we contact for reference? _____ Yes ____ No

Institution: _____ Phone: _____ Supervisor: _____

Full Address: _____ Salary: _____ Reason for Leaving: _____

_____   _____

Specialty Area: _____ Duties: _____

Unit Name: _____

Next Previous Employer: _____   Dates: From ____ to _____   May we contact for reference? _____ Yes ____ No

Institution: _____   Phone: _____   Supervisor: _____

Full Address: _____   Salary: _____   Reason for Leaving: _____

_____   _____

Specialty Area: _____   Duties: _____

Unit Name: _____

Next Previous Employer: _____   Dates: From ____ to _____   May we contact for reference? _____ Yes ____ No

Institution: _____   Phone: _____   Supervisor: _____

Full Address: _____   Salary: _____   Reason for Leaving: _____

_____   _____

Specialty Area: _____   Duties: _____

Unit Name: _____

Next Previous Employer: _____   Dates: From ____ to _____   May we contact for reference? _____ Yes ____ No

Institution: _____   Phone: _____   Supervisor: _____

Full Address: _____   Salary: _____   Reason for Leaving: _____

_____   _____

Specialty Area: _____   Duties: _____

Unit Name: _____

Next Previous Employer: _____   Dates: From ____ to _____   May we contact for reference? _____ Yes ____ No

Institution: _____   Phone: _____   Supervisor: _____

Full Address: _____   Salary: _____   Reason for Leaving: _____

_____   _____

Specialty Area: _____   Duties: _____

Unit Name: _____

Appendix 26-C

Sample Verification of Licensure and Status

List all states in which you currently or have in the past held licensure:

STATE	NUMBER	CURRENT?	EXP.DATE
_____	_____	YES__NO__	_____
_____	_____	YES__NO__	_____
_____	_____	YES__NO__	_____
_____	_____	YES__NO__	_____
_____	_____	YES__NO__	_____
_____	_____	YES__NO__	_____
_____	_____	YES__NO__	_____
_____	_____	YES__NO__	_____
_____	_____	YES__NO__	_____

(place additional information on separate sheet of paper)

COPIES OF ALL CURRENT LICENSES MUST BE PROVIDED

Have there ever, at any point in your professional career, been judgments or settlements made against you in professional liability case(s)?

YES_____   NO_____

-If "yes," state each instance in full detail on a separate sheet.

Have you ever had, or are you currently in the process of having licensure denied, revoked, suspended, limited, placed on probation, or voluntarily relinquished?

YES_____   NO_____

If "yes" explain each instance in full detail on a separate sheet.

Responses are true and complete. I understand that falsification of information is sufficient cause for dismissal.

Signature:_____   Date:_____

Source: Courtesy of University Hospital Consortium, Oak Brook, IL.

Appendix 26-D

Employment Health History

NAME: _____

          Last   First   Middle

SOCIAL SECURITY NO.: _____

DATE: _____

CHECK BELOW IF YOU HAVE OR HAVE EVER HAD ANY OF THE FOLLOWING:

YES	NO		YES	NO		YES	NO		YES	NO	
		Eye trouble			Cough			Ulcers			Dizziness, blackouts
		Ear trouble			Broken bones			Pneumonia			Loss of weight
		Back trouble			Gonorrhea			Gallstones			Shortness of breath
		Knee trouble			Bladder trouble			Jaundice			Swelling of ankles
		Skin trouble			Pleurisy			Epilepsy			High blood pressure
		Kidney trouble			Varicose veins			Syphilis			Nervous breakdown
		Stomach trouble			Chest pain			Convulsions			Loss of appetite
		Frequent colds			Heart trouble			Typhoid fever			Hernia or rupture
		Sinusitis			Diabetes			Hemorrhoids			Bone, joint deformity
		Head injuries			Arthritis			Tuberculosis			Tumors or cancer
		Asthma			Seizures			Rheumatic fever			Hepatitis
		Hay fever			Severe depression			Abdominal pain			Difficulty hearing
		Skin problems/rash			Glasses			Feelings of sadness			
		Heart murmur			Anemia			Unable to sleep			
		Stroke			Headaches			Numbness			
		Sugar in urine			Drinking problem						

Source: Courtesy of University Hospital Consortium, Oak Brook, IL.

Have you had:

	Yes	No	When
Mumps			
Rubella (German measles)			
Rubeola (7-Day measles)			
Tetanus booster			
Tuberculosis skin test			
Chest X-ray			
Regular physical exam			
Pap smear			
Chicken pox (Varicella)			

Have you ever been:

	Yes	No	When
Turned down for employment for medical reasons?			
Turned down for military service for medical reasons?			
Turned down for an insurance policy for medical reasons?			
Treated by a physician for anything other than a minor illness in the past three years?			
Restricted on your driver's license?			

OCCUPATIONAL HEALTH

	YES	NO	
Have you had needlesticks in the past?			If yes, explain.
Have you ever had a blood transfusion(s)?			If yes, explain.
Have you ever been exposed to a patient with a positive (+) HIV antibody?			If yes, explain.
Have you ever been exposed to a patient with hepatitis?			If yes, explain.
Have you ever been exposed to any other occupational health hazard?			If yes, explain.
Have you ever been exposed to toxic chemicals, fumes, mists, dusts, radiation or excessive noise?			If yes, explain.

The preceding information is true and complete. I understand that any misstatement or omission may be grounds for my discharge. I understand the foregoing medical history and results of the physical examinations will become part of my medical record and I authorize its release to UHC Recruitment Services and appropriate hospital personnel.

Signed: _____   Date: _____

Appendix 26-E

Sample Physician's Statement

Patient Name: _____ Date: _____

Address: _____

_____

The above-named patient has been examined by me and found to be in good physical and mental health, free from communicable diseases, and able to function as an RN at full capacity.

Date of Exam: _____

TB Skin Test: _____ Chest X-Ray:_____
             Date/Results   *(only if positive skin test)*   Date/Results

Rubella Titer_____ Rubeola Titer: _____
            Date/Results   Date/Results

Physician's Signature: _____ Address: _____

Physician's Name (Print):_____

Physician's License No.: _____

Please attach X-Ray results, TB Test results, copies of complete blood count and urinalysis.
Some hospitals now require proof of tetanus, hepatitis B and varicella vaccination.
If you have documentation of vaccination or titers, please attach it to this form.

Source: Courtesy of University Hospital Consortium, Oak Brook, IL.

Sample Affirmative Action Questionnaire

UHC Recruitment Services makes every effort to comply with Affirmative Action Guidelines. Submission of this form is **VOLUNTARY** and the information provided is kept confidential, for office use only. Refusal to provide this information will not affect your chances of being referred or hired.

We ask that you complete the following form and return it in the envelope provided. Thank you.

NAME: _____ SOCIAL SECURITY NUMBER:_____

DATE OF BIRTH:_____ SEX: **MALE / FEMALE** (circle one)

ETHNICITY GROUP: (check one)

_____ **American Indian or Alaskan Native**
A person having origins in any of the original peoples of North America and who maintains cultural identification, Tribal affiliation or community recognition.

_____ **Black**
A person having origins in any of the Black racial groups of Africa.

_____ **Asian or Pacific Islander**
A person having origins in any of the original peoples of the Far East, Southeast Asia, the Indian Subcontinent, or the Pacific Islands. This area includes, for example: China, India, Japan, Korea, the Philippine Islands and Samoa.

_____ **Hispanic**
A person of Mexican, Puerto Rican, Cuban, Central or South American culture or other Spanish culture or origin regardless of race.

_____ **White**
A person having origins in any of the original peoples of Europe, North Africa or the Middle East.

HANDICAP: YES / NO (circle one)   IF YES, PLEASE INDICATE _____

MILITARY STATUS: YES / NO (circle one) IF YES, PLEASE CHECK BELOW:

_____ Active Reserve

_____ Inactive Reserve

_____ Veteran

_____ Viet Nam Era Veteran

_____ Disabled Veteran

_____ Disabled Viet Nam Veteran

_____

Source: Courtesy of University Hospital Consortium, Oak Brook, IL.

Appendix 26-G

Sample Employer Reference Form

The person whose signature appears beneath mine has applied to UHC Recruitment Services for employment in the health care field and has submitted your name as a former employer for reference purposes.

The serious nature of our responsibility to our patients and institutions is such that any consideration of the individual by UHC is dependent upon receipt of satisfactory references. We would, therefore, appreciate your cooperation in replying to the questions listed below. Please be assured that your responses will be kept in the strictest confidence. Thank you in advance for this courtesy.

_____
Facilitator

I hereby authorize you to fulfill the above request for information.

_____
Applicant's Signature

Applicant's Name: _____   Soc. Security Number: _____

Position Held in Your Employ: _____

Employment Dates: From: _____ To: _____   Position: _____ Temporary _____ Regular Status

Reason for Leaving: _____   Eligible for Re-Hire? _____

PERSONAL EVALUATION:	ABOVE AVG.	SATISFACTORY	BELOW AVG.	POOR	COMMENTS
Quality of Work					
Quantity of Work					
Attitude					
Ability to Work in Stressful and or New Situation					
Dependability					
Cooperation					
Interpersonal Skills					
Ability to Accept Leadership Role					
Attendance and Punctuality					
Personal Appearance					

Hospital: _____   City: _____ State/Zip: _____

Signature: _____   Title: _____ Date: _____

Source: Courtesy of University Hospital Consortium, Oak Brook, IL.

Application Checklist

The contractual agreement between UHC Recruitment Services and UHC participating hospitals necessitates that the following documents be on file *before* a nurse is able to begin an assignment with UHC.

☐ Application
(With <u>complete</u> employment history
data, i.e., names, addresses
and telephone numbers)

☐ Competency Check List

☐ Notarized Documents Required
with I-9 Form

☐ Copy of Nursing   ☐ _____
License(s)   ☐ _____
(Include copies for
every state in which your license
is current.)

☐ BCLS Certification

☐ ACLS Certification

☐ Health History Form

☐ Physician's Statement
Test Results For:
____ TB
____ Rubella
____ Rubeola

☐ Federal Withholding Form

☐ State Withholding Allowance Form

☐ Other _____
_____
_____

Source: Courtesy of University Hospital Consortium, Oak Brook, IL.

chapter 27

Dealing with the Violent Patient

Susan Salpeter

INTRODUCTION

Violent and aggressive behavior has become more common in American society. Such behavior is not limited to inner cities. It is also increasing in areas where it had not been prevalent, such as schools. Health care institutions are not immune to the increase in violent behavior. The risk of such activity in any one institution depends in part on its location and patient population.

Although a hospital cannot be expected to totally control the behavior of its patients, it should be able to demonstrate that it has prepared for the possibility of violence. Hospitals that are not prepared face losses in several areas. If staff members are injured in caring for or subduing violent patients, the hospital faces workers' compensation claims. If other patients or visitors are injured, the institution may face civil liability. If the staff is overzealous and restrains a patient unnecessarily, the hospital may face charges of assault and battery. Violent patient behavior also has a negative impact on staff morale and public opinion. Staff and patients may be reluctant to work at or be treated in an institution they believe is dangerous. They also may become frustrated if they believe that their ability to provide appropriate care to nonviolent patients is compromised because of the presence of a violent patient.

PREPARING FOR THE RISKS

Hospital administrators and risk managers must prepare the institution to handle patients who may become violent.

There should be policies and procedures in place that address these situations. In addition, the hospitals should provide adequate education and training to those employees, such as nursing staff and security guards, who are likely to be involved in such situations. Education should include how to deal with violence in the patient care setting as well as the use of restraints and special considerations in caring for inpatient prisoners. By taking a proactive approach, violent behavior may be either prevented or handled in a way that will be the least disruptive for staff and patients.

UNDERSTANDING VIOLENT BEHAVIOR

To prevent violent behavior, it is important to understand the factors that contribute to violence in the medical center. Hospitals are frightening places for most patients. Their personal privacy is invaded and they must give up a degree of control over their bodies and their environment. Physicians, nurses, and other staff may come in and out of their rooms giving them exams, medications, and treatments. Patients are under stress because of their illnesses, fears of medical procedures, and an uncertain future because of health problems. The fear and anxiety patients experience make them less able to control their emotions and behavior. Many patients, especially the elderly who make up the majority of the patient population, become easily confused in the unfamiliar hospital environment.

Patients who exhibit tendencies toward aggressive or violent behavior should be assessed to determine whether there is an underlying condition. These conditions may be treatable.

DRUG ABUSE AND THE VIOLENT PATIENT

Violence is frequently associated with drug or alcohol abuse. Depressant drugs, such as alcohol, sedatives, or barbiturates, can cause impulsive feelings, reduce judgment, and lower an individual's inhibitions, leading patients to strike out. Stimulants such as amphetamines and cocaine can cause feelings of euphoria, suspiciousness, and even paranoia. They can also increase physical activity, irritability, and agitation. Hallucinogenics such as PCP commonly cause intense agitation and violent activity. Individuals under the influence of a combination of drugs have an even greater potential for violence, since one drug may potentiate the effects of another.

Drug use can also lead to violence in patients undergoing withdrawal. Individuals may become violent in their demands for drugs when withdrawal symptoms become uncomfortable and the patient seeks relief. Alcoholics may experience delusions, hallucinations, and agitation as a result of delirium tremens. LSD users may experience hallucinations, anxiety, and "flashbacks" several years after they have stopped taking the drug.

THE VIOLENT PSYCHIATRIC PATIENT

Certain psychiatric illnesses may make an individual more prone to violence. Paranoid disorders have been associated with assault. In the acute phase, paranoid individuals are very sensitive to any perceived slight and may strike out. Schizophrenic patients have disintegrated personalities that may increase their violent urges. Command hallucinations may induce patients to commit violent acts. During the manic phase of bipolar disorders, individuals can be irritable and belligerent. They are easy to provoke and can become aggressive.

UNDERLYING MEDICAL CONDITIONS MAKING A PATIENT VIOLENT

A patient's underlying medical condition can also affect the potential for aggressive or violent behavior. In addition to neurologic injuries or disorders, electrolyte imbalances, hypoglycemia, and other metabolic disorders can affect mental status and behavior. Renal and liver failure can result in uremia and hepatic encephalopathy. Cardiac and pulmonary disorders can cause hypoxia, which can lead to organic brain syndrome.

Individuals with these conditions are more prone to violence than the general patient population. However, any individual may become violent under certain circumstances. Patients may experience fear, anxiety, and frustration while hospitalized. Individuals who are by nature suspicious, aggressive, and impatient may not be able to control these emotions. If these feelings become overwhelming, they can be transformed into anger and violence.

IMPORTANCE OF EDUCATION FOR EMPLOYEES

To prevent violent episodes, hospital staff should be aware of and alert to verbal and nonverbal behavior indicating that patients may become violent. The staff can then intervene to prevent such episodes. Behavior may include angry or loud speech. Some individuals become quiet, but speak more intensely and forcefully. They may express anger or frustration, state that they are losing control, or threaten violence. Nonverbal behavior can also provide clues to impending violence. Patients may pace nervously, tense their muscles, change positions frequently, grimace, and clench and unclench their fists. They may also make threatening gestures toward the staff. Staff members often instinctively recognize such signals, and should trust and act on these feelings. At this stage, it may be possible to intervene and prevent a violent episode. It is helpful to have hospital security guards on standby.

DEFUSING THE VIOLENCE

In trying to defuse potentially violent situations, it is important to approach the patient in a way that will not worsen the situation. Employees must recognize that their own behavior affects the patient's behavior. They should not approach the patient in an aggressive, threatening manner. This can make the patient angrier and more frightened, increasing the potential for violence. The staff must try to help the patient overcome his or her frustration and anger, and to calm down. This can be accomplished using the verbal and nonverbal techniques described next.

Staff members should approach the patient slowly in a calm, self-confident manner. During this time they should assess the patient to determine the degree of danger present. Staff should not get too close to the patient. Although it is helpful to speak to the patient in private, staff members should never put themselves in danger. If a patient is extremely agitated, talk to the patient in a hallway. If the situation occurs in a patient room, the staff member should stand between the patient and the door to avoid becoming trapped in the room.

In approaching the violent patient, ask whether help or assistance is needed. In this way, staff members assume the role of the patient's advocate. Staff members should acknowledge the patient's feelings, and offer to help resolve the situation that is making the patient angry.

It is important for staff members to recognize that their body language can be threatening to a patient. The staff should not stand too close to or touch the patient. Standing face-to-face to a patient with arms folded across the chest may be perceived as threatening. Instead, hospital employees should stand at an angle to the patient with arms at their sides, fists unclenched, at least one arm's length away from the patient. It is important to make eye contact but this should not be continuous, since the patient may perceive it as a challenge.

If the patient does not respond to these interventions and continues to be aggressive or threaten violence, it is necessary to inform the patient that violent behavior is unacceptable. Some patients respond positively to firm instructions. Others may require a visual warning, such as having security officers come to the area. In some situations, these interventions will not be successful. The patient may be too confused or agitated to respond. The behavior may have erupted too quickly for staff members to use these techniques. Once violent behavior occurs, it is necessary to take immediate action to minimize injury to the patient and staff. The area where the incident is occurring should be cleared of other patients and visitors. There should be enough staff members present, including security officers, to effectively restrain the patient. A staff member should explain to the patient what is being done and why. Once the patient has been physically restrained, he or she may be placed in seclusion or given chemical restraints depending on the patient's underlying medical condition.

VIOLENCE IN THE EMERGENCY DEPARTMENT

The emergency department (ED) presents special considerations in the recognition and management of violent patients. It is open to the public 24 hours a day, seven days a week. Staff members do not usually know the patients, and therefore rarely know whether any underlying medical condition is causing or contributing to the patient's behavior. Emergency room patients are often intoxicated or under the influence of drugs. They may be victims of violence, and they or their families may want to strike out violently in response. Rival gang members injured in gang wars may want to continue their fighting. The ED staff must also be alert to the possibility that patients and visitors may be armed. When weapons are found special procedures must be taken to disarm the patient or visitor. See Exhibit 27-1 for a sample policy addressing the handling of weapons.

Exhibit 27-1
POLICY FOR CONTROL OF WEAPONS BROUGHT INTO THE HOSPITAL

Definition: Weapon refers to any firearm, knife, or device that could cause bodily harm or injury.

Policy: Weapons are never permitted in the hospital or on hospital property. Patients and visitors are instructed to register all weapons with the hospital security department. Whenever possible, if patients present for admission with a weapon it will be sent home with a family member. Patients being admitted through the emergency department (ED) or arriving at the hospital without a family member will have their weapon confiscated and stored in the hospital security department until they are discharged. Visitors will be advised of the need to check any weapon with hospital security prior to entering a patient care area. Visitors not complying with this regulation will be denied access to the hospital. Local authorities will be called if the visitor becomes disruptive.

Procedures

1. If a patient or visitor volunteers that he/she is in possession of a weapon, instruct the patient to wait outside the patient care area and call security.

2. If a weapon is found on a patient in the ED, the weapon should be confiscated immediately and security should be called.

3. If a patient or visitor is already in the patient care area and is found to have a weapon but is unwilling to surrender it, security should be called.

- Do not attempt to confront the patient/visitor.
- Explain the specific circumstance to security such as type of weapon, whether the patient/visitor is causing a problem or disturbance, or whether the patient/visitor is threatening to cause a problem in the patient care area or is making unusual/unreasonable demands of staff.
- After discussion with security, a decision should be made as to how to handle the situation, particularly a decision as to whether any patients or staff on the unit are in immediate harm. If this is the case, staff members will attempt to remove patients/visitors from the vicinity and advise them of the potential for harm.

USING SECURITY GUARDS IN THE EMERGENCY DEPARTMENT

Hospitals in high crime areas or urban settings should have security guards on duty and visible in the ED at all times. They should also consider installing panic buttons or alarms so that the staff can summon additional help. Because of the increased potential for violence, including armed violence in the ED, it is especially important to train staff in management of ED violence. Staff members should also be aware of their limitations. They must learn to recognize when security and/or police officers should be called for assistance.

Once a violent ED patient has been subdued, treatment should include an evaluation of whether there is an underlying physical or mental cause for the violence. The medical staff must also determine whether these individuals represent a threat to themselves or others, and to hospitalize them either voluntarily or involuntarily. Patients who are not a threat to themselves or others and do not require hospitalization should be encouraged to receive follow-up care or counselling to help them address specific problems they may have.

TRAINING THE HOSPITAL SECURITY STAFF

Hospital security guards assume many different functions. In many cases state law governs how much authority and responsibility a hospital security guard can assume.

Although many hospitals employ off-duty police officers, they should be aware that the scope of authority of a police officer may change when the officer takes a position as a security guard.

The hospital administration should decide whether or not security personnel should be armed. In most cases hospitals have elected not to provide hospital security guards with weapons. The importance of establishing cooperative working relationships with law enforcement agencies cannot be emphasized enough, as quick response from the local police can prevent serious problems in the health care setting when violence erupts.

THE APPROPRIATE USE OF RESTRAINTS

There are times during a patient's care where physical restraint becomes necessary but staff members should be advised that restraints are never appropriate if they are used merely for the staff's convenience. Patients who pose a threat to caregivers or to themselves may require restraints. Hospitals should develop policies to describe the situations in which the use of restraints is warranted, the role of the staff in monitoring the restrained patient, and the duration of time that the restraints can be used. Frequent evaluation of the patient (including the circulation of the patient limb distal to the restraint) should be enforced and documented frequently. When the patient's condition changes, making the restraints no longer necessary, they should be removed. See Exhibit 27-2 for specific details regarding the use of restraints.

Exhibit 27-2
POLICY CONCERNING MANAGEMENT OF DANGEROUS OR COMBATIVE PATIENTS

Purpose: Patients exhibiting behavior indicating that they are a danger to themselves or others must be managed in such a way as to minimize the threat of injury or harm. If restraints are necessary, they are to be used in a humane manner as a therapeutic measure to prevent patients from causing physical harm to themselves or others.

Procedures

1. Staff members should be aware of and alert to signs of potential violence.
2. If staff members determine that a patient is demonstrating behavior that indicates he or she may be violent, they should assess the level of danger presented. Security officers should be notified of the situation and put on standby to provide assistance as needed.

3. When speaking to patients exhibiting signs of impending violence, it is preferable to have one staff member approach the patient. However, under no circumstances should staff members place themselves in danger.
   - Staff members should not be alone in a room with an armed patient.
   - Staff members should always position themselves so that they have a means of exit.
4. If a patient becomes violent, adequate staff members should be present to restrain the patient. If possible, there should be five staff members present—four to hold the patient's extremities, and one to apply the restraints.
5. The decision to apply restraints will be made by the physician after personally observing and examining the patient. The head nurse or charge nurse may, in an emergency or in the absence of a physician, confirm in

continues

Exhibit 27-2 continued

writing the use of restraints after personally observing and examining the patient and determining that restraint poses no undue health risks. Orders must be confirmed by the physician within two hours by telephone or in person. Orders must be countersigned within 12 hours.

6. The order will state the purpose of restraints, the length of time restraints are to be used, and the clinical justification for the duration.

7. Staff will prepare the patient by explaining the reason for restraint, reassuring the patient that this is not a punitive measure and explaining expectations for removal, and advising the patient of his or her right to have a person notified of the restraint.

8. When applying restraints
   - For the combative patient, have adequate number of personnel.
   - Use padding between the cuffs and the patient's body. Check belts and cuffs for correct fit so that there is good circulation, yet not so loose that the patient can slip off the restraints.

9. The patient in restraints must be observed every 15 minutes. These observations should include an assessment of the security of the restraints and the circulation to the extremities. The findings must be recorded in the medical record.

10. The patient should receive nursing care a minimum of every two hours including
    - changing position
    - exercising extremities
    - offering nourishment and liquids
    - offering bed pan or urinal
    - checking for need for PRN medications
    - taking vital signs and recording in medical record

11. Documentation must include
    - the chart documenting the events leading up to the need for restraints, the time the restraints were applied, the justification for their use, observations of the patient's behavior, and the time the restraints were removed.
    - the Special Precautions Form, used to document the 15-minute checks and two-hour nursing care

CARING FOR PRISONERS IN THE HOSPITAL SETTING

Many hospitals have the responsibility of caring for prisoners who develop medical problems while incarcerated. If the hospital sees a large number of prisoners annually, it may wish to establish a designated unit to ensure that the safety and security of other patients within the hospital will not be jeopardized. Further, the hospital is obligated to ensure that its staff is protected from the prisoner and that the prisoner does not suffer harm or a violation of rights when security attempts to protect the rights of others.

The best way to prevent inpatient prisoner problems is to draft policies and procedures that clearly delineate the responsibilities of the staff (both hospital and law enforcement or prison employees) and the rights of the prisoner. A sample policy is provided in Exhibit 27-3.

The risk manager should also identify legal issues and problems that are likely to arise when prisoners become patients. In the ED, police officers may bring in arrestees. Police may ask staff members to draw blood or get other body fluid samples (gastric contents or urine) to prove that

the arrestee was under the influence of drugs or alcohol when the alleged crime was committed. Staff should be reminded that an arrest does not negate a person's rights, and thus, consent should be obtained from the prisoner prior to drawing blood or collecting samples. The risk manager and legal counsel should evaluate state laws that govern the hospital's operation. Policies addressing the collection of such evidence should be carefully drafted to comply with state law and should be kept where they can be easily accessed. Staff should also be educated on how evidence needs to be maintained, labeled, and transferred to the investigating authority in order to maintain the "chain of evidence."

Violent prisoners who require admission following care in the ED should always be admitted to a unit where they can be placed in a private room and where a guard can be assigned to protect other patients and staff. Also, if the prisoner/patient requires legal processing or if witness identification is to occur, the prisoner should be placed in a room that is as far away from the general patient population and staff as is safe. Preferably, a guard should be placed where other patients, visitors, and staff can prevent contact with the prisoner.

Exhibit 27-3
POLICY DEALING WITH INPATIENT PRISONERS

The following policy has been developed to help ensure the safety of all patients, visitors, and staff. Hospital personnel are urged to assist officers in discharging their duties, to the extent that those duties are compatible with the hospital's responsibility to the patient.

Procedures:

1. The hospital requires that all inpatient prisoners be guarded **at all times** by the custodial agency responsible for the prisoner. Exceptions to this, such as prisoners released on their own recognizance or on a medical furlough, will be reviewed, in advance, by hospital security and the custodial agency.

2. The admitting department will notify hospital security and the hospital administrator of every admission of an inpatient prisoner to the hospital and will provide a daily roster of all inpatient prisoners.

3. Hospital administration and the hospital public relations department will coordinate their efforts to ensure that any press releases regarding prisoners are appropriate and in accordance with the prisoner's rights and hospital policy.

4. The hospital security department will be responsible for coordinating checkin and checkout (including change of shift and relief) procedures for all police and corrections officers assigned to prisoners admitted as inpatients to the facility and will coordinate any security issues with the involved agency.

5. Officers, when assigned by external law enforcement and corrections agencies, are to remain within the prisoner's room on the inpatient units. In intensive care units (especially if the patient is in critical condition) the officer may sit outside the door of the prisoner's room. Officers are to leave prisoner's rooms only when relieved or on request of the physician or other appropriate health care provider.

   - If the officer on duty is requested to leave the room of the prisoner, the officer will assume a position to maintain visual contact with the prisoner, but of sufficient distance to protect the prisoner's right to confidentiality.
   - If bed curtains must be drawn or the door closed, the officer will assume a position that will prevent the prisoner's escape.
   - The officer will re-enter the room of the prisoner as requested by the physician or other appropriate health care provider or on departure of the physician or health care provider.
   - If the inpatient prisoner goes into the operating room (OR), the officer must remain in the room until the patient is anesthetized. Then the officer must leave the OR and wait outside the room. When the prisoner is transferred to the recovery room, the officer will accompany and remain with the prisoner.
   - Exceptions to the provisions requiring the officer to be present in the prisoner's room can be made due to the physical conditions in the room, or by infection control considerations. Exceptions will be approved by the senior management team of the hospital, including hospital security, administration, nursing, and the attending physician. Information on the reason for the exception should be shared with security and nursing personnel, and the duration for such exception should be noted. The decision should be re-evaluated on a daily basis.

6. External officers are to comply with all hospital policies.

7. All officers, when coming on duty, must read the *Universal Blood and Body Fluid Precautions* and *Correctional Officers Policy*.

8. All hospital personnel will be made aware that surgical and other medical instruments (as well as kitchen utensils) can be used as weapons by inpatient prisoners. Every possible precaution will be exercised to make such instruments inaccessible to the prisoner.

9. The hospital security department will assist external police or correctional officers as appropriate when requested. The hospital security department does not assume responsibility for the custody of the prisoner.

   - In the event of an extreme emergency that incapacitates the assigned external officer, the hospital security supervisor will be responsible for assigning personnel to protect patients, staff, and visitors pending arrival of appropriate relief coverage.
   - Hospital security does not provide relief coverage for external officers for purposes such as meals or personal breaks.
   - In the event that a patient prisoner expires while at the hospital, hospital security will assist in the external officers either getting access to the morgue or transfer of the body to the coroner.

10. To provide protection for physicians, nurses, hospital personnel, visitors, and other patients and to prevent the escape of the inpatient prisoner, the external officer shall use external restraints (which may include hand-cuffs or leg irons) unless they directly interfere with required medical care. The use of restraints must be approved by the patient's physician and must be used in compliance with hospital policy of the safe use of restraints.

11. Inpatient prisoners who must leave their bed and room for any purpose, such as visits to ancillary treatment areas, must be accompanied by the assigned external officer.

12. Law enforcement and corrections officials will not interrogate or conduct official proceedings involving an inpatient prisoner unless the attending physician is informed and grants consent. This is to ensure that the inpatient prisoner is medically able to participate in such activity.

13. No visitors shall be allowed in the room of the inpatient prisoner except those authorized by the custodial agency. The custodial agency, rather than hospital personnel, are responsible for screening all visitors. Admission of any representative from the press requires explicit concurrence from hospital administration.

THE COSTS OF VIOLENCE IN THE HEALTH CARE SETTING

The costs of violent activity in health care institutions can be high in both human and financial terms. Hospitals can take steps to minimize these costs by providing employees with education and training to teach them to prevent violent activity by intervening in situations where patients exhibit combative, aggressive behavior.

BIBLIOGRAPHY

Turner, J.T. 1988. *Handbook of Hospital Security and Safety.* Gaithersburg, Md.: Aspen Publishers, Inc.

Turner, J.T. 1984. *Violence in the Medical Center.* Gaithersburg, Md.: Aspen Publishers, Inc.

chapter 28

A Clinical Proactive Approach

Barbara J. Youngberg

The development of a proactive risk management program involves the integration of several pre-existing hospital disciplines and coordination among various hospital departments and administrative personnel. The more traditional focus placed an emphasis on risk transfer, such as the purchase of insurance, lawsuit management, and the successful defense of suits arising out of patient injuries.

A NONTRADITIONAL APPROACH

By contrast, proactive risk management identifies clinical areas of *potential* risk exposures and develops aggressive programs to optimize the care provided and utilize actual or near errors as learning experiences. This nontraditional approach requires that the risk manager no longer function in isolation. He or she must interact with other disciplines to acquire knowledge, understanding, and appreciation of the nature of "clinical risk." The traditional elements of insurance, litigation, safety and security issues, and staff education remain, but now the risk manager becomes concerned with the quality of clinical management.

In the past, risk managers have been slow to embrace this philosophy because they felt that quality of care issues were best left to the quality assurance professionals. Recent reviews of economic factors in the health care industry, however, suggest that the majority of dollars spent each year on risk-related activities are associated with significant adverse clinical incidents and staff errors, rather than with such issues as safety or security. Surely the development of a program that *prevents* injury rather than focuses on limiting liability once an injury occurs can be more cost-efficient.

ELEMENTS OF A PROACTIVE PROGRAM

The following elements are essential for an aggressive proactive risk management program:

- identification of the high-risk exposures in clinical areas of the hospital
- identification of key staff in clinical departments who can assist in the recognition of practice behaviors resulting in past patient and staff injuries or with the potential for future injuries
- identification of the types of clinical incidents that *always* result in departmental or interdisciplinary review
- coordination with appropriate hospital departments and their support in effecting changes deemed necessary as a result of departmental reviews (a process to initiate this action and follow-up also should be developed)

It is necessary for a successful proactive program to focus on quality care, rather than on patient injury! In other words, the program should emphasize elements of practice that could result in patient injury and not wait for the injury to occur.

Additional program requirements are often identified during the hospital's risk management self-assessment (see Chapter 4) and can be used to customize the risk management effort. For example, after completion of the self-assessment, a risk manager may find that there is no system in place for sharing information about "risky" physician behavior to the credentialing committee or no mechanism for tracking nurse performance over time. These omissions in the follow-up of risk management can make a program ineffective and must be addressed to guarantee success.

DEVELOPING DEPARTMENT-SPECIFIC GUIDELINES

Obviously, an aggressive proactive program will gain acceptance among staff members if they believe it is designed to optimize the care rendered to patients and to protect them from an unpleasant experience of becoming involved in a case of malpractice. The program will be even more accepted if the staff is allowed to set the clinical guideposts that form its core. Clearly, flexibility in the system is required so that it can conform to changes in clinical specialties. For example, any new technology in a clinical service should go through a period of monitoring and evaluation to identify previously unrecognized risk.

The proactive risk management program should be tailored to complement the pre-existing occurrence screen/incident reporting portion of the program. As indicated in the sample department-specific programs presented in Appendix 28-A, there is significant interface with the incident reporting system described in Chapter 5. A base manual provides clinical indicators for typically high-risk departments. Additional monitors become part of the manual through supplements.

Each individual department-specific program should operate under the following basic guidelines:

- Initially physicians and nurses identify areas of potential high-risk exposure within their respective clinical units. These areas include specific clinical indicators, as well as interdepartmental and interdisciplinary issues that could directly impact on the quality of care and result in patient injury.
- Staff then determines which of the above items require mandatory 100 percent review and which require monitoring to identify trends.
- Staff also suggests which items and resultant analyses are appropriate to drive department-specific educational programs.
- All department staff members are encouraged to participate actively in the program and assured that the results will be used to promote quality and not establish fault.
- Staff is advised that the program has a second focus of evaluating staff resources and can be used to justify the need for additional staff or perhaps more extensive training of present staff. Showing this type of specific data to the administration adds credibility to a department's request for more personnel or enhanced staff training.
- A proactive program aids in the coordination of services among departments and in the resolution of conflicts that may arise. It also helps to minimize the likelihood that an adverse outcome will result from multidisciplinary involvement in a patient's care.
- The indicators should focus on ongoing treatment, not necessarily on outcomes.
- Data collection and problem recognition should come from a number of sources, including physicians' and nurses' identification of problems and patients' feedback. It is important to recognize that *quality* is often defined very differently by a consumer than it is by a caregiver. In order to achieve total quality one must be aware of the many elements of the definition.

Appendix 28-A

Sample Proactive Risk Management Programs

AMBULATORY CARE DEPARTMENT

The following risk indicators should be monitored and tracked within the ambulatory care department. Risk indicators that are preceded by an asterisk (*) require 100 percent concurrent review. Those preceded by a plus (+) should have interdisciplinary review. All others should be tracked and evaluated through the case review process as staff deems appropriate.

* + Death of any patient in the ambulatory care area.
* + Complication of treatment resulting in unexpected or unplanned admission to the hospital.
  Serious patient complications as a result of diagnostic and/or therapeutic treatment rendered in the ambulatory care area.
  Unexpected return to the center or unplanned hospital admission for problems associated with initial visit.
  Medication, equipment, or treatment error resulting in patient injury or requiring transfer to the hospital.
  Failure to perform diagnostic test ordered or loss of results necessary to confirm diagnosis or determine treatment.
  Patient or visitor fall with injury.
  Patient refuses treatment or leaves the ambulatory care area "against medical advice" (AMA).
  Failure to perform a pregnancy test on any female (of childbearing age) who presents with a complaint of abdominal pain.

ANESTHESIA DEPARTMENT

The following risk indicators should be monitored and tracked within the anesthesia department (which includes the post-anesthesia recovery area). Risk indicators that are preceded by an asterisk (*) require 100 percent concurrent review. Those preceded by a plus (+) should have interdisciplinary review. All others should be tracked with case reviews as staff deems appropriate.

* + Neurologic sequelae following the administration of anesthesia.
* + Intraoperative or postanesthesia recovery (PAR) death.
* + Medication or transfusion error resulting in patient injury or additional treatment.
*   Improper airway management resulting in patient injury.
* + Unplanned admission to intensive care unit.
    Nerve or muscle damage due to improper positioning and limb restraint.
*   Any equipment malfunction or failure to use appropriate monitoring devices during anesthesia.
    Discharge of same-day surgery patient without responsible adult.
    Patient leaving same-day surgery against medical advice.
    Reintubation in PAR for respiratory distress.
    Mechanical trauma due to improper intubation.
    Patient injury during transfer from cart to operating room table or recovery room.

CRITICAL CARE DEPARTMENT—ADULT

The following risk indicators should be monitored and tracked within the critical care department. Risk indicators that are preceded by an asterisk (*) require 100 percent concurrent review. Those preceded by a plus (+) should have interdisciplinary review. All others should be tracked and evaluated through the case review process as staff deems appropriate.

* + Unexplained or unexpected death while in the intensive care unit (ICU).
* + Readmittance to ICU less than 48 hours following transfer from ICU to a general floor.
* Trauma incurred within ICU (e.g., falls, burns, procedure complications).
* Medication/transfusion error causing injury.
  + Transfer to ICU within 12 hours following admission to a general floor.
    No written consent or improper consent for procedure.
    Patient leaving ICU against medical advice.
* + Significant patient deterioration following "off-unit" special procedure (e.g., computed tomography scan).
* + All administrative issues related to do-not-resuscitate (DNR) orders.
* + Any security problems (e.g., patient or family disconnecting ventilator or tampering with infusion pump) resulting in patient harm or death or capable of having caused patient harm or death.
* + Any ethical dilemmas (e.g., patient/family disagreement related to DNR status) involving terminal or moribund patients.
* + Delayed response of code team or physicians when significant change in patient's condition or patient arrest occurs.
    Hospital-acquired infection.
* Infiltration from intravenous injection that results in tissue, muscle, or nerve damage.

DENTISTRY DEPARTMENT

The following risk indicators should be monitored and tracked within the dentistry department. Risk indicators that are preceded by an asterisk (*) require 100 percent concurrent review. Those preceded by a plus (+) should have interdisciplinary review. All others should be tracked with case reviews as staff deems appropriate.

Occlusal relapse (nonunion/malunion) following maxillofacial surgery.
Patient required blood transfusion following maxillofacial surgical procedure.
* + Intraoperative death.
  Failure to administer prophylactic antibiotics to patients with history of valvular heart disease, prosthetic valves, surgically constructed systemic-pulmonary shunts, or idiopathic hypertrophic subaortic stenosis.
  Unanticipated laryngospasm or airway obstruction during maxillofacial procedure.
  Intravenous sedation given in dentist's office without availability of any emergency equipment.
* Outpatient dental procedure performed that resulted in inpatient admission.
  Temporomandibular joint surgery performed on a patient without obtaining at least one of the following radiographic studies:
  Tomogram
  Magnetic resonance imaging
  Arthroscopy

DERMATOLOGY DEPARTMENT

The following risk indicators should be monitored and tracked within the dermatology department. Risk indicators that are preceded by an asterisk (*) require 100 percent concurrent review. Those preceded by a plus (+) should have interdisciplinary review. All others should be tracked with case reviews as staff deems appropriate.

Failure to perform eye examination and document results in chart prior to inception of ultraviolet light therapy.

* Adverse patient outcome, including increased erythema, skin burns, and/or corneal damage following ultraviolet light treatment.

Patient developed elevated triglyceride blood levels (> 700 mg) while receiving etretinate therapy.

Failure to obtain serum blood urea nitrogen, creatinine, and liver function test measurement prior to treatment with methotrexate.

* Patient developed renal/liver failure as a result of methotrexate therapy.

Excessive bleeding following excision of skin lesion(s).

Failure to obtain culture and sensitivity (C/S) or to follow up on C/S report on skin infections.

Failure to obtain pregnancy test on patient receiving Accutane® for the treatment of acne.

* Bovie burns to patient treated with electrosurgery for skin lesions.

EMERGENCY DEPARTMENT

The following risk indicators should be monitored and tracked within the emergency department (ED). Risk indicators that are preceded by an asterisk (*) require 100 percent concurrent review. Those preceded by a plus (+) should have interdisciplinary review. All others should be tracked with reviews as staff deems appropriate.

* + Death in ED.

* + Death prior to arrival in ED if the hospital has responsibility for transport service and personnel.

Patient remaining in ED for more than 12 hours.

Patient returning to ED within 48 hours for complaints of nonresolution of original presenting problem.

* + Acute trauma patient requiring surgery who remains in ED for more than 1 hour.

Patient who expires within seven days following discharge from ED.

* Patient presenting to ED following a suicide attempt who is sent home after stabilization, especially if the patient is not currently involved with a psychiatrist and a psychiatrist or psychologist was not consulted.

* Patient called back to ED because of an error in reading an x-ray or electrocardiogram or because of incorrect laboratory results.

* Patient discharged from ED without a complete set of vital signs or without being seen by a physician.

* Patient seen in ED following traumatic head injury who is discharged with abnormal level of consciousness or with abnormal neurologic signs.

Medication error resulting in allergic reaction or injury.

Treatment or procedure error resulting in patient injury.

No written consent or improper consent for procedure or treatment when consent is necessary.

ENDOCRINOLOGY DEPARTMENT

The following risk indicators should be monitored and tracked within the endocrinology department. Risk indicators that are preceded by an asterisk (*) require 100 percent concurrent review. Those preceded by a plus (+) should have interdisciplinary review. All others should be tracked with case reviews as staff deems appropriate.

* +   Unanticipated or unexpected death.
    Transfer to an intensive care unit within 24 hours following admission to endocrinology department.
    Patient developed neurogenic hypotension following thyroid needle biopsy.
    Patient developed respiratory distress following thyroid needle biopsy.
    Patient admitted to hospital with diabetic ketoacidosis that required more than 24 hours to control.
    Damage to radial artery following arterial blood sampling.

GENETICS DEPARTMENT

The following risk indicators should be monitored and tracked within the genetics department. Risk indicators that are preceded by an asterisk (*) require 100 percent concurrent review. Those preceded by a plus (+) should have interdisciplinary review. All others should be tracked with case reviews as staff deems appropriate.

*   No genetic consultation (or consultation offered and declined) for parents following delivery of child with multiple congenital anomalies.
    Absent record of genetic consultation performed (or offered and declined) for parents with family history of multiple congenital anomalies.
    Failure to afford genetic testing to mother with history of teratogenic environmental exposure.
    Failure to offer and/or provide counseling services to parents following birth of child with multiple congenital anomalies.
* +   Unexplained or unexpected death of infant with multiple congenital anomalies.

HEMATOLOGY AND ONCOLOGY DEPARTMENT

The following risk indicators should be monitored and tracked within the hematology and oncology department. Risk indicators that are preceded by an asterisk (*) require 100 percent concurrent review. Those preceded by a plus (+) should have interdisciplinary review. All others should be tracked with case reviews as staff deems appropriate.

    Persistent or delayed bleeding following bone marrow biopsy and aspiration (or bone marrow harvest) that required transfusion of red blood cells or platelets.
    Osteomyelitis following bone marrow biopsy and aspiration (or bone marrow harvest).
*   Cardiac puncture or hemopericardium following bone marrow biopsy and aspiration.
*   Chemotherapeutic agent extravasation resulting in tissue necrosis that required surgical debridement and/or skin grafting.
* +   Chemotherapeutic agents contributing directly to major organ or system failure or patient death.
    Cellulitis or infection at central venous catheter insertion site.
    Long-term infectious complications related to central venous catheter insertion.

HOME HEALTH CARE DEPARTMENT

The following risk indicators should be monitored and tracked within the home health care department. Risk indicators that are preceded by an asterisk (*) require 100 percent concurrent review. Those preceded by a plus (+) should have interdisciplinary review. All others should be tracked and evaluated through the case review process as staff deems appropriate.

* + Death within one week of client who was discharged from hospital to home health care (unless client was designated do-not-resuscitate).
* + Equipment failure resulting in client injury or death (e.g., ventilator or infusion pump malfunction).
  Incorrect use by client or client's family of medical equipment that results in client injury.
  Medication error resulting in client injury or death.
  Wound dehiscence or infection.
  Lack of follow-up by consultants (e.g., social workers, rehabilitation specialists) where ordered and indicated.
  Caregivers' deviation from agreed-upon plan of care, whether or not injury to client occurred.
  Inappropriate or inadequate vendor response in the provision of equipment or medication necessary to provide adequate home care.
  Client injury or exacerbation of client's condition resulting from improperly controlled or maintained environmental conditions (e.g., lack of heat or air conditioning, filth, lack of water or refrigeration).

INFECTIOUS DISEASE DEPARTMENT

The following risk indicators should be monitored and tracked within the infectious disease department. Risk indicators that are preceded by an asterisk (*) require 100 percent concurrent review. Those preceded by a plus (+) should have interdisciplinary review. All others should be tracked with case reviews as staff deems appropriate.

* Renal failure due to failure to monitor drug levels and blood urea nitrogen (BUN)/creatinine levels of patient receiving nephrotoxic antibiotics.
  Failure to offer or make available azidothymidine to patient with pneumocystis pneumonia.
  Extravasation of intravenous (IV) antibiotics into tissue that results in tissue damage.
  Failure to document in chart current weight of patient who is receiving IV antibiotics.
  Failure to stop or change antibiotics within eight hours after culture and sensitivity test indicates a resistant strain.

NEONATAL INTENSIVE CARE UNIT

The following risk indicators should be monitored and tracked within the neonatal intensive care unit (NICU). Risk indicators that are preceded by an asterisk (*) require 100 percent concurrent review. Those preceded by a plus (+) should have interdisciplinary review. All others should be tracked with reviews as staff deems appropriate.

* + Term baby admitted to NICU from the well baby nursery.
* + All neonatal deaths.
* + Neonate admitted with diagnosis of neonatal abnormality.
  Nerve, tissue, or muscle damage resulting from intravenous infiltration or from infusion of tissue-damaging medications.
* + Neonate requiring reintubation or tracheostomy following extubation.
* + Neonate who has a seizure prior to discharge from NICU.
  Medication or treatment errors causing patient injury.
  Equipment malfunction, with or without patient injury.
* + Nosocomial infection.
* + Neonate with excessive blood loss from catheter disconnects.
* + Transfusion errors.
* + Treatments performed within NICU without appropriate parental or guardian consent.
  Parent's or guardian's refusal of treatment, elopement or unauthorized removal of child from unit.
  Any significant neonatal injury resulting from delivery (skull fracture, brachial palsy, cord injury, etc.).

NUCLEAR MEDICINE DEPARTMENT

The following risk indicators should be monitored and tracked within the nuclear medicine department. Risk indicators that are preceded by an asterisk (*) require 100 percent concurrent review. Those preceded by a plus (+) should have interdisciplinary review. All others should be tracked with case reviews as staff deems appropriate.

* + Myocardial infarction, cerebrovascular accident, or death in patient within 24 hours following radiopharmaceutical administration.
* Severe chest pain and/or arrhythmia in patient receiving radiopharmaceutical administration.
   Absence in chart of correlation between nuclear medicine diagnostic studies and available pathology reports.
   Failure to document prescription and procedure in chart both in treatment plan and procedure note.
   Error in dosage or in drug administered with or without subsequent patient injury or side effect.
   Need to reschedule procedure due to lack of patient preparation.
   Extravasation of radiopharmaceutical drug that causes tissue damage.

OBSTETRICS DEPARTMENT

The following risk indicators should be monitored and tracked within the obstetrics department. Risk indicators that are preceded by an asterisk (*) require 100 percent concurrent review. Those preceded by a plus (+) should have interdisciplinary review. All others should be tracked with reviews as staff deems appropriate.

* + Maternal or infant death (unless fetus weighs less than 500 g).
* + Delivery of an infant, via planned cesarean section or following induction, weighing less than 2,500 g or with hyaline membrane disease.
   Apgar score of less than 6 at 1 minute or 7 at 5 minutes.
* Maternal injuries or complications related to delivery or anesthesia.
* + Infant injury related to delivery or anesthesia.
* + Infant transfer to the neonatal intensive care unit for complications that developed following delivery.
   Excessive maternal blood loss—defined as blood loss greater than 500 cc. It may also be defined as a drop in hemoglobin of 3.5 or more or a drop in hematocrit of 11 or more.
 + Infant who has a seizure prior to discharge.
   Delivery of an infant weighing less than 1,800 g in a hospital without a neonatal intensive care unit.
   Equipment malfunction.
   Second stage of labor greater than 2.5 hours.
* + Major congenital anomalies of the newborn (not anticipated prior to delivery).
   Emergency cesarean section that occurs more than 30 minutes from "decision to incision."
   Retained objects and/or instruments following obstetrical procedure.
   Medication or transfusion errors resulting in maternal or neonatal injury.
   Delivery attended by licensed physician without obstetrical privileges.
   Any high forceps delivery.

OPHTHALMOLOGY DEPARTMENT

The following risk indicators should be monitored and tracked within the ophthalmology department. Risk indicators that are preceded by an asterisk (*) require 100 percent concurrent review. Those preceded by a plus (+) should have interdisciplinary review. All others should be tracked with reviews as staff deems appropriate.

* * + Surgery performed on wrong eye.
* * + Wrong procedure or treatment performed.
* * + Retinal damage during surgery.
* * + Optic or other nerve damage intraoperatively or postoperatively.
* * + Instrument breakage or malfunction resulting in patient injury or potential harm.
    Incorrect needle, sponge, or instrument count that is unreconciled or omission of a count that is required by hospital policy.
    No written consent or improper consent for treatment performed.
* * + Transfusion or medication error resulting in patient injury.
    Patient or visitor injury or falls.
    Significant adverse drug reaction.

ORTHOPEDICS DEPARTMENT

The following risk indicators should be monitored and tracked within the orthopedics department. Risk indicators that are preceded by an asterisk (*) require 100 percent concurrent review. Those preceded by a plus (+) should have interdisciplinary review. All others should be tracked with case reviews as staff deems appropriate.

Dislodgment or complication of device, graft, implant, or prosthesis.
Periarticular cellulitis or sepsis following arthrocentesis.
* * Intraoperative fracture or dislocation.
* * + Hemorrhage or hematoma requiring transfer to the intensive care unit.
* + Disparity of preoperative and postoperative diagnoses of bone tumor.
Malunion following pinning and reduction of supracondylar humerus fracture that requires osteotomy.
* * Unexpected reapplication of cast following infection, neurological impairment, decreased circulation, or inadequate immobilization.
* * Development of pressure sores requiring skin grafts.
Infection following surgical treatment of scoliosis that requires incision and drainage.
* * + Intraoperative or postoperative myocardial infarction or death of patient.
Patient developed fat embolus postoperatively.
Development of pulmonary embolus postoperatively.
Renal or liver damage secondary to antibiotic drug therapy that was ordered (or continued) in absence of objective signs of drug reaction.
Patient remained in hospital for period longer than diagnosis-related group recommendation due only to delay in discharge planning.
Epidural morphine given to patient with known spinal deformity, urinary tract infection, or prostatitis.
Incident of pneumonia or atelectasis related to immobilization.
Development of compartment syndrome following closed intermedullary nailing of the tibia.

OTOLARYNGOLOGY DEPARTMENT

The following risk indicators should be monitored and tracked within the otolaryngology department. Risk indicators that are preceded by an asterisk (*) require 100 percent concurrent review. Those preceded by a plus (+) should have interdisciplinary review. All others should be tracked with case reviews as staff deems appropriate.

Patients admitted for epistaxis following outpatient treatment.
Patients readmitted for epistaxis following inpatient treatment.
* Development of orocutaneous fistula following head or neck surgery for cancer.
Patient developed pneumothorax following tracheostomy.
* Cerebrospinal fluid leak following removal of an acoustic neuroma.
Central neurological infection following otolaryngology procedure.
Injury of facial nerve during mastoid or parotid surgery.
* + Postoperative or intraoperative death.
Blood loss greater than 300 cc following tonsillectomy or adenotonsillectomy.
Patient developed hearing loss due to medication or procedure.

PATHOLOGY DEPARTMENT

The following risk indicators should be monitored and tracked within the pathology department. Risk indicators that are preceded by an asterisk (*) require 100 percent concurrent review. Those preceded by a plus (+) should have interdisciplinary review. All others should be tracked with reviews as staff deems appropriate.

* Misdiagnosis or improper treatment resulting from improper pathology interpretation.
* Failure to diagnose condition.
Lost specimen resulting in inability to reach a diagnosis.
* Subsequent interpretation differs significantly from initial results reported.
Specimen not usable due to delay in arriving in laboratory (e.g., frozen section, blood samples, etc.).
Unable to complete test due to patient refusal or lack of cooperation.

PHARMACY DEPARTMENT

The following risk indicators should be monitored and tracked within the pharmacy department. Risk indicators that are preceded by an asterisk (*) require 100 percent concurrent review. Those preceded by a plus (+) should have interdisciplinary review. All others should be tracked and evaluated through the case review process as staff deems appropriate.

* + Any patient who has a drug reaction due to the receipt of incompatible drugs dispensed by the pharmacy.
* + Patient death related to the receipt of prescribed drugs dispensed from the hospital pharmacy.
Failure of staff to follow recommendations for proper dosage resulting in patient injury or drug toxicity.
* + Allergic or idiosyncratic reaction to commonly prescribed medication.
* + Adverse patient reaction to drug due to improper packaging, labeling, or reconstituting of drug.
* Patient injury or death resulting from the pharmacy department's inability to fill an immediate (STAT) drug order in a timely manner.
* Contaminants found in intravenous fluids that contained additives mixed in the pharmacy.
Discovery that expired drugs have been administered to a patient.
Recall (by the manufacturer) of drugs that have been dispensed to inpatients or outpatients by the pharmacy.
Filling prescription for a pediatric patient without knowledge or documentation of the patient's weight.

PSYCHIATRY DEPARTMENT

The following risk indicators should be monitored and tracked within the psychiatry department. Risk indicators that are preceded by an asterisk (*) require 100 percent concurrent review. Those preceded by a plus (+) should have interdisciplinary review. All others should be tracked with internal department reviews as staff deems appropriate.

* * + Suicides and homicides occurring within inpatient units.
* * + Suicide occurring within one week following patient's discharge from an inpatient psychiatric unit.
* * + Homicide or other act of violence committed against a third party by a patient recently discharged from inpatient treatment.
* * + Patient transferred from psychiatric unit to a medical intensive care unit after medical problems went unnoticed following admission.
* Medication errors or adverse drug interactions.
* + Patient leaving unit against medical advice or patient failing to return from authorized leave of absence.
* No written consent or improper consent for treatment.
* + Allegations of sexual misconduct (whether made against hospital staff, other patients, or visitors).
* + Adverse reactions or injury from procedures not addressed or contemplated in consent form.
* Injury to limbs resulting from improper restraint.
* Patient injury resulting from fall.

PULMONARY MEDICINE DEPARTMENT

The following risk indicators should be monitored and tracked within the pulmonary medicine department. Risk indicators that are preceded by an asterisk (*) require 100 percent concurrent review. Those preceded by a plus (+) should have interdisciplinary review. All others should be tracked with case reviews as staff deems appropriate.

* * + Unexplained or unexpected death of patient.
* * Readmission occurring within 30 days following discharge of patient.
* Patient discharged from department with a hematocrit of less than 30 percent.
* * + Patient developed recurrent congestive heart failure within 7 days following discharge.
* Patient developed fever and/or signs and symptoms consistent with an infectious process within 7 days following discharge.
* Patient with central line or pulmonary line developed pulmonary embolus during hospitalization.
* * Complications secondary to invasive hemodynamic monitoring, such as:
  * radial artery thrombosis
  * hematoma, pleural effusion, or pneumothorax
  * ventricular arrhythmias, pulmonary infarction or emboli, or pulmonary artery hemorrhage
* * + Unplanned injury to organ or structure during invasive procedure.
* Unexpected transfer to operating room following bronchoscopy or central line placement.
* Respiratory depression or acute hypotension following administration of analgesics or sedatives.
* Patient developed laryngospasm, bronchospasm, or hypoxemia following bronchoscopy.
* Patient developed aspiration pneumonia during hospitalization.

RADIATION ONCOLOGY DEPARTMENT

The following risk indicators should be monitored and tracked within the radiation oncology department. Risk indicators that are preceded by an asterisk (*) require 100 percent concurrent review. Those preceded by a plus (+) should have interdisciplinary review. All others should be tracked with case reviews as staff deems appropriate.

* Radiation doses administered inaccurately (e.g., wrong dose, volume, field size, missing wedges) with or without subsequent patient injury.
  Radiation begun on patient prior to receipt of final pathology report.
  Failure to obtain and document a weekly weight on patients receiving radiation therapy.
  Failure to perform weekly blood tests on nonpalliative patients receiving radiation therapy.
* Significant burns to skin that require surgical debridement and/or grafting.
* + Patient death in radiation oncology department.

RADIOLOGY DEPARTMENT

The following risk indicators should be monitored and tracked within the radiology department. Risk indicators that are preceded by an asterisk (*) require 100 percent concurrent review. Those preceded by a plus (+) should have interdisciplinary review. All others should be tracked and evaluated through the case review process as staff deems appropriate.

* + Death in radiology department.
* + Cardiac or respiratory arrest in radiology department.
* + Complication of procedure performed in radiology department resulting in unexpected or unplanned admission to the intensive care unit (severe reaction to contrast, vascular perforation resulting in extensive bleeding, etc.).
* Postprocedure nerve or vessel damage.
  Instrument or equipment breakage or malfunction during procedure.
* Wrong patient studied in diagnostic radiology.
* Wrong procedure performed.
* No written or signed consent or improper consent in chart (when consent is dictated by hospital policy).
  Medication error resulting in patient injury.
  Radiographic report (final) that differs substantially from wet reading or initial impression.
  Patient fall resulting in injury.
  Aspiration during upper gastrointestinal series.
  Hematoma at the injection site requiring intervention.
  Extravasation of contrast media.
* + Renal dysfunction secondary to contrast dye injection.

REHABILITATION MEDICINE DEPARTMENT

The following risk indicators should be monitored and tracked within the rehabilitation medicine department. Risk indicators that are preceded by an asterisk (*) require 100 percent concurrent review. Those preceded by a plus (+) should have interdisciplinary review. All others should be tracked with case reviews as staff deems appropriate.

* + Failure to perform multidisciplinary team evaluation within 10 days of patient's admission to rehabilitation medicine department.
  Unscheduled readmission of patient to rehabilitation unit within 30 days following discharge.
* Readmission of patient within 90 days to an acute care facility with a medical problem related to the primary condition.
* Unplanned transfer to an acute care unit or intensive care unit from the rehabilitation unit.
  Deep vein thrombosis developing in patient with spinal cord injury.
* + Cardiac arrest or respiratory arrest within 10 days following successful weaning from mechanical ventilation.
  Development of pressure necrosis that requires skin grafting.

RHEUMATOLOGY DEPARTMENT

The following risk indicators should be monitored and tracked within the rheumatology department. Risk indicators that are preceded by an asterisk (*) require 100 percent concurrent review. Those preceded by a plus (+) should have interdisciplinary review. All others should be tracked with case reviews as staff deems appropriate.

* + Unexplained or unexpected patient death.
  Patient developed gastrointestinal bleeding secondary to steroid use.
* + Surgical intervention required for bleeding secondary to steroid use.
  Loss of function not documented during each inpatient or outpatient visit.
  Patient readmitted to hospital within seven days following discharge.

SAME-DAY SURGERY DEPARTMENT

The following risk indicators should be monitored and tracked within the same-day (outpatient) surgery department. Risk indicators that are preceded by an asterisk (*) require 100 percent concurrent review. Those preceded by a plus (+) should have interdisciplinary review. All others should be tracked and evaluated through the case review process as staff deems appropriate.

* + Intraoperative death.
* + Surgical complication resulting in unexpected or unplanned admission to the hospital as an inpatient.
*   Retained instrument, sponge, needle, or other item.
* + Postoperative nerve damage.
  Instrument or equipment breakage or malfunction during surgery.
*   Wrong patient operated on.
*   Wrong procedure performed.
  Lost surgical pathology specimen.
*   No written or signed consent or an improper consent in chart.
  No preoperative laboratory work in chart or improper laboratory work in chart.
*   Unplanned removal or repair of an organ or body part.
*   Incorrect sponge, needle, or instrument count.
* + Excessive blood loss.
  Improper discharge instructions in chart or no discharge instructions provided.
  Patient discharged from same-day surgery without responsible adult.
* + Lack of presurgical consult as required by department policy.
* + Unplanned admission to hospital within 72 hours following discharge home from same-day surgery.
  Medication or transfusion error resulting in patient injury or death.

SURGERY DEPARTMENT

The following risk indicators should be monitored and tracked within the surgery department. Risk indicators that are preceded by an asterisk (*) require 100 percent concurrent review. Those preceded by a plus (+) should have interdisciplinary review. All others should be tracked and evaluated through the case review process as staff deems appropriate.

* + Intraoperative death.
* + Surgical complication resulting in unexpected or unplanned admission to the surgical intensive care unit.
*   Retained instrument, sponge, needle, or other item.
* + Postoperative nerve damage.
  Instrument or equipment breakage or malfunction during surgery.

*   Wrong patient operated on.
*   Wrong procedure performed.
*   No written or signed consent or an improper consent in chart.
*   Unplanned removal or repair of an organ or body part.
*   Incorrect sponge, needle, or instrument count.
* + Excessive blood loss.
     Medication or transfusion error resulting in patient injury.

UROLOGY DEPARTMENT

The following risk indicators should be monitored and tracked within the urology department. Risk indicators that are preceded by an asterisk (*) require 100 percent concurrent review. Those preceded by a plus (+) should have interdisciplinary review. All others should be tracked with case reviews as staff deems appropriate.

* + Intraoperative or postoperative death following radical surgery for bladder malignancy.
* + Intraoperative or immediate postoperative myocardial infarction following urologic surgery.
     Patient developed sepsis following transurethral resection of the prostate.
*   Patient developed massive hemorrhage following retroperitoneal lymph node dissection.
     Patient developed pelvic abscesses, deep vein thrombosis, or pulmonary emboli following radical cystectomy.
     Patient developed pelvic abscesses, deep vein thrombosis, or pulmonary emboli following radical prostatectomy.
     Splenic injury during donor nephrectomy.
     Prolonged hospitalization due to inability to void following urological procedure.

chapter 29

Developing a Comprehensive Quality Management Program in Obstetrics

Marie Anne Dizon

INTRODUCTION

Controlling risks in the area of obstetrics has long been a challenge for health care risk managers. Historically, lawsuits involving birth injuries have been the most costly not only to defend but also in the ultimate verdict or settlement. Because of the emotions associated with injured babies and the high potential for multimillion dollar verdicts due to the high cost of providing lifelong care, many hospitals and health care insurers often decide to settle lawsuits based on elements of the case that have little relevance with provider negligence. Analyzing the issues in obstetrics that most frequently cause these claims and developing strong proactive strategies hopefully will allow for these claims to diminish and will allow for those filed to be more defensible.

Pregnancy and childbirth cases constitute a group of malpractice cases in which there is a possibility of some unfortunate results, even with the best of care. Defending care is often difficult as it is very complicated to prove that injuries resulted from the patient's condition or are unexplainable and not a consequence of the care rendered by the health care professional. The practice of obstetrics is high risk for the obstetrician, nurses, and other health care professionals involved with the patient. Regardless of the type of case (maternal or neonatal), the entire obstetrical team is the target for plaintiffs and their attorneys. Often, any delivery that is less than a perfect birth is presumed to have been a result of caregiver negligence. Therefore, health professionals should learn how to deliver high-

quality care by incorporating their knowledge of maternal–fetal medicine and nursing with proactive risk management and quality improvement strategies. Also, they should be given information relevant to the legal implications involved in perinatal care. Risk managers must work with all hospital staff that care for the obstetric patient and the child to ensure that the quality of care provided is maximized and that risks are kept to a minimum.

UNDERSTANDING THE CLINICAL RISKS IN OBSTETRICS

Obstetrics is a branch of medicine that concerns management of women during pregnancy, childbirth, and the puerperium.[1] Pregnancy and delivery are anxious periods for many women because of ill-founded fears and misinformation, and many disorders of pregnant women are aggravated by anxiety. Although pregnancy may be complicated, serious problems are uncommon with proper counseling and good natal care.[2] The public also has an expectation that healthy babies and noncomplicated pregnancies are a given right. This often leads to the belief that any unexpected problems are a result of provider negligence.

Although pregnancy is normally an uncomplicated process, many factors can jeopardize the likelihood of the mother giving birth to a normal healthy baby. Identifying these factors and intervening appropriately (managing the known risk) can help ensure that a healthy baby will be born. A high-risk pregnancy is one in which the life or health of the mother or offspring is jeopardized by a disorder coincidental with or unique to pregnancy. For the mother, the high-risk status extends through the puerperium, which is 29 days after delivery. Postdelivery maternal complications are resolved within a month of birth, but perinatal morbidity may continue for months or years.[3]

Serious biologic handicaps, health problems, obstetric disorders, and social deprivation may compromise the infant in subtle or more obvious ways. Early or late fetal damage may occur. The baby may be small for gestational age, preterm, or post-term. Infrequently, the infant may be preterm but of excessive size. In other instances, the post-term infant may be large. The management of these clinical risks constitutes unique perinatal problems and creates many challenges for the obstetrical and risk management team.[4]

The health care practitioner must identify early those women who may have a greater likelihood of pregnancy complications. Prudent ongoing evaluation during pregnancy will minimize unexpected serious complications. Accurate and complete recordkeeping of these evaluations and interventions is critical to allow not only for continuity of care but also for defending that care if questions arise. Providing an internal system that always allows for access of these records when care is provided is of equal importance. If abnormal trends develop, disorders can be anticipated, and prompt treatment may eliminate or reduce the difficulty. Everyone in the health care system should complement physicians' efforts in the promotion of maternal and fetal health, particularly in stressful social situations or during illness that may compromise both mother and infant.[5]

IDENTIFICATION OF RISK FACTORS

High-risk factors that contribute to perinatal morbidity and mortality are numerous. Exhibit 29-1 provides a reasonably inclusive list of criteria that should aid in the identification of high-risk women. (Risk managers may want to check this list against the history of a plaintiff filing a lawsuit to determine how to shape a defense.)

Almost 20 percent of all gravidas fall into the categories shown in Exhibit 29-1. These high-risk conditions account for 50 percent of all perinatal deaths and are associated with seven obstetrical complications:

1. breech presentation
2. premature separation of the normally implanted placenta
3. pre-eclampsia or eclampsia
4. multiple pregnancy

Exhibit 29-1
CLINICAL HIGH-RISK FACTORS—MATERNAL

1. History of any of the following:
   a. hereditary abnormality (Down's syndrome)
   b. premature or small for gestational age infant (most recent delivery)
   c. congenital anomaly, anemia, blood dyscrasia, pre-eclampsia, and other conditions
   d. severe social problem (drug addiction, teenage pregnancy)
   e. long delayed or no prenatal care
   f. maternal age less than 18 years or greater than 35 years
   g. exposure to rubella and cytomegalovirus
   h. greater than five pregnancies, especially with women past 35 years of age
   i. prolonged infertility or hormone treatment
   j. significant stressful or dangerous events in the present pregnancy (critical accident or excessive exposure to irradiation)
   k. heavy cigarette smoking
   l. conception within two months of a previous delivery
2. Diagnosis of any of the following:
   a. height under 60 inches or prepregnancy weight of 20 percent less than or over the standard for height and age
   b. minimum or no weight gain during pregnancy
   c. obstetric complications (pre-eclampsia, eclampsia, multiple pregnancy, hydramnios)
   d. abnormal presentation (breech, presenting part unengaged at term)
   e. abnormal fetal growth or fetus is disparate in size than that expected
   f. fetus of more than 42 weeks gestation

5. pyelonephritis
6. hydramnios
7. premature labor

Harmful drugs, viral infections, and irradiation pose additional risks to pregnancy. Although difficult to estimate, personal or social problems, lack of prenatal care and preventive therapy, lack of knowledge, poverty, and unwanted pregnancy may be potent factors that further compromise pregnancy and its outcome.[6]

In addition to these factors, the father's influences on early birth and other manifestations of high-risk pregnancy are largely speculative. Small-for-date infants are often reported, and the incidence of congenital anomalies may be slightly elevated when the father has diabetes mellitus or is drug addicted. Certain inheritable disorders such as $Rh_o(D)$ isoimmunization are traceable to the father.[7]

Fetal factors also may jeopardize the infant. These include congenital anomalies, short cord, cord entanglement or compression, hydramnios, abnormal presentation or position, immaturity, prematurity, and fetal infection.[8]

The neonatal period just after delivery, especially the few minutes exemplified by the 1- and 5-minute Apgar scores, may be critical for the neonate who must quickly and effectively adapt to extrauterine life. Problems of resuscitation, particularly establishing a patient airway and reversing narcotic overdosage by narcotic antagonists such as Narcan, may be vital. The early diagnosis and proper management of congenital anomalies, such as tracheoesophageal fistula and meningomyelocele, are equally important. The incidence of cerebral palsy, mental retardation, and other neurologic disorders largely depends on the skillful management of the intranatal and immediate neonatal period.[9]

Exhibit 29-2 provides a listing of risk factors identified before and immediately after birth that place the infant at high risk and demand special observation and treatment of the neonate.

IDENTIFICATION OF SOCIAL AND CULTURAL RISK FACTORS

In addition to the risk factors listed in Exhibit 29-2, race and socioeconomic status play a role in obstetrics and the delivery of care. Small parents usually have small babies, as evidenced by people of Oriental or Asian heritage contrasted with larger people of Anglo-Saxon Caucasian heritage. Further, Afro-American mothers as a group have smaller newborns than do Caucasian mothers. Although race has some bearing on the problem of the underweight infant, socioeconomic differences may be even more important in considering prematurity (a premature birth occurring before the end of the 37th week of gestation). Occupation of the father particularly relates to the incidence of abnormally early birth and low-birth-weight infants. Spe-

---

Exhibit 29-2
RISK FACTORS REQUIRING FURTHER EVALUATION

1. Maternal history of previously listed pregnancy factors, including:
   a. prolonged rupture of membranes
   b. abnormal presentation and delivery
   c. prolonged, difficult labor, or precipitous labor
   d. prolapsed cord
2. Birth asphyxia suggested by:
   a. fetal heart rate fluctuations
   b. meconium staining, particularly aspiration
   c. fetal acidosis—pH below 7.2
   d. Apgar scores less than 7, especially if present at five minutes
3. preterm birth less than 37 weeks gestation
4. post-term birth more than 42 weeks gestation, with evidence of fetal wasting
5. small gestational age infants (less than 10th percentile)
6. large gestational age infants (greater than 90th percentile) especially the large preterm infant
7. any respiratory distress or apnea
8. obvious congenital anomalies
9. convulsions, limpness, or difficulty in sucking or swallowing
10. distention or vomiting or both
11. anemia (less than 15 grams hemoglobin) or bleeding tendency
12. jaundiced in first 24 hours or bilirubin levels greater than 15 mg/dl

cifically, these problems are increased in persons with menial occupations and limited income. Clinic patients have a 50 percent higher incidence of low-birth-weight infants than do private patients. Moreover, women with only a grade-school education have twice as many growth-retarded newborns as do women who are college educated. Lack of money to purchase the necessities of life is a factor in poor health; thus, socioeconomic advantages tend to be equated with a healthier life and progeny.[10]

IDENTIFICATION OF ENVIRONMENTAL RISK FACTORS

In the preceding sections, medical, clinical, social, and cultural factors affecting pregnancy and defining it as a high-risk pregnancy were discussed. Additional factors warrant the critical attention of the practicing, prudent obstetrician and of other health care professionals. One of these is the dramatic increase in the number of drug-addicted or drug-dependent pregnant women, many of whom have limited access to prenatal care.

There has been a marked increase in cocaine use in the United States during the past few years, and cocaine has become more socially acceptable and more widely available to both the affluent and the poor. Thousands of women from middle and upper socioeconomic classes are addicted to cocaine. There is a lack of national data on maternal cocaine abuse, but unmistakable indications show the problem is growing. One New York City hospital recently reported that 10 percent of all newborns born there had a positive urine screen for cocaine.[11]

Women who use cocaine during pregnancy are more likely than nonusers to have spontaneous first trimester abortions. This finding is consistent with the implication of placental vasoconstriction induced by cocaine use. The incidence of abruptio placenta, usually occurring within an hour of cocaine administration, is higher among cocaine-addicted mothers. This finding is attributed to the acute hypertension caused by cocaine and the well-established relationship between hypertension and abruptio placenta.[12]

Cocaine use by pregnant women during the third trimester has been reported to induce a sudden onset of uterine contractions, fetal tachycardia, and excessive fetal activity within hours or even minutes of ingestion. For pregnant women, cocaine-induced tachycardia further strains the overworked maternal heart.[13] The teratogenic effect of cocaine on the developing fetus is relatively unknown at this time. Cocaine's profound impact on cardiovascular function can potentially place the exposed fetus in jeopardy for both short- and long-term adverse effects. Isolated reports and small sample studies suggest cocaine might be respon-

sible for many congenital anomalies. One infant studied exhibited cryptorchidism, prune belly syndrome, and hydronephrosis that may have been associated with maternal cocaine use.[14]

The consequences of cocaine exposure to the fetus are numerous. Infants born to cocaine-addicted mothers tend to be shorter, lower in birth weight, and have smaller head circumferences compared with infants of women who were drug free during pregnancy. Cocaine-exposed infants may show mild to moderate tremulousness, increased irritability, muscular rigidity, and startle response. These infants are difficult to console and state lability is pronounced. Further, elevated respiratory and heart rates, poor tolerance to oral feedings, diarrhea, and disturbed sleep patterns have been linked to cocaine exposure while in utero.[15]

Maternal prenatal cocaine use also places the infant at potentially higher risk for sudden infant death syndrome (SIDS). Abnormal sleeping ventilatory patterns implicated in SIDS have been noted in cocaine-exposed infants. In addition, perinatal cerebral infarction in infants exposed to cocaine just before birth has been reported. This finding tends to parallel reports of acute cerebral and myocardial infarction in young adults shortly after cocaine use.[16] Trends to decrease both maternal and infant mortality and morbidity, as well as prematurity, and the use of illegal substances have evolved through the years. Research and experience have led to the identification of factors that jeopardize the pregnant and postdelivery woman and the infant. This knowledge has permitted the development of increasingly effective preventive and therapeutic measures that could minimize the incidence of morbidity, disability, and death of the mother or infant. Frequently, the prudent nurse, conversant and familiar with deviations from normal, notes and reports potential or real high-risk factors. Physicians and nurses are in a position to be instrumental in the education of the general population in good health habits and good nutrition. This, in turn, could reduce significantly the incidence of high-risk pregnancy.[17]

Other environmental factors that should be considered when evaluating the potential for a high-risk pregnancy or a damaged infant include the living conditions of the mother. Does the mother live in an area where there is toxic waste or where levels of pollution are suspected or documented? Does the mother come from an economically depressed area where she may not be able to maintain adequate nutrition or pay for prenatal care? Is the mother from an environment where teenage pregnancies are common and associated with a high level of status?

Addressing the needs of the pregnant teenager also requires special efforts. Educational efforts targeted to this population require a different approach than those designed for adult professionals. Teenagers are not likely to perceive health habits and good nutrition and are more apt to eat junk foods. This diet attributes to a smaller birth-weight infant, a small gestational age infant, prematurity, and so forth.[18]

Additionally, teenagers and less educated young adults are unlikely to perceive health hazards as real and immediate dangers. Effective education for teenagers centers on dispelling the popular idea that cocaine use is normal and acceptable and that everybody uses drugs. Enlisting the aid of teenage peers to impart information to teen groups enhances the effectiveness of educational efforts and can be accomplished cost effectively via a videotaped presentation shown in a clinic waiting room.[19]

DEVELOPING TOOLS TO IDENTIFY AND ADDRESS RISKS

Developing tools to identify medical, socioeconomic, and cultural risks is an important part of any obstetrical program and can be of great value when attempting to defend care. The goals for care are prevention, detection, and treatment of threatening maternal and fetal disorders. Therefore, it is essential to screen those women who are jeopardized (high risk) from those who are not endangered (low risk). This is only effective when it imposes a relentless search for problems that may threaten the pregnancy during the prenatal, natal, and postdelivery period.[20]

Education, undoubtedly, is the most effective and ideal health care intervention. Many women are unaware of the potential danger inherent in poor nutrition, poor health habits, and in drug use. The key to any successful prevention effort is education—getting accurate information to those at greatest risk.[21]

As for cocaine use, educating the women can be exceptionally complex due to a mixed population. A substantial proportion of cocaine users are young, well-paid, well-educated, upwardly mobile professionals in their 20s and 30s. Young professionals tend to be fairly sophisticated, and for this reason nurses and physicians must make special efforts to deliver information straightforwardly and unemotionally.[22]

Educational efforts must rely on current preliminary data and will need to be updated as new information becomes available. Widespread knowledge is the best means to the long-term goal of prevention.[23]

In addition to educational intervention as a method to decrease the chance of having a complicated pregnancy outcome, access to prenatal care is also an effective way in fulfilling this goal. Providing prenatal care for all women, especially those at risk for poor pregnancy outcomes, greatly decreases the chances of having a low-birth-weight infant. Additionally, providing prenatal care to all women allows the physician to detect any fetal abnormalities that may pose an increased risk in maternal and fetal outcome.[24]

Considerable assistance can be obtained by consulting the professional societies governing obstetrical and maternal/child nursing practice. The American College of Obstetricians and Gynecologists (ACOG) has done considerable work in developing professional standards that address all aspects of obstetrical care. These guidelines should be reviewed before establishing any unit specific policies and procedures (see Exhibit 29-3). Also, keeping current with the many advancements in this clinical service is critical.

LIABILITY ISSUES ASSOCIATED WITH OBSTETRIC CARE

The definition of malpractice is straightforward. However, when there is catastrophic injury to babies, the black and white letter of the law often gives way to shades of grey. The elements of duty, breach of duty, injury proximately caused by the breach, and damages seem difficult for juries to interpret when a damaged child is the injured party. This is an important factor for professionals to know when working in the area of obstetrics. Ideally, issues such as the need to prove all elements of negligence before finding for the plaintiff and issues related to standards of care and reasonable performance should enable most practitioners to prevail if lawsuits are filed against them. However, the reality is that juries tend to be peers not of the physician or nurse but of the plaintiff. They often are unable or unwilling to send parents of a damaged child with catastrophic costs of care away from the courtroom empty-handed; thus, verdicts often are against the weight of the evidence. This is important to recognize when planning the defense in obstetrical cases.

All health care professionals—physicians, nurses, and other allied health care professionals—have a clear responsibility to keep current in all areas of their specialty, including the legal ramifications of their actions. Legal actions involving obstetric clients are not only significant in number but also often have the greatest dollar value of all malpractice suits.

With increasing frequency, nurses are held legally accountable as individuals for their actions. Now that health care has become more complex and nurses have assumed a more independent role as health care providers, nurses are accountable for their own actions, rather than having the hospital or employer assume that responsibility. Once the nurse–patient relationship is established, the nurse is legally accountable to the patient for nursing care and, within certain limits, the patient's well-being.[25]

Both physicians and nurses who perform in highly specialized areas of care like obstetrics or neonatology are

Exhibit 29-3
AMERICAN COLLEGE OF OBSTETRICIANS AND GYNECOLOGISTS—STANDARDS
FOR OBSTETRIC-GYNECOLOGIC SERVICES

ADMISSION POLICIES AND PROCEDURES

Obstetric patients with complications such as pregnancy induced hypertension, bleeding, premature rupture of membranes, multiple gestation, or other conditions requiring hospitalization before labor onset should be admitted to a designated antepartum area for labor and delivery. Obstetric patients with serious and acute complications should be assigned to an intensive care area such as the labor area. Ideally, obstetric patients with a medical or suspected surgical condition that complicates pregnancy should be assigned to the obstetric area. If such a patient is critically ill, however, admission or transfer to an intensive care unit away from the obstetric area may be indicated. When sufficiently recovered, the patient should be returned to the obstetric area, provided that her return does not jeopardize her care or the care of the other obstetric patients.

It is advisable for acutely ill patients who are likely to deliver a compromised or premature neonate to be cared for in a center with a neonatal intensive care unit. When feasible, antepartum transfer should be encouraged for these patients.

Written policies and procedures for the management of pregnant patients seen in the emergency department or admitted to nonobstetric services should be established and approved by the medical staff. These patients also should be seen by an obstetrician, and medical decisions concerning their care should be shared.

ANTEPARTUM ADMISSION

When warranted by the patient volume, a high-risk antepartum care unit should be developed to provide specialized nursing care and facilities for the mother and fetus at risk. When this is not feasible, written policies should be established for the care and transfer of pregnant patients with obstetric, medical, or surgical complications. The policies should specify where these patients should be assigned.

Obstetric services for high-risk mothers should be equipped to provide comprehensive ultrasound services on a 24-hour basis. This diagnostic service should be under the direction of a physician who has a special interest in obstetric diagnoses and complications. Technical personnel should be trained in the obstetric application of ultrasound. Also, equipment for electronic fetal monitoring, such as nonstress and stress testing of the fetoplacental unit, should be available for antenatal evaluation. Physicians using electronic fetal monitoring for antenatal surveillance must understand the indications, limitations, and interpretation of these tests.

INTRAPARTUM ADMISSION

Patients in labor, patients with premature rupture of membranes, and patients with vaginal bleeding should be admitted to the labor and delivery suite. Obstetric patients who are not in labor but who require special intensive care also may be admitted to this area, regardless of their stage of pregnancy. There should be a preadmission examining area in the labor and delivery area for triage of all patients.

Patients who may have a transmissible infection should be managed according to the established hospital policy.

LABOR SURVEILLANCE

When a patient is admitted in labor, the maternal and fetal vital signs, the frequency of contractions, and the status of the fetal membranes should be evaluated. A risk assessment should be performed.

Latent Phase

Low-risk patients in the latent phase of labor may be encouraged to ambulate. High-risk mothers and fetuses should be assigned immediately to a labor bed and followed in the same manner in which a patient in active labor is followed.

Active Phase

A patient in the active phase of labor should be admitted to a labor room, single labor–delivery–recovery room, or birthing room. Any new signs or symptoms that may significantly increase maternal or fetal risk, such as fetal heart rate abnormalities, the presence of meconium in the amniotic fluid, or excessive vaginal bleeding, should be evaluated by the obstetrician immediately.

Medical Induction or Augmentation of Labor

Induction or augmentation of labor may be initiated only after a responsible physician has evaluated the patient's condition, determined that induction or augmentation is beneficial to the mother or fetus, recorded the indication, and established a prospective plan of management. Only personnel who are familiar with the effects of the oxytocic agents and who are able to identify both maternal and fetal complications should be in attendance while these agents are being administered. An obstetrician should be readily available to manage any complications, including an emergency cesarean section, that may arise from the use of these agents. Before the administration of any oxytocic agents, the patient should first be examined vaginally by the obstetrician or obstetric nurse. The agent should be administered only intravenously, with a device that permits precise control of the flow rate. The fetal heart rate and uterine activity should be monitored very closely when oxytocic agents are being administered.

continues

Exhibit 29-3 continued

DELIVERY

When delivery is imminent, the patient should not be left unattended, nor should any attempt be made to delay the birth of the infant by physical restraint or anesthesia. Maternal blood pressure and pulse should be determined at least every 15 minutes and recorded. The fetal heart rate should be evaluated frequently, either by auscultation or electronic fetal monitoring. If internal monitoring is being used in patients who undergo cesarean delivery, the fetal scalp electrode and the monitoring equipment should remain in place until the abdominal preparation is complete. If external monitoring is being used in patients who undergo cesarean delivery, the fetal scalp electrode and the monitoring equipment should remain in place until the abdominal preparation is complete. If external monitoring is being used, it should be continued during the induction of regional anesthesia and terminated only when the abdominal preparation is begun.

POSTPARTUM PERIOD

Following the delivery, the mother should be closely attended for at least one hour. The mother's vital signs, including pulse, respiration, and blood pressure, should be recorded at least every 15 minutes during the first hour and thereafter until her condition is stable. Fluid intake and output should be recorded. The mother should be examined frequently to make sure that the uterine fundus is well contracted and that bleeding is not excessive.

After the patient has been transferred to her room in the postpartum care area, her vital signs, the status of the uterine fundus, and the degree of bleeding should be reassessed and recorded and should be repeated at regular intervals over the hospital stay. The postpartum hemoglobin (Hgb) or hematocrit (Hct) level should be checked the day after delivery. If ABO blood group and Rh type has not been done during the prenatal period, then it should be done along with the postpartum Hct/Hgb. The unsensitized Rh-negative patient who has delivered an Rh-positive infant should receive $Rh_o(D)$ immunoglobin within 72 hours of delivery, even if she received prophylactic $Rh_o(D)$ immunoglobulin prenatally. In addition, a postpartum mother found to be susceptible to rubella should receive rubella vaccine before discharge.

The postpartum mother with an infectious illness should be housed in a single room on the postpartum floor or in another area of the hospital. If the disease may be transmitted to the baby, the mother and the newborn should be separated until the disease is no longer communicable. Mothers with a temperature elevation known to be caused by a nontransmissible infection or a low-grade postpartum infection may be kept on the obstetric unit and need not be separated from their newborns.

Patient education also is an important element of postpartum care. Topics on self-care and baby care that can be discussed in either group or individual sessions include breast care, perineum and urinary bladder care, amount of activity allowed, diet, exercise, emotional responses, resumption of coitus, and signs and symptoms of common complications. Sessions in baby care include breast feeding and bottle feeding, infant growth and development, and parent–infant relationships, and so forth.

DISCHARGE PLANNING

Arrangements for postpartum follow-up evaluation should be made at the time of discharge, and the patient should be given information about what she should do if a complication or an emergency arises.

PROTOCOL GUIDELINE ON FETAL HEART RATE MONITORING

The intensity and method of fetal heart rate monitoring used during labor should be based on risk factors. Intermittent auscultation at intervals of 15 minutes during the first stage of labor and five minutes during the second stage is equivalent to continuous electronic fetal heart rate monitoring. When risk factors are present during labor or when intensified monitoring is elected, the fetal heart rate should be assessed by one of these methods according to the following guidelines:

a. During the active phase of the first stage of labor, the fetal heart rate should be evaluated and recorded at least every 15 minutes, preferably following a uterine contraction, when intermittent auscultation is used. If continuous electronic fetal monitoring is used, the tracing should be evaluated at least every 15 minutes.
b. During the second stage of labor, the fetal heart rate should be evaluated and recorded at least every five minutes when auscultation is used and should be evaluated at least every five minutes when electronic fetal monitoring is used.

For low-risk patients in labor, the fetal heart rate may be monitored by auscultation. The standard practice is to evaluate and record the fetal heart rate at least every 30 minutes following a contraction in the active phase of the first stage of labor and at least every 15 minutes in the second stage of labor.

Furthermore, the fetal heart rate should be evaluated immediately after spontaneous or artificial rupture of the membranes. The character of the amniotic fluid should be described. When meconium is present, careful monitoring should be initiated.

Source: American College of Obstetricians and Gynecologists, *Standards for Obstetric-Gynecologic Services*, Seventh Edition, American College of Obstetricians and Gynecologists, Washington, D.C., © 1989.

expected to perform as a reasonably prudent physician or nurse who is trained in that specialty area would perform. The standard of care for a practitioner working in a high-risk obstetric program is different from that standard of care for a professional delivering only low-risk healthy babies in a community hospital.

It is critical for the physician, nurse, and other allied health professionals to be thoroughly familiar with the policies and procedures of the facility where they practice, particularly those related to their area of practice. These policies and procedures should reflect the agreed-upon standard of care within that institution. If policies and procedures become outdated or do not reflect staff duties, they need to be changed. It is of equal importance that professionals working in the area of obstetrics understand the psychological components of this type of litigation, develop strong channels of communication with the patient and family, and always be sympathetic, empathetic, and caring.

Physicians and nurses involved in the care of women in labor have numerous legal responsibilities to these women and their babies. They must be knowledgeable about fetal monitoring and the proper actions they must take in maternal, fetal, or neonatal emergencies. Documentation of the skill and training of all members of the obstetrical team will be of great assistance if any of their skills are questioned.

MANAGING OBSTETRICAL RISKS—A PROACTIVE APPROACH

The safest environment for the mother and the baby during labor, delivery, and the immediate postpartum period is the hospital setting in which a team of professionals is available to respond to maternal and neonatal emergencies.

Medical specialty societies are continuing their efforts to develop guidelines to help hospitals provide quality care. The American College of Obstetricians and Gynecologists (ACOG) task force has developed a set of guidelines or protocols in the area of obstetrics and neonatology. These guidelines provide valuable guidance to the risk manager and the health care team in evaluating risks and in developing protocols to reduce these risks.

Potential Risk Exposures for Obstetrics

In addition to the clinical risks previously discussed, there are many additional areas related to health care professionals' jobs that frequently give rise to litigation. The risk manager should work with staff to recognize these areas and develop programs to respond to them. Some of the

most frequently seen problematic issues and a description of how they specifically relate to the area of obstetrics include:

- documentation
- consultation
- standard diagnostic testing
- transfer of high-risk patients/referrals
- identification and intervention in fetal distress

Documentation

A complete record can provide the practitioner and the risk manager with the most complete evidence of what actually occurred during pregnancy and delivery. Being able to corroborate testimony offered at trial with a record, which often was written years earlier, is very persuasive. The risk manager should stress this fact to the team of maternal child professionals and assist them in the development of tools, flow sheets, and forms that will facilitate and complement the written narrative.

As a rule, physicians and nurses do a great deal more than they are willing to document. A considerable amount of time and effort is expended in each case in thought processes, review of data, history taking, physician examination, procedures, patient discussions, family interactions, telephone calls, and so forth. But for some unexplainable reason, the health professional fails to take credit for this complete process not only for potential malpractice litigation but also for professional review organization activity and third-party payer scrutiny.

Documentation of patient care should be complete, concise, and legible. Document as if someone with less knowledge will read them; and documentation should be completed with the jury in mind. Using Joint Commission on Accreditation of Healthcare Organizations (Joint Commission) guidelines, good records should include demographic data, a history, a physical examination, orders, informed consent, clinical observations, test reports, and a conclusion at discharge.

Furthermore, documentation is equally important in the office setting. Orders for follow-up treatment, phone messages, phone conversations, phone prescriptions, return office visit dates, and failures to keep appointments are all tasks generally handled by the staff and conveyed to the patient in written form. Legible handwriting is important, and it is important to maintain a copy of these communications in the patient's file.

In 1987 the Minnesota Medical Insurance Exchange (MMIE) Obstetrical Risk Management Task Force was formed to review the current status of birth-related claims and the need for enhanced obstetrical risk management by physicians and hospitals. As a result, the task force developed a set of obstetrical risk management guidelines regarding perinatal documentation. The guidelines approved by the MMIE Risk Management Committee and Board of Directors are presented in Exhibit 29-4.

Once problems are identified and documented, they must be resolved in writing. In other words, the nurse must document not only the awareness of a problem but also the actions (interventions) and resolutions (outcomes).[26]

The following list are forms used for documentation of any obstetrical and neonatal charting. (Appendix 29-A provides an excellent example of a comprehensive prenatal flow sheet incorporating many of these elements.)

- health history summary
- initial pregnancy profile
- prenatal flow record
- weight change and urine estriol curves
- obstetric admitting record
- labor progress chart
- obstetric discharge summary
- postpartum progress notes
- initial newborn profile
- newborn flow record
- newborn discharge summary

Exhibit 29-4
DOCUMENTATION GUIDELINES

PRENATAL

Any record-keeping format used should include documentation of:

1. comprehensive health history
2. pertinent family and social history
3. comprehensive physician examination
4. results of necessary or indicated laboratory tests
5. identification of risk factors, and a plan for ongoing management of identified risk factors
6. gestational age determination, and a plan for ongoing management of identified gestational age problems
7. expected date of delivery (EDC), updated as appropriate
8. appropriate consultation or referral when indicated
9. any patient refusal of recommended tests, consultation, or referral, and discussion with the patient of the risks of refusal and alternatives to recommended actions

Included in the comprehensive health history are the following assessment factors:

1. interpersonal relationship of patient and baby's father, which can provide information indicating significant family problems that may affect outcomes
2. type of employment of the patient and the number of hours worked. (Long hours of standing may explain a poor pregnancy outcome, such as greater probability of still births. Prolonged standing also is associated with placenta infarcts and maternal floor infarcts, with a high fetal mortality of 17 percent that is **not** associated with the physician's management/conduct.)
3. history of psychological and or physical abuse (past, present, and current)
4. nutritional habits and general life styles, which may influence the pregnancy outcome. (Note prepregnancy weight, exercise, and so on.)
5. documentation of antepartum testing and results

6. frequency of fetal movement
7. history of congenital maternal/paternal defects
8. coital frequency and last episode. (There is evidence that orgasm at or near term may initiate labor and fetal heart rate decelerations have been observed. Coitus once per week in the last month of pregnancy can be associated with increased chorioamnionitis and subsequent increased fetal morbidity.)
9. other current physicians and medications prescribed
10. presence of environmental hazards (factories and nearby toxic spills), which can have adverse outcomes in pregnant women
11. habits (alcohol, smoking), including exposure to second-hand smoke, drugs, medications, and so on

ADMISSION

There are key elements to be noted when the patient is admitted to labor and delivery.

1. "Rule-in" fetal well-being. Rationale: Usually, physicians assume good fetal well-being until demonstrated otherwise. Because of the nature of their work, plaintiff attorneys will assume fetal distress unless the defense can demonstrate otherwise. Establishing maternal and fetal well-being help the physician establish that any alleged deviation from the standard of care had no bearing on the status of the mother or fetus.
2. Always note the time of admission and the status of mother and fetus at that time. Rationale: Recorded times can prove to be the primary factor in winning or losing a case. It would be beneficial to suggest to the staff that only the labor and delivery clocks be used.
3. Vital signs always should be recorded on admission. An electronic fetal monitor should be used for the first 30 minutes of admission for low-risk pregnancies; high-risk pregnancies should have continuous electronic fetal monitoring throughout labor.

continues

Exhibit 29-4 continued

4. Employ fetal blood scalp pH if there are any questions about fetal heart rate patterns.
5. If delivery is not required despite continued decelerations and/or scalp pHs, write a rate in the chart indicating time, date, observation, and judgment for decisions. Make sure to mention good versus poor variability. With poor beat-to-beat variability, an internal fetal monitor clip and/or scalp pH should be performed. If this is not done, document the reasons for not performing.

RUPTURE OF MEMBRANES

When the membranes are ruptured on admission, it is critical this be stated in the admission note. If meconium is present in the amniotic fluid, it is important to document on chart as "meconium present on admission." Rationale: This condition will be interpreted that a possible hypoxic injury to the fetus may have resulted when the patient was not under direct medical management. However, make certain that a clear distinction is made between meconium fluid or meconium staining.

Staining of the baby, membranes, and placenta has time elements attributed to it. The time factor demonstrates the passage of meconium before labor and/or delivery. This will require obtaining placental pathologic evaluation. If a hypoxic injury has been sustained by the fetus, the placental pathology may be able to show it occurred before admission.

LABOR AND DELIVERY

Throughout labor the physician should continue to require documentation of maternal and fetal well-being. Any change in either the fetus or mother requires a comment in the chart.

Fetal monitoring, electronic or by auscultation, should be performed throughout labor. Abnormal findings on any fetal monitor tracing should not be allowed to stand alone; however, explanations of the finding should be documented. Prolonged labors are frequently questioned if there was a poor fetal outcome. Establish that despite a prolonged labor both fetus and mother continued doing well. An internal electronic fetal monitor tracing would account for good fetal well-being if there was good beat-to-beat variability.

EMERGENCY CESAREAN SECTION

Some areas of concern in labor and delivery include use of oxytocin-like agents, epidural analgesics, prolonged second stage of labor, and forceps deliveries. The demonstration of one's judgment should be evident in the chart when faced with any decision involving these areas.

The second stage of labor prolonged more than two hours is seen by plaintiff attorneys as a breach of standards of care. However, this can be proven erroneous if it is shown that during that stage both the mother and fetus were monitored and showed no signs of distress. Document that the mother was comfortable; the mother showed no evidence of exhaustion; that she had both psychologic and physiologic support; that a good probability of a vaginal birth was anticipated; and finally, that the fetus showed no signs of distress.

The use of midforceps remains controversial; this should be clearly indicated by situations that require immediate termination of the pregnancy other than having a cesarean section. The best judgment should be used in doing such a procedure. If there is a poor fetal outcome, expect questions to arise about a midforceps procedure in lieu of a cesarean section as the alternative.

POSTPARTUM

During the postpartum period, the two areas of concern are maternal observation and observation of the newborn.

Maternal Observation

Maternal observation requires the recordings of the nurse that the observation was done. Two primary concerns during the postpartum period are to observe for postpartum hemorrhage and to note any changes that may be consistent with the development of postpartum pregnancy induced hypertension.

In the case of postpartum pregnancy induced hypertension, it must be recognized in order to be treated. In postpartum hemorrhage, "severe bleeding" suffices as documentation to the type of bleeding.

Neonatal Observation

With an unexpected neonatal outcome, the following concerns should be documented.

1. Record all cord blood gases obtained. Rationale: This demonstrates the presence of intrauterine hypoxia and/or ischemia.
2. It is recommended that the terms "neonatal asphyxia" or "birth asphyxia" not be used in documenting the newborn's condition. Rationale: These terms imply the baby's condition is directly associated with the birth, thus directly incriminating the physician. A better term to use is "depressed newborn."
3. Document Apgar scores for one minute, five minutes, and ten minutes when necessary. The Apgar scoring consists of color, tone, heart rate, reflexes, and respirations, and scores vary depending on the physiologic maturity of the fetus.
4. Document all observations noted on the newborn.

continues

Exhibit 29-4 continued

NURSING CARE GIVEN

A word of advice to nurses: Charting must not wait until the end of a shift or after the delivery is completed. Charting must reflect the status of the patient and should be done at the bedside. Large gaps in documentation make it appear the patient was not clinically evaluated during that time. Careful, defensive charting is the only evidence that a nurse provided quality care, acted appropriately, and clearly and quickly notified the physician. The charting must show that the standard of care was met and that a nurse followed the policies and procedures of the hospital. Rationale: If a case comes to litigation, the chart is the only valid record of events.

If the nurse is in the labor unit, fetal monitoring strips can be used to document observations. They are readily accessible, and the events can be recorded as they happen. If the nurse is in the nursery, the nursing progress record should be close by the crib or isolette. Normal as well as abnormal findings must be documented. It is important to chart signs and symptoms, not vague conclusions to a patient's discomfort. The charting must reflect the sequence of events and the clinical course of the patient during the entire hospital stay. Anyone reading the chart should be able to accurately reconstruct the events.

Source: Reprinted with permission from Richard W. Walker, "Obstetrical Risk Management: Establishing Documents of Defense," *Texas Medicine*, Vol. 86, Copyright 1990, Texas Medical Association.

These forms provide extensive information on maternity patients and their babies. Additionally, they offer many advantages.

- The forms can be completed in a checkmark fashion. Therefore necessary pertinent questions will not be missed.
- A checkmark system can be easily computerized.
- Carbon copies attached to the forms are sent to every health care provider who needs information on a particular patient.
- The forms accompany each patient from the time she first sees a physician until after she gives birth. Her medical history is itemized, and her current physical condition is constantly updated.
- The forms force physicians and nurses to think about potential problems, and as a result provide better care.
- If a lawsuit is filed, the forms provide a detailed patient record and a stronger defense.[27]

Consultation

Rapid advances in perinatal care in the past 15 years have produced dramatic improvements in neonatal survival and morbidity for high-risk newborns. Despite the growth of highly specialized fields of medicine such as perinatology and neonatology and their ability to enhance greatly the odds of delivering healthy babies out of circumstances that traditionally might have yielded disasters, the available specialty services are not employed in some cases where their use is prudent. Each year a small but significant number of infants are put in great jeopardy, or may even die, under circumstances that might have been avoided if the identifiable high-risk deliveries had been anticipated and

arrangements made for specialty services to be provided when needed. Some obstetricians may knowingly or unknowingly overreach their training and abilities and attempt to manage high-risk deliveries in settings inadequately equipped and staffed to yield the best chances for a good outcome. In too many cases, transfers are made **after** delivery when the infant is in great distress.[28]

Standard Diagnostic Testing

Laboratory tests are essential for the detection or confirmation of abnormal or disease processes. The physician and colleagues as well as other members of the obstetric health care team should keep apprised of the types of tests recommended at various stages of the pregnancy. Professionals must, however, remember that the patient has a right to decide whether these tests will be performed. To increase the likelihood that liability issues will not arise in this regard, the physician should be advised of the need to provide the patient with complete information about the recommended tests and specifically what the tests might be able to determine. Both the advantages and the risks should be discussed, and the results of this discussion should be documented. If written materials are developed to explain these tests, they should be reviewed so the health care professional is assured that the patient indeed understands the potential ramifications of refusing the test and the potential risks inherent in having the test performed.

Transfer of High-Risk Patients/Referrals

Rapid advances in perinatal care in the past years have produced dramatic improvements in neonatal survival and morbidity for high-risk neonates, especially the low-birth-weight premature. Much of these improvements have been accomplished through technologic innovation in monitoring the health of the fetus, both antepartum with the use of ultrasound, stress and nonstress tests, and amniocentesis, and intrapartum with the use of fetal heart rate monitoring, scalp pH determinations, and tests of fetal lung maturity. The medical knowledge of the obstetrician to intervene also has changed. Steroids are now used to hasten fetal lung maturity, and tocolytic agents can serve to halt premature labor, and broader indications prevail regarding the performance of cesarean section. The success of the above interventions is often predicated on the availability of high-quality neonatal intensive care, sophisticated infant ventilators and respiratory management, intravenous hyperalimentation, improved surgical techniques, exchange transfusions, and phototherapy. Along with these interventions have evolved the paired subspecialties of perinatology and neonatology.[29]

As part of the evolution of perinatal intensive care, there also has evolved a corresponding legal obligation to refer patients to more appropriate providers or facilities when circumstances indicate. The legal duty to refer is grounded on several principles. First, the duty to refer or advise the patient appropriately of the possibility of referral, applies when the obstetrician knows or, by using due care and diligence, should know that the medical problem is beyond his or her knowledge, training, or skill, or that the facilities and assistance are inappropriate or inadequate for the patient's foreseeable needs. Second, the duty to refer is determined by the practices of the community of references. Therefore, the physician would be held negligent for failing to refer or adequately inform a patient of the risks and alternatives when expert testimony establishes that a reasonably prudent obstetrician of similar knowledge, skill, and training would have done so under similar circumstances.[30]

The transfer of pregnant women, new mothers, and neonates between hospitals is recognized as an essential component of modern perinatal care. Transfer is one part of the system approach to improving obstetric and neonatal care. The decision to transfer a perinatal patient should be made by the primary obstetrician in conjunction with the consultant, which is usually a perinatologist. Transfer should be considered when the resources immediately available to the maternal, fetal, or neonatal patient are not adequate to deal with the perinatal patient's actual or anticipated condition.

The goal of interhospital transfer is to care for high-risk perinatal patients in a facility appropriate to their needs. A successful regional referral program is based on:

- risk identification and assessment of problems that will benefit from consultation and transfer

- knowledge of the available resources and the ways to gain access to them
- availability of an organized, appropriate, transport service that has adequate economic and political support
- recognition that care is continuous
- evaluation and analysis of performance

Regional perinatal care networks should have specific guidelines for the referral of high-risk mothers, as well as sick neonates, to regional centers for care.

See Exhibit 29-5 for a list of conditions that merit a pregnant woman's transfer to a perinatal center and referral to a perinatologist/neonatologist.

THE IMPORTANCE OF COMMUNICATION AND TEAMWORK

Lawsuits can occur because of any health care team member's action, failure to act, or attitude. Teamwork is essential in establishing an open, trusting relationship with the obstetrical patient and possibly between the patient's partner or family. Open communication between the patient and the health care professional, as well as between health care professionals, is crucial in keeping the patient well informed of pregnancy status. Any health care professional who puts procedures before people in the name of practice efficiency is undermining the quality of care provided, which leads to patient dissatisfaction. Often, the disgruntled patient is most likely to pursue litigation when there is a poor result.[31]

It is essential that all members of the health care team understand the important role they play in lessening the institution's risk. They must be taught not only the procedures but the rationale. The following are some basic rules and administrative tips to help an institution avoid some legal pitfalls, which can be created by an obstetrical unit that lacks quality standards of care.

Rule 1: Stay within the limits of delegation.

a. Before delegating any clinical tasks, check the legal requirements, hospital policy, and professional standards.
b. Be sure that everyone has valid qualifications for the procedures they are performing and that documentation clearly delineates each caregiver's experience and expertise.
c. Make sure employees are doing procedures in the manner required by the physician and that they know of the internal hospital mechanism for challenging superiors when quality of care issues arise.

Exhibit 29-5
CONDITIONS WARRANTING TRANSFER OR REFERRAL

MATERNAL TRANSFER

Medical-Surgical History

1. Moderate to severe chronic hypertension
2. Moderate to severe renal disease
3. Severe heart disease (class II to IV or history of congestive heart failure)
4. Class B to F diabetes
5. Previous endocrine ablation
6. Abnormal cervical cytology
7. Sickle-cell disease
8. Drug addition or alcoholism
9. History of tuberculosis or purified protein derivative (PPD) test reaction of more than 1 cm diameter
10. Pulmonary disease
11. Malignancy of any type
12. Gastrointestinal or liver disease

Obstetrical History

1. Previously diagnosed genital tract anomalies
   a. incompetent cervix
   b. cervical malformation
   c. uterine malformation
2. Two or more previous abortions
3. Previous stillborn or neonatal loss
4. Two previous premature labors or low-birth-weight infants (less than 2500 grams)
5. Two excessively large previous infants (greater than 4000 grams)
6. Maternal malignancy
7. Uterine myomas (5 cm or greater or submucous)
8. Ovarian mass
9. Parity of eight or more
10. Previous infant with isoimmunization

11. History of eclampsia
12. Previous infant with known or suspected genetic or familial disorders or congenital anomaly
13. Previous history of a need for special neonatal infant care or birth damaged infant
14. Medical indications for termination of previous pregnancy

Existing/Present Pregnancy History

Warrants admission to obstetrical ICU:
1. Severe pre-eclampsia or eclampsia
2. Hydramnios: polyhydramnios or oligohydramnios
3. Amnionitis
4. Premature rupture of the membranes more than 24 hours before labor
5. Uterine rupture
6. Placenta previa
7. Placenta abruptio
8. Meconium staining of amniotic fluid
9. Abnormal presentation
10. Multiple gestation
11. Fetal weight less than 2000 grams or greater than 4000 grams
12. Fetal bradycardia (longer than 30 minutes)
13. Breech delivery
14. Prolapsed cord
15. Fetal acidosis (pH 7.25 or less in the first stage of labor)
16. Fetal tachycardia (longer than 30 minutes)
17. Shoulder dystocia
18. Fetal presenting part not descending with labor
19. Evidence of maternal distress
20. Abnormal oxytocin challenge test (OCT)
21. Falling urinary estriol levels
22. Immature or intermediate L/S ratio or rapid surfactant test

Source: Reprinted from *Maternity Care*, 2nd ed., by Margaret Jensen, Ralph Benson and Irene Boback with permission of C.V. Mosby Company, © 1981.

Rule 2: Respect the patient's privacy.

a. Confidentiality of patient information is a given right and is often of heightened importance in the obstetrical patient.
b. Have a signed written authorization from patients to release information about their care to insurance companies, social services agencies, employers, schools, family members, and so forth.
c. Be sure all examining rooms are adequately soundproof.

d. Provide a mechanism for ensuring that areas surrounding clerical or intake staff are completely private so phone conversations and admitting discussions with patients are not overheard.
e. No conversations about patients should occur in corridors or common areas.

Rule 3: Respect patients as people.

a. Staff should know they provide an individual service, and when caring for the obstetrical patient, there are two patients with rights as well as a father who also may have rights.

Rule 4: Always tell the physician when a patient complains.

a. Listen carefully to the complaint and notify appropriate staff immediately.
b. Refer the obstetrical patient to other members of the health care team (finance department, social services department) who may be in a better position to deal with specific concerns or problems related to the delivery.
c. Develop a system for tracking patient complaints and for ensuring the problems or concerns are resolved in an appropriate and timely manner.

Rule 5: Always relay messages and instructions in an appropriate and timely manner.

a. For telephone calls a screening checklist should be designed, and staff should be trained to recognize urgent calls.
b. Message slips large enough to contain all vital information should be used.
c. Establish a message center so important messages are not overlooked.
d. Write instructions given to patient on sheets that can be placed in the patient's chart to create a permanent record. Provide documentation indicating the patient has been given the instructions and that she has an understanding of them.
e. Use preprinted forms for referral bookings, and keep a copy in the patient's chart.
f. Staff members should use a log to follow up on the instructions, to book specialist appointments or tests, and strike off the entry once the patient has been contacted.
g. Give special care to prescription renewals. Specific times should be established for calling pharmacies.

Rule 6: Provide documentation on the medical record.

a. Medical records must be complete, accurate, and current. All parts of the medical record should be available to the health care team for each clinic visit as well as at the time of delivery.
b. The complete medical record includes notes about each encounter with the patient, including telephone calls and prescription renewals.
c. Every cancellation, no-show, and incidence of non-compliance should be noted in the chart.[32]

Once these rules are discussed and are fully understood by the entire obstetrical and neonatal health care team, risk management becomes part of the daily routine.

In any area of clinical practice, the physician–patient relationship is of paramount importance since it governs the remainder of the interpersonal interaction. This component of care provided by any physician lays the foundation for the patient–physician relationship in encouraging teamwork with the patient. The following are some guidelines for physicians that help develop and promote the physician–patient relationship.

1. Develop the interpersonal interaction by encouraging the antepartum patient to bring a significant other to office visits. Explain the status of the pregnancy during the visits. Also explain how you, the physician, would like to go about doing things and encourage their input; ask for questions.
2. Be prepared to spend more time than usual with the patient, especially with primigravidas (first pregnancy). Stay seated throughout the visit because this gives the appearance of being patient and encourages the patient to ask questions.
3. Allow the patient to bring one or two other significant others to see the ultrasound viewing, especially if it is done in the physician's office.
4. **Always** share with the patient the laboratory findings and ultrasound findings regardless of the outcomes. Offer to give the result; explain all results in terms appropriate to the patient's level of understanding.[33]

Physicians can be effective communicators by addressing the concerns of patients, providing accurate and understandable information about the possible consequences of pregnancy complications, and motivating patients to use available resources and take appropriate action. Effective communication is a two-way process between the patient and the physician. An essential step in communication is to recognize that patient feelings are valid. Acknowledgment of the feelings, be it fear, anger, frustration, and sadness, is an important first step. It is equally important to support the patient's concerns when warranted, and to provide reassurances otherwise. Find out what the patient cares about and attempt to address those concerns first. It is important to separate the factual issues from the patient's feelings. Until the feelings are addressed, the patient will not be able to pay attention to the facts.[34]

Furthermore, information about pregnancy outcome and neonatal complication often is complex. Some recommendations for making complex information understandable are:

1. Pay attention to how much the patient knows and relate any new information to what is already known.
2. Use simple, nontechnical language.
3. Pictures and charts are useful in explaining anatomy, physiology, pregnancy, and neonatal outcomes.[35]

Aside from the importance of physician–patient communication, it is equally important for the nurse and physician to have open communication. Nurses are legally responsible to keep physicians informed of changes in a patient's status. After recognizing that a physician's intervention has become necessary, the nurse must provide the physician with specific information so the physician can make a reasonable medical judgment. It is vital to communicate what the nurse's expectations are. If the nurse believes the physician is needed on the unit, then this must be clearly communicated. In addition to being timely, the nurse's notification of physicians must be effective. That is, all necessary information has been gathered and clearly relayed to physicians.[36]

ESTABLISHING A RISK MANAGEMENT PROGRAM

According to the 1987 Government Accounting Office report, obstetrical related errors in medical malpractice were the highest in both median and average payments: $65,000 and $216,464 respectively. Obstetricians account for 5.2 percent of all physicians but are involved in 12.4 percent of all claims. These claims carry the highest severity of all medical closed claims. Of even greater concern is obstetricians' unawareness of liability risk management skills.

The purpose of an obstetrical risk management program is to identify the number of factors that identify a patient as one who is high risk. This definition is based on the patient's physical condition, social condition, or any number of other factors that may influence the ability to care for self or the child. The purpose of the program is to minimize the cost of loss from basic risk through identifying, measuring, and controlling these basic risks. This program should primarily be considered a means of improving and maintaining quality patient care.

Development of an obstetrical risk management program does not have to start from scratch. Rather, it can often result from a change of emphasis, reorganization, and better coordination of existing activities. Using quality assurance or generic screening indicators can provide an important foundation for a quality management obstetrical program. Such monitors will help a hospital to identify specific issues that could impact the quality of service provided. Quality in this context includes both technical and the personal components of service rendered. Service given must be technically proficient. Since health care is primarily a human service, it must be delivered in a personal, empathetic manner. Not only must the hospital's patients receive excellent service but they also must believe that quality care is being given.

For a proactive obstetrical risk management program to be developed and implemented, certain individuals in the organizations must be designated for specific responsibilities and critical functions. All individuals who have the authority to influence patient care outcomes directly or through others should be actively involved in risk management. This could include those professionals who provide clinical care as well as those within the health care setting that provide support care.

Where obstetrical risk management programs are motivated by the desire for improvement in patient care, physicians must take a leadership role. Without this involvement, a risk management program will be less effective regardless of how well it is organized. Decisions that expose hospitals to the risk of liability are made primarily by physicians. By their nature, these decisions involve the balancing of risk by professionals whose entire training has been focused on the question of evaluating when the risks inherent in diagnosis and treatment outweigh the risk of letting the symptoms of disease run their course. It would be extremely difficult for a risk manager to effectively intervene in the evaluation process without interfering in the practice of medicine. Risk management activities designed to reduce patient injury, improve patient care, and reduce physician liability require active participation of medical staff.

Medical staff should be encouraged to participate in decisions about their hospital's particular needs and be asked to assist in the process where future needs are identified and planned. The risk management program that the hospital decides to develop should meet the specific needs of the entire hospital setting. Physicians must be active participants from the start and be involved in selecting the type of quality management program that will support their practice. To gain their full participation, physicians should be kept apprised of the protection available to them under state and federal law regarding quality and peer review activities. Physicians should be represented on risk management committees as this will help them gain an understanding of the process and some of the impediments to controlling risk. Hospital administrators should support physician participation as related to these activities. Physicians need to be convinced that the committees exist primarily because of concern for better patient care and not simply to help the hospital fulfill insurance or accreditation requirements.

For risk management to be most effective, all members of the obstetrical team must believe that the underlying risk/quality management process is in place only to assist in or support the delivery of high-quality, patient focused care.

All members of the team should believe that everyone providing care wants to do the best possible job and may need the assistance and support of others to achieve the best possible result. For physicians, risk management should not be regarded as a punitive activity or as a discipline whose sole interest is in the resolution of lawsuits. Rather, they should see risk management as a process that assists them in identifying potential, current, problematic behaviors that could give rise to future injuries.

Aside from physicians, nurses and other professional and support staff should be involved as members of the obstetrical risk management team. Seldom does something occur within the hospital that can be attributed to only one person or one event. The risk management team must be as multidimensional as the problem it seeks to correct. It is often the case that nursing forms the first line of defense toward preventing such suits. The nurse is often the first person to see the patient and often is the one person who spends the greatest amount of time with the patient and family. Nurses should be advised, along with physicians, of those behaviors or comments that should raise suspicion that the patient is either concerned about the care she is receiving, concerned about her pregnancy, or holding back information that could affect the health of the child. The ability of the law to extend or limit nursing action requires that knowledge of the law be an integral part of nursing management. Awareness of the standards of care that the courts expect from nursing and a knowledge of the most common causes are the tools to begin a nursing risk management program that can minimize lawsuits. Standards of care have been published by the American Nurses' Association, the Joint Commission on Accreditation of Healthcare Organizations, and specialty organizations such as the Nurses Association of College of Obstetrics and Gynecology.[37]

DEFINING THE RISK MANAGEMENT PROCESS

The obstetrical risk management team or group should meet on a weekly basis to discuss potential problems that can arise either with patient care given, staffing problems, or with the patient's health status. If a bad pregnancy outcome should occur, the group should meet as soon as possible to discuss resolution of the incident. At this meeting, the risk manager can decide who talks to the family and who talks to the press. Remember that after a suit has been filed, it is too late to initiate conversation in an attempt to resolve a claim. However, if the risk manager and the obstetrical staff can react quickly after an incident and not fingerpoint, a potential lawsuit can be prevented.[38]

All health care providers are pursuing the same positive goals with regard to a patient's health and welfare. There-fore, multidisciplinary efforts toward these goals should be compatible and complementary.

DEVELOPING TOOLS TO SUPPORT AN OBSTETRICAL MANAGEMENT TEAM

In managing obstetrical risks, the obstetrical team must develop an early warning system that flags potential problems. Identify, in advance, which obstetric and labor delivery events should be reported or flagged. Exhibit 29-6 identifies the type of occurrences that most typically require mandatory reporting to the risk manager. Also, the medical staff must be informed that these events are always to be reported. To eliminate the defensiveness that might occur during risk management meetings, try to conduct an impartial discussion. Setting mandatory reporting standards before problems occur is essential: it allows for impartiality.[39] Also, Appendix 29-B, Clinical Indicators for Obstetrics, contains information on specific practices related to the provision of obstetrical care developed by the University Hospital Consortium. This information also can be used as quality screens to identify potentially problematic behaviors. This type of monitoring can help to focus on issues before they become problems. In Appendix 29-B a column has been provided to identify those types of situations that historically develop into risk management problems. To prioritize and facilitate programs that will reduce or eliminate risks, risk management obstetrical committees should establish a base of information. The committee must encourage employees to complete incident reports completely and objectively each time an incident occurs. The risk management committee can analyze the information statistically to ascertain the frequency and significance of certain events. Thus, they can identify high-risk areas and recurring incidents that need attention. The individuals involved in patient care should be encouraged to identify potential risks and to offer suggestions to eliminate or reduce the risks.[40]

The guidelines in Exhibit 29-6 are to be used to identify those events that would be automatically reported to the risk management committee. Within this committee there should be a disciplinary committee that reviews every aspect of a hospital's operations, not just obstetrics. The disciplinary committee would be responsible for deciding which problem cases are flagged to members of the obstetrics department, pediatrics department, and nursing department. Family practice should serve on the committee. These members would set rules for:

1. appropriate levels of care
2. hospital protocol
3. transfer policies

Exhibit 29-6
INSTANCES REQUIRING MANDATORY REPORTING TO THE RISK MANAGER

1. Maternal death
2. Fetal or infant death (if gestational age is greater than 6 months and gestational weight is greater than 1000 grams)
3. Low Apgar score (less than 5 at one minute and less than 7 at five minutes)
4. Infant skull fracture or palsy
5. A mother requiring a transfusion following delivery or excessive maternal blood loss (defined as blood loss greater than 500 cc, a drop in hemoglobin of 3.5 g/dl or greater, or a drop in hematocrit of 11 ml/dl or greater)
6. Attending physician who is not present during active labor or delivery
7. Emergency cesarean section that occurs greater than 30 minutes after fetal distress is noted
8. Baby born with multiple anomalies not anticipated before delivery

The following additional clinical situations also might be suggested for mandatory reporting. These situations relate specifically to the infant transferred to the neonatal intensive care unit (NICU) or high-risk nursery following delivery.

1. Term baby admitted to NICU from the well baby nursery
2. All neonatal deaths
3. Neonate admitted with diagnosis of neonatal abnormality
4. Nerve, tissue, or muscle damage resulting from intravenous infiltration or from infusion of tissue damaging medications
5. Neonate requiring reintubation or tracheostomy following extubation
6. Neonate who has a seizure before discharge from NICU
7. Medication or treatment errors causing patient injury
8. Equipment malfunction with or without patient injury
9. Nosocomial infection
10. Neonate with excessive blood loss from catheter disconnects
11. Transfusion errors
12. Treatments performed within NICU without appropriate parental or guardian consent
13. Parent's or guardian's refusal of treatment, elopement, or unauthorized removal of child from unit
14. Any significant neonatal injury resulting from delivery (skull fracture, brachial palsy, cord injury, and so on)

4. use of prenatal records
5. fetal monitoring
6. labor–delivery documentation
7. response to a delivery with complications occurring

In addition, the committee can recommend clinical reviews where a staff obstetrician rotates with other obstetricians to perform clinical reviews. This would allow the committee or staff reviewer to immediately examine potentially troublesome cases.

CONCLUSION

There will always be obstetrical malpractice suits. There will always be malpractice because health care providers are humans who are not perfect and predicting outcomes of treatment are close to impossible. Furthermore, lawsuits will continue because our legal system and society believe that anything less than a perfect result is indicative of provider negligence. We can lessen the possibility of a lawsuit by addressing our responsibility to the patient, to her treatment, and to the treatment of the neonate by providing the best possible level of care. Risk management and good patient care go hand-in-hand.

NOTES

1. *Taber's Cyclopedic Medical Dictionary*, 13th ed. (Philadelphia: F.A. Davis Company, 1977).
2. M. Jensen, et al., *Maternity Care*, 3rd ed. (St.Louis: C.V. Mosby Company, 1981), 315.
3. Ibid.
4. Ibid.
5. Ibid., 316.
6. Ibid., 316, 317.
7. Ibid., 317.
8. Ibid.
9. Ibid.
10. Ibid., 315, 316.
11. J. Smith, The Dangers of Prenatal Cocaine Use, *American Journal of Maternal/Child Nursing* 13 (May–June 1988): 174.
12. Ibid., 176.
13. Ibid.
14. Ibid.
15. Ibid., 177.
16. Ibid.
17. Jensen, et al., *Maternity Care*, 318.
18. Ibid., 246.
19. J. Smith, The Dangers of Prenatal Cocaine Use, 177.
20. Jensen, et al., *Maternity Care*, 318.

21. Ibid.

22. J. Smith, The Dangers of Prenatal Cocaine Use, 177.

23. Ibid.

24. C.S. Cagle, Access to Prenatal Care and Prevention of Low Birth Weight, *American Journal of Maternal/Child Nursing* 12 (July–August 1987): 235.

25. L. Chagnon and B. Easterwood, Managing the Risks of Obstetrical Nursing, *American Journal of Maternal/Child Nursing* 11 (September–October 1986): 308.

26. Ibid.

27. American Health Consultants Inc., Managing Your Facility's Obstetrical Risks, *Hospital Risk Management* 1988.

28. D. Richardson, et al., Referral Practices and Health Care Costs: The Dilemma of High-Risk Obstetrics, *The Journal of Legal Medicine* 6 (1985): 429.

29. Ibid., 428.

30. Ibid., 431, 436–437.

31. P. Milne, Be Cautious in the Office: Lawsuits Can Originate There Too, *Canadian Medical Association Journal* 139 (15 November 1988): 997.

32. Ibid., 997–998.

33. R. Walker, Obstetrical Risk Management: Establishing Documents of Defense, *Texas Medicine* 86 (June 1990): 32–33.

34. A. Gotsch and R. Kashdan, Risk Communication, *New Jersey Medicine* 85 (November 1988): 954, 957.

35. Ibid., 958.

36. Chagnon and Easterwood, Managing the Risks of Obstetrical Nursing, 306.

37. R. Luguire, Nursing Risk Management, *Nursing Management* 20 (October 1989): 56.

38. American Health Consultants Inc., Managing Your Facility's Obstetrical Risks, 1.

39. Ibid.

40. Ibid., 58.

BIBLIOGRAPHY

American Academy of Pediatrics and American College of Obstetricians and Gynecologists, *Guidelines for Perinatal Care.* 2nd ed. (Washington, D.C., 1988).

Brown, B. Jr., 1979. *Risk Management for Hospitals—A Practical Approach.* Gaithersburg, Md.: Aspen Publishers, Inc.

Craig, H.E., March 1986. Risk Management—Good Patient Care. *Minnesota Medicine* 69: 113.

Hayt, E., et al., 1982. *Law of Hospital, Physician and Patient.* 3rd ed. Chicago: Physician's Record Co.

Messenger, O., 15 November 1988. Risk Management in the Hospital: Medical Staff Must Be Involved. *Canadian Medical Association Journal* 139: 994–996.

Monagle, J. 1985. *Risk Management—A Guide for Health Care Professionals.* Gaithersburg, Md.: Aspen Publishers, Inc.

Palmer, S. and Gibbs, C., Fall 1989. Risk Management in Obstetric Anesthesia. *International Anesthesiology Clinics.* 27: 188–199.

Risk Management: The Widening Circle of Responsibility, Third Annual Summer Symposium (Chicago: American Society for Health Care Risk Management of the American Hospital Association, 3–4 August 1987).

Risk Management Review —MMIE OB Risk Management Guidelines Approved. *Minnesota Medicine* 71 (September 1988), 567–568.

Troyer, G.T. and Salman, S.L., 1986. *Handbook of Health Care Risk Management.* Gaithersburg, Md.: Aspen Publishers, Inc.

Comprehensive Prenatal Flow Sheets

Street Address					
City, State, Zip			Marital Status M D SEP S W		
Home Telephone	Contact Telephone		Spouse's Name		
Referred by	Preferred Language		Race - Ethnicity W B H I A O		

EDUCATION	Patient:	Enter Code Numbers	1- Elem Only 3 - HS Grad 5 - Coll Grad 2 - Parital HS 4 - Partial Coll 6 - Post Grad		
	Spouse:				
OCCUPATION	Patient:		Full Part Self Unempl — Employment Status (Circle) —		
	Spouse:		Full Part Self Unempl		
INSURANCE	☐ BC-BS ☐ Medicaid ☐ None Policy #: _____				
	☐ Private: ☐ HMO: ☐ Other:				

OB INDEX

Age	Term	Prem	Ab-Ect	Living

Birth Control Pills in Past Year
☐ Yes   ☐ No

LAST MENSTRUAL PERIOD	
☐ Normal Date:	
☐ Abnormal	
PMP:	EDC

MENSES — Onset X Int X Dur   CYCLE   ☐ Regular   ☐ Irregular

PAST PREGNANCIES

	EARLY LOSS (<20 WKS)				LIVE OR STILLBORN (≥ 20 WKS)									ASSOCIATED PROBLEMS
DATE			GEST AGE					VAGINAL			CESAREAN		Other/ Unk	
No.	Month	Year	Spont*	Ectopic	Elective*	Birth Weight	Sex	Age of Death**	Spont Vtx	Breech Forceps	CPD	Fetal Distress	Abn Pres	Repeat	
1															
2															
3															
4															
5															
6															
7															
8															
9															

*D&C MAb(Missed Ab) M(Molar) S(Suction) I(Intra-amniotic Injection) H(Hysterotomy)   **S(Stillbirth) N(Neonatal) I(Infant) C(Childhood)

HISTORICAL PROBLEMS

Prob. No.	+	Risk Value			PROBLEM NUMBER	SPECIAL COMMENTS	PRINT FOR DATA ENTRY
1		5		AGE ☐ <17 ☐ >35			
2		5		MULTIPARITY (5 or more ≥20 weeks)			
3		5		INDUCED ABORTION			
4		10		RECURRENT ABORTION (3 or more)			
5		10		PREMATURE (<38 weeks) ☐ LGA			
6		10		SGA (Small for Gestational Age)			
7		5		EXCESSIVE SIZE (>4000 grams or > 9 lbs.)			
8		10	PREVIOUS INFANTS	PERINATAL DEATH ☐ Stillborn ☐ Neonatal			
9		5		POST-NEONATAL PROBLEM ☐ Sudden Infant Death ☐ Neurologic ☐Developmental ☐ Serious Illness:			
10		10		NEONATAL JAUNDICE ☐ Rh ☐ ABO ☐ Physiologic ☐ Unknown ☐ Other:			
11		5		CONGENITAL DEFECT ☐ Chromosomal ☐ CNS ☐ Structural ☐ Cardiac ☐ Metabolic ☐ Other:			
12		5	GYN	HISTORY OF INFERTILITY ☐ Primary ☐ Secondary ☐ Untreated ☐ Treated: ☐ Clomiphene ☐ Other:			
13		10		STRUCTURAL ABN ☐ Anomaly ☐ Corr'd ☐ Myoma ☐ Myomectomy ☐ Incomp Cx ☐ Cerclage, Rmv'd ☐ Yes ☐ No			
14		5	OB	PRIOR C-SECTION ☐ Low Trans ☐ Low Vert ☐ Classical ☐ Unknown ☐Hysterotomy			
15		5		HEMORRHAGE ☐ Previa ☐ Abruptio ☐ Other 3rd Trimester ☐ Postpartum ☐ Transfusion			
16		5		PREGNANCY-INDUCED HYPERTENSION ☐ Req'd Hosp ☐ Req'd Early Delivery ☐ Dev'd Eclampsia			
17		10		CHRONIC HYPERTENSION (BP ≥140/90 non-pregnant) ☐ On Drug Therapy:			
18		10		HEART DISEASE ☐ Rheumatic ☐ Arteriosclerotic ☐ Surgical Correction Functional Class: ☐ Congenital ☐ Other ☐ Hx of CHF or Arrhythmia			
19		5		PULMONARY DISEASE ☐ Asthma ☐ Chronic Bronchitis ☐ Tuberculosis ☐ Other:			
20		5	MEDICAL SURGICAL	GENITOURINARY INFECTIONS ☐ Asymptomatic Bacteriuria ☐ Pyelonephritis ☐ Syphilis ☐ Cystitis ☐ Gonorrhea ☐ Genital Herpes			
21		10		RENAL DISEASE ☐ Glomerulo ☐ Chronic Pyelo ☐ Diabetic ☐ Collagen-Vas ☐ Calculi ☐ Other:			
22		10		DIABETES ☐ A ☐ B ☐ C ☐ D ☐ F-R ☐ Insulin, Pre-pregnancy Dosage:			
23		10		THYROID DISEASE ☐ Hypo ☐ Thyroiditis ☐ Hyper, treated with ☐ Surgery ☐ I¹³¹ ☐ Drugs:			
24		10		OTHER MEDICAL ☐ Phlebitis ☐ Embolus ☐ Hematologic ☐ GI ☐ Collagen-Vas ☐ On Drug Therapy:			
25		10		NEUROLOGIC ☐ Seizures ☐ Migraine ☐ Myasthenia ☐ MS ☐ Other: ☐ On Drug Therapy:			
26		5		PSYCHIATRIC ☐ Postpartum Depression ☐ Other: ☐ Hospitalized ☐ On Drug Therapy:			
27		5		PREVIOUS OPERATIONS ☐ Diag D&C ☐ Laparoscopy ☐ Appendectomy ☐ Cholecystectomy ☐ Other:			
28		10	HABITS	EXCESSIVE USE ☐ Alcohol ☐ Tobacco ☐ Marijuana ☐ Narcotics:			
29		5	FAMILY HISTORY	MATERNAL ONLY ☐ Hypertension ☐ Multiple Births ☐ Diabetes ☐ Other:			
30		5		MAT OR PAT ☐ Mental Retardation ☐ Congen Anom ☐ Congen Hearing Loss ☐ Hemoglobinopathy ☐ Allergies			

085944

PRENATAL HISTORY 1

PHYSICAL EXAMINATION   Date:

	Normal Yes No		Normal Yes No		Normal Yes No		Normal Yes No
BP		THYROID		ABDOMEN		VAGINA	
SKIN		LUNGS		EXTREMITIES		CERVIX	
EYES		BREASTS		NEUROLOGIC		UTERUS	
ENT		NIPPLES		PERINEUM		ADNEXA	
MOUTH		HEART		VULVA		RECTUM	

UTERINE SIZE VS. DATES ☐ Compatible ☐ Smaller ☐ Larger

PELVIS ☐ Adequate ☐ Borderline ☐ Inadequate   ☐ Clinical ☐ X-Ray   Characteristics:

ABNORMAL FINDINGS:
PRINT
FOR DATA ENTRY

SCREENING PROBLEMS

Prob. No.	+	Risk Value			
31		5		PRE-PREG WEIGHT ☐ < 100 lbs ☐ > 200 lbs	
32		10	ANATOMICAL	SIZE-DATE DISCREPANCY	
33		5		SMALL PELVIS	
34		5	Rh NEG	☐ Not Sensitized	
35		10		☐ Rh Sensitized ☐ Irregular Antibodies	
36		5	G-U TESTS	☐ Abn PAP ☐ Pos GC Culture ☐ Asymptomatic Bacteriuria	
37		5	POSITIVE LAB	POSITIVE SEROLOGY	
38		5		ANEMIA ☐ Mild (9-11 gms or 27-33%) ☐ Severe (< 9 gms or < 27%)	
39		5		ABNORMAL HGB ☐ SS ☐ AS ☐ SC ☐ Thalassemia ☐ Other:	

( ) ◄ **INITIAL RISK ASSESSMENT**
(Sum of Historical and Screening Problems)

Signature-Date:

CARE PLAN
Date

Lab Work ☐ Routine ☐ Additional:

Prescriptions ☐ Iron ☐ Vitamins ☐ Anit-Emetic:

☐ Nutritional Counseling: ☐ Social Service

EDUCATION AND DELIVERY PLANS

Anticipated Delivery ☐ Vaginal ☐ Cesarean

☐ Lamaze Birth ☐ Other:

Hospital of Delivery:

Childbirth Classes:

Support Person:

Anesthesia ☐ Yes ☐ No ☐ Uncertain   Type:

Breast Feeding ☐ Yes ☐ No ☐ Uncertain

Family Planning ☐ BTL   ☐ Papers Signed
☐ Other:

Pediatric Care:

SPECIAL CARE AND PROCEDURES

☐ Prenatal Hospitalization, Purpose:

☐ Genetic Studies ☐ AFP Screen ☐ Amnio ☐ Other:

☐ Diabetes Screen at   weeks

☐ Ultrasound Exam, Purpose: ☐ Serial Study

☐ Amniotic Fluid Study ☐ Serial △OD's   ☐ Lung Maturity

☐ Serial Estriols, start at   weeks

☐ Other Tests of Fetal Well-Being:

Additional Plans:

Consultations:

Referrals:

Allergies:

Medications:

085951

LABORATORY RESULTS

INITIAL DATA BASE
Date

TYPE ☐ A ☐ B ☐ O ☐ AB	URINE ANALYSIS	☐ Normal ☐ Abn:
Rh ☐ Neg ☐ Pos ☐ Du +		
ANTIBODY ☐ Neg ☐ Pos SCREEN Antr:	URINE Culture	☐ Neg ☐ Pos:
VDRL ☐ Neg ☐ Pos	PPD ☐ Neg ☐ Pos	
FTA ☐ Neg ☐ Pos	CHEST X-RAY ☐ Neg ☐ Pos	
RUBELLA TITER:	PAP ☐ Neg ☐ Inflam ☐ Dysplasia: ☐ CIS ☐ Invasive CA	
HCT/Hgb:		
SICKLE PREP ☐ Neg ☐ Pos	GC CULTURE ☐ Neg ☐ Pos	
Hgb ELECTROPHORESIS:	FATHER'S TYPE/Rh: ☐ Homozyg ☐ Heterozyg	

SCREENING

	Date	Weeks	Test	Result	
SERUM AFP				☐ Normal ☐ Abn
DIABETES				☐ Neg ☐ Pos
DIABETES				☐ Neg ☐ Pos

ULTRASOUND
☐ Previa ☐ Single ☐ Multiple ☐ Anomaly:

Date	Placenta	Abd/Thor	BPD	GA	Presentation

	GENETIC	Rh IMMUNIZATION
Date		
	Amniotic Fluid Result	△OD:
	☐ AFP ☐ Normal ☐ Abn	△OD:
	☐ CHROMO ☐ Normal ☐ Abn	△OD:
	☐ OTHER:	△OD:

BLOOD SUGARS

	FETAL STATUS
Date Fast 1 Hr 2 Hr 3 Hr	☐ Estriols ☐ HPL ☐ Non-Stress ☐ Stress ☐ Amnioscopy ☐ Other ☐ Lung Maturity

Date	Time	Result	Date	Time	Result	Date	Test	Result

ROUTINE REPEAT

ANTIB'Y TITER ☐ Neg ☐ Pos	URINE ☐ Neg
VDRL ☐ Neg ☐ Pos	CULTURE ☐ Pos:
HCT/Hgb:	GC CULTURE ☐ Neg ☐ Pos
HCT/Hgb:	

PRENATAL SCREENING AND PLAN 2

Pre-Pregnancy Weight	Height					

NUTRITION

ASSESSMENT	_ Acceptable _ Unacceptable _ Undetermined	_ Protocol _ Clinical

DIET THERAPY   ☐ WIC

OB INDEX

Age	Term	Prem	Ab-Ect	Living

Date of Positive Pregnancy Test

LMP	Quickening

Corrected EDC	EDC

PRENATAL VISITS

DATE	WEIGHT	SUGAR ALBU-MIN ACETONE	BLOOD PRESSURE 180 170 160 150 140 130 120 110 100 90 80 70 60 50	GEST AGE	FUNDUS	FETAL PRESEN-TATION	FETAL HEART	COMMENTS Return-Initials

DEVELOPING PROBLEMS

Prob. No.	+	Risk Value			
40		10	EARLY PREGNANCY	THREATENED AB ☐ Hospitalized ☐ Drug Therapy:
41				EARLY TERMINATION (<20 wks) ☐ Spontaneous ☐ Missed ☐ Induced ☐ Ectopic ☐ Molar
42		5		HYPEREMESIS GRAVIDARUM ☐ Hospitalized ☐ Drug Therapy:
43		10		INCOMPETENT CERVIX ☐ Cerclage ☐ Shirodkar ☐ McDonald, Date: ☐ Drug Rx:
44		10	INFECTION	TORCH/VIRAL ☐ Toxoplasmosis ☐ Syphilis ☐ Rubella ☐ CMV ☐ Varicella ☐ Mumps ☐ Hepatitis
45		5		FLU SYNDROME ☐ High Fever ☐ Gastroenteritis ☐ Hospitalized
46		5		GENITOURINARY ☐ Vaginitis ☐ Asymp Bacteriuria ☐ Cystitis ☐ GC ☐ Genital Herpes
47		10		PYELONEPHRITIS ☐ Hospitalized ☐ Recurrent ☐ Drug Prophylaxis:
48		10	MEDICAL-SURGICAL	GESTATIONAL DIABETES (This pregnancy) Rx: ☐ Diet ☐ Insulin:
49		10		THROMBOPHLEBITIS ☐ Hospitalized ☐ Embolus ☐ Anticoagulant Rx: ☐ Heparin ☐ Coumadin
50		10		CARDIOPULMONARY ☐ Asthmatic Attack ☐ Bronchitis ☐ Pneumonia ☐ Active TB ☐ Tachycardia ☐ Arrhythmia ☐ CHI-
51		10		OTHER MEDICAL ☐ Late Anemia ☐ Late Iso-Immunization ☐ Hematologic ☐ Neuro ☐ GI ☐ Renal ☐ Collagen-Vas ☐ Skin
52		5		SURGICAL ☐ Adnexal ☐ Appendectomy ☐ Other:
53		5	PSYCHO-SOCIAL	☐ Marital ☐ Coping and Support ☐ Unresolved Grief ☐ Family ☐ Other: ☐ Financial ☐ Relocation ☐ Prior OB Experience ☐ Sexual
54		5	ANATOMICAL ABNORMAL-ITIES	MATERNAL WEIGHT GAIN ☐ Inadequate (<15 lbs. at 36 Weeks) ☐ Excessive (> 30 lbs. at 36 Weeks)
55		10		UTERINE SIZE ☐ Suspected IUGR ☐ Multiple Pregnancy ☐ Polyhydramnios ☐ Myomata
56		5		FETAL LIE/PRESENTATION ☐ Breech ☐ Transverse Lie ☐ Oblique
57		5	ABNORMAL-ITIES OF FUNCTION	BLOOD PRESSURE ☐ Preg-Induced Hypertension Mild ☐ BP ≥ 140/90 or 1 30 mm systolic or 1 15 mm diastolic ☐ Proteinuria 1 + or 2 + ☐ Persistent Edema
58		10		☐ Superimposed Severe ☐ BP ≥ 160/110 or ☐ Proteinuria > 2 + (Both after 26 wks)
59		10		BLEEDING > 20 WKS ☐ Cervical ☐ Previa ☐ Low-lying ☐ Undetermined
60		5		HOSPITALIZED FOR LABOR OR RUPTURED MEMBRANES ☐ Suspected Premature Labor ☐ False Labor (>37 wks) ☐ PROM ☐ Pharmacologic Rx:
61		10		POST-TERM > 42 WKS (From original LMP or by other clinical parameters)
62				INTRAUTERINE FETAL DEMISE
63				PROTOCOL
64				DISPOSITION ☐ Moved ☐ Referred: ☐ Other:

(   ) ◄ **LATE PREGNANCY RISK ASSESSMENT (~ 36 WEEKS)**
(Sum of Initial Risk Assessment and Developing Problems)   Signature-Date:

085969

PRENATAL FLOW AND DEVELOPING PROBLEMS 3

Source: Courtesy of the University of Pennsylvania, Philadelphia, Pennsylvania.

Clinical Indicators for Obstetrics

UNIVERSITY HOSPITAL CONSORTIUM
QUALITY ASSURANCE CLINICAL INDICATORS
DEPARTMENT: OBSTETRICS

ASPECT OF CARE	INDICATOR	THRESHOLD	HIGH RISK/ VOLUME	I/O	MED STAFF MONITORING
Delivery, Generic	Transfer to ICU postdelivery (mother)	> 0%	HR	I	
	Unplanned readmit within 21 days (mother)	> 0%		I/O	
	Cardiopulmonary arrest (mother)	> 0%	HR	I	
	Delivery unattended by physician or certified nurse midwife	> 0%		I	
	Birth weight <2,500 grams post induction or planned C-section	> 0%	HR	I	
	Term infants admitted to ICU	> 5%		I	
	Term infants with Apgars <5 @ 5 minutes (Alt: Apgar score <3 @ 5 minutes when GA >34 weeks)	> 0%	HR	I	
	Initiation of antibiotics >24 hour post vaginal delivery	> 5%		I	DUE/IC
	Documentation of baseline fetal status (heart rate and response to contractions)	<100%			CP
	Monitoring consistent w/ACOG standards	<100%			CP

416

ASPECT OF CARE	INDICATOR	THRESHOLD	HIGH RISK/VOLUME	I/Q	MED STAFF MONITORING
	Pharmacologically induced labor for other than diabetes, premature ROM, pre-eclampsia, post-term gestation, intra-uterine growth retardation, cardiac disease, isoimmunization, fetal demise, chorioamnionitis, lethal fetal anomaly	> 0%		I	DUE
	Eclampsia	> 0%	HR	I	
	3rd"/4th" lacerations	> 0%		I	
	Endometritis	> 10%		I	
	Blood products administered (EXCEPTION: previa or abruptia)	> 0%		I	BUR
Vaginal Delivery	Return to delivery room for a) removal of retained placenta, b) control hemorrhage/drain hematoma	> 0%		I	
	Cord prolapse after artificial rupture of membranes	> 0%	HR	I	
	Uterine atony requiring C-section	> 0%		I	
Birth Injury	Newborn fractures	> 0%	HR	I	

ASPECT OF CARE	INDICATOR	THRESHOLD	HIGH RISK/VOLUME	I/O	MED STAFF MONITORING
Mortality	Newborn nerve palsy	> 0%	HR	I	
	Maternal death	> 0%	HR	I	
	Inhospital postpartum fetal death (>500 grams)	> 0%		I	
Antepartum External Cephalic Version (ECV)	Ultrasound to confirm lie	<100%		I	CP
	Gestational age confirmed by ultrasound	<100%		I	CP
	Documentation of fetal heart rate monitored during version	<100%		I	
	Version guided by ultrasound	<100%		I	
	Incidence of emergency delivery by C-section	> 5%		I	
	Version successful as evidenced by ultrasound confirmation of cephalic lie	< 60%		I	

ASPECT OF CARE	INDICATOR	THRESHOLD	HIGH RISK/ VOLUME	I/Q	MED STAFF MONITORING
Use and Performance of Cesarean Section (C-Section)	(Comparative Rate Indicators)				
	C-sections, as % of total deliveries	> 25%		–	
	Repeat sections, as % of total deliveries	> 8%		–	
	Repeat sections without attempted trial labor, as % of repeats	*		–	
	VBAC's, as % of previous C-section deliveries	< 14.5%		–	
	Sections for failure to progress, as % of all sections	*		–	
	Sections for fetal distress, as % of all sections	*		–	
	Sections for malpresentation, as % of all sections	> 10%		–	
	Length of stay post C-section delivery of more than five days	> 10%		–	
	C-section delivery occurs within 10 minutes of induction of general anesthesia	<100%	HR	–	

* Set thresholds based on number of deliveries, patient population, and experience.

ASPECT OF CARE	INDICATOR	THRESHOLD	HIGH RISK/ VOLUME	I/O	MED STAFF MONITORING
	C-section delivery is effected within 30 minutes of the decision to perform a C-section (EXCEPTION: Elective section)	<100%	HR	I	
	Prophylactic antibiotics are administered perioperatively (EXCEPTION: C-section performed before onset of labor or rupture of membranes)	<100%		I	DUE
Ectopic Pregnancy	Surgical intervention within four hours of diagnosis	<100%		I/O	
Invasive Prenatal Screening (e.g., Amniocentesis, Percutaneous Umbilical Blood Supply [PUBS], Chorionic Villus Sample)	Documentation of discussion with patients of test reliability limitations	<100%	HR	O	
	Infection	> 0%		O	IC
	Miscarriage/fetal demise	> 0%	HR	O	
	Undetected congenital abnormality	> 0%	HR	O	
Tocolysis	Management during treatment:				
	Bed rest	<100%		I/O	

ASPECT OF CARE	INDICATOR	THRESHOLD	HIGH RISK/ VOLUME	I/O	MED STAFF MONITORING
	Administration of IV fluids for hydration	<100%		I/O	DUE
	Assessment of gestational age	<100%	HR	I/O	DUE
	Ongoing monitoring of fetal status	<100%		I/O	DUE
	Urinalysis	<100%		I/O	DUE
	Intake and output monitoring	<100%		I/O	DUE
	Observation of pulmonary status	<100%		I/O	DUE
	Complications:				
	Pulmonary edema	> 0%		1	DUE
	Myocardial infarction	> 0%		1	DUE
Prenatal Care (Generic)	Documentation of:				
	1. Prenatal screening to include: a. O'Sullivan tests b. Rh factor c. hepatitis d. HIV risk	<100%		O	CP

ASPECT OF CARE	INDICATOR	THRESHOLD	HIGH RISK/ VOLUME	I/O	MED STAFF MONITORING
	2. Results of Alpha-Feto protein at 14 to18 weeks' gestation (or documentation of patient's refusal)	<100%	HR	O	CP
	3. Third trimester lab values to include: a. CBC b. antibody screens c. VDRL d. GCT e. HBsAg	<100%		O	CP

UNIVERSITY HOSPITAL CONSORTIUM
QUALITY ASSURANCE CLINICAL INDICATORS
DEPARTMENT: OBSTETRICS AND GYNECOLOGY

ASPECT OF CARE	INDICATOR	THRESHOLD	HIGH RISK/ VOLUME	I/O	MED STAFF MONITORING
Chlamydia Screening in New Clinic Patients	Documentation of risk factors (i.e., nonmonogamous; street drugs; V.D.; HIV risk)	<100%	HR	O	CP
	Chlamydia smear ordered in presence of one or more risk factors	<100%	HR	O	
Curettage in the Emergency Room	Documentation of: a. indications b. lab tests c. IV infusion d. medications e. vital signs f. patient disposition	<100%	HR	O	
Invasive Procedures: (e.g.: Endometrial Biopsy; Vabra Aspiration; Suction D & C; Cystoscopy and Urodynamics: Hysterectomy)	Documentation of: a. pelvic exam b. blood work (Hct: ABO type and Rh)	<100% < 100%		I/O	

ASPECT OF CARE	INDICATOR	THRESHOLD	HIGH RISK/ VOLUME	I/O	MED STAFF MONITORING
Mammograms	Records will include documentation of referral for mammograms or date of last exam for patients greater than 35 years of age.	< 90%	HR	O	

UNIVERSITY HOSPITAL CONSORTIUM
QUALITY ASSURANCE CLINICAL INDICATORS
LEGEND OF SYMBOLS USED IN TEXT

ASPECT OF CARE	INDICATOR	THRESHOLD	HIGH RISK/VOLUME	I/O	MED STAFF MONITORING
		Threshold indicates level at which review is required.	HR = High Risk		
			HV = High Volume		
			PP = Problem Prone		
				I = Inpatient	
				O = Outpatient	
					IC = Infection Control
					DUE = Drug Usage Evaluation
					BUR = Blood Utilization Review
					CP = Clinical Pertinence

Source: *UHC Compendium of Clinical Indicators* by University Hospital Consortium, Oak Brook, IL, 1991.

chapter 30

Risk Management in the Pediatric Setting

Barbara Grand Sheridan

INTRODUCTION

Many clinical areas in the health care setting can cause specific risk management problems because of the uniqueness of the population serviced and the special types of care provided. Studies analyzing claims from various hospital departments show that many risk management incidents occur in the neonatal and pediatric intensive care units. In these areas allegations range from misdiagnosis or inappropriate treatment resulting in death, to intravenous infiltrates, falls, and minor procedure complications. Although these incidents in many hospitals are not the most significant (based on the number of risk management claims and lawsuits), when they do occur, they can be devastating and costly. Additionally, many special legal, risk management, and quality issues are unique to these areas. Therefore, focusing on the potential for pediatric risk management problems and developing proactive strategies to solve these problems are important activities for health care professionals.

This chapter focuses on some clinical risks associated with the care of children on the pediatric, nursery, and intensive care units. In addition, issues related to the safety and security of the environment, the risk manager's role in child abuse and neglect, and other specific issues associated with the care of children are discussed. At the end of the chapter specific indicators are provided that can be used to evaluate proactively the process of care in the pediatric area and to help identify potential quality problems that could result in patient injury or harm.

HISTORICAL PROBLEMS ASSOCIATED WITH PEDIATRIC CARE

In the past, the major causes of morbidity and mortality in children were infections and malnutrition. For example, drug therapy for infections was nonexistent, and meningitis had a 75–100% mortality rate. The medical specialty of pediatrics has been revolutionized by the introduction of penicillin and vaccines. The practice of pediatrics today reflects tremendous strides in neonatology and its associated technology, which has profoundly impacted medical practice with corresponding increased public expectations.

RISK MANAGEMENT IN PEDIATRICS: WHAT ARE THE CHALLENGES?

Many malpractice claims are launched after a suboptimal outcome occurs that the patient or parent did not realize was possible. The core of the allegations is a misunderstanding of the difference between an adverse outcome caused by an inherent complication of a treatment or procedure and an adverse outcome caused by a breach in the accepted standard of care. Medical procedures and treatments have associated risks. Therefore, health care professionals must tell patients and parents that while all efforts are made to ensure quality of care within accepted standards, optimal outcomes are not guaranteed.

Medical malpractice lawsuits involving pediatrics are unique because of the prolonged statute of limitations for filing suit and because the projected cost of maintaining an injured child and projected loss of earning power can span several decades. Additionally, public opinion is that children deserve a heightened level of protection because they cannot protect themselves. This expectation and sympathy commonly felt for sick or injured children make defensive explanations and legal arguments about pediatric care difficult, particularly if a child has been seriously harmed.

To identify motivations for filing medical malpractice claims, studies indicate that patients or families who pursue litigation against physicians are not a homogenous group and that their motivations for legal actions are affected by their perceptions of their relationship with their physicians. Although some families have economic goals prompting them to file legal claims, erosion of the physician–parent relationship can also result in a malpractice claim.

Erosion of the physician–parent relationship can occur from dissatisfaction with physician–parent communication, a problem that exists in all specialty care areas. However, in pediatric care, parents often have heightened anxiety and concern for sick children who may be unable to articulate their problems and who often appear sicker than they really are. Also, there is an expectation that children are healthy and unlikely (or are too young) to die or suffer a catastrophic illness or injury; therefore, when children die or suffer, questions arise about the appropriateness of care. Thus, the issue of physician–parent communication can assume a greater significance than that experienced in other units. Two communication problems have been identified: failure of caregivers to listen, speak openly, or answer questions; and misleading statements and/or failure of caregivers to be honest. Institutions must emphasize and reinforce efforts to train physicians and nurses so pertinent information is effectively and honestly conveyed to patients, parents, and members of an extended family.

Patient care conferences involving providers and patient/family members can be an effective manner of communicating. A study involving the informational needs of parents of sick neonates identified the following characteristics of a successful medical conference:

- explanations that are meaningful and thorough
- conveyance that the physician was open and truthful
- opportunity to talk to the primary physician
- sense that the physician was concerned about the parents and the child's problems and concerns.

The risk manager should emphasize to all professional staff the importance of recognizing how parental stress can impact communication between parents and all health care team members. When necessary, staff should be encour-

aged to consult with social services or other support services to help the family cope with their child's illness and to support the family in understanding and reaching appropriate choices for care. Special attention should be given to families to ensure that parents feel they are active participants in the care provided to children, and parents should be given the opportunity to interact with their children as much as possible. Depending on a child's age, pediatric units can allow 24-hour parental stays, a policy that helps ensure that children receive optimal care. Asking or forcing parents to leave the room when children are distressed and need the comfort of parents can be detrimental to children as well as parents and can create a parental belief that the hospital is uncaring, inflexible, and is more concerned about hospital convenience than the needs of their children. Hospital policies that ensure flexibility in parental visitation and participation in care help diminish the anxieties and therefore any negative impressions associated with the facility and the caregivers.

MANAGING THE ENVIRONMENT WHERE PEDIATRIC CARE IS PROVIDED

Several innate differences between pediatric patients and the adult patients have risk management ramifications. Environmental issues, safety and security issues, and claims handling practices mandate that specific risk management controls be developed to limit the likelihood of potential problems.

Environmental Issues

Institutions are responsible for providing a safe environment for their patients. The duty to protect is shared with mentally competent adult patients who can identify situations that are potentially harmful and avoid the hazards. This duty is broadened in its application to pediatric patients because a positive obligation exists to protect pediatric patients from harm. A much higher standard is applied to pediatric care because of the increased vulnerability of children and because children cannot share the responsibility.

Risk managers should regularly inspect pediatric units to identify possible safety exposures and to ensure environmental safety. Evaluation should include the unit layout for identification of visitor access control and pediatric patient egress control. Ensuring a controlled environment also entails evaluation of door locks, stairwell door alarms, and a visitor pass system. Other child protection measures include evaluation of housekeeping practices to ensure that carts, solutions, supplies, and equipment are inaccessible to inquisitive children. Electrical outlets should contain protective adaptations for exposed outlets. Closet, stairway, and treatment room doors should be on automatic closure, and needle boxes should be safely secured.

To identify and intercept environmental hazards, regular reviews and critiques about the safety of the pediatric unit should be performed by housekeeping, safety, maintenance, nursing, and risk management personnel. Persons with expertise about pediatric development, such as childlife professionals, can be added to a health care team because they can identify specific equipment or items on a pediatric unit that would pose an "attractive nuisance" to children, generating further exploration by children. For example, adults not familiar with the inquisitive, exploratory nature of a toddler may not see a wastebasket as a source of potential high-risk activity, whereas a health care professional with pediatric development expertise would recognize that the disposable plastic bags in the wastebasket as well as the material disposed in the wastebasket would pose a threat of harm to a toddler.

Safety and Security Issues

Ensuring the security of the environment is also an important risk management concern. Although security issues are often focused in the nursery, similar issues can occur in any pediatric area. A profound change in hospital operational policies in nurseries and maternal child units has occurred over the past 15 years because of the increased focus on newborn/parental/sibling bonding. As a result, restricted access to these hospital units has been abolished, and visitation policies are less rigid including visitation policies pertaining to access to newborns and pediatric patients. The increased number of visitors to these units has created increased security risks for the institution, particularly the risk of kidnapping. The typical profile of a kidnapper is a nonviolent female who has an intense desire for an infant. In most cases she acts alone, putting on hospital clothing and posing as a health care professional (for example, a nurse or technician) to enter the nursery or a mother's room. The kidnapper usually has been on the unit previously, studying layout, traffic flow, and patterns of the infants as they are transported between the nursery and the mothers' rooms. Institutions can reduce the risk of infant kidnapping through several patient protection measures.

A thorough risk assessment should be undertaken every six months and should include an analysis of access and egress. Vulnerable areas such as those where access and egress can occur inconspicuously should be identified. Any security equipment such as alarms on locked nursery doors or video cameras on units should be evaluated to determine

if they are being used and are functional. Regular testing of such equipment should be enforced. An auditory cue such as a chime when the nursery door is unlocked and opened is recommended.

Access to the maternity or pediatric unit can be monitored via a visitor sign-in policy. If redesign is possible, situating the nursing station so each door on the unit can be visualized and so each visitor must walk past the nursing station to gain access to the unit is suggested. Definitive guidelines about individuals allowed to enter a unit or a room should be implemented. Staff attention to entry should be assessed. Also, employee identification is critical and can be accomplished via distinctive clothing. However, distribution of and access to such clothing must be tightly restricted to prevent visitors from freely and indiscriminately obtaining garments from laundry carts, closets, and breakrooms. Education and orientation of staff are cornerstones of nursery security. Knowledge of policies and procedures must be reinforced, such as the transport of all babies in bassinets, so hospital personnel are alerted if they see someone unfamiliar carrying an infant.

A risk management program can include the following seven components:

1. in-service training of all hospital personnel, teaching them about typical kidnapper profiles and patterns and the proper procedures to use when reporting suspicious persons
2. visitor control measures via restructuring of visiting hours and implementation of a visitor-control system
3. exit control via alarm systems, time-delayed opening locks, and an access card system
4. identification measures such as personnel identification badges, distinguishing uniforms, positive identification procedures by staff
5. patient tagging mechanisms such as electronic surveillance tags
6. security mechanisms such as designated patrols for visual identification
7. traffic design to enhance visual observations and flow-through traffic.

The nature and scope of parental instruction and participation in ensuring safety are beneficial and the following six precautions should be imparted to the parents:

1. Never leave the child unsupervised, especially in "rooming in" situations.
2. Contact the nurse if anyone approaches you about unscheduled tests or laboratory work.
3. Give the child only to personnel who are properly identified.

4. Know your nurses' names.
5. Call and notify the nursing station before anyone who is unfamiliar takes the infant.
6. Report anyone attempting to carry the infant.

After a kidnapping, several measures can be undertaken to diffuse the crisis situation. Media involvement is one effective method to recover a stolen infant; therefore, local media should be contacted. Staff should be briefed and counseled, and an official written statement should be disseminated to staff for responding to telephone calls from the public. The incident should be explained to other families on the unit by a hospital employee.

Making the environment safe for staff also should be an important consideration for the health care risk manager and administrative team. Violent situations related to the condition of a child or to family problems can occur, which can compromise both child and health care staff safety. One specific case illustrating this fact received national attention when a father, despondent over the vegetative state and the poor prognosis of his child who was a patient in the pediatric intensive care unit of a large urban hospital, held nurses at gunpoint while he disconnected his son from a hospital ventilator. Other less well-publicized instances where divorced or separated spouses attempt to force visitation or abduct their children have been reported and should convince hospital staff of the need to plan proactively for these situations. Education related to the recognition of families under stress and prompt referral to the social service department can help defuse some of these problems. Training of security personnel to recognize agitated visitors or visitors entering the hospital with weapons also can help minimize the likelihood that safety and security problems will occur.

Claims Issues

Policies for retention of pediatric medical records should be examined to ensure the availability of records in their original format throughout the extended statute of limitations, which often extends two years beyond the child reaching the age of majority. These records should be exempt from destruction until the applicable statute of limitations has been exhausted. Retention policies in radiology, EEG, and laboratory areas also should be examined and modified if necessary to maintain this information for a future pediatric claim.

Records pertaining to patients who have experienced a potentially compensable event should be securely stored, and the original record should be placed in a locked legal file. Chart mobility can be restrained by limiting access to these charts and by creating a copy for physician review or use for teaching.

TRANSFER/TRANSPORT

Institutions can be exposed to significant liability when the resources immediately available are inadequate to accommodate a patient's actual or anticipated condition. To reduce liability exposure in this circumstance, institutions must prospectively address potential elements of exposure. The liability issues generated by transfer/transport decisions can be categorized into exposures faced by the referring institution, those confronted by the transporting entity, and/or receiving institution. In the care of pediatric patients, transfers often occur because of the few number of hospitals that provide tertiary and quaternary care to children. Although advanced technology is available to treat neonates and children, cost and availability of such technology often necessitate transfer to another facility.

Multiple factors influence various policies and procedures of transfers and transports, and responsibilities must be prospectively delineated. Transfer of a patient can be limited to two entities (the referring and receiving hospitals) or can involve three or more entities. Policies and procedures depend on whether the receiving hospital provides transport services or whether the transferring hospital is responsible to arrange for the transport by private vendors. If private vendors are used for the transport, the scope of the referring hospital's responsibilities is broadened because of its responsibility for choosing a vendor and the possibility that the transport vendor does not provide specialized pediatric/neonatal personnel. Federal legislation such as the Consolidated Omnibus Budget Reconciliation Act (COBRA) provides that the referring hospital is responsible for the appropriate transport method and medical suitability of the receiving hospital. The referring physician must substantiate the necessity and appropriateness of the transport. The referring hospital must ensure that the skills and equipment available during transport will meet the anticipated needs of the patient. Institutions should investigate the use of transfer agreements, which can include the granting of temporary privileges to members of the transport team. All transport team members should have documented expertise in the care of high-risk pediatric patients. (For more information on transport programs see Chapter 34.)

Interhospital care should be available 24 hours via a program that identifies and explains elements such as the response time and the appropriate capabilities of personnel, patient care protocols and recordkeeping systems, ongoing personnel training and supervision, and periodic evaluations of operational aspects of the program (for example, patient response times, equipment maintenance logs, and effectiveness of communication). Further, the program should include the communication used (for example, telephone or radio contact during stabilization and transfer) between referring and receiving facilities. Also, copies of all medical records should accompany the patient, and a tube of maternal serum should accompany newborns.

Neonatal Transport

Advances in various technical aspects of perinatal care have altered the management of many conditions previously considered untreatable. The outcome of sick and low-birth-weight infants has been shown to be enhanced by management in a neonatal intensive care unit; therefore, the transport of known high-risk mothers and neonates constitutes a major area of decision making in modern perinatal practice. Community physicians should seek guidance from a neonatal referral center when they encounter complex clinical decisions, particularly those involving the provision of neonatal life-support systems.

Neonatal conditions requiring specialized care and possible transfer include:

- low birth weight (less than 1,500 grams). Although not all low-birth-weight infants require specialized care, some develop respiratory and/or nutritional problems requiring intensive management.
- respiratory distress syndrome, meconium aspiration syndrome, pneumothorax, and other forms of displaced air. If blood gas analysis is unavailable, infants with relatively mild respiratory problems requiring inspired oxygen concentration greater than 0.30 (30%) oxygen to abolish cyanosis or to maintain arterial oxygen saturation greater than 90% should be transferred to provide adequate blood gas monitoring. Infants with respiratory distress syndrome requiring a fractional concentration of inspired oxygen greater than 0.6 (60%) to maintain an arterial Pao_2 of 8.0 kPa should be transferred to the regional neonatal intensive care unit because of the high incidence of ventilatory failure, ventilatory assistance requirement, and possible pneumothorax. Infants with significant meconium aspiration requiring increased fractional inspired oxygen concentration greater than 0.3 (30%) should be transferred because they are likely to develop sudden and severe ventilatory problems in the initial 48 hours because of persistent fetal circulation.
- life-threatening congenital abnormalities that could require surgical management, such as diaphragmatic hernia, congenital heart disease, gastroschisis, esophageal atresia with tracheoesophageal fistula, and neonatal intestinal obstruction
- diagnostic problems
- management problems that could include neonatal convulsions refractory to treatment, sequelae of hy-

poxia persisting beyond two hours with evidence of multisystem involvement, feeding intolerance, severe jaundice that could require exchange transfusion, and/or metabolic disorder.

The responsibility of the regional neonatal intensive care unit is to provide transport facilities. The regional transport team functions as an extension of the intensive care unit and provides similar facilities. The medical director of the transport team should be a neonatologist or perinatologist. The pediatric transport entity must provide:

- personnel who possess the ability to assess and treat the infant and to use the equipment; personnel must have expertise in clinical assessment of the infant and possess strong neonatal intensive care unit skills; backup consultation should be available via telephone or radio
- facilities for adequate temperature control in any environment such as a transport incubator with warming characteristics sufficient to maintain the body temperature of an infant weighing less than one kilogram. This can be provided via a traditional convected air incubator (preferably with a double wall) or an enclosed unit using a servo-radiant heater.
- self-contained infant ventilator with an adequate supply of oxygen and air and a gas mixer
- continuous monitoring facilities for heart rate, core temperature, and inspired oxygen concentration. Portable units are also available for monitoring transcutaneous Po_2 and Pco_2, and oxygen saturation.
- equipment for resuscitation, intravascular infusion, chest drains and chest drain valves, Chemstrip or Dextrostix, and ventilator connections. Intravascular infusions must be controlled by a battery-powered infusion pump.
- drugs such as sodium bicarbonate, digoxin, dopamine, pancuronium, prostaglandin E, antibiotics, anticonvulsants, 10% glucose, and other intravenous solutions.

Pediatric Transport

Neonatal and adult emergency transport systems have generated much literature; however, recommendations for practice of pediatric critical care transport have not received a similar focus of attention. The premature neonate presents with predictable pathophysiology and responses to therapy; however, expertise in the diagnosis and management of the diversity of pediatric illnesses and injuries are more difficult to acquire. Many pediatric specialists in critical care and emergency medicine believe an increased morbidity in children transported by nonspecialized personnel occurs.

Consequently, team composition and transport staffing and training requirements of pediatric and nonpediatric teams are critical issues.

Team composition depends on the availability of large groups of individuals within each institution; the spectrum of physician expertise can be wide. Each critical care transport should be supervised by an attending physician who has expertise in pediatric critical care or emergency medicine. An extensive formal training program with a well-documented system of ongoing cognitive and procedural training emphasizing airway skills is mandatory for transport personnel. Educational models include the Pediatric Advanced Life Support (PALS) course (American Heart Association, American Academy of Pediatrics, 1988) and the Advanced Pediatric Life Support course (American Academy of Pediatrics, American College of Emergency Physicians, 1989). Specific policies and procedures, clinical protocols, and quality assurance programs should be developed.

Transport team members function as agents of the institution that defines and authorizes the members' responsibilities. Minimally, one team member on each transport should maintain certification in PALS or an equivalent certification. The team operates via an established chain of command with a designated medical director (pediatric critical care or emergency medicine specialist) overseeing the team and maintaining an active role in its function. The medical director approves protocols for team members and the communication center, provides expertise and responds to problems during transport, monitors team activities, and functions as a liaison and consultant to referring institutions and other physicians.

The institution and medical director must ensure transport team safety and are responsible for investigating vendors (air and ground) in maintenance, safety records, experience of drivers and pilots, and reliability of equipment. Written contracts should exist between the institution and vendors and should address specific insurance details.

CHILD ABUSE AND NEGLECT

The fact that children are abused and neglected is a well-recognized and documented phenomenon. Hospital personnel are often the first persons who can recognize that abuse and neglect are occurring and can intervene to protect the child and to see that the situation causing the abuse is addressed. This responsibility is critical and important to those caring for pediatric patients.

Child abuse and neglect are serious and pervasive problems. The responsibilities of pediatric care providers in the treatment of child abuse and neglect include detection, medical diagnosis, and treatment or referral. Comprehensive prevention strategies should be directed at increasing parents' or future parents' knowledge of child development and the demands of parenting. Issues addressed include parent–child bonding, emotional ties and family communications, and home and child management issues. Approaches to prevention should reduce the burden of child care, family isolation, and long-term consequences of poor parenting.

Pediatric care providers are in a unique position to detect injuries and behavioral problems resulting from child abuse and neglect because children are routinely examined and evaluated for wellness, illness, and behavioral conditions. The health care provider must conduct a complete physical examination on any child who may be a victim of abuse. During the diagnostic process, the provider should understand and assess the plausibility of historical and medical antecedents of the injury, determine the dimensions of continued risk to the child, and obtain the medical history of the child.

Physical signs of child abuse include:

- bruises and welts that are inconsistent with the history provided by the parent or child
- burns that include cigar or cigarette burns especially on the soles, palms, back or buttocks, immersion burns (stocking or glove-like on extremities, doughnut-shaped on buttocks or genitals)
- pattern burns that resemble an electrical appliance (e.g., iron, burner)
- fractures of the skull, ribs, nose, facial structure, or long bones, or multiple or spiral fractures in various stages of healing
- lacerations or abrasions such as rope burns on wrists, ankles, neck, torso, palate, gums, mouth, lips, eyes or ears, or external genitalia
- abdominal injuries such as bruises of the abdominal wall, intramural hematoma of duodenum or proximal jejunum intestinal perforation, ruptured liver or spleen, ruptured blood vessels, kidney or bladder injury, and pancreatic injury
- central nervous system injuries such as subdural hematoma (often reflects blunt trauma or violent shaking), retinal hemorrhage, subarachnoid hemorrhage (often reflects shaking).

Behavioral signs also can be recognized that are indicative or suggestive of abuse. Such signs might include:

- excessive or complete absence of anxiety about separation from parents
- constant desire for affection, attention, or recognition
- anger, isolation, or depression
- destructive or abusive behavior.

Physical neglect appears more prevalent than abuse and is defined as the failure of a parent or other person legally responsible for a child's welfare to provide for the child's basic needs and an adequate level of care. Neglect tends to be chronic and involves inattention to minimal needs for nurturance, food, clothing, medical care, safety, and education.

Physical neglect can be manifested by physical signs such as malnutrition, repeated episodes of pica, constant fatigue or listlessness, poor hygiene, severe diaper rash, and inadequate clothing for circumstances. Behavioral signs of neglect include lack of appropriate adult supervision, repeated ingestion of harmful substances, poor school attendance, exploitation, excessive child care or household responsibilities, drug or alcohol use, and role reversal where a child becomes a parental caretaker.

Signs of medical neglect include failure to receive adequate medical attention, lack of appropriate medical care in the presence of chronic illness, absence of necessary medications and immunizations, absence of dental care, and absence of necessary prosthetics including eyeglasses and hearing aids.

Emotional abuse is difficult to define and diagnose, and psychiatric consultation can help in documenting and investigating suspected cases. Emotional maltreatment can include excessive or unreasonable parental demands on children. Constant or persistent teasing, belittling, verbal attacks, and complete rejection can occur. Physical signs of emotional maltreatment can include delays in physical development or failure to thrive. Behavioral signs can include distinct emotional symptoms and/or functional limitations that can be causally linked to parental management, deteriorating conduct, increased anxiety, apathy or depression, and developmental lags.

Interviewing Process

The provider should investigate suspected abuse or neglect by interviewing the parents and child. The initial step is to gather historical data relative to the injury. If abuse or neglect is suspected, the provider must determine the risk level to the child. The child protection service agency must be notified.

If the child is interviewed for therapeutic or diagnostic purposes, the interviewer must be sensitive to the child's cognitive development and to the child's fear and apprehension about discussing the home situation. It may be preferable to interview the child without family members present. An audio or video recording of the interview can prevent the child from having to retell the story and can ensure accurate recordkeeping. Investigative aids such as anatomically correct dolls can facilitate communication with the child. When talking with younger children, experts recommend that the interviewer sit at the child's eye level and initiate questions with expressions such as "how come" instead of "why."

The following are recommended child interviewing techniques:

- Attempt to establish an empathetic trusting relationship.
- Conduct the interview in private.
- Ensure the child is interviewed by an experienced professional available in cases of severe physical and sexual abuse.
- Explain the purpose of the interview to the child in language appropriate to his or her developmental level.
- Always ask the child if he or she has any questions and answer these questions.
- Carefully explain to the child the reason and nature of his or her removal from the home if hospitalization is imminent.
- Ask the child to explain words or terms that are unclear to the interviewer.
- Use the child's own words and terms in discussing the situation whenever feasible.
- Acknowledge that the situation must have been difficult for the child and that the child was not at fault.
- Sit near the child, not across a table or desk.
- Sit at the child's eye level.
- Do not suggest answers to the child.
- Do not pressure the child to answer questions that he or she is unwilling to give.
- Do not criticize the child's language.
- Do not suggest that the child feel guilt or blame for the situation.
- Do not leave the child unattended or with unknown persons.
- Do not display shock or horror about the child or situation.

When interviewing parents or caretakers of children, the following techniques should be used:

- Inform the parents of the reason for the interview.
- Advise the parents of the physician's legal duty to report suspected abuse.
- Conduct the interview in private, or when indicated, with appropriate personnel (child protective service personnel).
- Attempt to be objective.
- Reassure the parents of your continued support.
- Explain further actions that will be required.
- Answer questions honestly.
- Do not attempt to prove abuse or neglect.
- Do not display anger, horror, or disapproval of the parents or situation.
- Do not pry into unrelated family matters.
- Do not place blame or make judgments.

Clinical, legal, administrative, risk management, and social service staff should always be responsible toward a child who is suspected of having been abused. Nine major management objectives of the provider who encounters child abuse or neglect are to:

1. Identify the child who may have been abused or neglected.
2. Provide emergency measures needed to prevent further injury.
3. Provide medical evaluation and treatment of injuries or conditions resulting from abuse or neglect.
4. Provide an accurate and complete medical evaluation consistent with the diagnosis of child abuse or neglect. If court evidence becomes necessary, a well-documented medical record can eliminate or reduce the time a physician spends in judicial proceedings. Documentation should include:
   a. a brief description of the nature and extent of injuries and the medical condition of the child; the location and nature of any injuries should be illustrated on a traumagram
   b. a record of all relevant behaviors and statements of the child and parents
   c. a complete medical and brief social history
   d. results of all pertinent laboratory and diagnostic studies, including X-rays, magnetic resonance imaging (MRI), and computerized tomography results.
5. Remain objective and nonjudgmental toward parents and child.
6. Establish or maintain a therapeutic alliance with the family.
7. Secure medical evaluation of other children in the household.
8. Report all suspected cases of child abuse and/or neglect following local laws and statutes.
9. Where permissible by law, the physician should hold any abused or neglected child when risk of further injury is present. This can be accomplished by hospitalization or foster home placement.

Reporting Requirements

Child abuse and neglect laws vary among jurisdictions; however, all such laws are universal in that all statutes include quick identification of the child suspected of abuse/neglect, designation of an agency to investigate reports, and provision of treatment services. Physicians, nurses, and social workers are granted immunity from civil and criminal liability if a report is made in good faith. Most jurisdictions impose a criminal or civil penalty for failure to report. Providers should obtain a copy of their jurisdiction's child abuse and neglect reporting laws. All suspected incidents of nonaccidental trauma, sexual abuse, neglect, and emotional cruelty by an adult, and all instances where a child is deprived of adequate nurturance, health, education, and safety should be reported.

A New Form of Abuse: Munchausen Syndrome by Proxy

Another form of pediatric abuse has recently received attention. This abuse is more difficult to detect and can be unusual in its presentation. Although written about in medical journals in 1977, this form of abuse called Munchausen Syndrome by Proxy has only recently received attention. Munchausen Syndrome is characterized by a parent's falsification of his or her child's illness in attempt to receive some secondary gain from the child's hospitalization. Normally, the parent presents the child for medical care disclaiming any knowledge about the origin or cause of the child's problems or complaint. Typically, it is the mother who fabricates or falsifies the child's history and induces the symptoms in the child. The child remains at risk for injury even while hospitalized because the parent can feel the need to simulate or produce illness in the child to continue the hospitalization.

In this form of abuse, the child becomes the victim of the adult (most often the parent's) behavior. In most cases reported the perpetrator of the abuse is the mother. The children can be injected with drugs, forced to ingest substances, suffocated, poisoned, or phlebotomized in attempts to create an illness that then requires medical evaluation and diagnostic intervention. Often the abuse must be repeated to "sustain" the complaint of illness.

Dr. Donna Rosenberg of the University of Colorado Health Sciences Center and the C. Henry Kempe, National Center for the Prevention and Treatment of Child Abuse and Neglect, conducted research on Munchausen's Syndrome by Proxy. Their study included 117 cases where the syndrome was identified. The abused child was not differentiated by sex (approximately half were female and half were male). About 98% of the abusers were biological mothers, and 2% of the abusers were adoptive mothers. Interestingly, the occupations of the abusers included 27% who were nurses and 20% who were mothers working at home. In many cases, other forms of abuse and neglect were also noted.

Some pediatric units are developing elaborate protocols for dealing with this unusual abuse. The protocols include hidden cameras or other electronic monitoring devices in the child's room or the development of educational and teaching programs for both parents and staff that not only describe the syndrome but also describe the legal ramifications of being found guilty of this abuse.

From a risk management perspective, this unusual form of abuse also can pose interesting legal challenges. The idea of placing cameras or other monitoring devices in the child's room can raise certain rights to privacy issues. Those risks must be carefully weighed against the benefits.

Sexual Abuse

Sexual abuse is most likely underdiagnosed and underreported by the medical community; consequently, it is often left untreated. Uncertainty about diagnostic criteria is a factor contributing to underreporting. Pediatricians and pediatric care providers will encounter sexually abused children in a variety of circumstances: during wellness or illness examinations, during evaluation for a behavioral condition when they are brought for evaluation by a parent who suspects sexual abuse has occurred, or when they are brought by a social service or law enforcement professional as part of an investigation.

Guidelines for the evaluation of sexual abuse in children have been prepared by the American Academy of Pediatrics for guidance of the primary care pediatrician. There are many ways that sexual abuse can present. Because abused children are commonly coerced into secrecy, a high index of suspicion is required. Presenting symptoms are often general (sleep disturbance, enuresis) and can be indicators of nonabuse-related stressors. Specific signs and symptoms of sexual abuse include rectal and/or genital pain, bleeding, or infection; sexually transmitted disease; and developmentally precocious sexual behavior. A complete history including behavioral symptoms and associated signs of sexual abuse should be performed. The diagnosis of child sexual abuse is based on the history; physical examination alone is infrequently diagnostic without a history and/or specific laboratory findings.

In many states the suspicion of child sexual abuse as a possible diagnosis mandates a report to the appropriate law enforcement or child protective services agency. Providers should be aware of state requirements regarding where and when to file a written report. If possible, the child should be interviewed alone, and the interviewer should use nonleading questions and avoid manifestations of shock or disbelief. A behavioral review of systems can reveal events or behaviors relevant to sexual abuse even without a history of abuse.

The physical examination should not lead to additional emotional trauma for the child. When the alleged abuse has occurred within 72 hours and the child provides a history that includes ejaculation, the examination should be performed immediately. With evidence of acute sexual assault or sexual abuse with ejaculation, forensic studies should be immediately performed. Rape kit protocols modified for child sexual assault victims should be followed to maintain a chain of evidence. When more than 72 hours has elapsed, the examination is not an emergency and should be scheduled at the earliest convenient time for the child, physician, and investigative team. The examination should include assessments of developmental, behavioral, and emotional status. Special attention should be paid to growth parameters and sexual development. Any signs of trauma should be carefully documented. Specific attention should be given to areas involved in sexual activity: mouth, breast, genitals, perineal region, anus, and buttocks.

In female children the genital examination should include inspection of the medial aspects of the thighs, labia majora and minora, clitoris, urethra, periurethral tissue, hymen, hymenal opening, fossa navicularis, and posterior fourchette. Physical findings consistent with but not diagnostic of sexual abuse are chafing; abrasions or bruising of the inner thighs and genitalia; scarring, tears, or distortion of the hymen; decreased or absent hymenal tissue; scarring of the fossa navicularis; injury or scarring of the posterior fourchette; scarring or tears of the labia; or enlargement of the hymenal opening.

In male children, the thighs, penis, and scrotum should be examined for bruises, scars, chafing, bite marks, and discharge. In both sexes the anus can be examined in the supine, lateral, or knee chest position, and the position can influence the anatomy. The presence of bruises around the anus, scars, anal tears (especially those extending into the perianal skin) and anal dilation are important to note. Sphincter laxity also should be noted.

In both male and female children, the presence of semen indicated by an acid phosphatase test, a positive gonorrhea culture, or serologic verification of syphilis makes a diagnosis of sexual abuse a certainty even without a positive history. Other physical or laboratory findings can be suggestive of or consistent with a history of sexual abuse. The differential diagnosis of genital trauma also includes accidental injury or physical abuse. This differentiation can require a multidisciplinary approach. Detailed records, drawings, and photographs should be retained. The submission of written reports to county and law enforcement agencies is encouraged.

Legal issues confronting providers in evaluating sexually abused children include mandatory reporting with penalties for failure to report; involvement in the civil, juvenile, or family court systems; involvement in divorce/custody proceedings; and involvement in criminal prosecutions. State laws require that pediatricians report all suspected and known cases of child sexual abuse. The failure of a pediatrician to recognize and diagnose child sexual abuse can lead to malpractice litigation.

ADDITIONAL ISSUES IN PEDIATRICS

Specific pediatric issues also exist that relate to the manner in which care is received. Although not clinical concerns, the issues of positioning of children and consent for treatment have recently received attention and have major clinical and risk management significance.

Positioning

Infant positioning is one area of focus, and the American Academy of Pediatrics Task Force on Infant Positioning has recently concluded that the weight of evidence implicates the prone position as a significant risk factor for sudden infant death syndrome (SIDS) and recommends that the prone position be abandoned for healthy and full-term infants in favor of the supine or lateral position. Pediatricians on staff should be consulted to determine the hospital policy about positioning of children (primary after feedings), and nursing personnel and families should be educated on the current state of debate. Specific patient populations with a higher incidence of aspiration, such as infants with reflux, should have included in their care plans specific instructions about positioning to minimize the likelihood of reflux or respiratory problems.

Consent

The task of determining the appropriate party from whom to obtain consent to treatment of pediatric patients can be confusing because of the impact of single parents, joint custody agreements, teenage parents, emancipated minors, mature minors, unmarried parents, and custodians/relatives without formal guardianship status. Although state consent laws vary, some common issues can be addressed.

Recognition that a consent issue exists is primary to averting a claim based on failure to authorize treatment. Parents can sue physicians for any unauthorized nonemergency medical treatment of a child. The risk manager should determine whether minors in the state are considered legally capable of giving consent and whether limitations and/or restrictive circumstances in which a minor can be legally capable in some specific situations but not in others exist. Knowledge of relevant requirements will facilitate the establishment of specific protocols to address the multiple situations that can be encountered.

The risk manager can be proactive by providing the admitting staff with accurate consent policies for pediatrics, repetitive in-service activities, and access to risk management staff when questions arise. Written guidelines are preferable. When special family circumstances such as custody battles exist, hospitals should have mechanisms to ensure that the physician and nurse have administrative support to ensure they will be able to provide medical services that are *in the best interest of the child*. Parental animosity or family fighting should never be allowed to compromise the care of a child. If a family situation becomes threatening to a health care provider, administration should seek to involve social services or legal counsel and ascertain the appropriateness of placing the child under custody of a state guardian who can ensure that parental hostilities will not negatively impact care of the child.

COMPLICATIONS OF DRUG ADMINISTRATION

Pediatrics is second to internal medicine as the most frequently implicated medical specialty in legal actions premised on drug-related events. The increasing complexity of pharmacologic intervention in pediatrics coupled with the narrow tolerance of the pediatric population to error makes this a significant area of exposure. Neonatal patients are a more homogenous group, are given a more limited number of drugs than older pediatric patients, and experience the lowest incidence of pediatric medication errors.

Medication complications are multidisciplinary and multifactorial and result in patient injury and increased health care costs in addition to liability claims. Medication complications can occur anytime during a hospitalization and can be made by anyone involved in the child's care. Complications include human errors made in the ordering, preparing, administering sequence and can include events that are not errors but that result in the incorrect administration of medication to patients (e.g., extravasation of an intravenous line resulting in late administration of drugs).

Studies have identified incorrect dosage as the most common medication error and overdosage as the most prevalent error. Inappropriate medication orders by a physician account for a minority of medication errors; however, they are associated with a higher risk for serious consequences than are errors related to dispensing and administering drugs. Studies have confirmed that first-year resident physicians have a significantly greater error rate than other physicians and that error rates for residents and fellows progressively decline with graduate years of training. The practice of relaying verbal orders also is a practice that can generate serious injury.

Risk management tactics for limiting exposures to such claims must address the multiple potential exposure factors that are encountered: errant drug and/or dosage order by a physician, errant preparation by a pharmacist or nurse, and inappropriate administration by a nurse or physician.

Twelve specific potential administration errors include:

1. *wrong time*—medication is not administered at the scheduled time
2. *dosing errors*—drug dosage or intravenous infusion is more or less than the ordered rate
3. *wrong drug*—incorrect drug is administered
4. *outdated medication*—intravenous solutions or parenteral nutrition is outdated
5. *contraindicated combination of solutions*—incompatible combination of agents are given in an intravenous solution
6. *wrong dilution*—a drug is incorrectly diluted
7. *wrong patient*—drug is given to the wrong patient
8. *omission*—a scheduled dose is omitted
9. *extra dose*—an extra dose is given
10. *unordered medication*—an unordered medication is administered
11. *incorrect route*—drugs are given by an inappropriate route
12. *interstitial intravenous line*—intravenous solutions extravasate into the interstitium.

Institutions can limit their exposure to such claims by analyzing medication incidents and identifying specific causes. Adaptation of medication incident reports can be beneficial. Development of or changes in operational practices then can be specifically designed to limit risk for medication errors. Procedural and educational initiatives such as accreditation procedures, physician assessment criteria, and educational programs can be developed based on such data, with the efforts targeted toward demonstrated deficiencies. Systems of checks and balances can be implemented, such as review of all medication orders by a pharmacist and double-checking of physician prescribing and pharmacy dispensing activities by nursing personnel. In hospitals with a large pediatric population, the hospital can have a pharmacist dedicated to the pediatric area who will be most familiar with dosing, complications, and contraindications of drugs for this special patient population.

Instituting and maintaining the following eight practices also can have an impact on the avoidable causes of drug-induced iatrogenic injury.

1. Regularly test all personnel who compute drug dosages.
2. Review and test personnel for knowledge of age/weight appropriate dosages.
3. Establish an allergy identification system.
4. Acquire a pharmacology computer program that provides automated dose checking, duplicate therapy checking, allergy checking, and drug interaction checking.
5. Avoid drug preparation on the nursing unit.

6. Integrate pediatric pharmacologists into the prescription, dispensation, administration sequence by close scrutiny of every order.
7. Use unit dose preparation by pharmacists.
8. Maintain a policy mandating that all orders must be written except in extreme emergencies.

TOTAL PARENTERAL NUTRITION

A related pharmacologic and caregiver issue is the potential of complications from total parenteral nutrition (TPN), that is, complications resulting from the infusate and the line inserted to deliver the infusate. Total parenteral nutrition was originally instituted to provide nutritional support to infants with surgically treatable gastrointestinal disorders who could not withstand enteric feeding; however, its use has now been extended to sick preterm infants. Identifiable reasons causing complications include:

- incomplete knowledge about nutritional requirements of premature or sick infants
- reference standards based on growth patterns of the fetus or healthy full-term infant
- inadequate monitoring tools for acute and long-term effects of parenteral nutrition
- toxic effects of total parenteral nutrition on multiple organ systems
- narrow margin between deficiency and toxicity of some TPN components
- human and technical errors in the multiple steps of ordering, preparing, and administering TPN

Pediatric patients receiving TPN should be carefully monitored by nursing and medical staff. Protocol for addressing the frequency of laboratory testing and the child's ability to tolerate this form of nutrition should be clearly described in the plan of care and documented as part of the medical record.

COMPLICATIONS OF TUBES AND LINES

The acuity of hospitalized pediatric patients has increased over the last decade, resulting in pediatric units now admitting children who once would have been admitted to the intensive care or other specialized units. In addition, advancements in drug and device technology have created an increased number of invasive procedures performed on children. Many of these treatments are administered through indwelling tubes and lines. The maintenance of these lines and the potential complications associated with them warrant heightened risk management and staff awareness. All complications of tubes and lines cannot be eliminated; however, many can be avoided if the following precautions are taken:

- proper training of those inserting lines
- awareness of potential hazards
- adequate preparation of the infant
- selection of the best materials
- compulsive attention to technique
- postinsertion care
- timely removal when complications occur.

Special Risks Associated with Tubes

Thoracic. A thoracic tube is often used as an emergency procedure when pneumothorax develops in an infant with stiff lungs. The incidence of lung perforation is high. Needle aspiration also can lead to lung perforation, and for emergency aspiration a cannula stylet is safer than a needle. Rapid re-expansion of a lung against a sharp trocar predisposes an infant to lung perforation, a complication that can be reduced by using a curved hemostat rather than a sharp trocar. Persistence of pneumothorax after tube placement should alert health care staff to the possibility of lung perforation or bronchopleural fistula. Other complications are reduced by appropriate technique and management.

Gastrointestinal. Gastrointestinal tubes are generally for feeding or bowel decompression. Complications are related to trauma or stress of the procedure. Most complications can be reduced by good technique including careful tube fixation. Perforation can occur with both PVC and silicone tubes, and the risk with PVC tubes is higher because they harden after insertion. Tube perforation should be considered when pneumoperitoneum occurs without other air leak syndromes.

Arterial and Venous Lines. Vascular line insertion is one common procedure performed on sick newborns; the major complications are trauma, infection, and thromboemboli. Thrombosis is a significant and frequent complication of any foreign object in the vessel lumen, and the major thrombogenic factor is damage to the endothelium. The risk of thrombosis is increased with end-hole catheters.

Peripheral Intravenous Lines. The major complications of peripheral intravenous lines are infection, infiltration, inadvertent arterial perforation, and complications of poor placement or improper restraint that can cause circulatory, tissue, or nerve injury. Complications are reduced by the elective rotation of infusion sites. Infiltration is reduced by providing good visibility at the placement site, frequent inspection for infiltration, and immediate removal of an infiltrated line. Damage is directly related to the toxicity and amount of the infusate and the time gap between injury and intervention. Dextrose, calcium, and vasopressors cause skin sloughs and full-thickness tissue necrosis. Any disruption of skin integrity will predispose a patient to infection.

Peripheral Arterial Lines. The arteries most commonly used for cannulation when the umbilical artery is unavailable are the radial, posterior tibial, and dorsalis pedis. The major risk of catheters in such vessels is ischemia due to vasospasm, embolus, or thrombosis. Preventive measures include determining the adequacy of peripheral circulation before catheter placement and testing distal perfusion of the limb after catheter placement. Immediate removal is necessary if ischemia is not relieved. Thrombosis is a later complication and can be impeded by using heparinized catheters in the wall. Heparin infusion can prolong lumen patency but the danger of overdosage and bleeding disorder exists. Hemorrhage due to perforation of the vessel wall or human error in managing the line or stopcock is particularly dangerous with arterial catheters.

Central Venous Lines. The subclavian and internal jugular veins are commonly used for parenteral nutrition. Complications of such central venous lines include insertion failure, insertion complications, and postinsertion complications. Further, central venous placement via peripheral vessels can result in complications such as occlusion, thrombosis, dislodgement, and failure to insert the line. Infection is the major concern and is more probable when pressure transducers are added to the line. Infection surveillance is mandatory. Hemorrhage, malposition, and infiltration of infusates are particularly worrisome with central venous lines. Malposition can cause cardiac arrhythmia. Complications are more common and serious when the line is not optimally situated in the distal superior vena cava. Thrombosis and emboli are more likely when the catheter tip is in a vein smaller than the superior vena cava. Rare complications include perforation of the superior vena cava or heart causing cardiac tamponade and perforation into the pleural cavity causing pleural effusion. Complications of these lines are reduced if their use is restricted to parenteral feeding, reducing the number of times the line is invaded.

Umbilical Venous Lines. Recognized complications of umbilical venous catheterization include endothelial damage, phlebitis, thrombosis, hepatic necrosis, hepatic abscess hemorrhage, and sepsis; therefore, their current use is restricted to exchange transfusion, central venous pressure monitoring, and emergency vascular access. The safest location is the thoracic portion of the inferior vena cava, and complications are higher when the portal, mesenteric, splenic, or intrahepatic veins are inadvertently catheterized. Liver damage is reduced if catheter position is confirmed before infusion. Complications are reduced by limiting the indications for and duration of use and by close attention to placement and management techniques.

Umbilical Arterial Lines. Umbilical arterial lines are frequently used for monitoring blood gases and mean arterial pressures in the newborn. Placement of umbilical arterial catheters is more difficult than that of umbilical venous catheters, thus increasing the likelihood of damage to the intima. A large catheter can cause changes to blood flow dynamics after the catheter is in place, which predisposes the vessel to intimal injury. Umbilical arterial lines are contraindicated in the presence of necrotizing enterocolitis, omphalocele, omphalitis, peritonitis, and vascular insufficiency of the lower limbs or buttocks. Many complications follow thrombus formation. Vascular complications include renal artery thrombosis, visceral infarction, intestinal ischemia, limb ischemia, and total aortic thrombosis. Consequences of these complications include organ failure, hypertension due to renal artery occlusion, extremity loss, and neurologic deficits.

Thrombosis is common in newborns and is not solely related to catheters; however, thrombocytopenia is associated with thrombosis in cases of intravascular catheterization. Perforation of an umbilical arterial line is a life-threatening complication and is more common when difficulty is encountered when inserting the catheter. Also, infection is a recognized complication of umbilical artery catheterization but the consequences are less serious than those of thrombosis. Vasospasm induced by catheter insertion is a significant procedural complication that has been successfully treated with tolazoline infusion, which has associated complications. Occlusion of umbilical artery catheters is not uncommon and has been reported to occur less frequently with continuous heparin infusion.

TELEPHONE TRIAGE AND TELEPHONE ADVICE

Pediatricians, pediatric nurse practitioners, and pediatric nurses are frequently asked over the telephone to dispense medical advice about various conditions. Giving advice based on telephone data can be hazardous from both medical and medicolegal perspectives. Major detriments to this practice are the difficulty in obtaining a clear history by telephone conversation and the hazards of making an assessment without the benefit of a physical examination. The situation of dispensing medical advice from an emergency room or pediatric unit is more hazardous than doing so from a clinic or office because the caller is often unknown and because many diverse individuals can answer the telephone.

Controversy exists about whether emergency department personnel and pediatric unit staff should provide medical advice in response to telephone requests or presentations of problems. Arguments favoring this practice include the service provided to the community and facilitation of the appropriate use of emergency services by telephone triage. Arguments opposing telephone management include the inherent difficulty in telephone assessment of illness severity, staffing requirements for such a system, and the medicolegal liability exposure. Although the advisability of such a practice is debatable, data exist confirming its widespread existence. Even hospitals with formal policies prohibiting this practice can provide this service in an informal manner. Many institutions that provide telephone advice have not established formal systems for handling these calls nor have they included or emphasized the subject in residency education.

Sometimes a concise history can provide sufficient information for appropriate triage and a lengthy, more inclusive history could be incorrectly interpreted or unnecessary. Concerns exist about the professional qualifications of individuals relaying advice and the appropriateness of their advice. Studies have shown many inadequacies in the histories elicited in this manner, and advice given over the telephone and quality control in this area are recommended. It is recommended that all institutions that continue this practice develop formal guidelines for this service. Such guidelines should address limiting the number of individuals responsible for handling telephone queries with formal training in telephone management provided and implementing medically sound protocols to guide the respondent. Many primary care physicians do not have the luxury of relying on a previously established relationship with the patient and parent to guide telephone decision making; therefore, expertise in telephone management is essential.

Additionally, written documentation of all advice given is mandatory, and periodic review of all calls to monitor the quality of the advice is warranted. Failure to document significant telephone calls can have a deleterious impact on the provider in a malpractice situation. A brief progress note usually suffices, but when the chart is unavailable a message slip facilitates documentation. Occasionally, phone calls are insignificant and do not warrant documentation; however, the following three guidelines can be beneficial:

1. Document phone calls in which positive test results are relayed to patients; note if the patient was advised to return or seek other medical attention or was instructed to take some specific action.
2. Document conversations where significant medical advice is given or history is obtained, particularly when the advice is considered an interim measure, the discussion relates to adjustments in medication, in cases involving common symptoms that if they persist could indicate more serious problems, or if speaking with an unfamiliar patient.

3. Document the substance of calls to consultants contacted for advice about a specific patient.

Recording information at the time it is received and transmitted eliminates future confusion. Notation devices should be carried with a beeper. Without written evidence, legal recall of conversations can become a question of fact to be decided by a jury. A void in written communication can enable a plaintiff's attorney to present a picture of a disorganized, uncaring provider. A growing number of clinics use a "call-back" program that is documented.

SPECIFIC CLINICAL ISSUES

Newborn Resuscitation

Immediate and adequate resuscitation of the apneic or hypoxic newborn is an urgent neonatal emergency. Appropriate and timely intervention can preclude death or neurologic damage; conversely, delayed, inadequate, or inappropriate action can culminate in death or impairment. The effectiveness of current methods of infant resuscitation underscores the necessity of adequate personnel and equipment wherever infants are delivered.

Factors that facilitate successful resuscitation include communication between the obstetric and pediatric services; anticipation that an infant requiring resuscitation can be delivered; adequate facilities and equipment in operating order; and the presence of an individual capable of intubation and other indicated procedures at all identified at-risk deliveries.

One of three newborns who require resuscitation at birth cannot be identified in advance of delivery; therefore, it is critical that an individual skilled in neonatal resuscitation be available for every delivery. Every institution that performs obstetric deliveries requires a resuscitation plan to provide immediate skilled help for the distressed newborn. This plan should include protocols for identification of high-risk deliveries and protocols for neonatal resuscitation. The plan must establish protocols to ensure the availability of appropriate resuscitative support (personnel and equipment) and should address the following:

- level of training, certification, and skill required of resuscitation team members; it is recommended that pediatricians who attend deliveries complete the specialized course in neonatal resuscitation that is cosponsored by the American Heart Association and the American Academy of Pediatrics; nursing personnel who participate in deliveries should become credentialed in neonatal resuscitation by completing the neonatal resuscitation program (NRP) promul-

gated by the American Heart Association; it is recommended that institutions without staff neonatologists establish a relationship with a neonatology group to provide on-call neonatology coverage on a 24-hour basis;
- identification of equipment and medications that should be available and protocols to ensure that equipment operates properly and that the medication supply is adequate;
- criteria for employing specific resuscitative methods; there should be a staged resuscitation plan based on Apgar scores and clinical manifestations; and
- protocol for the location of various types of deliveries (e.g., birthing room, delivery room, operating room).

Being aware of the prenatal history of the mother, the labor or intrapartum period, and the birth assessment of the child can help staff prepare for potential neonatal emergencies. Staff caring for neonates or receiving them in transfer from other hospitals should recognize that certain factors predispose a child to develop significant and emergent problems. Some of these factors are listed in Exhibit 30-1.

Documentation

A resuscitation form should be created and should include both the assessments and the interventions that occurred during resuscitation. Responses to interventions also should be documented. Timing of the interventions to establish a clear sequence of intervention is essential.

Resuscitation of the Meconium Stained Infant

Liability for improper resuscitation of the meconium stained infant is a major source of litigation. It is not always possible to predict whether aspiration of meconium has occurred even if the infant is covered with meconium at delivery. Infants at risk for meconium aspiration are those with evidence of fetal distress before delivery, those who are small for gestational age, or those who are postmature. Often inadequate medical record documentation of the resuscitative process compounds the liability problem.

A resuscitation plan should include guidelines about various interventions to be implemented. In the presence of meconium stained amniotic fluid, it is mandatory that the oropharynx be suctioned at the time the head is delivered to prevent aspiration; if thick meconium is present and the infant is depressed, the trachea should be cleared by endotracheal intubation and rapid suctioning.

Exhibit 30-1
FACTORS PREDISPOSING TO NEONATAL EMERGENCIES AND PROBLEMS

Neonatal Emergencies: Maternal Factors
　Diabetes
　Hypertension
　Pre-eclampsia
　Prolonged rupture of membranes
　Indications of maternal infection
　Drug addiction
　Maternal systemic disease
　Blood group isoimmunization

Neonatal Emergencies: Intrapartum Factors
　Meconium stained fluid
　Fetal distress
　Abnormal presentation
　Vaginal bleeding
　Cord prolapse

　Cesarean section
　Prolonged labor
　Recent analgesia
　Complicated operative delivery

Neonatal Problems: Fetal Factors
　Suspicion of fetal distress
　Prematurity (less than 37 weeks gestation)
　Postmaturity (greater than 42 weeks gestation)
　Intrauterine growth retardation
　Oligohydramnios
　Multiple gestation
　Congenital abnormalities
　Cardiac arrhythmias
　Hydrops fetalis

Documentation

Documentation should include the type of meconium seen, whether the infant is stained, and whether meconium is present under the infant's fingernails. The method of suctioning should also be documented (e.g., Delee, bulb). The medical record must clearly indicate that the cords were visualized and suctioned and that a catheter or endotracheal tube was passed below the cords to suction the upper bronchial airways; this should be performed before positive pressure oxygen is delivered to demonstrate that meconium was not pushed into the lungs during resuscitation.

Iatrogenic Complications of Neonatal Intensive Care

Neonatal intensive care relies heavily on mechanical devices and invasive procedures; iatrogenic disorders are a natural sequelae of such care. The adverse effects of diagnostic or therapeutic interventions are generally those of commission. A smaller infant means a narrower gap between helping and hurting and increases the difficulty to predict with certainty those patients destined for a more favorable outcome. Unintended adverse outcomes can be attributed to multiple factors including lack of provider skill, inherent hazard of the intervention, susceptibility of the host, or the extent of the affliction being managed. Although total prevention is impossible, techniques can be implemented so iatrogenic complications are decreased.

The first steps in reducing iatrogenic complications are the recognition that complications can occur and awareness of the various complications that can result from a particular

intervention. This awareness can modify the decision to intervene and increase the diligence in management when intervention is clearly indicated. (For a list of indicators to monitor high-risk conditions in the neonatal intensive care unit, see Chapter 28.)

Respiratory Complications

The evolution of assisted ventilation is a major reason for improved survival in the neonate; however, pulmonary complications are among the most common iatrogenic problems encountered in the neonatal intensive care unit. Common indications for assisted ventilation include:

- respiratory distress syndrome
- aspiration syndromes
- pneumonia
- postoperative support
- pulmonary immaturity
- hypoventilation (induced)
- sepsis
- central nervous system disorders
- lung anomalies.

Complications of assisted ventilation include air leak complications and endotracheal intubation complications. Air leak syndromes occur most frequently in preterm newborns and can be directly attributed to the use of mechanical ventilation techniques that apply a continuous distending pressure. Air leak syndromes include:

- pulmonary interstitial emphysema (PIE) (acute and chronic); PIE is the initiating event in all air leak syndromes and results from trapped interstitial air from the rupture of alveolar walls

- pneumothorax
- bronchopulmonary dysplasia; this is a deviation from normal lung development primarily caused by a combination of increased oxygen exposure and barotrauma over time.

Reducing Complications of Assisted Ventilation

Three major areas of reducing neonatal respiratory morbidity and mortality are prevention of preterm birth, reduction in the incidence or severity of neonatal respiratory disease by accurate assessment of lung maturity before elective delivery via pulmonary maturity index or by accelerating lung maturation, and technologic advances toward diminishing complications of mechanical ventilation. These include reducing the need for assisted ventilation, developing new methods of ventilation, providing agents that protect the lung from damage, improving nutritional support of the ventilated neonate, and using more accurate monitoring devices that permit more physiologic management of assisted ventilation.

The need for assisted ventilation can only be reduced if lung maturation can be accelerated or stimulated. Exogenous surfactants are the major source allowing lung maturation. When ventilation is necessary, the lowest pressures possible should be used. Advances in mechanical ventilators must reduce the barotrauma and oxygen toxicity caused by conventional ventilatory methods. High-frequency ventilation can accomplish this but has associated complications.

Extracorporeal membranous oxygenation (ECMO) has been associated with intraventricular hemorrhage (IVH) in infants less than 35 weeks gestation; therefore, it is recommended to forego this procedure in infants who have not reached that level of development. When ECMO is used in older gestation infants, the incidence of IVH can be reduced by avoiding thrombocytopenia, heparin overdose, and rapid changes in blood pressure. Additional complications of ECMO include jugular vein injury, equipment failure causing hemolysis, and oxygenation failure due to damaged tubing.

Complications Caused by Endotracheal Intubation

Acute complications of endotracheal intubation and suction catheters can be categorized into traumatic, mechanical, and physiologic; most chronic complications are consequences of trauma. Physiologic complications include changes in intracranial and mean arterial and cerebral perfusion pressures and are reduced by preoxygenation before intubation/suctioning. Blood pressure changes increase the risk of intraventricular hemorrhage.

The four major components of preventing complications of endotracheal intubation are proper technique, careful selection of equipment, adequate preparation of the infant, and monitoring the infant during the procedure. Endotracheal intubation complications can be substantially reduced by observing tube size, limiting the number and duration of intubations, reducing tube malposition by careful tube fixation, noting tube length at patient's nose or lip, and stabilizing the infant's head during handling. Endotracheal tubes in infants are generally noncuffed, making the risk of aspiration a potential hazard. Special positioning protocols should be followed, and frequent auscultation of the lungs of an intubated infant should be part of every assessment. Further, complications of suction can be decreased when guidelines are followed for appropriate suction pressure, length of catheter, and frequency and duration of suctioning. Unnecessary suctioning increases the risk of complications, and inadequate suctioning increases the risk of airway obstruction.

CONCLUSION

Many clinical and environmental risks associated with the care of pediatric patients have been discussed in this chapter. Good risk management requires that proactive strategies be used to evaluate those procedures and interactions that could give rise to quality problems. Working with the quality assurance or improvement team to identify problems that might inhibit the staff's ability to provide high quality of care is an important aspect of the pediatric risk management program. Appendix 30-A identifies examples of indicators that can be used to review and evaluate the quality of care provided to children for common admitting conditions. These indicators can be part of the hospitalwide quality improvement and risk identification program.

BIBLIOGRAPHY

American Academy of Pediatrics: Committee on Child Abuse and Neglect. 1991. Guidelines for the evaluation of sexual abuse of children. *Pediatrics* 87:254–260.

American Academy of Pediatrics and American College of Obstetrics and Gynecologists. 1992. *Guidelines for Perinatal Care*. 3d ed. Elk Grove Village, Ill. and Washington, D.C.: American Academy of Pediatrics and American College of Obstetrics and Gynecologists.

Black, J.A. and M.F. Whitfield. 1991. *Neonatal Emergencies Early Detection and Management*. 2d ed. Oxford, England: Butterworth-Heinemann, Ltd.

Council on Scientific Affairs. August 1985. AMA diagnostic and treatment guidelines concerning child abuse and neglect. *Journal of the American Medical Association*:254.

Folli, H.L., et al. 1987. Medication error prevention by clinical pharmacists in two children's hospitals. *Pediatrics* 70:718–722.

Guthrie, R.D., ed. 1988. *Neonatal Intensive Care.* New York: Churchill Livingstone.

Isaacman, D.J., et al. January 1992. Pediatric telephone advice in the emergency department: results of a mock scenario. *Pediatrics* 89, no. 1:35–38.

Kendig, J.W. July 1992. Care of the normal newborn. *Pediatrics in Review* 13, no. 7.

Lesar, T.S., et al. May 1990. Medication prescribing errors in a teaching hospital. *Journal of the American Medical Association* 63:2329–2334.

Vincer, M.J., et al. 1989. Drug errors and incidents in a neonatal intensive care unit; a quality assurance activity. *Am J Dis Child* 143:737–740.

Yanovski, S.Z., et al. April 1992. Telephone triage by primary care physicians. *Pediatrics* 89, no. 4:701–705.

Appendix 30-A

Sample Indicators for the Care of Pediatric Patients

The following clinical indicators can be used to evaluate the care rendered to pediatric patients with the common presenting conditions as listed.

Pneumonia

Documentation

1. History reflects:
   - change in breathing pattern
   - fever
   - chronic disease
   - medications
2. Physical examination reflects:
   - vital signs
   - breath sounds/rales/wheezing
   - cardiac exam
   - mental status
3. CBC with differential completed
4. Blood culture performed on children less than 2 years of age
5. PPD/tine test done if child is greater than 6 months and not undergoing steroid administration
6. Blood gases/oximetry performed if child has any of the following:
   - cyanosis
   - altered mental status
   - respiratory rate:
     - greater than 80 per minute if 0–12 months
     - greater than 60 per minute if 1–10 years
     - greater than 50 per minute if greater than 10 years
7. Chest X-ray done
8. Appropriate antibiotics are administered:
   - 0–1 month—ampicillin, ceftriaxone; ampicillin, gentamicin at admission
   - 1–3 months—ampicillin, ceftriaxone or, if mild, oral amoxicillin, Augmentin; erythromycin if chlamydia or pneumonia
   - 3 months–4 years—cefuroxime, ceftriaxone, ampicillin, amoxicillin, Pediazole

   - greater than 4 years—ceftriaxone, cefuroxime, erythromycin, amoxicillin
9. Intravenous fluids
10. Oxygen therapy for oxygen saturation less than 90%

Nonfebrile Seizure/Seizure Disorder

1. Drug levels of anticonvulsant medication drawn within 24 hours of admission for those antiseizure medications
2. EEG ordered within 24 hours of admission of a newly diagnosed seizure patient
3. Serum electrolytes and sequential multiple analyzer (SMA) for other blood chemistry determinations ordered within 24 hours of admission
4. Seizure precautions ordered by physicians at time of admission

Gastroenteritis

1. Daily weights done
2. Stool amount recorded for at least 4 hours after admission

Pulmonary Exacerbation of Cystic Fibrosis

1. Diagnosis is validated by the presence of at least two of the following:
   - increased cough
   - sputum production
   - fever greater than 100.4°F
   - weight loss
   - increased shortness of breath, difficulty breathing, or both
2. Sputum culture is obtained within appropriate time:
   - within 4 weeks if patient is followed through clinic
   - within 1 week of admission if not a clinic patient
3. Intravenous antimicrobial therapy is given for at least 3 days after admission if not a clinic patient
4. A pulmonary function test or pulse oximetry reading is obtained at least once per week
5. Weight checks are obtained at least once per week

Source: *UHC Compendium of Clinical Indicators* by University Hospital Consortium, Oak Brook, IL, 1991.

chapter 31

Risk Management in the Psychiatric Setting

Claudia Teich

INTRODUCTION

This chapter discusses the risk management issues associated with the care of the psychiatric patient. Incorporated into this discussion is a review of the legal aspects of various therapeutic measures, such as the application of restraints and the use of seclusion, often employed in the psychiatric setting. In addition to these topics, a review of the legal aspects of both the right to refuse treatment and informed consent in the psychiatric setting is provided.

A hospital staff prepared for the possible risk presented by a particular patient group will set a therapeutic tone of safety within the context of the patient care setting. Planning for what may be foreseeable problems in the care of a particular kind of patient is the clinical duty of all to whom such specialized care is entrusted. Therefore, a thorough understanding of one's professional responsibilities toward a patient includes an awareness of the legal basis of that care. This chapter begins with a brief discussion of professional and institutional liability. It is the role of the risk manager and psychiatric team to ensure that they understand, establish, and enforce operational policies and procedures that are consistent with the rights of the psychiatric patient and to create an environment that is both therapeutic and safe.

DEVELOPMENT OF PROFESSIONAL AND INSTITUTIONAL LIABILITY

The role of the nurse as a professional and independent health care provider has evolved only slowly since the establishment of the nursing profession during the Crimean War. In the last twenty years, however, the profession has witnessed a tremendous expansion of practice responsibilities and duties. Individual states have revised their nurse practice acts to keep pace with the true definition of nursing as it exists today. Yet with this increasing professional responsibility a widened scope of legal liability has also arrived. Other workers in the hospital setting such as aides and mental health workers also have experienced an expansion of their accountability. When an individual is trained as a caregiver, he or she must meet defined standards of care.

Although individual workers are not held liable for their actions, employers are liable. This theory of liability (discussed later in this chapter) is termed *vicarious liability*.[1] A few decades ago this concept of liability did not exist. Hospitals were viewed as charitable organizations immune to all liability. Today, however, the hospital is envisioned as a business concerned with maintaining a sound financial status. As a result of this comprehensive notion, hospitals are now responsible for developing patient care policies and procedures. Moreover, they are accountable for all whom they hire and train.[2] Therefore, institutions view risk management as an integral part of the efforts to achieve and maintain quality control.

RISK MANAGEMENT ISSUES IN CARING FOR SUICIDAL PATIENTS

Consider the following case of a wrongful death action brought by an administrator of an estate. The plaintiff sought to prove that the defendant's physicians and hospital were responsible for malpractice when the patient jumped to his death from the 11th floor of the hospital. Evidence showed that the decedent had suffered increasing depression and had entered the hospital for treatment for this disorder. The decedent was admitted to a unit of the psychiatric department. Although the patient had suicidal thoughts when he entered, the physician had not ordered any seclusion or restraints. A later order for transfer to a more secure environment had not been carried out.[3]

Patients who complain of suicidal thoughts or display overtly suicidal behavior present hospital staff with significant challenges with care and safety. Consequently, the staff must have an organized system for documenting and assessing such behavior. Yet a lack of consistent observation and omissions in communication among hospital staff have resulted in many examples that parallel the previously cited case. The initial phase of treatment presents the period in which observation and assessment are most critical for maintaining the patient in a safe environment and minimizing liability risk. The patient's signs and symptoms unfold slowly, thereby inhibiting the staff's ability to determine correctly the patient's risk for self-harm. Unfortunately, antidepressants and other drugs commonly used in the treatment of depression work slowly and cannot produce results for days or even weeks. From the start the staff must provide careful and thoughtful management of such cases. For example, they must immediately assess the need for one-to-one observation.

The case of *Johnson v. Grant Hospital* involves a woman who jumped to her death moments after leaving an area in which she had been secluded.[4] She had spoken of suicide during the previous day and evening. The nurse supervisor reported these observations to the patient's physician who then ordered seclusion for the remainder of the evening. In the morning the on-duty nurse was unaware of the patient's prominent suicidal ideation and placed her in the care of a new staff member. After the patient left seclusion in the company of staff, she found herself momentarily alone and within moments managed to jump to her death from a nearby window. She was 34 years old and the mother of two children.[5]

In litigating cases such as this, the courts look to whether one might foresee that the patient could or would take his or her life.[6] The basis of risk management entails that staff address questions of foreseeability with regard to potentially harmful patients. The court in the previously discussed *Johnson* case found the hospital staff liable for the patient's care regardless of the physician's orders about one-to-one observation.[7] The staff and physician must both maintain an exceptional level of diligence to their tasks when confronted with the suicidal patient. Among the methods available to the psychiatric staff are suicide precautions and seclusion.

CLINICAL AND LEGAL CONSIDERATIONS IN THE USES OF SECLUSION AND RESTRAINTS

Seclusion and restraints are effective methods of protecting patients. Their rate of use for controlling patient behavior varies widely, depending in part on the institution's treatment philosophy. Studies also have shown that geographical differences exist in the use of these control methods.[8] Large city hospitals tend to use physical methods of control more frequently than do smaller hospitals.[9] Whatever the treatment philosophy or location of the hospital, several legitimate indications for the application of these measures exist that include:

- prevention of imminent harm to the patient and/or others when no alternative method of control is likely to be effective
- prevention of serious physical damage to the hospital environment
- assistance in meeting the treatment plan's goals such as in the use of seclusion as part of a behavior modification program.[10]

Seclusion and restraints serve several therapeutic purposes in different patient populations. For instance, seclusion can be an effective technique in destimulating an anxious, aggressive, or violent patient.[11] Nevertheless, the user must be aware of the legal consequences of his or her actions when using restraints or seclusion even in situations that appear to justify the therapeutic use of such methods.[12] The legal criteria for employing these techniques entail the following:

- The physician (medical official) must write a proper order after he or she has personally examined the patient.
- The order must identify a specific period and cannot be written as "open-ended" or "as needed."

- The staff must make timely assessments of the patient's status while in restraints or seclusion and document these assessments in the medical record.
- The physician in charge must reevaluate the patient before extending the original order.[13]

In addition to these requirements, the individual states have enacted various statutory protections for the patient. For example, Illinois law permits a patient to notify a party(ies) of his or her choice concerning the seclusion.[14] In other states, statutes regulate the conditions under which restraints are used. Consequently, the mental health professional must be knowledgeable of the legal scope and ramifications such laws have in his or her locality. After the clinical indication for the legitimate use of restraints or seclusion occurs, the staff must be prepared to follow the appropriate legal guidelines that should be further reinforced by inclusion in the institution's procedure manual.

The four critical elements in preparing a patient for entering restraints or seclusion are:

1. The staff must remove other patients from the area of confinement and identify and remove any objects that can present hazards to the patient or others.
2. The staff must thoroughly search the patient's person for potentially injurious articles that include belts, lighters, pins, matches, and similarly dangerous materials or clothing.
3. One staff member has the main responsibility of assessing the patient a minimum of every 15 minutes.
4. The staff must systematically document the patient's medical status and behavior at the completion of each observational period.[15]

To place a patient safely in restraints, one must employ a precise procedure. If the staff are to perform these tasks competently and safely, they must have frequent training and review. Failure to follow appropriate policy and procedure and limited or absent training frequently lead to unnecessary episodes of physical and psychological harm to both patient and staff.

A sound procedure for applying restraints contains several elements. First, one staff member must be the designated leader. This individual directs how the patient is handled. Second, at least one staff member must handle each extremity while the leader assumes responsibility for stabilizing the head and neck. Another staff member raises the torso when the leader signals, while another staff waits, restraints in hand, in the seclusion area. When the patient has been successfully restrained, there is again a need to check the patient and the immediate area for potentially harmful items. At this time one also can reassess the need for medication.[16] Having completed these tasks, one notes the time, the patient's behavior that led to restraints, and his or her response to the restraint procedure. While in restraints, a patient cannot smoke or engage in other activities that are reasonably construed as constituting a hazard. The well-intended decision to allow a restrained patient greater liberty than prudent assessment warrants has frequently led to disastrous results.

When is restraint unlawful or when does restraint constitute false imprisonment? Patients have successfully brought suit for unlawful restraint as defined under the tort of false imprisonment[17]: an individual had been intentionally confined, detained, or restrained against his or her will and the imprisonment had been unlawful or false.

DISCHARGING PSYCHIATRIC PATIENTS

The decision to discharge a psychiatric patient requires as much care as the decision to admit such a patient. To evaluate a patient's readiness to reenter the family and broader social network requires structured planning with both the patient and individuals who play major roles in the patient's life. Many factors appear on the list of considerations. Among these considerations are financial issues that are more conspicuous now than in the past because of the current climate of managed care and governmental cost consciousness. These monetary factors have altered the notion of care delivery so the once leisurely process of assessment now finds itself often abruptly curtailed.[18] Psychiatric admissions last days instead of months.

Several legal cases have emerged to address the issues surrounding premature discharge. In *Wilson v. Blue Cross of Southern California*, the patient was discharged after a utilization review (managed care) company refused to certify more time for inpatient care.[19] The patient committed suicide shortly after discharge. The patient's mother and executor brought action against the health insurers for the patient's wrongful death. The court analyzed whether the denial for reimbursement of further hospital services engendered a substantial harm to the deceased.[20] In the court's opinion, when insurance benefits are denied, the treating physician must pursue whatever avenues of appeal the insurer offers and in fact has a duty to file the appropriate requests for an extension of benefits if the physician's judgment is that the patient's medical status requires that level of care. Further, the physician must document the process of continuing medical assessment in the chart.

An increasing number of corporations that provide their employees with health care benefits have adopted a utilization review policy. Concurrent review between the primary physician and the utilization reviewer has become a common process of current medical practice. When coupled with current limited benefit packages, the utilization review process forces the physician and staff to walk the narrow line between accelerating the care process while concomitantly remaining comfortably within the bounds of sound and safe practice.

CLINICAL MANAGEMENT OF VIOLENT PATIENTS

Patients who present with violent or physically aggressive behavior challenge the clinician. Several clinical features or risk factors are associated with such violence.

When taking a violent patient's history, the staff must especially note the following:

- history of violence
- violent environment
- impulsivity—previous violence toward friends and family or reckless behavior
- low intelligence
- paranoid ideation
- command hallucinations
- psychosis
- verbal threats of violence against another
- organic brain syndrome due to drug abuse
- personality disorder such as borderline or antisocial personality.[21]

Among the chief concerns is the type of unit on which to house such patients. Aggressive patients improve most rapidly in an environment that is restrictive and quiet, with seclusion rooms readily available. The staff should be experienced with this type of case as well as the use of restraints. On admission the caretakers will build their initial assessments and develop a care plan for the first 24 hours. Agitation, anxiety, and physical aggression toward people or property comprise the primary area of assessment.

One staff member has the assignment of individual care for the patient who will not be left unattended at any time. The initial goal must be to form a verbal relationship with the patient and to estimate his or her ability to respond appropriately to verbal direction. Teaching the patient to express his or her aggressive thoughts gives the patient an outlet for feelings. Yet caregivers must remember the need to remain at a respectful distance.[22]

Staff must *never* treat patients as though they are passive victims of their own aggressive behavior. Instead, the staff plans treatment for a patient in a manner that conveys the expectation for responsible behavior. Participation in unit responsibilities and attendance at patient groups and activities thus remain reasonable goals. Violation of the unit rules and expectations must have clear and immediate consequences of which the patient has been adequately fore-

warned. Observation of the patient's response to these environmental demands both highlights the patient's adaptive difficulties and instructs the patient about social milieu tolerations. This observational technique leads to inferences that in turn better predict the patient's future action. The more carefully one collects such data, the more accurate is the understanding of the patient's tolerance of complex stimuli and expectations. This heightened awareness becomes a key ingredient in the development of effective treatment plans, shortened hospital stays, and ultimately reduced patient suffering.

Impact of Violent Patients on Staff

Patients who become violent or who are otherwise intimidating evoke strong emotions in staff. These reactions are generally negative and set the tone for the unit. In fact, no staff can deny the real physical threats incurred in the care of such individuals. Overlooking this simple fact fosters a situation that can readily become uncontrolled. When confronted with such chaos, a staff member can feel frightened and opt for unnecessarily aggressive means of patient control. Ideally, the nurse or aide must project a firm but nonpunitive posture. Frequent patient care conferences lead to improved staff communication and encourage a unified treatment plan. Rotation allows another method of reducing the stress that a given staff member can accrue while caring for violent persons. Another concern is the need to have sufficient numbers of staff available on all shifts to meet the hospital's duty to provide patient safety.

Impact of Tarasoff on Caring for Violent Patients

The California Supreme Court first recognized that a duty to protect third parties was imposed only when a special relationship existed between the victim, the individual whose behavior created the behavior, and the defendant.[23] Therefore, the single relationship of a physician to his or her patient is sufficient to support the duty to exercise reasonable care to protect others from the violent acts of patients. Some jurisdictions have held that the need for public safety overrides all other considerations including confidentiality.[24] The psychotherapist has a duty to protect an endangered third party from a patient's violent and dangerous acts.

Some states have enacted statutes addressing the duty to protect doctrine. Generally, these statutes require that the victim be identifiable and that the therapist notify the police.[25] Typically, the focus is whether the violence was foreseeable. Information from inpatient hospital notes and therapist records can indicate whether the violence was foreseeable.[26] The therapist must address three factors about the likelihood of the violent act's occurrence: threat, means, and opportunity.[27]

In outpatient cases, most courts have held that the therapist's control over the patient is insufficient to establish a duty to protect without a foreseeable victim. The duty established by the case of Tarasoff generally operates when evidence is either expressed or implied that the patient is dangerous to a specific victim.[28] In inpatient cases, however, courts have held there is a duty to control the patient whether or not a specific victim is intended and if clinical data imply the patient's danger to others.[29] When the patient is in a hospital, a duty exists to evaluate constantly the patient's potential to harm others. Short-term assessments of the risk of violence are more accurate than long-term assessments.

RIGHT TO REFUSE TREATMENT

The right of psychiatric patients to refuse treatment has gained much attention from the legal system over the last few decades. In a landmark case, *Rogers v. Okin*, the court decided that in the absence of an emergency (e.g., serious threat of extreme violence or personal injury) any person who has not been adjudicated incompetent has a right to refuse antipsychotic medication.[30] In other similar cases, courts have held that competent adults have the right to refuse all forms of medical treatment, including treatment necessary to preserve life.[31] The concept of refusal is readily understandable for patients refusing interventions such as surgery or complex procedures; however, the same notion becomes far less ostensible in a psychiatric setting. While one can readily consider it inhumane to allow a human being to suffer the terror of a psychotic illness, one nevertheless must carefully question the wisdom of treating such people with a potent pharmacological agent that can affect them in untoward ways. Most mental health professionals consider that their highest purpose is to provide help for a person suffering from psychosis and consider unconscionable the failure to provide aggressive treatment. Thus, a patient who persists in refusing care places a heavy burden on the staff. Consider the following case in which a patient involuntarily committed to a hospital challenged the trial court's order that he forcibly receive medications for a maximum period of 60 days. On appeal the court reviewed the particular section of the state's mental health code and concluded that a recipient of such services can refuse treatment, including medication, unless such treatment is necessary to prevent the recipient from seriously harming self or others.[32]

The right to refuse medication pertains to the patient who is involuntarily committed to a psychiatric facility. Other courts reviewing similar questions, as raised in *People v. Orr*, found forcible treatment not a reasonable response to safety or security if less drastic means are available to achieve the same purpose.[33] The term *least restrictive alternative* is used to describe less intrusive methods of care.[34] Therefore, when considering the treatment plan, the psychiatric staff must entertain alternative interventions such as segregating a patient from other patients or employing less potent agents (minor tranquilizers).

LEAST RESTRICTIVE ALTERNATIVES

The least restrictive alternative of care gives the patient several treatment options. These provisions of care are based on the theory that deprivation of liberty solely to minimize danger to the ill person should not exceed what is necessary to his or her own protection. Thus, the patient cannot be confined in a hospital if care in an outpatient treatment facility can adequately provide effective treatment. Most state mental health codes have a least restrictive alternative doctrine.[35] The issue of least restriction does not focus solely on commitment versus noncommitment but also focuses on other forms of treatment. One such form involves the use of neuroleptic medication.

TREATMENT WITH NEUROLEPTIC MEDICATIONS

Neuroleptic or antipsychotic drugs have demonstrated prominent and consistent success in relieving the acute signs and symptoms of psychosis. This success has not come without its price in that all neuroleptic medications, except clozapine, have produced permanent and occasionally debilitating side effects in about 40% of recipients.[36] The term tardive dyskinesia (TD) names this class of side effects. TD entails the occurrence of syndromes of involuntary movements that can involve the tongue, neck muscles, torso, and extremities separately or in combination with any muscle group. The movements can mimic various disparate neurological disorders including parkinsonism. While most cases occur within the first 90 days of drug administration, the onset can develop any time during treatment. Some patient groups such as those with unipolar depression, organic mental disorders, and the elderly appear to have a greater risk of developing TD, although the increased risk can constitute nothing more than the medication's aggravation of preexisting but clinically unappreciated neurological disease.

Some researchers have reported that TD can be reversed if the signs are detected promptly. Nursing staff can provide early and thorough evaluation while the patient is in the earliest stages of a medication trial. Even before treatment begins, the physician needs to analyze the risk-benefit ratio of the therapy. The physician must consider the relative benefits and risks of the treatment for this particular patient, the likelihood of medication compliance, the probable duration of treatment, and the methods of monitoring outcome.

Neuroleptic treatment requires informed consent. In some states such as Illinois, the patient must receive a special consent form for any psychotropic drug treatment. The form describes the treatment and contains the patient's acknowledgement that he or she understands the potential consequences of taking the medication. Further, the patient receives a written description of the uses and side effects of the drug prescribed. If therapy begins without consent, the physician and staff incur potential liability involving battery, negligence, or both.

Legal advocates have offered the argument that the use of neuroleptic agents constitutes an Eighth Amendment violation. Naturally, such commentary appears fatuous to most mental health professionals who see a patient as suffering and often unable to exercise proper judgment. Informed consent carves a path between these two extremes.

For the mental health professional and the risk manager, consent to treatment requires a proactive approach. Except in cases of a valid medical emergency or a court order specifying care, every case must demonstrate a documented attempt to describe treatment and its alternatives to a patient.

INFORMED CONSENT

Since 1911 a series of legal cases have caused informed consent to become the obligation of the physician. The underlying principle is that each adult has a right to decide what can be done to his or her body. The legal process defines five essential elements of informed consent that include:

1. explanation of the proposed treatment in language a patient readily understands
2. possible risks and side effects inherent in treatment
3. potential for cure or success
4. alternatives to recommended treatment
5. explanation of disease course if treatment is withheld.

When adjudicating a case for lack of informed consent, the court will look for these elements to decide whether the patient has in fact given informed consent.

In the clinical setting, it can be extremely difficult to communicate with an anxious patient. Even more difficult is the task of relating adequate information to a psychotic patient. Nevertheless, the courts require mental health professionals to give a patient as much information as possible so the patient can decide. If a patient has lucid

periods, the physician must be available during these periods to inform the patient.

ROLE OF THE GUARDIAN

If no such opportunities arise, the courts can appoint a guardian whose judgment can substitute for a patient and whose additional duty is to consider the patient's best interests. The guardian can thus provide another avenue of balancing the patient's rights versus health care needs. The guardian's role is generally viewed as a temporary method of allowing for informed consent as well as the broader protection of the patient's rights.

CARE OF ADOLESCENT PATIENTS

The admission of adolescents to a psychiatric facility is a traumatic event for everyone involved. Caring for these young people challenges the staff members who manage treatment. Although various diagnoses can entail inpatient treatment at some point in their course, several behaviors are common to the disturbed adolescent. These include acting out or misbehavior, impulsivity, and moodiness. These behaviors are manifested as impaired judgment, poor school performance, fighting, arguing, running away, drug or alcohol abuse, shoplifting, pervasive indifference to others' needs or rights, suicidal preoccupations, and a persistent oppositional stance toward authority. The major goal of any treatment plan is to control the adolescent's behavior sufficiently so therapy and improvement can occur.

UNIT RULES AND REGULATIONS

Unit rules, regulations, and structure become the primary methods by which the patient, staff, and visitors receive safety and security. Several risk behaviors require special attention: aggression, elopement, drug abuse, and sexual activity. The unit structure must be developed to provide prompt response to these risks. For example, to respond to short-lived aggression often encountered in adolescents, the staff can use seclusion or the "quiet room." Intervention is immediate. Use of the quiet room for short intervals has a greater effect with adolescent patients compared with its use with adults. Following the use of seclusion, the staff must discuss the incident with the patient. Understanding the antecedents to the angry or aggressive behavior necessitates frequent conferences between patient and staff that establish bounds of behavioral control for the patient. A primary goal for managing aggressive behavior is to have the patient thoroughly learn and independently manifest or internalize the rules operative on the unit. Moreover, the quality of care an adolescent receives depends on the frequency and quality of communication between him or her and staff members. Unit policies, which must continually be reinforced, must require such interaction. On admission the staff confronts a patient with a complete outline of all unit policies and rules, leaving the patient with an understanding of what is allowed and not allowed in the unit. As a new admission, a patient gains privileges only gradually and in proportion to the severity of his or her illness and compliance with unit expectations. Because an adolescent patient can demonstrate variable signs and symptoms, the diagnosis cannot be immediately clear. Consequently, the staff can elect to observe the patient for a time, during which the diagnosis becomes clear. Unit structure prevails intact throughout all shifts that must be well-staffed to maintain this important function. Several rules and regulations find commonality in treatment facilities throughout the country and include:

- clear and consistent guidelines posted and presented to each patient
- constant supervision of the patient group
- thorough definition and consequences of violations
- doors to rooms fully open and the room visible, or doors closed and locked
- strict monitoring of contraband during all hours but especially when visitors are present.

Drugs, alcohol, and weapons readily emerge on the psychiatric unit from various sources. For instance, two major Chicago hospitals failed to check visitors of depressed patients. One brought a patient a gun with which the patient committed suicide. This incident occurred on a locked unit. A similar but more sinister episode occurred in another hospital where a patient used a smuggled gun to murder another patient. Thus, an aggressive policy of watchfulness cannot be underrated. While the smuggling of weapons is rare, the appearance of drugs and alcohol as well as cigarettes and matches happens every day.

SEXUAL BEHAVIOR

Sexually inappropriate behavior is the most universal problem among adolescent inpatients. Many young people who are emotionally troubled have conflicts regarding sexual behavior. These include questions of sexual identity and the incessant testing of the limits of propriety and adult tolerance. The literature on adolescent sexuality can teach staff members about expectations from the teenage patient. While the risks inherent in adolescent sexuality comprise many possibilities, the greatest concern to inpatient staff is

physical interaction and its attendant risks of pregnancy, disease, and assault. Therefore, unit policies must thoroughly state the limitations on room visiting, dress, and provocative behavior. Because the incidence of teenage pregnancy is of epidemic proportions, one can sensibly infer that the teenage patient already has been sexually active. Among females the risk for pregnancy grows when there has been a recent loss, sexually active peers, truancy, isolation from female companions, consorting with older males, and a family history of teen pregnancy. Substance abuse deserves special mention with regard to sexual activity because girls can be induced to trade sexual favors for drugs or can be forced into prostitution to obtain drugs or to pay off drug debts. While the same problems occur in males, their incidence is less common.

SUBSTANCE ABUSE IN INPATIENT UNITS

Substance abuse occurs widely among the teenage population. Drug and alcohol use can exist either as a manifestation of a more pervasive problem or independently as a disease entity. The mere confinement of a patient to an inpatient unit does not confer immunity from continuing substance abuse. After performing a thorough admission evaluation that includes blood and urine screening, the staff must remain aware of the signs and symptoms of abuse. Visitors including parents and siblings can become the source of illicit substances, although friends are the most common vehicle. As with adult patients, adolescents can encounter withdrawal syndromes, and detoxification planning must be part of the treatment protocol for the at-risk individual. Further, treatment does not stop after discharge, because aftercare is critical to a successful substance abuse treatment. When suspicious of ongoing substance abuse, the staff has an obligation to notify the adolescent's parents and perform whatever search is required to find the drug and perform the appropriate laboratory tests to confirm the patient's use. In general, the safety needs of the patient and peers significantly outweigh the question of violation of individual freedom, including the right to privacy. Moreover, the intoxicated patient cannot be properly treated. If parents or patients refuse to comply with the request for searches and screens, the patient should be immediately discharged from the hospital.

Both sexual behavior and substance abuse are linked to acquired immune deficiency syndrome (AIDS). The adolescent must learn the consequences of his or her behavior. In providing information, the hospital naturally serves to fulfill its role as a source of health information. Because the inpatient adolescent patient finds himself or herself at greater risk for AIDS, the educational program needs to incorporate AIDS teaching as an integral facet of its overall mission.

SEXUAL MISCONDUCT AND THEORIES OF INDIVIDUAL AND HOSPITAL LIABILITY

Most professionals encounter significant discomfort when broaching sexual misconduct with patients. Denial is often the first cry of many therapists even in the face of what constitutes a substantial number of therapist admissions of precisely such violations. More recently, several professional associations have endeavored to address the issues to uncover such misconduct, to develop a system of reporting suspected violations, and to follow up those reports with vigorous prosecution and significant penalties for the convicted. While statistics about this area of professional conduct vary considerably in their range and accuracy, the incidence of sexual impropriety appears to have waned since peaking in the late 1960s and during the 1970s. Both professional efforts to educate peers and unflattering media exposure have combined to depress this figure. Despite efforts to curb sexual contact between patients and therapists, such interactions probably will continue to occur to varying degrees and rates.

The most important warning sign indicating an erosion of the therapeutic relationship is the therapist's periodic crossing of the therapeutic boundary. The therapeutic boundary means behavior that indicates more than the respectful professional distance that must exist between patient and therapist for the work of healing to progress. Commonly, patients test this boundary, but the therapist is obliged to reinforce it or face unpleasant consequences. A common scenario for this process of erosion might be the following:

- The therapy sessions acquire a social tone.
- Therapist and patient address one another by first names.
- The therapist makes inappropriate self-disclosures to the patient.
- Hugging and other forms of touching emerge as part of the session.
- Sessions now occur at the end of the day.
- Cocktails or dinner follow the sessions.

Boundary violations, particularly when socializing occurs, can lead the therapist and patient to a sexual encounter. Although the literature has no profile of therapists inclined to engage in sexual contact with patients, it does indicate a model type: the male therapist between 40 and 50 years old whose marriage is troubled and who feels professionally burned out.

The American Psychiatric Association's Ethics Committee cautions their members that they hold a position of considerable power and sway in their patients' lives and must take precautions to keep a difficult and demanding situation within the expected therapeutic boundaries. In short, sexual involvement with a patient is both unethical and illegal. If uncertain as to how to handle a complex or confusing situation, a therapist is obliged to seek consultation from another professional, and, if necessary, to refer the patient to another professional better suited to handle this particular individual. The shame results from failing to act in a professional manner when confronted with difficult situations.

State Statutes

State statutes addressing the problem of sexual contact between professional and patient uniformly provide remedies to patients who have sexual encounters with therapists. For example, Wisconsin has statutes making sex with a current or former patient actionable for an unlimited time. Other states have statutes of limitations for complaining of such conduct. Sexual activity between therapist and patient is considered negligence per se. This means that any such contact is malpractice regardless of the condition or circumstance. The negligence per se rule creates a nonrebuttable presumption about a therapist's duty toward a patient. In court the plaintiff will need to prove that sexual contact occurred and that damage ensued.

Sexual encounters usually occur within the therapist's private office. The abuse also can occur in the inpatient setting. An Indiana case involved a 14-year-old retarded male who was sexually abused by a nurse's aide while he was a resident of the treatment facility. The boy's guardian sued the facility and the aide for compensatory and punitive damages. The aide was found to be liable for his actions; and the liability for those actions is based on the theory that all employees are accountable under law for their behavior whether licensed or not.

Hospital Liability

Numerous legal theories demonstrate the hospital's liability in addition to the individual malfeasor or tortfeasor. One such theory is the doctrine of *respondeat superior*. According to this doctrine, the hospital is *vicariously liable* for an employee's actions while performing his or her job responsibilities. A second theory of institutional liability is one of *corporate liability*. This emerging theory holds the hospital directly responsible for the safety of patients in the hospital environment. Today, it is frequently the hospital's burden to monitor and report information about impaired physicians and other licensed practitioners.

Reporting Process

Of the many possible violations of the standard of care for practitioners, sexual abuse remains among the most difficult to detect. California has created a brochure to help patients. The brochure takes the form of a code that instructs the patient about those situations that can precipitate into sexual encounters. Also, the brochure outlines the reporting process and what the complaining patient can expect to encounter after the complaint has been lodged.

Sexual misconduct entails several serious legal and ethical consequences for the violator. These include civil suit, breach of contract action, criminal sanctions, civil action for intentional torts of battery and assault, revocation or sanction of the professional license, and loss of hospital privileges. Even if a patient consents, the therapist is liable for malpractice as noted in the Wisconsin statute previously discussed. In the case of a child or adolescent, a patient's inability to offer legal consent opens the therapist to the charge of rape. Sexual misconduct devastates all involved.

Also, remember that sexual misconduct with patients is a crime in some jurisdictions. The criminality of sexual abuse is determined by one of two factors: the means of inducement to sexual activity and the age of the patient. The therapist can coerce a patient by using medication(s) and altering the patient's ability to resist unwanted advances.

Prevention of Sexual Misconduct

While vulnerable to unfounded allegations of sexual misconduct, therapists have means to protect themselves. First, a therapist must refer a patient if the therapist allows consistent boundary violations. Consultation with a trusted colleague can be a first step in this process or can result in a less drastic solution. Second, if a therapist suffers from serious personal problems, he or she must seek professional counseling. Third, health care workers on the inpatient unit must grasp their limitations in dealing with difficult or sexually provocative patients. For example, when adolescent or immature adult patients present themselves in a sexually provocative manner, the staff must be prepared to set firm and immediate limits. Any such provocations need to be documented with whatever actions the staff took to curtail them. Fourth, the hospital's policies must specifically sanction dating or other sexually toned contact with former patients in addition to the more obvious prohibitions against explicit sexual involvement.

Patients diagnosed as borderline personality disorder comprise a problematic group in regard to boundary violations and the risk of sexual involvement. These individuals characteristically idealize their therapists and exult in magnifying the importance of the therapist's role in their lives. An unwary practitioner can easily find himself or herself believing the patient's often unwarranted praise and be tempted to allow boundary violations to occur. The staff member who encounters this predicament should seek prompt consultation with a supervisor.

The following are useful guidelines for problematic patient–staff interaction:

- Conversations should occur in public areas, not in patient rooms.
- Patients must dress in a conservative, unprovocative manner.
- Staff members must not touch patients except as required by routine duties.

The media have reported on sexual abuse and harassment. Unfortunately, those in health care professions cannot avoid the risk of such accusations. While some stories are true and have assisted some in seeking help for legitimate grievances and problems, some stories serve to remind us that the innocent as well as the guilty can be accused. Rules for conduct with patients and awareness of the hazards of boundary violations help significantly to reduce the risks of exposure to unfounded accusations. Unfortunately, they do not eliminate them.

NOTES

1. B.R. Furrow and S.H. Johnson, *Health Law*, 2d ed. (St. Paul, Minn.: West Publishing, 1991), 134.

2. Furrow and Johnson, *Health Law*, 146.

3. *Dimitrijevic v. Chicago Wesley Memorial Hospital*, 236 N.E.2d 309, 92 Ill. App. 2d 251 (1968).

4. *Johnson v. Grant Hospital*, 286 N.E.2d 308 (1972).

5. Ibid.

6. Furrow and Johnson, *Health Law*, 221.

7. *Johnson*, *supra*, note 4.

8. R.I. Simon, *Psychiatry and Law for Clinicians*. (Washington, D.C.: American Psychiatric Press, 1992), 183.

9. R.I. Simon, *Clinical Psychiatry and the Law*, 2d ed. (Washington, D.C.: American Psychiatric Press, 1992), 374.

10. Simon, *Clinical Psychiatry and the Law*, 374.

11. Simon, *Clinical Psychiatry and the Law*, 374.

12. Simon, *Clinical Psychiatry and the Law*, 372.

13. Simon, *Clinical Psychiatry and the Law*, 374.

14. *Illinois Mental Health and Developmental Disabilities Code*. 1992. PA 80-1414, 2-108 (j).

15. *Illinois Mental Health and Developmental Disabilities Code*, 2-108(g).

16. *Illinois Mental Health and Developmental Disabilities Code*, 2-108(i).

17. W.L. Prosser and W.P. Keeton, *Prosser and Keeton on the Law of Torts*, 5th ed. (St. Paul, Minn.: West Publishing, 1984).

18. Furrow and Johnson, *Health Law*, 698,

19. *Wilson v. Blue Cross of Southern California*, 271 Cal. Rptr. 876, 222 Cal. App. 3d 660 (1990).

20. Ibid.

21. Simon, *Psychiatry and Law for Clinicians*, 134.

22. Simon, *Psychiatry and Law for Clinicians*, 134.

23. Simon, *Psychiatry and Law for Clinicians*, 137.

24. Simon, *Psychiatry and Law for Clinicians*, 137.

25. Simon, *Clinical Psychiatry and the Law*, 299.

26. Simon, *Clinical Psychiatry and the Law*, 301.

27. *Tarasoff v. The Regents of the University of California*, 551 P.2d 334 (1978).

28. Simon, *Clinical Psychiatry and the Law*, 299.

29. Simon, *Clinical Psychiatry and the Law*, 302.

30. *Rogers v. Okin*, 478 F. Supp. 1342 (1979).

31. Ibid.

32. *People v. Orr*, 531 N.E.2d 64 (1988).

33. Ibid.

34. Ibid.

35. Simon, *Psychiatry and Law for Clinicians*, 155.

36. P.S. Appelbaum, The Right to Refuse Treatment with Antipsychotic Medications: Retrospect and Prospect, *American Journal of Psychiatry* 145 (1988): 413–419.

BIBLIOGRAPHY

Appelbaum, P.S. 1988. The right to refuse treatment with antipsychotic medications: Retrospect and prospect. *American Journal of Psychiatry* 145:413–419.

Bednar, R. 1991. *Psychotherapy with high-risk clients, legal and professional standards*. Pacific Grove, Calif.: Brooks/Cole Publishing.

Clements, C.D., et al. May 1985. Assessment of suicide risk in patients with personality disorders and affective diagnosis. *Quality Review Bulletin*:140–153.

Fareta, G., and G.J. Grad. 1989. Special considerations in the inhospital treatment of dangerously violent juveniles. In *Juvenile Psychiatry and the Law*, eds. R. Rosner and H.I. Schwartz, St. Paul, Minn: West Publishing: 333.

Fiestra, J. 1990. *The law and liability: A guide for nurses*. 2d ed. San Diego: Delmar Publishers.

Furrow, B.R., and S.H. Johnson. 1991. *Health Law*. 2d ed. St. Paul, Minn.: West Publishing.

Goldman, M.H. August 1987. Risk focus. *Communique* 1.

Greenlaw, J., and V. Sermchief. 1990. Gonzalas and the debate over advanced nursing practice. *Law, Medicine and Health Care* 30:30–31.

Illinois Mental Health and Developmental Disabilities Code. PA-80-1414:2-102(a), 2-108(j) (1992).

Johnson v. Grant Hospital, 286 N.E. 2d 308 (1972).

Mills, M.J. 1988. The right of involuntary patients to refuse pharmacotherapy: What is reasonable? *American Academy of Psychiatric Law* 313:313–334.

Peterson, H.M. and R.B. Millman. 1989. Substance abuse juveniles. In *Juvenile Psychiatry and the Law*, eds. R. Rosner and H.I. Schwartz, New York: Plenum Press: 237.

Proctor, S.E. 1986. A developmental approach to pregnancy prevention with adolescent females. *Journal of School Health* 56:313–316.

Prosser, W.L., and W.P. Keeton. 1984. *Prosser and Keeton on the law of torts*. 5th ed. St. Paul, Minn.: West Publishing.

Reisner, R., and C. Slobogin. 1990. *Law and the mental health system*. St. Paul, Minn.: West Publishing.

Rogers v. Commerce of Department of Mental Health, 390 Mass. 489, 458 N.E. 2d 308 (1983).

Rogers v. Okin, 478 F. Supp. 1349 (1979).

Simon, R.I. 1992. *Clinical psychiatry and the law*. 2d ed. Washington, D.C.: American Psychiatric Press.

Simon, R.I. 1992. *Psychiatry and law for clinicians*. Washington, D.C.: American Psychiatric Press.

Stewart, J. 1991. Risk management in a psychiatric hospital: Wichita Falls state hospital. *Journal Quality Assurance* 22:22–24.

Strapes v. The Heritage House Childrens Center of Shelbyville, Inc. No. 41S04-8912-CV893, (Ind. Dec. 5, 1989).

Tarasoff v. Regents of the University of California, 551 P.2d 334 (1978).

Zuckermann, B.S. 1987. Mental health of adolescent mothers: The implications of depression and drug use. *Journal of Developmental Behavioral Pediatrics* 111:111–116.

chapter 32

Risk Management Issues Associated with Anesthesia

Barbara J. Youngberg

INTRODUCTION

The area of anesthesia has long been the focus of risk management concerns. Although the environment in which anesthetic is administered is usually a carefully controlled area, anesthetic agents and a patient's response to them can be unpredictable. Injuries sustained as a result of anesthetic administration and anesthesia can be serious with life-long and costly disabilities and even death. The costs of claims and thus the costs of insurance for anesthesiologists have resulted in the American Society of Anesthesiologists (ASA) being one of the first professional societies to develop and incorporate stringent proactive risk management standards that lessen the likelihood of patients suffering untoward events during the anesthetic administration. The Harvard Medical Foundation and several professional liability insurance carriers also have developed comprehensive guidelines for anesthesiologists. These guidelines address issues about:

- physical presence of anesthesiologist during anesthetic administration
- procedures during emergencies
- monitoring of patients receiving anesthetic, including regional anesthetics and conscious sedation, obstetrical anesthetic and nerve blocks, and general anesthetic recordkeeping.

Many of these standards for practice have been adopted by others and are frequently part of a hospital's clinical quality indicators developed for the review of anesthetic care provided to patients. Appendix 32-A provides examples of clinical indicators that can be used to monitor clinical care provided to patients. Also, Appendix 32-B provides examples of guidelines about the credentialing of anesthesiologists and the criteria for review of care.

ROLES OF THE ANESTHESIOLOGIST IN THE HEALTH CARE SETTING

Anesthesiologists can have several roles in the health care setting that extend beyond the operating room. In addition to providing anesthetic during surgical procedures, in many health care settings anesthesiologists also manage and control the care provided in the recovery room. Anesthesiologists also can be responsible for pain management in postoperative or terminally ill patients, who are usually admitted to an intensive care unit or to a general nursing (medical/surgical) unit.

Developing risk management strategies for the practice of anesthesiology to deal with all clinical risks, including equipment risks, is a challenging task. Given the many refinements in anesthetics and anesthesia care, the increased sophistication of equipment and monitoring devices developed for simultaneous use during anesthetic administrations, and the new developments in postoperative pain management, risk managers and anesthesiologists are constantly reviewing and refining indicators previously developed that had defined the prevalent standard of care to ensure indicators reflect current anesthetic practice. Also, the increase in the number of procedures requiring some form of anesthetic that are performed in outpatient or satellite facilities mandates that new risk areas be assessed.

RISK MANAGEMENT ISSUES IN THE OPERATING ROOM

Many allegations in malpractice cases relate to negligent administration of anesthetics or the negligent monitoring of patients under anesthesia. The difficulty in defending these cases is that often it is not provider error or negligence that has resulted in an untoward event. Rather, a patient has had an unpredictable response to the anesthetic administered. As such, even under the best quality of patient care, these untoward results have the potential to cause injury or death. The power of anesthetic agents and the often undisciplined reaction of the body's reactions to them make anesthesiologists' jobs risky and require the highest level of skill, including the use of mechanical support. Understanding what happens to a patient while under anesthesia provides comprehension of the inherent risks involved when administering anesthetics. During an operation requiring general anesthetic, a patient is sedated, paralyzed, intubated, and placed on a mechanical apparatus that assumes the breathing function. Because normal breathing is responsible for maintaining appropriate levels of oxygen in the blood and all vital body organs, when breathing disruption occurs, significant injury and death can soon follow. The responsibility of the health care professional administering general anesthetics is to ensure that an appropriate external support guarantees sufficient oxygen levels in the blood because a patient cannot self-breathe. Because there are many instances in the operating room where physicians or certified registered nurse anesthetists (CRNA) have little contact with patients after surgical procedures begin, their responsibilities to ensure appropriate patient care begin *before*

patients enter the operating room. During the procedure, the anesthesiologist relies on technology and intellect to assess the patient's well-being and response to the drugs given.

PREOPERATIVE VISIT

An important part of every anesthesiologist's job is to ensure a clear understanding of a patient's condition before any anesthetic is administered so that appropriate care can be given to the patient while under anesthesia. Reviewing the complete history and physical condition of patients and focusing on those medical factors that could influence a patient's ability to tolerate only certain anesthetics are essential components of the anesthesiologist's job. Determining the presence of any anatomic anomalies that could inhibit the ability to establish an airway is vitally important. Also, knowing if a patient has previously received anesthetics and understanding the patient's response to these administrations are important. Last, allowing patients to ask questions pertaining to how they will feel before induction, during the procedure, and after extubation is an important responsibility of the anesthesiologist. Informed patients with minimal anxieties helps ensure that patients are more relaxed and are comfortable with the person who is taking responsibility for their oxygenation during a surgical procedure. Sometimes, a patient may not want to discuss the risks of anesthesia or of anesthetic administration; these patients want minimum information. Regardless of how much information, if any, a patient wants to receive, hospitals can develop appropriate forms that allow for documentation of either participation in the informed consent or refusal to consent. Exhibit 32-1 is an example of a consent form, and Exhibit 32-2 illustrates a refusal to consent form. When a patient is resistant to information about the administration of anesthetics or anesthesia, the physician should consider whether this resistance is grounded in fear. If so, attempts to allay that fear are preferred before allowing a patient to refuse to be advised.

Exhibit 32-1
ANESTHETIC CONSENT FORM

Complete or imprint with Addressograph.

Name:_____

Room:_____

Medical Record:_____

Sex:_____ Age:_____ Physician:_____

ANESTHETIC CONSENT FORM

I _____ (patient) authorize the monitoring of vital bodily functions and the administration of anesthetics to_____ (patient or responsible party) under the direction of a staff member of the Department of Anesthesiology of_____
_____
(hospital). I have had explained to me and I agree to permit the administration of one or more of the following alternative forms of anesthetics (check all that apply) that may be suitable for the procedure I am about to have:

☐ *General Anesthetic*—including intravenous agents and inhaled gases, which will cause unconsciousness.

☐ *Regional Anesthetic*—including needle injections near major nerves, which will temporarily cause me to lose pain sensations in certain areas of my body.

☐ *Local Anesthetic*—including local anesthetic agents with or without intravenously administered sedatives.

I do not consent to the administration of _____
_____ (if no exceptions, place X on line) anesthetic. If my regional or local anesthetic is not satisfactory to me or my surgeon, I consent to the administration of general anesthetics.

I understand that during an operation, unforeseen changes in my condition can occur that would necessitate changes in the care provided to me. In that case, the anesthesiologist will act in my behalf with my safety as the first priority.

I am aware that the practice of anesthesiology is not an exact science and that no guarantees can be made about results of anesthetic administration or anesthesia. Common side effects of anesthesia include nausea and vomiting, headache, backache, sore throat or hoarseness, and soft tissue swelling. In addition, even minor surgery can have major unforeseen anesthetic risks. These risks and complications include, but are not limited to, dreams or recall of intraoperative events; corneal abrasions; damage to the mouth, teeth, or vocal cords; pneumonia; numbness; pain or paralysis; damage to veins, arteries, liver, or kidneys; adverse drug reaction; and, rarely, permanent brain damage, heart attack, stroke, or death. These potential risks apply to me whether I have a general, regional, or local anesthetic.

If I am pregnant, I understand that elective surgery should be postponed until after birth of the infant. Anesthetics cross the placenta and can temporarily anesthetize my infant. Although fetal complications of anesthesia during pregnancy are rare, the risks to my infant include, but are not limited to, birth defects, premature labor, permanent brain damage, and death.

I certify that I have to the best of my ability told the anesthesiologist obtaining consent of all major illnesses I have had, of all past anesthetics I have received and any complications of these anesthetics, of any drug allergies I have, and of all medications I have taken in the past year. Also, I have responded truthfully to any additional questions asked by the anesthesiologist.

The nature and purpose of my anesthetic and anesthesia management have been explained to me. I have had the opportunity to ask questions, and the answers and additional information provided have met with my satisfaction. I retain the right to withdraw this consent at any time before the administration of said anesthetic.

Comments:_____
_____
_____
_____

Physician:_____

Patient or Responsible Party:_____

Relationship of Responsible Party to Patient: _____

Witness:_____

Date:_____

Exhibit 32-2
REFUSAL OF CONSENT FORM

Complete or imprint with Addressograph.

Name:_____

Room:_____

Medical Record:_____

Sex:_____ Age:_____ Physician:_____

REFUSAL OF CONSENT FORM

Patient declines to be informed of anesthetic risk.

Although I have been given the opportunity to be advised of the nature, purpose, and risks of anesthetic administration and anesthesia, I decline to be so advised. No warranty or guarantee has been made about the results of anesthetic administration and anesthesia, and I fully understand that

general, regional, and local anesthetics have potential risks. I consent to the administration of anesthetics, but I refuse discussion of the specifics of such anesthetics or its risks.

Comments:_____

_____

_____

_____

_____

Physician:_____

Patient or Responsible Party:_____

Relationship of Responsible Party to Patient:_____

Witness:_____

Date:_____

ROLE OF THE ANESTHESIOLOGIST IN THE RECOVERY ROOM

In the recovery room, anesthesiologists often are responsible for assessing patients' readiness to be extubated or to be discharged to a general nursing unit such as a medical/surgical unit. Policies and procedures about patient management during the postanesthetic period should be developed jointly by the anesthesiology and nursing staff. They should address issues about assessment, monitoring, and discharge to a nursing unit.

Initial respiratory assessment should include:

- patient's level of consciousness on arriving in the recovery room
- patient's ability to take spontaneous breaths
- character and rate of these respirations
- ability to protect the airway (determined by presence of the gag reflex)
- patient's ability to sustain normal breathing.

Also, initial vital signs should be documented to establish a normal baseline. Intraoperative blood loss and blood replacement should be reviewed with the anesthesiologist or surgeon because excessive blood loss could inhibit a

patient from maintaining acceptable oxygenation. The assessment at discharge always should consider that after a patient leaves the recovery room area, he or she probably will be returned to a nursing unit (such as the medical/surgical unit). Thus, the patient will not have continuous monitoring of vital signs by health care professionals; if respiratory function decreases or level of consciousness diminishes, the patient could ultimately experience respiratory arrest.

Issues about monitoring of patients should specify when the use of certain monitoring devices should be implemented. Ensuring that recovery room staff receive proper education about using and troubleshooting monitoring devices is essential. Monitoring devices have the potential to cause harm, particularly if staff use another device and then misinterpret the information provided by the "substituted" device.

Although recovery room nurses are frequently the health care professionals who do the initial assessment of a patient's wakefulness and the ability to ventilate adequately, it is usually the responsibility of the anesthesiologist or CRNA to write the order discharging the patient from the recovery room. Thus, anesthesiologists and CRNAs must consider all assessment parameters that would support a patient's ability to cough, deep breathe, and, in general, to maintain an adequate and appropriate level of oxygenation after the patient returns to the nursing unit.

PAIN MANAGEMENT ON GENERAL NURSING UNITS

Managing a patient's pain after surgical procedures or when a patient's condition requires a continuous infusion of medication to ensure comfort presents many challenges for the anesthesiologist and for the nurse directly involved in the care of the patient. With the advent of the patient-controlled analgesic pump (PCA), patients now can manage their own pain by pushing a button that dispenses a dose of analgesic (usually morphine). Because this drug acts very quickly when administered intravenously, the patient receives almost immediate relief from pain. Also, because the effect is immediate compared with the time of waiting for an injection, the patient's pain does not reach the level where it becomes increasingly difficult to control.

Although this device has many benefits for patients, it is not without risk. Initially, the physician (often the anesthesiologist) will be asked to assess a patient to determine if he or she is an appropriate candidate for the use of the PCA pump. The patient's level of consciousness, ability to understand procedures for administration, prior responses to morphine or other analgesics, and patient's ability to use the hands to depress the machine buttons obviously must be considered. The physician's initial order must include the:

- initial dose of the drug to be given
- incremental dose the patient self-administers when experiencing pain
- maximum amount of medication the patient can self-administer over a specified period ("lockout" period)
- maximum amount given over a six-hour period.

Further, the hospital may have a policy that mandates physician's renewal of the order for PCA every 24 hours.

As a general policy, any unit that cares for patients on PCA pumps should educate all nurses about the signs and symptoms of patients who may be adversely reacting to the drug or for whom a cumulative effect of the drug seems to be causing neurological or respiratory depression. Whenever possible, patients controlling their own analgesics should be placed in an area that is easily accessible to the nurses' station or in a room that provides constant monitoring. An antagonist such as naloxone must be available, and nurses must know the current dosage and must have standing orders to administer it immediately if a patient's condition deteriorates.

In addition, problems with the use of PCA pumps have been identified when a patient has only one intravenous line and receives, in addition to the pain controlling drug, other regularly scheduled drugs (for example, postoperative antibiotics). When only one line exists, usually the nurse will "piggy-back" the additional medication into the patient's main intravenous line. If this additional drug is plugged into a port over the site where the pain-controlling drug is being infused, the patient can receive a bolus of the analgesic, causing sudden deterioration in respiratory status or level of consciousness. If supplemental drugs are to be given, the hospital may insert a heparin-locked line or add a connector to the main intravenous line, which has a port immediately above the intravenous insertion site. This would prevent any risk of the patient suddenly overdosing on analgesic when additional medications are received.

Further, some hospitals mandate that patients who control their own analgesics must also be monitored with pulse oximetry and ECG or apnea monitors. This practice allows for more careful monitoring of a patient's level of oxygenation, but adds greater responsibility to the health care professionals involved in the care of such patients. In other words, placing pulse oximetry on patients only measures the oxygenation level, and without a professional observing and reacting to these measurements, these devices have minimum benefit.

ROLE OF THE CERTIFIED REGISTERED NURSE ANESTHETIST (CRNA)

Certified registered nurse anesthetists (CRNA) are professional members of the anesthesiology team. Generally, these professionals are registered nurses who undertake additional study to work under the supervision of a board certified anesthesiologist to deliver anesthetic care. Although these professionals are highly skilled and trained, in most instances they work under the supervision of the physician–anesthesiologist. Hospitals using the services of CRNAs should have established protocols for these professionals that clearly delineate their clinical privileges and that accurately define the extent of supervision deemed appropriate. Generally, it is also prudent to provide liability insurance for the CRNA (or to require that CRNAs provide their own insurance) in the same limits required of the physician–anesthesiologist. The care provided by CRNAs to patients must be reviewed in the same manner as that provided by physicians.

EQUIPMENT ISSUES COMMON TO ANESTHESIOLOGY

As early as 1986, the ASA and the Harvard Medical Foundation agreed that certain devices used to track a patient's response to intraoperative anesthetics could be added to the list of previously accepted monitors. In 1986, standards and recommendations about the use of both end tidal CO_2 monitoring and pulse oximetry were provided. These devices would serve a proactive function and help anesthesiologists recognize gradual decreases in patients' levels of blood oxygenation and the possibility of ventilator disconnects. At that time, some of the standards were met with criticism by those who believed that the recommended "standards of practice" would add to the cost of anesthetic administration without improving on the safety. Since 1986, additional devices have been developed and are periodically recommended.

Much equipment has been developed to support not only the patient's ventilatory status during anesthetic administration but also to monitor the functions of the equipment and a patient's response. Naturally, equipment has certain advantages. However, practitioners should remember that costly and technologically advanced equipment can never replace the assessment and diligence of health care professionals when observing and providing care.

Risk management issues involving equipment have been addressed by many organizations, and suggestions for maintenance and preprocedure checkout have been developed. The Federal Food and Drug Administration (FDA) has developed specific guidelines for checking anesthetic equipment before use. These guidelines are provided in Appendix 32-C. Similar protocols should be developed internally by hospitals with concurrence of biomedical safety, risk management, and operating room and anesthesiology staff. Obviously, any problems related to equipment that result in patient injury need careful investigation, and the equipment must be removed from service if found to be defective. Reports under the Safe Medical Devices Act may also need to be completed. (See Appendix 24-C.)

When assessing the need to purchase equipment to support patients receiving anesthetics, hospital administration should ask the question, "Is the device or equipment going to enhance the professionals' ability to provide safe and competent care, or will it increase the distance of caregivers from patients, potentially minimizing caregivers' responsibility to assess and control care accurately?" If the answer to this question identifies the desire to further remove caregivers from patients, the purchase decision should be reevaluated.

ADDITIONAL SAFETY PRECAUTIONS WITH PEDIATRIC ANESTHESIA

Anesthesiology professionals who work with children are confronted with greater risks compared with those working with adults. The narrower margin for error due to differences in oxygen consumption, carbon dioxide production, fluid requirements, as well as risks of hypothermia, laryngospasm, and rapid desaturation, demand heightened awareness of anesthesiologists or CRNAs to avert anesthesia-related accidents in children.

Initially, consideration should be given to the special needs of pediatric patients undergoing anesthesia. A range of equipment in various sizes for securing airways, suctioning, and ventilating neonates, infants, or children is essential in both the operating room and recovery room. Proper calculation of pediatric drug doses also must be ensured through pediatric unit dose systems for commonly used drugs. A chart of pediatric drug doses for emergency resuscitation should be available in the recovery room area, especially if adult and pediatric patients receive care in the same area.

Specific Clinical Issues

Pediatric patients are often a greater risk for injury because some specific physiologic characteristics inherent in pediatric patients (primarily neonates and infants) heighten the potential for risk.

First, infants and children are at a disadvantage when it comes to defense against heat loss. As a general rule, infants and children cannot sustain body temperatures as well as adults in cold environments. This problem can be compounded by the higher ratio of surface area to body weight, resulting in greater heat loss through the skin. Premature infants are more vulnerable to heat loss, and the problems associated with this situation require higher environmental temperatures to maintain normothermia. In the operating room, the anesthesiologist generally measures "core" temperatures. These temperatures can be less sensitive to hypothermia than axillary or skin temperatures when a temperature change will register earliest. Early detection of hyperthermia provides the opportunity to intervene, preventing further heat loss and potential patient harm.

For surgical procedures involving limited surgical field exposure, conservative means of addressing heat loss can be used. This can include using warm blankets, wrapping extremities, and keeping the surgical suite slightly warmer than usual. In major surgical cases where there may be prolonged body cavity exposure to the environment, the anesthesiologist can consider heated humidification systems "in-lined" into the ventilator breathing circuit and to the blood traversing the pulmonary circulation. Obviously, the surgeon and the anesthesiologist should discuss matters about the appropriate body temperature and the methods used to maintain that temperature.

Providing anesthetic to premature neonates poses an additional challenge. In addition to knowledge about the transitional circulation found in the full-term newborn, an understanding of pulmonary circulation is particularly important when caring for critically ill neonates or preterm infants who can revert to a fetal circulatory pattern when pulmonary vascular resistance increases, accompanied by acidosis, hypercarbia, and hypoxemia. Anesthesiologists play vital roles in ensuring adequate pulmonary blood flow through the intraoperative choice of anesthetic agents, proper fluid management, and appropriate ventilator settings that control the rate, volume, and pattern of respirations. Documentation of special care taken to reduce the risk to an infant is helpful if problems develop.

Airway Concerns

More than half of deaths related to anesthetic administration are attributed to airway-related problems such as failure to ventilate adequately, esophageal intubation, ventilator disconnects, or failure to supply adequate amounts of oxygen into the ventilator circuitry causing accidental extubations. Many of these problems are preventable and can be controlled by using special alarm systems and other devices. Children present additional airway concerns.

First, the tongue of an infant is relatively large and occupies considerable space in the mouth and oropharynx, making intubation difficult. The larynx of infants and small children is high and anterior, with the narrowest portion of the airway in the cricoid region, which is nonexpandable. Last, the distance between the bifurcation of the trachea and the vocal cords in infants is not greater than 4–5 centimeters. Confirmation of correct tracheal tube placement needs to be verified and documented not only by auscultation but also by direct observation of chest examination during ventilation, a persistent humidified "flash" in the tracheal tube, and capnography when in doubt.

Mask ventilation in children needs to be accomplished with minimal encroachment on the soft tissue of the submental area; pressure here only displaces the soft tissue of the oral cavity closer to the palate, worsening intraoral obstruction.

Hospitals should consider delineating privileges for those providing anesthetics to both adults and children to include evidence of specialty training for those who care for children and neonates. Also, nurses working in recovery rooms not designated as areas for pediatric care should be provided with additional education to help them identify and respond to pediatric airway and respiratory emergencies.

AUTOMATED ANESTHESIA RECORDS

Considerable discussion exists about the value of automating all records that are part of a patient's surgical experience. In part, a fully automated system would provide an accurate chronological diary of the care given to a patient undergoing anesthetic administration and anesthesia as well as the patient's response to that care. Although the decision to fully automate recordkeeping during anesthesia can assist the risk manager in preparing a better defense in support of care provided, it offers another advantage: allowing the physician or CRNA to spend more time with a patient because less time is required in fulfilling cumbersome recording requirements.

Because the cost of these systems can be prohibitive, risk managers, physicians, administration, and quality professionals may want to analyze the current recording protocol within the organization. Also, they should attempt to identify the potential for problems, intermediary steps that could help to eliminate problems, and the benefits that could be achieved through an automated system.

IMPORTANCE OF DOCUMENTATION

Regardless of the system used in a health care setting that provides comprehensive documentation, anesthesiologists and other health care professionals should be aware of the heightened level of importance that documentation assumes for their specialty. Patients under anesthesia often react quickly to specific medications given to them. The need to create a chronological record that describes accurately the agents administered, the time each was administered, and the response that the patient had to the agent or intervention is critical to gaining an accurate understanding of the care provided. Periodic and regular assessments that describe the patient's condition and appropriate oxygenation help substantiate the anesthesiologist's consistent involvement in the care of the patient and attention so that quality of patient care is not compromised. Rapid intervention when assessments suggest a change in condition or a potential problem should also contain the time of intervention and the patient's response to that intervention. Documentation of a follow-up visit where an absence of complications is noted also demonstrates the anesthesiologist's continued concern and involvement in the patient's care. Exhibit 32-3 provides some suggestions for documentation that could assist in defending the care provided to a patient should such a defense be necessary.

Exhibit 32-3
DOCUMENTATION TIPS

To avoid allegations of negligence relative to the delivery of anesthetic, the following risk management recommendations should be considered.

1. Documentation of *preoperative* visit will be included in all patients' medical records. This document will include (at a minimum) the following:
   - review of results of preoperative studies
   - review of medical record and patient history
   - patient's medications and allergies
   - anesthetic history
   - review of physical status
   - anesthetic plan
   - ASA physical status
   - patient's consent to anesthetic
   - patient's current weight (necessary for correct calculation of drugs to be used).
2. Documentation of *intraoperative* management and monitoring of patients receiving general, regional, or monitored anesthetic care will include (at a minimum) the following:
   - monitoring of blood pressure, heart rate, ECG, pulse oximetry

   - dosage of all drugs and agents used and the time they were administered
   - type and amount of all fluids and blood products
   - description of techniques used
   - unusual events during anesthesia period
   - status of patient at conclusion of anesthesia.
3. Documentation of *postoperative* evaluation and patient's condition in the recovery room will include (at a minimum) the following:
   - documentation of vital signs and level of consciousness with times noted
   - intravenous fluids administered, including blood and blood products
   - all drugs administered with time and route of administration noted
   - any unusual events
   - no patient discharged with score <8 on Aldrete 10-point scoring sheet.
4. Documentation of anesthesiologist's postoperative visit occurring within 24 hours postoperatively will include assessment of patient's respiratory status and any complaints or concerns voiced by the patient, with a plan for how these complaints or concerns will be addressed.

USE OF INTRAVENOUS CONSCIOUS SEDATION

With an increasing number of procedures being done in a same-day surgical facility or outpatient facility, different techniques have been developed to help control the discomfort experienced by patients and the movement of patients that could impede a physician's ability to perform a specific procedure. Guidelines for the use of intravenous conscious sedation are found in Exhibit 32-4. Various drugs used singly or in combination are administered to patients to allay apprehension, supplement the analgesia induced by a local block, and provide a relatively quiet and controlled surgical field. By definition, conscious sedation is a minimally depressed level of consciousness that retains a patient's ability to maintain a patent airway independently and continuously and to respond appropriately to physical stimulation and/or verbal command. Although great value lies in the use of conscious sedation, the sedatives and analgesics used to provide conscious sedation have the ability to depress respiration to the point of airway obstruction or apnea. In other words, the optimum level of sedation can be exceeded or a patient can respond differently than anticipated to usual doses of drugs. Hypercapnia and hypoxemia

can ensue, and if unrecognized can potentially necessitate cardiopulmonary resuscitation. Seizures can result from local anesthetic toxicity and necessitate control of both seizures and ventilation. In some settings where conscious sedation is used, anesthesiologists are not present or readily available. When this is the case, careful policies and procedures should be developed for assessing patients and responding to emergencies. Also, all professional staff should receive education and in-service training about the drugs being used, their side effects, antagonists that can reverse the action of the drugs, and appropriate interventions should conscious sedation progress to deep sedation. An emergency cart or kit must be readily accessible and should include the drugs and equipment necessary to resuscitate a nonbreathing and unconscious patient and to provide continuous support until the patient is transported to a location where more definitive care can be given. A defibrillator must be available promptly. There must be documentation that all emergency equipment and drugs are checked and maintained on a scheduled basis.

Any patients receiving intravenous conscious sedation should be attended by at least two health care professionals—one performing the procedure (usually a physician or dentist) and the other a health care professional (generally

Exhibit 32-4
MINIMUM GUIDELINES FOR USE OF INTRAVENOUS CONSCIOUS SEDATION

- All health care professionals who are not from the anesthesiology department but who give agents used in conscious sedation will have Advanced Cardiac Life Support (ACLS) certification.
- All locations within the hospital or outpatient facilities where intravenous conscious sedation is administered will have full resuscitation equipment immediately available and the ability to ventilate patients with 100% O_2 and positive pressure.
- Except in designated special procedure areas, the medications cannot be administered by the individual performing the procedure.
- Monitoring of patients receiving intravenous conscious sedation will consist of, at minimum, an ECG, noninvasive blood pressure, and pulse oximetry obtained at least every five minutes. This monitoring will be performed by a registered nurse.
- Anesthesiology personnel will be available to respond to an emergency, at which time the case may be canceled and rescheduled for a later date with monitored anesthetic care, as indicated.
- Anesthesiology consultations will be requested at least 24 hours in advance of the procedure and will be done on all patients considered at risk.
- Patients will be provided with information about the risks/benefits of this anesthetic administration and the resulting anesthesia. This discussion and patients' consent will be documented.

a nurse) trained to monitor appropriate physiologic variables. Except with very light sedation, heart rate, respiratory rate, and oxygen saturation should be monitored continuously and recorded at least every ten minutes. A pulse oximeter is the minimum equipment to be available for use. A patient's color judged from appropriately exposed sites (e.g., nailbeds or oral mucosa) should be monitored visually on a continuous basis. Any restraint devices should allow exposure of sufficient sites for monitoring. The position of the head should be maintained to ensure a patent airway, and the patient should be checked for verbal responses repeatedly. At no time should a sedated person be left unattended.

The patient can be discharged from the facility after the procedure and does not need to be transferred to a special recovery area, provided cardiovascular and respiratory stability are ensured, the patient is alert, can sit unaided, and can ambulate with minimal assistance. The patient should be discharged to a responsible person who has been advised

of potential evidence of respiratory or neurologic depression. Guidelines such as those provided in Appendix 32-D are helpful in developing policies and procedures for caring for patients receiving sedation or anesthesia in the ambulatory care setting.

CONCLUSION

The practice of anesthesiology has received considerable attention by both professional societies, quality assurance professionals, and risk managers. Many proactive strategies have been developed to address issues of both potential risk and actual risk when patients are receiving anesthetics and while they are under anesthesia. Recent advancements in anesthesiology and changes in where anesthetic services are provided to patients may force many health care organizations to reevaluate policies and procedures to ensure that current issues and risks are being addressed.

Appendix 32-A

Indicators for Monitoring Clinical Anesthesiology Practice

The following indicators could be indicative of quality/risk problems in anesthesiology. It is recommended that when the following indicators are present that care be reviewed to ensure compliance with acceptable standards.

Aspect of Care	Indicator
Epidural Analgesic (postoperative)	Incidence of pruritus, nausea, vomiting, urinary retention, respiratory depression
	Incidence of inadequate analgesia
	Epidural catheter related to infection
	Incidence of hemodynamic events related to epidural local analgesics or epinephrine
	Cerebral spinal fluid leak
	*Peripheral nerve deficit after epidural catheter placement
Narcotics Usage	Oversedation requiring naloxone reversal
Equipment Problems	*Failure of ventilator or monitor
Spinal Anesthetic	Incomplete anesthesia
	Bleeding or hematoma at insertion site
	Two or more attempts at insertion
	Spinal headache
	*Peripheral nerve deficit
Airway Management	*Unplanned extubation
	*Traumatic dental injury to airway
	*Endobronchial intubation
	*Inability to intubate trachea
	Reintubation for respiratory insufficiency
Circulatory Management	Transient dysrhythmia
	Hypotension (systolic blood pressure less than 85 mm Hg for >30 minutes)
	Sustained hypertension (blood pressure increases >30% above preoperative level for >30 minutes)
	Hypothermia (<35°C in recovery room)

---

*Indicators that typically cause both risk management and quality problems.

464

Ventilation Management

Hypoxia/hypoxemia (O_2 saturation drops >10% from baseline)
  during anesthesia
*Aspiration during induction
*Aspiration after extubation
  Bronchospasm during induction persisting >2 minutes
  Pulmonary edema within 72 hours after anesthetic administration
*New onset aspiration pneumonia within 72 hours
  Laryngospasm requiring reintubation

Neurologic Changes

*Venous air embolism
  Seizure
*Coma
*Postoperative central nervous system complications
*Postoperative peripheral nerve damage

Traumatic Injury

  Ocular injury
*Electrocautery burn
*Position injury

Miscellaneous Aspects

  Parotid gland swelling <72 hours postoperative
  Bacterial pneumonia related to inadequate pulmonary toilet
  Patient injury during transport
  Delay in receiving blood products
  Prolonged length of stay in recovery room:
  —general anesthetic, >2 hours
  —epidural/spinal anesthetic, >3 hours

Appendix 32-B

Guidelines for Anesthesiologists: Credentialing and Review of Care

The following four guidelines should be considered when developing a proactive risk management program that seeks to control liabilities associated with anesthesiology practice.

1. *Credentialing of Anesthesiologists, CRNAs, Staff.* All persons providing anesthetics within the hospital or its satellites will be allowed to practice in a manner consistent with other attending medical staff. This applies to contract physicians and CRNAs, locum tenens staff, and all attending anesthesiologists.
2. *Presence of Anesthesiologist.* A person credentialed to administer anesthetics shall be physically present in the operating room with patients during the entire administration of general or regional anesthetics. If a CRNA or physician trained in the administration of anesthetics is primarily responsible for care, an anesthesiologist will be available by telephone and readily available if problems occur that require the physical presence of an anesthesiologist.
3. *Advanced Certification.* Advanced Cardiac Life Support (ACLS) certification is recommended for all professionals administering anesthetics.
4. *Review of Care.* A multidisciplinary review will occur whenever questions arise about whether anesthetic administration was responsible for or contributed to a patient's injury or death. This review will be given the same protection as that given to other hospital peer review activities.

Federal Food and Drug Administration Equipment Checkout Procedures

Anesthesia Apparatus Checkout Recommendations

This checkout, or a reasonable equivalent, should be conducted before administering anesthetics. Users are encouraged to modify the following 24 guidelines to accommodate differences in equipment design and variations in local clinical practice. Such modifications should have appropriate peer review. Users should refer to operators' manuals for special procedures or precautions.

*1. Inspect anesthetic machine for:
  —Machine identification number.
  —Valid inspection sticker.
  —Undamaged flowmeters, vaporizers, gauges, supply hoses, complete undamaged breathing systems with adequate CO_2 absorbent.
  —Correct mounting of cylinders in yokes.
  —Presence of cylinder wrench.

*2. Inspect and turn on:
  -Electrical equipment requiring warmup (e.g., ECG/pressure monitor, oxygen monitor).

*3. Connect waste gas scavenging system:
  —Adjust vacuum as required.

*4. Check that:
  —Flow control valves are off.
  —Vaporizers are off.
  —Vaporizers are filled (not overfilled).
  —Filler cans are sealed tightly.
  —CO_2 absorber bypass (if any) is off.

*5. Check oxygen (O_2) cylinder supplies:
  —Disconnect pipeline supply (if connected) and return cylinder and pipeline pressure gauges to zero with O_2 flush valve.
  —Open O_2 cylinder; check pressure; close cylinder; and observe gauge for evidence of high-pressure leak:
  —With the O_2 flush valve, flush to empty piping.

  —Repeat the above for the second O_2 cylinder, if present.
  —Replace any cylinder less than 600 psig (at least one cylinder should be nearly full).
  —Open cylinder that is less full.

*6. Turn off master switch (if present).

*7. Check nitrous oxide (N_2O) and other gas cylinder supplies:
  —Use same procedure as previously described in 5 above, but open and *close* flow control valve to empty piping.
  —*Note*: N_2O pressure below 745 psig indicates cylinder is less than ¼ full.

*8. Test flowmeters:
  —Check that float is at bottom of tube with flow control valves closed.

*9. Test ration protection/warning system (if present):
  —Attempt to create hypoxic O_2/N_2O mixture, and verify correct change in gas flows and/or alarms.

*10. Test O_2 pressure failure system:
  -Set O_2 and other gas flows to midrange.
  —Close O_2 cylinder and flush to release O_2 pressure.
  —Verify that all flows fall to zero; open O_2 cylinder.
  —Close all other cylinders and bleed piping pressures.
  —Close O_2 cylinder and bleed piping pressure.
  —*Close flow control valves*.

*11. Test central pipeline gas supplies:
  —Inspect supply hoses (should not be cracked or worn).
  —Connect supply hoses, verifying correct color coding.
  —Adjust all flows to at least midrange.
  —Verify that supply pressures hold 45–55 psig.
  —Shut off flow control valves.

*12. Add any accessory equipment to the breathing system:

---

*If an anesthetist uses the same machine in successive cases, the steps marked with asterisks(*) do not need to be repeated or can be abbreviated after the initial checkout.

—Add PEEP valve, humidifier, and so forth if they could be used (if necessary remove after step 18 until needed).

13. Calibrate O_2 monitor:
   —*Calibrate O_2 monitor to read 21% in room air.
   —*Test low alarm.
   —Occlude breathing system at patient end; fill and empty system several times with 100% O_2.
   —Check that monitor reading is nearly 100%.

14. Sniff inspiratory gas: there should be no odor.

*15. Check unidirectional valves:
   —Inhale and exhale through a surgical mask into the breathing system (each limb individually, if possible).
   —Verify unidirectional flow in each limb.
   —Reconnect tubing firmly.

†16. Test for leaks in machine and breathing system:
   —Close APL (pop-off) valve and occlude system at patient end.
   —Fill system via O_2 flush until bag just full but negligible pressure in system. Set O_2 flow to 5 L/minute.
   —Slowly decrease O_2 flow until pressure *no longer rises* above about 20 cm H_2O. Approximate total leak rate should be no greater than a few hundred mL/minute (less for closed circuit techniques).
   —*CAUTION:* Check valves in some machines; make it imperative to measure flow in the final step above when pressure *just stops rising.*
   —Squeeze bag to pressure of about 50 cm H_2O, and verify that system is tight.

17. Exhaust valve and scavenger system:
   —Open APL valve and observe release of pressure.
   —Occlude breathing system at patient end and verify that negligible positive or negative pressure appears with either zero or 5 L/minute flow and exhaust relief valve (if present) opens with flush flow.

18. Test ventilator:
   —If switching valve is present, test function in both bag and ventilator mode.
   —Close APL valve if necessary and occlude system at patient end.
   —Test for leaks and pressure relief by appropriate cycling (exact procedure will vary with type of ventilator).
   —Attach reservoir bag at mask fitting, fill system and cycle ventilator. Assure filling/emptying of bag.

19. Check for appropriate level of patient suction.

20. Check, connect, and calibrate other electronic monitors.

21. Check final position of all controls.

22. Turn on and set other appropriate alarms for all equipment to be used.

23. Set O_2 monitor alarm limits.

24. Set airway pressure and/or volume monitor alarm limits (if adjustable).

---

*If an anesthetist uses the same machine in successive cases, the steps marked with asterisks(*) do not need to be repeated or can be abbreviated after the initial checkout.

†A vaporizer leak can only be detected if the vaporizer is turned on during this test. Even then, a relatively small but clinically significant leak may still be obscured.

Guidelines for Sedation in Ambulatory Settings

POLICY

Increasing numbers of patients are being cared for in hospitals' ambulatory settings for diagnostic and therapeutic procedures. Many patients require sedatives, hypnotics, or general anesthetics to undergo such procedures. The safe use of sedation requires appropriate assessment, rational use of drugs, and appropriate care afterward.

PROCEDURES

Levels of Sedation

The following levels of sedation are considered:

- *Conscious sedation* is a minimally depressed level of consciousness that retains the patient's ability to maintain a patent airway independently and continuously and to respond appropriately to physical stimulation or verbal command.
- *Deep sedation* is a controlled state of depressed consciousness or unconsciousness from which the patient is not easily aroused, which may be accompanied by a partial or complete loss of protective reflexes including the ability to maintain a patent airway independently and respond purposefully to physical stimulation or verbal command.

Urgency of Procedure

The urgency of the procedure is considered based on the following definitions:

- *Elective.* Whenever feasible, procedures should be done when conditions are optimal for patient care. The most important factor is the probability that the patient's condition will worsen with delay; other factors involve the availability to key personnel, equipment, and facilities.

- *Emergency.* In some circumstances, diagnostic or therapeutic intervention is required immediately to provide for the patient's safety or comfort. Frequently, sedation and/or potent analgesic is necessary for primary pain relief during diagnostic or therapeutic procedures performed in an emergent or urgent basis. The risks and benefits of sedation/analgesia must be considered on an individual basis. Typically, the following factors should be considered:
  —Urgency of the need for analgesia.
  —Level of sedation required.
  —Risks inherent to providing sedation.
  —Risks associated with delay in therapy.

As examples, high dose IV narcotics are indicated for pain relief early in the evaluation and treatment of renal colic, while anesthetic for the repair of flexor tendon lacerations of the hand could reasonably be delayed to optimize total patient care.

NPO (Nothing by Mouth) Status—General Guidelines

Ideally, a patient should not have a full stomach if sedation sufficient to place the patient at risk for aspiration of gastric contents is to be given. The following guidelines are considered:

a. Elective—either conscious or deep
  - Adults and children over three years should be NPO for eight hours before elective procedures.
  - Children three years of age and younger can have clear liquids up to six hours before procedures.
b. Emergencies
  - *Conscious.* In an emergency, drugs given to relieve pain should be provided at doses that preserve the upper airway and respiratory effort. The patient should be monitored so timely intervention can be provided if sedation deeper than intended occurs.
  - *Deep sedation/general anesthetic.* The risks and benefits of the procedure, including the anesthetic

technique, should be documented in the medical record.

c. Concurrent Medications

Cardiac, antihypertensive, steroidal drugs, and other concurrent medications should be given by mouth with a sip (15–30 milliliters) of water no less than one hour before the procedure.

Equipment Immediately Available

- oxygen
- oxygen saturation monitor
- bag and mask, oral airways, laryngoscope, endotracheal tubes suction
- emergency drugs necessary for cardiopulmonary resuscitation
- intravenous line in place for patients receiving deep sedation.

Monitoring

1. During the procedure, vital signs (blood pressure, pulse rate, respiratory rate, and oxygenation saturation) should be monitored and recorded as part of the permanent record to document care.
2. The person performing the procedure must **not** be the person evaluating the patient's response to the drugs. The monitoring individual should have training in the evaluations of patients who are receiving sedative and hypnotic drugs. His or her primary responsibility should be the monitoring of the patient.
3. In the course of intravenous conscious sedation, the patient must be responsive to verbal stimuli at all times. If the patient becomes unresponsive to verbal command, he or she has entered deep sedation. Such an individual should receive appropriate airway management.

Guidelines for Drug Use

1. Special care should be taken to administer drugs in small increments with adequate time to assess the level of consciousness. The drugs involved include barbiturates, benzodiazepines, opiates, and dissociation agents.
2. At no time shall a sedated patient be left unattended.

Recovery and Discharge

1. The primary physician/dentist responsible for the procedure becomes responsible for determining that the patient is ready for discharge to a hospital room, recovery area, or home accompanied by a responsible adult.
2. Patients who have sedation should be given the post-sedation introductions.
3. Generally, patients should be able to ambulate (if ambulatory before the procedure and no surgical contraindications exist) and take fluids before being allowed to leave the hospital.
4. Any patient leaving the hospital should be discharged to a responsible adult and assisted in transport. The responsible adult should sign the post-sedation guide form acknowledging responsibility for patient at discharge.
5. A discharge note should be written, including condition of patient at discharge.

POST-SEDATION INSTRUCTIONS

The medications given today for your procedure will remain in your body for some time. You may feel dizzy or lose your sense of balance, your fine muscle control may be changed, and your judgment will be affected. Your reaction time, such as in driving a car, will be slowed. You may not recognize any of these changes. For your safety we have some strict instructions:

1. Do **not** *drive*.
2. Do **not** use potentially *dangerous appliances or equipment* (stove, lawn mower, garbage disposal).
3. Be alert to any *dizziness*—move slowly, take your time, and remember that sudden position changes can cause nausea.
4. Do **not** make any important *decisions*—you may change your mind tomorrow.
5. Do **not** drink *alcoholic beverages*—the drugs can cause your reaction to alcohol to be dangerous.
6. If you have **any** questions, *ask your physician*, _____ who can be reached at _____.
7. Do **not** eat if you feel nauseated or sick to your stomach; remain on clear liquids and soft foods today.
8. Be sure and ask your physician about taking or continuing any medications.

You should be completely recovered from these medications by tomorrow.

Signature of Responsible Adult:_____

chapter 33

Risk Management Issues in the Emergency Department

Paul A. Craig

INTRODUCTION

Most of the general risk management issues in the emergency department (ED) affect virtually all EDs, regardless of size or sophistication, and occur because of the essential nature of emergency medicine. Patients are usually acutely stressed and some face life-threatening crises. Information flow is frequently limited in context of the ED; the staff rarely have a preexisting relationship with patients and treatment decisions frequently must be made with minimum or no knowledge of patients' prior medical history. The scope of treatment is usually limited to acute care, whether it involves a prescription for sore throat, a stitch and a bandage, or intubation and thoracotomy. Follow-up care is limited or frequently nonexistent.

Many of the particular issues in ED risk management arise out of the relative position each ED occupies in the health care system or community network. Each level of specialization and each level of participation in paramedic systems and trauma networks present certain unique risk management considerations. The basic community ED, the paramedic resource hospital ED, the trauma center ED, and the teaching hospital ED each face risk management problems particular to the level of care the hospital has elected to provide. These particular problems are dictated, at least in part, by the ED's structural relation to other providers, other departments, and other agencies or institutions.

This chapter concentrates on the risk management issues that can be generalized across the levels of care and strata of community participation. It begins with an overview of basic structural issues concerning staff credentials, documentation, and chart reviews common to all EDs. The chapter then walks through various risk management issues in the sequence encountered by the ED patient, from the initial triage examination though admission, transfer, or discharge. This is followed by a discussion of infection control issues and a brief discussion of particular risk management issues inherent to specialized EDs: paramedic resource hospitals and trauma centers.

Although there are several issues related to the security and safety of patients and staff in the ED due to the threat of violence and the types of patients frequently cared for in the ED, this subject was previously discussed in Chapter 27 so will not be discussed again in this chapter.

BASIC STRUCTURAL CONSIDERATIONS/STAFF CREDENTIALS AND DOCUMENTATION

Emergency departments, from urban trauma centers to rural community hospitals, are often the stages for unpredictable human events. Adequate ED intervention requires the response of qualified health care providers. The Joint Commission on Accreditation of Healthcare Organizations (Joint Commission) creates three levels of EDs and requires that hospitals classify themselves from Level I (comprehensive, with at least one physician experienced in emergency medicine on duty 24 hours a day) to Level III (with a physician from the staff roster available within 30 minutes).[1] This chapter assumes the comprehensive Level I ED as the standard model. Although the board-certified ED physician is becoming a regular sight, there are still wide variations in emergency medical and emergency nursing credentials across the country among Level I EDs.

It is recommended that ED physicians be board certified in emergency medicine. At a minimum, all ED physicians must have experience and training in a specialty relevant to emergency care and should be certified in Advanced Cardiac Life Support (ACLS). Advanced Trauma Life Support (ATLS) certification or other advanced airway and trauma resuscitation training is recommended for ED physicians who have not been trained through emergency medicine residencies. Medical directors of EDs should be board certified in emergency medicine.

Further, it is recommended that all ED nurses be ACLS certified. ED nurses should have regular in-service programs covering general topics in emergency nursing, and nurses should be encouraged to obtain specialty certification in emergency nursing.

In the often hectic pace of EDs, chart documentation is usually neglected and scantily performed at best. An effective ongoing risk management and quality assurance program requires regular focused chart audits to promote diligence in documentation. In a similar vein, regular monitoring of emergency equipment checks is necessary to ensure Joint Commission compliance. A standing departmental in-service program should be established to highlight the results of chart audits and monitoring of incident reporting. Problems identified through this process should become the focus of quality improvement activities. Exhibit 33-1 provides a list of indicators typically monitored in the emergency department that could give rise to quality improvement activities.

Exhibit 33-1
INDICATORS TO MONITOR EMERGENCY DEPARTMENT PRACTICE

- Patient seen in emergency room who has either been discharged from the hospital or seen in the emergency department within the past week. *Exception:* Condition on previous encounter well documented with instructions to return at a specified interval or for a specified reason.
- Patient discharged or admitted to hospital without being seen by a physician.
- Patient arrives dead on arrival (DOA) and has been either discharged from the hospital or seen in the emergency department within the past seven days.
- Patient dies in the emergency room or within 24 hours of admission.
- Patient refuses treatment or hospitalization or leaves against medical advice (AMA).
- Final x-ray report differs substantially from the emergency department diagnosis, or x-ray interpretation in the emergency department, or both. *Exception:* Unimportant incidental findings unrelated to the patient's complaint, e.g., degenerative process related to aging or normal anatomic variance.
- Unexpected abnormal diagnostic test results returned to the emergency department after patient discharge.

- Patient or visitor fall resulting in injury.
- Transfusion error.
- Treatment or procedure errors (e.g., wrong patient or wrong treatment/procedure).
- No written consent or improper consent for procedure or treatment, when consent is necessary.
- Complaints from patient, family, or both.
- Cardiac arrest. *Exception:* Patient admitted with cardiac arrest or with diagnosis of myocardial infarction and a monitor.
- Respiratory arrest.
- Patient presenting with a complaint of head trauma discharged with an altered state of consciousness or a neurological deficit.
- Patient discharged from the emergency department after having received parenteral analgesic without appropriate documentation of instructions and dispositions contained in the record.
- Patients who return within 48 hours of being seen in the emergency department without instruction to do so.
- All transfers.
- Medication error.

TRIAGE: INITIAL SCREENING EXAMINATION

The performance of an appropriate initial screening examination and the related triage concept are cornerstones to effective ED risk management. Not uncommonly, the "first come, first served" principle is inappropriate in the context of the ED. Triage entails sorting patients and setting treatment priorities according to medical need.[2] It is not the basic principle of triage or the concept of sorting among patients that creates risk management nightmares. It is well documented that patient outcome is improved by a systematic approach to triage.[3] Risk management problems arise out of who performs the triage examination, the adequacy of the initial examination, and the criteria used for prioritization.

The first person each ED patient should see is someone with appropriate formal nursing or paramedic training. No ED patient should be registered or administratively processed *before* a triage examination by a health care professional. The Joint Commission requires that *every* ED have procedures in place so that *all* persons seeking emergency care are initially assessed by "qualified individuals" and that "the priority with which persons seeking emergency care will be seen by a physician . . . be determined by specially trained personnel using guidelines provided by the emergency department. . . ."[4(p. 19)]

The area where triage examinations are performed must be in proximity to the ED entrance and should be readily accessible to the registration area. However, the area should provide for a sufficient degree of privacy. Certain patients, such as infants and persons with cardiac or respiratory conditions, may need to be partially undressed for an adequate examination to be conducted.

The triage examination involves "the provision of immediate brief medical evaluation of all incoming patients and the determination of the problem, the type of service needed, and the appropriate referral."[5] The extent of the examination is limited by its purpose, which is to screen for emergency medical conditions. Based on the triage examination, the ED staff determine which patients must be given more immediate priority and which patients can be processed in order of arrival.

At a minimum, for an adequate triage examination, a full set of vital signs must be obtained; a focused history of the acute complaint and contributory medical history must be obtained; and medication and allergy history must be documented. Weight should be documented in all pediatric patients. The triage examination should not involve an exhaustive evaluation. However, based on a patient's presenting complaint and appearance, a more detailed examination can be necessary. For instance, this could include a brief auscultation of lungs or examination of circulation, movement, and sensation to an injured extremity.

After the triage examination is completed, priority of treatment is based only on medical need. No patient with an emergency medical condition should have care delayed to obtain insurance information or to obtain health maintenance organization (HMO) authorization. Prioritizing patient care based on ability to pay, or other social utility, presents a significant potential for liability.[6] The days when any hospital could perform a "wallet biopsy" before giving emergency care have passed.

Federal Emergency Medical Treatment and Active Labor Act (EMTALA or COBRA) Part I

An ED's general obligation to screen for emergency medical conditions has been codified in the federal Emergency Medical Treatment and Active Labor Act (EMTALA), also called medical COBRA.[7] EMTALA is often termed an anti-dumping act (see Chapter 21 and Exhibit 21-1). Although the legislative history of EMTALA indicates it was intended to deter hospitals from transferring or dumping uninsured or indigent patients, its broad language reaches beyond these groups of patients. The Act applies to any hospital that receives federal Medicare or Medicaid funds. EMTALA provides for two types of enforcement mechanisms: governmental administrative action and private lawsuits. There is no requirement that a private plaintiff be a Medicare or Medicaid recipient. Several federal courts have decided that plaintiffs are not required to claim that they were uninsured or indigent to bring suit under the statute.[8]

EMTALA has two prongs. The first prong requires a hospital ED to conduct adequate examinations for emergency medical conditions. "The term 'emergency medical condition' means (A) a medical condition manifesting itself by acute symptoms of sufficient severity (including severe pain) such that the absence of immediate medical attention could reasonably be expected to result in (i) placing the individual (or, in the case of a pregnant woman, the woman or her unborn child) in serious jeopardy, or (ii) serious impairment or bodily functions, or (iii) serious dysfunction of any bodily organ or part. . . ."[9(p.18)]

The second prong, discussed later in this chapter, dictates what a hospital must do once an emergency medical condition is discovered. Therefore, a hospital can violate EMTALA in two ways. First, it can fail to detect the nature of the emergency condition through inadequate screening procedures. Second, it can transfer or discharge a patient without stabilizing an emergency condition.[10] The screening process only begins at triage, and it does not end until an ED physician completes a thorough evaluation. (Chart documentation for EMTALA compliance is discussed later on page 479, Exhibit 33-3.)

Language Barriers

EDs across the country are treating increasing numbers of non-English-speaking patients, or patients who can speak only limited English. Although the problem of language barriers is not new to hospitals, evidence shows the language gap is growing.[11] Studies have demonstrated that language barriers can create gross misunderstandings between providers and patients.[12] Particularly in the acute setting of EDs, linguistic barriers compromise the delivery of quality health care and expose providers to liability risks at several levels. The most obvious risks involve the areas of diagnosis, discharge instructions, and informed consent.[13] The Joint Commission now mandates that "When required frequently in the emergency care area, there is a means of communicating in the languages of the predominant population groups served by the hospital's emergency department. . . ."[14(p. 18)]

The liability risk resulting from a language gap is frequently compounded by a scarcity of trained interpreters. The risk may be compounded by critical translation errors where other patients or untrained employees are used to interpret on the spot. Hospitals in areas from New York to Seattle have developed innovative strategies to reduce the risk presented by language barriers and the use of untrained interpreters.[15] Any practical plan involves several fundamental elements that can involve ambitious efforts. The goals of any effective program involve the prompt availability of quality interpretation services and the maximization of limited resources.

In EDs serving concentrated limited English-speaking populations, recruitment of bilingual volunteers and staff, who will be present in the department, is strongly recommended. As a quality control mechanism, volunteers and nonprofessional staff should be required to attend a training course, leading to certification in medical interpretation. A pool of interpreters, with posted hours of availability and speed of accessibility, should be created. Most hospitals attempt to accomplish this within the confines of their own institution. However, in urban areas, cooperative pooling of resources among hospitals can more likely create a roster of interpreters available 24 hours. Finally, in some areas, hospitals may subscribe to fee-for-service language clearinghouse services. For instance, in New York and Chicago a "language line" service is available by phone.[16] Exhibit 33-2 is a sample policy for health care professionals serving limited English-proficient patients.

Exhibit 33-2
**SAMPLE POLICY FOR HEALTH CARE PROFESSIONALS SERVING
LIMITED ENGLISH-PROFICIENT PATIENTS**

INTENT

To promote access to interpreters for limited English-proficient patients in health care facilities. This policy is based on the premise that clear and accurate health care information is essential to quality health care delivery and consistent with civil rights, patients rights, and informed consent provisions required under federal and state statutes as well as by standards promulgated by the Joint Commission on Accreditation of Healthcare Organizations (Joint Commission).

DEFINITIONS

Health Care Interpreter: Ideally, the health care interpreter should be an individual employed for the express purpose of providing interpreter/translator services to limited English-proficient patients and specially trained to perform in the role of interpreter/translator. The health care interpreter should have proficient knowledge and skills in English, as well as in the language of the patient, and employ that training in a medical or health-related setting. In addition to language proficiency, the skills of the health care interpreter should include the cultural sensitivity and mastery of the medical and colloquial terminology, which make possible the conditions of mutual trust and accurate communication leading to effective provision of health care services. The health care interpreter should maintain an unbiased, professional demeanor and seek to translate with a high level of accuracy.

Community Volunteer: An individual not employed or formally trained as a health care interpreter but who can at times act as interpreter for a patient. It is essential that high standards of language, cultural, and medical proficiency be applied to the performance of volunteer interpreters (see above definition). At minimum, volunteer medical interpreters should be provided with orientation and training in the essentials of interpretation.

Employee Volunteer: An individual employed by the health care facility in a job title other than health care interpreter but who is called on to provide interpretive services on an ad hoc basis. It should not be assumed that an employee has interpreter skills even if he or she holds an otherwise professional

continues

Exhibit 33-2 continued

title. All volunteer employee interpreters should be held to high standards of performance and be provided with an orientation to interpreting and ongoing training.

Cultural Competence: Culturally competent health care organizations are those that truly seek to understand the cultural and linguistic differences among staff and patient populations, and recognize that these differences can and do lead to obstacles in the delivery of quality health care. Such organizations actively seek to increase their understanding of these issues and to build their internal capacity to deliver health care that is culturally and linguistically sensitive. These organizations understand that the bilingualism is *not* synonymous with biculturalism; therefore, they seek to hire staff representative of the patient population to be served and thus can negotiate bicultural work assignments. Culturally competent organizations understand the interplay between policy and practice and are committed to policies, procedures, and programs that enhance services to diverse clienteles.

Language Barriers: Those communication obstacles that result from a patient's inability to comprehend either spoken or written English.

Cultural Barriers: Those communication obstacles that result from a patient's inability to understand a medical or health idea or concept because of cultural differences between the patient and the health care provider.

POLICY

To ensure access to health care information and services for limited English-proficient patients. Health care facilities should use the following guidelines.

1. Annually review existing policies regarding interpreters for patients with limited English proficiency. If such policies do not exist, policies will be developed and will include procedures for providing trained health care interpreters whenever a language or communication barrier exists.
2. Procedures will be designed to maximize efficient use of trained health care interpreters and to minimize delays in providing interpreters to patients. Interpreters will be available 24 hours a day.
3. Develop and post information (notices) about interpreter services.
   a. Notices will advise patients and their families of the availability of trained health care interpreters.
   b. Notices will include the procedures for obtaining an interpreter and the telephone numbers where complaints may be filed concerning interpreter service

problems, including but not limited to a (TDD) number for the hearing impaired and the numbers of the regulatory agencies at the federal, state, and local levels.
   c. Notices should be posted at a minimum, in conspicuous locations such as the emergency department, admissions department, entrance areas, and outpatient areas.
   d. Notices will inform patients that interpreter services are available on request, will list the languages for which interpreter services are available, will instruct patients to direct complaints about interpreter services to the appropriate internal department and/or external regulatory agencies.
   e. Notices will be multilingual.
4. Identify and record a patient's primary language/dialect and need for interpretive services on admitting forms, patient medical chart, hospital bracelet, bedside notice, and nursing care. Documentation should include whether the patient's interpretive needs were met.
5. Prepare and maintain as needed a list of in-house health care interpreters. Health care interpreters as well as community volunteers and employee volunteers will be provided with an initial orientation in health care interpretation. In addition, all interpreters will be provided with annual continuing education aimed at improving interpreter skills and professionalism.
6. Provide training to other appropriate health care personnel on the use of interpreter services.
7. Notify employees of the health care facility's commitment to provide trained health care interpreters. This should be a facility-wide policy, initiated and monitored by administration.
8. Employees hired specifically for their bilingual skills or employees used intermittently as interpreters will be compensated for their interpreter work.
9. Review all standardized written forms, legal forms, waivers, documents, and informational materials to determine which should be translated into languages other than English.
10. Review all such forms for medical, cultural, and linguistic accuracy after they have been translated.
11. Provide visual and audio information for limited English-proficient patients in the event that they are illiterate in their native language.
12. Encourage community liaison groups to assist the health care facility and the limited English-proficient communities to ensure the adequacy of the health care interpreter services.

Source: Courtesy of Wendy L. Siegel, Chicago Institute on Urban Poverty, Travelers and Immigrants Aid, Chicago, IL.

INFORMED CONSENT AND RIGHT TO REFUSE TREATMENT

Informed Consent

The doctrine of informed consent resulted from an older concept of "medical battery." The doctrine stems from the simple idea that a medical procedure cannot be performed on a patient without the patient's permission or consent.[17] It has evolved to focus on the issue of whether a patient's consent to a procedure was actually informed so as to constitute genuine knowing consent. In its current form, the doctrine requires the treating physician to discuss the foreseeable *risks, results, and reasonable alternatives* with a patient before performing any invasive procedure.

Emergency department informed consent claims are rarely brought independently of malpractice claims and are fairly difficult to prove. In most states, as in any malpractice claim, a plaintiff must first prove a breach of the relevant professional standard of care regarding disclosure. Informed consent plaintiffs frequently have a difficult burden proving proximate cause. A plaintiff must prove more than that he or she would have refused to undergo a procedure if the plaintiff had been adequately informed of the risks involved. The plaintiff also must prove that an objectively reasonable person standing in his or her shoes also would have refused the procedure. The types of procedures performed emergently in EDs are not frequently interventions that a reasonable person would ordinarily refuse.

From the perspective of hospital liability, it is important to note that in many states the duty to actually obtain informed consent falls exclusively on the treating physician, not the hospital. A hospital has no independent duty to obtain a patient's informed consent. (Note that a hospital can always be vicariously liable for physicians that are its employees or agents, such as interns, residents, and salaried physicians. ED physicians *can* be hospital employees, but are typically independent contractors. Usually, surgeons and other private physicians are independent contractors.)[18] The hospital does have a duty to provide adequate procedures for obtaining written consent, and the hospital must periodically review staff physicians to determine that they adhere to hospital policies. Also, the hospital must supply proper consent forms. Forms must be in simple language, and it is strongly suggested that written forms be available in the native language of the predominant local non-English-speaking populations.

The informed consent doctrine has an emergency exception. If it were not for its limited scope in the context of EDs, the exception might swallow the rule. Under the emergency exception, where informed consent cannot reasonably be obtained without substantial risk to the person's life or body part or system, the life-saving or limb-saving treatment can be performed without informed consent. However, the scope of treatment is limited to only that which is reasonably necessary in the emergency.

As a general rule, an unemancipated minor cannot give consent for treatment. In this area, the emergency exception is of particular relevance, and no minor should ever have emergency treatment delayed to obtain parental consent. However, nonemergency treatment, which is not life saving or limb saving or reasonably necessary to prevent serious dysfunction to any body part or system, can in a physician's discretion, await parental consent. Parental consent can be in person, in writing, or by telephone to be followed up in writing later.

Right To Refuse Treatment

The corollary of the doctrine of informed consent is the fundamental idea that any competent adult has the personal autonomy to say "no" to medical treatment, even if the physician believes the treatment is in the person's best interests. ED staff must be cognizant of patients' rights to refuse care. Competent adults have the right to refuse even life-saving treatment.[19] In the context of the ED, a minor usually is not regarded as having the right to refuse life-saving treatment. However, some states have adopted the "mature minor doctrine" under which an unemancipated minor can have a limited right to refuse life-saving treatment but only after a judicial determination of maturity. This situation is unlikely to be encountered in the ED setting.[20]

There are several significant limitations to the right to refuse treatment of particular relevance to the ED. First, a person must be competent to knowingly refuse treatment. If a person is intoxicated, postictal, or has just suffered head trauma or loss of consciousness, he or she may not be competent to refuse treatment. Before any person refuses treatment that the ED staff believes is reasonably necessary, the ED physician must document a "mini-mental exam" that delineates the person is alert and understands the foreseeable *risks* of refusing the treatment proposed.

When a Patient Leaves against Medical Advice

When a patient leaves the ED against medical advice (AMA), exactly what treatment was advised should be thoroughly documented in the medical chart. It is important to document the patient's mental status and objective behavior as well as what attempts were made to secure consent. Written instructions and recommendations for follow-up including an open-ended invitation to return to the ED should be given to the patient. While it is recommended that the patient sign for the instructions, it is not uncommon for patients to refuse to sign forms when leaving AMA. A refusal to sign an AMA form is not fatal. Although it is important to document that the instructions were tendered to the patient who refused signature, it is more important to ensure the patient actually receives the instructions.

DIAGNOSIS, TESTING, AND ANCILLARY SERVICES

Retrieval of Prior Medical Records

The Joint Commission mandates that prior records, including previous ED visits, be made available whenever possible when requested by the ED physician.[21] It is recommended that inquiry about prior hospitalizations and ED visits routinely be made by the ED staff and recorded on the medical chart either at triage or on registration. Where ED charts are computer-generated and the ED is on-line with medical records, prior dates of treatment should routinely be documented. The nursing staff should anticipate the need for prior records and have them obtained early in the ED visit any time it is clinically indicated. Prior treatment records are invaluable help in uncovering pertinent information that a patient may or may not recall or relate on any particular visit to the ED. Prior laboratory tests and results, prescription information, and other data are of particular assistance in making a diagnosis that could otherwise be missed.

Documentation of Diagnostic Considerations

Most ED medical malpractice suits have classically been attributable to misdiagnosis.[22] Charting deficiencies in three particular areas frequently contribute to the likelihood of misdiagnosis: prior history, focused examination about the chief complaint, and failure to document follow-up results from laboratory tests or x-ray studies, particularly those reported after the patient left the ED. The failure to diagnose abdominal pain,[23,24] myocardial infarction (MI),[25–27] and meningitis or sepsis in children[28,29] all yield significant liability potential. The following analyses of misdiagnosed abdominal pain and missed MI are illustrative of the importance of this issue.

The accurate diagnosis of abdominal pain is a clinical challenge and usually is made based on systematic physical examination with a careful acute history. Reliance on laboratory and x-ray results is often not helpful. Therefore, with this chief complaint, proper documentation focuses particularly on the physical examination and history of the acute illness. Documentation of the examination should demonstrate the systematic ruling-out thought process. This is an area in which documenting negatives is particularly helpful.

The documentation of "no tenderness or rebound, no masses, positive bowel sounds, and strong peripheral pulses" supports the ruling out of entities such as appendicitis or an abdominal aortic aneurysm better than a normal complete blood count (CBC), abdominal x-ray, and the notation "abdomen benign" (which arguably describes the same physical examination). In addition, a body temperature must always be recorded. Any time the history includes vomiting, the patient's tolerance of oral liquids observed in the ED should be documented before discharge. Discharge instructions about follow-up examination are important to avoid missing pain of a periodic nature.

The diagnosis of MI relies heavily on the combination of acute history, focused risk factor history, and the venerable ECG. The profile of the typical missed MI includes a patient under the age of 49 with atypical chest pain where no ECG was obtained.[30] In the ED, a single measurement of cardiac enzymes usually is not helpful.[31] Cardiac enzymes frequently are reported after the patient leaves the ED. Unless the ED carefully controls an exhaustive daily system to track late-reported laboratory results, the tests are not clinically useful and can constitute a liability "smoking gun."

Laboratory Studies

The Joint Commission mandates only that routine laboratory studies, including microbiologic studies, be available.[32] All pertinent laboratory tests ordered during an ED visit should be transcribed in the progress notes, as well as on laboratory sheets, to indicate they were reviewed and analyzed. The problem of late-reported laboratory studies, such as blood or urine cultures, must be addressed by a carefully documented follow-up system reviewed by professional staff. By their very nature, these tests will be reported *after* ED patients are discharged from the ED. Therefore, the ED must have a system for calling back discharged patients with positive culture results and notifying patients' physicians or clinics. Carefully maintained logs with entries that include the name and phone numbers of persons notified should be kept by the ED.

TREATMENT

The essential issues regarding ED treatment involve the establishment of policies concerning which providers can treat patients in the department, a definition of the scope of treatments performed in the ED, and the regular monitoring of patient responses to treatments and intervention. Frequently, staff physicians want to examine their private patients in the ED. Policy should dictate that an ED chart be generated for all patients, that vital signs be documented whenever possible, and that a notation be made that the patient was or was not examined by the ED staff.

Detailed policies explaining what types of treatment can be undertaken by the nursing and paramedical staff must be established. Policies should govern modes of intravenous access, application of orthopedic devices, and other interventions that can be the physicians' responsibility in other settings. Particular attention must be given to standing orders, which can be initiated by nurses in their professional judgment without direct physician supervision. Although standing orders are common and useful in the ED, the appropriate implementation of standing orders should be regularly monitored by nursing management and the ED medical staff.

Written policies should delineate specific procedures that are not routinely performed in the ED. The classic example is the incision and drainage of deep abscesses. Although procedures of this type can appear simple, they present liability risks that are better managed in a more controlled and regulated environment.

The key element often missing in ED chart documentation is evidence of ongoing monitoring in response to treatment. It is not uncommon for ED nursing staff to document a thorough initial assessment only to fail to periodically monitor the patient during the remaining ED visit. Documentation must be appropriate to the presenting complaint. Vital signs and at least a brief notation about mental status and overall condition should follow administration of significant medications or any invasive procedures. Before admission or transfer of any patient, vital signs and summary overview of condition must be documented. Any abnormal vital signs, even in an otherwise apparently stable patient, including elevated body temperature must be repeated before discharge.

DISPOSITION: ADMISSION, TRANSFER, AND DISCHARGE

Admission

When a patient is admitted to an institution, the interface between departments must be governed by written policies concerning interdepartmental reports and transfer of the medical record, laboratory reports, and x-rays results. Generally, the ED retains control and liability until the patient is safely nestled in bed. Policies must address gray areas such as when patients go to radiology or magnetic resonance imaging (MRI) scans and are transported directly to their destination without returning to the ED. Vital signs, a summary overview of the patient's condition, and status of presenting complaint should always be redocumented shortly before admission. With any critical patient, close monitoring should continue to be documented while out of the ED and during transportation, where possible.

EMTALA (COBRA) Part II

If a patient presents to an ED and is found to have an emergency medical condition or is in active labor, the second prong of EMTALA is activated, and the act imposes a statutory duty to stabilize the condition within the hospital's capacity before transfer to another facility or discharge. A patient is stabilized when sufficient treatment has been provided to ensure that no material deterioration of the patient's condition will result from a transfer to another facility.[33] An unstabilized patient can be transferred only if the patient or responsible party makes an informed request in writing or if the ED physician certifies that the medical benefits of treatment at the other facility outweigh the risks of transfer.[34,35]

A thoroughly documented medical record is essential. Exhibit 33-3 provides an example of a documentation form. The ED physician must summarize the risks and benefits expected of transfer and document that the receiving hospital has available beds and has accepted the patient. All pertinent medical records, including x-rays, must be sent to the transferee hospital. The transfer must be made by qualified personnel. Unless prior agreement has been made with a transport team from a tertiary care center, the responsibility for the patient remains with the transferring physician and hospital.

Hospitals will reduce their liability exposure by developing written transfer policies that detail 1) when a patient is stabilized within the particular hospital's capabilities; 2) under what types of conditions unstabilized patients are to be transferred; and 3) that providers are to undertake the transfer, by what available mode, and to what facilities transfers are authorized for particular conditions.[36]

Preexisting Transfer Agreements

Notwithstanding the strictures of EMTALA, hospitals are free to enter standing transfer agreements with other entities that are rationally designed in the patients' interests. Standing transfer arrangements between general hospitals and specialty units, such as trauma and burn units and perinatal networks, are not at odds with the rationale behind EMTALA. This is particularly true where sophisticated transport teams are sent out by a tertiary care center to hospitals with lesser treatment capacities.

Exhibit 33-3
MODEL DOCUMENTATION FORM

Institution Name
Address
City, State, Zip Code
Phone

TRANSFER DOCUMENTATION

This document is to be used in conjunction with the <u>Guide for Inter-Hospital Transfer of Individuals</u> published by the Metropolitan Chicago Healthcare Council. *Complete all six sections of this form.*

Date: _____   Medical Record No. _____

---

1. MEDICAL SCREENING EXAM

A medical screening exam of _____
(name of individual)

was completed by _____ at _____
(time)

The examination revealed that the individual had an emergency medical condition, which in the case of pregnancy includes a woman having contractions where (1) there is inadequate time to effect a safe transfer to another hospital before delivery, or (2) transfer may pose a threat to the health or safety of the woman or the unborn child.
☐ Yes   ☐ No

---

2. DEMOGRAPHIC INFORMATION

Name: _____   Sex: ☐ M ☐ F

Address: _____

Phone No.: _____   Age: _____   Date of Birth: _____

Next of Kin: _____   Phone: _____

Personal Belongings: ☐ Sent with patient   ☐ Given to _____
                                                ☐ None

List: _____
_____
_____

Transferring/Releasing Physician: _____

Family Physician: _____   Phone No: _____

continues

Exhibit 33-3 continued

<table>
<tr><td colspan="2" align="center">3. REASON FOR TRANSFER
Complete Part A, B, C, <u>OR</u> D and Sign Below</td></tr>
</table>

PART A

☐ Emergency—Unstable

I have examined

_____
(name)

and certify that, based on the information available at the time of transfer, the medical benefits reasonably expected from the provision of the appropriate medical treatment of the individual's emergency medical condition at another facility outweigh the increased risks to the individual, and in the case of labor, to the unborn child from effecting the transfer.

This certification is based on the following summary of the risks and benefits of transfer of the unstable condition:

Risks: _____
_____
_____
_____

Benefits: _____
_____
_____
_____

NOTE: Be sure to complete the portion of Medical Records section pertaining to on-call refusals or failures to appear; if any, *Sign below.*

PART B

☐ Emergency - Stabilized or
☐ Non-emergency (check one)

I have examined

_____
(name)

and find that the individual either did not present an emergency medical condition, or that any such condition has been stabilized such that no material deterioration in the individual's condition is likely, within a reasonable degree of medical certainty, to result from this transfer. *Sign below.*

PART C

☐ Individual's Request

Transfer was requested by the individual or the legally responsible person acting on the individual's behalf pursuant to the attached <u>Consent/Request to Transfer</u> form. *Sign below.*

PART D

☐ Refusal to Consent to Examination/Treatment/Transfer

The individual or the legally responsible person acting on the individual's behalf, after being informed of the risks and benefits of the recommended further examination, treatment, or transfer to another facility, refused to consent to such examination, treatment or transfer. *Sign below.*

_____   _____
Physician's Signature   Print Name

_____   _____
Qualified Medical Person's Signature   Print Name
(only at the direction of a consulting physician when no
physician is present in the Emergency Department)

continues

Exhibit 33-3 continued

---

4. TRANSFER INFORMATION

Individual transferred to: _____   _____

Hospital/Facility   Unit/Room

Accepting/Receiving Physician: _____

Name

_____

Service or Specialty

☐ House Staff   ☐ Attending/Private   ☐ Attending/Emergency Department

Time of first request for transfer: _____   Time transfer accepted: _____

The following was done at the request of the receiving facility/physician prior to transfer:

☐ None

List: _____

_____

_____

Medical diagnosis at transferring facility: _____

_____

Summary of treatment rendered at transferring facility: _____

_____

Individual to be transferred via (check one):

☐ ambulance   ☐ ALS ☐ BLS   Provider Name _____
☐ helicopter   Provider Name _____
☐ aircraft   Provider Name _____
☐ other (specify): _____
☐ private auto (or taxi)

Health care personnel to accompany individual during transfer: ☐ No   ☐ Yes

Name: _____

☐ RN   ☐ MD   ☐ Other (specify)   _____

Accompanied by relative, friend, etc.:   ☐ No   ☐ Yes

Name: _____

continues

Exhibit 33-3 continued

5. MEDICAL RECORDS

Records sent: (This includes all medical records, or copies, related to the emergency medical condition for which the individual presented, available at the time of transfer.)

☐ E.D. record   ☐ X-ray films
☐ Progress Notes   ☐ ECG
☐ Nurses' Notes   ☐ Other (list) _____
                                            _____
                                            _____

Individual's condition at time of transfer:

☐ Good   ☐ Fair   ☐ Serious   ☐ Poor

Vital signs at time of transfer:

Blood Pressure _____ Pulse _____ Respirations _____ Temperature _____

> In the case of an individual with an unstable emergency medical condition requiring the services of an on-call physician to provide necessary stabilizing treatment, the following on-call physician(s) failed or refused to appear or was otherwise unavailable prior to the individual's transfer to provide such treatment:
>
> Name: _____
>
> Address: _____
>
> ☐ This section does not apply in this case.

6. SIGNATURES

Physician's Signature _____   Print Name _____

Nurse's Signature _____   Print Name _____

Time patient left transferring facility: _____

Source: Copyright 1990, Metropolitan Chicago Healthcare Council.

The principal risk management issue involved in such standing agreements is to clearly designate the point where liability passes. Without preexisting contractual agreement, the presumption is that the transferring hospital remains liable. Generally, it would appear that when a transport team arrives and takes control of an unstable patient, the liability risk would also pass. However, gray areas will arise that should be explained in hospital policies and procedures.

Discharge Instructions

Written discharge instructions for follow-up care must be given to every patient. They must include, at a minimum, the name, address, and telephone number of a particular referral provider (which can be a return to the ED); a specific recommended time limit for follow-up (e.g., within 24 hours or one week) with an expressed invitation to return sooner if symptoms worsen; and instructions about medications and treatment indicated. Discharge instructions must be written in simple common language, without "medicalese" or medical abbreviations, and should always be translated in writing for non-English-speaking patients. The instructions should be written on a separate sheet and signed by the patient or representative in acknowledgment of receipt.

A copy of the discharge instructions must be retained and attached to the ED record. Incredibly, in ED malpractice suits it is frequently found that no discharge instructions are attached to the permanently filed ED record. This compounds problems of proof regarding the standard of treatment and the defense that the patient may have been contributorily negligent in failing to follow the recommended course of treatment.

INFECTION CONTROL

The ED is a high-risk area for occupationally transmitted hepatitis B and HIV exposure.[37] Regular in-service programs are necessary to ensure that all providers routinely follow the Universal Precautions issued by the Centers for Disease Control (CDC).[38] (See Chapter 15.) The American Hospital Association (AHA) also has issued recommendations for health care practices regarding HIV infection.[39] These recommendations address issues about the following topical areas:

- informed consent
- patient counseling
- use of test results
- confidentiality
- nondiscrimination

- HIV education and health care workers
- organization of care within hospitals
- cost of transmission and prevention
- reporting of contact tracing
- balance between public and private financing
- role of the private sector
- role of the public sector
- adequacy of public and private benefits
- public information and education
- research priorities

SPECIALIZED EMERGENCY DEPARTMENTS

Paramedic Resource Hospitals

Paramedic resource hospitals coordinate the prehospital personnel and have ongoing responsibilities for paramedic telemetry radio communication and training. In many states, the prehospital systems are shielded from liability by a certain statutory "qualified immunity."[40] Under these paramedic statutes, the ED professional staff who direct paramedic personnel cannot be liable to patients for standard medical malpractice and only can be liable to a patient in the prehospital setting if their acts are considered "willful and wanton" or totally inconsistent with their training.[41]

Trauma Centers

The principal risk management issues involving trauma center EDs involve response time and coordination of the trauma team and other surgical specialists; the timely availability of operating rooms (OR) and OR teams; and the allocation of control of the trauma patient between the trauma service and the ED staff. Some of these issues are governed by state and local regulations, particularly the issues about routing trauma patients to the trauma center from the scene of a mass casualty incident. However, the coordination of internal triage and allocation must be governed by hospital policies and procedures.

Trauma hospitals represent themselves as having certain levels of expertise and readiness and, in public perception and in law, can be held to a higher standard of care than other facilities. The administration of a trauma hospital should be committed to receive all trauma patients within its capacity. Hospital liability issues have occurred when hospitals' facilities and personnel have been either unavailable or at overcapacity conditions and patients have arrived in reliance on the hospital's expert capabilities.

The in-house trauma service, operating room, and radiology should be notified before the arrival of any serious trauma patient. It is recommended that the team assume control from the beginning to minimize any delays in getting the patient to the OR for definitive treatment in a controlled environment. This allows the ED staff to effectively and efficiently operate the rest of the ED. The nursing personnel involved in trauma resuscitation must have a clear chain of command established to minimize the confusion attendant to trauma resuscitation.

CONCLUSION

The emergency department is a complicated area that is fraught with risk. Recognizing the potential for quality and liability issues to arise and developing proactive strategies to address those issues will help ensure that patients receive high quality care and that providers of that care are protected.

NOTES

1. Joint Commission on Accreditation of Healthcare Organizations, *1993 Joint Commission Accreditation Manual for Hospitals*, Section ES 1.3 (Oakbrook Terrace, Ill.: Joint Commission on Accreditation of Healthcare Organizations, 1993).

2. S. Frye-Revere, Emergency Rooms: The Triage Metaphor Error, *Journal of Health and Hospital Law* 24, no. 370 (December 1991): 370–372.

3. R. Yurt, Triage, Initial Assessment, and Early Treatment of the Pediatric Trauma Patient, *Pediatric Clinics of North America* 39, no. 5 (October 1992): 1083–1091.

4. Joint Commission, *1993 Joint Commission Accreditation Manual for Hospitals*, Sections ES 1.2 and ES 2.2.4.

5. E. Zwicke, Triage Nurse Decisions: A Prospective Study, *Journal of Emergency Nursing* (May/June 1992): 32.

6. P. Craig, Health Maintenance Organization Gatekeeping Policies: Potential Liability for Deterring Access to Emergency Medical Services, *Journal of Health and Hospital Law* 23, no. 135 (May 1990): 135–146.

7. *Emergency Medical Treatment and Active Labor Act*, 42 U.S.C.A., ¶ 1395dd (1992).

8. *Deberry v. Sherman Hospital*, 741 F. Supp. 1302 (N.D. Ill. 1990).

9. *Emergency Medical Treatment and Active Labor Act*, 42 U.S.C.A. ¶ 1395dd(e)(1) (1992).

10. Ibid.

11. Patients Say "Ah" in Many Languages, *The New York Times*, 31 December 1992: Section B.

12. Chicago Institute on Urban Poverty/Travelers and Immigrant Aid, *Concept Paper: Insuring Access to Health Care Services for Immigrants and Refugees: A Multilingual Model for Training Health Care Interpreters in the Chicago Metropolitan Region* (Chicago: Chicago Institute on Urban Poverty/Travelers and Immigrant Aid, October 1992), 3.

13. Chicago Institute on Urban Poverty/Travelers and Immigrant Aid, *Concept Paper*, 4.

14. Joint Commission, *1993 Joint Commission Accreditation Manual for Hospitals*, Section ES 1.5.

15. Ibid.

16. Ibid.

17. K.D. Peters, Illinois Law on Informed Consent Medical Malpractice Actions, *Illinois Bar Journal* (March 1988): 372.

18. *Pickle v. Curns*, 435 N.E.2d 877 (1982).

19. *Cruzan v. Missouri Department of Health*, 110 S. Ct. 2841 (1990).

20. *In Re E.G. a Minor*, 549 N.E.2d 322 (1990).

21. Joint Commission, *1993 Joint Commission Accreditation Manual for Hospitals*, Section ES 6.1.

22. J.J. Trautlein, Malpractice in the Emergency Department: Review of 200 Cases, *Annals of Emergency Medicine* 13, no. 9 (September 1984): 709.

23. M.W. Tan, A Proactive Approach to "Missed Appendicitis" Claims, *Forum* (July/August 1989): 6–8.

24. J.D. Dunn, Study Reveals High-Risk Areas of Emergency Medical Practice, *Malpractice Digest* 14, no. 1 (Spring 1987): 1–4.

25. C.H. Herr, The Diagnosis of Acute Myocardial Infarction in the Emergency Department: Part I, *Journal of Emergency Medicine* 10, no. 455 (1992): 455–461.

26. R.A. Rusnak, Litigation Against the Emergency Physician: Common Features in Cases of Missed Myocardial Infarction, *Annals of Emergency Medicine* 18 (October 1989): 19.

27. Dunn, *Malpractice Digest*, 1.

28. E. Su, The Sepsis Workup for the Febrile Child, *Journal of Emergency Medicine* 10, vol. 445 (1992): 445–453.

29. Dunn, *Malpractice Digest*, 1.

30. Rusnak, *Annals of Emergency Medicine*, 22.

31. Ibid.

32. Joint Commission, *1993 Joint Commission Accreditation Manual for Hospitals*, Section ES 3.1.

33. *Emergency Medical Treatment and Active Labor Act*, 42 U.S.C.A., ¶ 1395dd (1991).

34. Metropolitan Chicago Healthcare Council, *Complying with COBRA: A Reference Handbook* (Chicago: Metropolitan Chicago Healthcare Council, 1990).

35. L. Singer, Review and Analysis of Federal "Antidumping Legislation": Practical Advice and Unanswered Questions, *Journal of Health and Hospital Law* 22, no. 145 (May 1989): 145–149.

36. Singer, *Journal of Health and Hospital Law* , 148.

37. E. Reed, Occupational Infectious Disease Exposures in EMS Personnel, *Journal of Emergency Medicine* 11, no. 9 (1993): 9–16.

38. Recommendations for Transmission of HIV and HBV, *40 Morbidity and Mortality Weekly Report*, No. RR-8 (Atlanta, Ga.: Centers for Disease Control, 12 July 1991), 1–9.

39. American Hospital Association, *Recommendations for Health Care Practices and Public Policy* (Chicago: American Hospital Association, 1992), 1–17.

40. ILL. REV. STAT., Ch. 111 1/2 Par. 5517(a) (1992).

41. *Johnson v. University of Chicago Hospitals*, 61 U.S.L.W. 2400 (7th Cir. 1992).

Chapter 34

Developing a Quality Aeromedical Transport Program

Judi Barager-Kemper, Donald E. Barker, Jan Davis, and Louise White

INTRODUCTION

The development of a quality aeromedical transport program includes the appropriate selection and training of a flight team, providing quality in-flight care, complying with air medical standards guidelines and regulations, and transport safety. Developing standards and appropriate indicators to monitor on-going program quality and effectiveness is equally important. Because little methodological work in this field was found in the literature, the University of Kentucky Hospital Aeromedical Service adopted the 10-step model of the Joint Commission on Accreditation of Healthcare Organizations (Joint Commission) for monitoring and evaluation. Capitalizing on multidisciplinary expertise, the hospital embarked on a project to develop and implement a quality improvement program.

This chapter provides a brief description of the University of Kentucky program, including important operational features. Program philosophy, management, and design are discussed. The process of indicator development is described and an example of a multi-indicator aspect of care presented. Broad strategies are also discussed to assist the reader in understanding the rationale utilized to develop this program. It is anticipated that the information can be used as a foundation for developing similar programs tailored to meet the unique needs of individual hospitals.

DESCRIPTION OF AN AEROMEDICAL TRANSPORT SERVICE

The University of Kentucky Hospital, a 461-bed tertiary care teaching facility and Level 1 trauma center, commenced aeromedical transport service to Central and Eastern Kentucky in 1987. This single-aircraft service has averaged approximately 1,200 flights per year to sites within a 150-mile radius of the city of Lexington. The helicopter is housed atop the hospital's critical care complex with direct access to the operating room, emergency department, and adult, pediatric, and neonatal intensive care units.

The aeromedical transport service provides emergency and critical care treatment for adult, pediatric, and neonatal patients during interhospital transport (90 percent of flights) and transport of patients from accident scenes within the service area. Patient types include medical, surgical, and obstetrical emergencies. Of approximately 110 flights per month, 40 percent involve cardiac patients; 40 percent, trauma patients; 3 percent, neonatal patients; and 17 percent, patients with miscellaneous other medical and obstetrical emergencies. Neonatal flights are attended by a specialized neonatal transport team consisting of two neonatal transport nurses. A majority of cardiac flights are attended by a cardiologist. All flights are attended by a flight nurse and a flight paramedic.

When evaluating the need for an aeromedical transport program at an institution, certain questions should be asked. The answers to these questions will shape all aspects of the service to be provided. A multidisciplinary team should analyze the answers to best develop an appropriate strategic plan. Hospital planners, physicians, nurses, marketing staff, legal counsel, and possibly representatives from the community or targeted referral base should be included.

What will be the radius of the service area? The answer to this question involves several considerations: (1) the impact that the radius of service will have on a decision about the type of aircraft to be purchased or leased, (2) the availability of a similar service offered by a competitor, and (3) the types of transport anticipated (e.g., hospital to hospital, emergency scene rescue) that may require multiple training courses for the transport staff and different marketing approaches. An additional consideration may be the potential impact that an aeromedical program could have on the community where the hospital is located. A large urban hospital planning frequent helicopter transports may be faced with significant resistance from the community if people are upset by the noise of the aircraft. A careful review of local noise abatement statutes is required in advance so that community problems can be averted.

What types of patients will be targeted for aeromedical transport? Does the hospital intend to focus on increased patient volume for specific preexisting hospital specialty services (e.g., cardiac, burn, transplant, neonatology) or will the hospital accept all patients for transfer? How will a referral network be developed to identify the targeted patient population, and how will referring physicians be approached? As part of the process of identifying and contacting referral sources, the hospital should also address a plan for patient feedback and the educational resources that will be available to referring hospitals and physicians.

Flight Team

The flight team at the University of Kentucky consists of specially trained critical care/emergency flight nurses and flight paramedics. Flight nurses and paramedics are in constant communication with a medical control physician throughout each mission. To enhance in-flight safety, as well as safety of ground personnel, each mission is flown with two pilots.

Specific invasive procedures, such as tube thoracostomy, pericardiocentesis, surgical airway, central venous access, and cut downs, may be performed by flight nurses according to approved protocols. Cardioversion and laryngotracheal intubation may be performed by a flight nurse or paramedic.

In choosing personnel for a flight team, a hospital must consider the types of patients that will be transported, as well as the official position of the particular state regarding expanded roles of the nurse, paramedic, and physician's assistant. In some states. it may be necessary to include a physician on every transport of a critically ill patient. The hospital must also determine how its flight team will be trained and ensure that its skills remain sharp. Protocol for the handling of radio communication that enables the flight team to remain in contact with specialists on the ground is also advised, but it should never replace the need to develop a highly skilled and specially trained flight team.

Aircraft

The aircraft used by the University of Kentucky is a Sikorsky S-76 twin–turbine engine helicopter. This aircraft is recognized as one of the fastest and safest in the industry. A state-of-the-art navigation system and an isolated cockpit with two pilots provide optimum safety. The cabin is designed for two patients with full body access and four medical attendants. It is equipped with advanced life support medical technology, including a ventilator, invasive monitoring devices, a full array of specialty equipment for life-saving procedures, intravenous pumps, pulse oximetry, and a balloon pump or isolette as needed. A backup aircraft is also available.

In setting up an aeromedical program, a hospital should evaluate the merits of owning an aircraft versus leasing it from a company that will be responsible for maintenance, insurance, and other requirements. The advantages and disadvantages of various aircraft models, as well as the decision to use fixed-wing aircraft or rotorcraft transport, must also be considered. In planning a flight program, it is essential for the risk manager or hospital attorney to be involved in insurance and liability issues that could result in additional unbudgeted costs for the program.

The helipad or airstrip must be located to facilitate access to the hospital. Specific guidelines developed by the Federal Aviation Administration and standards developed by the Association of Air Medical Services identify areas that must be considered prior to reaching decisions regarding aircraft and helipads or landing strips (see Appendixes 34-A and 34-B).

PROGRAM DESIGN

Structure of the Aeromedical Service

In keeping with its mission to provide exemplary emergency patient care, the University of Kentucky Hospital Aeromedical Service has developed a multidisciplinary monitoring and evaluation program for timely collection and analysis of objective data pertinent to the structures in which care is provided, the process of services delivery, and patient outcome. The program includes evaluation of medical care, appropriateness of transport, operational aspects of service delivery, and operational safety. The medical director, the flight team, and the administrative director of the program have accomplished a working relationship and program philosophy that facilitate cooperation and integration of the monitoring and evaluation program with service management. The program is structured to ensure open communication, ongoing data collection, frequent evaluation of findings, and appropriate delegation of responsibility for action and follow-up.

The quality assurance plan for the aeromedical service was written in accord with the Joint Commission's 10 steps for monitoring and evaluation. Responsibility for program management is shared by the medical director, the administrative director, and the chief flight nurse. Program leadership is supported by three working committees:

1. The Aeromedical Quality Assurance Committee is chaired by the medical director and includes the administrative director; chief flight nurse and assistant chief flight nurse; paramedic representatives; physician representatives from the surgery, medicine, pediatrics, and neonatology departments; director of nursing; trauma nurse coordinator; nursing director of the emergency services department; and a pharmacist.
2. The Aeromedical Operations Committee is chaired by the administrative director and includes the chief flight nurse, the medical director, and the lead pilot.
3. The Aeromedical Staff Quality Assurance Committee is chaired by the assistant chief flight nurse and is composed of designated flight nurses and paramedics.

Each committee is charged with evaluation of the quality of the aeromedical service. For example, findings pertinent to in-flight patient care are included in proceedings of the Aeromedical Quality Assurance and Aeromedical Staff Quality Assurance committees and are disseminated to the staff at staff meetings. Operational safety matters are presented to and discussed by the Aeromedical Operations Committee. Recommendations for improvement are forwarded to either or both of the other committees when indicated.

A mechanism to obtain feedback from the service receiving a patient from the flight team can be useful in an aeromedical monitoring and evaluation program. The flight team gets valuable information about the stabilization and treatment of the patient during transport that influences the interventions required when the patient is admitted. Additional feedback may be sought from and provided to referring hospitals regarding initial stabilization or "first-response" initiatives. This feedback can be part of the education offered to hospitals within the network in exchange for referrals.

Medical Staff Oversight

The hospital requires all clinical services to provide quarterly summaries of quality assessment activity to the Clinical Management Council, a subcommittee of the Medical Staff Executive Committee. This oversight body is chaired by the chief of staff. Membership includes the chiefs of surgery, medicine, pediatrics, neurology, and obstetrics/gynecology; the hospital director; and the director of quality assurance and utilization review.

The council provides written recommendations to the medical director of acromedical services and to the administrative director of the program. Council comments are reported to the Medical Staff Executive Committee on a monthly basis and to the governing body on a bimonthly basis (see Figure 34-1).

In addition to formal lines of accountability, individual cases are frequently referred to monthly patient care conferences of the surgery department and to a multidisciplinary trauma committee comprised of several physician and ancillary service representatives. These less formal referral relationships facilitate critical physician evaluation of patient care.

INDICATOR DEVELOPMENT

Led by the medical director, a board-certified general surgeon with specialty board certification in surgical critical care, the University of Kentucky Hospital Aeromedical Service developed and implemented a comprehensive monitoring and evaluation program. In addition to subjective review of all flights performed by nurses and physicians, the service focuses on selected aspects of care via systematic objective monitoring and evaluation. Exhibit 34-1 displays these aspects of care and the content that the indicators are designed to measure.

Because little work relating to the reliability and validity of indicators applicable to aeromedical services has been published to date, the hospital's aeromedical service leadership devotes considerable energy to developing and testing service-specific indicators. Topics for indicator development are raised by the Aeromedical Quality Assurance Committee, which delegates responsibility for indicator development and approves indicators for testing. A representative from the hospital's quality assurance department provides consultative service to the aeromedical service staff.

Prior to implementation, indicators are evaluated and tested for availability of the data, practical measurability,

Figure 34-1
ORGANIZATIONAL STRUCTURE AND REPORTING RELATIONSHIPS, UNIVERSITY OF KENTUCKY HOSPITAL AEROMEDICAL SERVICE

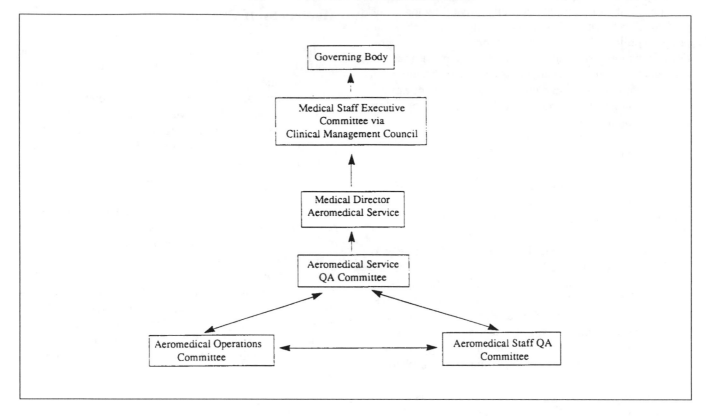

and content validity. Thought is given to delegation of data collection responsibility to the staff level that is best positioned for timely, complete, and accurate collection of the data. Peer review at all staff levels has been adopted to enhance individual accountability for patient care and to maximize continuous learning and program improvement.

Team Management of Cardiac Patients

Transport of cardiac patients accounts for approximately 40 percent of all flights. Therefore, in-flight team management of the cardiac patient was determined to be an important high-risk, high-volume aspect of care. The following indicators were developed to facilitate monitoring and evaluation of this service.

1. Integrity of airway is addressed to include the following:
   A. Breath sounds
   B. Respiratory rate
   C. Respiratory pattern
   D. Continuous pulse oximetry
   E. Oxygen administration at minimum 4 liters per minute
   Threshold: 100 percent
2. Perfusion status is addressed to include the following:
   A. Color
   B. Pulses
   C. Mental status
   D. Skin moisture
   E. Blood pressure, pulse, and respirations at least every 15 minutes
   F. Presence of at least two large-bore intravenous lines
   G. Presence or absence of nausea and vomiting
   Threshold: 100 percent
3. Cardiac status is addressed to include the following:
   A. Heart sounds
   B. Heart rhythm
   C. Continuous electrocardiographic monitoring
   D. Cardiac strip of treatable dysrhythmias
   Threshold: 100 percent

Exhibit 34-1
INDICATOR CONTENT FOR SELECTED ASPECTS OF CARE IN AEROMEDICAL SERVICE

INDICATOR CONTENT

Aspect of Care	Structure	Process	Outcome	Necessity	Safety	HR	HV	PP
Appropriateness of Transport				X		X	X	
Patient Deterioration During Transport		X	X			X		X
Initiation of Invasive Procedures		X	X			X		X
Medication Initiation		X					X	
Timeliness of Flight Acceptance	X	X					X	X
Timeliness of Aeromedical Response	X	X		X		X	X	
Team Management of Cardiac Patient		X	X		X	X		
Maintenance of Technical Skills		X				X		
Availability of Equip/Supplies	X							X
Operational Safety	X	X			X	X	X	
Death/Discharge within 48 hours		X	X	X		X		

HR = high-risk services
HV = high-volume services
PP = problem-prone services

4. Presence or absence of pain is determined. If pain is present, its status is addressed to include the following (exception: Glasgow Coma Score (GCS) < 9):
   A. Character
   B. Radiation
   C. Severity scaled 1–10
   Threshold: 100 percent

5. Safety is addressed to include the following:
   A. Stretcher safety straps
   B. Hearing protection
   Threshold: 100 percent

6. Medication administration includes the following:
   A. Reason for intervention
   B. Route

C. Dose
D. Time
E. Effectiveness
Threshold: 100 percent
7. Deviation from protocol occurred at the direction of the cardiologist on board.
    Threshold: 5 percent (in the event of deviation from protocols established for use by nurses and paramedics, specific orders are documented and reported)
8. Other treatment protocols or procedures were initiated. (A threshold is not applicable to this indicator. It was designed to prompt evaluation of other protocols.)

Responsibility for data collection on this aspect of care has been delegated to flight nurses and paramedics. Flight records of all cardiac flights are reviewed. To the extent possible, data collection is concurrent. The assistant chief flight nurse and designated paramedic are responsible for organizing and monthly reporting of data to the Aeromedical Staff Quality Assurance Committee. Conclusions and recommendations of this committee are then presented for discussion to the Aeromedical Quality Assurance Committee chaired by the medical director.

Professional societies can also provide valuable information regarding the evaluation of aeromedical services and can assist in the development of standards that relate to the overall operation of a quality flight program. Exhibit 34-2 contains examples of process indicators developed by the Association of Flight Nurses and the Association of Air Medical Services.

DEVELOPMENT OF PROTOCOL FOR RECORDKEEPING AND ADMINISTRATIVE DETAILS

The hospital must draft documents that clearly define the scope and services to be offered by an aeromedical transport service that delineate how patient care is provided during transport. A comprehensive flow sheet and mechanism for recording vital assessment information, as well as for maintenance of rhythm strips, fetal monitoring strips, and other supplemental items collected during transport, can be vitally important later during a review or defense of the care that was rendered in flight. Obviously, staff members who develop transport forms and documentation protocol should keep in mind the stressful nature of the service. Critically ill patients often require intensive monitoring and multiple interventions within a space that is less than ideal. Transport records should be designed to minimize the amount of longhand necessary for documentation. Comprehensive checklists can substantially decrease the amount of transcription required and improve the accuracy of record-keeping during transport. The participation of the flight team and in-house counsel or risk management staff in the development of documentation can ensure that it is accurate and sufficiently adequate to defend the in-flight care of patients. Formal documents may also be needed to address issues related to the transfer of authority during patient care and to describe the point at which liability and accountability attach to each specific caregiver. These issues often are the focus of medical negligence cases and can be minimized if spelled out clearly in advance.

CONCLUSION

Quality assessment in aeromedical services is a relatively new venture. The value of clinical and operational evaluation and the potential for future quality improvement require the individual expense and personal commitment of the program's leadership and a fully integrated program structure. The program at the University of Kentucky Hospital has been designed to foster active participation of all members of the flight team in its management. Accountability and formal lines of communication are clearly defined in writing and have been shared with and approved by representatives from all functional levels in the organization. This procedure has proved to be an effective management strategy and should continue to facilitate and promote dynamic management and continuous improvement of the aeromedical service.

Exhibit 34-2
PROFESSIONAL SOCIETY INDICATORS

AAMS Resource Document

Clinical Standards/Indicators/Thresholds

NFNA PRACTICE STANDARD III: PLAN OF CARE - Realistic goals and a prioritized plan of care are based on nursing diagnosis.

Support Standard: The flight nurse shall derive a valid plan prioritizing the patient's needs based on actual or potential threats.

NFNA PRACTICE STANDARD IV: INTERVENTION - Nursing interventions are performed in a planned sequence to support the patient experiencing single or multiple system failure.

Support Standard: The flight nurse shall implement nursing care based on current scientific knowledge and within his/her scope of practice.

A. AIRWAY

	THRESHOLD
1. Airway secured by endotracheal, nasotracheal, or cricothyroidotomy on all trauma patients with Glasgow Coma Score (GCS) of 6 or less.[3]	90 - 95%
2. Appropriate size ET tube placed according to documented patient age and weight, as noted in ACLS (Advanced Cardiac Life Support) and PALS (Pediatric Advanced Life Support) standards/guidelines.	90 - 95%
3. ET placement confirmed by at least two methods and documented initially and during transport on all intubated patients.	
4. Overall successful tracheal intubation on patients where the procedure is attempted.[4,5,6,7]	75 - 90%

B. MEDICATIONS/BLOOD PRODUCTS

1. Medications administered by air medical personnel appropriate for weight and age of patient.	95 - 99%
2. Complete documentation of medication administration including dose, route, time of administration and effectiveness where appropriate.	95 - 99%
3. Appropriate and safe administration of blood products as evidenced by:	
a. Documentation of blood unit # and type of blood product.	95%
b. Hemoglobin and hematocrit documented prior to transport if available.	90%
c. Documentation of patient response to blood product administration, including V.S.	95%

C. VENOUS ACCESS

1. IV access is obtained and patent.	95 - 99%

D. ONGOING PATIENT ASSESSMENT

1. ROTOR - Vital signs assessed and documented a minimum of every 15 minutes and every 5 minutes when patient condition warrants (vital signs include blood pressure, pulse, respirations).	95 - 99%
2. FIXED WING - Vital signs assessed and documented every 15 minutes x 2 and then every 30 minutes or as appropriate for patient stability (vital signs include blood pressure, pulse, respirations).	95 - 99%

E. TRAUMA CARE

1. Immobilization of cervical spine on all patients with suspected injuries above the clavicle.	95 - 99%
2. Air medical personnel's assessment for potential life-threatening injuries is consistent with the mechanism of injury and actual injuries identified by the receiving physician.	80 - 90%

NFNA PRACTICE STANDARD I: DATA COLLECTION - The assessment and collection of patient health data is systematic and continuous. The data is documented and communicated to appropriate members of the health care team.

Support Standard: Data collection shall be recorded in a systematic and retrievable manner.

AAMS STANDARD VII: The quality and appropriateness of patient care provided by air medical services shall be continuously reviewed, evaluated, and assured through the establishment of a quality control mechanism.

Interpretation: A patient record shall be maintained documenting patient care rendered by the ACM* and disposition of the patient at the receiving institution and kept on file for a period of time to include that of the statute of limitations.

F. DOCUMENTATION

1. Documentation by air medical personnel in compliance with the flight service's policy and procedure for documentation.	80 - 95%

Operational Standards/Indicators/Thresholds

AAMS STANDARD II: The ACMs* shall be well organized, properly directed, and staffed according to the nature and extent of health care needs anticipated and scope of services offered.

AAMS STANDARD VIII: The air medical service must strive for full integration into existing emergency medical systems and interhospital transfer networks.

Interpretation: The air medical service must ensure continuum of care and expedition of treatment of patients using standard protocols whenever possible.

continues

Exhibit 34-2 continued

A. TIMELINESS OF CARE

	THRESHOLD
1. Ground times of 20 minutes or less on flights to accident scenes with the exception of:	90 - 95%

    a. Entrapment

    b. Cardiac arrest

    c. Multiple victims

    d. Victim remote from landing zone

2. True bedside preparation time of 30 minutes or less on interfacility transports excluding neonatal and IABP flights or for other reasons as determined by the specific flight service.	90 - 95%

AAMS STANDARD IV: The aircraft must have appropriate equipment in order to assure the maximum safety of the ACMs* and the patient(s).

NFNA AIRCRAFT SAFETY STANDARD III: PATIENT SAFETY - The flight nurse must assume responsibility for the patient's safety since the patient has an altered ability to meet this need.

    Support Standard: The flight nurse will ensure proper preparation and unloading of the patient for transport.

B. SAFETY

1. All patients secured to the aircraft stretcher with two or more straps during loading, transport, and unloading.	95 - 99%

AAMS STANDARD IX: An organized and structured plan must be developed to access the air medical service, provide flight following and communicate pertinent data between the requesting agency, airborne flight crew, and receiving agency.

AAMS STANDARD VI: A designated person must be assigned to receive and dispatch all requests for air medical services.

    Interpretation: Continuous flight following must be maintained and documented. This should include, but need not be limited to, voice communication to base, specifying location and ETA, no less than every 15 minutes.

2. Completion an documentation of flight following by communications personnel no less than every 15 minutes.	95 - 99%

AAMS STANDARD V: The helipad must be designated and located so as to facilitate safe and effective transfer of patients.

    Interpretation: The helipad must comply with local, state and federal requirements.

3. Weekly fuel samples of on-site fueling reservoirs will meet minimum quality control standards.	95 - 99%

AAMS STANDARD VIII: The air medical service must offer sufficient training and education to ensure safe conduct around the helicopter by all potential users.

NFNA AIRCRAFT SAFETY STANDARD I:
EDUCATION - Performance is dependent on knowledge and understanding of general aircraft safety, Federal Aviation Administration (FAA) rules and regulations pertaining to safety in and around the aircraft, and specific features of the aircraft.

    Support Standard: The flight nurse shall receive written and verbal instruction throughout orientation and prior to assuming independent responsibility.

4. Documentation of semi-annual safety training of all air medical personnel based on specific format safety program designed by the individual flight service.	95 - 99%

AAMS STANDARD VII: All ACMs* must be trained and capable of performing program missions.

    Interpretation: Training specific to general aircraft safety must include environmental survival.

5. Documentation of geographically appropriate survival training in accordance with the service's policy and procedure manual.	95 - 99%

AAMS STANDARD I: The air medical helicopter operating VFR must establish weather minimums based on the topography of the service area and weather history known to exist in the area.

    Interpretation: Operational policy dealing with climatic changes affecting flight must be established and adherence ensured through periodic flight review.

6. All cases in which a patient is transported after another air medical service has refused the flight to the same receiving hospital because of weather restrictions will be reviewed and evaluated.	95 - 99%

AAMS STANDARD III: Staffing the air medical unit shall be commensurate with the mission's patient care needs afforded by the airborne facility. The aircraft, by virtue of medical staffing and retrofitting, becomes a patient care unit.

AAMS STANDARD IV: All training and experience requirements must be commensurate with the mission profile and airborne environment and must be documented and approved by the service medical director and in the service's policy and procedure manual.

    Interpretation: Continuing education - Competency and currency must be ensured through relevant in-service education programs and appropriate affiliations. The didactic for such programs should be based in part on the results of the review and evaluation of the quality and appropriateness of care and should include, at least, annual education programs relating to safety, infection control, stress management, and skills maintenance specific to the air medical component.

continues

Exhibit 34-2 continued

NFNA PROFESSIONAL STANDARD I:

QUALIFICATIONS - The flight nurse shall be competent and current according to the established Flight Nurse Standards of Practice.

Support Standard: Registered nurses shall meet specified qualifications prior to assuming the independent role of the flight nurse.

Support Standard: Flight nurses shall demonstrate a continuing advancement of knowledge through didactic and skills education.

NFNA EDUCATIONAL STANDARD II: CONTINUING

EDUCATION - To ensure current competency in the care of the critically ill or injured patient, the flight nurse must engage in a continuing education program pertinent to critical care and emergency nursing.

Support Standard: The flight nurse shall maintain competency in psychomotor skills by participating in ongoing laboratory and clinical experience.

C. CERTIFICATION AND TRAINING

1. Documentation of current professional licensure and/or other appropriate certifications for all ACMs* as mandated by the specific air medical service's policy and procedure manual. — 100%

2. ACMs* will have regular skills maintenance training in compliance with the air medical service's scope of care and skills maintenance policy. — 95 - 99%

Utilization Review Standards and Indicators

AAMS STANDARD II: The air medical crew shall be well organized, properly directed and staffed according to the nature and extent of health care needs anticipated and the scope of services offered.

Interpretation: The air medical service shall accept medically necessary calls from authorized personnel and will not discriminate against any person because of race, creed, sex, color, age, religion, national origin, ancestry, or handicap.

AAMS STANDARD VIII: The air medical service must strive for full integration into existing EMS systems and interhospital transfer networks.

Interpretation: The air medical service must strive for appropriate utilization of its services.

A. UTILIZATION APPROPRIATENESS

** NOTE: The following indicators for ROTOR WING transports should be used to trigger an evaluation to determine the medical necessity or appropriateness of an air transported patient. These indicators **do NOT preclude the use of air transport** for a given patient, but are intended to help "weed out" those patients for whom ground transport might have been more prudent or air transport might have been carried out more appropriately.

Review of all patients:	THRESHOLD
1. Who are discharged home directly from the Emergency Department, or discharged within 24 hours of admission after transport to the receiving hospital.	*tbd*
2. Transported without an IV line, oxygen or monitor.	*tbd*
3. In which CPR is in progress on liftoff in the aircraft.	*tbd*
4. Who is NOT a direct admission to a critical care unit of a hospital (i.e., patients admitted to a non-acute ward).	*tbd*
5. "Scheduled" transports	*tbd*
6. Air transported more than once for the same illness or injury within a 24-hour period.	*tbd*
7. Transported from the accident scene with a trauma score of 15 or greater, or fails to meet area-specific triage criteria for a Level I trauma patient.	*tbd*
8. Transported interfacility, and the receiving facility is not a higher level of care than the referring facility.	*tbd*
9. Transported from an accident scene to any hospital that was not the closest appropriate and available trauma center (depending on local or regional trauma plans).	*tbd*
10. Flown initially by fixed-wing and transported from the airport to the receiving facility by helicopter.	*tbd*

tbd = To be determined by the individual flight service

* NOTE: ACM (air medical crew member) was a term incorporated into the AAMS standards in the early 1980's. Presently the term is being evaluated for its application to air medical personnel and to differentiate it from the term "flight crew member."

References

1. *Minimum Quality Standards and Safety Guidelines,* Association of Air Medical Services, Pasadena, Calif. 1988.

2. *Accreditation Manual for Hospitals* (JCAHO), Chicago 1989.

3. Rhee KJ, O'Malley RJ: The Effect of an Airway Algorithm on Flight Nurse Behavior. *Journal of Air Medical Transport* 1990; 9(1):6-8.

4. Jacobs LM, Berrizabeitia LD, Bennet B, et al.: Endotracheal intubation in the prehospital phase of emergency medical care. *JAMA* 1983; 250(16):2175-2177.

5. Shea SR, MacDonald JR, Gruzinski G: Prehospital endotracheal tube airway or esophageal gastric tube airway: a critical comparison. *Ann Emerg Med* 1985; 14(2):102-112.

6. Obrien DM, Danzi DF, Sowers B, Hooker EA: Airway management of aeromedically transported trauma patients. *J of Emerg Med* 1988; 6:49-54.

7. Syverud SA, Borron SW, Storer DL, Hedges JR: Prehospital use of neuromuscular blocking agents in a helicopter ambulance program. *Ann Emerg Med* 1988; 17(3): 236-242.

continues

Exhibit 34-2 continued

Quality Assurance Resource Document Addendum

Clinical Standards/Indicators/Thresholds

NFNA PRACTICE STANDARD III: PLAN OF CARE— Realistic goals and a prioritized plan of care are based on nursing diagnosis.

Support Standard: The flight nurse shall derive a valid plan to prioritize the patient's needs based on actual or potential threats.

NFNA PRACTICE STANDARD IV: INTERVENTION- Nursing interventions are performed in a planned sequence to support the patient experiencing either single or multiple system failure.

Support Standard: The flight nurse shall implement nursing care based on current scientific knowledge and within his/her scope of practice.

B. MEDICATIONS/BLOOD PRODUCTS   THRESHOLD

Pediatric

1. IV fluids and rate

   a. IV rate appropriate according to PALS standards for fluid bolus and maintenance rates.   95%

      1) Fluid bolus - 20 cc/kg crystalloid solution, repeated as indicated.[1]

      2) Maintenance fluid rate adjusted to current disease process:

	24 Hour Period
0-10 kg	100 cc/kg
11-20 kg	1000 cc + 50 cc/kg over 10 kg
Over 21 kg	1500 cc + 20 cc/kg over 20 kg[2,3]

   b. Documentation and use of IV infusion pump or Buretrol for all pediatric inter-facility transports in order to maintain accurate volumes.   90%

   c. Medication dosages in pediatric patients are consistent with pediatric advanced life support (PALS) guidelines.   90% - 95%

Neonatal

1. Documentation of administration of prophylactic eye drops, vitamin K, and PKU status by referring facility or flight nurse completed.   95% - 99%

2. Amount of blood out in cc's documented.   95% - 99%

C. VENOUS ACCESS

Pediatric

1. Intraosseous (IO) insertion

   a. Unsuccessful IV attempts prior to IO insertion documented.   95%

   b. Number of IO attempts documented.   95%

   c. Intraosseous location and documentation appropriate (i.e., -3 cm below the proximal tibial tuberosity; distal 1/3 of femur; or medial malleolus).[2(p852)]   95% - 99%

Neonatal

1. Venous and Arterial Access

   a. Documentation will include:

      1) IV, umbilical arterial catheter (UAC), umbilical venous catheter (UVC), and arterial lines secured with tape or suture.   95% - 99%

      2) Position of UAC and UVC lines by chest and abdominal X-ray.   95% - 99%

      3) Appropriate IV fluids and rate are administered according to patient age, weight, diagnosis and type of IV line.   90% - 99%

D. ONGOING PATIENT ASSESSMENT/INTERVENTION

Pediatric

1. Recent temperature (less than 1 hour old) recorded on pediatric patients up to 10 years old.   95%

2. Pediatric Glasgow Coma Scale used for neurological evaluation of children less than 2 years old when indicated for suspected head injury or alteration in mental status from other medical causes.[2(pp12-13),3(p757)]   95%

Neonatal

1. A complete maternal history will be obtained at the referral hospital by patient interview and/or maternal chart review.   90%
   a. Maternal age.
   b. Gravity/parity.
   c. Rupture membranes
      1) Time.
      2) Fluid color.
      3) SROM vs. AROM.
   d. Previous complications with pregnancy (both past and previous pregnancies).
   e. Prenatal care.
   f. Type of delivery.
   g. Maternal drugs, smoking, ETOH.
   h. Blood grouping.

2. Parental permission for transport obtained.   95% - 99%

continues

Exhibit 34-2 continued

3. Parent teaching in regard to patient condition, reason for transport, and information about receiving hospital provided is documented. — 90% - 95%

4. Transport isolette for 5 kg or less neonates or infants with acute illness. — 95% - 99%

5. Vital signs documented a minimum of every 15 to 30 minutes (*temperature*, pulse, respirations, BP, SaO_2, if available, or determined by flight program's patient care guidelines/standards, procedures, and protocols). — 95%

6. Documentation includes first time void and stool on newborns. — 95%

7. Blood cultures obtained and labeled, appropriately with central or peripheral IV source prior to antibiotic administration. — 95% - 99%

Pediatric/Neonate
1. Serum Glucose Level

   a. Recent Chemstrip or serum glucose completed (within the last 30 minutes) and documented on all interfacility transported patients less than 3 years old. — 95%

   b. Repeat Chemstrips completed every 15 minutes when acute systems suggest hypoglycemia. — 95%

   c. Glucose administered in pediatric/neonate patients with Chemstrip or serum glucose levels less than 40 for children less than 3 years old.[3(p1919)] — 95%

   d. Dextrose solution administered to pediatric/neonate patients up to 10 years old will be no greater than D25W.[1(p53),3(p1919)] — 95%

2. Initial assessment includes fontanel assessment.

Maternal
1. Fetal heart tones documented every 15 minutes per external monitor and/or doppler. — 95%

2. Fetal monitor strip evaluated at *least* at the referring facility and the following documented: — 90%

   a. When fetal monitor strip was obtained (i.e., referring facility, during transport, or at receiving facility).
   b. Variability.
   c. Presence or absence of decelerations.
   d. Description of fetus response to contractions.

3. Recent or initial maternal temperature documented on patients in preterm labor or when ruptured membranes present. — 90%

4. During transport, the maternal patient is positioned in either lateral position (preferably left) to avoid supine hypotension in the mother and fetal distress in the infant. — 95%

5. In patients with ruptured membranes, a vaginal exam is done by sterile speculum unless patient is in active labor. — 90%

6. Uterine contraction assessment and documentation will include: — 95%
   a. Frequency.
   b. Duration.
   c. Maternal response.

E. TRAUMA CARE

Maternal
1. During transport of the *pregnant trauma* patient more than 20 weeks gestation, the backboard/scoop is tilted to the left. Placement of a towel roll under the right or left hip is *only* done when LS and thoracic spine is cleared radiologically for fractures. — 95%

NFNA PRACTICE STANDARD I: DATA COLLECTION— The assessment and collection of patient health data is systematic and continuous. The data is documented and communicated to appropriate members of the health care team.

Support Standard: Data collection shall be recorded in a systematic and retrievable manner.

AAMS ROTORCRAFT STANDARD VII: The quality and appropriateness of patient care provided by air medical services shall be continuously reviewed, evaluated, and assured through the establishment of a quality control mechanism.

Interpretation: A patient record shall be maintained, documenting patient care rendered by the air medical personnel and disposition of the patient at the receiving institution and department on file, for a period of time to include that of the statute of limitations.

F. DOCUMENTATION
Neonatal
1. Copies of most recent X-rays obtained unless there is a significant change from previous X-rays. — 90% - 99%

Neonatal/Maternal
1. Copied chart of maternal and neonatal history obtained. — 90% - 99%

Maternal
1. Obtained copies of fetal monitoring strips if abnormal. — 90%

2. Documentation of referring hospital last vaginal exam (VE) or flight nurse VE includes: — 90% - 95%

   a. Dilatation.
   b. Effacement.
   c. Presenting part.
   d. Abnormalities.
   e. Sterile technique utilized.

continues

Exhibit 34-2 continued

Adult/Maternal/Neonatal/Pediatric
1. Patient care documentation reflects nursing   95% - 99%
   assessment, plan, intervention, and evaluation.

Operational Standards/Indicators/Thresholds

AAMS ROTORCRAFT STANDARD II: The ACMs shall be well-organized, properly directed, and staffed according to the nature and extent of health care needs anticipated and scope of services offered.

AAMS ROTORCRAFT STANDARD VIII: The air medical service must strive for full integration into existing emergency medical systems and interhospital transfer networks.

Interpretation: The air medical service must ensure continuum of care and expedition of treatment of patients using standard protocols whenever possible.

A. TIMELINESS OF CARE   THRESHOLD
  Neonatal
1. Emphasis on timeliness of neonatal inter-   80% - 90%
   facility care is placed on quality of stabilization;
   therefore, in-house time limits reflect acuity
   of neonate, procedures done prior to transport,
   and equipment/drugs used during transport.

AAMS SAFETY GUIDELINE IV: The aircraft must have appropriate equipment in order to assure the maximum safety of the air medical personnel and the patient(s).

NFNA AIRCRAFT SAFETY STANDARD III: PATIENT SAFETY: The flight nurse must assume responsibility for the patient's safety, since the patient has an altered ability to meet this need.

Support Standard: The flight nurse will ensure proper preparation and unloading of the patient for transport.

B. SAFETY
  Neonatal
1. Neonate will be secured in the isolette with   99%
   safety belt throughout entire transport.

2. Transport isolette will: 99%

   a. Have a minimum of one hour battery supply.
   b. Have adequate heating capabilities using
      electrical or battery power.
   c. Be secured in the aircraft with FAA approved
      restraints during all transports.

Adult/Pediatric/Neonatal/Maternal
1. All patient transports in *dedicated, medically*   99%
   configured rotor-wing or fixed-wing aircraft
   will have a 500 watt or greater inverter on
   board for medical equipment (i.e., for isolettes,
   invasive monitoring, pacers, intra-aortic balloon
   pumps, suction units, pulse oximeters, infusion
   pumps, and external fetal monitors).

References
1. Chameides L (Ed): *Textbook of Pediatric Advanced Life Support.* American Heart Association, 1988 p 47.
2. Blumer, JL (Ed): *A Practical Guide to Pediatric Intensive Care.* 3rd ed, St. Louis, C.V. Mosby, 1990 p 547.
3. Oski FA (Ed): *Principles and Practice of Pediatrics.* Philadelphia, J.B. Lippincott Co, 1990 p 58.

Source: Courtesy of Association of Air Medical Services, Pasadena, CA.

BIBLIOGRAPHY

Association of Air Medical Services. September 1990. Position paper on the appropriate use of emergency air medical services. *Journal of Air Medical Transport:* 29–33.

Eastes, L., and J. Jacobson, eds. 1990. *Quality assurance in air medical transport.* Orem, Utah: Association of Air Medical Services.

Joint Commission on Accreditation of Healthcare Organizations. 1990. *Accreditation manual for hospitals, 1991.* Oakbrook Terrace, Ill.: Joint Commission on Accreditation of Healthcare Organizations.

Joint Commission on Accreditation of Healthcare Organizations. 1988. *Monitoring and evaluation of the quality and appropriateness of care: A hospital example.* Oakbrook Terrace, Ill.: Joint Commission on Accreditation of Healthcare Organizations.

Appendix 34-A

Aircraft Standards and Safety Guidelines

STANDARDS

Fixed Wing

The following minimum Standards and Safety Guidelines, presented here in outline form, have been developed by the Association of Air Medical Services to serve as reference for the development and continuing operation of an air medical service. The Standards are intended to ensure the quality of patient care and the safety of both crew and patient(s).

Standard I

The aircraft designated for the air medical mission must be evaluated carefully, considering the geographic area to be served, the type of missions it is to perform and the crew and equipment it must carry.

Standard II

The air medical crew shall be well organized, properly directed and staffed according to the nature and extent of health care needs anticipated and the scope of services offered.

Standard III

Staffing the fixed-wing air medical unit must be commensurate with the level of care offered.

Standard IV

All training and experience requirements must be commensurate to the critical care, advanced life support, specialty care, and basic life support airborne environment and must be documented and approved by the program medical director and in the program's policy and procedure manual.

Standard V

Policies and procedures addressing patient transport issues involving communicable diseases, infectious processes, and health precautions for emergency personnel as well as for patients must be written and readily available to all members of the air medical service. Additional medical and agency resources pertinent to the area of infection control must be identified and made available in the policy manual to all members of the air medical team.

Note: Provider members will receive a complete copy of the Standards and Safety Guidelines upon acceptance of membership. Other members and interested parties may purchase a copy from the AAMS National Office.

Source: Courtesy of Association of Air Medical Services, Pasadena, CA.

Standard VI

A significant commitment of resources is required of the sponsor of air medical service(s). Appropriate services shall be rendered within the defined capabilities of the service to ensure continuity and smooth transition of care.

Standard VII

The quality and appropriateness of patient care provided by the air medical service shall be continuously reviewed, evaluated, and assured through the establishment of a quality control mechanism.

Standard VIII

The air medical service shall strive for full integration into existing emergency medical systems and interhospital transfer networks.

Standard IX

An organized and structured plan must be developed to access the air medical service, file flight plans, provide flight following, initiate overdue aircraft procedures, and communicate pertinent data between the agency, the airborne flight crew, and the recipient agency.

Standard X

A professional and community education program must be developed that will promote proper air medical service utilization.

Standard XI

The air medical crew will approach the mission where hazardous material is suspected or known to exist in such a manner so as to ensure the safety of the crew and aircraft as the primary consideration. A structured program for responding to the patient(s) involved in a hazardous material incident must be in place, with policies and procedures clearly outlined and available for the pilot and medical crew prior to lift off.

Rotocraft

Standard I

The Aircraft designated for the air medical mission must be evaluated carefully, considering the geographic area to be served, the type of missions it is to perform and the crew and equipment it must carry.

Standard II

The air medical crew shall be well organized, properly directed, and staffed according to the nature and extent of health care needs anticipated and the scope of services offered.

Standard III

Staffing the air medical unit shall be commensurate with the mission's patient care need afforded by the airborne facility. The aircraft, by virtue of medical staffing and retrofitting, becomes a patient care unit.

Standard IV

All training and experience requirements must be commensurate with the mission profile and airborne environment and must be documented and approved by the program medical director and in the program's policy and procedure manual.

Standard V

Policies and procedures addressing patient transport issues involving communicable diseases, infectious processes, and health precautions for emergency personnel as well as for patients must be current with the local standard of practice. Information must be written and readily available to all members of the air medical service. Additional medical and agency resources pertinent to the area of infection control must be identified and made available in the policy manual to all members of the air medical team.

Standard VI

A significant commitment of resources is required of the sponsoring institutions. Appropriate services shall be rendered within the hospitals, the defined capabilities of the sponsoring hospital, and/or other hospitals within the service region.

Standard VII

The quality and appropriateness of patient care provided by the air medical service shall be continuously reviewed, evaluated, and assured through the establishment of a quality control mechanism.

Standard VIII

An air medical service must strive for full integration into existing emergency medical systems and interhospital transfer networks.

Standard IX

An organized and structured plan must be developed to access the air medical service, provide flight following, and communicate pertinent data between requesting agency, airborne flight crew, and recipient agency.

Standard X

A professional and community education program shall be developed that will promote proper air medical service utilization.

Standard XI

The air medical crew will approach the mission where hazardous material is suspected or known to exist in such a manner so as to ensure the safety of the crew and aircraft as the primary consideration. A structured program for responding to the patient(s) involved in a hazardous material incident must be in place, with policies and procedures clearly outlined and available for the pilot and medical crew prior to lift off.

SAFETY

Rotorcraft

Guideline I   *Weather Minimums*

Weather: The air medical helicopter operating VFR must establish weather minimums based on the topography of the service area and weather history known to exist in the area.

Guideline II   *Rotorcraft Pilot Duty Time and Training*

Pilots: The helicopter pilot, flying air medical missions, must call upon many resources, experiences, and skills. The mission frequently involves night flying and unprepared landing sites. The pilot shall be summarily prepared, certified, and trained.

Fixed Wing

Guideline III-A *Fixed Wing Pilot and Mechanic Training*

Pilots: The nature of the air medical mission requires that the aircraft and pilot be mission-ready so as to be able to move air medical personnel and patient(s) safely and expeditiously.

Rotorcraft

Guideline III   *Rotorcraft Mechanic Duties and Training*

Maintenance: The helicopter mechanic is vital to mission readiness.

Guideline IV   *Rotorcraft Equipment and Configuration*

Aircraft: The aircraft must have appropriate equipment in order to ensure the maximum safety of air medical personnel and patient(s).

Guideline V   *Helipads*

Helipad: The helipad must be designed and located so as to facilitate the safe and effective transfer of patients.

Guideline VI   *Communications and Flight Following*

Communications: A designated person must be assigned to receive and coordinate all requests for air medical services.

Guideline VII   *Air Medical Personnel Safety Training*

Medical Personnel: All air medical personnel must have initial *annual* and *recurrent* safety training and be capable of performing program missions.

Guideline VIII   *Rotorcraft Safety Education Programs*

Pre-Hospital and Hospital Personnel: The air medical service must offer sufficient initial and recurrent training and education to ensure safe conduct around the helicopter by potential users.

Appendix 34-B

Federal Aviation Administration Guidelines for Air Ambulance and Emergency Medical Service/Helicopter Operators

ADVISORY CIRCULAR

Subject:
EMERGENCY MEDICAL
SERVICES/HELICOPTER (EMS/H)

Date:
Initiated by: AFS-250

AC No:
Change: 135-14A

1. PURPOSE. This Advisory Circular (AC) provides information and guidance material that may be used by Air Ambulance and Emergency Medical Service/Helicopter (EMS/H) operators. Items of both mandatory and advisory nature are included. The words "required" and "must" are used to designate items mandated by regulations (either explicitly or implicitly), while "should" is used to indicate items of an advisory nature. It must be emphasized that this AC diminishes neither the force nor the effect of the Federal Aviation Regulations (FAR). The regulations, of course, are always controlling. This document does not interpret the regulations; interpretations are issued only under established national Federal Aviation Administration (FAA) procedures.

2. CANCELLATION. AC 135-14, Emergency Medical Services/Helicopter, dated October 20, 1988.

3. FOCUS. These guidelines are applicable to EMS/H operations under FAR Part 135 and are recommended for EMS/H operations conducted by public service and other operators.

4. RELATED FAR SECTIONS. FAR Parts 1, 27, 29, 43, 61, 65, 91, 135, and 157.

5. RELATED READING MATERIAL. Additional information may be found in the following AC's (as revised) and other listed publications:

a. FAA Documents:

(1) AC 27-1, as revised, Certification of Normal Category Rotorcraft.

(2) AC 29-2, as revised, Certification of Transport Category Rotorcraft.

(3) AC 91-32, as revised, Safety in and around Helicopters.

(4) AC 91-42, as revised, Hazards of Rotating Propeller and Helicopter Rotor Blades.

(5) AC 120-27A, as revised, Aircraft Weight and Balance Control.

(6) AC 120-49, Certification of Air Carriers.

(7) AC 135-5, as revised, Maintenance Program Approval for Carry-On Oxygen Equipment for Medical Purposes.

(8) AC 150/5390-2, Heliport Design.

NOTE: Copies of (1) through (8) may be obtained free of charge from the U.S. Department of Transportation, Distribution Requirements Section, M-443.2, Washington, DC 20590.

b. Other Documents.

(1) Pamphlet—DOT/FAA/PM-86/45, Aeronautical Decision Making for Helicopter Pilots. Copies may be purchased from National Technical Information Service, 5285 Port Royal Road, Springfield, VA 22161. Order number is ADA178050. Microfiche is available for purchase.

(2) Pamphlet—DOT/FAA/DS-88/7, Risk Management for Air Ambulance Helicopter Operators. Copies may be purchased from National Technical Information Service, 5285 Port Royal Road, Springfield, VA 22161.

(3) Pamphlet—National EMS Pilots Association, Preparing a Landing Zone. Copies may be purchased from the National EMS Pilot Association, P.O. Box 2354, Pearland, TX 77588.

(4) Helicopter Association International Pamphlets (HAI)—HAI Safety Manual, HAI Fly Neighborly, HAI Heliport Development Guides, and Association of Air Medical Services and HAI EMS Guidelines. Copies may be purchased from HAI, 1619 Duke Street, Alexandria, VA 22314.

(5) NFPA Publication 410–1980: Fire Protection/Aircraft. Copies may be obtained from National Fire Protection Association (NFPA), Battery Park, Quincy, MA 02269.

(6) Air Ambulance Guidelines, DOT HS 806703. Revised May 1986, U.S. Department of Transportation, National Highway Traffic Safety Administration. Copies may be obtained from U.S. Department of Transportation, Distribution Requirements Section, M-443.2, Washington, DC 20590.

6. BACKGROUND. The use of helicopters as swift transportation of wounded personnel from the battlefield to medical facilities for immediate care during the Korean and Vietnamese conflicts resulted in a substantial drop in the death rate of U.S. servicemen as compared to previous wars. This dramatic use of helicopters as a medical tool spread to the civil community. Today, helicopters are a vital tool within the medical field, providing a means of transporting critically injured people in urgent need of medical assistance. The EMS/H industry continues to expand. Each year thousands of patients are transported while being attended by medical teams trained to accommodate specific needs of the patients. EMS/H aircraft are equipped with the latest state-of-the-art medical monitoring and support systems to ensure proper care while en route. In response to the dynamic growth of this industry, the FAA has issued this AC providing information and guidelines that will further assist EMS/H operators in their operations. This AC provides guidance to operators conducting or planning EMS/H operations.

7. DEFINITIONS. This paragraph defines terms used for the purpose of this AC. Other definitions may be found in FAR Part I, "Definitions and Abbreviations," and the "Pilot/Controller Glossary" supplement to the Airman's Information Manual.

   a. Aeromedical Director. A licensed physician within an air ambulance service or EMS/H operation who is ultimately responsible for patient care during transport missions. The aeromedical director is responsible for assuring that appropriate medical personnel and equipment are provided for each patient.

   b. Air Ambulance and/or EMS/H. A helicopter designated for the transportation of ambulatory patients or other patients requiring special care including, but not limited to, basic life support (BLS) or advanced life support (ALS). An air ambulance or EMS/H is equipped with the medical equipment (portable or installed) necessary to support these levels of care in flight with trained medical personnel.

   c. Air Ambulance Service and/or Emergency Medical Service (EMS). The use of an aircraft in transportation, for carriage of ambulatory or other patients requiring special care, including BLS or ALS, during flight, and/or transport of body organs for medical reasons. An air ambulance or EMS aircraft may be used to transport patients deemed by medical personnel to require other special service not available on regular commercial air carrier or charter flights. NOTE: The service of providing transportation for body organs and no passengers can be considered a cargo operation.

   d. Certificate Holding District Office (CHDO). The FAA Flight Standards District Office (FSDO) with responsibility for management of the air carrier's certificate and which is charged with the overall inspection and surveillance of the certificate holder's operations.

   e. Flightcrew Member. A pilot, flight engineer, or flight navigator assigned to duty in an aircraft during flight time is considered a crewmember.

   f. Helicopter Hospital Emergency Medical Evacuation Services (HEMES). The operation of a helicopter, based at a hospital, to transport patients in an emergency medical evacuation service only. Operations of this type can operate under FAR Section 135.271 provided that all of the conditions prescribed therein are followed.

   g. Levels of Medical Care.

      (1) BLS. Refers to the air-medical provider offering airborne patient transports staffed by a minimum of one medical person who is experienced and qualified by training, certification, and current competency in BLS care. This medical person practices through the orders of a physician-medical director and is supported by a medically configured aircraft capable of providing BLS systems (such as oxygen, suction, electrical supply, lighting, and climate control) to the patient. As used in this statement, BLS consists of a medical person capable of recognizing respiratory and cardiac arrest, starting and maintaining the proper medical procedures until the victim recovers or the medical person stops procedures, or until ALS is available. In air-medical transports, BLS includes air-to-ground communications to ensure continuity of care. ("Standards for CPR and ECG," *JAMA*, February 18, 1974.)

      (2) ALS. Refers to the air-medical provider offering airborne patient transports staffed by a minimum of two medical personnel who are experienced and qualified by training, certification, and current competency in emergency critical care. The medical personnel practice through the orders of a physician-medical director and are supported by a medically configured aircraft capable of providing life support systems (such as oxygen, suction, electrical

supply, lighting, climate control, pressurization, etc.) to the patient. The following elements are recommended for ALS:

   (i)   BLS.

  (ii)   Using adjunctive equipment and special techniques, such as endotracheal intubation and closed chest cardiac compression.

 (iii)   Cardiac monitoring for dysrhythmia recognition and treatment.

 (iv)   Defibrillation.

  (v)   Establishing and maintaining an intravenous infusion lifeline.

 (vi)   Employing definitive therapy, including drug administration.

(vii)   Stabilization of patient's condition.

NOTE: ALS includes: (1) air-to-ground communications to ensure continuity of care, and (2) the capability of constant monitoring and life support until the patient has been delivered to a continuing care facility. ("Standards for CPR and ECG," *JAMA,* February 18, 1974.)

h. Local Flying Area. An area designated in nautical miles by the operator that takes into account the local geographic terrain features. (The local flying area should be determined between the operator and Principal Operations Inspector (POI) based upon the operating environment in which EMS operations will be conducted.)

i. Medical Personnel. A person trained in air-medical environment and assigned to perform medical duties during flight including, but not limited to, doctors, nurses, paramedics, respiratory therapists, or emergency medical technicians. Medical personnel may also be trained and assigned to perform other duties by the certificate holder.

j. Principal Avionics Inspector (PAI). An FAA inspector assigned by the FAA Administrator to oversee the avionics functions of the certificate holder.

k. Principal Maintenance Inspector (PMI). An FAA inspector assigned by the FAA Administrator to oversee the maintenance functions of the certificate holder.

l. POI. An FAA inspector assigned by the FAA Administrator to oversee the operations functions of the certificate holder.

m. Public Aircraft. An aircraft used only in the service of a government or political subdivision. It docs not include any government-owned aircraft engaged in carrying persons or property for commercial purposes.

NOTE: Public Law 100–223, December 30, 1987, Section 207. Public Aircraft Defined Section 101(36) has been amended thus: "for the purposes of this paragraph, 'used exclusively in the service of' means, for other than the Federal Government, an aircraft which is owned or operated by a government entity for other than commercial purposes or which is exclusively leased by such government entity for not less than 90 continuous days."

CONTENTS

CHAPTER 1. CERTIFICATION

1. GENERAL. Aircraft operators desiring to commence Air Ambulance or EMS/H operations as a FAR Part 135 air carrier who do not hold a FAR Part 135 air carrier certificate should refer to AC 120-49, Certification of Air Carriers, dated November 23, 1988, for methods and procedures to follow in the certification process. The FSDO located in the area where applicant desires to locate its principal business office will assist the applicant in becoming certified. This chapter refers to added steps that may be required to obtain a FAR Part 135 certificate for EMS/H operations.

    NOTE: For those operators presently conducting operations under FAR Part 135, new or revised operations specifications may be required prior to initiating EMS/H operations.

  a. Inspections. Inspections will be conducted at the principal base of operations, and will include items such as:

    (1) Maintenance facilities, equipment and records (including installation of special/medical equipment), lease agreements, and contract maintenance records.

    NOTE: Lease agreements are considered proprietary documents and will be treated accordingly by FAA personnel.

    (2) Manuals to ensure they contain information required by FAR Section 135.23.

    (3) Recordkeeping system.

    (4) Aircraft to be used in air transportation service.

    (5) Each certificate holder is responsible for the airworthiness of its aircraft (FAR Section 135.413). Operator and/or contract maintenance facilities may be inspected for compliance with appropriate FAR. This particular inspection will be accomplished to determine the adequacy of tools, spare parts, special tools, and that properly trained personnel are available.

  b. Additional Equipment/General. The applicant should identify, in the initial application, any specialized equipment that may be used in EMS operations. The equipment should be installed in the aircraft in an acceptable manner (using data approved by the aircraft manufacturer, an EMS equipment manufacturer, or the FAA Administrator). The FAA may approve add-on equipment installation after evidence of airborne test results are submitted from the aircraft operator, the Department of Transportation (DOT), Department of Defense, or an independent testing organization. Any equipment installed aboard the aircraft should comply with the data in AC 43.13-2A, Acceptable Methods, Techniques, and Practices—Aircraft Alterations. Chapter I, paragraph 2(d) and 3, and Chapter 12, paragraph 243(a), and withstand the following static loads in accordance with AC 43.13-1A, Acceptable Methods, Techniques, and Practices—Aircraft Repair:

    (1) 9.0G forward. 6.6G downward, 3.0G upward, and 1 .SG sideward; and

    (2) tie-down, 13.5G forward, 9.9G downward, 4.5G upward, and 2.25G sideward.

    (3) Supplemental Type Certificate (STC) or Field Approval. All items of additional equipment must be installed in accordance with the applicable FAR. The installation of additional equipment may require an STC or field approval by an airworthiness aviation safety inspector. It should be noted that the requirements for field approval

are the same as for an STC. If the certificate holder is unsure of the requirements on the proposed equipment, he or she should contact the PMI before installation is initiated.

(4) Maintenance Test Flight. Certificate holder should ensure that the installation of all additional equipment is compatible with all previously installed aircraft systems. Aircraft navigation and communication equipment may have to be recalibrated after installation of any additional medical equipment. Before returning the aircraft to service after the installation of additional equipment, flight tests may have to be accomplished to determine if there is radio frequency/electromagnetic interference (RFI/EMI) with any navigation, communication, or flight control systems. The flight tests should be accomplished in visual meteorological conditions. Tests should include all installed equipment as well as items of carry-on medical equipment intended to be used for patient transport. Results of the flight tests verifying acceptability should be entered into appropriate permanent records of the aircraft.

NOTE: Medical monitors may also be affected by the aircraft's electronic equipment; therefore, the medical monitors should be checked for accuracy by medical personnel before use with a patient.

c. Equipment Recommended for EMS/H Operations.

(1) Aircraft-Approved Searchlight. A searchlight to be manipulated by the pilot, having a minimum movement of 90° vertical and 180° horizontal and capable of illuminating a landing site. The pilot should not have to remove his or her hands from the aircraft flight controls in order to operate the searchlight.

(2) Radio Capable of Air-to-Ground Communications. To ensure safe and satisfactory completion of transportation and to coordinate with emergency personnel on the scene (i.e., local or state police, fire department, etc.).

(3) Restraining Devices. To prevent patients from interfering with the flightcrew or the helicopter flight controls.

NOTE: Child restraint seats provided must meet DOT/FAA restraint and securing criteria.

(4) Intercommunications System (ICS). An ICS should be provided for flightcrew and medical personnel to communicate with each other aboard the helicopter.

(5) Wire Strike Protection System.

NOTE: If a minimum equipment list has been approved, the items listed in (1) through (5) above should be included.

(6) Stretchers (Litters). Stretchers must be in compliance with FAR Sections 27.561 and 29.785. Restraining devices, including shoulder harnesses, must be available to ensure patient safety.

NOTE: Patient life support systems which include litters/stretchers, berths, incubators, heart pumps, etc., not normally included in the type design of the aircraft, must also be installed in accordance with the applicable FAR- and FAA-approved data.

d. Additional Equipment for EMS. The following additional items of equipment are recommended for EMS operations:

(1) Medical Oxygen System. A medical oxygen system including bottles, lines, gauges, regulators, and other system components that has been installed by approved data on an aircraft becomes an "appliance." If a single servicing port is installed in accordance with AC 27-1, as revised, Certification of Normal Category Rotorcraft, or AC 29-2A, as revised, Certification of Transport Category Rotorcraft, the system may be serviced by any person trained by the certificate holder. An oxygen bottle installed in a rack in the cabin area having its own regulator, hose, and mask feeding directly to the patient may be removed and serviced by any person trained by the certificate holder. If servicing is accomplished by removing and replacing bottles or by disconnecting lines, regardless of the type fitting, it must be accomplished by an appropriately certified mechanic or repairman.

(2) Supplemental Lighting System. Some aircraft may require additional lighting since standard aircraft lighting may not be sufficient for adequate patient care. An emergency lighting system with a self-contained battery pack may be incorporated to allow for continued patient care and for emergency egress from the aircraft in the event of a primary electrical failure. A means to shield the cockpit from light in the patient area should be provided for night operations.

(3) EMS Electrical Power Installation. All wiring, electrical components and installation procedures must conform to the requirements of FAR Parts 27 or 29. An electrical load analysis must be performed to preclude an overload on the aircraft generating system. The system should be designed to provide the pilot a fast means of shedding electrical load in an emergency situation.

(4) Motor-Driven Vacuum Air Pump. Motors and/or pumps must be installed in accordance with FAR Parts 27 and 29. Any motor-driven device should be installed in such a way as to preclude contact with any flammable fluid, gas, or foreign materials that may cause heat buildup and possibly fire. Aircraft should be flight-tested with electrical motors running to check for RFI/EMI interference.

(5) Defibrillator. Extreme care should be taken when using a defibrillator on an aircraft. A suitable means of isolating the patient from the airframe must be incorporated to prevent inadvertent electrical shock to the flightcrew and other passengers. Defibrillator must be ground-tested for proper operation before use in flight.

(6) Incubators. Incubators, balloon pumps, or other large carry-on medical equipment must be restrained in an appropriate manner to the following ultimate load factors:
  (i) 3.0G upward, 6.6G downward; and
  (ii) 9.0G forward, 1.5G sideward.
NOTE: If the equipment manufacturer does not provide pull test data to confirm that specific equipment can withstand the above loads, the certificate holder must demonstrate the above loads on each specific piece of equipment, or use an approved restraining device. Aircraft cargo straps or safety belts provide a satisfactory restraint in many instances. Also, mechanical (metallic) fasteners may be used for attachment.
NOTE: The incubator lid latches should withstand appropriate loads (approximately 15 pounds and any significant lid load). The operator should ensure the unit has minimum movement when secured if straps or belts are used. If the incubator includes features requiring electrical power, operation should be evaluated to assure there is no interference with aircraft instruments and equipment that are required by the FAA airworthiness certificate. The operator should provide padding for the infant for forward and downward loads and movement. Mattresses and all padding used should be in accordance with AC 25.853-1, Flammability Requirements for Aircraft Seat Cushions dated September 17, 1986, and FAR Sections 27.853 or 29.853.

e. Additional Equipment Installation. Some equipment is installed in the aircraft for the purpose of patient care only. This equipment should be installed, using approved data, in racks that meet the g-loading requirements of an emergency landing. The racks should be removed and replaced by a certified FAA mechanic, but the medical equipment in the racks used for patient care should be installed so that it may be removed readily to accompany the patient. Instructions for removal and replacement should be contained in the operator's manual required by FAR Part 135.

(1) The certificate holder must ensure that the installation of all additional equipment is compatible with the aircraft systems. FAR Section 135.91(a)(1)(iv) requires that all installed equipment, including portable devices, be appropriately secured. The structure supporting the equipment must be designed to restrain all loads (up to the ultimate inertia specified in the emergency provisions/emergency landing conditions) required by FAR Parts 27 and 29. Equipment installed aboard the aircraft should meet the static and dynamic loads specified in AC 27-1 and AC 29-2, as revised.

(2) The installation of additional equipment by an STC or field approval. Normally the STC should provide instructions and operational supplements, weight and balance data, and instructions for continued airworthiness.

(3) Each installation must be evaluated at the time of its approval. This is to determine if a mechanic is required to perform installation or if other personnel can be trained for removal or replacement of these items. Frequent removal and replacement may constitute maintenance and require a certificated mechanic.

(4) If the installation does not require tools and can be done in accordance with approved data and procedures in the operator's manual, any person trained by the certificate holder may be authorized to install the equipment.

2. RECORDS.

a. Maintenance Records. Each certificate holder must comply with the maintenance recording requirements of FAR Section 135.439 and/or 91.417. When aircraft are sold, the certificate holder must comply with FAR Section 135.441 and/or 91.419, Transfer of Maintenance Records.

b. Flight Records. Records required by FAR Section 135.63 must be kept at the certificate holder's principal business office, or at other operational locations approved by the Administrator. The following records should also be maintained at operational bases located at other than the principal business office:

(1) Flight crewmember's flight time and rest records. The flight time and rest records must contain information to show compliance with the flight, duty, and rest requirements of FAR 135, Subpart F. The records should indicate whether operations are being conducted in accordance with FAR Sections 135.267 or 135.271.

(2) A copy of the most recent competency and/or proficiency flight check. For each pilot assigned to that particular location, a copy of the current flight proficiency check should be available.

(3) Current airworthiness documentation. In order for the pilot to determine the acceptability of the helicopter prior to each flight, airworthiness documentation must be available.

(4) Flight following records. Flight following records of each flight will be maintained for a minimum of 30 days in accordance with FAR Part 135.

3. OPERATIONS SPECIFICATIONS.

a. Additional Requirements. FAR Part 135 certificate holders may use EMS procedures authorized with appropriate operations specifications. The operations specifications may contain conditional authorizations that apply to individual operators. The approving authority for the operations specifications will be either the POI, PMI, or PAI of the FAA CHDO having jurisdiction over the certificate holder. The operations specifications include the following items:

NOTE: If a FAR Part 135 operator does not provide full EMS/H services requiring medical personnel or special medical equipment but only occasionally transports body organs, that operator may not be required to comply with all provisions of the EMS/H automated operations specifications.

(1) Bases of operation. Location of all bases of operation where EMS/H activities will be performed.

(2) Exemptions. As appropriate.

(3) Deviations. As appropriate.

(4) Area of operation. The area of operation (local and cross-country) for an EMS/H certificate holder will be identified on the operations specifications issued by CHDO.

(5) Special authorizations.

b. Automated Maintenance Operations Specifications. Operations specifications are indicated in AC 120-49. However, in addition the following are items that should be considered:

(1) Special/medical and navigation communication equipment, if appropriate to the operations being conducted.

(2) If the helicopter is being maintained under an Approved Aircraft Inspection Program, the operations specifications must include the make, model, and registration number of the helicopter on that program.

c. Weight and Balance. A weight and balance program using average weights for crewmembers, medical personnel, and patients should be developed regardless of the size of the helicopter used. This approved program will be listed in the certificate holder's operations specifications.

4. FACILITIES. The facilities include the business office required by FAR Section 135.27, maintenance area, and operational area. Items to be checked during FAA inspections should include the manual as required by FAR Section 135.21, as well as the operator's use of business names, aircraft, advertising, area of operations.

a. Maintenance. Maintenance facilities should be large enough to house the largest type of helicopter used by the certificate holder, adequately lighted, and equipped to perform required maintenance. Additional specialized equipment may be required for the EMS equipment installed in the aircraft. Contract maintenance will be performed in accordance with the procedures outlined in the operator's manual.

b. Operations. The operations facilities should have an area for flight planning, scheduling, flight following, training, and recordkeeping.

c. Flightcrew Place of Rest. In accordance with FAR Section 135.271, an adequate place of rest will be provided for flight crewmembers assigned EMS/H duty at or in close proximity to the hospital at which the HEMES assignment is being performed. The place of rest should be in an area away from the general flow of vehicle and pedestrian traffic, allowing a quiet, restful atmosphere. The place of rest should provide adequate facilities including but not limited to, a shower, a closet, a bed with sheets, and the space environmentally controlled for comfort. The place of rest should be available on a continuous basis for flight crewmembers.

d. EMS/H and HEMES Heliports. FAR Part 135 EMS/H heliports should meet criteria established in AC 150/5390-2, Heliport Design. These heliport criteria have been established to ensure the highest level of safety for established heliports.

5. MANUAL. Although FAR Section 135.21 does not require an operations manual for a certificate holder with only one pilot, it is recommended that each certificate holder conducting EMS/H operations should prepare a manual for such operations. The manual should be available in each helicopter and at each dispatch location. The following items are suggested for inclusion in the operations manual as well as items identified in FAR Section 135.23:

NOTE: This list does not relieve a certificate holder from including other items in the operations manual as required by FAR Part 135.

a. Names of all EMS/H management personnel who have authority to act for the certificate holder. The aeromedical director will not exercise control over EMS air ambulance missions unless he/she is listed in the manual required by FAR Section 135.21 as a person authorized by the certificate holder in accordance with FAR Section 135.77.

b. The front page of the certificate holder's operations and maintenance operations specifications.

c. Accident and incident notification procedures to include the local FAA, National Transportation Safety Board, and FAA CHDO telephone numbers.

d. Refueling procedures for normal and emergency situations.

NOTE: Refueling with the engine running, rotor turning, and/or passengers on board is not recommended. However, emergency situations of this type can arise during an EMS/H operation. Specific and rigid procedures should be developed by the operator in accordance with the POI to handle these occurrences. Such "hot refueling" procedures will be covered in the operator's training program.

e. Type of medical oxygen system installed including bottles, lines, gauges, regulators, other system components, and the approved method of servicing.

f. Instructions for the removal and replacement of equipment installed for the purpose of patient care only. This equipment should be installed in racks by approved data that meet the g-loading requirements in an emergency. The racks that hold the equipment should be removed and replaced by a certificated FAA mechanic, but the medical equipment used in patient care should be installed for easy removal by medical personnel if it is needed to go with the patient, and the medical personnel should be trained accordingly.

NOTE: Patient life support systems, which include litters/stretchers, berths, incubators, heart pumps, etc., not normally included in the type design of the aircraft must also be installed in accordance with approved data. These approved data normally include installation and removal instructions and should contain operational supplements, weight and balance data, and instructions for continued airworthiness.

Removal and replacement of these items may be repeated on a frequent basis and may or may not constitute maintenance. Each installation must be evaluated at the time of its approval to determine who is authorized to complete the installation. If the installation is simple, does not require tools, and can be done in accordance with approved data and procedures contained in the operator's manual, any person trained by the certificate holder may be authorized to install such equipment.

FAR Section 135.91(a)(1)(iv) requires that all equipment installed, including portable devices, must be appropriately secured. The supporting structure to which the equipment is to be attached must be designed to restrain all loads up to the ultimate inertia specified in the emergency provisions/emergency landing conditions required by the FAR.

g. Hospital flight following and flight release procedures.

h. In-flight emergency and emergency evacuation duties for EMS/H crewmembers and medical personnel.

NOTE: Items listed in (a) through (h) above do not preclude a certificate holder from including other items in the operator's manual required by FAR Part 135.

CHAPTER 2. TRAINING PROGRAM

6. GENERAL. This chapter outlines recommended training for all EMS personnel including flight crewmembers and medical personnel.

a. Flight Crewmember. The unusual requirements of the EMS/H mission means that aircraft may be dispatched in less than ideal weather conditions; i.e., night, low ceiling and/or low visibility, and into remote areas. Because of these adverse conditions, the pilot should be trained in the basic instrument flying skills to recover from inadvertent Instrument Meteorological Conditions (IMC).

NOTE: This training does not authorize or condone operating an aircraft in IMC without proper Air Traffic Control (ATC) clearance. Its purpose is to provide pilots with an additional margin of safety when conducting life-saving missions. An operator's training program should include night operations into similar or like conditions that are normally encountered in EMS operations.

b. Medical Personnel. Medical personnel assigned duty during flight should be trained in the use of aviation terminology. Medical personnel should use aviation terminology to avoid confusion or misunderstandings of instruction from the flightcrew during the EMS mission.

(1) Medical personnel should be trained to properly use, remove, replace, and store medical equipment installed on the aircraft.

(2) Medical personnel should also be trained in physiological aspects of flight prior to being assigned flight duty.

(3) Medical personnel should be trained in aircraft evacuation and patient loading and unloading.

NOTE: The training program should consider the particular aircraft being used, and its safety features. A practice evacuation using emergency exits should be accomplished.

NOTE: If the certificate holder desires to use medical personnel to help advise the pilot of wires, obstructions, and other traffic during takeoffs and landings at EMS/H sites, those duties should be assigned by the certificate holder. Personnel assigned those duties should receive appropriate formal training.

c. Ground crew and other ground personnel (i.e., nurses, paramedics, etc.). EMS operations require stringent safety around the aircraft especially during arrivals, departures, loading, and unloading. The FAA recommends that each certificate holder and hospital develop a training program that encompasses, in addition to their normal training program, the following:

(1) Loading and unloading the helicopter with the rotors and/or engine running.

(2) Loading and unloading with the helicopter shut down.

(3) Use of visual cues for positioning and parking the helicopter (i.e., standard hand signals. communications, etc.).

(4) A program coordinated with local authorities (i.e., fire and police departments) to deal with fuel leaks on the heliport, helicopter fires, and other situations requiring emergency responses.

(5) Personal safety in and around the helicopter for all ground personnel (i.e., high winds from rotor during landing or takeoff, danger of tail rotor).

(6) Procedures for day/night operations into and out of an unprepared landing site for the recovery of a patient.

(7) The safe handling of oxygen equipment by all involved personnel. All personnel authorized to refill oxygen should be trained in the use of the recommended cascade system. If liquid oxygen (LOX) is used, the specific nature of LOX should be addressed.

NOTE: The FAA recommends that this program involve a licensed airframe and power plant mechanic to teach the correct procedures for handling oxygen equipment.

d. Maintenance Personnel. In addition to meeting the requirements of FAR Part 65, Certification: Airmen Other Than Flight Crewmembers, maintenance personnel should be trained by the manufacturers of aircraft modification equipment, or in other maintenance training programs approved by the Administrator.

(1) Inspection of installation as well as the removal and reinstallation of special medical equipment should be a part of this training.

(2) Supplemental Training. Training on servicing and maintenance of medical oxygen systems, along with characteristics of medical oxygen versus aviator breathing oxygen, should be included in the training program.

NOTE: Recurrent training is recommended for all maintenance personnel.

e. Cockpit Resource Management (CRM). Regardless of the type of operations conducted (Instrument Flight Rules or Visual Flight Rules), a training program should be established for CRM and the use of checklists. Pilots should be trained in "challenge and response" methods of checklist use. First officers should be trained to assist the pilot as directed. Cockpit procedures should be devised that deal with emergencies where one pilot is designated to fly the aircraft while the second pilot tends to the emergency.

f. Judgment and Decisions. The decision-making process should have input from all elements involved in an EMS operation. Aeromedical directors, helicopter operators, the flightcrew, medical personnel, and ground crew contribute to this process. The degree of input from each of these elements will depend upon the type and complexity of each mission.

(1) Management personnel, including the aeromedical director, should be familiar with appropriate FAR and FAA guidelines related to safe operations. Management personnel should participate in the certificate holder's training program to gain knowledge concerning EMS/H operations.

(2) An essential element in flight operations is the timely decision to conduct a particular flight (or continue a flight as planned). To reach a decision, each participant in the decision-making process must be familiar with helicopter operations pertaining to the mission being planned.

(3) All personnel assigned to EMS/H should be trained in the operational aspects of each type of helicopter being used. Training should include, but is not limited to, the range of each helicopter versus number of crewmembers/passengers carried, equipment installed versus carry-on equipment, weather capabilities, safety around helicopters, and safety in landing areas.

(4) The certificate holder should be thoroughly familiar with the operational characteristics of each helicopter and the qualifications of each flight crewmember.

(5) Pilot judgment may be defined as: The mental process by which the pilot recognizes, analyzes, and evaluates information regarding himself/herself, the aircraft, and the external environment. Good pilot judgment can be developed as part of a flightcrew training program. Pamphlet DOT/FAA/PM-86-45, Aeronautical Decision Making for Helicopter Pilots, is recommended to improve aeronautical decision making. The pamphlet covers the concepts of judgment and decision making and is designed to be reviewed under the supervision of a flight instructor.

(6) A final decision to conduct a flight, or to continue a flight as planned, should be made by the pilot in command based on his/her judgment. The decision should not be based solely on the condition of the patient.

(7) The final step is the decision to conduct the flight in a safe and timely manner.

CHAPTER 3. OPERATIONS

7. GENERAL. This chapter outlines recommendations regarding the conduct of FAR Part 135 EMS operations with helicopters.

   a. EMS/H Flight Following. In order to ensure a safe, orderly execution of an EMS/H mission, each operating site should have a flight locating system. Several factors, including the potential 24-hour demands of EMS/H missions, surrounding terrain, and variable weather conditions, affect the safety of EMS flight operations. The following is provided to help ensure safe mission accomplishment:

   (1) Flightcrews should have procedures to notify the flight following center of specific aircraft departure times and estimated time of arrival.

   (2) Flight following and/or communications should be maintained with the helicopter during each mission at specified intervals (i.e., 15/30 minute intervals).

   (3) A communications system is established to ensure that medical personnel and crewmembers can communicate with the hospital and ground personnel at the patient transport site.

   (4) A qualified, trained individual is designated as a communications specialist to receive and coordinate flight requests for EMS/H operations.

   (5) An intercommunications system is available for communications between medical personnel and the flightcrew.

   b. Weather Minimums. Each EMS/H flight following location should establish a local flying area and a cross-country flying area. VFR weather minimums should be specified for day and night local, and day and night cross-country. VFR minimums should be no less than in Table 1.

   NOTE: For operations in controlled airspace, refer to FAR Sections 91.155 and 91.157.

   (1) Each EMS/H certificate holder should develop a system of obtaining weather information prior to releasing any flight.

   c. Landing Sites.

   (1) Criteria should be established to ensure each airport approved helicopter landing site has been evaluated by qualified personnel and the heliport or landing site meets the guidance contained in AC 150/5390-2, Heliport Design Advisory Circular. The site evaluation should include the following:

      (i) Identification and/or removal of obstructions.

      (ii) Assessment of area lighting.

      (iii) Notation of helicopter ingress/egress limitations.

   (2) A system should be established to familiarize pilots with all heliports serviced by the hospital/certificate holder. A method considered acceptable would be photographs, drawings, and other descriptive means to identify the helistop or heliport and any obstructions.

   d. Flight Controls. The flight controls of a helicopter should not be left unattended by crewmembers while the rotor is turning.

   e. Flight Time and Rest Requirements. Each operator will maintain a record that distinctly shows the difference of flight time, rest time, and off-duty or unassigned time, in accordance with FAR Part 135. It should be noted that in addition to FAR Section 135.263, there are two basic flight and duty time FAR sections applicable to EMS operations.

   (1) FAR Section 135.267 titled, Flight time limitations and rest requirements: Unscheduled one- and two-pilot crews, allows the flight crewmember to conduct any flight or other duties as assigned such as training, testing, routine transport missions, etc., while on duty/assignment. For an assignment conducted under this section, flight crewmembers must receive rest in accordance with FAR Section 135.267 (at least 10 consecutive hours of rest during the 24-hour period that precedes the planned completion of the assignment).

   NOTE: FAR Sections 135.267 or 135.271 should be identified in the company training program and operations specifications and specify which FAR the operator has chosen to comply with for his/her particular operation.

   (2) The rest requirements for HEMES under FAR Section 135.271 differ from the requirements of flights conducted under FAR Section 135.267. During operations in accordance with FAR Section 135.271, provisions must be made for 8 consecutive hours of rest during any 24 consecutive hour period. If the flight crewmember does not receive the required rest period, that pilot must be relieved of the assignment. The certificate holder should

Table 1
VFR WEATHER MINIMUMS

| | Uncontrolled Airspace | | | |
| | Non-Mountainous Terrain | | Mountainous Terrain | |
Conditions	Ceiling	Visibility	Ceiling	Visibility
Day local	800 ft.	1 mile	1000 ft.	3 miles
Day cross-country	1000 ft.	2 miles	1200 ft.	3 miles
Night local	1000 ft.	2 miles	1200 ft.	3 miles
Night cross-country	1300 ft.	3 miles	1500 ft.	3 miles

establish a recordkeeping mechanism to show that only bona fide emergency flights are conducted during these FAR Section 135.271 assignments. While a flight crewmember is assigned to HEMES under FAR Section 135.271, he/she may not be assigned to any other duties.

(3) For programs providing 24-hour consecutive EMS/H coverage, it is recommended that no less than four pilots per aircraft be assigned. EMS/H programs with high activity levels or those with unusual circumstances may require higher pilot-to-aircraft ratios. Sufficient staffing levels should be established to promote operational safety standards.

(4) Each certificate holder should provide relief for each person performing maintenance from duty for a period of at least 24 consecutive hours during any 7 consecutive days, or the equivalent thereof, within any 1 calendar month. The requirement of the certificate holder should be the same for contractor/vendor maintenance.

f. Weight and Balance. Each operator should develop a control system for weight and balance that shows the aircraft will be properly loaded and will not exceed limitations during flight. A control system may include the following:

(1) A loading schedule, composed of graphs and tables based on pertinent data for use in loading that particular aircraft in a rapid manner for EMS/H operations, should be prepared.

(2) An index type weight and balance program using average load weights may be established in accordance with AC 120-27A, as revised. If an index-type weight and balance is used, the manual should contain the procedures for using, managing, and updating.

(3) These programs should include assorted aircraft occupant and equipment configurations (i.e., one or two pilots, two medical personnel, two patients, large carry-on equipment, balloon pumps, fuel in the most critical center of gravity location, etc.).

g. Procedures for Flight Into Instrument Meteorological Conditions (IMC). An operational procedure for inadvertent flight into IMC should be developed for inclusion in the certificate holder's operations manual. The procedures should address the applicable FAR pertaining to IFR including operations in an ATC radar environment as well as inadvertent IMC in isolated areas or a non-radar environment.

NOTE: This procedure should in no way be construed as authorizing or condoning actual IFR flights without meeting all IFR requirements.

The FAR Part 135 certificate holder/operator might choose to request the use of a discreet transponder code from the local ATC facility for use when conducting EMS/H operations in that area. This would provide positive identification during an EMS/H operation at all times. This procedure may be established with a Letter of Agreement between the operator and its local ATC facility.

h. Night Experience. The pilot in command must meet the requirements of FAR Part 61 and should complete a company night training program before conducting any night operations. Procedures for maintaining night currency in EMS/H operations should be developed and specified in the company training program. Such night training should be tailored to the operations of a certificate holder considering the experience level of EMS pilots, the area of operations, and the management and safety policy for that operator.

i. EMS/H Heliports. Because of the operating environment (night, weather, and emergencies), EMS operations require a high degree of safety. FAR Part 135 EMS/H operations should only be conducted from heliports that meet the criteria established in AC 150/5390-2. For operations over congested areas, ingress/egress routes to EMS/H heliports may have to be identified for compliance with FAR Section 91.119.

CHAPTER 4. SAFETY

8. GENERAL. The commitment to safety must start at the top of an organization. The single most important element of a successful safety program is the commitment of senior management. Safety cannot be dictated—it must be practiced. Managers must display a prudent, safe attitude by being involved in safety training. The following safety program recommendations are unique to EMS/H operations:

   a. Safety Program. The safety program should be developed considering coordination, when necessary, with organizations that may be essential to the safe completion of an EMS/H mission. The operator may coordinate with one or more of the following organizations: ATC, hospitals, police and fire departments, and search and rescue organizations. An operator might hold briefing sessions with another organization prior to undertaking a specific EMS mission addressing topics concerning the aircraft operations.

   b. The certificate holder should designate a safety officer. This individual should be familiar with each aspect of an EMS/H operation with particular emphasis on the safety requirements involved in the operation of helicopters. This individual should plan, organize, and disseminate information about the safety program to all involved persons.

   c. The program should encompass at least the following areas: safety in and around helicopters, site evaluation/preparation, weather analysis, communication equipment and procedures, facilities, and other areas deemed appropriate by the certificate holder and local FSDO.

Index